LAWYERS AT WORK

LAWYERS AT WORK

by

Herbert M. Kritzer

ꟼP

LAWYERS AT WORK

by

Herbert M. Kritzer

ꟼP

QUID PRO BOOKS

New Orleans, Louisiana

Published in 2015 by Quid Pro Books, as part of the *Contemporary Society* Series.

ISBN 978-1-61027-283-4 (pbk.)
ISBN 978-1-61027-289-6 (hardcover)
ISBN 978-1-61027-297-1 (ebook)

QUID PRO, LLC
5860 Citrus Blvd., Suite D-101
New Orleans, Louisiana 70123
www.quidprobooks.com

qp

Publisher's Cataloging-in-Publication

Kritzer, Herbert M.
    Lawyers at work / Herbert M. Kritzer.
        p. cm. — (Contemporary society)
    Includes bibliographical references and index.
    ISBN 978-1-61027-283-4 (pbk.)

1. Practice of law—United States. 2. Lawyers—United States. 3. Law firms—United States. 4. Justice, Administration of. I. Title. II. Series.

KF310.W23 K41 2015   347.93'56—dc22
                                                      2015717859

Author photograph on back cover inset provided courtesy of the University of Minnesota Law School/Tim Rummelhoff photographer, copyright © 2009, used by permission. Cover design © 2015 by Quid Pro, LLC.

CONTENTS

LIST OF TABLES

LIST OF FIGURES

To David, Joel, Bill, and Austin

without whom none of the work in this book
would have come to exist

PREFACE

This volume contains a set of papers on a topic that surprisingly to me became the central focus of my research over the last 35 years. I am grateful to Alan Childress, the publisher of Quid Pro Books, for entertaining the idea of bringing together many of the separate articles I have published on lawyers and their work.

With the exception of Chapter 1, some version of all of the chapters has appeared previously. Each chapter notes the original publication, but I would like to acknowledge and thank the publishers of *Arizona Law Review, American Bar Foundation Research Journal, Civil Justice Quarterly* (Thomson Reuters), *DePaul Law Review, Journal of Empirical Legal Studies, Law & Society Review, Social and Legal Studies* (Sage Publications), *Texas Law Review, Vanderbilt Law Review*, and *Washington University Law Quarterly*. Two chapters previously appeared in books, one edited by June Starr and Mark Goodale and published by Palgrave/St. Martins, and the other a chapter from my book, *Risks, Reputations, and Rewards*, published by Stanford University Press (copyright © 2004 by the Board of Trustees of the Leland Stanford Jr. University; all rights reserved; used with permission of Stanford University Press, www.sup.org). I am grateful to both of these publishers for permission to reprint those chapters in this volume. Chapter 8 was coauthored by Frances Kahn Zemans; she kindly granted permission for it to appear in this volume.

I have a significant debt to the senior collaborators on the Civil Litigation Research Project—David Trubek, Joel Grossman, William L.F. Felstiner, and Austin Sarat—which constituted the beginning of this work, and became the source of many of the theoretical and empirical questions that I have explored over the last 35 years. The large law and society community at the University of Wisconsin during my 30 years in Madison provided a wonderful environment to pursue this work, as did the broad acceptance at UW of interdisciplinary research. I have continued to enjoy a supportive environment in the years since I left Madison, first at William Mitchell College of Law and now at the University of Minnesota Law School.

My wife, Amelia Howe Kritzer, has lived through this work with me, at times taking on extra burdens while I was traveling in connection with the Civil Litigation Research Project or immersed in observational work. When this work started our family was young and growing, and today we have grandchildren older than any of our children were in 1980 when the Civil Litigation Research Project was going full tilt. Today, our youngest child, who was born during the time I was working on litigation project, is now a member of the profession I have spent so many years studying while his older sisters are pursuing their own careers as a writer and as a chemist.

My research work related to the legal profession has been supported by a range of funders including a large contract with the U.S. Department of Justice, several grants from the National Science Foundation (SES–8320129, SES–8511622, SES–9212756, and SBR–9510976), a grant from the Project on Scientific Knowledge and Public Policy, the Canada Studies Program, by several small grants from the Research Committee of the University of Wisconsin–Madison Graduate School, the University of Minnesota Law School, and the University of Minnesota Grant-in-Aid Program.

Finally, I owe the largest debt to the many lawyers who have taken the time to talk to me about their work, and particularly to that smaller group of lawyers who allowed me to shadow them as they went about their work over periods of from several days to a month.

H.M.K.

February, 2015

LAWYERS AT WORK

PART I

THEORY AND METHOD IN THE STUDY OF LEGAL PRACTICE

1

REFLECTIONS ON THEORY AND METHOD

If someone had told me in 1974 as I completed my graduate studies in political science that a major focus of my scholarly work over the next forty years would be lawyers and their work, I would have thought that person was nuts and would have said as much. I had no particular interest in lawyers, and saw my research interests as centered on the behavior of political elites. The evolution of my interests toward lawyers and their work arose largely as a result of opportunities that came my way after I joined the Political Science Department at the University of Wisconsin-Madison, an institution with a strong tradition of interdisciplinary work related to law and legal institutions. One element from what I had originally seen as my area of interest carried over to my research on lawyers: a focus on behavior. Unlike most work in the sociology of professions generally and the sociology of the legal profession more specifically, my research has not been directed toward the role and place of lawyers in the social system but on what lawyers actually do, how they do it, and why they do what they do.

In considering these questions I have both drawn on existing theories and developed new frameworks for understanding lawyers' work. The extant theories I have used or adapted come largely from sociology and economics. The theoretical work has generally either been to structure empirical projects or come in reflection on completed empirical projects. Those empirical studies have relied on diverse methods: surveys, interviews, coding of institutional records, experiments, and observation, usually combining two or more methods for collecting data. This introductory chapter briefly reviews the range of theories I have employed and methods I have used.

I. THEORIES FOR THE STUDY OF LAWYERS AND THEIR WORK

A. LAWYER AS BROKER

My research related to lawyers started with my involvement in the Civil Litigation Research Project (CLRP) which ran from the University of Wisconsin in 1979–81 under the leadership of David Trubek. This project, which was funded by a contract with the U.S. Department of Justice, had as its central goal the analysis of the costs of litigation and several forms of alternative dispute resolution. The data we collected came from institutional (largely court) records, and interviews with lawyers and their clients.[1] Soon after the data collection was completed, there was a change in Washington—Jimmy Carter was out and Ronald Reagan was in—and the new leadership of the Justice Department had no interest in continuing the study. Thus, after relatively minimal analyses had been completed (see Trubek et al. 1983b) funding ended, and most of the senior staff shifted their attention to other endeavors. I was left with a complex dataset that had cost about $2 million to collect, and faced the challenge of what, if anything, I might do with it beyond several eventually published articles for which analyses had already been completed (see Grossman et al. 1982; Kritzer and Anderson 1983; Kritzer et al. 1985; Kritzer et al. 1984a; Kritzer et al. 1984b).[2]

In the months after the funding ended, I agreed with the other senior staff to take a cut at drafting a book manuscript using the rich data we had jointly worked to collect. However, after having completed a version of that book, there was a consensus that what I had managed to come up with was not particularly interesting, in no small part because it lacked any kind of meaningful theoretical framework. The other members of the group had by then become immersed in other research activities or administrative duties, and none expressed an interest in continuing the collaboration. It was clear that either I figured out something I was interested in doing with the data or it was time for me to move on to other work.

It took me a couple of years to come up with a workable theoretical framework, and a sabbatical leave to draft a book manuscript. The book contrasted the image of a professional as defined in key aspects of sociological theory with what I labeled a broker. The argument I posed was that the work of lawyers handling ordinary civil litigation was more akin with what one would associate with a broker than with a professional as defined by sociological theory. This distinction involved the set of elements summarized in Table 1.1.

Table 1.1: The Professional and the Broker

Dimension	Professional	Broker
Centrality of the fee-paying relationship	low	high
Nature of expertise	technical/formal	insider/informal
Position occupied by professional/broker vis-à-vis other actors	[unspecified]	intermediary between client and other actors
Autonomy/client control	professional controls	client instructs/ broker responds

---

[1] See Kritzer (1980–81) for a discussion of the research design and methods employed by the project.

[2] I obtained some funding from the National Science Foundation (SES-8511622) to prepare the CLRP data for archiving, and eventually those data were deposited with the Interuniversity Consortium for Political and Social Research (ICPSR Studies No. 7994 and No. 9743).

This framework was the basis of my book *The Justice Broker* (1990) in which I used the CLRP dataset to examine the work of lawyers in ordinary litigation under the two lenses of the professional and the broker, and argued that the analysis showed that much of the work of ordinary litigation, including many cases in total, could readily be handled by nonlawyers with appropriate training and/or experience.

B. DIMENSIONS OF ADVOCACY

The major conclusion of *The Justice Broker*—that much of ordinary litigation could be handled by persons with less training than a lawyer—was challenged by some of the reviews who correctly asserted that it was essentially speculative on my part because I did not have any actual evidence about the performance of nonlawyers handling litigation-type work. To answer this critique I designed another study that directly compared lawyers and nonlawyers appearing as advocates. I could not do this using actual court cases because nonlawyers are barred by unauthorized practice rules from appearing on behalf of another person in court. However, there are a range of tribunals that operate similarly to courts where nonlawyers can appear. As I thought out how to do this study, I developed a more refined theoretical framework that focused on three core dimensions, each with three subdimensions, of the work of the advocate (Kritzer 1998b:14-20).

Expertise

The three subdimensions of expertise are:

Formal training vs. insider knowledge

> *Should expertise be defined in terms of formal training and credentials (e.g., a law degree or a license as a certified public accountant), or should it be defined in terms of knowledge, particularly people knowledge, gained from day-to-day practice and experience dealing with particular types of issues in a specific setting?*

Generalist vs. specialist

> *Should expertise be defined in terms of a broad base of knowledge that recognizes the possible interrelationships among a wide range of issues (e.g., an unemployment compensation dispute over what constitutes grounds for discharge for misconduct may be directly relevant to a pending criminal charge or to a discrimination claim), or should it focus on detailed knowledge of the rules and regulations governing one specific area (e.g., unemployment compensation)?*

Substantive vs. process

> *Does the core expertise consist of the substance of law, regulations, etc. governing decisions in a specific forum (or a specific type of case), or does it consist of the hearing/advocacy process itself?*

Representative-Client Relationship

The three subdimensions of representative-client relations are:

Pre-existing vs. ad hoc

Are representatives retained on a one-shot, issue-specific basis, or does the representation extend across cases and issues, and include structuring pre-dispute activities to avoid problems or to position the client for favorable outcomes (i.e., is the representation antici-patory or simply responsive)?

Broker vs. alter ego

Are representatives there solely to reflect the interest of the client, or are they recognized as having interests of their own which may not be entirely consistent with those of the client (e.g., the outside, retained representative who is concerned with earning a fee versus the inside representative whose future is directly tied to the future of the party represented)?

Agency vs. fiduciary (delegate vs. trustee)

Are representatives expected simply to act on behalf of the interest of the client as the client defines that interest, or are representa-tives expected to exercise independent judgment as to what is and is not in the client's interest?

Accountability and Control

The three subdimensions of accountability and control are:

Regulated vs. unregulated

Is the representative answerable to some licensing or disciplinary authority?

Client-centered vs. forum-centered

Is the representative's allegiance primarily to specific clients, or is it to the forum in which the representative appears on a regular basis?

"Shareholder" vs. nonshareholder

Does control flow in part from the representative's having a direct stake in the outcome (i.e., the contingent fee lawyer who will re-ceive a share of the winnings, or the civil rights attorney who will receive a fee award set by the court), or is the representative's in-terest not directly related to the outcome of the specific case?

The research employing this set of dimensions examined advocates in four very different forums: unemployment compensation appeals, social security dis-ability appeals, Wisconsin state tax appeals, and labor arbitration hearings. The results (see Kritzer 1998b) clearly demonstrated that the nature of expertise that advocates brought to their work was of more importance than whether the advocate had the formal qualifications of a lawyer.

C. POSTPROFESSIONALISM

One of the ideas that developed as I was finishing the study directly comparing lawyer and nonlawyer advocates was that at least some of the ability of nonlawyers to be effective flowed from broader political and technical developments. I saw three developments that were important:

- Lawyers (and other professions) were losing some of their ability to limit competition from nonprofessionals.
- Increasing specialization meant that nonprofessionals could acquire the specialized expertise necessary to be effective in many narrow areas of law-related work.
- The rationalization of knowledge combined with the tools of information technology allowed nonprofessionals to access information that previously was effectively the exclusive domain of a particular profession.

This theoretical argument, which I label "postprofessionalism," is developed in detail in Chapter 14 of this volume.

D. DIMENSIONS OF LAWYER/CLIENT RELATIONSHIPS

A second follow-up study to CLRP focused on lawyer/client relations. One of the issues that swirled around CLRP was the increased concern in the corporate world about legal expenses, particularly in litigation (Banks 1983; Wessel 1976). I hypothesized that this would be a lesser concern in England because of the availability of formal procedures for the review of legal bills (called "taxation"). While my original idea was that the project would be carried out in England during a year at a university near London, the plan to be in England fell through and I relocated the project to Toronto because Ontario had a similar set of formal procedures. The project relied on semi-structured interviews with large-firm lawyers and officials at their corporate clients. After only a small number of interviews, it was obvious I had committed a "Type III" error—I was asking the wrong question (see Kirk and Miller 1986:29-30); very different elements were driving the lawyer-client relationship, and when I distilled my research notes I recognized that there were three identifiable elements: professional, business, and personal. I detailed the resulting analysis in a short article (Kritzer 1984b) which is reprinted in this volume as Chapter 4.

E. PORTFOLIO THEORY

One of the frequent criticisms of contingency fee practice is that it gives lawyers an incentive to take weak cases in the hope of getting quick settlements. While there are certainly a few lawyers who approach their work in this way (see Engstrom 2009, 2011), my work on CLRP led me to have doubts that this kind of approach to running a legal practice made sense. For several years I thought about designing a project that would try to get at the questions of how lawyers screen cases and what the likelihood is that lawyers take a case offered to them by a potential client. In the midst of a lunch discussion about future research with a friend it occurred to me that the questions I was asking about case screening were potentially part of a much larger study broadly focused on contingency fee legal practice.

As I started thinking about how to frame and design such a project, I realized that lawyers handling contingency fee cases were in a sense managing a portfolio of investments in which the time and expenses expended on each case constituted the investments, and the fees received when each case was resolved were the returns. Sometimes the fees produced a positive return on the investment and sometimes a negative return, with the latter occurring either when no fee was received because no recovery was obtained or when the fee feel below the lawyer's opportunity cost. The complete losers are comparable to a stock investment where the company goes bankrupt and hence the investment is a complete write-off with the situation of fees falling below the lawyer's opportunity cost comparable to selling a stock at a loss. This thinking led me to portfolio theory, an idea that produced a share of the 1990 Nobel Prize in economics for Harry Markovitz. The core ideas of "modern portfolio theory," which focuses on assessing risk and the use of diversification to hedge risk, became the framework for my study of contingency fee practice and the resulting book (Kritzer 2004b). One chapter from that book appears as Chapter 5 in this volume with several other aspects of the book summarized in an article (Kritzer 2002c) which appears as Chapter 12.

F. FEE REGIMES

From the time I worked on CLRP the issue of how various fee arrangements influenced the work of lawyers has been a central question in much of my research (see Kritzer 1984c; 1987 [Chapter 9 in this volume]; Kritzer et al. 1985). When I was asked to prepare a paper on the impact of fee arrangements on lawyer behavior for a symposium at the University of Texas School of Law, I began thinking about how to frame a discussion of this very broad topic. In the resulting paper (Kritzer 2002b [included in this volume as Chapter 11]) I focused on two elements of fee arrangements: who actually pays the lawyer's fee and how that fee is computed. Subsequently, I refined that framework by adding a third element, how fees are regulated and/or reviewed, and came to describe the three elements together as constituting "fee regimes." I first presented this framework at a symposium during a visit to Australian National University in Canberra, and subsequently as a talk at the University of Minnesota Law School. A review of civil litigation costs and fees undertaken in England by Court of Appeal judge Sir Rupert Jackson (Jackson 2009) became the motivation to turn the talk into an article which was published in the English journal *Civil Justice Quarterly* (Kritzer 2009 [included in this volume as Chapter 10]). The core argument that I make in the article is that the three elements of a fee regime interact such that modifying only one of the elements can produce unpredictable results because such changes lead to unanticipated changes in the other two elements.

G. Craft

As I discuss in Chapter 3, I have long been intrigued by the idea of "craft." I trace this interest to my experience as a teenager working at the ceramic supply business owned by my next-door neighbors, one of whom had trained as a potter and the other as a sculptor. I heard them interact with customers and talk about the time it took to master their respective crafts. Over the various projects I have done that have involved interacting with and observing lawyers as they work, it became clear that they were engaged in work that can fairly be described as a kind of craft. A problem was that I was not sure exactly what that meant. When I was asked to participate on a panel at a professional meeting focused on what the organizers labeled "judgecraft," I saw the opportunity to formulate a theoretical approach to understanding the idea of craft, or more specifically the work that craftspersons undertake which I came to label "craftwork." The eventual article (Kritzer 2007) identified six elements that defined craftwork and applied those elements to the work of judges. However, from the start of this effort, my interest was less in judgecraft and more in how the elements of craftwork could be applied to understanding the work of lawyers; hence Chapter 3 is a revision of the original paper on judgecraft which retains the original six elements while shifting the sketch of how the elements can be applied from the work of judges to the work of lawyers.

H. Other Theoretical Frames

The various theoretical approaches described above cover much of my work on lawyers but do not include all of the theories or theoretical approaches I have employed. In a broad sense much of the work has been concerned with the role of incentives, which are particularly prominent in the discussions in Chapters 9 and 11 in this volume. Two other frameworks represented in this book are commodification (see Chapter 6) and local legal culture (see Chapter 8). For the various frameworks discussed previously, I can claim some originality, either in the central ideas or in their application. However, I do not make such a claim for these other frameworks. I mention them primarily to emphasize the broad range of theoretical approaches I have used in the course of my research and writing on lawyers and their work.

II. METHODS

As the discussion in the previous section should make clear, I have been eclectic in my use of theory. The same can be said for my selection of research methods. My training and original methodological orientation was highly quantitative. For the first 34 years of my teaching career, I was in positions where I had been hired in significant part because of my ability and willingness to teach quantitative methods. I was brought on board as a participant in the Civil Litigation Research Project primarily because of my skills in quantitative methods. The majority of my research projects over the years since CLRP have involved quantitative elements, including surveys, coding and analysis of institutional records or decisions, the analysis of data obtained from agencies and archives, and simple experiments. However, over this same period my work has also often included significant qualitative elements with two projects relying exclusively qualitative methods (see Chapters 4, 6, and 7 in this volume).

My first significant experience with qualitative research came in my study in Toronto (referenced in the previous section) which was based entirely on semi-structured interviews. My studies of advocacy, contingency fee practice, insurance defense practice, and my current project on legal malpractice all have used semi-structured interviews as one significant source of data. However, as discussed in Chapter 2, observation has been the most fruitful of the qualitative methods I have employed.[3] Observation is very intense, extremely time consuming, and not always possible to arrange; I had plans for an observational study of government lawyers, but that study never came to fruition because I was unsuccessful in locating an agency that would agree to let me observe.[4]

My basic principle in selecting the research methods to use for a particular project is to identify which approaches will yield the information and insights I am seeking. The use of multiple methods is frequently crucial, and for most projects I have been able to employ multiple methods combining qualitative and quantitative approaches where possible. In all three projects where I have undertaken observation of lawyers at work, I have supplemented those observations with semi-structured interviews as a vehicle for insuring that what I have observed is not peculiar to those lawyers I have observed; in two of those projects there were major quantitative elements in addition to the observational work and the semi-structured interviews. While the quantitative elements have allowed me to be sure that the patterns I thought I was seeing in the observation were in fact generalizable, the more important understandings tended to come from the observational elements which provided a depth to the analysis that could not be obtained from the quantitative materials.

III. ORGANIZATION OF THE BOOK

I have selected twelve journal articles plus two book chapters for inclusion in this collection. One of those book chapters is drawn from my book on contingency fee practice, *Risks Reputations, and Rewards* (Kritzer 2004) and one of the journal articles was subsequently integrated into my book on negotiation and settlement, *Let's Make a Deal* (Kritzer 1991b).

I have organized the material into four parts: theory and method (including this introduction), lawyers at work, impact of how lawyers are paid, and legal practice in the 21st century. While I have made a few cuts to avoid too much repetition, some repetition remains. At a number of places I have either updated references to reflect eventual publication of items, or revised some discussions

---

[3] I should note that in some of my research not related to legal practice I have done what might be described as "light" history, looking at news reports and some primary documents. Generally this has been part of some larger project with the historical materials playing a supporting or supplementary role.

[4] I did find one agency where the acting head was amenable to the project, but that fell through after someone else was appointed to head the agency, and it did not seem advisable to approach someone who was just taking charge about a project of the type I had in mind.

to capture developments since the original publication of the article. Articles that originally appeared in law reviews have been revised to use social science style in-text citations, thus eliminating many of the footnotes that appeared in the original publication.

IV. GOING FORWARD

As this collection is assembled I am engaged in a continuing project on legal malpractice with a focus on how claims of malpractice are handled by insurers and the lawyers who prosecute and defend those claims. As is true of much of my work on lawyers and legal practice, this project combines qualitative methods (semi-structured interviews) and quantitative methods of various sorts. One of the central puzzles in this research is the sharp differences in how claims of legal malpractice are dealt with compared to claims of medical malpractice. There are a variety of potential answers to this puzzle, some institutional, some economic, and some cultural; it is not yet clear what balance might exist among the possible answers, not is it clear that it will be possible to come to any solid conclusions about that balance.

As noted above, Chapter 3 in this volume, "Craft and Legal Practice," is a revision of an article focused on the work of judges. As revised it represents early thinking about a possible book length application of the idea of craft to the work of lawyers. This book would draw on my previous research along with studies by other scholars who have observed lawyers at work or interviewed lawyers about how they go about their work. A major question about this potential project is the range of types of legal practices it would include. There is substantial extant research on criminal work, divorce, and civil litigation but relatively little on transactional practice. There is less work on in-house practice and surprisingly little on government practice other than the most senior positions. Thus, the rich literature that could be used to explore how craft functions in legal practice is both extremely broad and limited in important ways. The first challenge in carrying the work forward will be in making the hard choices about the range of legal practice that will serve as the basis for the analysis.

2

LAWYERS IN THE MIST: DEEP HANGING OUT IN LAW OFFICES[1]

INTRODUCTION

In recent years there has been increased attention to the value of qualitative research and the methods for conducting that research in a rigorous manor. We now have available excellent discussions of issues of design (King et al. 1994; Yin 1994), data collection (Douglas 1985; McCracken 1988; Spradley 1979, 1980), and analysis (Feldman 1995; Miles and Huberman 1994; Silverman 1993; Strauss 1987). My interest in this essay is on data collection.

There are three archetypical methods of generating qualitative data: reading (relying on existing texts, typically from archival sources), talking (interviewing), and watching (observation).[2] Historians have been very candid about the issues and dilemmas of their data sources, and historiography provides a wealth of guidance regarding the issues involved in relying upon archival materials (Barzun and Graff 1992; Bloch 1953). Users of field interviews and of observational techniques have devoted less attention to the limitations of the information their methodologies produce.[3] Consequently, I will concentrate my attention on talking versus watching as methods of data generation.

A great deal of socio-legal research (as well as sociological and political science research) relies upon open-ended interviews. These interviews typically focus on a combination of factual and attitudinal issues. Sometimes they are a kind of personal oral history interview, in which respondents are asked to reconstruct past events, with the added element of asking for the reasoning behind specific actions. The duration of the interviews is most often in the range of one to three hours. Interviews can be an efficient way to collect data. For one hour interviews, it can be possible to conduct four or five interviews per day if

---

[1] This chapter originally appeared as pp. 143-159 in June Starr and Mark Goodale (eds.), *Practicing Ethnography in Law: New Dialogues, Enduring Practices* (New York: Palgrave/St. Martin's, 2002); it is reprinted here with the permission of the publisher.

[2] Dingwall (1997:53) describes the three modes as "reading the papers," "asking questions," and "hanging out."

[3] See the essays in Miller and Dingwall (1997) for a significant exception to this. Also, there is a large literature in anthropology dealing with the limits of and issues involved in ethnographic fieldwork (see, as one relatively early example, Agar 1980; other work in this genre include Hammersley 1992; van Maanen 1988).

the respondents are close together geographically and their schedules happen to allow the appropriate scheduling.

Much less research relies upon observation (or observation combined with interviewing[4]). This is not surprising.[5] Observation is extremely time consuming, and much of the time spent doing the observation can be relatively unproductive given that it is not possible to restrict the observation to activities or events relevant to the research, and that much of the observation may involve extremely repetitive activities. Even if time is not a constraint, for many of the phenomena of interest to socio-legal scholars it can be difficult to obtain the access necessary to conduct observation. For example, when Sarat and Felstiner (1995) were first beginning to plan their observational study of divorce lawyers and clients, it was not at all clear that they would succeed in obtaining the access that the research required (Chambers 1997: 214-19; see also Danet et al. 1980). In addition, because of the time required, observational methodologies tend to limit the number of data sources in ways that can raise questions about generalizability.

Because of the difficulties of observation, it is not surprising that researchers (perhaps with the important exception of anthropologists, who will find nothing of what I say in what follows the least bit surprising) more often opt to collect data through interviews, attempting to capture through the interview process the kind of information that would be obtained if observation could be carried out. Researchers pay surprisingly little attention to the limitations of the pure interview methodology, even though at least some of these limitations are well documented (see, for example, Briggs 1986; Converse and Schuman 1974), perhaps because few researchers have the opportunity to compare directly the results obtained with the two methodologies. When such comparisons are possible, the differences can be striking.

I. AN EXAMPLE

Let me illustrate this with an example from my research on contingency fee legal practice in Wisconsin. The design for this research involved three major components: a structured mail survey of Wisconsin practitioners, observation in three different firms (one month in each firm), and a series of semi-structured interviews with contingency fee practitioners around the state. Of interest here are the latter two components. In designing the research, I was very aware of the issues of generalizing from what amounted to three observational case studies (even if those settings were specifically chosen to insure variability). The specific goal of the interviews, which were conducted after the completion of the observation, was to assess the generalizability of the observational data. To do this, I sought to design questions that would try to provide information that was as

---

[4] While in this essay I tend to dichotomize between observation and interviewing, many, perhaps most, observational studies include a significant interview component. Thus it is probably more accurate to distinguish between studies that rely heavily on observation supplemented by interviews and studies that rely exclusively on interviews.

[5] In Dingwall's (1997:52) words, "Researchers cannot make the field fit their lives, [nor is it] easy to make your life fit the field."

14

comparable as possible to the kind of information I obtained from the observation. Among other things this involved:

- a question asking the respondent to give me a tour of what he or she did the previous day (i.e., the kinds of cases dealt with, telephone calls, etc.);
- a question asking the respondent to describe the most recent case closed, what the matter was, how the client came to the lawyer, the issues raised by the case, how it was resolved;
- a question asking the respondent to describe what would happen if a potential client contacted his or her office about a particular hypothetical case.

Given that I had already conducted the observation when I did the interviews, I knew very clearly the type of information I was seeking. I found that I was unable to get information that was even marginally comparable about details of events and processes.

A. OBSERVATION OF A DAY'S WORK

One can see the clarity of the problem by looking at an sample of my (edited) observational notes of one day in one of the three firms in which I observed, and one of the better (if not the best) responses I got to the first of the listed questions above. The lawyer observed in the example below, whom I will call Alex Stein, works in a small firm (under five lawyers) that largely (but not entirely) specializes in personal injury cases, including workers' compensation. This firm handles routine, run-of-the-mill type cases, most of which are under $50,000 (no one in the firm has ever handled a case that led to a judgment or settlement of over $500,000, and the two senior lawyers have been in practice for over 15 years). The day that follows was toward the end of my time observing in the firm; it is reasonably typical, although there was more in the way of settlement discussions than on most days, and there was less in the way of client in-take activities. [To assuage the curiosity of readers, I have included as bracketed comments some information on the final outcome of two of the cases dealt with during the day.]

> At 7:00 A.M. Alex Stein called my home to tell me that he wasn't going to his gym this morning, and wanted to get into the office early; he asked me if I would like him to pick me up and give me a ride (it's −24° out this morning, and I don't refuse). On the ride in, Alex told me that he had worked on the brief [for a case he is appealing] last night for 4 hours; he had sat down to do one paragraph and ended up revising one subsection.
>
> When we arrive at the office (about 8:00 am), Alex immediately went to work on the brief. He dictates changes. This takes 30-40 minutes, during which he declines to take one or two phone calls. He gives the dictation tape to his paralegal/secretary, Jim Allen, at 8:55.
>
> At 9:00 he turns to the mail and telephone messages. In the mail was a police report for the accident of one new client, medical records for another couple of cases (including one which prompts Alex to make

an observation about the high charge for copying a bill), and a motion (and accompanying brief) from the opposing lawyer in a non-PI case he is handling as co-counsel with another attorney.

In reaction to one of these bills Alex comments on a $55,000 medical bill in a workers' comp case. The medical insurer in that case has agreed to pay Alex a fee (20%) if he can recover the medical costs from the workers' comp carrier. In fact, the case was referred to Alex by the medical insurer; it would not have been worth his while to pursue the case just for the benefits that would come to the client. Alex comments on the potential for conflicts of interest between the insurer and the client in cases like this. The client comes first.

At 9:30, Alex calls Bob Strong, a client for whom he had been nego-tiating a settlement the day before. [This call, and most others, is handled on the speaker phone.] He gets some additional info on Strong's work situation, work duties, and prior medical treatment. Strong tells Alex that he had no related symptoms prior to the auto accident; his former job (he had been dismissed for absenteeism last month) was on a limited term basis [meaning that he received no benefits], even though it had lasted 3 or 4 years. Alex has Strong de-scribe his job duties; this produces a somewhat confused discussion, but the thrust is that most of the work was light duty such as sorting mail, with occasional assignments (perhaps 2–3 times a month) that involved moderate to heavy over-the-head lifting (getting this infor-mation from Strong is not easy, but Alex does eventually get it). Strong missed virtually no work before surgery. Alex explains the ad-juster's concern, "It is just as likely that the client's problem with his neck is related to work as to the accident." Alex observes to Strong, "It's not clear what happened here." Alex tells Strong that the situa-tion is difficult, repeatedly telling him that the issue is whether the surgery is really related to the auto accident, and the difficulty of es-tablishing proof. "This is a very iffy case in terms of litigation ... I'm concerned whether this is provable in a court of law." During this conversation Alex discussed with Strong the option of filing for bank-ruptcy to avoid paying other outstanding debts which would absorb most or all of any settlement Strong might receive.

The call ends at 10:00 A.M. (having lasted 30 minutes). Alex comments, "This case is going to be a tough one"; Alex comments that Strong mentioned some leg problems that aren't in the record; Alex's view is that Strong does not have good recall on this. Alex tells me more about the bankruptcy option; under Wisconsin law, you can keep up to $25,000 of an injury settlement. Alex is very skeptical about this case; clearly he doesn't want to take it to litigation. Alex says that if the adjuster makes a low offer and Strong rejects it, Alex will encour-age Strong to get another lawyer.

Jim [the paralegal] comes in with the revised brief. Alex spends 15 minutes or so reviewing it.

Alex's partner comes in with a question about whether there can be multiple independent medical examinations (IME's) when there are multiple insurance carriers. After responding, Alex discusses a drunk driving case with his partner, wondering about whether the facts of the case might restrict the availability of punitive damages. Alex decides he needs to check the statutes; there is also the question of who is responsible. Later checks the statute and finds a clear answer to his question.

At 10:30, Alex called Carl Hopkins, a client in another case [a workers' compensation case], to check in. Hopkins' employer has no work available given the restrictions on what Hopkins can do given his injuries. Alex mentions he has another client from the same employer (but at a different location) ... Hopkins comments that "it's rough work." Hopkins has a question about a recruitment bonus he got for finding another employee: he is supposed to get a bonus of $xxx if the new employee stays xx months. The employer is hedging on whether he will pay this bonus because Hopkins is not currently working. Alex tells Hopkins that he is probably entitled to the bonus, but that Alex can't really do anything; he advises Hopkins to go to small claims court if it becomes necessary. Hopkins is concerned about problems he might encounter if he went back to work at the employer. Alex strongly repeats the warning "don't quit." Alex tells Hopkins about a case he had settled earlier in the week where the employee had quit and the problems quitting created. Alex tells Hopkins "don't do anything without talking to me." He mentions the upcoming IME, and Hopkins asks "What should I expect?" Alex describes how the company that will do the IME operates, stating that "the doctor is looking for ways to save the company money." Alex tells Hopkins that he needs to emphasize how the injury happened. About the specific doctor who will do IME, Alex comments "there are worse doctors around ... he's on the conservative side ... I'm not looking for great things from him ... be polite ... show him deference." The call lasted about 30 minutes.

Alex calls back the adjuster, Stan Davis, in Bob Strong's auto accident. Alex gives Davis some information that Davis had requested (Strong's work history, medical treatment, work situation). Alex explains that his client does not have health insurance because of his LTE [limited term employee] status. Alex emphasizes that he has no independent information, but is simply taking what Strong has said at face value; Alex offers to make Strong available ... "if you want to interview him, I'm willing to make him available." Davis mentions that he is looking through his notes. Alex says "there is nothing I am aware of [that explains the injury other than the accident]. I've asked him eyeball to eyeball ... there's nothing I'm aware of that would be an intervening cause." Davis comments that "it's a hard one to swallow ... that the auto accident is the sole cause ... [Davis is clearly having difficulty coming to a decision about what to offer, and Alex is not doing anything here to push him ... Alex is laying back to see what he will say]." Davis offers $30,000 "to get rid of this one." Alex is stunned; he was expecting $5,000 or $10,000 as an opening offer (and he would have been happy to get it and get out of the case). Alex does not hesitate in leaping to it "let's probe this one ... if causation was not an issue is my demand of $50,000 appropriate?" Davis concedes that if there were no causation issue, the $50,000 demand would be reasonable, but goes on to say that he still has problem with the case. Alex says, "I appreciate the problem you have but here is my problem." Alex goes on to describe Strong's outstanding $17,000 medical bill, and the problem of getting providers, as opposed to insurers, to take a reduction; Alex goes on to say to Davis that "I know where you are coming from." The call ends at 11:05 having lasted 25 minutes.

Alex comments to me that Strong needs to seriously consider the bankruptcy option. He then immediately calls Strong, and tells him about the offer commenting that it is "double what I thought he would offer ... a neck surgery with a good result is worth about $50,000 [if there is no causation problem]. We would have serious problems proving the case [at trial]." Alex gives detailed description of conversation with the adjuster (including adjuster's reluctance to come up with a number). Alex recommends a counter at $42,500 and hopes for a $35,000 settlement. Then goes on to tell Strong that "I think you've got to make some tough decisions." Alex goes through various options mostly related to bankruptcy. He offers to take a fee reduction (rather than 1/3 of total, he will take 1/2 of what's left after paying the outstanding medical bills and expenses; this would probably be about $9,000 rather than $12,000 if the settlement is $35,000). Alex comments to Strong that he wants to be sure that he (Strong) gets at least as much as Alex gets. Alex goes on to brag a bit ... "I've done a fine piece of work on this case. I handled the adjuster the right way." Alex again talks about the bankruptcy option which would avoid payment to the medical providers, commenting that "I hate to write off the doctor's bill because he made the case for you ... but business is business and the doctor probably makes at least $400,000 a year." Alex asks Strong about other debts. He then suggests some other options such as talking to the medical providers to see if they would their reduce bills to avoid getting nothing at all if Strong filed bankruptcy. Alex asks for authority to demand $42,500 and to settle for whatever he can get, and Strong grants him this authority. He again emphasizes the problems with the case, commenting that "it's not a good risk at all." Alex mentions the downside of bankruptcy. The call lasted about 15 minutes. Alex tells me that he will wait until Monday to call Davis back because he wants Davis to think that Strong really had to think about the offer and that perhaps that Strong had some reluctance. I ask Alex how much time he has spent on this case; he estimates 20 hours, but reminds me that 90 minutes hours ago he was ready to walk away from it. [This case settled for $35,000, with Alex taking a fee of $10,000 rather than the one-third that the contingency fee retainer called for; the client did decide to file for bankruptcy.]

At 11:40, Alex receives a call from a chiropractor [a couple of days earlier Alex had a rather heated conversation with the receptionist at the chiropractor's office]. Alex describes what happened. He had called the office wanting to insure that medical records pertaining to his client were sent to him before being sent to third party insurer in order to be sure there were no errors in the records (he describes the example of an error he recently discovered in the records of another medical provider). Overall the conversation with the chiropractor goes very well; the chiropractor has no problem sending records to Alex for review before sending them to insurer, but will not erase records, only note corrections. That is fine with Alex. The chiropractor says that he normally sends a draft of his report to the lawyer before doing the final version; Alex is delighted. Overall, it is a very good conversation. Alex comments "wasn't he great." The call lasts 12 minutes. Alex tells Jim (his paralegal) to call the client to let her know that things are smoothed over, and that her husband doesn't need to straighten out the situation with the chiropractor.

At 11:55 another client, Sue Edwards, calls. Alex had been waiting for the doctor's report which finally has come in. Alex tells Edwards that on first glance report looks good. Edwards has a notice from DILHR [the agency responsible for workers' compensation]; Alex tells her to send the notice to him and he will deal with it. They discuss the case a bit; Edwards is concerned that her post-injury wage potential is reduced. Alex explains that because she is back at work at her former employer that he can't do anything about the larger labor market even though Edwards is concerned about what might happen if employer were to close up the local operation. The call lasts eight minutes.

For about 15 minutes, Alex works on miscellaneous tasks such as looking at his mail, sorting through and balancing a checking account, etc.

At 12:22, adjuster Bob Fox calls regarding a claim. Alex had demanded $75,000; Fox had previously acknowledged that case was in the $50,000–$75,000 range. Fox offers $62,500 on a take it or leave it basis, saying that he will not budge. When Alex indicates that he "would like to counter it," Fox essentially says that he would be wasting his time. Alex talks about the problems of getting the subrogation claims reduced, but he gets no encouragement from Fox. This is an underinsured motorist (UIM) claim, so if they can't agree on a settlement it will go to arbitration; Alex raises that possibility, but Fox says that going to arbitration is no problem as far as he is concerned. The call ends at 12:27 (5 minutes). Alex tells me that the "offer is imminently fair" (there were two accidents and there is some uncertainty about which accident caused what). Alex thinks that Fox might be serious that $62,500 is all there is (i.e., take it or leave it), but Alex says he will test it. [The case did settle the following week; Alex was able to move the adjuster up only $500 to $63,000. He did succeed in getting the subrogation claim reduced to $11,000 which was a considerably larger reduction than he had expected to be possible.]

From 12:30 to 1:35 Alex leaves the office for lunch.

When he gets back at 1:35, his partner is on the phone with an adjuster. The adjuster would like to talk to Alex. It turns out that the adjuster wants status reports on several cases, which Alex provides.

Alex had tried calling Sarah James, a potential client involved in an accident caused by a drunk driver, several times before lunch, and tries again now; the line was busy earlier, and is still busy.

Alex has a call from another lawyer on the "lawyer-to-lawyer hotline." Alex is listed as knowledgeable on a particular area. The conversation lasts about ten minutes.

Alex looks at the opposing brief in a non-PI case for which he is serving as co-counsel. The defendant is asking for dismissal on several bases. Alex does not think the other side has a strong argument.

At 2:00 P.M., Alex calls another lawyer to discuss a brief he has been working on. The lawyer has little to say "I think it [2nd argument] is splendid ... I think it's a darn good job." He has no substantive comments. The call ends at 2:10.

Alex returns a call from the Larry Gavin, the other driver in a case he is handling as a UIM claim. Gavin wants to know what's happening. He specifically asks about the injuries suffered by Alex's client, information which Alex does not want to provide. Gavin asks for the name of Alex's client's insurer which Alex is reluctant to give out because he is concerned Gavin might make a claim against his client (Gavin ran a stop sign, but Alex's client might have been speeding). It turns out that Gavin needs to get documents from the insurer in order to get his driver's license back under Wisconsin's financial responsibility law. Alex explains that his client cannot sign a release because that would jeopardize the client's UIM claim. Alex agrees to call his client's insurer to tell them that Gavin wants to get in touch, and then insurer can contact Gavin.

Alex and his partner are talking about letters from doctors. Alex notes that a doctor he met with a few days earlier charged $87.50 for a 10 minute conference. His partner tells of a $187 bill from a doctor for a 15 minute conference. Neither is really complaining, because in these cases the doctors' letters were central for making the case.

At 2:30, Alex finally got through to Sarah James (the potential client injured by a drunk driver). Alex tries to explain something about one of the potential issues in the case; James gets confused and thinks Alex is telling her that no damages are available. Alex clarifies. James had expected to be downtown in connection with the arraignment of the drunk driver, but it turns out she doesn't need to come. Alex had suggested that would be a good time to meet (and he hoped to get a signed retainer at that time). Alex offers to come out to James's home (which is just outside of town). James says that if the doctor on Monday says she can get out, she would just as soon come downtown. They leave it that they will talk on Monday or Tuesday after the doctor's appointment. James asks about a crime victimization form which she has filled out and returned; Alex tells her that it raises no problems. The call lasted about 12 minutes.

At 2:48, Alex takes a call from a doctor to whom Alex has written to for a report (Alex is not at first sure who the doctor is). Alex is sympathetic, but not sure what to say. Alex coaches him on the "magic language." Alex is careful not to push doctor on substance of opinion but on *how* to say it. Alex emphasizes that the magic words are that the accident was "a substantial factor"; doctor says "I think I'm willing to say that." The call ends at 2:52. Alex tells me after the call "That's a surprise." Alex tells me the background of the case, and that he did not expect to get a favorable opinion from the doctor. He has 20–25 hours into the case, and it's "just warming up."

Alex tells me that this current active cases seem to him to be a bit more complex than average. He has lots of routine stuff in the hopper but not at the top. Alex comments on the normally routine nature of workers' compensation claims; for those cases the key is "staying on top of them."

Alex tries calling his co-counsel in the non-PI case; the other lawyer is not in, so Alex leaves a message asking him to call back.

Alex calls another lawyer to talk about the bankruptcy issue confronting his client Bob Strong. The discussion suggests that it might be best for Strong to file bankruptcy before consummating the settlement. Alex says he will try to call Strong immediately and make it a conference call. However, there is no answer at Strong's number.

At 3:45 Alex gets another call from a lawyer on the lawyer hotline. The other lawyer has a question having to do with claim of an adult child; the case is complicated by the fact that the accident happened out of state. Alex is clearly thinking stuff through as he goes. Alex talks about some cases he's had involving recovery by adult children in wrongful death claims. The call lasts about 13 minutes.

Alex makes notes on his extensive things to do list.

Jim brings in the completed brief which is ready for printing.

Alex reviews the status of medical bills in a couple of cases, and then cleans off his desk (it's about 4:30). [This is a bit earlier than his usual 5:30 departure, but he arrived at the office about an hour earlier than usual.]

He goes over to EconoPrint to drop off the brief to be printed.

While this day's activities differed in some ways from most of the other days I spent in the firm, the overall pattern is reasonably typical. In the course of the day, Alex Stein dealt with at least 20 different cases, often moving quickly from one matter to another (for Stein to keep anything resembling accurate time records would have been virtually impossible). A very large portion of the day was spent on the telephone with incoming calls often disrupting the activity that Stein was working on; Stein had conversations with clients, potential clients, adjusters, medical providers, and other lawyers. No clients actually came into the office (most clients came in only for the intake interview and then to receive the settlement check, with most contact taking place via telephone).

B. AN INTERVIEW RECONSTRUCTION OF A DAY'S WORK

How well can the image captured by the observation be recreated using an interview format? I attempted to do this by using a standard type of question described in the literature on ethnography: what Spradley (1979) calls a grand tour question. As noted above this is probably the best response I was able to get to my question, and its follow-ups.

Q: I spent the last few months literally following lawyers around. If I had spent yesterday following you, that is, if I had spent the day with you as a "ride along," can you give me a tour of what I would have seen in the course of the day?

A: Let me just refresh my memory by looking at my calendar of yesterday. I do recall several things that did take place. I have a fairly substantial case that I am trying to negotiate a settlement on right now. I set up a conference with another attorney involved in the case. I talked to my client. There are several subrogated carriers involved and I am trying to work out a reduction in the amount that they are asking in subrogation. I was successful in getting all of them to take at least a 50% reduction, but I want a 60% reduction. Talking to them, and then getting back to my client took up several hours of the day yesterday.

Q: How many calls did that involve, do you have a sense? A dozen?

A: Six, seven, eight—somewhere in that range. It was several calls...

Q: Did you settle that case yesterday?

A: Not quite. We are awfully close now. We are in the range now that I think it can be done, and we will work that one out. And there were two other calls, two other claims representatives...

Q: Different cases.

A: Different cases. I am working on settlements there. I recall sitting down with my associate yesterday and reviewing two P.I. cases that he has. I was trying to give him an idea of what would be a reasonable demand range, a reasonable settlement range, and a reasonable jury range if we were to go to trial on those cases. They are coming up to trial rather quickly. In addition I did some things on a couple of worker's comp. cases. I worked on compromise agreements for them, and got one compromise agreement done. I am preparing the actual formal compromise agreement for that case. On another one I prepared a proposal to try and work toward a settlement on a compromise agreement.

Q: On a worker's comp.?

A: On a worker's comp. as well. And another case I got out the request for attorney's fees from the Social Security Administration.

Q: Did you have any calls from new clients yesterday? Potential new clients?

A: In the personal injury field?

Q: Or worker's comp. or Social Security, any of the contingent fee fields?

A: None of those three.

Q: What other kinds of matters did you work on yesterday? You said you did some family cases yesterday.

A: Yes, because I had a hearing today that took the morning, so I was doing a lot of work on that. And I had some people come in, we are working on a final Marital Settlement Agreement to dispose of some remaining issues. I took care of that, and worked on several Marital Settlement Agreements; actually I did three of those yesterday.

Q: Three different cases?

A: Three different cases.

Q: How many different matters would you say, total, both contingent fee and otherwise, did you touch yesterday?

A: Different number of cases?

Q: Yes.

A: At least fifteen.

Q: Fairly typical?

A: Pretty typical. I usually work a ten or eleven hour day. I am usually here at 7:00 A.M. and I leave at 6:00, and I don't take lunch.

Again, I should emphasize that this is one of the better answers I was able to obtain. Perhaps that was in part due to the respondent's referring to his calendar as a means of refreshing his memory. Yet, while the interview response is not inconsistent with the kind of flow reflected in the field notes, it gives none of the sense of continuity and discontinuity that comes out of the observation. It is certainly possible that a more skillful interviewer than I could have gotten more detail from the respondent, but I doubt whether that would have moved the information that much closer to the depth obtained from the observation.

II. IMPLICATIONS

Few experienced researchers (and probably no anthropologists) will be surprised at the differences I described above. The fact that you will see more detail than you will be able to get an interview respondent to describe seems virtually self-evident. There are, of course, some things that interviews may tap more directly than will observation, particularly things related to expressions of motivation. However, for understanding the nature of a social or political or legal process, nothing is ultimately going to replace actually seeing the process in operation. But, beyond the accuracy of description, do the differences between interview data and observational data really matter?

The best answer to this question must come from a comparison of analyses of data based exclusively on interviews and data based on observation (usually supplemented by interviews with those observed). To do this, one needs matching pairs of studies that look at more or less the same phenomenon using

23

the two different methodologies. I have identified three such pairs of studies, all of which involve lawyer/client relationships:

Divorce: A number of researchers have studied the relationship between lawyers and clients in the context of divorce. Drawing on their extensive observation of divorce lawyers interacting with their clients, Felstiner and Sarat find a great deal of ambiguity in the power relationship, with issues of dominance and control constantly in flux and subject to implicit renegotiation (1992:1495-98; see also, Sarat and Felstiner 1995). In contrast, Mather et al. (2001), who conducted extensive interviews with divorce lawyers, found that the lawyers reported that they largely controlled the direction of their cases, and on the best way to handle them. The researchers found that lawyers report trying to avoid taking cases where the client will insist on things that they lawyer views as unrealistic or undesirable. The researchers use the metaphor of passenger and driver, arguing that the driver (the lawyer) largely determines both the destination and the route to that destination, with the passenger (the client) at best being allowed to do a little backseat driving (Mather et al. 1995).

Corporate Practice: Drawing on 18 months of ethnographic field work in an 80 lawyer corporate law firm in Chicago, Flood finds that corporate lawyers vary in their degree of responsiveness to their clients (i.e., how willing they are to simply execute their clients' instructions). The lawyers are most responsive to those clients who are seen as having substantial long-term fee potential; a key element of this finding is the variation among clients, even for a corporate law firm (Flood 2013:156-58). In contrast, Nelson finds that lawyers in the four corporate law firms (also in Chicago) where he conducted extensive interviews report their clients largely call the shots; there is no sense of any type of systematic variation in how the lawyers in the four firms studied differentiated among clients (see also Heinz 1983; 1988:250-59).[6]

Personal Injury Plaintiffs' (Contingency Fee) Practice: Drawing upon my observational work, I found that contingency fee practitioners are attentive to the interests of their clients, in significant part because the lawyers rely heavily on satisfied clients as sources of future clients (Kritzer 2004b:62-63). In contrast, two interview-based studies, Hunting and Neuwirth (1962:107-09) and Rosenthal (1974:95-116), found that personal injury clients had little say in the settlement of their claims, although Rosenthal found that lawyers were more responsive to active clients.[7]

In all three of the pairs of studies, the interview-based research presented a clear-cut, relatively unambiguous image of lawyer/client control in the settings studied. The images involved can be readily explained in theoretical terms, which leave the authors confident about their analyses. In contrast, the observa-

---

[6] Nelson is quite sensitive to the softness of his information on lawyer-client relations given that it was based entirely on the reports of his lawyer-respondents. The limitation here is the method of semi-structured interviews, and many users of the method recognize its inherent limitations.

[7] It is worth noting that Rosenthal had originally wanted to do an observational study, but did not succeed in obtaining the needed access (Rosenthal 1974:179-80); he was able to conduct interviews with both lawyers and clients.

tional studies present more nuanced images which tend to contradict the more straightforward results of the interview-based analyses. It is possible that these differences reflect actual differences in patterns in the behaviors studied; I have no way of ruling out this possibility.

However, my experience doing both the observation and the interviews lead me to the conclusion that the differences arise, at least in part, from the nature of the data each method produces. Reviewing the kinds of questions I asked, and the answers I obtained, that relate to client control, I easily see that I could have been led to the conclusion that the lawyers have many tools of control and use them in ways that work against their clients' interests. However, the observation made clear the ways in which the lawyers work hard to satisfy their clients. For example, in the case of Bob Strong described in the observational notes, Alex Stein could readily have decided to try to settle it quickly by sharply reducing his demand. Instead, his approach was to keep his higher offer on the table and let the adjuster make the first move. During the observation, the lawyers I spent time with generally pursued this strategy rather than simply looking for the quickest way out of the case (which is what the interview research on personal injury practitioners tends to emphasize). The reason for this is not that the lawyers are altruistic professionals (although this has some role), but that the lawyers recognize their own long-term self-interest as being served by producing satisfied clients who stay satisfied *and who consequently refer friends and acquaintances in need of legal representation to the lawyers*; the lawyers do not want clients to go away and later realize that their lawyer sold them short in the settlement process (see Kritzer 2004b:67).

This became clear only during the observation as I watched the lawyers interact with their clients and with potential clients. I saw one lawyer repeatedly spend significant time talking to persons about cases which the lawyer had quickly realized was not something he was interested in. This was not productive time for him in the sense of generating a fee but it was extremely important in attracting future clients. I saw another lawyer take much more time with potential clients referred by prior clients, and even take one case he had doubts about because it had been referred by a prior client; his goal was to do whatever he could to encourage former clients to make referrals and he believed that once a client had made such a referral paying particular attention to those referrals was a way of encouraging the former client to make future referrals. A third example was one lawyer's "exit" process after a case was resolved: the lawyer would hand the client the check, and his business card, and say to the client something like, "Hopefully, you won't need me again. ... If you know anyone who does [need me], please send them in."

It is hard for me to see how I might have designed interview questions that would have turned up these kinds of patterns unless I had anticipated them in advance. In the interviews, the preconceptions of the researcher will determine the questions, and if the literature says that lawyers tend to dominate their contingency fee (or divorce) clients, the questions are likely to be framed in ways the produce responses consistent with that literature. While the observer does not enter the observational setting as a *tabula rasa*, what he or she sees will inevitably differ in important ways from initial expectations. While the observer may fail to see some things because of various preconceptions, he or she will discover more that is unexpected than will the typical interviewer who imposes more structure on the data collection process.

Writing on the limitations of interviews focuses on a combination of the problem of communication—the difficulty respondents have in understanding questions, the difficulty interviewers have in understanding answers, and the impact of cultural norms vis-à-vis interpersonal communication more generally (see Briggs 1986), and the problem of bias and social desirability—responses reflecting what the respondents want the interviewer to think about the respondent rather than providing the information solicited by the interviewer. That is, "the products of an interview are the outcome of a socially situated activity where the responses are passed through the role-playing and impression management of both the interviewer and the respondent" (Dingwall 1997:56, citing Cicourel 1964; see also Melia 1997). The point of this essay is somewhat different: interviews by their nature get only the information the interviewer solicits (with some relatively rare exceptions), and then only in a highly edited or abbreviated form (see Dingwall 1997:59; see generally Garfinkel 1967). The most skillful interviewers can mitigate this problem to a limited degree, but the difference between what can be seen during observation versus what can be heard during an interview will remain large. Of course, observation does not allow the seeing of what is unseeable, and an interview can bring out to some degree the inner views, thoughts, and feelings of participants that the observer will typically not see. However, many types of observational settings do allow the watcher to ask question that provide some of that which is unseeable.

The implications of this for socio-legal studies (and other empirical social science research) are obvious. We must be constantly aware of the strengths and weaknesses of the data that we employ. Qualitative researchers often criticize quantitative researchers for relying upon data that are overly structured by the researcher. Yet, the largest portion of qualitative research relies upon interviews which involve very much the same type of structuring. Dingwall puts the problem very neatly when he notes that "interviewers [regardless of whether the interview is structured, semi-structured, or unstructured] *construct* data, observers *find* it [emphasis in original]" (1997:60); "in an interview study, we can pick and choose the messages we hear and that we elicit, [while] in observation we have no choice but to listen to what the world is telling us" (*ibid.*, 64). This does not mean that the researcher sees everything or that the researcher does not see selectively, but rather that the nature of the constraints imposed by the researcher differ markedly depending upon the data collection strategy employed.

3

TOWARD A THEORY OF CRAFT[1]

INTRODUCTION

The work of lawyers is highly varied. It can involve criminal matters, corporate matters, regulatory issues or private disputes of various types. Some lawyers handle a wide range of types of matters although increasingly lawyers have tended to specialize (Heinz et al. 2005:30-38). Lawyers work in a wide range of settings, from firms with literally thousands of lawyers to solo practices to government and corporate offices. While law school provides the foundation for persons to enter the legal profession, the actual practice of law is something that is ultimately learned by doing. This continues to be true even as law schools increase their efforts to provide skills training. Essentially, during the early years of practice, the new lawyer learns the *craft* of practice. That is, legal practice is in reality a kind of craft, albeit one that involves working with one's head rather than one's hands. This chapter seeks to theorize the concept of "craft," or alternatively "craftwork," and then goes one to examine how such a theorization suggests questions for the empirical study of lawyers and their work?

The first question one must ask is, what is "craft"? We regularly speak of craft in a wide variety of contexts. My search of a major university library catalog in 2014 for books with titles starting with the phrase, "The Craft of ..." yielded 122 unique entries (i.e., excluding duplicates for books that went through multiple editions). The titles of the books ranged from *The Craft of Argument* to *The Craft of Wood Carving*. The item most relevant to craft vis-à-vis lawyers is *The Craft of Justice*, a study of the key actors in the criminal courts: prosecutors, defense lawyers, and judges. This book does not conceptualize craft but it does offer a definition: "Craft is practical knowledge of how others perform their work and of the relationships involved in this work. It combines personal experiences with the lessons learned by others so that legal practitioners can organize their work and manage their relations" (Flemming et al. 1992:195). Unfortunately, this only suggests that craft is how someone does

---

[1] This is a substantial revision of an article originally appearing in *Social & Legal Studies* 16 (2007), 321-40, as part of a symposium on "judgecraft"; the revision shifted the focus from judgecraft to the craft of legal practice. I would like to thank Richard Moorhead, David Cowan, Carrie Menkel-Meadow, and two anonymous reviewers for their comments on an earlier draft of the original version of this chapter; I would also like to thank Cyrus Tata for inviting me to present that original version article at the University of Stratheclyde, and his colleagues who attended that presentation and provided me with a variety of useful comments.

his or her job, and how doing that job involves the use of practical knowledge and prior experience. We need a conceptualization of craft that has some theoretical richness.

I. TOWARD A CONCEPT OF CRAFT

I did my graduate study at the University of North Carolina in the early 1970s. About 60 miles from Chapel Hill there is an area that has been the home of indigenous potters since the 18th century. These were for most of their existence "production" potteries where basic set pieces were "turned" on the wheel and finished with interesting glazes. For most of the pieces produced, the emphasis was on functionality; these were pieces of pottery that were to be used in ordinary daily life.

Starting around 1970 potters not native to the local area began to locate in this region of North Carolina. Many of these young potters had trained in university-based art departments. For these potters, there was a greater emphasis on decoration, and they saw their work less as producing utilitarian objects to be used day-to-day, and more as creating pieces that would be displayed as decoration or art. What is it that distinguishes the craftsperson from the artist, and what does that begin to tell us about "craft" as a concept?

Howard Becker (1978:864) provides a useful discussion of the distinction between art and craft. Central to Becker's discussion is the transition between art and craft, and how that transition informs the conceptual distinction between the two. Becker starts with what he calls the "folk" definition of a craft: "[A] body of knowledge and skill which can be used to produce useful objects: dishes one can eat from, chairs one can sit in, cloth that makes serviceable clothing, plumbing that works, electrical wiring that carries current."

Importantly, Becker does not limit the notion of craft to the production of objects: "From a slightly different point of view, [craft] consists of the ability to perform in a useful way: to play music that can be danced to; serve a meal to guests efficiently; arrest a criminal with a minimum fuss; clean a house to the satisfaction of those who live in it" (p. 864). Becker identifies two key elements in this definition: the fact that knowledge and skill are used to produce a product or service that is *useful* and the fact that the work is done for or on behalf of *someone else* to fulfill that person's need for a useful object or service.

However, more is needed to label something a craft. According to Becker (1978:865), in addition to function and the end user,

> [C]raftsmen accept a[n] ... aesthetic standard: virtuoso skill. Most crafts are quite difficult, with many years required to master the phys-ical skills and mental disciplines of a first-class practitioner. One who has mastered the skills—an expert—has great control over the craft's materials, can do anything with them, can work with speed and agili-ty, can do with ease things that ordinary, less expert craftsmen find difficult or impossible. ... The specific object of virtuosity varies from field to field, but it always involves an extraordinary control of mate-rials and techniques. Sometimes virtuosity also includes mastering a wide variety of techniques, being able not only to do things better than most others but also to do more things. Virtuoso craftsmen take

pride in their skill and are honored for it in the craft and sometimes by outsiders.

The aesthetic inherent in craftwork provides an important standard by which one craftsperson can assess the work of another. Importantly, while the layperson may be able to recognize differences in quality among producers, it often takes a practicing craftsperson to be able to identify what it is that distinguishes a first-rate job/product from an adequate or typical job/product.

Becker (1978:866) applies the notion of "beauty" as a criterion for assessing craft activities, and goes on to distinguish between "ordinary" craftspersons and the "artist" craftsperson. The key distinction between the two groups is the importance of the aesthetic element, the concern about "beauty." The ordinary craftsperson wants to see that a job is well done, and the desired function is achieved; however, the ordinary craftsperson may not be concerned about whether the result is beautiful, or as a possible alternative concept, "elegant" (p. 866). The artist-craftsperson, in Becker's analysis, is still concerned about functionality and usefulness, but seeks to achieve a standard that goes beyond achieving those goals. In Becker's analysis, the artist-craftsperson produces work that has "some claim to be considered 'art' by the custodians of conventional art—collectors, curators, and gallery owners." The nexus between the artist-craftsperson and the end user is weaker in Becker's analysis, and the artist-craftsperson looks beyond the end user (and other craftspersons) for recognition of his/her work.

However, one can imagine a somewhat milder distinction among craftspersons which moves beyond the end-user (or customer/client) but not all the way to the "custodians of conventional art." Imagine a tiler installing a new ceramic floor in your kitchen. The ordinary craftsperson will want to be sure that the job is done right: that the underlayment is properly installed, that the tiles are lined up in precise lines, that the grouting is evenly colored and applied properly, that any cut tiles look right, that the proper capping tiles are used, and so on. The resulting floor will be functional and attractive. The artist-craftsperson will go at least one step further, and want the result to be more than functional and attractive. The artist-craftsperson will seek out touches that will make the resulting floor beautiful or elegant. This may involve suggesting something more than a simple square tile, perhaps a pattern of tile of some sort or including some distinctive tiles intermixed to produce a more elegant result. The floor will still be intended as something to be walked on and used in everyday life, but the discerning observer will notice that there is something special here, something more than just a good, solid floor. That is, there is an audience beyond the customer/client; someone coming into a kitchen and seeing this tile work will more likely take note and comment on its beauty or elegance.

In Becker's (1978:867) analysis, the larger distinction comes when the craft becomes art or, in his words, "art invades craft." Key here is that artists turn to the medium of the craftsperson to produce artistic expression, although one can imagine craftspersons moving themselves into the art world. The goal is now the expression of the creator, whether we label the creator artist or craftsperson. Usefulness or functionality is secondary, if it is important at all. While a piece of work may be created as a "commission," choice lies primarily in the hands of the creator rather than working to specification (beyond perhaps the most general statement of where the piece of work will be placed or what it might be placed with). The audience is the world of art, not the world of use. Becker gives the example of a group of artists gaining control of a ceramics department in an art school and insisting that no "high-fire" pottery be made in the department; high firing is necessary to insure that clay objects be useful for household purposes (holding water, withstanding daily use, etc.).

Interestingly, along with the devaluation of utility, the artist working in what is traditionally viewed as a craft may devalue the "old craft standards of skill" (Becker 1978:867). Work that a craftsperson might see as "sloppy" becomes elevated to art. Where the craftsperson values the ability to produce objects repeatedly, the artist focuses on the uniqueness of each object; the craft skill to turn on the potter's wheel a set of matching bowls as part of a dinner service is not important to the artist because the artist has no interest in producing something as functional as a dinner service. For the artist, it is better that no two objects be alike because art generally does not involve duplication but creation.

II. DIMENSIONS OF CRAFTWORK

From this discussion, we can distill the central elements of a usable concept of "craft," or perhaps better, "craftwork." By "craftwork" I mean the nature of the work that is done within the context of a craft. In identifying this series of elements, my goal is to describe a set of factors that are applicable to a wide range of work rather than to specify elements that are specific to legal practice. In the following section, I then seek to briefly apply these dimensions to the work of lawyers.[2]

A. CRAFTWORK PRODUCES SOMETHING THAT HAS UTILITY

As discussed earlier, the product of craftwork is something that others value for its utility. The traditional craftsperson produced something tangible such as a piece of clothing or a door. However, we do not need to limit craftwork to the production of objects; it can also include the production of a service ranging from serving a meal to performing a complex medical procedure or presenting an opening or closing argument to a jury.

B. CRAFTWORK HAS AN IDENTIFIABLE CUSTOMER OR CLIENTELE

The work is done on behalf of the customer or clientele. Craftwork is typically done to two levels of specification. One level is set by the customer or client and the other level is set by the norms of the craft. The client may recognize the absence of some aspects of the internal norms but will probably miss the more subtle aspects of it.

---

[2] See the original published version of this chapter for my application of the dimensions to the work of judges, or "judgecraft."

C. CRAFTWORK INVOLVES PRODUCING A CONSISTENT PRODUCT

As noted previously, craftwork involves producing objects repeatedly in contrast to the work of an artist who focuses on the uniqueness of each object. Thus, the product of craftwork has the characteristic of consistency. That consistency could range from the ability to fashion a set of matching dinnerware on a potter's wheel to producing a delectable chocolate soufflé in a restaurant kitchen.

D. CRAFTWORK INVOLVES AN INTERNAL AESTHETIC

While laypersons can draw broad distinctions among the products of craftsperson, the core aesthetic of the craft is internal to the craft community. There are important yet subtle distinctions that few outside the community can see or recognize. The members of the craft community appreciate what to the layperson would be "little things" that do not affect the functionality of the product or service provided by the craftsperson. Thus, if one is looking at a piece of homemade clothing and comparing it to a piece of handmade clothing produced by a skilled seamstress or tailor, the layperson is not likely to notice how precise the stitching is or whether a particular technique had been used in part of the construction of the garment. The trained tailor or seamstress, on the other hand, will notice these things and recognize the difference between a garment made by a "pro" and one made a layperson.

One can also see this idea of internal aesthetic in areas where the product is "intangible." Take the following statement by a professional musician I know:

> Playing music for a living, it is easy to take for granted what we do. We find ourselves watching the clock on gigs, and complaining on our breaks of being underpaid and overworked. In private, we joke about the clueless audience members who come up to the stage and rave about our performance — "You guys are the best band I've ever heard!"; "How do you get that sound?!" or, "Y'all bad!" We laugh at them because we obsess over the quality of our individual performance, and thus we only think about how much better we *could* have played.

Thus, while the consumer of a craftsperson's work makes judgments about the quality of that work, for the craftsperson the more important assessment comes from norms developed within the community of craftspeople. What may seem excellent to the consumer may not be seen in such a light by the craftsperson or other members of the craft community.

Craftspersons regularly go well beyond what is necessary to accomplish a given task. Frequently this may involve aspects that come to resemble a ritual in that it is done not because it is a necessary part of the work but because it serves an internalized function that the craftsperson finds satisfying or useful. An example for a musician may be tuning and retuning an instrument well beyond anything anyone would recognize as being out of tune. Hughes (1971:322) observes that the amount of ritual varies among occupations, with it being strongly developed in those where there "are great unavoidable risks" such as medicine. However, as the musician example above illustrates, ritual is not limited to situations of risk. There is of course the question of where ritual ends and superstition begins.

E. CRAFTWORK INVOLVES AN IDENTIFIABLE SET OF SKILLS AND TECHNIQUES

Each area of craftwork is defined by a set of skills and techniques. Some of this involves "knowledge" which can be systematized and conveyed through written or verbal instruction. For example, for a tailor or seamstress, there are a variety of types of stitches that can be used, some appropriate in limited situations and others appropriate in large numbers of situations.

While there may be innate talents or abilities, the true skill of craft is specialized in nature and comes only with time and practice, typically obtained under the tutelage of a person who has previously mastered the craft. The specialized skills required for many areas of craftwork are usually learned through some type of training process. However, even where there is a natural talent, the development of the talent to the level of craft typically involves some form of training. Thus, one would distinguish between the untrained singer who can pick up a tune by ear versus the trained singer who can read the music and quickly grasp the style of a piece; or, the difference between the "natural" actor versus someone who has had systematic training in performance. The traditional mode or training is that of apprenticeship: the apprentice cabinet maker, the apprentice potter and so on. However, the training need not involve a formal apprenticeship; it can be in the form of more formal teaching if that teaching focuses heavily toward "hands on" work by the pupil.[3]

The level of skill involved in craftwork is such that a significant amount of what the accomplished craftsperson does cannot readily be described by that craftsperson. The person simply does it and does not think about it. Can the master potter tell the novice what it is that she does to produce a pot with extremely thin walls? Can the master carpenter explain how he knows the precise way to position a door frame for proper alignment? Can the skilled lawyer tell the young associate precisely what she did that wowed the jury in the summation of a case?

Atul Gawande (2002:21-22) describes his experience as a surgical resident learning how to place a "central line" which involves inserting a small catheter through the chest to provide direct nourishment and/or medication. His first couple of times doing this ended in failure, with the task being taken over by a more senior resident. On the third occasion, he successfully carried out the procedure, and then observed,

> I still have no idea what I did differently that day. But from then on, my lines went in. Practice is funny that way. For days and days, you make out only the fragments of what to do. And then one day you've got the whole thing. Conscious learning becomes unconscious

---

[3] I have taught quantitative, statistical analysis for forty years; in that teaching, I continually emphasize that the only way students will come to understand both how to do and how to understand quantitative work is by actually doing it, and ideally doing a lot of it.

knowledge, and you cannot say precisely how. ... When everything goes perfectly ... you don't think. You don't concentrate. Every move unfolds effortlessly. You take the needle. You stick the chest. You feel the needle travel — a distinct glide through the fat, a slight catch in the dense muscle, and then the subtle pop through the vein wall — and you're in. At such moments, it is more than easy; it is beautiful.

This quote illustrates that at least some aspects of craftwork become "automatic" in that the craftsperson simply does them without thinking about them.[4] Certainly some aspects remain conscious. In the case of the surgeon, this includes such things as checking that instruments are available, proper sterilization, and so on. However, other aspects are not conscious, because while carrying out the work, the craftsperson does not think explicitly about all the steps; she or he simply does many of them.

F. CRAFTWORK INVOLVES SIGNIFICANT PROBLEM SOLVING

While craftwork is often repetitive, it also regularly involves unanticipated problem solving. Something does not work as expected, or something goes wrong, and the craftsperson has to make adjustments on the fly. For a musician or actor this might involve a missed cue. For a lawyer, it could involve an unexpected answer during questioning of a witness. For a nurse, it could be a failure of a patient to respond as expected to some aspect of treatment. The craftsperson needs to be able to improvise in ways that both serve the ultimate goal and which draw upon the craftsperson's skill and experience.

Drawing the line between the very routine and craft can be tricky. A key element here comes in terms of the possibility of having to deviate from the routine. In the factory setting, a worker might encounter a defective part in something he or she is assembling; however, all that is necessary is to discard the defective part and get a replacement. In contrast, in craftwork the deviations from the routine are more challenging even when the emphasis is on routinization. Gawande (2002:38-41) describes a medical clinic, Shouldice Hospital in Toronto, which specializes in hernia repair:

In most hospitals [a hernia repair] takes about ninety minutes and might cost upward of four thousand dollars. In anywhere from 10 to 15 percent of cases, the operation eventually fails and the hernia returns. ... At Shouldice, hernia operations often take from thirty to forty-five minutes. Their recurrence rate is an astonishing 1 percent. And the cost of an operation is about half of what it is elsewhere.

This clinic has an exceptionally high success rate because the staff does nothing but hernia repairs. Each surgeon repairs between 600 and 800 hernias a year. With this level of experience, the surgeons at the clinic still encounter complications, but very seldom are the complications so novel that significant conscious thought is needed to come up with a work-around.

---

4 Compare this to "know how is in the action" (Schön 1983:50) or to Michael Polyani's phrase, "tacit knowing": in Polyani's phrase, we attend from its impact on our hand to its effect on the things to which we are applying it (quoted in Schön 1983:52).

Table 3.1: Elements of Craftwork

	External	Internal
Production	Consistency	Skills and Techniques
Functionality	Utility	Problem Solving
Evaluation	Clientele	Aesthetic

G. SUMMARY

This discussion identified a set of six factors that combine to distinguish craftwork from other kinds of activities, either work that falls below "craft" such as the kind of production that occurs in a factory setting where each worker does a very narrow range of repetitive tasks, or that which achieves the status of "art." The six factors can be grouped into two dimensions, those that are external to the craftsperson by their focus on the product and/or the client and those that are internal to the craftsperson by their focus on the producer. The former include utility, clientele, and consistency while the latter include aesthetics, skills and techniques, and problem solving. We can further organize the six factors to produce a two-dimensional table as shown in Table 3.1. The distinction between craft and non-craft production turns primarily on the three internal factors while the distinction between craft and art turns primarily the external factors.

III. CRAFTWORK IN PROFESSIONAL OCCUPATIONS

Central to the analysis above is the idea that craft is linked to the nature of work that is performed. There are a number of sociological perspectives on professions, ranging from the functionalist work of Talcott Parsons (1954a) to the relational work of Eliot Freidson (1986; 2001), Terence Johnson (1972), and Andrew Abbott (1988), to the economic analysis of Magali Larson (1977) and the relatively recent work linking professions and gender (Witz 1992). Most of these perspectives focus on the relationship of the professional to society and/or to the professional's clientele. Despite the recognition that the world in which professionals go about their work has changed and is continuing to change,[5] there is surprisingly little research focused on the actual *work* of the professional, particularly since a profession is an occupation, and in that regard, "consists

---

[5] One major theme regarding this change, recognized in the 1970s, is what is variously labeled "deprofessionalization" or "deskilling" (see Haug 1973; Toren 1975). While some authors have linked this specifically to the entrance of women into a number of professions which were traditionally male preserves (see Sommerlad and Sanderson 1998), I have elsewhere cast the issue as "postprofessionalism" (Kritzer 1999 [see Chapter 14 in this volume]), which I see as tied in significant part to changing technology that is doing for professional work what the factory did for traditional craftwork. Closely related to this is the fact that professional work is increasingly being carried out in the context of bureaucratic structures that are not entirely unlike a modern factory setting. In the context of legal practice Nelson et al. (2005) have described this shift as one from professional dominance to organizational dominance.

of a bundle of several tasks ... [not all of which] require the same degree of skill ... [and not all of which] have the same prestige" (Hughes 1971:313).

A. THE SURGEON AS CRAFTSPERSON

Consider Gwande's (2002:39-40) description of one of the surgeons at Shouldice Hospital as the surgeon did a hernia repair:

> Though we chatted during the entire operation, Dr. Sang performed each step without pause, almost absently, with the assistant knowing precisely which tissues to retract, and the nurse handling over exactly the right instruments; instructions were completely unnecessary. ... Dr. Sang injected the skin with a local anesthetic in a diagonal line. ... With a No. 10 blade, he made a four-inch slash along this line in a single downstroke. ... Sang swiftly cut down through the outer muscle layer of the abdominal wall, exposing the spermatic cord ... Sang slowed down for a moment, checking meticulously for another hernia, along the area where the cord came through the inner abdominal wall. Sure enough, he found a small, second hernia there—one that, if it had been missed, would almost certainly have caused a recurrence. He then sliced open the remaining muscle layers beneath the cord, so that the abdominal wall was completely open, and pushed the bulging abdominal contents back inside. ... He sewed the wall back together in three separate muscle layers, using fine wire, making sure that the edge of each layer overlapped like a double-breasted suit. After Sang closed the patient's skin with small clips and removed the [sterile] drapes, the patient swung his legs over the edge of the table, stood up, and walked out of the room. The procedure had taken just half an hour.

From this account it should not be surprising that Gawande refers to Shouldice Hospital as the "hernia factory." There is a striking similarity to the "production" handcraft pottery which can turn out one piece after another that are to the same design, or to Amish furniture makers who produce the same table, by hand, again and again and again.

B. "PROFESSIONALISM" AND CRAFT

One hears the term "professionalism" used in the context of a wide range of occupations, both those that we commonly label as "professions" (medicine, law, teaching, social work, etc.) and those that we do not (cook or waiter in a restaurant,[6] truck driver, plumber, secretary). One can see the terms professional and professionalism as distinguishing amateur from amateurism. The first pair of terms, professional and amateur, distinguishes between someone who engages in an activity for the pleasure of it rather than the money (i.e., a musician who plays simply for the love of music rather than as a means of earning a livelihood). The contrast can also be used in reference to the quality of the work performed. This is the more common usage in reference to the second

---

[6] See Bruni (2005) for the nature of the craft and professionalism involved in the work of waitstaff in better restaurants.

pair of terms, professionalism and amateurism, with the former denoting a commitment to quality and care, with the latter often used in a derogatory manner ("amateurish") to reflect on both the skill and the result produced by the non-professional.

Used in this way, the term professionalism is closely linked to craft. Specifically, when we speak of someone completing a task in a "professional" manner, or when someone speaks of being professional about how she does her work, the reference is to a commitment to standards that are associated with the particular work or task. That is, the word professionalism is used to convey something about how well the worker performs his or her job, not about the position of the occupational group as a whole on a continuum of professionalism. The nature of those standards will typically be similar to the kinds of elements, both external (consistency, utility, and clientele) and internal (skills and techniques, problem solving, and aesthetic), that I associate with craftwork.

"Professional work," as distinct from either work carried out in a "professional manner" or the worker's status as a professional rather than an amateur, has some special features that differentiate it from the work of occupations not falling within what those sociologists would label as one of the professions. A central distinguishing feature of professional work in this sense is the nature of the knowledge involved. Schön (1983:30) describes the dominant model of professional *knowledge* as "the application of scientific theory and technique to the instrumental problems of practice." This suggests that what makes work "professional" is that it involves using knowledge that is based on "science." Schön defines science broadly such that it includes law, reflecting a view that law is based in the same general ideology of "technical rationality" as is areas such as medicine (pp. 28-30).

However, as I have elsewhere argued in my own research on lawyers' work in litigation (Kritzer 1990) and on legal advocacy (Kritzer 1998b), the work of lawyers and legal advocacy more generally involves expertise and activities that go well beyond the "formal" knowledge and activities associated with science-like training. In the earlier of that work (Kritzer 1990; see Table 1.1 in this volume), I distinguish between what I have labeled formal legal activities (the kinds of things imparted by formal legal training) and informal legal activities (the kinds of things that are learned by doing litigation and have more of an 'insider' nature). My later work (Kritzer 1998b; see also Chapter 1 in this volume) refined the dimensions of expertise into: (a) formal training vs. insider knowledge; (b) generalist vs. specialist; (c) substantive vs. process. These kinds of distinctions are useful in beginning to think about the skills and tasks involved in professional work more generally, and how those might be recast into the idea of craftwork.[7]

---

[7] There is at least one article that develops a "craft perspective" and applies it to a professional setting: specialist social workers (Eisikovits and Beker 2001). The authors of that study arrayed their analysis along two dimensions, one of which I would label inputs (techniques, social arrangements, and habits of mind) and the other I would label outputs (sustained effort, product, practical product, and durable product). There is some overlap with the dimensions I define, but there are also some major differences.

Consider another example from the world of medicine: the practitioner who sees lots of ill children. Here is someone who has had a lot of formal training and a lot of on-the-job training. The work involves both diagnosing and treating the child *and* interacting with the parent (more often than not the mother) who brings the child in to see the physician. Over the years, I have known a number of young physicians who began their practice before they themselves had any children. Without exception, they have told me that their understanding of parental concern and how to deal with the parents (particularly interpreting the parents' reports of their children's condition and symptoms) changed significantly after they had their own children and had experienced being on the parental side of the diagnostic relationship. What this example brings home is that the "craft of pediatrics" involves both technical skills and interpersonal skills, particularly interpersonal skills involving persons other than the patient. It involves what Bensman and Lilienfeld (1991:iv) have labeled "habits of mind."

The interest here, however, is not medicine, it is the workaday world of lawyers. Take the following passage from an interview I conducted with a lawyer as part of a study of how lawyers deal with scientific and expert testimony in light of U.S. Supreme Court rulings on the standards courts should apply in deciding whether to admit such testimony (e.g., *Daubert v. Merrill Dow* [1993]). In the course of the interview the lawyer described how he went about defending a challenge to one of his side's experts:

> Having thought about bringing these motions with some regularity over the span of 11 years, and never having brought one, I felt pretty confident that our opponents had acted in one of the many situations that we routinely consider and reject. The federal judge involved has been on the bench quite a while. He's a very good lawyer. He's a good writer. And he's had his turns through the court of appeals, and he has left behind a written legacy. And I was able to, not only argue from the theory of *Daubert* and [Federal Rules of Evidence] Rule 702, I was able to take what the expert actually had opined, show what the method was that he had applied to the facts of the case, and the conclusions he's reached, and then reach into this judge's rich written, published record—*the case law of the judge*—and find similar cases where he had permitted just this kind of testimony. ... There would have been no opportunity to endorse our expert in front of the judge that way had they not filed that motion. The judge rejected it, almost of out of hand, at a pretrial hearing. ... It was our opportunity to take an awkward situation and make our man shine.

Here the lawyer relies upon knowledge about the judge's own prior views, what the lawyer called "the case law of the judge," to frame his argument about why his expert's testimony should not be limited or excluded. Moreover, he drew upon his experience thinking about when he would or would not challenge an expert from an opposing side. Interestingly, this lawyer had never actually challenged an opposing expert because, as he put it,

> [W]hen the expert really sucks, that's a gift from heaven. And [we] think long and hard before we deprive our client of the opportunity to show a jury how half-baked the opposing expert is on an important

issue in the case by taking it away from the jury. ... It's counter-intuitive: the worse their expert is, could be the better for us.

What the above example shows is a kind of problem solving that demonstrates what I would describe as a high level of craftwork. It shows a kind of *subtle* expertise about the litigation process that goes well beyond the mechanics of the process.[8]

IV. THE CRAFT OF LAWYERING

Does the theorization of craft, or more specifically craftwork, have any utility for the analysis of lawyering? Does it serve to identify questions and issues that are significant for understanding the work that lawyers do? Here I assess that potential by very briefly looking at each of the six dimensions: consistency, utility, clientele, skills and techniques, problem solving, and aesthetic.

A. CONSISTENCY

The ability to produce consistent products that yield consistent outcomes is a central aspect of the work of a lawyer in private practice. Achieving consistent results is important for two reasons. For those who are responsible for generating and retaining clients, consistent results are what clients and potential clients are looking for. This does not necessarily mean that a lawyer has to win every case given that lawyers may be given a losing hand in some, perhaps even many, cases or matters, or may confront a decision maker who is not sympathetic to the case the lawyer must present; nonetheless, clients do not want to retain lawyers who do not have a record of consistently providing good service and good results. Business clients who have repeat business will be in a better position to assess consistency than will be one-shot individual clients, although both types of clients can seek out information about a lawyer's or law firm's reputation for getting good results. For junior lawyers in the roll of an associate or an employee in a private law firm, consistency in the quality of the that lawyer's work product will be one factor that senior members of the firm will consider in making decisions on partnerships or other forms of long-term employment.

Consistency will also be important for lawyers in other types of employed settings: in-house, prosecutors, public defenders, and other types of government positions. In many such settings the lawyer's work is driven by organizational policies and maintaining consistency with those policies is important for the success of both the individual and the organization. Thus, from the individual practitioner's perspective, opportunities for advancement in those settings will turn on experience and consistent performance. Such performance may also create opportunities for the individual beyond the organizational setting where the person is currently employed.

---

[8] See Blasi (1995) for an extended discussion of the role of problem solving in legal practice. While Blasi does not specifically use the term craft in his discussion, what he describes closely aligns with the earlier discussion.

B. Utility

It would seem hardly necessary to ask whether lawyering has utility, although there are the inevitable comments about lawyers making things more rather than less difficult. Clearly experts in law are a necessary part of any political or social system that prides itself on the rule of law.

C. Clientele

Clients are central to what lawyers do. Without clients most lawyers would be out of business.[9] There can be questions as to who *is* the client. For example is management or the shareholders the clients of lawyers working within or on behalf of a corporation? Is the client of a government lawyer the official who hires the lawyer (or within whose domain the lawyer works), the senior officials appointed by someone holding elective office, or the people who elected the governmental leaders? When one party hires a lawyer on behalf of another party and the former is paying the lawyer's bill, as is commonly the case for insurance defense lawyers, is the hiring party a client or is only the person who has the legal problem that lawyer is hired to deal with the client (see Silver and Syverud 1995:273-80; Kritzer 2012)? There are certain situations where one can ask whether there actually *is* a client? One such situation arises in some class actions, perhaps most commonly in securities class actions, where it is effectively the lawyers who initiate and control the case (Hensler et al. 1999:71-72); a second situation might arise with a cause lawyer when the client may simply be a device for getting a policy question before a court and the lawyer's primary commitment is to the cause rather than to the specific client (see Scheingold and Sarat 2004:9).

D. Skills and Techniques

Three core skills, common to all legal professionals, are legal reasoning, legal analysis, and legal writing.

Presumably, one of the key functions, if not *the* key function, of legal education is to train future lawyers in the closely related skills of legal reasoning and legal analysis. Despite a substantial literature on legal pedagogy, debates over the form and structure of legal training continue in many countries around the world. One can ask the question of how legal reasoning varies across legal systems, and what that means for legal pedagogy. Should training in common law legal reasoning be conducted differently than training in civil law legal reasoning or Islamic law legal reasoning, or is there an underlying common element that should exist across training in all systems? Even within a given broad legal system, does legal reasoning differ in its emphasis such that a system of training that is strong on problem solving is more important in one country and a system that is strong on form and precedent is more important in another? Is the Socratic method better for imparting one style of legal reasoning while a treatise-oriented system works better for another?

---

[9] See Kritzer and Krishnan (1999) for an analysis of the methods through which at least some lawyers seek to bring in clients.

As is true of all forms of writing, legal writing is in many ways an archetypical example of something that can only be learned by doing. Arguably it is closely related to both legal reasoning and legal analysis because the ability to clearly and succinctly express the analysis reflects the quality of the analysis itself, and often writing out the analysis leads to clarifying and deepening the analysis that has been done. I once asked a training partner at a large law firm what skills he frequently found lacking in newly hired associates; despite the fact that the prestige of this firm allowed for a great deal of selectivity in its hiring, the partner replied that the biggest problem he saw was deficiency in writing skills. Importantly, it was not so much a deficiency in technical legal writing as it was problems with basic writing skills. While in theory writing is something that can be taught in a setting such as law school, it requires an extremely labor-intensive form of teaching as well as a willingness of the student to devote a great deal of time and effort his or her writing. One result is that for many law students, legal writing is a skill that is ultimately learned on the job.[10]

Lawyering requires many other skills, although many of the specific skills may depend on the specific nature of a lawyer's practice. Those skills may include formal advocacy before an adjudicator; negotiation in transactional, regulation, and litigation settings; client interviewing and counseling; and/or case evaluation. While law school curriculums increasingly include classes intended to teach these skills, the mastery of them comes only through practice over a period of years, just as is the case for traditional craftwork skills.

E. PROBLEM SOLVING

Problem solving is central to lawyering. People and businesses go to lawyers to solve problems, including solving the problem of how to avoid having problems in the future.

Cases often do not fit into nice, neat boxes that the law envisions. Part of what lawyers have to do is translate a client's lay description of a problem into one of the categories of problems for which the law provides a remedy (see Felstiner et al. 1980–81). As part of this "transformation" process, lawyers often have to figure out if an alternative way of looking at a problem might serve a client. One common example is taking some sort of injury situation and identifying an underlying products-related problem that might yield a much higher level of compensation than could be obtain from the more obvious tortfeasor; this would be the transformation of a problem from a simple auto accident to a products liability issue, or perhaps the transformation from a workers' compensation claim to a products liability tort claim.

During my research on contingency fee legal practice, I observed an interesting transformation in the other direct, from tort to workers' compensation. One contingency fee lawyer with whom I spent time (Lawyer Two) received a referral from another personal injury lawyer (Lawyer One) of a case involving a man who had suffered a moderate injury at work that required surgery; something

---

[10] This is assuming that it is learned. My own experience reading documents prepared for filing in court is that a substantial number of lawyers never really master writing.

went very wrong during the surgery which left the man with severe breathing problems and a very shortened life expectance. Lawyer One was a highly respected lawyer who handled medical malpractice cases; however, after extensive work on the case Lawyer One had not succeeded in finding any basis for a medical malpractice claim. Because the statute of limitations would soon preclude bringing a claim, Lawyer One referred the man to Lawyer Two with the hope that Lawyer Two might see some basis for a malpractice claim that Lawyer One had not be able to find. One thing that differentiated the two lawyers was that Lawyer Two handled high-value workers' compensation cases as well as the kinds of cases that can become lawsuits. While Lawyer Two was also unable to find any basis for a malpractice claim, he realized that since the medical injury occurred in the course of treatment for a work injury, the man had a substantial workers' compensation claim because he was now permanently totally disabled and was consequently unemployable. While the compensation available through this avenue was a fraction of what might be obtained if there were a viable medical malpractice claim, it was still a sizeable amount that would be a significant help to the man and his wife.

In another study I observed a social security disability (SSD) appeal hearing handled by a lawyer (whom I will call Jim) who particularly liked to take on the kinds of challenging cases that other advocates who handled SSD cases tended to decline. The particular case involved extreme obesity and a back condition, and had actually been declined by another advocate I had observed because of problems getting the kinds of medical records and other evidence that advocate felt she would need to prove the case. In the hearing Jim took the position that this was "a listings case" which meant it was presumptively disabling.[11] One of the issues was the date of onset, and the problem here was establishing the claimant's weight on specific dates. Getting information on weight was a problem because of the limits on the scales in most doctors' offices. Furthermore, there was one medical report showing the claimant's weight at 315 pounds, which was well under the listings' requirement. Jim elicited the following points through his client's testimony:

- The claimant had injured his back in 1985 when he had been pinned against a tree by a car. When he attempted to resume normal activity nine months later, his back gave out when he tried lifting something in his garage.

- The claimant made an attempt to resume work in 1988 by trying to start a "cottage industry." He had previously been a musical instrument maker with a local manufacturer of brass instruments. He could not work in the factory because the physical setup was incompatible with his condition. He tried to set up a shop at home where he could assemble horns, but he

---

[11] Under the Social Security law there is a "Listing of Impairments" consisting of medical conditions that are presumptively disabling. Cases that fall under this list are referred to as "listings cases." One such condition at the time of my research was extreme obesity; in 1999 that condition ceased to be included in the listings (see http://www.disabilitysecrets.com /conditions-page-2-45.html, last visited September 28, 2014).

found that he could only work for an hour or so a day, and his output was so minimal that he was producing very few finished horns.

- Until 1987, the claimant's weight had been around 290 which would not qualify under the obesity listings given his height. After some additional surgery in April of 1987, he stopped smoking and started gaining weight. After the surgery, he started "topping out" on the scale at his doctor's office, which went only to 350 pounds.

- The lawyer asked the claimant about one of the medical records among the exhibits, a report from a visit to a chiropractor in 1989, which showed the claimant's weight as 315. The claimant explained that that must have been an error in transcription; he was topping out on the chiropractor's scale, and the typist must have misunderstood "350" as "315." The client further reported that during this period the only way medical personnel could get an actual weight for him was to send him to the shipping department at the hospital, and have him weighed on the shipping scale.

Testimony also covered in great detail the nature of the claimant's back pain, the efforts he had made to deal with it, and his ability to function on a daily basis. To further establish that the claimant's weight in 1989 was as he testified, the lawyer brought along some photographs to enter into evidence. The photo showed both the claimant and his daughter, and the lawyer used the apparent age of the daughter in the photo as a way of establishing when the photo had been taken (Kritzer 1998:144-45).

F. AESTHETIC

This is one of the more challenging elements when one thinks about lawyering. What are the aesthetic elements? I would include in this an element of creativity: being willing to try to come up with different ways of thinking about a problem. In the example above of the lawyer who commented, "When the expert really sucks, that's a gift from heaven," it was clear as he made the statement that he derived elements of pleasure in describing this approach. There is an aesthetic element to presenting an argument, either written or oral and either formal or informal. Key aspects of this aesthetic would be the linked characteristics of parsimony and clarity, to which one might also add creativity.

V. CONCLUSION

In this chapter I have sought to theorize the ideas of craft and craftwork. My purpose is to develop "craft" into something more than a shorthand for how people do their work. My argument is that craftwork involves a set of elements which, when taken together, can provide a framework for not just describing how professionals do their work, but can yield insights into how they might do their work better. Some of this would involve training, some would involve introspection. To the degree that such analyses lead to prescriptive insights, they would build on the seminal work of Donald Schön.

I do not want to suggest, however, that prescription is my goal. Rather, prescription would be a useful benefit of better analyses of the work of lawyers and other professionals. While I do see the framework I have described as first and foremost serving an analytic function, I do not want to suggest that the framework provides a "complete" way of understanding the work of lawyers or any other professional. For any profession there are going to be elements that cannot be well captured by any single analytic approach. A good example regarding lawyers is the exercise of judgment. While the craft framework captures many elements of judgment, I doubt that it captures all elements. Nonetheless, given that the idea of craft is invoked, the failure of my framework, or potentially alternative conceptualizations of craft, to be comprehensive, does not detract from the advantages of being able to think about and apply the concept in a rigorous, systematic way.

PART II

LAWYERS AT WORK

4

THE DIMENSIONS OF LAWYER-CLIENT
RELATIONS: NOTES TOWARD A THEORY
AND A FIELD STUDY[1]

INTRODUCTION

There have been a number of studies in recent years that call into question
traditional thinking about the lawyer-client relationship, which has usually been
characterized in two different ways. First, the lawyer has been viewed as the
advocate of the client's interest (Brazil 1978; Simon 1978): the lawyer serves as
the client's alter ego (Johnson 1980–81), seeking to do what the client would
want done if the client fully understood the legal ramifications of the situation
or problem. Second, the lawyer has been thought of as a professional with the
autonomy to define the client problem without depending on the client's
definition of what is going on (Parsons 1962; Smigel 1964; but see Carlin 1962:
184-200). Other studies, both theoretical and empirical, cast doubts on both of
these views of the way lawyers relate to their clients.

A number of studies have considered the impact on lawyer behavior of the
various forms of fee arrangements that lawyers make with their clients. The
thrust of the theoretical studies is captured in Johnson's consideration of this
question (Johnson 1980–81; see also Clermont and Currivan 1978; Franklin et
al. 1961; MacKinnon 1964; Rosenthal 1974; Schwartz and Mitchell 1970). The
primary point of these analyses is that what is in the lawyer's economic interest
may not be in the client's interest; the lawyer may want to put in more or less
work on a case than the client would like. A comparative analysis of percentage
fee versus hourly fee lawyers seems to bear out a part of Johnson's analysis; for
the relatively modest cases (under $6,000 at issue), which, even after excluding
small claims, make up more than 50% of the civil cases in American courts
[circa 1980], the contingent fee lawyer devotes significantly less time than does
the hourly fee lawyer (Kritzer et al. 1985). These various analyses call into
question the conception of the lawyer as the client's alter ego.

[1] This chapter originally appeared as a research note in the *American Bar Foundation Research
Journal* 1984, 409-25; it was a revision of a paper presented at the 1983 Annual Meeting of the
Law and Society Association, June 3–5, Denver, Colorado. The research was supported by a
grant from the University of Wisconsin Graduate School. I would also like to thank Judge
James Felstiner, who provided extremely valuable assistance at a crucial stage of the research.

What about the professionalism view of lawyer-client relations? According to this view, the lawyer defines the situation and, consequently, determines what is to be done. That is, the lawyer has autonomy of action and thus dominates the lawyer-client relationship. The status of the lawyer comes from the ability to structure the relationship. This clearly implies that the high-status lawyer has the most autonomy. In their seminal study of stratification in the Chicago bar, however, Heinz and Laumann (1982:336) forcefully argue that, in fact, the high-status lawyers serving the corporate hemisphere of the legal services market have relatively little autonomy, while the lawyers engaged in "personal plight" practice (e.g., handling the legal problems of individuals and small businesses) are the ones with the greater degree of autonomy. Heinz and Laumann use Terence Johnson's (1972) distinction between "patronage" and "collegiate" occupations to suggest that high-status lawyers depend heavily on the patronage of their clients to maintain their practices. Heinz cited research by Nelson showing the infrequency of corporate lawyers' rejecting assignments from clients as indicative of the client's dominance in the lawyer-client relationship (Heinz 1983; see also Nelson 1981; Nelson 1983). Thus, it appears that the legal profession is strangely turned on its head with regard to status and autonomy.

But is it really? In his study of corporate lawyers in four Chicago law firms, Nelson argues that emphasizing autonomy in analyzing lawyer-client relations may be misdirected because "the great mass of lawyer-client relationships do not generate questions of lawyer-client independence. In concentrating on the unusual event [of lawyer-client conflict] we may tend to ignore the more pervasive role that lawyers play for clients, the role of the committed advocate" (Nelson 1983:325). Two other studies of lawyer-client interaction, both concentrating on "personal plight" lawyers, provide results that contrast with each other and that may help us understand more systematically what accounts for the nature of lawyer-client relationships. Hosticka's study of lawyer-client interaction in two federally funded legal services offices found that it was in fact the lawyer who structured both the interaction with the client and the definition of the problem (1979:603):

> During the initial period of interview clients supply information, while lawyers receive information. While the lawyers supply little information during the first phases of the interview, they maintain a high degree of control over the process. This pattern is established from the moment the lawyer meets the client in the reception area.

> The interview setting further communicates the superior status of lawyers. All interviews take place in a small room containing a desk and two or three chairs. ... The lawyer sits behind the desk and the client sits opposite or at the end of the desk. The shape of the initial part of the conversation is dictated by the forms that the lawyer proceeds to fill out.

Yet contrast this image of lawyer dominance[2] with what Maureen Cain found in her study of "family" solicitors in England. In her observation of solicitor-client interaction in 82 cases, she found that the client typically chose the "desired outcome" and that the exceptions to this are typically the one-shot clients: "Most clients tell the solicitor what they want and he sets about getting it for them ... none of the recurring clients, those who bring regular business, had his objective rejected" (Cain 1979:343).

One might argue that there really is no inconsistency in these findings, since the kinds of clients that Hosticka is describing probably most resemble the one-shot clients described by Cain. Likewise, the personal injury clients that Rosenthal (1974) describes might be one-shotters as well, though we cannot be sure. In fact such an observation goes a long way toward explaining the difference between the Cain and Hosticka findings, and probably would help us account for the distinction between Heinz and Laumann's two hemispheres; but what is the theoretical significance of the distinction between one-shot and repeat-player clients (Galanter 1974)? Does it have to do with the status of the clients, the status of the lawyers, or something else? Is there a fundamental problem with Terence Johnson's distinction between patronage and collegiate occupations (as suggested both by Heinz and Laumann and by Cain)? Or is there some broader theoretical aspect of lawyer-client relations that these scholars have overlooked?

All the studies discussed above attempt to define what constitutes a professional (in terms of status and control). As with most theoretical frameworks, this one takes a complex reality and simplifies it into a set of essential elements; and as with most theoretical frameworks, this abstraction process ignores some important pieces of the real world. In fact, the relationship between lawyers and clients is multifaceted, and only by considering a number of the dimensions underlying the relationship can we begin to account for what Heinz and Laumann, Cain, Hosticka, and others have reported. In the rest of this chapter, I will suggest one set of dimensions that might be used to describe lawyer-client relations and then report on research conducted in Toronto that shows the utility of those dimensions.

I. THE THREE DIMENSIONS OF LAWYER-CLIENT RELATIONS

The dimensions that we describe here are not necessarily definitive, either in fully describing lawyer-client relations or in representing the only way to cut the "pie." Also, while the dimensions I suggest are conceptually distinct, they are not independent of one another.[3]

---

[2] This notion of lawyer dominance was also an underlying theme in Rosenthal's important study (1974) of lawyer-client relations. His findings are consistent with Hosticka's argument that the lawyer tends to dominate the interaction (1979). Rosenthal emphasized the importance of client control as a means of overcoming the lawyer's dominance. Likewise, Hosticka argues that it is the most persistent clients who receive the greatest attention from legal services lawyers (see also Menkel-Meadow and Meadow 1983).

[3] In a factor analytic sense, one would think of the dimensions as oblique rather than as orthogonal.

The first of the dimensions is the professionalism dimension, in which the concern is the traditional notion of the professional's ability to act autonomously. At the heart of this autonomy is possession of expert knowledge (Wasserstrom 1975:16-17):

> [T]he professional is the possessor of expert knowledge of a sort not readily or easily attainable by members of the community at large. Hence, in the most straightforward of all senses the client, typically, is dependent upon the professional's skill or knowledge because the client does not possess the same knowledge.
>
> Moreover, virtually every profession has its own technical language, a private terminology which can only be fully understood by members of the profession.

Professional autonomy has many different facets: an ability to control the lawyer-client interaction, an ability to define the nature of the problem, an ability to define the nature of the task to be done, or an ability to define the way that a task will be done.

At the heart of the idea of autonomy is the image of the actor who is an independent player in the relationship. This independence, perhaps more appropriately called lack of dependence, can function at some levels of the relationship but be absent at others. For example, one might distinguish between the strategy for handling a legal problem and the tactics used to accomplish that strategy. A lawyer might have little autonomy in deciding on the general strategy of action to be taken but have a great deal of autonomy regarding the tactical details; for example, one can imagine a tactical decision to persuade an opposing party to settle by smothering that party with discovery demands, which would give the lawyer(s) making that decision a free hand in deciding what kinds of discovery requests should be made, in what volume, and with what frequency.

One could envision an autonomy scale that took into account the number of ways that a professional is autonomous. Such a scale could include a combination of "areas of autonomy" and "levels of autonomy." The major difficulty in operationalizing an autonomy scale would be that some situations would have more potential for autonomous action; for example, a request to perform a routine task such as preparing a simple will presents less room for variation in autonomy than does even a moderately more complex task such as drawing up a trust agreement. In any case, some professionals (both lawyers and persons in other professions) may have more autonomy than others, and the degree of autonomy may depend on the other dimensions of the professional-client relationship.

The second dimension of the lawyer-client relationship is the business dimension. Despite what the rhetoric of the profession might be, few professionals are selfless actors seeking solely to advance their professional horizons or the well-being of humankind; professionals are workers who are engaged in an activity to earn a living. Professionals, like other workers, are concerned about both the size and the security of their livelihoods. For lawyers, the business dimension is reflected in the lawyer-client relationship in terms of the dependence of the lawyer on the client for both current and future income.[4]

The corporate services lawyer is usually not concerned about who is going to pay the bill for the services currently being rendered, but the importance of the repeat client is central, since the number of potential corporate clients is severely limited. What this means is that corporate lawyers depend on a relatively small client base for a large portion of their incomes (Nelson 1983: 306-07) and must take care to ensure the good will of the current set of clients.

The personal services lawyer is in a very different situation. This lawyer's remuneration is often more or less independent of the current client. This is most obvious in third-party payment situations (such as that described by Hosticka), but it is also true if the client has paid in advance or if the lawyer will be compensated in a manner over which the client has little control (i.e., through the contingent fee, where the check from the defendant is made payable to both the lawyer and the client, or to the lawyer only, and the client effectively is paid by the lawyer after the lawyer has deducted the fee). Even if the lawyer must be paid directly by the client, if the lawyer's practice is not dependent on repeat business, then the current client has relatively little leverage.

I recognize that I have probably overdrawn the contrast between this aspect of law practice for the two types of lawyers, and that few lawyers (or other professionals) are unconcerned about having repeat clients or about their reputations among past and potential clients. Despite the contrast, I realize that the degree of concern about client good will, and the business ramifications of that good will, are important concerns to all lawyers.

The third dimension of lawyer-client relations is the social dimension. Lawyers and their clients often interact outside the professional setting. In fact, for the personal services lawyer, social settings often provide the contacts that eventually lead to business. In the corporate services sector, the ostensible concern about the social dimension was for many years used to justify discriminatory practices in hiring and retaining young lawyers in corporate law firms (Smigel 1964:36-61). The presence of a social relationship as well as a professional relationship can carry over into lawyer-client interactions, modifying both the norms of the usual professional-client interaction, and the norms of the usual business relationship.

As I suggested in the introduction to this section, the three dimensions, while separable, are not unrelated. The nature of the relationship in one dimension will likely affect the nature of the relationship in one or more of the other two dimensions. At the same time, it is not really possible to collapse the three dimensions into a single continuum, because a variety of combinations among the dimensions are possible. Let us now turn to some "data" that demonstrate the utility of separating the three dimensions when we examine lawyer-client relationships.

---

[4] In his seminal study of lawyer-client interaction in the context of plea bargaining essentially Blumberg (1967) argues that the business dimension of the relationship is uppermost in the lawyer's mind in dealing with the client, at least until the client has paid the lawyer's fee.

II. THE RESEARCH SETTING

The following research was undertaken to examine only one of the three dimensions described above (though at the time of the research I had not identified the three dimensions). The work began as an offshoot of the Civil Litigation Research Project (Trubek et al. 1983a; Trubek et al. 1983b). During the course of that research, we became aware that American corporations were significantly changing the way they bought and used legal services; this was largely attributed to the high and unchecked cost of legal services. Specifically, large American corporations were significantly restructuring their relationships with their outside law firms. The current research sought to determine whether there would be less change in corporate behavior if the legal system included some method of formally reviewing legal fees and the amount of work represented by those fees.

The site selected for this research was Toronto. In Ontario's legal system, a client who believes that a lawyer's bill is excessive has the right to ask that the bill be reviewed ("taxed") by the taxing officer, who is a court official charged with reviewing legal fees.[5] While I did not expect that a large portion of clients would ask that their solicitors' accounts be "taxed," my hypothesis was that since taxation required some standard for appropriate levels of effort and appropriate fees, these standards would create norms and expectations regarding reasonable levels of both effort and fees.

During July 1982, I conducted 60 interviews in Toronto, each averaging about one hour, with corporate lawyers, court officials, government officials, corporate executives (both lawyers and nonlawyers), and journalists who regularly cover legal affairs as they affect business. The interviewees were identified in several different ways. First, I contacted most of the companies listed in the top 50 of the *Financial Post 500* that were headquartered in Toronto, with some care taken to avoid overloading my group of respondents with representatives of the oil companies that dominate the top of the list. Second, a judge in a family court in the Toronto area provided introductions to attorneys in many of the major firms in the city and to executives in a number of middle-sized corporations with offices in Toronto; in addition, I had several other personal contacts through my work with the Civil Litigation Research Project. Lastly, interviewees suggested other people to talk with, or the interviews gave me ideas for people to contact. Table 4.1 provides a breakdown of the positions occupied by my respondents. I have divided law firms into three sizes: large (over 50 attorneys), medium (21–50), and small (2–20). Most of the corporate lawyers I spoke with were litigators, though I also spoke with several managing partners who were not engaged in litigation work. The *Financial Post 500* (June 1962, p. 161) listed the ten largest law firms in Canada, and I spoke with one or more partners in each of the six top Toronto law firms on that list.

---

[5] The term taxed is a term of art in the Ontario system. Essentially it means to set the fee at a level consistent with an existing, albeit fuzzy, standard.

Table 4.1: Field Study Respondents

Position	Number
Partner, small law firm (2–20 partners) (S)	2
Partner, medium-sized firm (21–50 partners) (M)	6
Partner, large firm (more than 50 partners) (L)	14
Inside lawyer (I)	23
Corporate or organizational official (C)	8
Legal affairs reporter (R)	2
Court officials	2
Government lawyers	2
Law professors	1

The questions posed to the interviewees tended to focus on problems related to the costs of legal services and particularly on costs (and rules about costs) in litigation. While many of the questions dealt with lawyer-client relations, the interviews were not broad-ranging discussions of the day-to-day interactions between lawyers and clients. As is often the case with research, I found little support for the hypothesis that had originally motivated the research: "taxation" and the standards established by the "taxing" officer have relatively little relevance for the interaction between corporations and their outside law firms. At the same time, respondents' comments suggested the importance of viewing lawyer-client relations as multidimensional.

III. ANALYSIS

A. THE BUSINESS DIMENSION

The first thing that struck me about what my respondents said was the central role of what sociologists of law call "continuing relations." Macaulay, in his study of the real world of contractual relations between businesses, argued that the formal contract was generally less important than the need or desire of business organizations to maintain good ongoing relations with one another (Macaulay 1963). This same theme came out again and again in response to questions regarding what would happen if there were a disagreement over a bill. In the words of the house counsel (inside lawyers):[6]

> We've never considered taxing because we have an ongoing business relationship. (50-I)

---

[6] The numbers in parentheses following each of the quotes are my interview identification numbers. The letters that follow the interview numbers indicate the position occupied by the respondent: L–large-firm lawyer, M–medium-size-firm lawyer, S–small-firm lawyer, I–inside lawyer, C–corporate official, R–legal affairs reporter.

[Taxation] is a factor that doesn't belong in a longstanding relationship between a client and his lawyer. (58-I)

If we went and taxed our main law firm, it would not be the gentlemanly way of doing business; if we did it, we would not be dealing with the firm for very long. (53-I)

Questions about the bill do come up, but the relationship has been there a long time. ... The nature of the business relationship precludes taxation. (56-I)

Going to the taxing officer would completely destroy our relationship. ... It would probably be the last case. (41-I)

The continuing relationship serves to control litigation costs. (6-I)

The continuing relationship is more important than taxation. ... [The] continuing relationship will establish common expectation of fees. (10-I)

Or, in the words of large-firm, outside lawyers:

If it's a regular commercial client, you do everything possible to keep the client happy. (35-L)

You don't maintain your client-solicitor relationship if you inflate your accounts or take advantage of a situation. (32-L)

We would never allow taxation to happen with a good business client; if we did, it would destroy the relationship. (24-L)

Adjustments to bills that are challenged are made most of the time in order to keep the client happy. (25-L)

These quotations are quite explicit about the importance of the business dimension of lawyer-client relationships; yet several respondents were even blunter, specifically describing the relationship in business terms:[7]

I doubt that potential review has an effect on bills; it's more a factor of the business relationship. (24-L)

Taxation standards don't affect billing; more of a business judgment. (18-I)

The practice of law is less and less a profession and more and more a business. (59-L)

The legal business is still a gentlemen's business. (13-R)

---

[7] To some degree, the business dimension of the relationship simply reflects the need of the corporate client to conduct its affairs in a businesslike manner. This showed up in several of the interviews in references to the clients' need to be able to attribute their outside legal fees to "cost centers" within the corporation:

I have never had a client question a bill personally except for requests for information to allow the client to allocate to cost centers. (55-L)

Clients have a growing need to attribute everything to cost centers. (24-L)

While most of my respondents were quite sensitive to the business aspects of the lawyer-client relationship, several client respondents perceived a gap in the business sensitivity between lawyers and clients:

> Some of the more elaborate offices in Toronto are large law firms; there is a real clash on the horizon as corporations try to slash expenses. (4-I)

> Those guys in the major downtown firms are pricing themselves right out of the market. (50-I)

B. THE PROFESSIONAL DIMENSION

The more traditional professional-client dimension came out in my interviews in two very different ways. Interviewees first commented on the need to be able to trust one's lawyer. In the words of an inside lawyer:

> Trust is the important factor in the relationship, and if you trust them, you don't quibble about fees. (58-I)

Interviewees also commented on lawyers' reluctance to discuss explicitly with their clients the business aspects of the relationship. This reluctance typically came up in response to questions asked by clients about hourly rates or requests by clients for detailed billing (i.e., time by person by hourly rate). Inside lawyers and corporate officials told me:

> Law firms don't want to send us hourly rates. (53-I)

> It created a great ruckus the first time we asked for detailed time billing. (26-C)

On the other hand, outside lawyers reported:

> I could count on one hand the number of times corporate clients have asked about hourly rates. (3-M)

> We refuse to render bills on a straight hourly basis, but the pressure is rising ... it's a losing proposition. (24-L)

The professional-client relationships of the persons I interviewed are more accurately described as professional-professional relationships: they take place between the outside lawyers and the house counsel. As in the United States (Galluccio 1978), there is a movement in Canada to shift more and more of the legal activities of a corporation to inside staff.[8]

> One sees, particularly in larger companies, and particularly those with roots in the U.S., a desire to internalize legal services. (34-L)

> In the last 10 years there has been a great growth in in-house legal staffs, particularly in the banks. (58-I)

---

[8] Interestingly, the representative of one of the companies that I contacted reported that it was the outside lawyer who had "suggested hiring a young lawyer in-house to handle routine matters as a way of saving money." (57-C)

Before looking at the nature of the relationship between inside and outside lawyers, let us pause and look briefly at the professional role of lawyers who serve as house counsel or on house counsel staffs.[9] Is a person on the legal staff of a corporation a lawyer who happens to be employed directly by a corporation or a businessperson who happens to have a law degree? Several respondents suggested that in-house lawyers "tend to become more businessmen who happen to be lawyers ... rather than lawyers who happen to be employed by business" (42-M). Whether this is true was not clear from my interviews, but the observation should temper the image of the outside counsel/house counsel relationship as one that is purely collegial in nature.

The idea that the inside lawyer is a legally sophisticated businessperson came out in several outside lawyers' comments to the effect that inside lawyers know what to look for in examining the bill submitted by outside counsel:

> You tend to be more explicit in billings to inside counsel. (25-L)

Likewise, inside counsel tend to be very sensitive to the business aspects of their legal practice:

> In-house counsel are getting to be more result oriented; they are less likely to fight about principles. (37-L)

What is the nature of the relationship between inside and outside counsel? In thinking about this, at least in Ontario, it is useful to keep in mind the idea of the divided bar. While there is not a formal distinction between barristers and solicitors in Ontario, the distinction was mentioned by many respondents in describing the inside-outside attorney relationship. One should also note that while the barrister is usually thought of as the courtroom lawyer and the solicitor as the office lawyer, the barrister also serves as the specialist whom a solicitor may consult on a very specific question, even if it has nothing to do with a court action.

The persons I spoke with in Toronto typically described the relationship between inside and outside counsel in two general ways. The first view was that inside counsel served essentially a liaison function:

> The house counsel serves as a conduit to the company; all instructions come from the house counsel. (36-L)

> I use house counsel as a source of information and as a liaison. (35-L)

> The main function of house counsel is information gathering; ... key contact for decision making vis-à-vis most major decisions. (32-L)

---

[9] Previous research has shown the status differential that exists [circa 1984] between in-house and outside corporate lawyers (see Slovak 1980). This was borne out in the comments of a number of my respondents:

> As an inside lawyer I have to convince people that I am not a second-class lawyer. (58-I)

> People in house-counsel positions are not necessarily the brightest, most up-to-date people. (51-L)

Most house counsel at most serve a liaison function if outside counsel is retained. (59-L)

One of the big advantages of inside counsel is in defining what the problem is ... particularly keeping an eye on the business objectives and knowing the inside actors and their needs. (48-I)

The second major way of describing the relationship was in terms of barrister (or "counsel") functions versus solicitor functions. These descriptions came from both in-house and outside lawyers:

In litigation, in-house tend to be solicitors, not barristers. (59-L)

In-house does solicitor work, not counsel work. (30-S)

House counsel rarely just turn a matter over; [they] more often serve a liaison function, and sometimes there is a solicitor-barrister relationship (though most serve a liaison-reviewer function). (55-L)

I have never been involved with house counsel on a co-counsel basis, though a barrister-solicitor relationship is not uncommon. (38-L)

Five to ten years ago house counsel served a liaison function. Today it is not unusual for client's house counsel to junior the outside lawyer, or for there to be a solicitor-barrister relationship. (47-L)

In litigation it is the responsibility of the inside lawyer to manage the case. ... [The inside lawyer] may provide in some cases a solicitor function [and] occasionally will serve as the outside counsel's junior. (50-I)

In-house lawyer serves as solicitor; out-house serves barrister functions. (27-I)

In a litigious matter, inside-outside relationship is solicitor-barrister in form. (58-I)

These last four quotes suggest an apparent trend toward greater involvement by house counsel, who may serve as co-counsel or as the outside lawyer's assistant, or "junior," particularly in litigation as explicitly suggested in the following:

Inside counsel serves as co-counsel and as liaison with the corporation. (5-I)

On major matters, inside counsel works along with outside counsel as co-counsel. (28-I)

Sometimes I will use a member of the house counsel staff as a junior. (19-L)

C. THE SOCIAL DIMENSION

What about the third dimension of lawyer-client relationships? In my interviews, I did not explicitly inquire about social relationships between lawyers in the major corporate law firms and executives in the major corporations that they serve; hence, the information I have on that dimension is very sketchy.

What I did hear about the social dimension of the relationship tended to come out in references, often by relatively junior inside lawyers or by middle-level corporate officials, to the longstanding link between the senior management of the company and senior partners at the company's outside law firm:[10]

> The senior partner [at outside firm] and chairman [of the corporation] are old buddies. ... I have never questioned one of the bills; I have never felt a need to and I'm not sure it would ever happen because of the close connection between the law firm's senior partner and the chairman of the board. (12-I)

> When disagreements over bills arise, I usually win except with a firm which has a senior partner on the board ... there's a little pressure to put more of the outside work with that firm. (21-I)

> We have a very loose arrangement with the outside firm because a partner at that firm has been looking after the company's affairs longer than most of the management has been here. (52-C)

> The senior outside counsel has been senior counsel for 20-25 years, and on the board of directors for 15 years or so. (57-C)

These comments are at best suggestive of the social dimension of lawyer-client relations in the corporate world. It is perhaps more interesting and perhaps suggests more about the social dimension that I obtained many of my interviews through a family court judge in suburban Toronto who knew socially both a large number of senior partners at the major corporate law firms and a large number of senior corporate executives from companies headquartered in Toronto. The social network appears to be relatively small, which tends to support the argument that substantial social contact occurs between the outside lawyers and the executives of the corporations that they serve.

Yet another aspect of the social relationships that seemed to exist within the network I was studying is that both sides of the lawyer-client relationship were dominated by members of the bar (the majority of persons I spoke with who worked for corporations were solicitors—of the 31 corporate officials I interviewed, only 8 did not have legal training). More important, most of these persons had received their legal training either at Osgoode Hall Law School or at University of Toronto Law School. Furthermore, because of the prestigious nature of the positions occupied by my respondents, it is likely that the vast majority came from the upper echelons of their law school classes. Given these circumstances, I suspect that many social relationships were established well before the persons involved reached their current positions.

---

[10] Interestingly, only one respondent reported that a concern about potential conflicts arising from the presence of outside counsel on the board of directors led to a change of law firms:

> We changed law firms because of the potential conflict of interest arising from the presence of a senior partner from the old firm sitting on the board of directors. (14-C)

IV. DISCUSSION

The purpose of this research has been first to suggest a multidimensional framework in which lawyer-client relationships can be described and understood and then to illustrate the validity of the framework, drawing on interviews with lawyers and clients from the corporate hemisphere of legal services. I have suggested three dimensions that can be used to analyze lawyer-client relations: the professional dimension, the business dimension, and the social dimension. I have also pointed out that these dimensions, while conceptually distinct, are not independent of one another. In this concluding section, I will explore the notion of salience as applied to the three dimensions and then close with a brief reinterpretation of the patronage status of the corporate hemisphere described by Heinz and Laumann.

The multidimensional image of lawyer-client relationships deepens the ability to interpret the relationships that one observes on a day-to-day basis. At the same time, many relationships may appear to be essentially unidimensional; that is, a given relationship may look to the observer as a rather straightforward business transaction, with little or no professional or social content. In fact such an interpretation may well be appropriate; there are relationships in which only the business dimension is salient. In effect, this means that one should not try to read more into a relationship than is really there. One must consider not only where a particular relationship falls in terms of the dimensions that I have defined but also which of the dimensions are salient for the interpretation of that particular relationship.

The notion of salience is helpful when I turn back to the observation of Heinz and Laumann, that in the corporate hemisphere the lawyer and client appear to have a patronage relationship in which the lawyer tends to be relatively subservient to the client. In interpreting a range of interactions between a particular client and a particular lawyer (or law firm), the salience of the three dimensions may vary depending on the transaction involved. A great deal of the work the outside firm performs for the corporate client, while requiring a high level of expertise,[11] may be relatively routine, may have been done repeatedly in the past, and may have been defined very specifically by the client. In this kind of relationship, the business dimension may be most salient (perhaps tempered a bit by the social dimension); the client delivers a set of specifications to the outside lawyer for the work that is to be done, and the law firm delivers the finished product (much the same way the corporation orders widgets from a widget supplier). In other situations, perhaps best exemplified by a major lawsuit, the corporation depends more on the expertise of the lawyer because it lacks experience with the substance or the procedure involved. Here,

---

[11] In a certain sense, one might argue that it is the routinization of the unusual that marks the professional's craft. You go to a medical specialist not so much because you expect a unique solution for your medical problem but because you hope that for the specialist your problem is relatively routine. This is most clear in the area of surgery; one wants a surgeon who has done the operation many times before, not one for whom the surgery represents a new challenge (though in some very unusual situations, there may be no surgeon for whom the operation is "routine").

the professional dimension of the relationship becomes highly salient, tempered perhaps by both the business and social dimensions.

One can speculate about the salience of the various dimensions in types of legal practice other than the servicing of large corporate clients. For example, which dimension is most salient for a personal injury practice or a divorce practice? This is not easy to answer, because the relative importance of the dimensions probably depends on a variety of factors in addition to the nature of the practice: pre-existing relations between lawyer and client, sophistication of client, complexity of the legal task, arrangements for compensating the lawyer for services (i.e., contingent fee, fixed fee, fee schedule, hourly fee).

The complexities involved in determining which dimension is dominant in the relationship can probably be best illustrated by personal experience. After the death of my mother, my father needed a lawyer to handle the probate of her estate. The lawyer who had drafted the will was ruled out because his practice had changed substantially in the years since the will had been drafted. Although I do not have legal training, just before my mother's death, I had a new will of my own drafted. During the preparation of that will, I asked my lawyer many questions that were relevant to my mother's situation. Moreover, I had spent some time reviewing recent changes in the state law governing my mother's estate in order to answer some questions that came up regarding what could be done to minimize the legal difficulties that might arise after her death.

Through four different sources my father and I identified four lawyers to approach regarding the estate. Two of these referrals came from personal acquaintances; two were recommended through other professionals we had dealt with. Because of the relative simplicity of the estate, we sought a relationship that was dominated by our business concerns: obtaining a particular set of services (that were relatively sophisticated) for the minimum cost. All four lawyers tentatively proposed handling the estate on the basis of a standard fee schedule published by the local probate court. Because this fee schedule would yield what we believed to be an excessive fee in the case of my mother's estate, we wanted to negotiate an hourly fee. In the end, we chose a lawyer who was knowledgeable (some of the lawyers we spoke with did not seem to be familiar with all the issues I had discovered in my research) and who was agreeable to an hourly fee arrangement. After that lawyer was retained, we continued to give him fairly specific instructions as to what we wanted done and at several junctures raised questions about his advice. In summary, while we were open to his professional advice, we limited his range of professional autonomy in light of our own business concerns.

In other circumstances, we might have chosen a lawyer we knew through a prior social relationship, or who we perceived to be the most professionally sophisticated (one of the lawyers we rejected seemed to be more expert in probate than the one we retained). In addition, if we had retained the lawyer based on some other fee arrangement, our attitude toward the business dimension of the relationship might have been very different. Thus, we ranked the salience of the dimensions as business first, professional second, and social third; other rankings might have been chosen depending on the particular participants and the specific circumstances.

I began this essay with the problem of autonomy; let me return to it briefly before closing. The idea of the three dimensions suggests that autonomy takes on different forms depending on which of the dimensions is salient for the relationship. We are most used to thinking about autonomy, which I previously equated with the notion of independence, as it relates to professional decision making (i.e., decisions regarding questions that are accepted as part of the professional's area of expertise). I have argued that the social and business dimensions can impinge on this type of autonomy. One can turn that idea around and speak of autonomy in the business domain or in the social domain. For example, certain types of business relationships between lawyer and client free the relationship from a concern over the business aspects of their interaction: a lawyer who is to receive a fee based on a standard fee schedule need not worry about how to calculate the fee or how to justify the fee to the client; likewise, clients need not worry about the meter running if they should decide to raise a particular issue or question with their lawyer.

On the social dimension, it is easier to see the implications of lack of autonomy. A lawyer who has a strong social relationship with a client may have difficulty restraining the client's demands, either regarding the timing of action or the nature of action. For example, the lawyer may need to make decisions dictated by business concerns (i.e., the need to devote attention to a case involving a major, lucrative client when another client, who is also a close friend, demands action) or by professional concerns (i.e., the case involves an issue that should not be brought to trial but the client is demanding vindication). Yet, the attorney does not want to harm the personal relationship by "telling it like it is" (i.e., "I am sorry but I have a more important case to work on for the next few weeks," or "This case is a sure loser; your demands are not realistic"). Likewise, an individual who has retained a friend to perform a legal service may find it difficult to express dissatisfaction with the lawyer's work because of a fear of disrupting the personal relationship. Thus, the idea of autonomy can be extended beyond the professional dimension to any other dimension that one identifies as salient in accounting for the lawyer-client relationship.

In closing let me raise one final, intriguing question suggested by the distinction between the business and professional aspects of lawyer-client relations in the corporate world. That has to do with the nature of services typically provided by corporate law firms. My impression, based both on the work of the Civil Litigation Research Project and the interviews I conducted in Toronto, is that much of the work of corporate law firms is relatively routine, though very pricey, "paper pushing."[12] Corporations are willing to pay high prices to have such work

---

[12] Cf. Nelson (1983:317-18): "The vast majority of tasks which lawyers in these [large corporate] firms are called on to perform involve legal technical questions among parties of roughly equal status and resources. In the preparation of securities offerings, in arranging a leverage leasing transaction, in planning an estate, lawyers are not called on to deal with questions of good and evil (beyond considerations of simple honesty which pervade all human affairs)."

done because of the amount of money involved in the transactions the work concerns (e.g., paying $60 per hour associates, or perhaps even $100 per hour partners, to proofread the prospectus for a $100 million bond offering). In a real sense, corporations are often buying from their outside law firms something that might be best described as a business service (as distinguished from a professional service), and where this is true, it should not be surprising that the nature of the interaction between lawyer and client is more of a business relationship than a professional-client relationship.[13] The distinction between a business service and a professional service is not clear, yet it makes some intuitive sense. I would suggest that a professional service is one that is marked by a high level of knowledge and training, and that training involves a substantial intellectual component; furthermore a professional service is one that cannot readily be delivered by a person lacking that formal training. A business service may require training (e.g., servicing a copying machine), but that training can typically be accomplished in a relatively short period. I am suggesting that there are substantial aspects of legal practice that are less than professional in nature and that can be delivered by a person without formal professional training.

This can best be seen in the increasing use of paraprofessionals (paralegals) to carry out many of the tasks that were previously performed by lawyers. This trend reflects in part the (business) demand from clients that the cost of legal services be reduced (or at least be prevented from rising as fast as it has in the past). The related trend is the increasing concern of major corporations about the business implications of how they purchase and consume legal services. This was the very phenomenon that originally motivated the above research, though the analysis presented here moves off in a somewhat different direction.

Thus, what is important for understanding the changing nature of lawyer-client relationships in the corporate world is not the presence or absence of formal structures that might serve to control that relationship (e.g., rules that govern the fees that lawyers can charge their clients), but rather the inherent complexity in the lawyer-client relationship and the ability of one side or the other to determine which dimensions of the relationship will be most salient.

---

[13] [It is important to note that this observation was made based on research done in the early 1980s; it is likely that during the intervening years many large corporations have moved much of the routine work sent to outside firms to in-house legal staffs. And, the hourly rate figures would be multiples of those charged in the early 1980s.]

5

THE WORK OF THE
CONTINGENCY FEE LAWYER[1]

The research presented in this chapter is based on my study of contingency fee legal practice. It draws primarily on observation I did for one month in 1996 in each of three Wisconsin law offices. The lawyers I observed are referred to by pseudonyms. Each lawyer's practice was different: one was a lawyer at a specialist plaintiffs' firm, another was one of two plaintiffs' specialists working in a medium-sized general practice firm, and the third was a "litigation" specialist (broadly defined to include criminal, family, and civil work) in a small general practice firm. The observation is supplemented by interviews with other contingency fee practitioners, defense lawyers, and claims adjusters. The chapter also makes some references to a survey of Wisconsin contingency fee practitioners carried out in the fall of 1995 (see Chapter 12 in this volume for more details on the research design and data collection).

INTRODUCTION

Those who have studied the criminal justice system often speak of two contrasting models or images of the system (e.g., Packer 1964). One model, the adversary or due process model, views the system as operating in an adversary mode with the twin goals of arriving at the truth and protecting the rights of the accused; the core presumption of the system is that defendants are presumed innocent until proven guilty. The other model, variously called the "crime control model" or the "dispositional model," views the system as operating in a processing mode where defendants are presumed guilty and the goal is determining appropriate sanctions given a defendant's record and the current offense. These two models coexist side by side, with lawyers sometimes acting in terms of one model and sometimes in terms of the other model; some actors tend to lean more toward one model than the other, although the dispositional model is probably dominant.

While these models do not translate directly to the civil justice system, or apply specifically to contingency fee legal practice, my observation makes it

---

[1] This chapter originally appeared as Chapter 4 in *Risks, Reputations, and Rewards: Contingency Fee Practice in the United States* (Stanford University Press, 2004); it is reprinted here with the permission of Stanford University Press.

clear that there are two very different approaches to handling the work of contingency fee cases that have some parallels to the to criminal justice models. I label these the "litigational" approach and the "case-processing" or "dispositional" approach. Under the former, the lawyer, while recognizing that most cases will settle, presumes that cases should be prepared as if they were going to go into suit and will eventually be tried. Under the latter, the lawyer works from the presumption that cases should be prepared for settlement, given that virtually all cases will settle, most without a lawsuit ever being filed.[2] Just as with the criminal justice system dispositional model's assumption that most defendants are guilty, the case-processing approach assumes that liability is not the major issue. As with the dispositional model's focus on finding an appropriate sanction, the case-processing model of civil justice focuses heavily on determining an appropriate settlement amount. In the criminal justice system the adversary and dispositional models exist side by side, and the same is true of the litigational and case-processing models in the civil justice system. Lawyers sometimes pursue one approach and at other times the other approach, and the approach can change within a given case. While I suspect that the case-processing approach is the more dominant of the two, at least for relatively routine cases, my research does not provide any systematic evidence on that question. Moreover, in some types of cases—medical malpractice, products liability, mass torts, discrimination, and large stakes business cases (securities, business torts, antitrust, etc.)—the litigational approach probably dominates.[3]

Some lawyers intentionally intermix the two types of approaches in a way that directly reflects the portfolio nature of contingency fee practice. For example, one lawyer I interviewed, who is a highly regarded trial attorney, disposed of as many as 200 cases per year. Most of these cases were handled, *processed*, entirely by his staff, none of whom were attorneys. These cases served to cover the overhead of the practice and to attract a large number of clients, a small number of whom had significant cases that the lawyer himself handled in a litigational mode. He estimated that two-thirds of his gross fees come from perhaps a dozen of these cases; in other words, 5% of his cases produce two-thirds of his revenue. In addition to covering the firm's overhead, the large number of cases was needed in order to produce a flow of potential clients from which he could find the small number of cases that produced significant fees and established relationships that led to both repeat representation and referrals. To handle the high volume of cases that are processed, his large staff is organized by task—people who specialize in dealing with medical records, others who obtain police reports and the like, still others who draft demand letters and actually negotiate with insurance adjusters. While many of

---

[2] In their study of divorce lawyers, Lynn Mather et al. (2001:110-31) describe two styles of advocacy that parallel my distinction between "dispositional" and "litigational" styles. In the latter, the lawyer relies more heavily on the formal tools of litigation, such as formal interrogatories, while in the latter the emphasis is on finding less formal ways of sharing information and getting the case resolved.

[3] Typically the literature, both scholarly and popular, on such cases portrays an intensive litigational style (see, e.g., Mintz 1985; Sanders 1998; Stern 1976; Vidmar 1995).

these cases are best described as "processed" rather than litigated, about 20% of cases lead to a lawsuit being filed, and the lawyer tries five to ten cases a year.

I spoke with lawyers at several high-volume firms. While those firms tend to be oriented toward case processing, they are also structured to handle litigation. This may involve a division of labor, with some lawyers overseeing cases as long as they are in the processing mode and other lawyers handling cases that have moved into the litigational mode. These firms typically rely heavily on staff to handle many of the processing aspects, such as collecting and reviewing medical records, obtaining and reviewing police reports, initial case screening, and the like. The most processing-oriented volume firms are structured so that the modest cases do more than simply cover overhead costs; this is accomplished by creating procedures that provide efficiencies which in turn keep costs low.

What little we know about how lawyers handle contingency fee cases comes in the form of personal accounts of lawyers handling cases (Stern 1976) and the occasional journalistic retelling (Harr 1995). Moreover, the accounts that do make it into print almost always focus on the spectacular or unusual case, not the day-to-day routine case that constitutes perhaps as much as 99% of the cases lawyers handle on a contingency fee basis. Not surprisingly, these published accounts portray the litigational approach, not the case-processing approach. In part, this is because the cases meriting journalistic attention, or looming large enough in lawyers' memories to be discussed in memoirs, are precisely the types that get litigated rather than just processed for settlement.

In this chapter I look at how contingency fee lawyers handle cases, except for the settlement process itself. As will be clear from the discussion that follows, the three lawyers I observed differ in where they fall in the litigation/case-processing continuum. While all three lawyers at times process and at times litigate, the balance differs sharply. Chuck Brown is very litigation-oriented, Steve Clarke is very case-processing-oriented, and Bob Adams falls somewhere in between. To some degree, this reflects the kinds of cases each of the lawyers handles. Brown handles mostly larger cases involving significant damages; he prides himself on taking and winning large recoveries in cases that other firms decline as too risky. Adams and Clarke handle a lot of very routine cases, most of which would not be economical to take to trial; in some proportion of the cases they accept, they have explicit understandings with the client that they will handle the case for purposes of obtaining a settlement only.

I will focus on three general tasks that lawyers must deal with after they have accepted a case: obtaining and managing information, managing the relationship with the client, and managing the relationship with the opponent. As the discussion that follows will show, whether the lawyer is case-processing-oriented or litigation-oriented appears to be linked to how the lawyers handle each of these tasks. For lawyers taking both approaches, there is a concern about the amount of time being invested in a case. That is, in line with portfolio theory, the lawyer must be constantly thinking about the size of the investment in relation to both the likelihood of a return and the likely size of the return; in addition to the instant case, the lawyer must keep in mind the implications of how he or she handles the case for the reputation that will have long-term impacts for future cases.

I. INFORMATION: INVESTIGATION AND RESEARCH

Regardless of whether the lawyer is processing or litigating cases, civil litigation of the type handled by contingency fee lawyers is fundamentally about information. The rules of civil procedure devote substantial attention to the formalized "discovery" processes for obtaining and exchanging information. More generally, the rules of procedure structure the information process by requiring the parties to define claims and issues about which information will be needed.

A. FACTUAL INVESTIGATION AND RESEARCH, OUTSIDE FORMAL DISCOVERY

A large proportion of cases, particularly routine personal injury cases, involve relatively little factual investigation. Over the three months I spent observing in lawyers' offices, there was not a single occasion on which a lawyer went out to inspect an accident scene or to collect evidence. The lawyers went out of the office for court and hearing appearances, for depositions, and meetings with experts (e.g., on one occasion one of the lawyers went to the office of a medical provider to discuss the report the physician had been asked to prepare). Most of the investigation that did occur took place over the telephone and often involved more background work than anything else.

> In a workers' compensation case involving an employer's unwillingness to accommodate a work restriction, the lawyer had an extensive discussion with a union representative over whether the employer had in the past made accommodations for other employees and whether the union contract contained any restrictions that might have made it difficult to make accommodations.
>
> In a case involving a claim that arose because of delays in medical treatment owing to the failure of a shipping container used to transport biological materials, the lawyer contacted several companies to obtain background information about the type of container that was used and the shipping process involved in handling certain types of biological materials; the lawyer also obtained additional information from industry literature on shipping containers.
>
> In a case involving an injury resulting from involvement in a medical study at an institution in another state, the lawyer contacted various people trying to determine who were the key people on the research project. He later looked at information available online at a site at the National Institutes of Health that had information on grants.
>
> In a case involving an injury at a construction site, the lawyer spoke to people in the industry about the standard procedures used at similar sites and to other workers at the site where the injury occurred to determine whether particular procedures had been followed. Both the lawyer and his paralegal reviewed a number of industry safety publications trying to find material that might be useful to challenge

opposing testimony about the standard of care expected on construction sites.

On a couple of occasions, the lawyer making the phone call did not reveal the
true purpose of the call or that he was a lawyer; usually this was because of a
concern that if the caller revealed that he was a lawyer, the person at the other
end of the call would immediately be suspicious and would be reluctant to
provide even the most routine information. For example, in one case, the lawyer
needed information about a key piece of equipment that was crucial to his
client's claim. One point concerned the weight of the equipment when crated for
shipment. To get this information, he called the manufacturer and pretended
to work for a company involved in a billing dispute with a common carrier that
had transported a piece of that equipment and hence needed to know what the
normal shipping weight was.[4]

The closest any of the lawyers came to engaging in field investigation during
my observation involved a slip-and-fall case. The client claimed to have fallen
walking into a store in a nearby town because gravel was scattered across the
walkway. The lawyer had determined that the landscaping around the establishment used decorative gravel and considered having a law clerk who doubled
as an investigator make the rounds of the landscaping companies in the town to
see if any had recently done any work at the store. Before this was actually done,
the case settled for a modest payment. In another case, involving a slip and fall
on ice, this same lawyer did have his law clerk speak to someone at a building
inspection office about whether there had been complaints regarding sump
pump discharge onto the site that would have created unusual and excessive ice
buildups, although this investigation was done before my observation began.

That none of the lawyers I observed personally undertook any field investigation during my time in their offices does not mean that they never did such
investigations. One of the lawyers related going to the site of the accident in one
of the cases he was working on while I was in the office, but this field investigation occurred prior to my period of observation. This same lawyer described to
me doing field observation in other cases he had handled. While neither of the
other two lawyers described any field investigation they had done, they both had
at least some cases where I would be surprised if they had done no field
investigation. My point is not that contingency fee lawyers do not undertake
field investigation, but rather that it is not a significant part of their day-to-day
work in terms of the amount of time devoted to such investigation.[5]

The only other factual research, outside of formal discovery, that I saw
involved reviewing various kinds of literature.[6] For example, in a medical

---

[4] Clearly the lawyer was deceiving the person he called. Deception can raise ethical questions
(see Hazard 2000), but the harmless deception here almost certainly did not rise to that level.

[5] In fact, in an accident case involving a member of my immediate family, I accompanied the
lawyer we retained on a visit to the site of the accident.

[6] Here I focus only on contingency fee cases. In the firm where the lawyer I was shadowing
had a general trial practice, I did observe instances where the lawyer instructed a law
clerk/investigator to handle specific investigative tasks such as obtaining maintenance
records on an intoxilizer involved in a drunk driving case he was defending.

malpractice case, the lawyer handling the case had amassed an extensive collection of more than 170 articles from medical journals relating to various aspects of the case.[7] He spent time both reviewing those articles and identifying additional articles he thought might be relevant. Most of this effort was background research rather than trying to answer specific questions related to the case. Similarly, while reviewing files from a workers' compensation case in which the claim involved repetitive stress syndrome, the lawyer at some point consulted an electronic "medical adviser" for information on repetitive stress. In the construction accident case mentioned above, the lawyer had obtained copies of company brochures and the like for the general contractor on the site and reviewed these for ideas about potential witnesses and experts.

In retrospect, the sparseness of active factual research should not have been surprising. In most routine cases, the lawyer obtains an account of what transpired from the client, plus any reports on the incident that might have been prepared by or filed with government authorities. Little investigation is necessary because what happened is often not in dispute, or in the case of workers' compensation claims, fault is not at issue. Early in the case, often at the first meeting with the client, the lawyer will collect names of witnesses to be prepared to contact them if there is a dispute over what happened; some lawyers will contact witnesses regardless in order to obtain their account of what happened before it fades into memory, although potential witnesses may not be lined up until just before trial (or hearings in workers' compensation).

In one of the offices, the lawyer was scheduled to try a case the month following my observation and was engaged in a combination of preparing for trial and trying to settle the case during my time in his office. Part of his preparation, at this late date, involved trying to line up witnesses who could testify to the psychological trauma experienced by his client in the wake of the incident precipitating the case. From the telephone conversations with the potential witnesses, it was clear that these were not simply calls checking back with persons who had previously been contacted, but rather initial contacts with persons suggested by the client.

One fact-related issue that the lawyers did address early in handling the case involved preserving, or even creating, evidence. Most often this involved photographs of damage and injuries, particularly lacerations. The lawyer may instruct the client to take photographs or possibly have someone from the firm or an investigator take photographs. For small routine cases, the lawyers I observed relied upon the clients to handle this task. One other way in which the lawyer may instruct the client to create evidence is by having the client keep a diary of what normal activities the client could not engage in and any pain or discomfort the client experienced. Several of the lawyers I interviewed reported that their firms had investigators on staff who would routinely take photographs of damaged vehicles, injuries, and accident sites; however, this was true only of firms that had high-volume personal injury practices. In one of the firms where

---

[7] This lawyer told me that he also spoke at length on a number of occasions with medical experts about the medical issues in the case (i.e., standards of care, normal procedures, etc.).

I observed, a paralegal would be sent out to take photographs in substantial cases.

The nature of the investigation depends upon the type of case and whether the lawyer is handling the case in a litigational or case-processing mode. As noted earlier, medical malpractice cases are generally handled in a litigational mode; this is because lawyers perceive defendants in medical malpractice cases as always resisting the claim regardless of how meritorious and clear-cut it is. In these cases the lawyer will conduct much of the investigation through formalized discovery procedures, such as taking depositions of hospital staff persons.

B. FORMAL DISCOVERY

By definition, formal discovery occurs after the lawyer has initiated a lawsuit. In most offices, only a minority of cases end up in suit, and thus formal discovery may be infrequent. There are several types of exceptions to this. The first is workers' compensation claims, which are always filed with the state agency responsible for adjudicating workers' compensation disputes. The discovery in workers' compensation typically involves medical examinations by physicians retained by the workers' compensation insurance carrier and vocational assessments by specialists retained by the insurer.[8] The second exception can involve medical examinations conducted on behalf of the defending insurance company in cases other than workers' compensation claims before a formal action is initiated, although this is relatively rare. A final exception would be the taking of a sworn statement before a court reporter, something that was suggested by one of the lawyers in connection with a case he hoped to settle without filing suit.

In all three offices I attended at least one deposition. In Steve Clarke's office only one deposition occurred the entire month I was there. In Bob Adams's office I attended two depositions, although both involved cases in which Adams was being paid by the hour rather than on a contingency basis; in one case he was defense counsel, and in the other, a dispute over remodeling of a home, he was representing the plaintiff.[9] In Chuck Brown's office, I observed five depositions, three of which involved the same case and were done back-to-back. Only one of the depositions I observed was initiated by Brown. None of the depositions was very long, all lasting less than an hour. The approach to depositions varied by office; it was clear that in Brown's office they were both more routine and more important than in the other offices. In Steve Clarke's office, depositions were relatively rare simply because very few of Clarke's cases were ever filed in court. The one court filing that happened the entire month I was in the office involved a case in which the statute of limitation was fast approaching and it was evident that the case would not be ready for settlement because the client was still receiving medical treatment. Clarke did not view the filing as anything

---

[8] Vocational assessments can also be done as part of social security disability appeals handled on a contingency fee basis.

[9] In this latter case, there was a second deposition, the spouse of the first deponent, but I had a scheduling conflict and could not stay for that deposition.

more than a pro forma move to protect the claim, and he spoke of the opposing side as seeing it in the same way. A significant portion of Clarke's time was spent on workers' compensation cases, which do not normally involve formal depositions because the rules governing the process do not allow for discovery (other than medical examinations and assessments by occupational specialists) except in rare instances where a physician needed for a hearing is unavailable.[10] The one deposition that did occur during my month with Clarke involved a tort claim arising from a workplace accident; the deponent was Clarke's client. The day before the deposition, Clarke had the client come in for preparation. Both the preparation and the deposition itself were unusual because the client could remember virtually nothing about what had caused his head injury; Clarke focused the preparation on things the client should avoid saying and on the importance of taking his time and being sure that he understood the question. At the start of the deposition, the opposing lawyer, who was conducting the questioning, did not realize the problem he was encountering. After about thirty minutes, the lawyer realized the deposition was not yielding any information and asked Clarke what was going on. When Clarke explained the situation, the deposition was adjourned.

As noted previously, depositions were much more a part of the routine for Chuck Brown. He went into the depositions very well prepared. As I previously noted, three of the depositions involved a single case dealing with third-party liability in an injury that occurred in the workplace. The three deponents, all of whom were Brown's witnesses concerning the circumstances of the accident, had previously given depositions, and Brown had unsuccessfully tried to block the opposing party's request to take another deposition; the judge overseeing the case had issued an order that the new depositions not be repetitive, but Brown was expecting them to be repetitive, given a communication he received from opposing counsel. He went into the depositions with detailed knowledge of the previous depositions and with the transcripts of the prior depositions available on a laptop computer he brought along. As the first deposition proceeded, Brown began pointing out to opposing counsel that he was asking questions covered in the previous deposition, giving the exact text of the question that he located on his laptop. Essentially the same thing happened in the second deposition, which started soon after the first one concluded. Brown had previously told me that rather than instructing the witness not to reply to repetitive questions, he might simply state an objection and then later move to have the entire deposition deemed inadmissible as in violation of the judge's order.

The importance of depositions to Brown's litigation-oriented practice was also evident in a deposition involving one of his clients. That client had been injured in an auto accident in which several passengers had filed suit against the driver and the driver's employer; the client was to be deposed by the lawyer for one of the other passengers as a witness in that passenger's lawsuit. While the

---

[10] Workers' compensation cases do not involve issues of fault, further mitigating the need for discovery; in some cases there is a dispute over whether the incident allegedly causing injury actually occurred, and in others there is a dispute over whether there is any permanent disability.

information that his client was likely to provide was not particularly important, Brown saw the deposition as extremely important because it was the first look the lawyer for the common defendant would get at the client as a potential witness at trial. Brown met with the client several days before the deposition, both to go over some interrogatories and to discuss the upcoming deposition. Brown advised the client that his physical appearance at the deposition would be important (the client was a bit "artsy" in his appearance, with a long ponytail down his back); Brown explained to the client that it would be good if he would come to the deposition dressed to reflect his professional occupation. When the client arrived at Brown's office thirty minutes before the scheduled deposition, he was sporting a neat haircut and was dressed in a jacket and tie. The brief preparation session involved helping the client recall such things as times and distances; Brown used a stopwatch to help the client think about how long certain colloquies might have taken. The deposition itself proved to be uneventful, reviewing the events of the accident with Brown remaining largely silent, breaking in only when his client expressed an answer as a "guess" or in terms of "probably."

The importance of depositions to Brown was further evident in another case in which he wanted the court to strike one of the opposing party's proposed witnesses. In preparing the motion to strike the witness, he drew upon the witness's deposition testimony. One afternoon, I sat and watched as Brown devoted a substantial block of time to editing the draft motion, most of which involved searching through the electronic version of the witness's deposition to find citations from the deposition to insert. The next day, he devoted another block of time to working on the motion, much of which was spent creating an extract from the deposition to attach to the motion.

It is possible that the three practices where I observed were atypical vis-à-vis depositions. I think not; if anything, the discussion above may suggest that there is more deposition-related activity than is in fact the case in most practices. In my follow-up semi-structured interviews, I asked each of the contingency fee lawyers, "Walk me through what you did yesterday. ... What would I have seen if I had sat in this office from the time you got here until you left for the day?" Not a single lawyer made reference to a deposition; only two made any reference to formal discovery, one about needing to plan who was going to do what concerning discovery in one case, and the other about the failure of the opposing party to conduct any discovery in a case scheduled to go to trial in two weeks. This pattern is generally consistent with other empirical research that has shown that most civil cases involve only modest amounts of formal discovery, if there is any formal discovery at all (Connolly et al. 1978; McKenna and Wiggins 1998; Mullenix 1994a, 1994b; Trubek et al. 1983b; Willging et al. 1998). At the same time, one must be cautious in not dismissing the importance of discovery in some subset of cases. For Chuck Brown discovery was crucial to his practice and to many of the cases he handled, and he was constantly thinking in terms of how a client or witness would perform in a deposition and how particular deposition responses might help or hinder a case. However, Brown's practice was far from typical.

C. MEDICAL RECORDS

By far the biggest factual issue in the cases I observed concerned damages and the related issue of causation—whether the medical condition associated with the claim for damages was caused by the defendant or, in workers' compensation cases, was attributable to the claimant's employment. Most of the cases involved personal injury, the result of which was that damages turned on a set of interrelated questions: What was the nature of the claimed injury? What evidence was there of pre-existing conditions related to the injury or the client's current condition? What evidence was there that the injury was caused by the accident? A significant amount of effort goes into obtaining and reviewing medical records. In all three offices where I observed, much of this work was handled by paralegals. From the interviews with other practitioners, it was clear that delegating this task to staff was common and perhaps typical.

The detail in medical records can be extremely important. Lawyers and their staffs closely review records with a variety of issues in mind. An incident from a case handled by Steve Clarke illustrates this. The issue dealt with a single letter, the letter *s*, in a medical provider's case notes. This case involved a soft tissue injury; in noting the source of the injury, the physician had at one point referred to the "accidents" rather than to the "accident." If the injury had resulted from more than one accident that fact would raise questions about whether the accident which led to the claim was the cause of any of the injuries, or the degree to which the client's condition was attributable to pre-existing conditions. There was only a single accident, and the lawyer was able to get the medical provider to correct the record before it was forwarded to the insurance company's claims adjuster. While this is the kind of error the lawyer wants to catch, this particular error was actually identified by the client when he reviewed the records.

In part for this reason, most lawyers insist on reviewing medical records before they are sent to the opposing party. Clarke had a sharp exchange with the office of a medical provider that had sent records directly to an insurer without having received a release to do so; Clarke discovered the problem only when the adjuster with whom he was dealing sent copies to Clarke. The medical provider's office manager, who explained that the records had been sent because the third-party insurer would not demand a fee reduction as would the patient/client's HMO, became extremely upset when Clarke demanded that this not be done in the future and explained his concern about errors in the medical records, citing the case discussed above.

One of the first things all three of the lawyers I observed did upon being retained by a new client was to revoke any releases the client might have previously signed at the request of the opposing party's insurer. Again, this was usually to allow the lawyer to review the records for errors and for extraneous information which could be used to damage the client's claim. However, Bob Adams's practice differed somewhat; he allowed medical records to be sent directly to insurers but made sure that the provider was acting on a restricted release that he drafted rather than the kind of blanket release that the insurer typically used. This was also true of several of the lawyers I interviewed, although the dominant practice was that the lawyer would review records before forwarding them on to the insurer.

All of the foregoing involves the handling of medical records prior to a suit being filed. Once a suit is in progress, the rules concerning discovery govern access to medical records. Opposing lawyers can then obtain any medical records that they can argue are potentially relevant to any aspect of the case. Some of the lawyers I interviewed reported that they had encountered insurance companies that insisted upon direct access to medical records before discussing a settlement; the lawyers varied in how they responded to such demands, some allowing access because the insurer would get access through formal discovery if the case got into suit, while others refused such demands, telling the insurer that if that was the way the insurer wanted to play it, the lawyer would simply go ahead and file suit and start taking depositions.

Although records of medical treatment are important in assessing damages, such records are probably even more important concerning issues of causation. Given the nature of the injury, how does it relate to the precipitating incident? What other conditions pre-existing the incident, or other factors coexisting with the incident, might account for the client's injury or disability? A client may be claiming back injury but have a history of back complaints. The lawyer will often try to ascertain during intake or soon thereafter directly from the client whether there are complications lurking in the medical records by simply asking about the client's health history or prior injuries.

Alternatively, a client may have a number of pre-existing medical conditions that make it difficult to sort out what is and is not related to an accident. For example, Steve Clarke agreed to represent a woman who had been in an auto accident in which her car was rear-ended. While there was little issue over liability, the woman had a host of pre-existing medical conditions, including chronic fatigue syndrome. Clarke explained to the client that "this is not going to be easy to sort out"; he went on to say that "while there is a claim here, given the complexities, [he could] handle the case only to obtain a settlement, because the pre-existing conditions would complicate things in a way that it would be very expensive to bring in all of [the client's] doctors to testify to try to sort things out."

Medical records can also reveal other types of facts about clients that make it difficult to pursue a case. For example, one lawyer I interviewed had accepted a client who claimed she was injured in a fall from a stairway in her apartment house. Allegedly this occurred because of poor lighting and a low railing, and the lawyer contemplated a negligence claim against the landlord. During the intake interview, the lawyer had asked the client whether she had had anything to drink, and the client reported a single beer. When the lawyer obtained the client's hospital record, the lawyer discovered an unrelated visit to the emergency room around the time of the injury when the client had told the hospital staff she had consumed two beers, but the hospital laboratory reported a blood-alcohol level of .26. The lawyer withdrew from representing the client.

As noted above, the lawyers differ somewhat in how they process medical records. Some lawyers delegate the responsibility largely to paralegals. Of the lawyers I observed, this was most true of Steve Clarke. Other lawyers distinguish between their routine cases and their nonroutine cases, with paralegals handling the former and lawyers the latter; this tended to be the case with Chuck Brown. Others, particularly those who do not have practices specializing in personal injury (and hence do not have paralegals with significant experience in reviewing medical records), do much of the review of the records themselves. One important distinction is between medical records and medical bills; some lawyers handle the records review themselves but leave the sorting out of medical bills, between those related to the injury and those unrelated, to a paralegal or secretary. High-volume practices depend the most on staff to process and review medical records. Some lawyers have a staff member prepare a treatment chronology to be used both in arriving at a valuation for an initial demand and for use in the damages portion of a demand letter or brochure; other lawyers prepare summaries or chronologies themselves in order to become familiar with the records.

Lawyers often need to have medical providers prepare reports that speak directly to issues of causation and long-term impact, issues that are frequently unclear in the medical records that are produced in the normal course of medical treatment. Medical providers differ in their willingness to cooperate in preparing such reports. Some do not want to be bothered; some provide the reports grudgingly, often in a form or language that is not as helpful as the lawyer would like; and some want to be as helpful as possible. Sometimes there are very specific issues that the lawyer needs to have addressed, such as allocating causation among several sources, the implications of which the medical provider does not understand. A lawyer may try to educate the provider about why this is necessary and how best, from the client's perspective, to approach it. Often the issue turns on whether the report contains the "magic words," referring to a specific turn of phrase or some specific statement of degree of certainty.

The importance of having a "good report" from the treating physician was clearly illustrated throughout my research. One example involved an auto accident one of the lawyers I interviewed had recently closed. The client had suffered a soft tissue neck injury when another driver pulled out in front of him and struck the car the client was driving. The client had medical bills totaling $2,500 and lost wages of $3,200; if the client had no lasting effects from the injury, one might expect this case to settle in the range of $10,000 to $15,000. However, the treating physician's report stated that the client-patient had suffered injuries that would result in lifelong pain and consequent limitations on his activities, which lowered the client's work life expectancy. When the lawyer received the doctor's report describing the permanency, he contacted the insurance adjuster, explained that "we have permanency," and asked for a certified copy of the insurance policy in order to ascertain what the limit was. The adjuster refused,[11] and the lawyer sent a letter demanding $75,000,

---

[11] Once a lawsuit is initiated, the insurance policy is "discoverable"; before formal court action is initiated, the insurer is not obligated to provide a copy of the policy, although I was told that most insurers will do so.

attaching the report; the adjuster responded with an offer of $20,000. The case settled for $35,000.

Lawyers will do what they can to get physicians to write reports that use terminology that is favorable to a client. One lawyer I spoke to went so far as to state that he would draft reports for physicians because physicians did not understand what needed to be in the report. This was exceptional. Most lawyers will try to explain the importance of certain types of statements; in a sense they will try to put words in the physicians' mouths but they do not try to manipulate the physicians' medical conclusions. Words like "permanency" or "continuing pain" or "permanent restrictions" do more to bolster the case than do words such as "possible limitations" or "uncertain prognosis." For the lawyer, the good medical provider is one who will both provide good treatment for the lawyer's client and use the "magic words" in their reports on the treatment and condition of the client that trigger desired responses from insurance adjusters and defense lawyers. I accompanied Steve Clarke on a visit to a doctor's office to discuss the situation of a workers' compensation client who had pre-existing medical conditions that complicated the case. Clarke explained to the physician that the issue was whether an upcoming surgery was connected to a work injury; he told the physician that the independent medical examination had concluded that while the work accident had temporarily aggravated the client's condition, the current situation was not due to the work accident. The physician immediately stated that while there is no definitive way to determine whether the client's current condition was due to the accident, the client had been stable before the incident and had definitely worsened after the accident. The upcoming surgery was specifically to deal with that worsened condition. The physician then proceeded to pick up his recorder and dictate a letter to the lawyer giving his opinion that the current condition necessitated surgery, that the client's current condition was a result of an aggravation of the client's pre-existing medical condition, and that the aggravation was due to the work injury.

D. INFORMATION: SUMMARY

Litigation centers on information. Much of the work of litigators, including those working on a contingency fee basis, involves collecting, sorting, and evaluating information. However, in most cases handled on a contingency fee basis, little of this information processing involves "investigation" in the sense of on-scene assessments, digging for details or obscure facts, or interviewing witnesses. Most of the information is available directly from the client or in documents generated through routine processes by medical providers and law enforcement personnel.

Where possible, lawyers seek to manage the information that the opposing side receives. Lawyers are most able to manage information prior to the initiation of formal litigation because once a lawsuit is filed, the rules of formal discovery limit the lawyer's information management capability. Much of the information involved in personal injury claims is very routine and is frequently not in dispute. Lawyers, particularly those in specialized personal injury practices, often rely on staff to collect, sort, and manage the information that forms the basis of the eventual settlement demand (or trial, in the few cases where trials occur).

II. MANAGING THE CLIENT

A. ORGANIZING CLIENT MANAGEMENT

Managing the relationship with the client is an important part of the lawyer's work, both to handle the instant case and to further the client's likelihood of recommending the lawyer to others in the future. In my observation, I saw examples of two distinct approaches to this part of the practice.

Steve Clarke (relatively high-volume, routine cases, processing-oriented) handles almost all of the client contact himself. Calls that came in from clients were routed to him unless he was unavailable. His paralegal would handle calls from clients only when Clarke was unavailable; I never saw him refer a call to his paralegal. Clarke had organized himself to be able to respond to calls from current clients efficiently. He used [in 1996] an entirely paper-based filing system and maintained the files of current cases in lateral files which he could access without getting out of his chair. If a client called in and he needed a bit of information he did not have in his head, he could grab the file and talk intelligently about the case, such as telling the client what he was still waiting for. Clarke also initiated a lot of status calls to his clients. If he had not heard from someone for a while, he would call the person. While he did not have a formal tickler system to maintain client contact, he did regularly review his pending files to see if it was time to check in with the client. Clarke had a high volume of calls in the course of most days, and he was able to move among clients and cases with ease, partly because of his filing system and partly because of his memory of cases. On several occasions he was able to remember off the top of his head details about clients' injuries and treatment that the client did not recall. Clarke also went beyond strictly business interactions; one client who called in to report on his post-surgery progress expressed his thanks to Clarke for the plant Clarke had sent to cheer him up.

Chuck Brown (low-volume, focus on high-value cases, litigation-oriented) bifurcated his client contact between routine cases and high-value cases. His paralegal handled most of the client contact in the routine cases, and he handled much, if not most, of the contact in high-value cases. His paralegal would often be present at the client intake meeting, and she would handle the completion of routine forms such as releases and the like at the conclusion of that meeting. This served to introduce the client to the paralegal and create the image of there being a team working on the case. For routine cases such as workers' compensation or soft tissue injuries, the paralegal would handle most of the work, sometimes even drafting the demand letter. On the rare occasion when a call from a client in a routine case got through to Brown, he was not particularly conversant with the status of the case because he was not involved in the day-to-day work of handling it. He and his paralegal did maintain an online case status log, which he could, and did, consult from the computer workstation next to his desk. After telephone calls from clients, he would assiduously update the information in the online system to record the call and note any changes to the status of the case. Brown did handle client contact in larger or more complex cases, particularly when significant events such as hearings or depositions were approaching. The combination of lower volume and delegation meant that Brown's office was a much quieter place than was Clarke's; where Clarke might receive or make twenty-five or more telephone calls in the course of a day, a busy telephone day for Brown would involve half a dozen calls.

The interviews showed that both approaches to client contact were common. In very high-volume offices, delegation was the norm, although many smaller offices also delegated routine contacts to support staff. Part of the rationale for this was that it was more cost-efficient for staff to handle calls (hence helping to control the lawyers' time investment in each case), but lawyers also commented that it made it easier for the client to get through immediately to someone knowledgeable about the case. Lawyers would often be tied up in meetings with other clients, or be out of the office, and have to try to return calls. Other lawyers try to handle the client contact as much as possible themselves. Still others distinguish between routine and nonroutine contacts or cases.

One general point to be distilled from both my observations and interviews: relatively little client contact involves face-to-face meetings. For many, possibly most, cases, the lawyer and client meet only twice: to establish the lawyer-client relationship by signing a retainer agreement and to end the immediate relationship with the delivery of a settlement check. The rest of the contact between lawyer and client is conducted either over the telephone or by written communication from the lawyer to the client. The key exceptions to the pattern of minimal face-to-face contact come in either high-value, complex cases or cases that get at least to the stage of formal processes such as the taking of depositions; for most lawyers, a minority of cases meet either of these criteria.[12]

B. Signing the Retainer

The first aspect of client management is establishing the formal attorney-client relationship by signing the retainer agreement. While some lawyers seek to do this as quickly as possible, others see the process as somewhat more of a transition. The survey included the question, "When do you normally ask a potential client to sign a retainer agreement?" The response options and the resulting percentages are as follows:

At the first in-person meeting	43%
After the first meeting but before any independent investigation	22
After some minimal independent investigation	24
After more than minimal independent investigation	6
Other (including volunteered responses that "it varies")	5

---

[12] The pattern of limited face-to-face contact is by no means specific to American personal injury practice; Boon (1995:258) describes a similar pattern for at least an important part of personal injury practice in England.

The last of these responses typically came from lawyers who distinguished between routine cases such as auto accidents, when the lawyer asked the client to sign a retainer before obtaining accident reports or conducting any independent investigation, and more complex cases such as medical malpractice, when the lawyer wanted to do some significant preliminary evaluation such as reviewing medical records and seeking the opinion of an independent expert.

Not only is there considerable variation in when lawyers have clients sign contingency fee retainer agreements, but there is a systematic pattern to that variation, as shown in Table 5.1. Personal injury specialists are much more likely to have clients sign a retainer at the first in-person meeting (65%) than either general practitioners (36%) or other lawyers (31%). Some of this difference may reflect the fact that for the personal injury specialists there is no ongoing relationship with the potential client, while for the other lawyers, particularly the general practitioners, there often is an existing attorney-client relationship and the retainer agreement serves primarily as a fee agreement rather than to establish the relationship. However, it also reflects the importance to contingency fee lawyers of getting clients "signed up."

Table 5.1: When the Retainer Agreement Is Normally Signed

	All Respondents (%)	Personal Injury Specialists (%)	General Practitioners (%)	Others (%)
At the first in-person meeting	43	65	36	31
After the first meeting but before any independent investigation	22	12	32	24
After some minimal independent investigation	25	14	24	33
After more than minimal independent investigation	6	2	3	9
Other (including volunteered responses that "it varies")	5	8	5	4
N	494	161	102	231

$\chi^2 = 27.27$ (8 df, $p < .001$)

Some lawyers have a client sign what effectively is an option for the lawyer to handle the case, which gives the lawyer the authority to conduct investigatory activities but allows the lawyer to decide to drop the case depending on the result of that investigation. Others simply have the client sign a regular retainer agreement but make clear that the results of the lawyer's investigation may result in a decision not to pursue the case. Still others undertake investigatory activities with no retainer in place and then have the client sign the retainer once the lawyer has made the decision to pursue the case.

C. TREATMENT COUNSELING

The perceived linkage between medical expenses and compensation for pain and suffering raises the possibility that treatment is undertaken for nonmedical reasons. In some states with no-fault systems, which is not the case for Wisconsin, payments for pain and suffering will be made only if the medical expenses exceed some threshold amount; this creates an incentive to get above that threshold. A number of studies provide evidence that in at least some situations accident victims receive "unneeded" or "excess" medical services (Abrahamse and Carroll 1999; Carroll et al. 1995; Insurance Research Council 1996). The assumption underlying the supposed excess medical service is that insurance companies use the amount of the medical bills as a guide to deciding on compensation for pain and suffering; "three times specials" is sometimes quoted as a rule of thumb (Ross 1980:100; Wolfram 1986:528n21). The logic of maximizing medical treatment to maximize compensation is clear, assuming that insurance companies do use simple rules of thumb or view medical expenses as a simple surrogate for amount of pain and suffering.

I would not expect the lawyers I observed or interviewed to admit to counseling clients to get medical treatment purely for the purposes of increasing the value of a claim.[13] While I have little doubt that some lawyers do engage in activities that lead to questionable medical services, what I saw and heard raises some important questions about what critics have labeled "excess" treatment. The lawyers confronted several issues with regard to advising clients about obtaining medical services, all of which might legitimately lead to clients obtaining more medical services than they would obtain without the advice of a lawyer. These issues include the need to document that an injury has occurred, the reluctance of some clients to obtain medical treatment—or the inclination to simply grin and bear it—and the desire to have the client find an effective treatment modality. The lawyers also recognize that some treatment modalities raise more questions with insurers than do others. A frequent theme I heard, both as I observed and in my interviews, is that clients need to have an injury documented by a physician. In the words of two of my respondents:

> I usually tell my clients that I don't necessarily encourage them to go
> to the doctor just because I am handling the case. But I do tell them

---

[13] At least one of the lawyers I interviewed who does primarily insurance defense along with an occasional plaintiff's case specifically commented that he did not see cases that he felt were particularly abusive, even if there was some over-treating.

the facts of life: insurance companies do not take cases seriously unless the claimant has received medical treatment. ... I have clients [who] I know are legitimately hurt, but when I talk to the insurance adjuster, all the adjuster wants to know is how many times the client has been to the doctor.

I have to have the medical testimony of a doctor; it doesn't do much good for the client to sit there and tell me about all of the things that resulted from the accident. I tell the client to go to a doctor and tell the doctor, because the doctor is the person who has to provide a report and possibly testify.

A somewhat similar situation arises with a client whose injury lingers but who does not continue in medical treatment. In the words of one lawyer,

If I've got a client in shortly after an accident, within a week or two, they may ask me about treatment. I will tell them, if you continue to have problems, seek medical care, because what's going to happen if you don't is either you're going to have a lapse in treatment or you're going to have no treatment, and then there's going to be no documentation of the injuries. If, when it comes time to settle, you come into my office and tell me that you've been suffering for six months but you've got only one month's worth of medical records showing treatment, I will tell you that your case is worth one month's worth of treatment. The last thing I want to encourage is for the client to try to milk up the claim a little bit, but they need to have the treatment indicated by the injury.

A third problem with documentation can arise if a treating physician simply does not want to prepare reports or go to court if necessary. My sense is that most treating physicians will provide support for their patients, but lawyers did remark on the need to have clients go to a different physician if the treating doctor was known as someone who would not be supportive in the claims process.

While a lawyer could try to steer a client to providers who would over treat and thus build up medical expenses, I did not see any clear evidence of this, nor would I expect to. I saw a lot that clearly went in the opposite direction. For example, during my observation in Steve Clarke's office, one potential client called in about a minor accident she had been involved in several days earlier. Clarke asked if she had obtained any medical treatment; the caller said she had not but that she had a prior appointment scheduled with her doctor later in the week (the call came in on Tuesday). Clarke suggested that she might not want to wait until Friday to get medical treatment. He went on to tell her that if she was feeling fine by Friday, she might want to just call the insurer and that they might pay her a few hundred dollars; no lawyer would be needed. However, if the problem did not clear up by Friday, she should get back in touch.

The concern about avoiding clearly unnecessary treatment was also evident in the frequent comments about excessive treatment by chiropractors. Generally the lawyers were wary of chiropractic treatment because they knew that insurance companies tend to be skeptical of such treatment, and hence often heavily discount chiropractic fees in assessing the significance of the injury. Lawyers are careful to avoid blanket characterizations, but several lawyers had stories about chiropractors contacting them about mutual referral arrangements. One lawyer I interviewed did report initiating contacts with chiropractors to obtain referrals. Lawyers did not rule out chiropractic treatment, but they were concerned about the issues such treatment raised in the settlement process. Some of the lawyers saw chiropractic treatment as having more credibility with juries than with insurance adjusters.

Lawyers try to make it clear to their clients that once the case is settled there is no second bite at the apple. If a client indicates that she is still experiencing symptoms related to the injury caused by the accident, it is important that she go back to her doctor, to obtain additional treatment, to document a condition that is likely to continue, or to assess the client's current medical status. Lawyers appear to be concerned that their clients obtain the medical treatment they genuinely need, even when the client is inclined to "grin and bear it." This can mean referring the client to a different type of medical provider—a neurologist, an orthopedic surgeon, a pain management clinic, a physical therapist, or in some circumstances a chiropractor. Clients will sometimes ask the lawyer for advice either on what type of provider to see or for a specific recommendation of an individual provider; some lawyers will refer to an individual physician, while others provide the client with a list of possibilities, and some decline to name names.

Most of the "delay" in resolving cases I became aware of was related to medical treatment issues. The lawyers were extremely sensitive to the need for clients either to recover fully from their injuries or to reach a "healing plateau"—that is, to recover as much as they are going to recover. If lawyers believed that further recovery was possible, they would counsel clients not to settle yet and to seek additional treatment that might help the client's condition. If the client seemed to have reached a healing plateau, then the lawyer would seek to have the treating physician provide a report stating that a plateau had been reached and giving a prognosis concerning the possibilities of future improvement.

D. MANAGING CLIENT BEHAVIORS

One issue that lawyers confront is that a client can do things that jeopardize the client's claim. The lawyer needs to manage aspects of the client's behavior to keep this from happening. Two common issues came up during the observation.

The first related specifically to workers' compensation cases. When a workers' compensation claim involves a permanent partial disability, it is common that the current employer will no longer have work that the claimant is able to do. It is much better for the claim for an employer to inform the claimant that the employer has no work that the claimant is able to do than for the claimant to quit his or her job with the employer. Many claimants are tempted to quit, and employers may do things to try to encourage them to quit. The lawyers advise clients not to quit because doing so can jeopardize the claim or reduce its value. Quitting creates problems because employers have the option of accommodating an employee who becomes disabled, and if the employer can find an accommodation that does not significantly reduce the employee's wage rate, the employer avoids having to compensate the employee for lost potential income.[14] The employee quitting makes it easier for the employer to argue that an accommodation would have been made if the employee had stayed.

A second way that a client's claim can be jeopardized is if the opposing party documents behaviors inconsistent with the claim. In particular, if a client is claiming a disability that prevents something like heavy lifting, catching the claimant engaged in activities such as shoveling snow, or vigorous recreation such as touch football or basketball, will call into question the claimed disability. It does not matter whether the client realizes afterward that he pays with significant pain or discomfort for having engaged in the activity. When one lawyer warned a new client of the consequences of being caught engaging in such activities, the client reported that he had done a little snow shoveling ... but had then "paid for it." Being captured on a surveillance tape only a single time will be sufficient to damage the claim. Surveillance is undertaken by workers' compensation insurers because of concerns about fraud, and these concerns are not entirely without a basis, as reflected in one exchange I observed between a lawyer and a client:

> During one conversation, the client mentions the possibility of work-ing under the table. The lawyer immediately says, "I don't want to hear about it," and goes on to warn the client that if he does do some-thing like that, the insurer is very likely to find out about it and even might catch the client on video. If the insurer finds out, the client will lose the workers' compensation case. The client acknowledged that he is very fearful of surveillance; he has heard of it happening to people he knows and won't even do stuff around the house because of this concern.

On the other hand, workers' compensation cases often involve claimants who are used to a high level of physical activity, and controlling the urge to get out and do things, even if there is a cost in pain to be paid later, can often be very difficult. While the issue of surveillance seemed to come up most often in the workers' compensation context, it can arise in any situation where a client is claiming a permanent disability.[15]

E. MANAGING CLIENT EXPECTATIONS

Many if not most clients know that relatively few cases ever get to trial. Even so, the process of settling cases takes place in the shadow of what might happen should the case go to trial; unfortunately, the only way to know for sure what would happen at trial is to go to trial. Lawyers believe that they have some idea of what would happen, both from their own direct experience and from the attention they pay to the trials in which they are not directly involved (either by

---

[14] In Wisconsin, strictly speaking, the employer need only come up with a position that pays 85% of the original wage rate.

[15] See "Surveillance Tape Crucial in McDonald's Defense Win," *National Law Journal*, June 18, 2001, p. A12.

word of mouth or from sources such as jury verdict reporters). The only sources of information for most clients are news reports, which are wildly biased toward the largest cases (see Bailis and MacCoun 1996; Chase 1995), word of mouth from their social circle (which is likely to be based largely on the biased media reports), and the assessments of their lawyers. This provides the lawyers with a substantial measure of control over the client's expectations, and in this section I discuss how the lawyers go about managing the clients' expectations (see Kritzer 2004b:169-76, for a discussion of how the client's expectations are dealt with during the settlement process).[16]

Managing the client's expectations about the likely case outcome typically begins at the very first contact and involves three key strategies by the lawyer: avoiding creating expectations, deflating expectations, and emphasizing uncertainty. Exactly how and when lawyers deploy these strategies depends in part on when the client first contacts the lawyer. That is, if the client contacts the lawyer very soon after the accident, it is easy to avoid answering specific questions because the client is just beginning his or her recovery period; on the other hand, if the client waits some months until recovery is complete, the situation presented to the lawyer may be more clear with regard to injuries, although it may be less clear with regard to other factors relevant to resolving the case.

1. Avoiding Creating Expectations

While a number of the lawyers I spoke with remarked that they knew of lawyers who would create expectations of substantial recoveries early in a case, the lawyers I observed and spoke to generally avoided talking about specific amounts of potential compensation during initial interviews or early in the case. Surprisingly, given the popular image of the litigious American, in few of the initial lawyer-client discussions that I observed did the client (or potential client) specifically ask the lawyer how much they might be able to recover. Furthermore, the lawyers were generally careful to avoid bringing up the subject of what the case was worth. When it did come up, it was likely to be in the context of some limitation on damages, such as the schedule of damages under workers' compensation or the damage cap that applies to governmental defendants in Wisconsin. This pattern was also clear from the interviews. In response to my question, "What do you do to try to establish a client's expectation [regarding amount of compensation]?" lawyers told me things like the following:

> I try to avoid the subject as much as possible because I never really know until the end how much a case is worth. It depends on a lot of factors. A lot of my clients try to pin me down.

> At the outset I don't promise or guarantee them anything.

> I don't want to get clients thinking at the initial conference that somehow or another we are talking about boxcar figures, because

---

[16] See Mather et al. (2001:96-98) for a description of this same process in the divorce context.

then it is very difficult to talk settlement when you want them to be reasonable.

When I see people, I first tell them that I do not know what your case is worth. Anybody who tells you that they know is just making it up, because your bills are not in, we don't know how long your treatment will take, we don't know how well you will recover. We don't know all of these things.

I probably do stuff specifically not to establish expectations. ... I try not to build up any expectations. [If they ask,] I tell them that I'm not going to be able to give them that information. I can only give them my version of what goes into how the decision is made.

I don't give [clients] any numbers right off the bat because you have no idea. You don't have enough [information] at the first meeting. If you say any number, it sticks in their head and then that's what their expectation is forever. So, I always try to keep their expectations down.

Lawyers might try to find out if a client has some amount in mind, but the goal here is primarily to determine whether there is a need to head off unrealistic expectations. "You have to start feeling them out from the beginning to find out if all of a sudden they have an inflated value of the case. You have to find out where they are at."

2. Deflating Expectations

As noted previously, the nature of the news coverage of jury verdicts and compensation for injuries creates a biased image of the outcomes of compensation claims. This does not stop potential clients from taking news reports as indicators of what their claims might be worth. One lawyer reported that "some clients bring in clippings of somebody who was malpracticed upon" and won a large jury verdict. Another lawyer commented, "It is amazing how many clients come in and say that they are not trying to get rich off this case but think they should get $100,000 for a whiplash or a slip-and-fall." Still another described the situation of a woman with some questionable soft tissue injuries who insisted that her case was worth $700,000.

An unrelated national survey I conducted in 2000–2001 (Kritzer 2001c) included the following open-ended question: "In addition to deciding guilt and innocence in criminal trials, juries are used in the U.S. to determine liability and the amount of money to be paid in compensation for damages in noncriminal cases. From what you know, can you give me an estimate of the typical or average amount of money that juries award as compensation in a personal injury case of the type that arises from auto accidents, injuries from defective products, medical negligence, and the like?" A total of 1,524 respondents answered this question in some way, with 40% replying that they did not know what the typical or average amount was. The median for those who did respond was $100,000, and 23% gave estimates of $1 million or more. In comparison, an analysis of jury verdicts in tort cases from a sample of the seventy-five largest counties in 1996 found that the median verdict was $31,000 and that only 6% were $1 million or more (DeFrances and Litras 1999:8).

If the client comes in with inflated expectations, it is important for the law-yer to try to shift the client to a more realistic perspective. Sometimes the context of the injury provides a way for the lawyer to lower expectations. For example, under workers' compensation statutes, there are strict limits on the amount of compensation available to persons injured on the job when there is no third party involved. Lawyers can use the limits imposed by those statutes to make clear the range of compensation that is likely to be available. In effect, the workers' compensation limitations themselves tend to lower expectations. One of the lawyers I observed frequently commented to a new client that his or her injury would have been "worth a lot more" if the case was not limited by the workers' compensation statute.

While the caps under the workers' compensation statutes tend to lower ex-pectations, other types of damage caps, or debates about caps, actually tend to increase expectations. While very few injury claims result in compensation payments of $250,000 or more, this is a common figure for caps for various types of damages.[17] The existence of such caps can create expectations, particu-larly when the lawyer needs to advise the client of the limits of recovery. This kind of "anchoring" effect is well documented in social psychological research (Kahneman et al. 1982; Plous 1993; Tversky and Kahneman 1974:1128-30), including research applied specifically to the legal system (see, e.g., Babcock and Pogarsky 1999; Guthrie et al. 2001:787-94; Hastie et al. 1999:463-65; Hinsz and Indahl 1995:1013-15; Pogarsky and Babcock 2001; Robbennolt and Studebaker 1999). In Wisconsin, anchoring can happen in a variety of contexts, but, as noted above, it is most common in cases involving a governmental unit as the defendant (e.g., an auto accident caused by the negligence of a governmental employee operating a government-owned vehicle).

When a cap of $250,000 applies to a case, it can be necessary for the lawyer both to advise the client of the limit and then to immediately move to prevent that from anchoring an expectation. For example, I sat in on discussions with one potential client who had been seriously injured ("I'm lucky to be alive") in an auto accident involving a state car, where the driver of that car was unambig-

---

[17] A good source of information on the size of claims is data collected by the Insurance Research Council (IRC). I reanalyzed data collected for the IRC's 1992 and 1997 (see Insurance Research Council 1994, 1999) studies of closed automobile injury claims and found that 99.5% (1992) and 99.8% (1997) of claimants represented by lawyers receive bodily injury compensation of less than $250,000; if one includes all claims regardless of legal representation, 99.9% received payments of less than $250,000 (only one unrepresented claimant in either study received a payment exceeding $250,000). Among the Wisconsin claims in the studies (n = 582 for 1992 and n = 695 for 1997), there was not a single one that involved a payment of $250,000 or more. The absence of significant numbers of large payments reflects a combination of the modest nature of most claims and the absence of large numbers of auto insurance policies with limits of $250,000 or more. However, even where there is a source that can pay a large amount of compensation, such payments are rare. For example, the Texas Department of Insurance (TDI) collects, or at least at one time collected, data annually on closed commercial liability claims. For calendar year 1994, TDI reported a total of 53,437 paid claims, of which only 2.5% involved payments of $250,000 or more (computed from information in Texas Department of Insurance 1995 and reanalysis of the TDI data).

uously at fault for the accident; the injuries involved broken ribs and other internal trauma and resulted in seven days of hospitalization including three days in intensive care. In the course of the discussion, the lawyer explained that because the other driver was a state employee operating the vehicle in the course of his employment, the claim against the state was capped by statute at $250,000. The problem was that as soon as the lawyer mentioned the $250,000 cap, that had the likely effect of getting the client thinking in terms of that amount. To counteract this, the lawyer engaged in what I came to recognize as a common method of deflating a client's expectations; the lawyer said to the client, "Hopefully, you don't have a $250,000 claim, because that would mean that you had some serious *permanent* injuries; for your sake, I hope this claim is *not* worth $250,000." One of my interviewees described this strategy very clearly: "I always start out explaining that if, for example, their child had suffered a broken leg, the case would be worth a lot more if instead the child had been left crippled by the accident. ... Isn't it better that the child is not crippled, because it's far better to have a healthy child than to have a big case. You try to get them thinking about things in perspective. ... If the child had two broken legs, the case would be worth more, but aren't you glad it's only one?"

The many-year campaign of the insurance industry to portray the tort system as in crisis and out of control (see Daniels 1989; Daniels and Martin 1995; Galanter 1993; Sanders and Joyce 1990; Haltom and McCann 2004) has, in some ways, made the situation of unrealistic expectations worse. As one lawyer described his experience: "It is not unusual that somebody comes in and says, 'Well, I won't take a dime less than $500,000.' We say, 'Well, that's interesting, but the last one we tried that we had that involved these injuries and these similar facts, we got an initial offer of $5,000. We were delighted that we were able to eventually get $16,000.' It is a constant problem because people really believe the insurance industry propaganda that you get $500,000 for showing up."

A final way for a lawyer to deflate a client's expectation is to quote what the lawyer knows is likely to be a lowball figure. That is, a lawyer may simply tell the client that a case is worth less than the lawyer thinks will eventually be recovered. In the words of one lawyer, "I always tell them that it is worth less than what I think I'm going to get, and then when I get the settlement they are ecstatic, I look good, and everybody is happy. Now is that honest? Probably a little tinge there of not being totally honest with the client. Does it work? Yes!"

3. Emphasizing Uncertainty

As I noted previously, neither lawyers nor clients tend to bring up the question of specific valuing of a case during the initial meetings. The lawyers tend to emphasize to the client the need to get through the recovery period in order to determine the nature of treatment the client needs and whether the injury has any continuing consequences. When the client does raise the question of how much the compensation might be, the lawyer usually explains that the amount will depend upon how well the client recovers from the injury and whether any complications come up. The lawyer also explains that the amount the client will end up with depends upon how much will have to be paid to medical insurers to satisfy subrogation claims.[18] Typically the most that the lawyer will say is that "we should be able to get you some money." If a client presses the question, the lawyer may go through a list of the elements that will ultimately determine the amount of compensation, with the emphasis on whether there is any permanent impact.

F. Assessing Who's in Charge

The discussion above raises the specter of extensive manipulation of clients for the lawyers' benefits. The issue of control in the lawyer-client relationship is important, both from the perspective of those who study the legal profession and from the practical perspective of the fairness of the legal system. In the mid-1970s, Douglas Rosenthal (1974) published a book focusing on lawyer-client relations in personal injury cases; the title of that book, *Lawyer and Client: Who's in Charge?*, states the issue directly: Do lawyers use their knowledge and position to manipulate their clients, or are clients able to exert control over their lawyers to ensure that the work carried out on their behalf genuinely reflects their needs and interests? Law and economics scholars typically express this issue in terms of the "agency problems while sociologists of law focus on the issue of "power" in the lawyer-client relationship (Felstiner and Sarat 1992). Underlying all of the discussions is the observation that the interests and needs of lawyers and clients often conflict, and consequently a fully autonomous, self-interested lawyer will make decisions that a fully informed client would reject (Clermont and Currivan 1978; Johnson 1980–81; Schwartz and Mitchell 1970).

Empirical studies of lawyers and their clients differ in their answers as to the locus and nature of control. Some find that the clients, at least in some situations, exercise a reasonable amount of control:

- John Heinz and Edward Laumann (1982:360-74) found that corporate lawyers are quite responsive to their corporate clients but largely autonomous of their personal services clients.
- Maureen Cain (1979:334-35) found that most of the solicitors she observed had their objectives defined by their clients and that the solicitors generally provided the service the client requested.
- Jerry Van Hoy (1995:705) found that, because of the high level of routinization in franchise law firms, lawyers (and secretarial staff) do dominate clients, but the standardization imposed by management "helps to protect clients with basic problems who might otherwise be subject to unscrupulous practices."

---

[18] Subrogation refers to the claims that other parties might have to part of a recovery. For example, medical bills from an accident may be paid by the injured person's health insurer. If that person then collects damages from the tortfeasor, the medical insurer will want to be reimbursed for some or all of what it paid to medical providers. In Wisconsin, subrogation is taken very seriously. The insurance companies' claims systems kick out subrogation liens almost automatically in many situations.

However, many more studies report that lawyers dominate the relationship:

- Roger Bryant Hunting and Gloria Neuwirth (1962:107-9) found that accident clients had little say in the settlement of their accident claims; Rosenthal (1974) found that lawyers were more responsive to active clients but that largely it was the lawyer who was in charge.

- Carl Hosticka (1979:604) found that, in the legal services setting, lawyers seldom even asked their clients what the client wanted the lawyer to do.

- In criminal justice cases, studies have repeatedly found that defense lawyers see themselves as moving guilty clients through the system rather than seeking to get the clients' input and defining goals and strategies in terms of those inputs (see Blumberg 1967; Casper 1972; Flemming 1986; McConville et al. 1994; McIntyre 1987:153-62; Nardulli 1986) and that to do otherwise can produce problems for the client (see Mann 1985; Simon 1991).

- In consumer bankruptcy, lawyers generally sell what amounts to a product (a Chapter 7 filing, or a Chapter 13 filing), often on a take-it-or-leave-it basis, while doing relatively little to determine what is best for the individual client (Neustadter 1986).

- Lynn Mather, Richard Maiman, and Craig McEwen (1995; see also Mather et al. 2001:87-109) found that divorce lawyers reported that they largely controlled the direction of their cases and the best way to handle them. The researchers found that lawyers try to avoid taking cases in which the client insists on things that the lawyer views as unrealistic or undesirable. They use the metaphor of passenger and driver, arguing that the driver (the lawyer) largely determines both the destination and the route to that destination, with the passenger (the client) at best being allowed to do a little backseat driving.

Still other studies find more ambiguous patterns:

- Ann Southworth (1996) reported that lawyers in civil rights and poverty practice vary substantially in the degree to which they respond to and defer to clients and that these variations depend upon certain characteristics of the lawyers.

- John Flood (2013:156-58) found that corporate lawyers are more responsive to those clients who are seen as having substantial long-term fee potential.

- Drawing on extensive observation of divorce lawyers interacting with their clients, William Felstiner and Austin Sarat (1992:1495-98) found a great deal of ambiguity in the power relationship, with issues of dominance and control constantly in flux and subject to implicit renegotiation.

My research makes it clear that there is not a simple answer to the question of control in the lawyer-client relationship (see also Felstiner 2001). While lawyers may try to manage the relationship in a number of ways (Reed 1969), both professionalism and long-term concerns about a continuing portfolio of contingency fee cases create the conditions for lawyer deferral to clients.

G. LAW TALK

A second important question in the way lawyers and clients interact is the image of the legal system that lawyers present to their clients. Sarat and Felstiner (1989) coined the term "law talk" to describe divorce lawyers' routine portrayal of the legal system to their clients as "relegating rules [and other formalisms] to the background" and as "stressing instead the peculiar patterns of individual legal actors" (pp. 1684-85). To what degree do contingency fee lawyers engage in similar patterns of law talk with their clients?

At one level there are certainly parallels between Sarat and Felstiner's divorce lawyers and the contingency fee lawyers I observed and interviewed: both groups of lawyers emphasized indeterminacy and uncertainty in the process. Contingency fee lawyers portray the formal adjudication process as highly risky, and this portrayal is used as one argument to convince balky clients to accept a settlement offer rather than going to trial. However, a major difference is that divorce clients come into the legal process from a different position than do contingency fee clients; divorce clients would like to preserve the financial position and their parent-child relationships that existed prior to the initiation of the divorce proceedings, something that is extremely unlikely to occur. In contrast, many contingency fee clients can expect to achieve something akin to the status quo ante; if the client achieves a full medical recovery by the time settlement looms on the horizon, the payment received to settle the claim becomes something of a future benefit as much as compensation for prior economic and noneconomic loss. Furthermore, the relationship between the claimant and the defendant is impersonal in most cases, particularly when the defendant is for all practical purposes an insurance company, and the emotionality inherent in the divorce proceeding and the resulting need for formal vindication is usually absent.

The reality is that, unlike all divorce clients, the majority of contingency fee clients do not become involved in formal legal processes. Most cases are settled before a lawsuit is filed, and even when a lawsuit is filed, many if not most of those cases settle relatively early in the process, either because the filing of the suit was simply to protect a claim against a looming statute of limitation, or because an opponent was not revealing key information such as the name of the insurance company that would have to pay any damages, or because the filing was primarily to make clear to the opposing party or insurance company that the claim was serious.[19] Furthermore, the lawyers are able to focus their discussions of uncertainties on juries, which do not exist in divorce cases and which clients easily accept as involving a high degree of chance.

---

[19] Filing probably has more significance for the contingency fee lawyer than for the client; as I discuss below, the filing of a case will bring in a lawyer on the defense side who is being paid by the hour, and that lawyer will have an incentive to spend time on the case which will require the contingency fee lawyer to spend time. While there are some circumstances when the defendant may hold back on preparing a case even after a court filing (i.e., as I discuss below, the filing is simply to deal with a statutes of limitations problem), contingency fee lawyers tend to view the defense lawyers' "running the clock" as the dominant pattern.

There were very few occasions when I heard the lawyers speak critically of court officials or officials who adjudicated workers' compensation claims. At the same time, the lawyers did express frustration at times about not being able to deliver some benefit more quickly to a client. For example, Wisconsin's workers' compensation system provides for some interim payments; however, these payments must be ordered by an administrative law judge. Consider the following telephone interaction with a workers' compensation client who had had a prehearing the previous week:

> The client explained to the lawyer that he is in a major financial crunch; there is a lot of tension with his wife, who is working much overtime to bring in money. The lawyer responded, "I kind of don't know what to tell you," and went on to explain that there was nothing the lawyer could do for a while because they had to give the opposing party a chance to do its thing. "The administrative law judge is not going to make them pay until they have an opportunity to complete an independent medical examination. ... That's the way the system works." The lawyer went on to acknowledge that "they [the opposing party] are stalling. ... That's the way they play the game. ... This [opposing] lawyer does it on every case. ... They aren't going to do anything for you." The lawyer was clearly frustrated and commented that "maybe it will get to the point that the workers' compensation department is ready to throw the book at them."

To the degree that there is something like law talk going on here, it is directed to the opposing side and how the opposing side uses the rules either for its own benefit or to the client's detriment. During my observation, it was not uncommon for the lawyer I was shadowing to make a disparaging comment about an opposing lawyer, but there were few such comments in the presence of, or to, clients.

Lawyers do make statements about the uncertainty of the legal process to their clients. Lawyers bring up these uncertainties most often in discussing the pros and cons of accepting a settlement offer. As I discuss elsewhere (Kritzer 2004b:171-74), it is likely that lawyers devote more emphasis to uncertainty when they want a client to accept a settlement that is on the table. Lawyers also regularly tell prospective clients who call with dubious cases that the legal system does not offer the kinds of remedies that the client might think he or she is entitled to. However, this is not so much a matter of "law talk" as it is a problem of dealing with the misperceptions created by a combination of popular culture and the sustained campaign of insurers and other advocates of so-called tort reform to convince the American public that redress through the tort system needs to be sharply limited.

Overall, "law talk," as conceptualized by Sarat and Felstiner, does not appear to be a major part of the interaction between contingency fee lawyers and their clients.[20] The interesting question is whether the relative lack of law talk

---

[20] It is certainly possible that the relative lack of "law talk" I find in contingency practice reflects differences in data collection methods. I observed fulltime in lawyers' practices while Sarat and Felstiner specifically observed, and tape-recorded for analysis (I did not tape-record during my

indicates that contingency fee practice (particularly personal injury plaintiffs' work) is fundamentally different from other types of legal practice in terms of the way lawyers talk about the legal system to their clients, or alternatively, that law talk is largely a phenomenon that is specific to the divorce setting, reflecting the particular problems lawyers and clients confront in divorce cases.

III. WORKING WITH OPPOSING PARTIES

The third major element in the day-to-day of contingency fee work is dealing with opposing parties. Mostly this means interacting with and responding to defense lawyers and insurance adjusters.[21] Many of these interactions take place within the context of ongoing relationships where the contingency fee lawyer has repeated contacts over a number of cases.

A. DEFENSE LAWYERS

A central theme both in the observations and in the interviews was reciprocity: "what goes around comes around" (compare to Mather et al. 2001:127-30). While recognizing that the litigation process is designed to be adversarial, the lawyers clearly preferred positive working relationships with their adversaries. This is not surprising given (1) a human inclination to have a pleasant work environment and (2) the expectation of repeat contact with opposing actors. While the amount of repeat contact in the general civil arena is much less than in criminal court work groups (Eisenstein and Jacob 1977) or criminal court communities (Eisenstein et al. 1988), there is still enough, particularly in a moderate-sized legal community such as Madison, Wisconsin, that there is an incentive and a desire to maintain positive relations. In the larger community of Milwaukee, the higher volume of cases handled by many firms creates incentives to maintain positive relationships as a means of facilitating case processing.

One can overstate the importance of reciprocity. It does not mean rolling over and playing dead in the face of a demand. It does mean (1) playing relatively straight and (2) not engaging in activities that are simply intended to hassle the other side. The lawyers I observed and spoke with did express concerns about opponents who engaged in activities simply to delay; in reference to one opposing lawyer, Steve Clarke commented, "This lawyer is a jerk. He could care less about my client. ... If he can stall off in paying benefits, he will." While the overall norm appears to be one of reciprocity, some defense lawyers and adjusters had reputations as being difficult to work with, or in some cases, even as untrustworthy. An extreme example of this was described by one interviewee:

---

observation), lawyer-client meetings. I am convinced that there is little evidence of law talk in my field notes or the transcripts of my interviews; as a check, I had a research assistant read the Sarat and Felstiner article and then read all of the notes and transcripts to see if he could identify significant and widespread examples of law talk. He came up with essentially the same examples that I found in my own analysis.

[21] I include in this group risk managers who function essentially as adjusters but are employed directly by a defendant such as a government agency or large corporation.

I had one particularly bad experience with an attorney. It wasn't so much being jerked around, the guy was just a liar, could not trust a word that he said. He was very friendly, at first. And as time went on it became clear that you could not trust a word that he said, and to the point where you couldn't trust a settlement offer that he would give me on the phone: "My clients gave me authority to $50,000." "OK, I'll take it." "I didn't mean I wanted to settle it for that, I was giving you, I mean, I meant ... or something along those lines." So it got to, actually at that point in the negotiations we were getting ready to go to trial.

This was about two or three years ago that I was dealing with this guy. He has this reputation with other lawyers. In fact I've gotten a couple of calls from people who said, "I've dealt with this guy; he does some weird stuff—I heard that you had dealt with him in this case, what was your experience?" I tell them, "My experience is, get everything in writing. If he wants to extend a deadline, you put it in writing. Because he will tell you later that he didn't agree to it."

At that point, we were trying to settle this age discrimination case, so I was still doing it with him, three years ago, I guess. He said, $50,000, and I asked, "Is that a firm offer, is that a settlement offer of $50,000?" He said, "Yes." "OK," I said. I take it to my client. This was like on a Saturday before a Monday trial; we are preparing for trial, and the client was here, so I said OK. We go to appear before the judge for the pretrial—actually a magistrate, it was $50,000 at the time over here—and I said my clients are going to accept that offer. And he says, "Well I have to check with my..." I said, "Wait a minute. You gave us an offer, and we are accepting it." Fortunately I hadn't already stopped preparing, because I didn't trust the guy, but that is the kind of person that he was. So, in dealing with that kind of thing, I mean, that kind of situation, I was just calling the guy a liar to his face. I said, "I can't trust you."

Contingency fee lawyers expected defense lawyers to engage in a vigorous defense on behalf of their clients. It was only those lawyers who behaved in an untrustworthy manner or engaged in scorched earth tactics that generated wrath from the contingency fee practitioners.

With this said, there was a common view among contingency fee practitioners that once a defense lawyer had a case, that case would not settle until the opposing lawyer had put in some minimum quantity of time that the defense lawyer had to bill to his or her client. That is, while the contingency fee lawyer's incentive was toward efficiency (i.e., only put in time that is productive in achieving a result), the contingency fee lawyers saw the defense bar as having a very different set of incentives which led to patterns of behavior that served neither the interests of the contingency practitioners nor the defense bar's own insurance company clients. The lawyers I observed and spoke with viewed this as a normal part of what defense lawyers did, although there seemed to be a some animosity for those defense lawyers who did this to an extreme, which the plaintiffs' lawyers referred to as "churning."[22] For example, one lawyer com-

---

[22] [How accurate this view is in an overall sense is unclear; see the discussion of insurance defense practice in the next chapter in this volume.]

mented that the opposing lawyer in a particular case worked for a firm which had recently opened a Madison office. In order to attract insurance company clients, the firm cut deals with insurers at rock-bottom rates, but then "had to churn their files to generate adequate fees." Another lawyer I spoke with described a particular defense lawyer as the "queen of churn." A lawyer whom I interviewed in his role as a defense lawyer, but who did handle some plaintiffs' cases on a contingency basis, commented that "the Milwaukee [defense] firms need to churn their files a little more."

There were some exceptions to the expectations that formal filing inevitably meant a defense lawyer wanting to run the meter for some minimum period of time. Typically these involved situations in which a plaintiffs' lawyer had to file a case to avoid problems with statutes of limitations. This happens when a client is still in treatment as the statute's deadline approaches. The claimant's lawyer will make it clear to the adjuster that the filing does not represent any effort to escalate the case. In Wisconsin state court, the plaintiff has ninety days to serve the complaint on the defendant; a plaintiff's lawyer may send a copy of the complaint to the adjuster after filing and tell the adjuster that the copy is for information purposes only and that he will hold off on service in the hope that the case can be settled within the ninety-day period required for service. One lawyer told me about a case in which the ninety-day period was ending and so service had to be completed; in that case, the lawyer notified both the defending insurance company and the judge to whom the case was assigned that the plaintiff was waiving the forty-five-day limit on time for the defendant to file a response, explaining that the plaintiff was still in treatment and that the case should settle once treatment was completed. In all of these situations, the goal of the plaintiff's attorney is to avoid the case being referred to an outside defense lawyer who will want to start "running the meter."

B. INSURANCE COMPANIES

For most contingency fee lawyers, dealing with insurance companies through the adjusters (see Ross 1980) who work for those companies constitutes a large part of their work. For personal injury claims, the adjusters both evaluate cases and negotiate settlements for those cases that do not get into formal litigation. As one would expect, the contingency fee lawyers want to influence how the adjusters evaluate cases because that evaluation influences the amount of money the company is going to be willing to put on the table when settlement is discussed. In a sense, the lawyer wants to "help" the adjuster dispose of the case in a favorable way, and this involves doing whatever the lawyer can to get the adjuster to see the case in the same way the lawyer sees it. An important part of this involves giving the adjuster the information he or she needs to justify a settlement to supervisory personnel (see Ross 1980:61-63).

One example of "helping" the adjuster involves the practice in insurance companies of setting a "reserve" when a claim is lodged. The reserve is the adjuster's estimate of the likely case payout. For the lawyers it is important to get the reserve set at an appropriate amount for several related reasons. First, adjusters work within a hierarchical setting, with the level of settlement authority depending on a particular adjuster's experience and position. Second, adjusters are evaluated at least in part based on their judgment in setting reserves; it does not look good for an adjuster to set a reserve at a relatively low amount, only to find later that a case settles for a much higher amount. Finally, once an adjuster has a reserve amount in his or her head that is the general framework within which the adjuster will be thinking about the case. It takes some effort to move an adjuster significantly once the mind-set is established. This latter point has essentially the same type of "anchoring effect" discussed earlier in this chapter with regard to client expectations. While for the client the lawyer wants to avoid unrealistically high expectations, with the adjuster, the lawyer is concerned about an assessment that is too low. Not surprisingly, most lawyers are more than happy to help the adjuster justify setting a high reserve, although at least one lawyer I spoke with viewed the issue of reserves as the insurance company's problem and not his.

The need to be cognizant of the reserve setting process influenced other aspects of how the lawyer processed a case. This was nicely illustrated by one of the lawyers I observed after a telephone conversation with an adjuster:

> For a long time I followed the practice of not requesting medical records until the client was more or less finished treating, because I had noticed a pattern where the style/content of records changed once [the] doctor knew a lawyer was involved; often the doctor seemed less sympathetic. To avoid this, I would not ask for records while treatment was ongoing. However, this practice created problems when I submitted cases for settlement. The adjuster had no idea what was going on and had set a small reserve on the case. When he got hit with large specials [medical expenses and wage loss], he would be thrown for a loop. Now I ask for medicals as a case progresses, and I keep the adjuster informed of the case progress and treatment my client is receiving.

Even with this approach, the lawyer found himself at times making demands that greatly exceeded the reserve the adjuster had established. In one case, the lawyer demanded the policy limits of $300,000, when the adjuster had reserved only $120,000. Before submitting the demand, the lawyer had observed to me that the adjuster probably had under-reserved the case, and in a phone conversation after the demand was received, the adjuster commented, "I have it under-reserved."

Adjusters have differing styles in their interactions with the lawyers. Some of the differences appear to be individual, while others reflect company cultures. At the individual level, some adjusters are easier to work with and more accommodating than are others. As Steve Clarke commented after a lengthy conversation with one adjuster with whom Clarke had had a lot of dealings, "He doesn't jerk you around a lot"; in regard to another adjuster, Clarke commented, "He's a good guy. ... A lot of people think he's a cheap jerk, but I've found that he's quite reasonable if you deal with him straight."

An example of how adjusters can be accommodating came up while I was observing in Clarke's practice. This involved a case submitted for settlement near the time that the statute of limitations was due to run; the delay reflected a long period of recovery on the part of the client. The adjuster handling the case called Clarke's office to tell him that they would not be able to complete their review and evaluation before the statute ran out; he went on to say that they would waive the statute for one month should it turn out that, after they completed their evaluation, no settlement could be reached within that extra month and Clarke had to file suit.

Of course, there are other adjusters with negative reputations. This was reflected in a variety of comments during the observation and interviews:

> There's an adjuster that I deal with who is a stupid jerk if I talk to him on the phone or negotiate with him on the phone. If I correspond with him, they are nasty, short, snippy letters.

> Some adjusters are just jerks, and there's a couple of them that I won't even deal with. I'll talk to them a couple of times and if they prove themselves as living up to my past experience, I'll put it into suit. There's one guy from [insurance company]; ... I deal with other people in [insurance company] and I have no problem. Some of them are tough, but this guy's such a jerk, and he said personal things about my clients. I will not listen to this stuff; I put it into suit.

Overall the tenor of the observation and interviews was that most people on the other side were reasonable people to deal with, given an understanding that they were there to oppose you.

Apart from the individual adjusters, some insurance companies have long-standing reputations as being difficult to deal with: refusing to make settlement offers, making clearly lowball offers, and the like. These variations are more problematic for lawyers who are oriented toward processing cases than for lawyers who are more oriented toward litigation. For the latter group, needing to file suit and use the formalized processes of litigation is more a part of their day-to-day routine. For example, Chuck Brown, whose practice is litigation-oriented, described the problems he had with one large insurer which for a period of time was giving only "lowball offers"; Brown said that at one point he just put all of his cases involving this insurer into suit and advised the other personal injury lawyers in his firm to do the same. Eventually, he got a call from one of the adjusters at the insurance company; the adjuster wanted to know why Brown was putting all of the cases into suit. Brown responded that he did not like the offers he was getting. The offers then seemed to get better, at least for a while, and Brown backed off from putting all of the cases with that insurer into suit; however, Brown reported also that the offers may have shifted back toward lowball again. This lawyer's experience with this particular insurer was by no means unique; a number of the lawyers I interviewed specifically mentioned this same company as one that was difficult to deal with, although at least one lawyer I spoke to described this company as "good to deal with," identifying one other large national company as much harder to deal with ("traditionally been cheap, and they still are").

Another way that contingency fee lawyers routinely interact with insurers involves what are called "independent medical examinations" (IMEs). Such examinations are more or less standard practice in workers' compensation cases and frequently occur in other kinds of personal injury cases that get into suit. These examinations of the lawyer's client are conducted by a physician chosen by the insurance company that is liable for the claim.

Lawyers view these examinations not as "independent" medical examinations but as "adverse" medical examinations. They view the primary purpose of the exam, particularly in workers' compensation cases, as to find reasons not to pay compensation or to dispute the level of disability found by the client's own physician. Lawyers explain to their clients that the insurer is entitled to have such examinations done and that the examination is done in aid of the insurer's case, not the client's case. One of the lawyers told me about a skit that was performed at a meeting of workers' compensation practitioners.

> A reporter has come to interview the doctor, but the doctor mistaken-ly thinks the reporter is a patient who has come for an IME. The doctor tells the patient to strip to the waist. Without looking at the reporter, the doctor starts dictating a report about this and that. After completing the dictation, the doctor takes the tape out of the recorder, places it in a microwave oven sitting on a counter near his desk, presses a few buttons, waits ten seconds, and then pulls out a thirty-page report.

While one might mark this skit up to the cynicism of the contingency fee practitioners handling workers' compensation cases, it is noteworthy that the skit was performed by *defense* lawyers who represent workers' compensation insurers.

The lawyers are particularly skeptical of physicians working for companies that specialize in providing medical examinations for insurance companies, believing that these companies are hostile to the lawyers' clients because the companies believe that findings of their doctors will affect whether the company will continue to receive business from the insurer. While not all doctors doing independent medical examinations work for such companies, the lawyers still see the incentives of future business as affecting the doctors' conclusions. One lawyer told me that he tried to neutralize doctors working independently by actually having them on occasion do examinations for his side of the case; he remarked that one such doctor had just done an IME for an insurer in one of his cases and that the doctor had "just given an incredibly fair IME" in that case.

Is the generally cooperative approach described above peculiar to contingency fee lawyers in Wisconsin? Would I have found similar patterns had I conducted this research in New York City or Chicago or Dallas or Los Angeles? Older studies that focus on, or at least touch on, practice in such areas (Carlin 1962; Ross 1980), as well as studies of settlement negotiation (Hyman et al. 1995; Kritzer 1991b) , are not inconsistent with an emphasis on cooperation, at least when such cooperation is reciprocated. Moreover, the investment image of contingency fee practice provides a theoretical expectation that contingency fee lawyers should prefer to find ways of resolving cases that allow them to control the amount of time they are investing in those cases; controlling time investment is facilitated by cooperation. None of this says that highly competitive, conflictual cases are necessarily rare, and many of the lawyers I interacted with could tell stories about cases that involve little or no cooperation from the opposing side, its insurer, or its lawyer.

IV. WHAT IS MISSING HERE?

In reading this chapter, one might naturally ask, where are activities such as legal research, or drafting legal documents such as briefs, motions, and pleadings? From my observations, these activities consume small portions of the time of contingency fee lawyers. Chuck Brown, whose practice is the most litigation-oriented of the three I observed, did devote roughly the equivalent of one day during the month I was in his office to drafting motions in connection with two of the cases he was working on. Steve Clarke, whose practice is the most case-processing oriented of the three lawyers, also spent about that amount of time, or perhaps a bit more (he reported to me having spent one evening working on a brief), drafting a brief in connection with a case he was appealing and drafting a complaint in connection with a case that he had to file because the statute of limitation deadline was coming up. Each of the two lawyers did do some legal research, half a day's worth at most, in connection with these and other cases. For Chuck Brown this involved working from electronic search tools his firm licensed; for Steve Clarke, the primary research tool he used was the telephone, calling individuals who could quickly answer technical questions concerning very specific legal and procedural issues.[23] For these two lawyers, at most 10%, and probably closer to 5%, of their time during the month was devoted to legal research and drafting. The third lawyer I observed, Bob Adams, undertook neither drafting nor legal research himself; several drafting and research tasks did come up during the month, but in every instance he delegated those tasks to his paralegal.

V. CONCLUSION

The distinction between litigational and case-processing styles of practice points to some important differences in what contingency fee lawyers do in their day-to-day work. A practice dominated by the litigational style is likely to involve more formal discovery activities, while a lawyer whose practice is dominated by the case-processing style will try to handle fact gathering in less formalized ways. In part this is because lawyers employing the litigational style are more likely to file cases and thus bring into play the rules of civil procedure. However, the differences between the two styles of practice is less in what the lawyers actually do than it is in the mind-set of how the lawyers see what they do and in the ways they imagine their opponents understanding what it is that they are doing. Regardless of which style the practice takes, the lawyer's time is largely consumed by gathering and processing information, managing the relationship with the client, and managing the relationship with the opposing party.

---

[23] Parikh (2001:172-95) explores in detail "advice networks" among personal injury plaintiffs' lawyers in Chicago.

My interviews suggest certain types of exceptions to these generalizations. In some types of high-volume practices, there are lawyers who focus specifically on immediate trial preparation and trial itself. The three primary tasks I focused on in this chapter may be delegated to staff, or there may be lawyers within the firm who handle those activities. For example, one lawyer I interviewed, who disposes of approximately 200 cases per year, focuses his personal attention on perhaps ten to fifteen of those cases. These are the cases that get close to trial or are among the five to ten that he actually tries in a given year. Most of the work for the bulk of his cases is handled by staff, leaving the lawyer to focus on trial work and motions practice. Alternatively, a lawyer may specialize in cases with a relatively high probability of filing and trial (e.g., medical malpractice cases), where motions practice and trial preparation are much more central to the typical case.

Regardless of the type of practice a lawyer has or the style of practice a lawyer adopts, the investment nature of contingency fee practice puts a premium on efficiency. Lawyers want to run their practices efficiently because they profit from efficiency. This stands in contrast to lawyers working on an hourly basis, where one could argue that inefficiency, to the extent that clients will tolerate it, leads to increased profit. This emphasis on efficiency is evident in high-volume, case-processing-oriented practices where tasks are routinized and assigned to staff whenever possible. It is also evident in litigational style practices. In the words of one lawyer in a litigational style practice, "We pride ourselves on being really cost-efficient. We think about every penny we spend." During my observations, the lawyers I was with frequently expressed frustration with costs they incurred in handling cases; while these costs would largely be passed on to the clients, this would not be true if a case did not yield a recovery. It was in the lawyer's own economic interest to be careful about the costs being incurred.

One of the problems for the contingency fee lawyer is that the incentives of lawyers on the other side run directly counter to their own. Defense lawyers billing by the hour increase their revenue by engaging in precisely those activities which effectively reduce the return to contingency fee lawyers. This flows logically from the investment nature of contingency fee practice and the fact that the contingency fee lawyer wants to control the size of the investment. One of the reasons that settlement before filing is so attractive to contingency fee lawyers is that adjusters, unlike defense counsel, have a significant concern about efficiently disposing of cases, because they are evaluated in part on the basis of how quickly they close files (Ross 1980:59-61).

The need to control investment, both in terms of time and in terms of expenses, is a central aspect of contingency fee practice. Those lawyers who specialize in contingency fee work tend to be very sensitive to the issues of efficiency. A constant concern for the lawyers is finding the balance between controlling costs and doing what is necessary to get a good result, both from the client's perspective and from the lawyer's perspective.

6

THE COMMODIFICATION OF INSURANCE DEFENSE PRACTICE[1]

INTRODUCTION

There is a vibrant and growing empirical (and theoretical) literature regarding the plaintiffs' bar in the United States (see, e.g., Daniels and Martin 1999, 2001, 2002, 2015; Kritzer 2001a, b, 2004b; Rosenthal 1974; Van Hoy 1999). Much of this research has focused on the implications of the contingency fee structure for the work of lawyers representing individuals who pursue injury and other kinds of monetary claims. The interest in this work reflects both the growing political salience of the plaintiffs' bar and the argument that the contingency fee structure may create perverse incentives that produce significant conflicts between lawyers and their clients, and between lawyers and societal interests.

In contrast, there is relatively little research, either empirical or theoretical, focused specifically on the lawyers who routinely stand opposite the plaintiffs' bar: the insurance defense bar. Laurence Ross (1980) has written a seminal book on claims adjusters. However, while Ross discusses the adjusters' relationships with claimants' lawyers, he does not discuss adjusters' relationships with outside counsel hired by the insurance company to represent insureds once a claim is in suit. There is also some theoretical and empirical literature related to hourly fee arrangements (Johnson 1980–81; Kritzer et al. 1984b), which are the dominant way by which insurance defense lawyers charge for their services, but

---

[1] This chapter was prepared for presentation at the Vanderbilt University Symposium on Empirical Legal Research, February 18, 2006, and subsequently published in the *Vanderbilt Law Review* 59 (2006), 2053-94. An earlier version, based on very preliminary analyses of the data, was presented at the 2005 W. G. Hart Workshop, Institute for Advanced Legal Studies, London, June 28–30, 2005, and at the Annual Meeting of the Law and Society Association, Las Vegas, Nevada, June 1–5, 2005. The chapter has been reformatted to conform to the citation style used in this book. Funding for this project was provided by the Project on Scientific Knowledge and Public Policy under an unrestricted grant from the Common Benefit Trust, a fund established pursuant to a court order in the Silicone Gel Breast Implant Products Liability litigation; data collection was made possible by a sabbatical leave from the University of Wisconsin. I would like to thank all of the lawyers who spoke with me, and particularly the lawyers at "Etling, Burke & Howe, LLP" who welcomed a stranger into their midst for three and a half months in the fall of 2004. I would also like to thank Tom Baker for making available to me comments from lawyers he interviewed, some of which, with his permission, I incorporated into this chapter.

that literature does not focus on lawyers doing insurance defense work.[2] And there is at least some recent interest in the implications, particularly the legal and ethical implications, of shifts in insurance defense practice toward alternative billing arrangements and the use by insurance companies of in-house or captive-firm counsel (Barker 2004; Silver 1997). However, none of the past work provides a good empirical or theoretical picture of insurance defense practice, either as it might have existed thirty to forty years ago or as it now exists.

In this chapter, I present an analysis of insurance defense practice using the heuristic of a commodity.[3] Essentially, I argue that many, perhaps even most, insurance companies have come to view the more routine work of insurance defense as something to be purchased in a marketplace where there are a large number of interchangeable providers (Taylor 1991). Loyalty between buyer and seller, to the extent that it had been an important element of the relationship, has faded. Today, insurance companies frequently shop for the best deal, which may include producing insurance defense services in-house rather than purchasing those services from an outside firm (Mack 1995). As is true of any commodity seller, insurance defense firms seek to differentiate their product from their competitors; how successful they are in doing so is hard to ascertain. Insurance defense firms also seek to maintain the kinds of person-to-person loyalties that were probably the mainstay of insurance defense practice thirty to forty years ago, but insurance companies increasingly have adopted policies and changed management structures and in so doing have made this personal loyalty much more difficult to maintain.

The observation that insurance defense lawyers have less independence from their clients than might be expected given the professional ideal is consistent with Heinz and Laumann's recognition that lawyers working in the corporate services sector functioned more in line with a "patronage" image rather than the "collegiate" image of the autonomous professional (1982:35-61). This distinction is based upon Johnson's typology of collegiate and patronage occupations, with the latter being those occupations in which "the producer defines the needs of the consumer and the manner in which these needs are catered for," while a patronage occupation is one in which "the consumer defines his own needs and the manner in which they are to be met" (1982:360, quoting Johnson 1972:45-46). My argument is that the insurance industry has been able to push beyond even the patronage mode of lawyer-client relationship and thus achieve a level of control and dominance that is relatively unique in the provision of legal services.

I. RESEARCH DESIGN AND DATA COLLECTION

In the fall of 2003, Professor Les Boden of the Boston University School of Public Health brought together a group of researchers, whose work focused on

---

[2] There have been studies of areas of private practice where hourly fees are commonly charged, but these studies focus on lawyers who do work for individuals rather than corporations, and hence do not include insurance defense work (see Mather et al. 2001; Seron 1996).

[3] The idea that insurance defense has become a commodity practice has been expressed previously (see Cox 1997).

civil justice issues, to brainstorm ideas for research on the impact of the *Daubert* decision (*Daubert v. Merrill Dow Pharmaceuticals*, 509 U.S. 579 [1993]). Professor Boden was a member of a group based at George Washington University called the Project on Scientific Knowledge and Public Policy ("SKAPP"),[4] which described its goals as follows:

> [To engage] scholars and scientists in the study of scientific evidence and its application in the legal and regulatory arenas in order to enhance the scientific community's understanding of how science is used in public policy and legal proceedings; to inform decisionmakers about the nature of scientific inquiry and opinion; and to advance the public's understanding of the role of scientific evidence in government programs that seek to protect public health and the environment.

I proposed a project that I called "*Daubert* in the Law Office." The idea of this project was to observe for a period of months in a law firm in the Twin Cities area with a book of business that included cases where *Daubert* issues were likely to arise. Some initial explorations of this idea led me to decide to focus on the defense side and to design the project to have two tracks, one focusing on *Daubert* and one focusing on insurance defense practice broadly defined. I eventually found a law firm that was willing to allow me "hang out" at their offices. During my time in the office, I was formally designated as a paralegal,[5] and I took on any tasks assigned to me that were within my competence, logging any time devoted to paralegal tasks in the firm's timekeeping/billing system.

The firm, which I call "Etling, Burke & Howe" ("EBH"), consists of sixty to seventy lawyers and is divided about evenly between a transactional practice and a litigation practice. The litigation and transactional groups are quite separate; it is almost as though there is an office sharing arrangement that includes sharing infrastructure support (information technology, overhead, human resources, etc.). There is some tension between the two groups: the transactional group is able to charge considerably higher rates to its clients, but has both a higher overhead and a somewhat lower collection ratio; in contrast the litigation group charges lower rates, but the insurance clients generally pay their bills, at least after auditing.

Over three and a half months during the fall of 2004, I spent about two weeks with each of five different lawyers, plus shorter amounts of time with two other lawyers.[6] These lawyers did a variety of types of insurance defense work,

---

[4] Major support for SKAPP was provided by the Common Benefit Trust, a fund established pursuant to a court order in the Silicone Gel Breast Implant Products Liability litigation, with additional support from the Alice Hamilton Fund and the Bauman Foundation. DefendingScience.org, http://www.defendingscience.org/About.Us.cfm (last visited Aug. 31, 2006).

[5] The paralegal designation brought me under attorney-client privilege rules; assigning me some actual work served to avoid challenges that this designation was simply a fiction. The tasks I performed included some memo preparation, assisting on drafting of briefs, assisting at depositions, review of discovery materials, and assisting lawyers in preparing for presentations.

[6] During my observation, which typically was from 8 A.M. until 5 or 6 P.M., I kept notes on steno pads. Each evening I transcribed and expanded those notes using my word processor. After an initial detailed review and highlighting of those notes, I completed a systematic coding of those

including workers compensation, auto accidents, products liability, professional liability, and other personal injury; the auto work included traditional liability, uninsured and underinsured motorist ("UM/UIM") claims, and no-fault claims ("Personal Injury Protection" or PIP) where the insurer and the insured disagreed over whether treatment was reasonable and necessary. In addition to insurance defense work, the firm also handled insurance subrogation cases and insurance coverage matters, plus some commercial litigation.

I chose to do this research in a single firm rather than multiple firms because of the potential for conflicts.[7] Originally, I was concerned that the firm did some commercial litigation in addition to the insurance defense litigation, and, as a result, if I were to observe at another firm with a similar book of business, there would be a chance that the second (or third) firm would be representing an adverse party in a case that I saw at EBH. In fact, I underestimated the problems that might have arisen if I had observed in multiple firms: a large number of cases I saw involved multiple insurers who had adverse interests. In some types of cases, the issue was essentially one of subrogation where an insurer was trying to recover payments made to its insured from another insurer. In other types of cases, there were multiple defendants; this was particularly true in construction defect cases where the general contractor who, after being sued by an owner, brought in subcontractors and materials suppliers, each of whom had its own insurer. In some types of cases, a single defendant might have had multiple insurers on the risk over a period of time, and there were issues regarding whose risk it was and/or how to share out the risk.[8]

One of the potential problems of observing in a single firm is that the firm's practice may have been atypical. To assess the generalizability of what I observed, at least its generalizability to insurance defense practice in the Twin Cities area, I conducted a series of interviews with insurance defense practitioners in other firms.[9] I identified potential respondents in a variety of ways. I started by asking key people at EBH who their main competitors were. A second source was the membership roster of the Minnesota Defense Lawyers Association, which was posted on MDLA's website.[10] The final source was suggestions from respondents (i.e., I asked each respondent if there were other firms I might want to contact). A total of seventeen interviews were completed with insurance defense practitioners other than those at EBH.[11]

---

notes using qualitative analysis software (NVivo) which allowed me to group and review notes related to a given theme or issue.

[7] In an earlier study of contingency fee practice (see Kritzer 2004b:20-21), I observed for a month in each of three different law firms

[8] In fact, there was at least one case on which I observed some activities at EBH that I later heard about from a lawyer I interviewed.

[9] One of the seventeen interviews was completed with a Wisconsin practitioner based in Milwaukee. I also conducted some less formal interviews of lawyers at EBH with whom I did not spend a significant amount of time.

[10] Minnesota Defense Lawyers Association, http://www.mdla.org/members-alphalisting.html (last visited May 10, 2005).

[11] I also conducted an equal number of interviews with lawyers whose practices involve cases likely to raise *Daubert* issues.

I developed the questions I asked during the interviews after an initial review of my observational notes. All but two of the interviews were recorded and then transcribed. For the two interviews where the respondent declined to be recorded; I took extensive notes during the interview and then transcribed and expanded those notes within an hour or two of the interview. I coded the observational notes and the interview transcripts according to the same framework.

II. ANALYSIS

A. THE BUSINESS REALITIES OF INSURANCE DEFENSE PRACTICE

Insurance companies are large consumers of legal services. Given the quantity of such services they buy, these companies want what is akin to wholesale prices for those services unless they are confronting exceptional circumstances (i.e., the threat of a very large loss, probably eight figures or more). Because of this volume, insurance companies are able to secure hourly rates that are well below those that are paid by other commercial clients. Relatively few insurance defense lawyers in the Twin Cities are able to charge rates in excess of $160–$170 per hour [circa 2004].[12] More typical rates are in the range of $110–$120 per hour for associates and $140–$150 per hour for the most senior partners; at some firms, the rates charged by associates start out as low as $90 per hour. To put these rates in perspective, the going rate for auto mechanics in the Twin Cities at the time of my research was about $80 per hour,[13] and for plumbers it was as much as $150 per hour.

Insurance companies are able to get these wholesale rates because they often have limited loyalty to their outside lawyers. Insurance defense lawyers can raise their rates only cautiously because insurance companies can easily move the work, either to competing firms or to in-house/captive offices (see Cox 1997: A17; Mack 1995:C38). For much commercial work there is a cost to changing lawyers, in that the current lawyer will have a lot of working knowledge of the client's affairs that will take time to replicate in the new firm. The nature of insurance defense work, however, is such that there is little if any such cost involved. Insurance companies have in place detailed litigation policies that can be handed to the new firm, and in many cases the authority of local claims staff is so constrained that the personal relations that might exist between outside counsel and those staff persons, particularly when combined with litigation policies, has little impact on the handling of cases.

---

[12] Only one firm reported that they were able to charge over $200 per hour for partners, and that firm had taken the stance that they would only do insurance defense work if the client was willing to pay the rate they demanded. Not surprisingly, the firm was doing less and less such work, and the work it did was not the "run of the mill" insurance type case.

[13] This is the nominal rate for mechanics; the time that is charged is based on the "book" time, and good mechanics can consistently beat the book time which means that their real rate is something more than $80 per hour (probably more in the range of at least $100–$120 per hour). Moreover, this figure is for labor only, and does not include the markup on parts; my guess is that a good mechanic probably generates close to $150 per hour net of the wholesale cost of the parts he or she installs.

I do not suggest that loyalty is completely absent in relationships between law firms and insurers.[14] The degree of loyalty will vary from insurer to insurer, and some insurers may genuinely treat outside counsel as nothing more than a commodity. However, even in the presence of significant loyalty between an insurer and a law firm, the commodity nature of the market for these services sharply constrains the fees that can be charged to the insurers, and forces the law firms to put up with demands that they find both costly and annoying (e.g., reducing bills they view as entirely reasonable, bearing costs that would normally be the client's responsibility, etc.).

B. ALTERNATIVE FEE ARRANGEMENTS AND THEIR IMPLICATIONS

The purchasing power of the insurance companies is such that threats to leave or move work in-house can lead law firms to consider "deals" with the insurers that shift risks from the insurer to the lawyer. As one lawyer described the situation to me, "[I]nsurance companies became resistant to paying by the hour [because] they didn't trust the counting of hours and wanted some protection against inflated prices arising due to the slowness of the lawyers."[15]

The result is a variety of alternative fee arrangements.[16] Most of the insurance defense lawyers I spoke with indicated that the issue of alternative methods of billing had come up with their insurance company clients, although only about one-third acknowledged currently doing any work on an alternative fee basis. About an equal number of firms reported either that they had done some such work in the past, had considered offering alternative fee arrangements, or had successfully resisted adopting such arrangements when asked to consider them by one or more insurance company clients. Of those lawyers who reported that their firms in the past had alternative billing arrangements but no longer used them, some reported that the decision to drop the alternative

---

[14] In fact, at least one lawyer I spoke with felt that loyalty between insurance companies and their outside lawyers had increased: "[D]espite many examples of a lack of loyalty, my view is that loyalty has improved over time, not worsened. Most clients do recognize the substantial benefits of long term relationships with their lawyers and do not take lightly the decision to switch horses."

[15] As this quote makes clear, the billing arrangement inevitably impacts the principal-agent relationship (see Cumming 2001:253-58; Hay 1997:44; Miller 1987:193-95; Spiegel 1979:122). The goal of different fee arrangements is to structure the incentives in that relationship with the purpose of trying to align the lawyer's interest with the fee payer's interest. Every fee arrangement inevitably produces a mixture of positive and perverse incentives (see Johnson 1980–81:569-602; Kritzer 1994:188-89). One irony in the desire of insurance companies to move away from the billable hour is that they may have been the primary force in creating this billing arrangement for insurance defense work. One of Tom Baker's respondents observed, "We didn't bill by hours when I started. We billed by task. We didn't keep time. ... The insurance company said, 'Hey, we don't want to pay you $50 for a motion. You tell us how long it took you to do the motion and we'll pay you whatever your hourly rate is as long as it is reasonable.' And we didn't like it but they were the clients. [But] we went along with it and it turned out that we liked it. Because we didn't know how much time we were spending on half of this stuff. We found out. We were shocked. Even today I'm shocked to find out it's 5 o'clock in the afternoon. I thought it was like 2 o'clock. Where did the day go?"

[16] A senior partner at one law firm told me that the firm had entered into its first alternative fee arrangement in the mid-1980s.

arrangement came from the insurance company and some reported that it was a firm decision.

The simplest alternative billing arrangement is some sort of flat fee: the firm receives a fixed amount (plus expenses) for handling a case. Such arrangements make sense when cases are fairly predictable and routine. Thus, the most common type of case involving flat fees was a PIP case where the firm represented the insurer in a dispute with the insured over no-fault benefits. Under Minnesota law, most of these cases are resolved through arbitration if they cannot be settled. Much of the preparation for the arbitration is done by the paralegal, and the lawyers I observed could handle them with a few hours of arbitration preparation, plus time spent trying to negotiate a settlement. The arbitration hearings themselves were very quick (typically an hour or less). Given that most of these cases involve disputes over what medical treatment should be covered by the insurer, a significant part of the lawyer's time goes into setting up independent medical exams (IMEs) and preparing medical records to be provided to the physician conducting the IME. In sum, the time required for these cases is quite predictable, so lawyers can handle such cases on a fixed fee basis. Moreover, even if the firm does not make as much on each file as it might under an hourly fee, such fixed fee arrangements can increase the volume of work and serve as "loss-leaders" for other, more profitable work.

The fixed fee arrangement, however, creates some other problems. Given that the full fee is payable even if the case settles after it is referred to the lawyer but before arbitration, insurance adjusters may be reluctant to refer cases that they think will settle. One effect of this reluctance is that adjusters sometimes delay referring cases, and this can result in a case being poorly postured when the lawyer finally receives it. One lawyer I spoke to emphasized this as a recurring problem. He said that his firm was negotiating with one of its insurance company clients to modify the arrangement so that adjusters could consult with the firm on an hourly fee basis prior to referring the case, with any fees generated being credited against the fixed fee if the case were to be turned over to the lawyer. Another lawyer told me that his firm avoided this problem by having an understanding with insurers concerning files referred on a flat fee basis: if the lawyer felt the case could be handled very quickly, the firm would handle it on an hourly basis rather than charge the normal flat fee.

I was told of other attempts to use flat fee arrangements in traditional tort cases or in UM/UIM cases. Most of these arrangements seem to be short-lived, with neither the insurer nor the firm particularly satisfied with the results. According to the lawyers, the insurers tend to resent paying flat fees and then having cases settle quickly; one result is that the mix of cases referred to lawyers, which had been the assumed mix when the deal was struck, tend to change with fewer of the "quick" cases, i.e., the "slam dunks," being referred. This result is not surprising. Suppose an adjuster has $10,000 on the table and the plaintiff is demanding $20,000. If the fixed fee that will be payable if the case goes into suit or to arbitration is $5,000, the adjuster will find it advantageous to try to settle the case for any amount $15,000 or less. Another lawyer in a firm which had briefly done auto liability cases on a fixed fee basis reported that they had found the firm lost money under the arrangement because the claims representatives would not settle once a case was referred to the firm; according to the lawyer, the claims representatives' view was that "it doesn't cost us anything to take the case to trial, so why settle?" That is, the insurer did not have to worry about the cost of defense, and, as a result, the law firm found that they were trying more cases than ever before.[17] While the arrangement was entered into in good faith with the management of the insurance company, the problem arose with the lower level staff who processed cases on a day-in, day-out basis.

Alternative billing arrangements are not limited to flat fees. Other fee arrangements I saw or was told about include:

> Flat fee with opt out for a specified percentage of cases (i.e., the firm can designate up to xx% of cases that it handle on an hourly fee rather than a flat fee basis).

> Mixed flat fee/hourly fee, in which the case is handled on a flat fee up until some specified stage of the case (e.g., the start of depositions or the start of trial), and then shifts to hourly.

> Time-capped flat fee, in which a case is handled on a flat fee with a cap on the amount of billable time covered by the flat fee, such that if the cap is exceeded, the fee shifts to hourly for time beyond the cap.

> Simple phase billing, in which an agreed upon amount is paid for each stage of a case (opening and answering, initial motions, depositions, pretrials, etc.); usually these arrangements shift to hourly once trial starts.

> Multi-track phase billing, in which cases are identified as simple, medium, and complex, with different phase billing amounts for simple and medium, and straight hourly billing for complex cases.

> Mixed hourly and "unit" billing, in which some activities are done on an hourly basis and some on a "unit" or per diem basis (i.e., a specific amount for a deposition, a specific amount for reach day of trial).

> Open-file billing, in which the firm receives a set amount for each month a file is open, typically with some minimum to account for the flurry of activity involved in opening a file (e.g., $250 per month with a three month minimum).[18]

From the viewpoint of the law firm, the firm provides an additional service to the insurer by accepting some of the risk posed by unpredictable legal expenses.[19] However, the market position of the insurers is such that they often,

---

[17] Another lawyer, who told me that her firm had tried a "flat fee up until trial arrangement" for such cases, reported that her firm found that the adjusters had less inclination to settle early, and that many more cases progressed closer to trial.

[18] A lawyer I interviewed at one of the firms with this kind of arrangement told me that the firm arrived at the per-month fee by analyzing the average monthly billing per case for a particular client and then setting a fee commensurate with the historical average.

[19] The firms can limit the risk by including provisions, such as the number of trials per year, in their agreements with insurers (with trials above the agreed upon figure handled under a traditional hourly fee arrangement).

if not usually, can get this additional service essentially at little or no cost from the firm.

One major dilemma that these arrangements present is that, as with any billing or fee arrangement, the incentives of the payer and the payee of the fee depend on the arrangement (see Johnson 1980–81; Kritzer 1994, 2002b). Behavior is at least modified by the incentive structure, even if there is an agreement that cases will continue to be referred as before and that lawyers will continue to handle cases as before. I discussed above some of these incentives with regard to the flat fee. It is easy to imagine the incentive-related effects that go with other arrangements (e.g., for open-file billing, there is an incentive to keep a file open at least until costs have been covered).

This is a particular problem when the client is not the insurance company paying the lawyer's bill but the insured whose policy requires the insurer to cover the cost of defense. One lawyer specifically commented, "I think that they [the insurer] were uncomfortable with the obligations made in their policies to their insureds; uncomfortable in that a flat fee arrangement might curb what a lawyer should be doing for an insured, a premium payer." While in most cases, claims are well within policy limits, and hence the insured simply wants to have the insurance company deal with the case and be involved only when necessary,[20] alternative billing arrangements can be extremely problematic if there is any risk of the case going to trial and resulting in a verdict that exceeds insurance coverage. Thus, if the incentive structure discourages the defense lawyer from undertaking the same level of pretrial preparation that lawyer would undertake if being paid on an hourly fee, the lawyer may be subject to claims of malpractice from the insured, and possibly to disciplinary action from the regulatory body responsible for the legal profession. One lawyer described this issue very well:

> To me, there is an inherent conflict; an immediate and apparent conflict on the flat fee basis. You can imagine this scenario: Insured has a $50,000 limit, and you've agreed to a $5,000 flat fee. You're now at $4,995; you propose to take some depositions, and some other things. The insurer is all for it because now you are on your own nickel. Let's say the case comes back with a verdict of $125,000. The insured, your client, to whom you owe due diligence, fealty, and loyalty, now says:
>
> "What happened?"
>
> "We got a bad result."

---

[20] One lawyer described to me his typical relationship with the insured who is the actual client. When the lawyer receives the file from the insurer, he writes to the client to introduce himself and to alert the client that the case is in suit. The lawyer may have a telephone conversation with the client to get the client's side of what happened, although if the insurer's file contains a statement from the client, the lawyer may rely on that during the preliminary stages. The lawyer typically will not actually meet the client until it is time for the client's deposition at which time he will have the client come in an hour or two before the deposition for preparation. Unless the case actually goes to trial, the only other contact the lawyer will have with the client will be when he sends the client a letter informing the client that the matter has been resolved.

"How come you didn't do any discovery after May 16?"

"I didn't think it was necessary."

"What billing rate did you have?"

"I had a flat fee."

"When did you hit the flat fee cap?"

"May 14."

Thus what it creates is an immediate conflict, because the age old conundrum for insurance lawyers has been the proscription against, in the rules of ethics, being paid by someone other than your client. The American Bar Association and the insurance industry created some rules of agreement back in the late 1930s, canons of understanding between the insurance carriers and the profession. This was allowed because it was the only way you could do it and get the benefit of the agreement by the insurance company to pay for the defense lawyer. But that problem becomes more acute as you start altering the billing arrangements.

Another lawyer I interviewed told me of a case where he was sued by a defendant for failing to provide a vigorous defense:

Several years ago, I defended a client [an insured] who, while drunk, drove the wrong way down a divided expressway and crashed head on into an oncoming car. The driver of the other car suffered serious injuries requiring lifetime medical care. My client had a $100,000 limit policy, but the plaintiff refused to settle for the policy limit because she wanted a judgment reflecting the actual amount of damages even if it was uncollectible. The case went to trial, and the jury returned an award for multiple millions.

A couple of years later, my client turned around and sued me for failing to provide a vigorous representation. He claimed that I should have argued that the design of the expressway entrance was defective—if the entrance had been properly designed, it would not have been possible to get on the highway going the wrong way, and thus the government was at fault for defectively designing the expressway. During discovery, the former client's lawyer found something in my file that suggested I had handled the case on a flat fee basis; the lawyer advanced the argument that this was evidence that I had failed to provide zealous representation. Fortunately, as it turned out, I had in fact told insurer that the case was too big and complex to handle on fixed base and it was actually handled on an hourly basis.

One obvious solution to this kind of problem would be to limit the use of alternative fee arrangements to matters where the lawyer represents only the insurance company, as is the case in no fault claims and UM/UIM claims, or to claims that clearly fall well below any policy limits.[21]

---

[21] Thinking about the lawyer who reported that his firm had found itself trying many more cases under the flat fee arrangement because the insurance representatives had less incentive

The lawyers at Etling, Burke & Howe appeared to feel that how they handled a case was influenced, at least somewhat, by the fee arrangement under which they were working. Under arrangements where they do not bill the client for their time, there is an incentive to increase efficiency. Thus, if there is a choice between using a formal discovery process to obtain needed information and trying to get that information without the time and expense of a formal process, under alternative billing arrangements the lawyer may be more inclined to use an informal process. Under some of the arrangements there is an incentive to move files along as quickly as practical given the issues in the case. One EBH lawyer who often worked under alternative fee arrangements commented to me that he has had plaintiffs' lawyers say things like, "[T]hanks for getting this done so quickly."

Another lawyer whom I accompanied to a judicial settlement conference commented as we walked to the courthouse that he had no incentive to keep the case going because it was a flat fee case (he also commented that the plaintiff's lawyer probably wanted to get it settled because that lawyer's investment in the case already well exceeded any fee the lawyer could expect to get). However, I do not want to suggest that the alternate fee arrangements lead defense lawyers to roll over and play dead in the negotiation process. Given the continuing nature of the relationship with the insurance company clients, the lawyers have an inherent interest in getting "good deals" for their clients. In addition to concerns about how they are perceived by their repeat clients, litigators tend to be competitive. One lawyer I spoke with told me that in a case he was trying to settle, he had settlement authority of $10,000 and had received a demand for that amount; nonetheless, the lawyer said he would haggle with the opposing lawyer and see if he could get the other side to accept a lower amount in settlement. Thus, while the fee arrangement may affect the inclination of the defense lawyer to hold out for a marginally better deal, the effects are to be found at the margins.

Another kind of incentive effect of various fee arrangements concerns who within a firm should do various tasks. Under an hourly fee arrangement, the obvious incentive is to have as much work done by "timekeepers" (i.e., staff who track and bill for their time) as possible, provided that the client is willing to pay for the work. Typically, the insurer's litigation guidelines specify some tasks that they will not pay for on the assumption that the work should be handled by clerical staff (e.g., scheduling depositions, arranging for a court reporter, sending forms requesting medical records, etc.). Even within such guidelines, however, there is a lot of discretion reflecting how tasks might be characterized. For example, what is involved in requesting medical records? If it is simply filling out a form requesting all records between two dates, attaching a release from

---

to settle [discussed above], one also could argue that even if there were absolutely no risk of a verdict exceeding coverage, the insured has to endure the time and psychological costs of trial, which would otherwise be avoided through settlement. Of course, there is also the situation of the insured who feels strongly that she or he has no liability or responsibility for what happened and wants to be vindicated through trial, but under the traditional fee system does not get the opportunity because the insurance company makes a business decision that it is best to settle the case.

the plaintiff, and mailing it to the medical provider, it makes sense to label it a clerical task. However, if what is involved is reviewing medical records received to date, identifying gaps in the medical records or issues that require additional investigation (e.g., possible pre-existing conditions), and preparing a request that specifies in some detail the records being requested, this is more than a clerical task. Thus, while the goal under alternative fee arrangements is to push work down to the lowest level person who can do it efficiently, the goal under an hourly fee is to push tasks upward in the fee hierarchy. This must be done with some sensitivity, both to formal guidelines and to the continuing relationship and the desire for future business; a lawyer does not want the insurer to develop a view that the lawyer is "overstaffing" a case, either in the sense of spending too much time on the case or in the sense of having tasks done by more expensive personnel than is necessary.

While an hourly fee creates an incentive to push work up to timekeeping and higher priced staff, under a non-time-based arrangement the incentive is the opposite: to have the work done by the least expensive personnel that can do an adequate job. The firm wants to keep costs as low as possible because any difference between costs and fee is either profit or loss; the lower the costs, the higher the profit (or the lower the loss). Thus, even if an insurer being billed on an hourly basis would pay to have a paralegal complete a task (e.g., preparing a treatment chronology), if the task could be done by a secretary paid $20–$25 per hour rather than a paralegal paid $30–$35 per hour,[22] and if the time were not being directly billed to the insurer, it would be advantageous to have it done by the secretary. Similarly, if there were an investigatory task that could be done either by the lawyer or by the paralegal (or a law clerk or an investigator), the incentive as to who should do the work would depend on the billing arrangement.

In some ways these seem like straightforward choices, assuming that there are significant cost differentials for different types of staff. The difficulty arises when a firm does work on a variety of fee arrangements. If company X pays by the hour while company Y pays on an "open-file" basis, the firm would like to have work distributed differently depending on whether the file is from company X or company Y. However, from a management perspective, this work distribution is extremely difficult to bring about. At Etling, Burke & Howe there was a drive to increase the ratio of timekeepers to secretaries as a way of reducing overhead. However, this only reduces overhead under the hourly arrangement where secretarial staff is a pure cost and produces no income; under alternative arrangements secretarial staff can be a profit center if the secretary is able to do work that under an hourly arrangement would be assigned to a more costly timekeeper.[23]

---

[22] The cost of secretarial time may not be less than that of a paralegal. A senior, experienced secretary may well be paid more than a relatively junior paralegal; in fact, the average salary of paralegals at EBH is only about 10% more than the average salary of legal secretaries at the firm, and many experienced secretaries are paid more than relatively junior paralegals.

[23] From a firm management perspective, it is not easy to distribute work in the optimally efficient manner. Doing so requires tracking the time and costs of all elements involved in handling cases, including the time which secretaries devote to specific cases.

C. Marketing: Getting and Keeping Business

As with any business, insurance defense firms prosper only as long as they have a continuing flow of work that is reasonably predictable. Traditionally, firms did many things to maintain a good flow of work from their insurance company clients. One element of this was to be very cognizant of the insurers' expectations vis-à-vis costs. While the natural incentive under an hourly fee is to bill as much time as possible in a given case, this is not true if one is dependent on current sources (and payers) for future cases; under that circumstance, the lawyer has to take care that the bills do not seem out of proportion with what other firms are charging or the adjusters' expectations. I saw repeated examples at EBH of lawyers making efforts to reduce expenses in a way that benefited their insurance company clients, and often that involved putting off to the last minute billable activities in anticipation of a hoped-for settlement.

Historically, the adjuster with whom the lawyer interacts has played an important role in the dance of expectations, and lawyers and firms have worked hard to maintain good working relationships. Law firms often entertain the adjusters with whom they work through happy hours, meals, tickets for sporting events, golf outings, hunting and fishing trips, and the like.[24] Social aspects are important to keep the relationships well-oiled. However, many insurance companies have moved to limit the role of the front-line adjusters in these relationships. This has happened in a variety of ways. Insurers have centralized claims offices so there are no local personnel (making social events difficult) or have greatly limited the authority of local offices.[25] Many insurers have begun enforcing existing but long ignored policies that restrict adjusters' participation in these activities. At least some firms have tried to work around these policies by wrapping meals or other "goodies" into seminars on recent developments that are relevant to the adjusters' work.

---

[24] One other issue that has developed relates to gender. Many of the traditional marketing activities are geared more toward traditionally male interests (sporting events, golf, hunting, fishing, etc.) than what some would see as female interests. This made sense in a time when most adjusters were male (Ross 1980:28). However, the adjusters with whom the lawyers work are increasingly women. One lawyer estimated the percentage of women adjusters to be as high as 90%, and no one I asked gave a figure less than 50%. Some firms have adjusted their entertainment activities to include theater tickets and even have designed events so there was a choice between playing golf at a resort and spending time at the resort's spa. At least one female attorney with whom I spoke expressed discomfort over social situations in which she found herself taking a male adjuster (or a group of male adjusters) to dinner or out for drinks; wait staff would always present the bill to the male. Another woman attorney reported that in discussions about marketing activities in her firm, she presented statistics to her male partners which showed that over 90% of hunters are men.

[25] Limited authority at the local level is by no means a new development (Ross 1980:172-74). However, other changes may have further reduced the discretion of adjusters, whether local, regional, or national. Specifically, many insurers now employ a computer-based system for assessing claim value; the most widely used such system is known as Colossus, which was developed by Computer Sciences Corporation. See Colossus Brochure, http://www.csc-fs.com/downloads/pcbroch/colossusbroch56404500.pdf (last visited May 24, 2006). Colossus has been controversial among the plaintiffs' bar (see DeShaw [undated]; see also Heckman 2003).

Even with such limits in place, it is clear that defense lawyers continue to value relationships with adjusters with whom they work on a regular basis. The lawyers I observed at Etling, Burke & Howe routinely spent a bit of time during most telephone conversations with adjusters engaging in some informal social chat about family, activities, sports teams, and the like. While in most cases this amounted to only a minute or two at the beginning of a call, on occasion it went on for some time. After one fairly lengthy bit of social chat I overheard with an adjuster, the lawyer commented that this adjuster tended to go on and on, and to maintain the relationship the lawyer felt it necessary to engage in the long conversations even though he could not bill the time. Lawyers at EBH also continue to engage in more traditional activities to nurture client relationships, such as taking adjusters to lunch, distributing tickets to sporting events, and purchasing small gifts for adjusters around Christmas or at other opportune moments. An example of the latter involved an adjuster who was making her first trip to London; the lawyer went to a local book store to purchase a couple of travel books on London as a gift for the adjuster (an expense that would be billed to the firm's marketing account).

Most of the other lawyers I interviewed reported that they or their firm engaged in these same types of marketing activities, although the lawyers also reported that the amount and nature of such activities have changed over time.[26] Some lawyers said that there was more emphasis on one-on-one activities. Others suggested that certain types of entertaining have become less common. Some of these changes may reflect specific concerns on the law firm side. For example, one lawyer commented that his firm had substantially reduced the emphasis on alcohol because of an increased concern about liability issues. While at one time the two- or three-martini lunch might have been an aspect of the firm's entertaining of adjusters, that is no longer the case; nor does the firm sponsor "happy hour" gatherings with adjusters.

D. BILL AUDITING AND LITIGATION GUIDELINES

Insurance companies have sought to develop systematic methods of monitoring the billing practices of the outside lawyers they employ. One aspect of this monitoring is the controversial use of outside auditing firms where the bills submitted by the law firm are reviewed and frequently reduced (no one reported to me an instance in which the audit increased the payment). Lawyers in a number of states have attacked such auditing practices as violating attorney-client relationships and the lawyers' ethical responsibility to the client (see Brennan 1998c; Conley 2001; Van Duch 1999c). Outside auditors have an incentive to cut the lawyers' bills as a justification for the fees they are paid by the insurers; if they do not find cuts greater than their own fees, insurers may see the auditors' services as not worth their cost, although if the lawyers limit their billing in anticipation of the audits, the savings might be realized even in the absence of specific cuts made by the auditors.

---

[26] One lawyer reported that at one time "you were supposed to wine and dine so many hours a month; it's not part of our firm's practice, and I don't think it's part of any firm's practice, at least not openly."

Even if outside auditors are not used, insurers may require lawyers to submit bills through an on-line system, either one provided by an outside vendor or one created and run by the insurer itself. One lawyer complained to me that a major insurance company client had started using an outside vendor but required that the submitter of the bill pay the vendor's fee. That is, every time the law firm submitted a bill for a case, it had to pay the outside vendor a fee of $20. This created a disincentive to submit bills for small amounts of time because the billing fee of $20 could take a nontrivial chunk out of the amount being billed: when aggregated across a large number of cases, $20 fees quickly add up to a sizeable amount. One side result is to encourage firms to carry small amounts of outstanding time across billing periods in order to avoid repetitive billing fees. This effectively allows the insurers to secure an interest-free loan from the law firm; while any one such "loan" is small, the total amount of such interest-free loans outstanding at a given time many be quite significant when the client is a large insurer with many files out at law firms.

Another way that insurance companies have sought to control outside counsel has been to define what counts as billable time. Insurers do this by establishing formal guidelines that specify procedures that defense counsel must follow and identify a list of things that the insurer will not pay for or will pay only at a reduced rate:

> Clients have gotten more frugal, and they demand more explanation for what you're doing. That's the biggest change. They'll pay for less. For example, they'll say, we'll pay you half time to travel. I don't care that you have to drive to somewhere way up north because we ask you to take the case. You can't fly there; you have to drive. But they're only going to pay you half time for that. Or clients won't pay for voice mail, even though you have to pick up the file and you have to figure out why you're calling, and dial, and you make notes; it's usually six minutes or more there anyway. And it seems to get more stringent as the years go by.

In addition to specifying what can be billed, the typical set of guidelines require the lawyer to provide a written report periodically to the insurer and to obtain approval for key steps in the litigation process (e.g., obtaining independent medical examinations, hiring experts, scheduling depositions, and the like). Some insurers require the lawyer to prepare a litigation budget for each file the insurer refers to the lawyer.

The lawyers I spent time with and interviewed saw these guidelines as a necessary evil and found ways to work within them such that conforming to the guidelines became part of the lawyers' routines. No lawyer I spoke to reported that they encountered significant resistance to proposed litigation plans (i.e., taking depositions, doing medical exams, etc.); occasionally an adjuster might suggest holding off on an activity (e.g., a medical exam or a deposition) in the hopes that the case might settle without incurring that expense. The more frequent problem that lawyers mentioned was simply getting the adjuster to respond to the request to proceed with some activity; lawyers attributed this to the heavy caseload most adjusters carried and to the trust they felt existed between the adjusters and themselves. The solution that most lawyers arrived at was to tell the adjuster that they planned to proceed as outlined unless they heard otherwise from the adjuster. In the words of one lawyer:

> For the most part, at least these days, I'm working with insurers with whom I've got a lot of trust, and I write up a report, and say, "This is what I think we should do, and if you disagree call me," and I don't get any calls.

One lawyer told me that a particular adjuster told him to put a memo in his (the lawyer's) file indicating that he had received verbal approval to proceed so that if a question came up during an audit, they were covered. While getting adjusters to respond was often an issue, lawyers typically reported that some adjusters were quick to respond, either because it was just the adjuster's style or because the lawyer and adjuster had not had a lot of prior experience working together. One lawyer reported that one of the companies he worked with had a form that the adjuster was supposed to sign and return approving the plan proposed by the lawyer. Still, even when an adjuster wanted to discuss some aspect of what the lawyer was proposing, or wanted some additional justification, lawyers reported that the adjuster almost always approved the course of action the lawyer had proposed.

While one might expect lawyers to complain about being required to prepare budgets, I heard few objections. Some lawyers told me that they dealt with the budget issue by updating the budget regularly as the case progressed. One lawyer commented that it was sometimes a problem to increase a budget as a case progressed, not because of the adjuster but because of the adjuster's superiors; the lawyer found that he often had to write elaborate letters justifying the increase in the budget. Other lawyers told me that they simply gave the adjuster a "high side" budget to reduce the likelihood that they would have to increase it to avoid these kinds of problems. Perhaps the most interesting comment on budgets was from a young lawyer who told me that he was very suspicious and hesitant about budgets initially but had come to realize that being required to prepare budgets forced him to think through cases more thoroughly when they initially came in. Of course, sometimes the insurer's demand for a budget seems a bit absurd:

> I settled one case right off the bat, before I did the budget. I submitted the bill last month, and they wrote back, "We can't pay this because you haven't submitted the budget." Well, it's kind of ridiculous, so I have to sit down and for 20 minutes go through what the budget would be in a case that's closed, and probably didn't cost them more than $300, $400 in attorneys' fees, and the budget is going to say $5,000.

One lawyer pointed out how the budget can be extremely useful for the insurer from a business perspective other than as a means of controlling the relationship between the lawyer and the insurer:

> If I tell them that my litigation budget on this file is $10,000, and they could settle it for five [$5,000], it is a pretty easy decision for them.

114

So when I'm recommending settlement in my initial evaluation in this range, they say, "Yes, it makes sense from a defense side. Let's go in and do that." So I do think that they're worthwhile.

Billing guidelines (i.e., what can and cannot be billed) raise fewer problems than one might expect. One specific area that did seem problematic was the policy of some, perhaps many, insurers that they would not pay for internal meetings (i.e., meetings where two or more lawyers met to discuss a case). This creates some problems when a senior lawyer assigns a junior to work on a case, and they need to meet to discuss the case. It can also create problems when a case raises different kinds of issues which are handled by different lawyers, and the lawyers need to meet to coordinate their activities. I did not sense that this was a major problem but rather that it was more of a nuisance; I suspect that the time was still billed, but was not described as a meeting.

The other problem that the billing guidelines create, when combined with auditing by the insurers, is the need to adequately describe activities so that whoever reviewed the bills would not question whether it was a billable item. Part of this involves the need to identify an appropriate code for the specific activity involved and another part involves the need to provide a narrative description of the activity. One lawyer I interviewed told me about a particularly extreme example: The lawyer called the representative of the insurance company to find out what billing code to use in connection with some work he had done; this work saved the insurer $40,000 by providing a basis upon which to deny coverage. The representative he talked to asked what exactly he had done. The lawyer explained that he had spent one hour thinking through the client's situation and had come up with the idea which the insurer subsequently used in a letter it sent to the insured denying coverage. The contact told the lawyer that there was no billing code for "thinking."

A more common example is requesting medical records. Simple requests to medical providers to send medical records are deemed to be clerical tasks that should be completed by clerical staff who are not timekeepers (i.e., it is not a billable task). However, preparing a request for medical records can be billable if it is more than clerical. For example, a paralegal can bill his time for this task if the billing notation says something like, "reviewed medical records received to date; identified possible prior treatment that might be related to claimed condition; prepared specific request for medical records for relevant treatment and time period." This work is seen as involving judgment rather than simply performing a clerical activity. Law firms have to train staff, both junior lawyers and paralegals, to use the appropriate descriptions and catch phrases that will reduce the likelihood that a billed item will be questioned.[27] It is important to note that lawyers did not necessarily see the documentation/description

---

[27] The training is not only an issue for new staff; there is also the issue of teaching old dogs new tricks. One young lawyer who was a shareholder in a small, relatively new insurance defense firm commented that at her previous (larger) firm, many of the older lawyers had substantial difficulty adjusting to the demands of the insurers for documenting exactly what they were doing. Where previously they might simply have recorded "prepare for deposition," they now had to detail what this preparation involved, or the insurer would refuse to pay for the time.

requirements as a bad thing; one lawyer commented, "Part of [the auditing process] was really good for us, because it made us describe what we did, and the more we describe what we do, the easier it is for people to pay that bill." Another lawyer commented that "it now seems natural to put down the detail of what you are doing in the time records."

While the lawyers have accommodated the demands of their insurance company clients in terms of billing, prior approvals, and general oversight, they do have mixed feelings about these developments. When I asked one lawyer about the major changes he had seen over the last ten years, he replied:

> Oh man, much more oversight by the insurance companies. Much more concern with the bottom line. Much more control, or attempt to control the case, by the insurance companies, rather than to rely on my judgment. I feel like I'm being second-guessed a lot more. And it's getting to the point where it's almost an adversarial relationship. Adversarial isn't the right word. But it's like the companies who are hiring us to do the best job for their insureds don't trust us enough to do the best job. They have to second-guess what we're doing. We're not going to pay for this because we don't think it was necessary. But we aren't going to pay for this because we don't think it took you as long as it did.[28]

While these kinds of changes are attributed to cost consciousness on the part of the insurance companies, they may also reflect consolidation within the insurance industry, and the problems that such consolidation creates for management and control:

> The insurers have become hierarchical. There's less control locally. And, we saw, perhaps beginning about 10 years ago and capping about five years ago, a consolidation within the industry. Companies were merging, and so they necessarily had to become more hierarchical. And so the relationship with the local adjuster has been de-emphasized. And the adjusters themselves in these companies are probably feeling it as well. More need to document what they're doing. Less decision making that they can exert. And depending on the client-base, that could be more so as far as how they handle the case.[29]

One might ask whether any firms or lawyers had such negative experiences with one or more insurance companies that they decided to decline future

---

[28] One of Tom Baker's respondents expressed much the same view: "I can look back 33 years and if I look back 33 years to 1966 we pretty well had the freedom to handle, and I did some litigation in 1966. ... We had the freedom to handle a case the way we wanted to. We would report to the company and we knew the people at the company pretty well, or the senior partner knew them personally. So we had pretty much freedom to handle that case the way we chose."

[29] A number of lawyers commented on the declining role/decreased authority of local claims people (see above for a discussion of the possible role of Colossus). The consolidation probably has also affected personal relationships between senior partners and senior insurance company executives. One lawyer commented, "The biggest changes were just the nuance of the relationship between a more personal relationship where the firm, the rainmaker in the firm, had a personal relationship with the claim manager or the vice president of the company."

business from those companies because the work was not worth the hassle. Only two or three lawyers reported having "fired" a client insurer for these kinds of reasons. At one firm I was told that there were insurers they would not work for, but this was because the firm would not agree to the rates that the insurer was demanding. A senior partner at another firm told me:

> Firms like ours do not get into bidding wars for absurd fee agreements, and we often walk away from business opportunities we regard as unprofitable. We have fired a number of clients over the years because of pricing issues.

There were also firms that I was told had abandoned routine insurance defense work, but this too was more because of the fees insurers were willing to pay as opposed to issues such as billing or litigation guidelines. In fact, even large corporate clients often (perhaps usually) have guidelines for billing and litigation activities that their law firms must abide by, although they may be less manic over details than the insurance companies.

1. The Tyranny of Time

Despite the growth of alternative billing methods, time and timekeeping are central to insurance defense practice. Every lawyer I spoke with reported that the expectation at their firm was that lawyers would bill at least 1800 hours per year; in some firms this expectation was formalized while at others it was an informally accepted goal. Lawyers reported having billed between just under 1800 hours to over 2200 hours during 2004. The time billing expectation creates two problems: putting in the time and recording it in billing records.

The lawyers I spent time with made many remarks about needing to keep pushing to get enough hours billed; they would remark that they were "getting behind" and needed to find ways to make up time.[30] This often meant working at home in the evening, coming in on weekends, or starting the work day as early as 6:00 am. It also was reflected in comments complaining about having to spend time on activities that the lawyers did not feel they could bill. Some of this time was spent on overhead activities, such as preparing for seminars which were part of the firm's marketing activities, reviewing billing records, attending internal firm meetings, or preparing personal business plans for the coming year. Some of it was time spent on cases that the lawyer simply felt could not be billed to the client.[31] An example of the latter involved a lawyer who had a very

---

[30] At least one lawyer I spent time with specifically commented that my presence was "slowing me down;" I suspect that some of the other lawyers felt this way as well even if they did not verbalize their concerns. This was an issue that I was very sensitive to, and I tried to refrain from asking questions except during natural breaks (i.e., trips to get coffee). Even so, my presence frequently prompted lawyers to talk about what they were doing or to ask me questions about how I would evaluate something.

[31] In some situations it was the firm and not the lawyer who felt the lawyer could not bill all of the time. The management at EBH looked closely at both the hours billed and the revenue generated by each lawyer. This can be a particular problem when there are alternative fee arrangements. A lawyer under pressure to bill 1800 hours may 'flog' files that are billed on a non-hourly basis because the lawyer does not have to be concerned about the insurer auditing

peripheral role in a case but was the only person available when a call came in from a client inquiring about the status of a court filing in the case. The lawyer spent over an hour trying to track down what had happened because no one else (no lawyer, no paralegal, and no secretary) was in the office or reachable who could quickly provide the information. The lawyer commented to me as he worked on this task that he was going to have to "eat most of this time."

A key issue for everyone in this system is recording the time spent working on client matters. One of the more senior lawyers I spoke with talked at length about the problems of getting lawyers who are supposed to record time to do it accurately and to get it all down even when they are expected to bill a certain amount of time. He related his own problems tracking his time:

> At the end of the day, I review the time I have recorded, and it often seems an hour or more short. And I can't figure out where the missing time went.

This is a problem even for lawyers who tend to spend concentrated periods of time on a single file rather than jumping among up to a dozen files in the course of a day.

Lawyers have a variety of strategies to deal with this problem. Some lawyers simply keep the billing/time-record software open in a window on their computers and try to immediately record every bit of time on every case as it happens. One lawyer I spent time with uses a computer program called Time Stamp, which resembles a chess clock. This program allows him to click among files; at the end of the day he can look at the "clock" and record his time during the day. One problem he encounters is being sure to open a clock for a file if an unexpected telephone call comes in; another is being sure to "hit the button" to switch among files. At the end of the day, he still has to reconstruct what he has done on each file that he recorded time on.

Even with a good strategy to track time, there are issues of what to record and what to let slide by, as well as how to record time. That is, who defines what an hour is? The standard minimum billing unit is a tenth of an hour (six minutes). It was common for lawyers to record that minimum for any activity even if the activity, sending a quick email or a telephone call, required only a minute or two. But there is still the question of how to count the time spent playing telephone tag (i.e., do you record one tenth of an hour if you try to call an adjuster or opposing counsel or expert and end up leaving a voice mail message?) or reading an email that does not require a reply (is this worth a tenth of an hour?). Imagine the following sequence on the "Smith file": at 9 A.M. lawyer Jones gets a call from the adjuster asking about the status of the case, and Jones tells the adjuster that he is waiting to hear back from the plaintiff's lawyer on a date for the plaintiff's deposition. The call lasts two minutes. At 10:30 the plaintiff's lawyer calls to say that he can make the plaintiff available on a specific date; Jones checks his calendar and agrees to that date; the call lasts two minutes. At 1 P.M., Jones's secretary brings in the mail, and in it Jones

---

his or her time. However, this is a very significant concern for the firm which wants lawyers to generate revenue equal to (or, preferably, greater than) their hourly rate for 1800 hours.

finds a long awaited medical record for the Smith file, and spends eight minutes looking at it. He does nothing else on the Smith file that day. How much time should Jones record for the file? Should he aggregate the time and record two tenths of an hour, or should he treat each bit of time as a separate billable item and record four tenths? Would it be different if the tasks were done consecutively so that the lawyer spent a total of twelve minutes during a single time stretch? Should time be broken out by task or by client?

From the viewpoint of a lawyer who needs to accumulate 1800 billable hours in the course of a year, billing for distinct tasks increases the amount of time that might be billed in the course of a day. It may be possible to actually bill eight hours during a period of eight hours in the office if there are a lot of tenths that actually only involved a minute or two. In the course of an hour, a lawyer might try to return a dozen phone calls, completing only three, each of which lasts fifteen minutes. For each of the three completed calls he might bill three tenths of an hour and for each of the nine voice mail messages left, he might bill a tenth. The total would be eighteen tenths of an hour billed for a sixty minute period.

As I spent time with the lawyers at Etling, Burke & Howe it became clear that tracking and billing time is a learned skill. This was most evident as I watched one lawyer work with a paralegal who had been promoted from a position as a secretary. In the earlier position as a secretary, the employee had not needed to track time. As a paralegal, she was now a timekeeper and the firm expected paralegals working full time to bill 1600 hours per year or roughly thirty-two hours per week.[32] The new paralegal was having trouble even coming close to this target in the time she recorded. Part of the problem was that she was not sure what she could and could not bill for; some of the problem was simply keeping track of activities in the course of the day. The lawyer supervising the paralegal was meeting with her every day or two to go over what she had billed and discussing what she had not billed that she should have.

E. HANDLING CASES/WORKING WITH ADJUSTERS

The activities involved in handling insurance defense cases vary depending upon whether the case is personal injury (tort or UM/UIM), no-fault, workers' compensation, or property damage. Typically, lawyers have to assess cases in terms of liability, causation, and damages (or, in the alternative, the insurance company's exposure). Initial activities on a case involve opening the file (checking for conflicts and getting a file number for billing purposes) by completing some internal forms, preparing and serving and/or filing answers to complaints,[33] notifying the insured that the lawyer has been retained, beginning to

---

[32] One issue EBH was struggling with was new overtime regulations which meant that paralegals who worked more than 40 hours in a week had to be paid at time and a half. The firm could not pass on overtime costs to clients, so paralegals had to meet their billing targets within the 40 hour per week limitation.

[33] I say "serving and/or filing" because under the rules of civil procedure in the Minnesota state court, complaints and answers are not filed with the court until some action by the court is required; pleadings are simply served on the relevant parties. Lawyers in Minnesota speak in terms of a case being "in suit," which means that a complaint has been served.

collect relevant documents such as medical records and police reports, and preparing an initial assessment for the insurer.

The next phase of the work involves more formalized investigatory activities such as taking the plaintiff's (or claimant's) deposition, scheduling medical examinations, retaining experts to investigate and opine on causation issues (in products-related cases), and assessing damages more systematically. In personal injury cases there may be substantial delay between the time a file is received by the defense lawyer and the completion of this phase if the plaintiff's medical condition has not stabilized. A key issue during this phase is selecting physicians to conduct independent medical examinations, along with choosing other experts relevant to the case. Lawyers draw heavily upon their accumulated experience and connections when selecting experts. The lawyer may contact an expert used in the past whom the lawyer knows does not quite "fit" the instant file and ask that expert for suggestions. In products-related cases, the lawyer may ask the client to suggest a reputable expert.

Once the file is "mature," the case is ripe for settlement. In some situations there may be ongoing settlement negotiations as the file develops, but those negotiations may not involve the defense lawyer; that is, there may be negotiations between the plaintiff's lawyer and the insurance adjuster even as the defense lawyer works on the case.[34] Sometimes the adjuster will tell the defense lawyer to hold back on developing the file because the adjuster hopes to reach a settlement without incurring substantial litigation expense (this may arise if a case is filed to protect against a statute of limitations problem or if the adjuster had held off making good offers to see how serious the plaintiff's lawyer was).

Typically the defense lawyer does not receive any settlement authority until the file is well-developed (i.e., IME's have been completed, depositions of the plaintiff and defendant have been completed, and the defense lawyer's experts have provided at least an informal report). This does not mean that early settlement discussions never happen, but there does not appear to be pressure from the adjusters to move quickly to settlement except when the settlement discussions continue between the adjuster and the plaintiff's lawyer, although there may be cases in which the lawyer's initial assessment of the case leads the adjuster to seek a settlement before the lawyer does much work on the case. When the lawyer does receive settlement authority, that authority is likely to be at the low end of the lawyer's evaluation of the case.[35] That is, if the lawyer tells

---

[34] One lawyer reported that often in the week before trial he will let the adjuster handle the negotiations with the plaintiff's lawyer so he can focus on preparing for trial.

[35] One of Tom Baker's respondents was very adamant about the relatively limited role of defense lawyers in the settlement process: "If you do anything in your article, would you please enlighten all the people in law school, 98%, not 98%, 50% of the plaintiffs' attorneys, that the days of our having anything to do with settling the cases are long gone, long gone. ... All the new kids think we can just pick up the phone and tell the people to settle cases. When I first started out, that's the way it was. My boss used to pick up the phone and scream and yell, 'You idiot.' As a matter of fact I'll go you one further. I at one time had authority to settle for 2 different insurance companies. I had the authority to settle any case at all under $100,000. I did. I never did it. I'd always call and verify but I could. Those days are long gone. And with most of the companies they don't even want our input because they don't want to see afterwards if there was one of those bad faith things. 'Your own lawyer recommended you.' So they don't even ask

the adjuster that the exposure if the case goes to trial is $30,000, and that a good settlement would be perhaps $15,000, the lawyer's initial authority in the case is likely to be in the range of $3,000 to $5,000. As the settlement negotiations progress, the lawyer usually has to go back to the adjuster for increases in authority. For example, in the judicial mediation I attended, the offer on the table was $50,000 and the plaintiff's demand was $60,000; the defense lawyer's authority was $52,000. The judge asked the plaintiff's lawyer if $55,000 would settle the case, and the lawyer replied in the affirmative. The judge then asked the defense lawyer to find out if the adjuster would go to $55,000; the lawyer left the room, called the adjuster, and got approval for $55,000, thus settling the case.

In the most extreme situation, the adjuster essentially authorizes each specific offer that the defense lawyer extends to the plaintiff. One lawyer told me about a case that got to the eve of trial:

> Prior to suit, the plaintiff's demand was $50,000 and the adjuster's offer was $5,000; after the case went into suit and the plaintiff's doctor had been deposed, the adjuster authorized the lawyer to offer $10,000. The plaintiff reduced his demand to $40,000 but no further offers were made until a week before trial when the adjuster authorized the defense lawyer to offer $20,000. The plaintiff's lawyer responded that he had no authority to accept anything less than $40,000, but would "look at" an offer of $35,000; the defense lawyer reported to the adjuster who said, "let them stew." The defense lawyer contacted the plaintiff's lawyer and asked for a firm demand under $40,000.[36]

> Two days before trial, the defense lawyer reported to the adjuster that she had heard nothing further from the plaintiff's lawyer and told the adjuster to expect a trial result between $15,000 and $50,000. When

---

you. You just report, go down to the pre-trial, tell us what the demand was, tell us what the judge said, blah, blah, blah, this that and the other thing."

Another of Baker's respondents observed, "More and more [settlement activity] is going in-house. Just like counsel is going in-house more and more. I mean, a lot of these firms basically just tell the lawyers, 'Don't get involved in any negotiations, you just push the papers through, we'll take care of all the negotiations.'"

A third commented, "In the old days, even 20 years ago, we would tell the insurance company what the exposure in the case was and that means what they could expect for a reasonably fair verdict if they got hit. And then what a reasonable settlement value was. And I would say 95% of the time they went along. Then you went into settlement discussions and you conduct the discussions. They weren't even there. You would report to them on the phone what you thought and what the judge said and you'd give them a recommendation and they'd go along with it 98% of the time. If the case could be settled, it was. If it wasn't, it wasn't. Today sometimes they don't even ask us what the exposure is or what a reasonable settlement value is. But there usually are settlement discussions and we usually get back to them. Very often they ask. They are more proactive today, especially in the larger cases than they used to be. That's my feeling. I don't think I'm in control as I used to be."

[36] This example illustrates the risk aversion of at least some adjusters. I was struck by the fact that the lawyers were often more inclined to go ahead to trial than were the adjusters with whom they worked. This was by no means a universal pattern, but there were several cases I saw at EBH where the adjusters were very anxious to get a case settled and avoid the risks of trial.

the defense lawyer came in the day before trial, she found a voicemail from the evening before from the adjuster in which the adjuster said they were rethinking. The defense lawyer called the adjuster who said his supervisor had said to go ahead and up the offer; the defense lawyer told the adjuster that she thought that "it's going to take 40." The adjuster instructed the defense lawyer to offer $35,000, which the lawyer proceeded to do.

Two hours later the plaintiff's lawyer called and said they wouldn't go below 40. The defense lawyer called the adjuster; she told the adjuster, 'The plaintiff knows you want to settle, and they won't take less than $40,000." The adjuster authorized the lawyer to offer the $40,000, and the case settled for that amount.

In some situations the lawyer may have substantial authority to negotiate a settlement within a broad range. This seems to be particularly true at a mediation. In fact, it is often the case that the lawyer first obtains settlement authority on the eve of mediation, and that there have been no settlement discussions between the defense lawyer and the plaintiff's lawyer before the mediation. Regardless of when the defense lawyer first obtains settlement authority, the lawyer will make a first offer that is very low within that authority, but may be able to settle the case within the authority he or she has at the outset. I sat in on a mediation where the lawyer came in with $100,000 in authority. The sequence of demands and offers went as follows:

Round	Plaintiff's Demand	Defendant's Offer
1	$315,000	$20,000
2	$285,000	$25,000
3	$200,000	$50,000
4	$180,000	$57,500
5	$165,000	$62,500
6	$160,000	$65,000
7	$140,000	$75,000
8	$120,000	$75,000
	(but says he would accept $110,000)	(but says he would settle at $100,000, though refuses to settle at that amount)

When the offer stood at $65,000, the defense lawyer contacted the adjuster, who shortly was going to be leaving her office, and asked to have his authority increased to $125,000 in the event that he needed more than $100,000 to settle the case; the adjuster agreed to the increase. The lawyer told the adjuster that he hoped he would not need to use the additional authority. About ninety minutes later, the case settled for $100,000.

While in the above case the lawyer worked essentially within his authority, it is not unusual for an adjuster to actually attend a mediation. In this situation, the defense lawyer and the adjuster jointly assess offers. Even when the adjuster is not present, the lawyer may go back to the adjuster to discuss each move rather than working within the authority granted previously by the adjuster. Whether there is anything systematic that explains how much discretion lawyers receive from the adjusters in the settlement process is unclear. Certainly some of it has to do with the constraints under which the adjuster operates (i.e., company policy regarding granting settlement authority to outside counsel). One might be tempted to say that it is a function of the lawyer's experience and hence the degree of trust that the adjuster has in the lawyer's judgment; however, I saw the same lawyer work both within a context of extensive leeway (having substantial settlement authority in a case) and within a context of substantial constraint (having to obtain specific authorization for each move).

If mediation and settlement negotiations fail to resolve a case, the lawyer must prepare for trial. This involves a detailed review of materials in hand, the preparation of exhibits, the preparation of a "trial book" (i.e., a notebook outlining the case the lawyer will make at trial, containing key documents, bits of transcripts, medical reports, etc.), taking testimonial depositions of medical and other experts (including treating physicians), taking testimonial depositions of other witnesses who will not be able to appear in person at trial, and some intensive contact with witnesses the lawyer will call in person at trial. The lawyers I spent time with delayed much of this preparation for as long as they could. Importantly, this was not mere procrastination. Rather, as mentioned previously, it was a more calculated decision to avoid incurring costs that the insurer would have to pay. The goal was to keep insurers happy by limiting costs, if at all possible. The result was that the day or two before trial was very intense because so much had been put off. In the simplest cases, the lawyer might even wait until the night before trial to really work intensively on it, particularly if there were ongoing settlement discussions during the day. For the lawyers, a trial starting on a Monday was almost ideal in terms of cost controls because little negotiation would occur over the weekend; if the case did not settle on Friday, the lawyer would have two days to get ready for the Monday trial.

One final point regarding the lawyers' relationships with the insurance companies who retain them: those insurers sometimes ask the lawyers to do things that the lawyers have significant doubts about.[37] For example, one lawyer I spent time with refused, under the instructions of the insurer, to turn over some materials that the insurer claimed were privileged. The lawyer told me that the insurer always resisted requests for these types of materials even though once the plaintiff's lawyer brought a motion to compel, there was no doubt that the materials would have to be surrendered. From the insurer's perspective this was a matter of principle and they would continue to insist that counsel resist the requests even when advised that they would lose any motion to compel. In another small case involving a dispute over the necessity of medical treatment an insured had obtained and was claiming under no-fault Personal Injury Protection (PIP) coverage, the insurer was insisting that the lawyer demand that

---

[37] These examples are based on observations at EBH. I tried to devise questions that I could use in interviews to access the generalizability of these patterns, but almost none of the lawyers I spoke with would acknowledge these types of happenings. It is possible that this is unique to EBH, but I very much doubt that is the case. I suspect that many of the other lawyers had similar experiences but either my questions were inadequate to the task, or lawyers simply will not acknowledge these kinds of experiences. The only way to find out about them is to be present when they occur.

the claimant appear in person at the PIP arbitration hearing even though the insurer could agree to allow the claimant to appear by telephone (he now lived out-of-state), and the expense of travel to attend the hearing would greatly exceed the amount in dispute.[38] The lawyer expressed serious qualms about demanding that the claimant appear in person; she saw the insurer's demand in this regard as unreasonable, albeit within the insurer's rights under Minnesota's no-fault statute.[39]

Another lawyer at EBH expressed frustration to me after a no-fault arbitration hearing about handling cases where the insurer had no good defense. The lawyer believed that the insurer had made a business decision to fight such cases as a means of deterring certain classes of claims even though the insurer should have known that the claimant who persisted with the claim would prevail. A different lawyer described a case he was working on as a "virtual sure loser"; in the lawyer's view the type of case involved could be won only when the claimant would present so poorly that the claimant would have a total lack of credibility.

Sometimes insurers make demands that the lawyer can readily refuse on clear ethical grounds. For example, one lawyer told me about a telephone conversation that she had recently had with an adjuster whose supervisor had just decreed that the company would not pay on the file unless the defense counsel called the claimant's treating physician to see what the physician had to say about the case. The lawyer was able to essentially laugh off this demand by explaining that it would be unethical to call the treating physician of a represented claimant. Furthermore, while the claimant had signed a release for medical records, the claimant had not signed a release authorizing the physician to speak with anyone other than his own lawyer, and under the Health Information Protection Act (HIPA) it is illegal for a physician to discuss a patient's medical situation unless specifically authorized to do so.

F. WORKING WITH OTHER PARTIES

Insurance defense lawyers spend significant time interacting with lawyers representing the plaintiff and lawyers retained by insurance companies to represent codefendants. Just as is the case for contingency fee practitioners (Kritzer 2004b:234-41 [see Chapter 5 in this volume]), defense lawyers value cooperative relationships. This does not mean they expect the other lawyers to be less than vigorous advocates for their clients; it does mean that they value honest dealing and willingness to accommodate reasonable requests in the course of the litigation. As was true for plaintiffs' lawyers, defense lawyers reported that they found some opposing lawyers reasonably easy to work with and others to be more difficult. Interestingly, in the case of defense lawyers, these

---

[38] Not only would the travel exceed the amount being claimed, the claimant's share of the arbitrator's fee was almost equal to the amount in dispute (although the arbitrator could make an award that placed the entire burden of his/her fee on the insurer). The cost to the insurer of forcing the issue to arbitration was more than 10 times the amount at issue.

[39] The lawyer also observed that these types of demands may serve to "drive a wedge" between the insurance company and the arbitrators. The implication is that in the long run the insurer may be less able to get positive decisions from arbitrators who see this behavior.

other lawyers could be either lawyers representing the plaintiff or lawyers representing other defendants. I encountered a surprising number of comments about the difficulties that the opposing plaintiffs' lawyers were probably having with their clients (e.g., that the client had unrealistic expectations about the value of her case, or that the client was being difficult in scheduling an IME).

A very significant portion of the interaction the lawyers had with lawyers representing other parties involved lawyers representing other insurance companies. In other words, a significant proportion of tort and workers' compensation litigation consists of insurance companies fighting among themselves. As briefly mentioned when I discussed my decision to observe at a single firm, this fighting among insurers happens in two ways.

First, a good bit of litigation involves matters of subrogation in which one insurer has paid out on a policy and is now trying to recoup its payment from the insurer of an alleged tortfeasor. Aside from health insurers seeking to recoup medical payments, the most obvious example of such litigation involves significant property loss cases. Consider the case of a business that has suffered a significant fire loss; the business's insurer pays off on its policy, both for the physical loss and the lost business revenue. The investigation of the fire suggests that the source of the fire was around an area where a number of pieces of electrical equipment were plugged in, and while not definitive, the fire inspector concludes that there was probably a short-circuit in the outlet, and the circuit breaker that was supposed to cut off failed to do so. Further investigation indicates that the circuit breaker was recently installed, and it may not have been installed correctly. The business's insurer files suit, in the name of the business owner, against the electrician who installed the circuit. The lawyer hired by the electrician's insurer then brings in the manufacturer of the circuit breaker as a codefendant; the insurer for the manufacturer retains another lawyer. You now have a case involving three insurance companies, one trying to collect from a second, and the second pointing a finger at the third. While nominally the parties are the business, the electrician, and the manufacturer, in reality this is a fight among the three insurers as to which of the insurers should be responsible for paying for the loss caused by the fire.

The second situation involving fights among insurers was partly included in the above example: the finger-pointing among defendants or insurers. I saw two fairly common situations where this arises in fairly extreme ways. The first involves workers' compensation cases. Consider the following situation:

> A workers' compensation claim is filed. The claimed injury is an ag-
> gregation of a prior injury, and the aggregation is something that
> would have probably developed over time (rather than being the re-
> sult of a clearly identifiable incident such as an accident on the job).
> The condition of the claimant is such that she requires significant
> medical treatment and will be off from work for several months. The
> prior injury occurred ten years ago at a previous employer, Company
> X, who at the time was covered by Insurer A. Six years ago, the claim-
> ant left Company X and went to work for Company Y doing the same
> type of work. Two years ago, the claimant was hired by her current
> employer, Company Z. These were all small construction companies,

and each frequently changed insurers in order to get the best insurance rates; over the ten year period at issue the employers and insurers were:

Year	Employer	Insurer
1	X	A
2	X	A
3	X	B
4	X	B
5	Y	C
6	Y	D
7	Y	D
8	Y	E
9	Z	F
10	Z	G[40]

The insurers for Company Z might claim that the current condition is not an aggravation but simply a normal progression of the original injury, and hence it should be the responsibility of Insurer A. Insurer A might argue that the current condition has nothing at all to do with the original injury but was in fact a result of the claimant's recreational activities; in the alternative, Insurer A might argue that given the cumulative nature of the injury, all seven insurers should share in the payment with the shares proportional to their time on the risk. The insurers for Company Y (C, D, and E) might claim that the injury was due to a specific incident at Company Z; Insurer F might agree with that position and point specifically to an incident in Year 10, thus arguing that Insurer G should bear the full cost of the new claim.

I asked two different workers' compensation specialists what percentage of their files involved multiple insurers trying to resolve responsibility and/or shares. Their estimates differed substantially, with one giving an estimate of 10%, and one estimating the figure to be 25–35% (omitting asbestos cases which always involve multiple insurers).

The other setting where this type of finger-pointing routinely occurs involves construction defect cases. There are a large number of cases in Minnesota where homeowners are claiming that construction defects have led to moisture intrusion, which causes significant damage and can make houses uninhabitable if there is significant mold growth. In these cases the homeowner typically sues the general contractor, who brings in subcontractors (stucco, framer, roofer, window installer) and materials suppliers such as window manufacturers. Many of these parties have multiple insurers over time, and the law has been unclear as to whether liability (and thus coverage) depends upon the date the work was performed, when the damage was discovered, when the damage occurred, or some combination.[41] The result is that these construction defect cases involve

---

[40] One could make the situation even more complex by presuming that employer Z was represented in year 10 by insurer D who had previously insured employer Y for two years.

[41] There appears to be some case law in Minnesota that favors the theory that damage from moisture intrusion is deemed to be a "continuing event" and thus that all insurers on the risk from the date the owner took possession from the builder are liable, and the damages should be split proportional to the time each insurer was on the risk. See *Wooddale Builders, Inc. v. Md.*

anywhere from three to ten insurers. In some cases, the insurers for a single party may agree on a joint defense and on how to share the payment of any damages; in other cases there is no such agreement and every insurer may retain its own defense counsel.

Finger-pointing among insurers can also arise in traditional personal injury cases. A good example would be a construction accident where a new type of scaffolding being used collapses. The scaffolding might be manufactured by a company in England, for example. A U.S. vendor is responsible for selling, providing manuals and safety materials, and training purchasers. The scaffolding may be rented from an equipment supplier which contracts with a company that actually erects the scaffolding at the building site. Part of the scaffolding system might include a hoist that can handle some specified weight limit. The scaffolding collapses when a workman employed by the insulation contractor is working on it, and at the same time the roofing contractor is hoisting a batch of roofing shingles. It is not hard to imagine the finger-pointing that would go on:

> The general contractor has overall responsibility for the site and the work, so it gets sued.

> The insulation contractor can't be sued because it was the employer of the injured worker, but its workers' compensation carrier files a subrogation claim.

> The roofing contractor is sued alleging that its workers overloaded the hoist.

> The company that erected the scaffold is brought in under the allegation that the scaffolding was not properly erected.

> The company that owns the scaffolding is sued under the allegation that it failed to insure that the company it hired to erect the scaffolding knew what it was doing.

> The U.S. vendor of the scaffolding is sued for failing to adequately warn the company that bought it about the hoist's limitations, and for failing to provide proper training.

> The foreign manufacturer is sued for manufacturing and selling a product that was faultily designed.

There is no question that something happened that should not have. While there may be a dispute about appropriate damages (assume that the injury is such that the worker will no longer be able to work in construction, and will be unable to engage in active recreational activities that had been an important part of his life), this case would be more an issue of resolving who should pay what portion than it would be a matter of the plaintiff demonstrating that he was entitled to significant compensation.

The transaction costs associated with these cases are very high because of the number of parties and lawyers involved. One could make an argument that a

---

Cas. Co., 695 N.W.2d 399, 404 (Minn. Ct. App. 2005). However, the lawyers I spoke with seemed to see the coverage issue as more ambiguous than this suggests.

significant portion of the costs associated with tort litigation arise not from demands by injured parties but by fights among insurers over who should pay and/or how to apportion the payment among multiple insurers. How much might be saved in transaction costs borne by insurers and their insureds if there was some system whereby insurers did not fight over these issues and there was some simple rule determining which company should bear the loss? In fact there is a history of such agreements, called "knock-for-knock" agreements (Jacob et al. 1996:129), in some settings where insurers essentially waive subrogation rights on the grounds that over a large of number of cases things will balance out, and it is best to avoid the transaction costs of fighting over responsibility in individual cases. The problem here is akin to a prisoners' dilemma: if all casualty insurers were to abide by a knock-for-knock type policy, most insurers would gain;[42] however, as soon as one insurer seeks to invoke its subrogation rights, other insurers will feel compelled to do so as well. The breakdown is particularly likely in the case of a very large loss, which would look bad on the insurer's books and place the company management in an awkward situation with shareholders and potential investors.

II. RESPONDING TO COMMODIFICATION

The idea that insurance defense practice has evolved into a "commodity" area of legal practice has been expressed before. In a 1997 *National Law Journal* article (Cox 1997:A1), law firm consultant Harvey Goldstein described insurance defense as a "commodity practice," which he compared to wills and trusts work. The nature of the practice and the nature of the market for such work allow insurance companies to "nickel and dim[e] the firms to death." A good example of this "nickel and diming" is the requirement discussed above that firms use an online system for submitting bills, and then require that the firms pay a fee to the system vendor each time they submit a bill.

Insurance companies have long been able to demand good rates from their lawyers simply because of the amount of legal services that they buy. However, the emphasis on the bottom line, combined with trends such as company consolidation and the growth of in-house (or captive firm) legal staffs led to a major shakeout in insurance defense practice starting in the early 1990s (see Taylor 1991). Some of the larger firms in the Twin Cities that were known as insurance defense firms have essentially abandoned that area and shifted their focus to other areas.[43] As part of my interviewing process, I asked respondents

---

[42] This does not necessarily resolve the subrogation issue that can arise when there are insurers who specialize in different lines of insurance (e.g., casualty versus health versus workers' compensation).

[43] This is by no means unique to the Twin Cities area. Several of Tom Baker's respondents commented about getting out of insurance defense work or limiting that work in particular ways: "We still do for some carriers the slip and fall, rear end collision, that kind of work. But that's a dramatically slower part of our practice than it once was. Considering the amount we have to pay to start an associate, it is not cost effective for the firm to do insurance defense work in those situations where we have to go to special discount built in. We can't. And the discounts are fairly substantial. ... And the auditing business. So it's a double whammy in that regard. When I first started I would say that half of our litigation department was in insurance defense work. And I would say that much, much, much smaller, it is a much smaller

to name insurance defense firms that I should be sure to contact. The name of one firm came up repeatedly, but my efforts to schedule an interview at the firm ran into problems (I was turned down by several lawyers I contacted). I finally contacted the managing partner of the firm, who agreed to meet with me; however, when in the course of our telephone conversation I mentioned that many people had suggested his firm as one that I should contact, the managing partner expressed chagrin that other practitioners were describing the firm as an insurance defense firm. He explained that the firm had shifted its focus to other areas and that insurance defense work was a very small part of the firm's current book of business.

The strategy of some of the smaller firms that did insurance defense was to develop expertise in specific, more specialized areas in which cases involved higher stakes. One area that many firms seek out is medical malpractice defense, particularly for large, self-insured medical providers. Another area involves specialized motor vehicle accident cases such as claims against trucking companies, claims against taxi companies, or claims against companies that provide specialized transportation services (e.g., medical transport, employee transport, etc.). As discussed above, a third area that was booming in the Twin Cities (as of the time of my research in 2004) was construction defect cases involving moisture intrusion. This area at times seemed like it was, at least temporarily, a full-employment program for insurance defense lawyers because each case involved a number of parties and often multiple insurers for many of the parties. As part of my interviews with insurance defense practitioners, I asked each to tell me about the most recent case they had settled; the most common type of case that was described was a construction defect case.

For the larger firms that want to continue in the insurance defense area, one possible business model is to develop a diversified defense practice that includes a combination of more routine insurance defense (both liability and workers' compensation) and more complex cases involving medical and professional negligence, products liability, major construction defects (beyond the moisture intrusion cases) plus areas not involving insurance defense such as intellectual property litigation or other kinds of commercial litigation. The rationale is that a larger firm can use the routine work to help cover firm overhead in areas such as accounting and billing systems, human resources, technology support, and the like. While the routine work may not generate significant profits that accrue to the partners, it can be done on a break-even basis. The routine work serves as a training area for younger attorneys,[44] and provides a pool of staff resources that

---

percent. Transitioning to commercial litigation from tort litigation. Litigation is what we're the strongest in. So we needed to have a better balance in our firm between tort litigation and commercial litigation. But it was a no brainer with the factor of, that if you ask an insurance company to pay you $300 an hour, they're going to have some second thoughts."

[44] One of Tom Baker's respondents, when asked about whether the development of staff counsel had impacted him and his firm, commented, "Not at all, because I'm handling major cases ... I need to bring in some of the smaller cases to train the younger lawyers and there was a period of time with the in-house counsel we were not getting the smaller cases and that impacted on my ability to train them. Now we're getting a sufficient number of the smaller cases that I can train them."

can be mobilized for larger, more profitable cases, which require a team of lawyers and for which higher hourly rates can be charged. Given that many of the insurers that have large numbers of small matters also have commercial lines of insurance that produce some large claims, the relationships that a firm develops and maintains handling routine work can lead the insurer to refer larger files to the firm. In a sense, the goal here is to develop a portfolio of cases some of which come to the firm in a steady and predictable way and thus provide a stable cash flow, plus a set of less predictable cases that are more episodic, but which can be billed out at higher rates because of the complexity and stakes involved. This is not unlike the portfolio of cases I have elsewhere described for contingency fee practitioners (Kritzer 2004b:10-11).

Finally, in my interviews I sensed at least some frustration about the declining importance of relationships between lawyers and local adjusters, particularly among lawyers with substantial experience. They remember a time when their relationships with local claims personnel were central to their work. These local people not only steered work to them but also could provide support if questions arose about bills and litigation strategy. Local claims people have become much less important, both losing decision-making authority and being displaced by centralized billing and audit systems; in some cases they have simply disappeared as insurers have consolidated claims operations at regional, or even national, offices. At a personal level, lawyers may feel that their work is not appreciated; they are just a cog in the claims machine—a cog that can be easily replaced if a cheaper one comes along. One lawyer expressed this very clearly when asked what has changed in his practice over the last ten years:

> I could talk a long time about this. It's one of the great disappointments I have in my practice. Two main areas: loyalty and gratitude. It's not that we don't get the gratitude from the insureds, the small guy. We continue to get that, and it's one of the great things about doing this work. ... The gratitude issue that is a problem for me is the adjusters, the supervisors—and this blends into the loyalty issue—they don't care. It doesn't matter. You might spend all night, all week trying the case. ... In the first ten years I practiced, there were a dozen occasions, I might get a letter from a corporate executive of the [insurance] company thanking me for the job I had done. ... That hasn't happened in ten years; I haven't seen it.

> Nor has there been the loyalty we used to have. It seems to be more a matter of numbers, of budgets. ... I understand that it's a business; I understand that it's corporate, [but] there are a lot of personal elements involved here. I have some clients that I have worked with for twenty years. Those guys are generally appreciative, but the heat that they're under from their companies now versus ten years ago, it's night and day. ... We could do the best job possible for a company today, get the best verdict possible, and that would mean nothing in terms of loyalty for the next case. If another firm came along and offered them five dollars less per hour, that's where they'd go.

Not all of the attorneys I spoke with saw the loyalty issue in this way. Many had established and maintained longstanding relationships with one or more insurers, even when the firm did not offer (or would not agree to) rock-bottom rates. Moreover, while the lawyers quoted above refer to insurers changing firms as solely a function of rate competition, other factors may be involved such as dissatisfaction with the work done by a firm. At EBH, one lawyer told me of a client they had lost, not due to rates but due to company consolidation (i.e., the claims manager which came from Company A which had merged with EBH's client, Company B, had worked with another firm), coming back to EBH after becoming dissatisfied with the work of the other firm.

Another lawyer told me how the loyalty that existed between the firm and one of its major insurance company clients had positioned the firm to develop creative alternative fee arrangements that persuaded the insurance company to keep their substantial business with the firm rather than moving to a staff counsel operation:

> We had represented XXXX for around 35 years at the time this issue arose. A lot of people at XXXX went to bat for us and helped convince the very few people who wanted to create a staff counsel office not to make the switch. Some of the people we worked with called us in the early stages of XXXX's planning, and that's how we got wind of their plan in the first place. I remember well the tension in the air at the meeting where I presented our proposal to the company, a proposal our friends at the company helped us formulate to meet anticipated objections. The people who liked us simply overpowered the one person at that meeting who was determined to create the new office; they were well prepared at that meeting and they provided enormous assistance in warding off this attempted change in counsel.

The lawyer went on to explain that while under the new fee arrangement the firm's revenue per hour from this company had dropped slightly, the firm had captured much more of the company's work so that their total revenue from the company was now several times what it had been previously.

One difficulty in reaching strong conclusions on the loyalty theme is that I do not have solid information on how practices have changed over time; I only have the perceptions of long-time practitioners. Moreover, perceptions about the impact of some changes in the insurance industry can cut both ways. For example, has the shift from control of allocation of files to law firms from the local claims staff to regional or national claims offices increased or decreased loyalty to firms? I observed one lawyer at EBH speaking with a claims adjuster with whom he had worked for a number of years who was moving to another company; at the conclusion of the call, the lawyer commented on his belief that this move might enable the firm to get some work from the adjuster's new employer. On the other hand, a senior partner at EBH commented that:

> The control of the business by centralized authority rather than individual adjuster, as it used to be, improves loyalty. When I started practicing, cases often went to the lawyer who gave the adjustor the best perks. We used to talk about taking an adjustor to lunch "to pick up a file." With centralization came a reduction in the number of law firms who could do the work, less discretion by individual adjusters, and greater loyalty. Now when an adjuster leaves the company, we

still keep the business, and when a new adjuster shows up, he's required to use us even though he has strong personal ties elsewhere.

The two perceptions are not entirely inconsistent because the lawyer I observed might have been dealing with an adjuster who did not work at a company with highly centralized policies, and the adjuster's new employer might not have centralized policies either. The difficult question to answer is not whether there has been some change, but how much change there has actually been.

III. CONCLUSION

Insurance defense has never been the most lucrative field of practice for American lawyers. However, the absence of high fees and the resultant high income was offset by stability and predictability. Lawyers and law firms established relationships with specific insurance companies, and barring major changes (mergers of insurance companies or droppings of lines of insurance by the companies), lawyers and firms could rely upon a steady stream of business over a period of many years. Unlike contingency fee practitioners who always had to worry about where the next client would come from, insurance defense lawyers knew that more files would be arriving next week.

The working environment for insurance defense practice has changed radically between 1980 and 2005. Insurers became even more conscious of costs and were (and possibly still are) constantly looking for ways to reduce their expenditures on defense counsel. That may mean moving work in-house, it may mean seeking alternatives to hourly fees, it may mean putting work out to bid, and it may mean changing firms if a better price can be obtained. Insurance defense practitioners now live in a highly competitive world where they must be prepared to lose a major source of work at any time. They also must be prepared to live with being "nickeled and dimed" again and again and again by the insurers who send work to them.

These kinds of changes are not unique to the field of insurance defense. They are generally consistent with the changes that have been occurring within what has been called the corporate hemisphere of the bar (Heinz and Laumann 1982: 319-85; Heinz et al. 2005:29-37). The corporate world has become much more cost conscious vis-à-vis the legal services it buys. Corporations have built up in-house counsel operations both as a means of direct cost saving (i.e., in-house lawyers can do the work cheaper than outside counsel) and as a means of intelligently monitoring the work of outside counsel both for cost and quality (Nelson and Nielson 2000:458-59; Rosen 2002:670-71). What distinguishes insurance defense work from other legal services provided to corporations by law firms is the relatively low rates that insurers are able to obtain from the firms to which they refer work. The reason that other types of corporate work have not become "commodity" in nature is probably that the corporation is likely to incur some significant costs in shifting work from one firm to another because the current firm has acquired significant knowledge specific to the corporate client. The more routine, commodity nature of insurance defense work means that insurers do not incur these costs in changing legal service providers.

7

DAUBERT IN THE LAW OFFICE:
ROUTINIZING PROCEDURAL CHANGE[1]

INTRODUCTION

Polemicist Peter Huber popularized the term "junk science" to describe questionable expert testimony offered in the course of litigation (Huber 1991).[2] Although Huber's catchy phrase has garnered a lot of public attention, the tension between scientists and other experts, and the legal process, is longstanding. Golan (2004) documents this tension going back well over 200 years in common-law countries.[3] Although most writing about experts in the litigation process focuses on what transpires in the courtroom, the relationship between lawyers and the experts they need to make or defend cases starts well before anyone stands before a judge (see Prichard 2005).[4]

What happens in court is the culmination of a long process of interaction among lawyers, parties, fact witnesses, and expert witnesses. In this chapter, I

[1] This chapter originally appeared in the *Journal of Empirical Legal Studies* 5 (2008), 875-906. An earlier version was presented at the 2006 Annual Meeting of the Law and Society Association, Baltimore, Maryland, July 5–9. Funding for this project was provided by the Project on Scientific Knowledge and Public Policy under an unrestricted grant from the Common Benefit Trust, a fund established pursuant to a court order in the silicone gel breast implant products liability litigation; data collection was made possible by a sabbatical leave from the University of Wisconsin. I thank all the lawyers who spoke with me, and particularly the lawyers at "Etling, Burke & Howe, LLP," who welcomed me for three and a half months in the fall of 2004. I also thank Les Bodin and the anonymous reviewer for their helpful comments on a previous version of this article, and the faculty of the University of Iowa College of Law for the opportunity to present and discuss the results of this research.

[2] Undoubtedly, questionable science is offered in the courtroom (as well as to administrative agencies, congressional committees, and policymakers in many other settings), but the significance of the problems discussed by Huber has come under question (see, e.g., Chesebro 1993).

[3] Saks and Faigman (2005:106) report that the earliest recorded case involving such testimony in England was in a 1610 murder trial, and they go on to observe that "the use of such witnesses was not regarded as a novelty even in that case."

[4] Prichard nicely describes the conflicting perspectives of contemporary lawyers and the technical (in Prichard's case, engineers) experts they retain to testify. Fundamental to the tension Prichard describes are differing perspectives on uncertainty and on error, with the engineers viewing uncertainty and error as inevitable while lawyers need to limit uncertainty and treat error in a way that produces "a clear-cut case for the client" (2005:27), engineers "continually look at weaknesses, short comings, problems with the product in an effort to make it work better." The engineers' goal of "criticizing a project [in order] to improve it ... conflicts with [the defense lawyer's goal of] making a clear-cut case that the product was safe" (*ibid.*, 28).

consider what leads up to the *Daubert* challenge: How do lawyers make decisions about challenging experts? What role do clients play in this process? How important are factors such as the cost of preparing challenges? What types of cases are most ripe for such challenges? Given the "junk science" debate, it is not surprising that *Daubert* is most associated with the type of science-based cases that produced that decision. However, as I will discuss below, the *Daubert* processes that I saw and heard about came from much more mundane cases, and none involved the kind of innovative or questionable science that has been at the core of the debate launched by Huber's polemic.

What I show in this chapter is that *Daubert* has become another arrow in the lawyer's large quiver. The *Daubert* arrow gets pulled out to be used against a wide range of targets in a wide range of cases. In many of these cases, the *Daubert* motion is not the hugely expensive procedural move that it is thought to be. Although *Daubert* motions are not "cheap" to prepare (I did see one motion that probably cost less than $500 in lawyer's time), many involve costs that make such motions practical in low six-figure cases and possibly even in high five-figure cases. Moreover, as I will show, *Daubert* echoes through a number of aspects of the litigation process, and has thus become part of the routine for lawyers who handle cases involving a variety of types of technical experts.

I. BACKGROUND

Through much of the 20th century, the admission of expert testimony in most U.S. jurisdictions, including the federal courts, was governed by what is known as the *Frye* test.[5] Under the *Frye* test, judges were instructed to focus on whether the testimony being offered had "gained general acceptance in the field in which it belongs." In practice, this meant that judges considered a combination of the credentials of the expert and the body of knowledge on which the expert was to base his or her testimony. The result was that courts typically adopted the standard of the scientific or technical field from which the expert came (Saks and Faigman 2005:107). The judge, in deciding whether to admit testimony, needed only to determine whether the expert had appropriate qualifications, and whether the testimony accorded with accepted wisdom within the expert's field; the judge had no need to assess what underlay the testimony. This meant that methods that had gained general acceptance could be the basis of testimony even if there was little or no scientific validation of the method employed, while innovative findings that relied on sound scientific method but had not yet gained "general acceptance" would not be admissible.

In its landmark decision, *Daubert v. Merrill Dow* (509 U.S. 579 [1993]), the U.S. Supreme Court radically altered the standards governing the admission of expert testimony in federal (and many state courts—see Bernstein and Jackson 2004; Kritzer 2008a). The Court drew on the Federal Rules of Evidence, particularly Rule 702:

---

[5] See Golan (2004) for a discussion of the *Frye* case, which involved the admissibility of testimony based on a polygraph test, and Lepore (2015) for *Frye*'s interesting origins and people.

If scientific, technical, or other specialized knowledge will assist the trier of fact to understand the evidence or to determine a fact in issue, a witness qualified as an expert by knowledge, skill, experience, training, or education, may testify thereto in the form of an opinion or otherwise.

The Court observed that nowhere did this rule enshrine the principle of "general acceptance."[6] The Court ruled that it was the judge's role to serve as gatekeeper by making "a preliminary assessment of whether the reasoning or methodology underlying the testimony is scientifically valid and of whether that reasoning or methodology properly can be applied to the facts in issue." The purpose of this inquiry is that "under the Rules the trial judge must ensure that any and all scientific testimony or evidence admitted is not only relevant, but reliable." Thus, while factual issues are normally left to the jury, because this was an issue of admissibility, it was the judge's responsibility to make what amounts to a factual determination about what the Supreme Court referred to as the "reliability" of the proffered testimony. The Court went on to enunciate a set of guidelines ("[W]e do not presume to set out a definitive checklist or test. But some general observations are appropriate...") that have come to be referred to as the "*Daubert* factors."

1. "[W]hether a theory or technique ... can be (and has been) tested."
2. "Whether the theory of technique has been subjected to peer review and publication."
3. "The court ordinarily should consider the known or potential rate of error."
4. "Widespread acceptance can be an important factor in ruling particular evidence admissible, and 'a known technique that has been able to attract only minimal support within the community,' [citation omitted] may properly be viewed with skepticism."

Rule 702 was subsequently modified to essentially reflect the *Daubert* decision's focus on "reliability."

If scientific, technical, or other specialized knowledge will assist the trier of fact to understand the evidence or to determine a fact in issue, a witness qualified as an expert by knowledge, skill, experience, training, or education, may testify thereto in the form of an opinion or otherwise, if (1) the testimony is based upon sufficient facts or data, (2) the testimony is the product of reliable principles and methods, and (3) the witness has applied the principles and methods reliably to the facts of the case.

As Saks and Faigman (2005:110) observe, *Daubert* "changed [the] focus from *Frye*'s deference to the experts to a more active judicial evaluation of a

---

[6] The Court did not say that "general acceptance" was irrelevant: "Widespread acceptance can be an important factor in ruling particular evidence admissible, and 'a known technique that has been able to attract only minimal support within the community,' [citation omitted] may properly be viewed with skepticism."

particular field's claims of expertise." Moreover, while *Daubert* itself referenced only "scientific" testimony, the same principles quickly came to apply to any kind of technical expertise that had an underlying technical or scientific basis (*Kumho Tire v. Carmichael*, 526 U.S. 137 [1999]).

II. *DAUBERT* IN THE LAW OFFICE

In the approximately 15 years since the *Daubert* decision, legal scholars and sociolegal scholars have studied and discussed the application of *Daubert* principles in the federal (and some state) courts. Research has considered the application of *Daubert* and the other cases in the *Daubert* Trilogy (*Daubert*, and *Kumho*, plus *General Electric v. Joiner,* 522 U.S. 136 [1997])[7] to a wide range of cases, both civil and criminal, as well as the broad patterns in court decisions drawing on *Daubert* principles (see Buchman 2007; Cheng and Yoon 2005; Dixon and Gill 2001; Dobbin et al. 2002; Gatowski et al. 2001; Krafka et al. 2002; Risinger 2000). Thus, the focus of research on *Daubert* is on what happens in court.[8]

However, the cases that arrive at the stage of a formal *Daubert* decision are the veritable tip of the iceberg. *Daubert* should have very substantial anticipatory and strategic impacts. That is, lawyers should be thinking about and working with experts in ways that anticipate possible *Daubert*-related issues that might be raised. For example, the deposition process, including both preparation and execution, can become a crucial element in determining whether an opposing expert is challengeable on *Daubert* grounds. In addition, *Daubert* could be used in ways unrelated to the admissibility of testimony; specifically, the possibility of a *Daubert* issue might serve as a discovery vehicle, allowing a lawyer in a deposition setting to explore questions with an expert that might otherwise not arise, or a *Daubert* motion might be part of a settlement strategy. Considering *Daubert* issues may also influence how lawyers work with their clients, both reflecting the costs of raising a *Daubert* challenge and the need to work with the client's employees in assessing the potential of a *Daubert* challenge. One might also expect that over time, as lawyers understand the implications of *Daubert*, the actual incidence of formal *Daubert* motions and hearings will decline, a phenomenon that may already have occurred in the kinds of medical-legal products cases that led to the *Daubert* decision. None of the various types of effects enumerated above can be ascertained through a study of *Daubert* limited to what comes to and takes place in the courtroom.

Essentially, *Daubert* and its subsidiary principles do not exist in isolation. Studies that focus on court rulings on *Daubert* motions fail to illuminate the ways *Daubert* has become a part of the repertoire of the federal litigator. The evidentiary considerations enumerated in *Daubert* and its progeny interact with procedural rules and other legal principles. Thus, to understand how *Daubert* influences the litigation process in federal court, one needs to examine how

---

[7] *Joiner* set "abuse of discretion" as the standard of review to be used by the court of appeals when it reviewed trial court decisions on the admissibility of expert testimony under *Daubert*.

[8] For a summary of this literature, see Saks and Faigman (2005:106).

litigators think about *Daubert* as they consider the range of options they face in the course of litigating cases. As I will show in this chapter, *Daubert*'s impacts extend well beyond the core scientific areas that were originally addressed in the *Daubert* decision; while this is not surprising given *Kumho*, the types of cases where *Daubert* looms largest may be surprising, as may the types of experts most frequently targeted by *Daubert* motions.

A. RESEARCH DESIGN

To examine the more subtle, behind-the-scenes impacts of *Daubert*, I undertook a research project involving extended observation in a law firm whose book of business included cases in which *Daubert*-type issues can arise.[9] The firm, which I call "Etling, Burke & Howe" (EBH), is located in the Twin Cities of Minnesota and has a roster of 60–70 lawyers.[10] The firm is divided about evenly between a transactional practice and a litigation practice. Most of the litigation practice is insurance defense, including auto, construction, products, medical malpractice, other kinds of professional negligence, premises liability, major property loss, and workers' compensation. The litigation and transactional groups function quite separately; often, it appears as if these are two separate firms sharing infrastructure support (information technology, overhead, human resources).

Over three-and-a-half months during the fall of 2004, I spent about two weeks with each of five different lawyers, plus shorter amounts of time with two other lawyers. During most of this time, the work of the lawyers did not focus on *Daubert*, but the design of the project was such that I shifted to focus on *Daubert* at any time *Daubert*-related things were happening. In the course of the fall, *Daubert* motions came up in four different cases and *Daubert* issues were directly or indirectly discussed in at least two additional cases. My role in the law firm was that of a paralegal and, as such, I undertook various tasks, which included assisting at a deposition of an opposing expert who was eventually the subject of a *Daubert* challenge, assisting in the drafting of *Daubert* motions involving two different opposing experts, reviewing other depositions of witnesses who were challenged or were being considered for possible challenges, researching industry materials related to possible challenges of experts, discussing with lawyers the viability of *Daubert* motions in some cases, and preparing an extended memo concerning the *Daubert* prospects in

---

[9] I chose to do this research in a single firm rather than in multiple firms because of the potential for conflicts. My concern flowed from the fact that the firm did some commercial litigation in addition to defense litigation and there was a chance that a case that I saw at EBH might turn up at any similar firm where I might have observed, with the second firm representing a client adverse to EBH's client.

[10] To find a firm with a practice that was likely to include multiple cases involving *Daubert* issues, the research had to be done in a relatively large city. I chose Minneapolis-St. Paul as the research site for personal reasons. The Minnesota state courts rely on a standard known as *Frye-Mack* (*State v. Mack*, 292 N.W.2d 764, 768 (Minn. 1980); see also *Goeb v. Tharaldson*, 615 N.W.2d 800, 814 (Minn. 2000), reaffirming the *Frye-Mack* standard), which falls somewhere between the traditional *Frye* test and the federal *Daubert* standards. Importantly, Minnesota has not adopted the abuse of discretion standard set out in *Joiner* for review of trial court decisions on admissibility of expert evidence.

one case. I also was able to observe an oral argument in connection with a *Daubert* motion.

Subsequent to the observation, and after an initial review of the observational notes, I undertook a set of 13 interviews of lawyers in the Twin Cities area whom I could identify as having handled *Daubert* motions; an additional three interviews were conducted in Wisconsin (Madison and Milwaukee).[11] Some of these lawyers were counsel in recent cases identified as part of the research I did while at EBH, some had been recommended to me by knowledgeable people in the Twin Cities area, some I found by doing Google searches, and some were recommended by other interviewees.

In addition, I did 18 interviews of individuals I had identified as lawyers whose practice focused on insurance defense;[12] as part of that interview, I asked if the lawyer had had any experience with *Daubert*, and found that two of the respondents had. I then asked these lawyers many of the questions I asked the lawyers identified specifically in connection with *Daubert*. Thus, the interview base that supplements my observations is drawn from a total of 15 interviews. Most of the interviews were tape recorded and then transcribed; for the small number where respondents declined to be recorded, I took extensive notes, which I proceeded to expand within a couple of hours of the interview itself.

III. SOME GENERAL OBSERVATIONS

A. FAMILIARITY WITH *DAUBERT*

One issue that I observed both at EBH and in the course of interviews is that many lawyers who lacked significant experience with *Daubert* tended to equate *Daubert* with the qualifications of the expert rather than the *Daubert* "factors" associated with assessing the specific testimony. For example, one of the lawyers at EBH, a mid-level partner with whom I spent a lot of time, repeatedly expressed skepticism about the possibility of getting a particular opposing witness excluded because the witness had substantial experience with the product in question (albeit most of it as an expert testifying as to its defects). A second EBH lawyer whom I observed (a mid-level associate) had a products case in which the expert had produced a report that clearly failed to meet *Daubert* standards, but the lawyer had not thought about *Daubert* because in his mind the expert was clearly qualified.[13] When I had lunch with one of these lawyers some weeks after I concluded my observation, he told me that he had thought that *Daubert* focused on the expert's qualifications; it was only in the course of the fall, by working on a couple of *Daubert* motions, that he realized that the core of *Daubert* concerned the expert's opinion and how it was derived.[14]

---

[11] On two occasions two lawyers participated in the interview.

[12] Based on the same fieldwork, and drawing on these 18 interviews, I have also analyzed the nature of contemporary insurance defense practice (see Chapter 6 in this volume).

[13] The issue of *Daubert* arose when the lawyer showed me the expert report, which he described as "shitty," and I asked about the possibility of challenging the expert.

[14] The lawyer also told me that he had not realized that it was unnecessary to depose the expert in order to pursue a *Daubert* challenge.

B. TYPES OF CASES INVOLVING *DAUBERT* CHALLENGES

As mentioned previously, four cases at EBH involved *Daubert* motions during the fall of 2004. Two of these cases arose from workplace accidents and lawsuits against the manufacturers of equipment involved in the accidents; one case concerned fire causation and involved the manufacturer of a small home appliance and one case was a commercial contract case involving a business decision made by the defendant. In addition, there were two cases in which *Daubert* was either explicitly mentioned as a possibility or in which discussions with an expert were clearly intended to avoid a *Daubert* challenge; the former was a professional malpractice (nonmedical) case and the other was an intellectual property case.

In the course of my interviews, I asked each respondent about his or her most recent case where a *Daubert* motion had actually been filed;[15] I also asked about the most recent case in which a *Daubert* motion had been considered but not filed. Table 7.1 lists the kinds of cases involved. As the table shows, the most common type of case I encountered was fire causation.[16] However, what is most

Table 7.1: Types of Cases Involved in *Daubert* Motions

	Motion Filed	Motion Not Filed
Fire causation	5	1
Toxic/chemical/mold exposure	3	1
Personal injury involving defective machine	3	3
Auto accident (causation of injury)	1	0
Intellectual property	2	1
Commercial contract	1	0
Professional negligence	0	1
Medical product (device or pharmaceutical)	0	1

---

[15] Ideally, one would like to be able to come up with some measure of the rate of occurrence of *Daubert* motions or, even better, of *Daubert* issues. Unfortunately, there is no way of ascertaining the number of cases involving issues that might be the subject of a *Daubert* motion; that is, while one in theory might be able to come up with a measure of the number of *Daubert* motions filed, to obtain a rate one must have a denominator. In theory, any case involving an expert witness could raise a *Daubert* issue.

[16] In my original design for this research, I included examining the issue of how *Daubert* had changed lawyers' relationships with the scientific and technical experts they employed. I found little evidence of that because lawyers litigating cases that involve highly technical and scientific matters have long immersed themselves in those technical and medical details. The one area where I found evidence of a changed relationship involved a lawyer who specialized in cause and origin cases (fire, explosion, structural failure). His own background was highly technical, and he prided himself on how *he* trained his experts so as to avoid *Daubert* issues. This lawyer in fact conducted what amounted to training exercises for some of the experts he might potentially use: "I'll be conducting several tests of flashovers in Roanoke. There will be experts there that I will probably use in the next four or five years."

striking by its minimal presence is medical products, including either devices or pharmaceuticals. One obvious question is whether this reflects peculiarities of my sample or broad patterns in how *Daubert* has been used.

I contacted one respondent specifically because I saw a news article that indicated that he represented a major medical device company in product liability cases. However, when I interviewed him, he told me that he had not actually filed a *Daubert* motion in more than five years. For the products made by his client, federal preemption had become the key defense (see Nagareda 2006); he reported that he was often able to get claims dropped against his client by pointing out to the plaintiffs' lawyer that the device had "premarket approval" (PMA) from the Federal Drug Administration, and this PMA approval preempted claims concerning testing and/or general defects.

> One of the reasons I haven't had to get to the point of filing *Daubert* motions recently is that many of my cases are implicated by the FDA statutes and preemption. Federal preemption has become a huge defense that I have used very successfully. It's been applicable in a lot of my cases. A lot of the devices [against which] I defend claims are FDA approved, and there's very strong preemption. So, we rarely [have] a device that isn't FDA approved, and where I really worry about an expert coming in.

This respondent went on to say that it was still possible for plaintiffs to bring some claims even in the face of preemption.

> There are ways around preemption. Even if you have a device that's FDA approved, if the evidence suggests that the device wasn't manufactured in accordance with the FDA's requirements—if it's manufactured differently, or labeled differently, or didn't undergo the testing that's required under the protocols that were approved by the FDA—[you can get] around it, and plaintiffs who are sophisticated and smart will understand that. They can get around preemption. If you have a problem there, you try and resolve the case. I don't want to see my clients spend all the time and money going to trial.

The issue of preemption came up in another interview as well, although not specifically in connection with medical device and pharmaceutical cases (although this respondent did say her practice involved such cases). When asked whether *Daubert* had changed the kinds of cases being brought by plaintiffs, she responded:

> I'm sure there are cases where [the plaintiff's lawyer] can't find [an expert] to give a general causation opinion. I generally think that in a lot of the cases I see, the plaintiff's strategy has changed to allege more things like consumer fraud. It's probably more of a result of preemption than it is of *Daubert*. But it might be a *Daubert* phenomenon too. It's harder for them to prove the basic strict liability and negligence claims, so they're a little bit more likely to bring consumer fraud type claims.

I went back and recontacted a couple of respondents to ask specifically about preemption in medical device and pharmaceutical cases. One of these respondents told me that he did not handle such cases and referred me to one of his partners who did. When asked whether preemption had supplanted *Daubert* in medical device and/or pharmaceutical cases, she responded that she thought it had, provided that the product had gone through the full PMA process; she indicated that it was less clear when something less than a full PMA review had been involved (which can occur when some relatively small change is made to a product and the manufacturer asks that only the changes be reviewed[17]). Even with a full PMA review, a plaintiff may be able to argue that the information provided to the FDA by the manufacturer was incomplete or otherwise corrupted in some way the PMA process; in these cases, preemption may fail and *Daubert* becomes clearly relevant.

The second respondent I recontacted had described his practice as involving a lot of pharmaceutical and medical device cases, as well as toxic tort and other types of product liability work. The specific case he described to me as the most recent case in which he had filed a *Daubert* motion was a toxic tort case. He viewed preemption as less important because many medical devices that become the subject of litigation undergo something less than the full PMA process that in many circuits can lead to preemption.[18] He reported that he continued to regularly file *Daubert* motions in pharmaceutical and medical device cases.

What this discussion shows is that the use of *Daubert* interacts with other developments that might undercut the need for experts. The development of the federal preemption doctrine appears to have had this impact in the medical products area. In the area of fire and explosion causation, *Daubert* also interacts with how courts have responded to the issue of spoliation of evidence. One lawyer who specialized in fire and explosion cases talked about the need to get his experts, whether he was on the defense or plaintiff side, to the site quickly to avoid any spoliation questions. A lawyer handling a major property loss case at EBH spoke about how quickly after the event he was on the scene to be sure that key evidence important for his case (and his experts) was preserved. The link with *Daubert* is that the ability of an expert to produce and defend an opinion in

---

[17] This involves what is often referred to as the FDA's 510(k) process. "PMA review typically requires 1,200 hours of rigorous testing for device safety. In contrast, §510(k) review focuses on 'substantial equivalence' and is completed in an average of twenty hours." *Brooks v. Howmedica, Inc.*, 273 F.3d 785, 795 (8th Cir. 2001).

[18] In *Medtronic, Inc. v. Lohr*, 518 U.S. 470 (1996), the Supreme Court ruled that this abbreviated process, known as the "§510(k) Process," was not adequate to invoke preemption. As of 2008, five circuits had ruled that full PMA process serves to invoke federal preemption. See *Horn v. Thoratec Corp.*, 376 F.3d 163, 169 (3d Cir. 2004); *Martin v. Medtronic, Inc.*, 254 F.3d 573, 584 (5th Cir. 2001); *Kemp v. Medtronic, Inc.*, 231 F.3d 216, 226–27 (6th Cir. 2000); *Mitchell v. Collagen Corp.*, 126 F.3d 902, 913 (7th Cir. 1997); *Brooks v. Howmedica, Inc.*, 273 F.3d 785, 795-96 (8th Cir. 2001). My respondent also was of the belief that even a full PMA process would not lead to preemption in at least some circuits, although he was not sure how many circuits had ruled against preemption. I was able to identify only one, the Eleventh, that had ruled in that way; see *Goodlin v. Medtronic, Inc.*, 167 F.3d 1367, 1377 (11th Cir. 1999).

these cases depends on the evidence available to the expert and to those who might consider challenging the expert.

C. TYPES OF EXPERTS

Daubert was initially directed to scientific testimony. Typically, the kinds of cases involved dealt with either the synthesization and summarization of an extant body of scientific findings or the reporting of original research undertaken to test the linkage between a product and an alleged injury. With *Kumho*, the analysis described in *Daubert* was extended to a wide range of technical experts. Table 7.2 lists the types of experts involved in the cases I saw at EBH, or about which I spoke to respondents. With the possible exceptions of the three economists and the business practices expert, none of the experts involved would have been engaged in original research of the type dealt with in *Daubert*, and neither the three damages experts nor the business practices expert would have been relying on their own original research for their opinions but, rather, on fairly standard methodologies.

Table 7.2: Types of Experts Involved in *Daubert* Cases

Medical	4
Engineering	10
Fire causation[a]	1
Business practices	1
Economist (damages)	3

[a] This expert was probably an engineer by training, although that was not specified during the interview.

Most striking here is the dominance of engineering experts. Are such experts overrepresented in *Daubert* motions compared to the frequency of such experts appearing in court? Without some measure of the frequency of using various kinds of experts, there is no way to know this. However, I suspect that experts with engineering backgrounds are quite common (see Prichard 2005), perhaps second or third in terms of frequency of appearance, behind only medical and damages (economics) experts. However, this is purely speculative; I know of no research systematically estimating the relative numbers of various types of experts appearing in civil cases.

D. OUTCOMES

I have information on a total of 21 motions filed either by lawyers while I was at EBH or by interview respondents.[19] Just over half (11) of those resulted in

---

[19] In addition, one lawyer told me of having prepared a *Daubert* motion that was not filed because the parties reached a settlement before the motion could be filed. Another lawyer told me of a case where he considered drafting a *Daubert* motion, but before doing so "provided the opposing counsel reasons [he] would win," and the opposing counsel dismissed the lawyer's

a trial court ruling granting the motion in whole or in part, including one that was initially denied and then granted in part at trial; six were never ruled on because the case settled or the plaintiff agreed to dismiss the case against the moving party, and four were unsuccessful.[20] Table 7.3 summarizes these results.

Table 7.3: Outcome of *Daubert* Motions

Successful, upheld on appeal	4
Successful, no appeal	6
Initially unsuccessful, but partially granted at trial	1
Unsuccessful	4
Dismissed from case before decided	1
Case settled while motion pending	5

One of these motions was filed in a state court in a state that relies on *Daubert*. In addition, there was one motion brought against a client of EBH while I was doing my observation; that motion was eventually denied by the court. My "sample" of *Daubert* motions is unlikely to be representative of all such motions. Of the motions the lawyers report having been ruled on, 10 of 15 were granted (this does not count the one that was initially unsuccessful but was partially granted at trial). A study of *Daubert* decisions producing opinions reported in the Westlaw database found that in the late 1990s (July 1996 through June 1999), only 54% were granted (Dixon and Gill 2001:54). Another study looked only at federal tort cases reported in the LEXIS database that involved expert testimony issues between January 1983 and August 2003; in 56% of the cases in that study, the expert testimony was excluded (Buchman 2007:681) over the entire period, and 57% in the years since *Daubert*.[21] A last study for comparison focused on toxic tort cases; that study, which identified 163 rulings on expert testimony using the LEXIS database, found that testimony was excluded or limited in 79% of the decisions (Robinson 2004:98).[22] Except for the last of these other studies, the success rate for *Daubert* motions was lower than was the case for the motions identified in my study; however, the

---

client from the case. A third lawyer told me about an MDL (multi-district litigation) case in which he was involved. A *Daubert* motion had been decided at the national level limiting the testimony of a particular witness. Back at the local level the opposing plaintiffs' lawyers tried to go beyond what the MDL proceeding had allowed. Eventually, the opposing lawyers "saw the error of their ways" and abided by the national decision.

[20] In two cases, I did not obtain information on the type of expert; hence, 21 cases are included here compared to the 19 experts included previously.

[21] Personal correspondence (electronic) with the author, Aug. 12, 2005.

[22] This same study also looked at *Daubert* rulings concerning expert testimony in federal criminal cases (fingerprints, handwriting, DNA, and the validity of eyewitness testimony).

difference between the success rate in my study and that in those studies with a lower success rate is not statistically significant.[23]

IV. DOING *DAUBERT*: THE LARGER LITIGATION CONTEXT

In this section, I discuss a number of aspects of how *Daubert* is used. The core point is that *Daubert* does not exist in isolation but that it interacts with other aspects of the litigation process. Some of this relates to the specific types of cases in which *Daubert* motions arise, some aspects relate to procedural rules, particularly rules governing expert discovery, and some to the role of settlement processes in litigation.

A. THE *DAUBERT* FACTORS

Daubert lays out a series of factors that trial judges might use in assessing the "reliability" of an expert's proposed testimony. The Court used the term "reliability" in the sense of whether or not one should "rely" on the expert's testimony, not in the sense that most scientists or social scientists use the term "reliability." Within the scientific community, the standard term for what the Court referred to as "reliability" is "validity." The Court listed several factors that might be pertinent in determining validity.

- Whether the theories and techniques employed by the scientific expert have been tested;
- Whether they have been subjected to peer review and publication;
- Whether the techniques employed by the expert have a known error rate;
- Whether they are subject to standards governing their application; and
- Whether the theories and techniques employed by the expert enjoy widespread acceptance.

The extension of *Daubert* to the broader class of technical experts introduced other elements into the consideration. Specifically, in the area of machine and product design, one begins to encounter issues related to "reasonable alternative design." Although the *Restatement (Third) of Torts* (Section 2, Subdivision 3) requires only that a plaintiff provide a "reasonable alternative design" to avoid a "foreseeable risk"[24] (i.e., it does not require that the alternative design be prototyped or tested), defendants now regularly argue that under *Daubert* it is insufficient to simply provide a design. *Daubert*, the defendants argue, requires that the plaintiffs prototype and test the alternative design to prove that it will

---

[23] The differences remain statistically nonsignificant if I treat 11 of 15 as granted (i.e., include the one initially denied but then partially granted at trial). Notwithstanding tests of statistical significance, if the success rate in my study is in fact higher than the universe of reported cases, it may in part reflect bias in what cases get reported. However, I suspect it also reflects bias in the cases described by my respondents, all of whom work for law firms oriented toward nonroutine litigation, more like the toxic tort area where the success rate was in fact somewhat higher than in my cases, although that difference was not statistically significant either.

[24] "A product is defective in design when the foreseeable risks of harm posed by the product could have been reduced or avoided by the adoption of a reasonable alternative design ... and the omission of the alternative design renders the product not reasonably safe."

work, that it will eliminate or reduce the risk, and that it will not introduce new risks.

In my interviews and observation, I sought to determine what specific issue concerning the proposed testimony was the focus of the challenge.[25] The most common of these issues are listed in Table 7.4.

Table 7.4: Most Common Issues Challenged by a *Daubert* Motion

Failure to test or adequacy of testing	10
Lack of prototyping	4
Absence of peer review	3
Lack of foundational evidence	7
Methodology	2
Qualifications	6

"Methodology" refers to situations where the expert was unable to describe the methodology used to arrive at the opinion the expert was advancing. "Lack of foundational evidence" essentially refers to the alleged failure of the expert to provide systematic evidence in support of his or her opinion. For example, in a toxic tort pollution case, the expert may have failed to provide evidence in support of an opinion that the source of contamination of a lakebed was a particular alleged polluter. It is not sufficient to show that the polluter was located within the watershed that fed the lake and that the polluter used or produced the toxic substances found in the lakebed. The expert must have evidence that showed how the toxic substance got from the defendant to the lakebed and must also have evidence that eliminated other possible sources of the pollution.

The qualifications issue was typically raised in conjunction with other challenges to the expert. For example, an expert might have testified that warnings were inadequate. A challenge might be raised that the expert lacked the requisite expertise in designing and testing warnings, and that the expert had failed to test an alternative warning that the expert claimed would have been more effective. In the motion that was brought against one of EBH's experts, the plaintiff had asked that the expert's testimony be limited such that the expert could not opine on the causal aspects associated with the alleged damages and thus be limited to opining on the quantum of damages. Specifically, the plaintiff argued (unsuccessfully in the end) that only someone with specialized expertise in the particular commercial area would be qualified to discuss causation, and the background of the expert in question was too general. In fact, the lawyer handling the case had tried to find an expert with industry-specific experience but was not able to do so, and decided to use the challenged expert to obtain a

---

[25] The total number of issues here is 30 because some cases involved more than one issue.

perspective from a broader viewpoint.[26] Much of the discussion about how to respond to the motion to limit the expert's testimony focused on how to characterize the issue in the case, whether it concerned a business decision that had to focus on a very specific kind of setting (which is what the motion claimed) or a more general kind of business decision to which someone with no industry-specific expertise could speak.[27]

Noteworthy by its absence from the list in Table 7.4 are challenges that focused specifically on the failure to provide an estimated error rate. This probably reflects in significant part that many of the cases I heard about involved issues of alternative design in product liability cases, and the Eighth Circuit has not viewed the error-rate prong as relevant in such cases (see *Pestel v. Vermeer Mfg. Co.*, 64 F.3d 382, 384 [8th Cir. 1995]). This makes sense because the concept of error rate does not work well in the context of design cases. The logic underlying the error-rate prong in *Daubert* comes from statistical hypothesis testing where one commonly speaks of Type I error (concluding that there is a relationship when there is not; i.e., seeing something that is not there) and Type II error (failing to conclude that there is a relationship when such a relationship does exist; i.e., failing to see something that is there). Not all testing is statistical, or can be statistical. For example, in a fire causation case, the issue might be whether the alleged cause of the fire can be shown to produce conditions that could lead to ignition. Presume that the alleged source is an electric skillet, and that the initial ignition material was a wood cabinet above the skillet. Testing would probably involve measuring the temperature that could be achieved on a surface above a skillet that was left turned on for a period of time. Although the measurement of the temperature might be subject to a certain amount of error, and the test might be repeated a number of times, what would constitute an error rate in the sense of a test of a statistical hypothesis?

B. GOALS AND SIDE BENEFITS

The ostensible purpose of a *Daubert* motion is to exclude an expert's testimony, either in whole or in part, but a *Daubert* motion can play other roles as well. Sometimes, a *Daubert* motion is filed with these other goals clearly in mind; at other times there are secondary benefits should a *Daubert* motion not be granted. Some of the goals are closely linked to excluding an expert, such as limiting the expert's testimony and by doing so getting some claims dismissed even if other claims go forward. However, some of the additional goals depart from the exclusion of experts or of aspects of testimony.

---

[26] The lead lawyer commented, "it would not be fatal to our case if [the expert] is struck, but our client won't be happy." One difficulty the EBH lawyers faced in replying to the plaintiff's *Daubert* motion was the need to avoid any arguments that would undercut their own summary judgment motion. Specifically, if they challenged the specific nature of an opposing expert's expertise, the other side might then have challenged one of EBH's experts on the same basis.

[27] At some point, the associate who drafted the reply brief in this case commented: "It muddies the waters."

As is true of many procedural and legal moves, a *Daubert* motion can be filed as part of a settlement strategy. The broader process here is what Galanter called *litigotiation*: "the strategic pursuit of a settlement through mobilizing the court process" (1984:268). Through a *Daubert* motion, the moving party may want to show the opposing party some key weaknesses in that party's case.[28] For example, in one case I observed at EBH, a motion was filed just before a scheduled mediation. Although the lawyer believed that motion had a good chance of success, his immediate goal was to settle the case on favorable terms for his client. In thinking about making the motion, the lawyer had commented to me, "I will probably bring the motion to knock down the value of the case"; he went on to discuss how he valued the case, and the value at which he thought his client would be willing to settle. Without the *Daubert* motion, he thought the opposing side would probably want at least 50% more than his client's resistance point; if the *Daubert* motion was seen as having a 50–50 chance, that would probably bring the opposing side down to his client's range. In fact, the mediation was successful and the outcome was right at what he thought his client would agree to; by the lawyer's estimate, he settled the case for about two-thirds of what he thought the other side was shooting for and the savings was about 10 times the cost of preparing the *Daubert* motion.

This kind of strategy was also described by several of the people I interviewed. One respondent observed:

> I filed the motion about a month before a mediation. The plaintiff's demand was $2 million, and there was no liability defense. The plaintiff had had a number of surgeries so far. We ended up settling the case for $300,000. An excellent result.

Other respondents also specifically mentioned the potential impact of the *Daubert* motion on settlement discussions.

> If I think the other side is having some client control problems, and the parties are trying to settle the case, a strong *Daubert* motion, even if it fails, will help educate the other side about the obstacles that it's going to face at trial. And maybe temper their expectations and their hopes, and maybe get the case to a point where the parties can come together and get it settled.

> It was either going to produce a settlement, or it was going to get the judge scrutinizing the plaintiff's claim at this point, where ... especially in federal court, they're just not reluctant to throw stuff out.

> If there's going to be a big gap between the time it's filed and whenever it gets decided, maybe there's some time in there for the other side to negotiate and maybe you can convince them that you've got a good case, and they've got a lousy case, and they come back to you with a more reasonable settlement position.

---

[28] As suggested by Galanter's idea of litigotiation, this is by no means unique to a *Daubert* motion; it can be the goal behind many motions *in limine*.

Another respondent described filing a motion just before a mediation with the hope that "it might scare the hell out of the plaintiffs."

An additional common goal, beyond excluding the expert, is to prime the judge to the issues. In some cases, this meant that even when a motion was initially denied, the judge at trial would reopen the *Daubert* issue and exclude some or all of an expert's testimony.

> I always view these motions as, even if we lose, we [are] educating the court to the issues.

> Education of the court was an important part of our motion. Even if we had lost in whole or in part our motion, and ended up in trial where we have then had, if we get to trial and these experts are on the stand where we would be battling them to some extent question-by-question to limit them if we can't keep them out essentially all together. So I think part of what we were thinking was that if we didn't succeed in whole and we only succeeded in part, that having educated the trial judge in advance of the trial would pay us dividend at trial.

> I firmly believe that litigation is an accretion process with the judge, and that as you go along, hopefully you are educating her about your case, and that even if you don't win this one, you're setting up some ultimate victory down the road. And maybe at trial, she might revisit the issue; maybe you'll get some limiting instructions, or something like that from her; maybe you'll convince her once she sees the expert testify, "Hey, I'm entitled to a directed verdict here."

Not all the lawyers saw this priming as a positive because it also primed the defendant and the defendant's experts so that they could come into trial better prepared.

> The downside is that you sort of educate your opponent about what your [own] expert has to say and how you're going to cross-examine and attack the [opposing] expert at trial. You're showing your hand in a larger sense.

Another lawyer, who sought to exclude a damages expert, commented: "Very rarely do I find you want to prime the judge on damages issues." However, another respondent whose motion dealt with a damages expert indicated that there had been some discussion of the motion serving to prime the judge.

A third function beyond excluding or limiting expert testimony that several respondents mentioned was that the *Daubert* motion served to extract additional information from the opponent about the opponent's case.

> There are certainly instances where I might file a *Daubert* motion as sort of a later discovery effort, where I want to get the expert to flesh out the basis for the opinions.

> You can find out other things about the other side's case, and if you've got a good motion that has a chance of winning, isn't a slam dunk, but has a good chance of winning, that can always be a by-product.

Thus, the motion served as a kind of supplemental discovery device.[29]

Finally, while not a goal of a *Daubert* motion, a majority of the lawyers agreed that the *Daubert* factors provided something of a framework that they frequently used in deposing or cross-examining experts.

> Depositions of experts have become a huge issue. In the old days, they were simply literally informational ... what's this guy going to say. Now, they're tactical and developing a record for a *Daubert* analysis.

> It significantly alters the way you conduct expert discovery and expert depositions. You ask about the typical *Daubert* factors that courts tend to look at. And while you asked about some of those pre-*Daubert*, you didn't ask about all of them, and not quite as formalized way.

> There's a list of *Daubert* questions that we ask everyone. "Have you done any testing?" "Is it replicative type work?" Yeah, so ... I wouldn't say it's a complete outline, but it is a portion of what you have to do now.

In fact, only two respondents explicitly said that *Daubert* had not had a *significant* impact on how they conduct expert depositions, and one of those acknowledged that it had had some impact.

> No, it really hasn't. You may have different questions. There will be different terms. There will be different sequences.

C. *DAUBERT* AND DISCOVERY: DEPOSITIONS AND REPORTS

There is an important interaction between *Daubert* and the Rule 26 requirement that experts provide a written report containing[30] "a complete statement of all opinions to be expressed and the basis and reasons therefore; the data or other information considered by the witness in forming the opinions; any exhibits to be used as a summary of or support for the opinions" (FRCP 26(a)(2)(B)). How do the factors listed in *Daubert* that a judge might consider in assessing the "reliability" (i.e., validity) of the opinion interact with the report requirement? *Daubert* and the Rule 26 requirement should interact to force experts to produce more complete, more detailed reports. What if the expert's report fails to provide any information (or sufficient information) to assess the "reliability" of the expert's opinion? Can a motion for exclusion under *Daubert* be filed based on the expert's report alone?

In fact, at least in the Eighth Circuit, challenges are regularly filed based solely on the report, and such challenges are often successful. In three of the four cases involving *Daubert* motions I saw at EBH, the challenged expert had not been deposed. One of these was the case mentioned earlier in which one of

---

[29] There are a variety of techniques that lawyers might use as a form of discovery beyond what the rules technically allow. A *Daubert* motion is one such technique. Another method that I observed in an earlier study (Kritzer 1998b) is that lawyers might use a related administrative proceeding as a discovery device in a larger case.

[30] [The exact wording of this Rule has changed since the original article was published.]

EBH's experts was challenged and where the opposing side had not deposed the EBH expert involved. In a second case, the EBH lawyer had tried to schedule the expert's deposition in advance of when he wanted to file the motion (which was timed in connection with a scheduled mediation), but was not able to work out a schedule with the opposing side. In the third case, the expert's report was nothing more than two paragraphs, one stating that there were design flaws and one stating that there were inadequate warnings and instructions; the report provided no specifics with regard to the design flaw or what the alternative design(s) might be, nor did it provide any alternatives for warnings and instructions.

A senior partner at EBH commented to me that *Daubert* "has diminished the amount of discovery we do on experts; 8 of 10 times we don't depose the expert in a federal case. Instead, we rely on the expert's report. The deposition might give away your case, particularly how you will attack the expert's testimony at trial." My sense is that the lawyer was underestimating the frequency of expert depositions; even so, the combination of Rule 26 requirements and *Daubert* probably has had some impact on the frequency of such depositions.

Most of the cases described in the course of my interviews *did* involve depositions of the challenged expert; however, in a small number of cases, the lawyer reported that in retrospect, he or she could have done the *Daubert* motion without the deposition.

> The report probably would have been sufficient on its own to trigger the motion. We could have done it without the deposition. The deposition was confirmation.

More typically, the lawyers felt that the deposition was a crucial part of the preparation of the *Daubert* motion, and frequently it was the critical piece.

> I think that at their deposition testimony they to some extent hung themselves by being confronted with the problems with their methodology and their sort of changing opinions over time.

> At the deposition he admitted that he could have done testing, and his response was, "That's really expensive and difficult, and these are freak occurrences, and who knows if I could replicate it."

> To me, the deposition is the place where you get to really go through and discuss the different *Daubert* factors, and whatever other factors you want to talk about.

> You can really dig down, and you get those nice little quotes that become the basis of the summary judgment—the motion to exclude, but also the summary judgment motion.

In some cases, the significance of the deposition reflected major inconsistencies between what the expert stated in his or her report and what transpired at the deposition.

> Both were equally critical in this situation because in the deposition, he contradicted his report. It had to do with failure analysis of a com-

ponent, and in his report, he came up with a theory of failure analysis that in the deposition examination he backed off on one theory and analysis and went towards another one.

There were inconsistencies between the report and his deposition, so I would say that both were important.

One of the challenges of the deposition, as one of the lawyers I spent time with at EBH explained, occurs if you have a case in which it is not obvious to the opposing party that you will be filing a *Daubert* motion. How do you get answers to key questions without revealing too much of your strategy? In the particular case the lawyer and I were discussing, the expert had produced a prototype but had done no testing. The lawyer wanted to get the fact of no testing on the record, but did not want to prompt the expert to go out and now do some thorough testing. Ultimately, the lawyer decided that he needed to ask the question very explicitly, and the expert did subsequently do some very minimal testing.

Prior to the changes to Rule 26, advance information on the expert's opinion was available only through interrogatories and depositions. As the discussion above suggests, *Daubert* and the discovery rules interact in important ways. This makes it somewhat difficult to sort out the effect of one versus the other, a point made by one of the lawyers I interviewed.

It's a little harder to distinguish how much the changes regarding the experts have resulted from *Daubert* and how much have resulted from the amendments to Rule 26, because we now have to make so much more detailed disclosures of our experts than we used to. So the reports tend to be a little bit more detailed than they were in the past.

D. COSTS

The range of costs involved in preparing *Daubert* motions is quite wide. Of the three cases filed by EBH lawyers during my time at the firm, one cost well in excess of $20,000, one cost approximately $5,000, and one was only about $500. The latter motion, which was clearly an outlier, was a small part of a larger motion to dismiss, which, in its entirety, cost several thousand dollars. There seemed to be categories of costs that I would group as $2,500 to $10,000, $10,001 to $20,000, and more than $20,000.[31] Table 7.5 sets out the distribution of estimated costs. Clearly, while preparing a *Daubert* motion can be very costly, there is substantial variability reflecting the level of fees a firm charges, the familiarity of the lawyer with *Daubert*,[32] the complexity of the evidence, and the legal issues involved in the motion.

---

[31] The figures I am quoting above do not take into account the cost of appeals.

[32] Part of the reason the motion at EBH that cost about $5,000 came in at that cost was that the lawyer had just been involved in preparing the motion that cost over $20,000 and, consequently, had a lot of recently acquired familiarity the Eighth Circuit's case law on *Daubert*.

Table 7.5: Distribution of Estimated Costs of *Daubert* Motions

$2,500 to $10,000	5
$10,001 to $20,000	6
More than $20,000	8
Unable to estimate[a]	2

[a] Although two lawyers could not provide an estimate, it was clear from their comments that a lot of time was involved; both these cases were at least in the middle category, and probably in the highest category.

Most of the time, regardless of whether the motion was in the highest or lowest cost category, several lawyers in the firm worked on the motion. Occasionally, a single lawyer would do all the work, or perhaps get relatively minimal research assistance from an associate ("I may have had an associate help out" or "another lawyer did a little research").[33]

V. PREPARING A *DAUBERT* MOTION

A. CLIENT ROLE

Clients play a surprisingly small role in the preparation of a *Daubert* motion; this even extends to the decision whether or not to pursue a *Daubert* motion. In none of the three motions I saw prepared at EBH did the client play a significant role. Presumably, the client in at least two of the cases agreed to the expenditure of time and resources.[34] In one case, the time involved was so minimal that the lawyer did not feel it necessary to get specific approval for including the *Daubert* challenge in a larger motion. In one of the cases, involving a product that had gone out of production many years earlier, the client probably suggested possible experts who might be retained on the defense side, and at least one of those experts was asked to read and respond to the reports and depositions of the expert who was ultimately challenged. However, the expert would have been

---

[33] I asked the lawyers whether there was anyone in their firm who was the "go to" person on *Daubert* issues. About half said there was no *Daubert* specialist; of the remaining, about half (a quarter of the total) said that they were probably the "go to" person in the firm when a *Daubert* issue arose.

[34] When I asked the lawyer who handled the case in which the preparation of the motion cost something over $20,000 what role the client had played in the decision to challenge the expert, the lawyer responded that there was "very little consultation—I called the client and recommended the motion after I took [the expert's] deposition, and the client agreed. That was it." The lawyer handling the motion that cost about $5,000 was very concerned about the cost/benefit considerations, and knew from the start that the stakes in the case could not justify an expenditure anything like the $20,000+ that the *Daubert* motion in the other case cost; in thinking about whether to proceed, he had estimated the cost of the motion in the range of $5,000-7,500.

asked to do that in preparation for his own deposition even in the absence of the *Daubert* challenge.

A senior EBH lawyer told me that he thought he had a possible *Daubert* issue in a professional malpractice case he was handling. He had just deposed the expert, and when the expert was asked the basis of his opinion, the expert replied that "it was his opinion" as an experienced professional in the field. However, the lawyer ultimately decided not to challenge the expert, or to even raise the idea with the client. The stakes in the case were relatively low (mid six figures), the case was in a different circuit, which would have necessitated some significant research expense, and the client was very sensitive about the costs of the litigation. Moreover, in this case, EBH was representing the plaintiff and consequently excluding the expert would not have been the basis for a potentially case-winning summary judgment motion.

When I asked the lawyers I interviewed if they had ever had the experience of a client rejecting a recommendation to file a *Daubert* motion, very few of the lawyers reported such an experience. One lawyer told me of a decision not to pursue a *Daubert* issue and explained it as a decision made in consultation with a client. The client had previously been involved in a case in which counsel had filed an unsuccessful *Daubert* motion against the same expert who was now appearing in the instant case. The client felt burned on the previous motion and did not want to risk repeating the experience. Two lawyers reported that they had been told not to pursue a *Daubert* motion they recommended when it was an insurance company paying the bill; one of those lawyers told me that he had found that when an insurance company was covering the litigation costs, there was a greater reluctance to incur the cost of a *Daubert* motion,[35] which is generally consistent with insurers' desire to tightly control the costs of litigation (see Kritzer 2006 [Chapter 6 in this volume]).

Many of the respondents indicated that the decision to file a *Daubert* motion was essentially theirs, although in some, perhaps most, cases the client was asked to approve going ahead with the expenditures involved.

> It was understood that no motion, or no briefing, that required a reasonable amount of work was going to be undertaken until the client was consulted.

In some cases, the lawyer described the clients as "sophisticated players," fully conversant with *Daubert*, who essentially assumed that a *Daubert* motion would be filed if it were appropriate.

> I think the client is a sophisticated enough client that they knew and expected that we would file a *Daubert* motion from the outset.

> They're very familiar with *Daubert*, very familiar with the idea of defending a product and a product line, and so the suggestions early on were, what will we do in terms of the other side's experts? What can we do?

---

[35] A fourth lawyer told me that he knew that had happened in the past, but he was not able to recall any specific cases.

Even with a client that had inside legal counsel, the preparation of the motion and brief was handled by the outside lawyer; inside counsel might be asked to review the brief, but I got no sense of significant comments or input coming from inside counsel. As said by one respondent:

> This was very much a trial strategy kind of decision made by outside counsel with recommendations to inside counsel, but [inside counsel] was very hands off.

On the occasions when the client did play a role, it was usually on the technical side. Inside technical experts often educate the lawyer on the technical aspects of the case, including providing extensive data that may be relevant for a *Daubert* challenge.[36] Those same experts may be used to critique the report prepared by the opposing experts.

> [Inside expert] played a role in evaluating the other [opposing] expert's opinion, and they played a role in helping to determine whether or not that opinion had been developed following the scientific method, and whether it's supported by good science in terms of testing, in terms of methodology, and in terms of the knowledge in the field.

In some cases, the inside technical experts might be asked to assess the work of an outside expert retained on behalf of their employer and, occasionally, inside experts do serve as testifying experts, although they have potential credibility problems with the jury because it is their employer (and possibly their product) that is under attack.

B. TO FILE, OR NOT TO FILE: THAT IS A QUESTION

As suggested by some of the discussion above, the decision whether or not to file depends in significant part on a cost-benefit analysis. How much is at stake in the case (both the instant case and in terms of potential future cases)? What will it cost to prepare a *Daubert* motion? What is the chance of success? When I asked lawyers about decisions not to file, these factors were frequently mentioned. Specific points that came up included:

- A concern that filing a motion against a particular expert might weaken motions against a more crucial expert.
- A concern about the inclination of the judge assigned to the case (i.e., with a particular judge, the prospects for a successful motion were perceived to be relatively low).
- While the lawyer did not feel that the expert had met the *Daubert* criteria, the expert had done enough in the way of testing or prototyping that it had substantially dimmed the prospects of a successful *Daubert* motion.
- The lawyer was able to have the case dismissed on other grounds before it was time to file a *Daubert* motion.
- Timing issues, such as being brought into the case too late to get a motion together.

---

36 Compare to Prichard's (2005) discussion of the role of in-house engineering experts.

- A strategic decision that the opposing expert would probably actually help the lawyer's case more than hurt it.

One lawyer went on at some length on this last point.

> This might sound counter-intuitive, but when the expert really sucks, that's a gift from heaven. And I think, and I think my colleagues think, long and hard before we deprive our client of the opportunity to show a jury how half-baked the opposing expert is on an important issue in the case by taking it away from the jury and filing a motion that puts it strictly in the hands of a judge. ... The worse their expert is, the better it could be for us.

It is worth noting that this lawyer was typically involved in cases where excluding an expert was unlikely to lead to a motion for summary judgment.[37]

Clearly, whether or not excluding an expert would effectively end the opposing party's case is an important consideration in deciding whether it is worth the cost, a point that may explain at least part of the reason that the defense is much more likely to bring a *Daubert* motion than is the plaintiff. Recall the one case at EBH where a senior lawyer told me about an expert he felt could be challenged on *Daubert* grounds, but where he chose not to do so. Although there were cost considerations involved in this decision, it was also the case that EBH was representing the plaintiff, and that while excluding an expert might weaken the defendant's case, it would not be the kind of case-determining result that can occur when the court excludes a plaintiff's expert.

Typically, relatively little time had been invested in the *Daubert* consideration in cases where a decision was made not to proceed; one lawyer reported having spent on the order of 10–15 hours ($3,000 to $4,000), and another reported that he thought some significant time had been expended but could not be more specific. This does not take into account the costs involved in deposing the opposing expert who might have been challenged because that deposition would probably have been done regardless of the possible *Daubert* motion.

I specifically asked the lawyers whether, in their own minds, there was any minimum likelihood of success required before they would proceed with a *Daubert* motion. There was little consistency in the responses. Several lawyers pegged this at 50–50; a couple put it as low as 25–75; and one put it at 70–30. The most common answer, however, was that it depended on how much was at stake or whether other purposes might be served by the motion.

> I start with what's the financial reality. It's the economic distribution of the risk again. If the case is quite large, and you could get hit with 8 to 10 million, then how can you control that? How can you control that and bring them to the table. I would think that in a lot of cases where there is an education aspect for the trial judge, even if the probability of success in your mind is one in three would still justify

---

[37] This lawyer was the only respondent who told me that he had had a client that wanted him to pursue a *Daubert* motion where he had counseled the client not to do so. He explained this advice on precisely these grounds.

bringing the motion because you can have some benefits even if your motion is denied.

Well that's a hard question because there are reasons to go forward with a motion that aren't based on that, a significant high probability of success. We do a cost-benefit analysis. Going to trial in these cases is so costly that if you can do anything to prevent the possibility of trial, that's probably worthwhile. Also, even if we lose, it better frames the issues for settlement once the *Daubert* issue is out of the way.

My threshold on that's pretty low. If I thought we had a 25% chance of success, I'd bring the motion. Maybe even less than that. It doesn't have to be 50–50; it can be way below that because you don't have anything to lose. You're in the same spot even if you lose the motion.

[I]t's kind of like what Potter Stewart said on obscenity, "I can't tell you what it is, but I know it when I see it." ... It just depends on the case. I haven't had a case where it was multi-million dollars, ten million dollars, and "oh my god," But in a case where we had *Daubert* sitting out there, but if I had a case where it was 10 million bucks or 20 million bucks on the line, and it's no holds barred. If I had a 30 per—As long as I didn't think that I was going to alienate the judge by taking an extreme position, then I would bring my *Daubert* motion.

C. IMPACT OF *DAUBERT* ON THE RESPONDENTS' OWN USE OF EXPERTS

A senior lawyer at EBH told me that "the selection, vetting, and the way you deploy your expert has substantially improved in quality" as a result of *Daubert*. While I was observing at EBH, I sat in on meetings with experts in a number of federal cases. In all those meetings, it was evident that the EBH lawyers (and at least some of the experts) were very cognizant of the *Daubert* factors, and the need to provide reports that clearly demonstrated appropriate methodologies and testing. Whether this was specifically the result of *Daubert* or reflected what defense lawyers like to claim has long been their ability to retain top-class experts in their cases,[38] I have no sure way of ascertaining. Still, it was clear that the EBH lawyers wanted to be sure that their expert's testimony could not be excluded on *Daubert* grounds. In discussing an upcoming deposition with one expert witness, a senior EBH lawyer commented to the expert, "I don't want them to have the opportunity to exclude your testimony. You must be able to state your views with a reasonable degree of [field] certainty."

When I asked my interview respondents whether *Daubert* had affected their own use of experts, I received responses that indicated a firm belief that there had been some changes. Those changes seem to fall along two lines. First, while

---

[38] Defense lawyers often assert that they are able to obtain top-class experts. Presumably, this reflects the willingness of their clients to pay for such experts. Even if this is true when the cost of the litigation is being borne by the defendant directly, it is less clear that it is true when the cost is being borne by an insurer. One indication that it might not be true when an insurer has a role in managing the litigation is reflected in the fact that in subrogation cases, it is often experts retained *on behalf of an insurer* seeking to recover part of a loss who face *Daubert* challenges. This was the situation in at least one of the *Daubert* motions I observed at EBH.

lawyers have generally taken care in retaining experts (see Prichard 2005:127-30, 54-74), respondents indicated that they took even more care in selecting experts as a consequence of *Daubert*.

> Well, you have to be a lot more careful, depending on the case. If you have a big case, and you are in federal court, you need to spend a lot more time and effort finding a witness who will withstand attack.

> You have more experts being used.

> Choose them more carefully. And I say choose them more carefully, I really do mean that. It's not as though the subject is industrial engineering. I just don't want an industrial engineer. I want someone who has done this particular thing; who understands this particular thing, because the expertise can be too broad. I think that's the main thing we do. We choose them more carefully. We try to be more specific.

The second kind of change involves the preparation of experts. Lawyers take a lot more care in getting experts to write appropriate reports and be prepared for testimony.

> In the old days, people used to joke about it ... you wind people up and march them in and then sit back and they just talk. That doesn't happen.

> I think that what goes around, goes around. What's good for the goose is good for the gander. I think ... the one time when plaintiffs filed a motion against our expert, it was a learning experience. I think I've learned to challenge our own experts more so than I have in the past to insure that we never face that situation again. We're going to be able to defend them in spades, with a great level of confidence.

> I would say that *Daubert* has been a boon for the expert witness industry. They have the opportunity now ... there's the billing for going to the scene, there's the billing for evidence, there's the billing for going over the files. I think it's affected how I prepare them, but not very much. It hasn't changed the kind of expert I hire.

> We prepare our experts more.

More generally, the lawyers I spoke with seem to view the impact of *Daubert* as having improved the overall quality of expert testimony.

> I would say that there has been an increase in the quality of testimony, at least in the cases I do.

VI. SUMMARY AND CONCLUSION

Understanding the impact of a change in the litigation system such as that wrought by the *Daubert* Trilogy requires looking beyond what transpires in court. The decisions of judges constitute the tip of the *Daubert* iceberg. Equally, perhaps more, important impacts happen in the lawyers' offices as the lawyers decide whether to pursue cases and how to prepare the cases they do pursue.

My research focused largely on the defense side, which typically brings *Daubert* motions to exclude or limit plaintiffs' experts. Consequently, I am not able to say how *Daubert* has impacted the plaintiffs' bar or the cases plaintiffs' lawyers bring, or consider bringing, on behalf of injured persons.

Looking at *Daubert* from the defense perspective, it is evident that *Daubert's* influence has rippled through the litigation process. It interacts with discovery rules as those rules pertain to experts, and with other evidentiary concerns such as spoliation. It has become part of the broader process of litigotiation. It has had major impacts in some types of cases, and less impact than many observers expected in others—the latter because other developments have displaced *Daubert* in a way that many cases do not get to the stage where *Daubert* is likely to play a role.

8

LOCAL LEGAL CULTURE AND THE CONTROL OF LITIGATION[1]

INTRODUCTION

The rules governing the filing and prosecution of lawsuits constitute a key component of gatekeeping in the civil justice system. The rules of civil procedure, as they are typically called, can serve to encourage or discourage litigation, either by direct restrictions or by manipulation of incentives. As the debate about litigiousness waxes and wanes, rules of procedure are changed to reflect current perceptions of problems and issues. In 1983, Rule 11 of the Federal Rules of Civil Procedure was modified to rectify what was perceived to be an increased filing of motions and pleadings that were not grounded in fact or law. By 1990, these changes had produced an acrimonious debate among federal litigators, legal academics, and federal judges.

The 1983 changes modified and strengthened the existing provisions of Rule 11 to create a presumption that lawyers who file pleadings or motions without ascertaining that they are well grounded in fact and/or law will be sanctioned by the Court. The language of the Rule is reasonably straightforward:

> The signature of an attorney or party constitutes a certificate by the signer that the signer has read the pleading, motion, or other paper; that to the best of the signer's knowledge, information, and belief formed after reasonable inquiry it is well grounded in fact and is warranted by existing law or a good faith argument for the extension, modification, or reversal of existing law, and that it is not interposed for any improper purpose, such as to cause unnecessary delay or

[1] This chapter, which was coauthored with Frances Kahn Zemans (and is included here with her permission), originally appeared in *Law & Society Review* 37 (1993), 535-57; an earlier version was presented at the Annual Meeting of the Midwest Political Science Association, Chicago, April 9–11, 1992. It is drawn from a study of the use of the 1983 version of Rule 11 of the Federal Rules of Civil Procedure; a third major contributor to that study was Professor Lawrence Marshall. The research was conducted under the auspices of the American Judicature Society and was made possible by the generous financial support of the M. R. Bauer Foundation, the West Publishing Company, the Ninth Circuit Attorney Admission Fund, the Illinois Bar Foundation, the Dallas Bar Foundation, the Indiana Bar Foundation, and the Aetna Foundation, Inc. The original Appendix from the published article has been omitted here; several references have been updated to reflect papers that were subsequently published.

needless increase in the cost of litigation. ... If a pleading, motion, or other paper is signed in violation of this rule, the court, upon motion or upon its own initiative, shall impose upon the person who signed it, a represented party, or both, an appropriate sanction, which may include an order to pay the other party or parties the amount of reasonable expenses incurred because of the filing of the pleading, motion, or other paper, including a reasonable attorney's fee.

The intention of the 1983 amendments to Rule 11, which shifted from permitting sanctions to effectively mandating sanctions,[2] was to reduce the filing of supposedly frivolous cases, claims, and motions.[3] There is no doubt that Rule 11 had an impact; if nothing else, the number of sanctions imposed increased sharply: between 1938 and 1976, Rule 11 sanctions were imposed in only 3 reported cases (out of 19 reported cases in which Rule 11 motions had been filed); between 1983 and 1989, trial judges imposed sanctions in 379 reported cases (Federal Judicial Center 1991).[4]

The debate over Rule 11 led the Advisory Committee on Rules of Practice and Procedure of the United States Judicial Conference to hold hearings in 1990 to determine whether a new set of amendments to Rule 11 was warranted. The criticisms of the 1983 version of Rule 11 included:

- disparate impact on plaintiffs and defendants
- particularly negative impact on civil rights plaintiffs
- stifling of innovation in the law
- limiting access to justice
- generation of unnecessary "satellite litigation" and its attendant costs
- placing too much power in the hands of federal judges
- lack of uniformity in enforcement
- use of the rule by some federal judges to punish litigants who file cases with which the judge disagrees politically.

The critics included persons from many segments of the bar, from personal injury and civil rights plaintiffs' attorneys to big firm commercial litigators.[5]

---

[2] The amendments also shifted from a standard of conduct that focused on what was known to one that focused on what should have been known.

[3] Ironically, no one bothered to ascertain whether there were in fact significant numbers of frivolous cases, claims, or motions; it was simply asserted that this was a problem and that some solution was needed to the problem.

[4] Reported cases can give a very distorted image of what is occurring in the courts (Siegelman and Donohue 1990; Olson 1992), and we present this figure recognizing that fact; Wiggins et al. (1991:7) point out that 58% of Rule 11 opinions were published by just ten districts, and 38% were published by only two districts. Nonetheless, the sheer magnitude of the difference before and after 1983 is striking.

[5] Interestingly, while many big firm commercial litigators were included among the vocal critics of the rule, the large corporate clients of those litigators were either silent or were generally supportive of the rule as evidenced by testimony presented to the Advisory Committee on the Civil Rules (testimony by Alfred Cortese, 19 Feb. 1992, Atlanta; copy on file with the authors) and written comments on the proposed changes filed by the American Insurance Association (comments dated 31 Oct. 1990; copy on file with the authors).

To assess many of the claims about the use and impact of Rule 11, we undertook a survey of federal litigators in three circuits. The survey, which was conducted during the spring of 1991, sought information both on visible Rule 11 activities (actual sanctions, motions, and in-court warnings) and on those Rule 11 activities that take place outside of court. The research design targeted federal practitioners[6] in 11 federal judicial districts, some dominated by major metropolitan areas, others including larger regional cities, and others essentially nonurban in character.[7] Up to three mailings consisting of a 12-page questionnaire and a cover letter from the chief judge of the relevant circuit were sent to 4,496 practitioners;[8] 3,358, or almost 75%, responded.

One of the intriguing results from our previous analyses of these data (Marshall et al. 1992) is the possibility that local differences existed in Rule 11 impacts and practices. Studies of several aspects of judicial practices have argued that local differences cannot be accounted for by simple reference to external factors such as caseloads, judicial structures, or local rules. These studies (see Church et al. 1978; Eisenstein et al. 1988; Schiller and Manikas 1987; Sherwood and Clarke 1981) advance what came to be called the "local legal culture" perspective (Church 1982, 1985); that is, local patterns of practice reflect in part informal norms and expectations that regular players in the system (lawyers and judges) have developed and have come to accept as "how we do things."

The concept "local legal culture" can take on two subtly different meanings. The first is that it simply reflects the complete set of norms and attitudes that govern the operation of a court system. Some of these norms are reflected in formal rules (e.g., time limits, discovery limits); others are the natural outgrowth of structural factors such as caseloads, numbers of players involved in the system, and the like; and still others are not traceable to formal procedure or structure but simply reflect a perception of "how we do things here." The second meaning of "local legal culture" is limited only to the last subset of norms and attitudes, those that do not reflect the internalization of structural and contextual differences. In a real sense, this latter, more narrow meaning constitutes a "residualization" of what could be a very broad, general concept. Nonetheless, it is this latter, residual definition that we have adopted for our analysis.

---

[6] Federal practitioners were identified by selecting a sample of cases from each of the 11 districts and extracting from the docket sheets (either manually or electronically) the names of the lead attorneys on both sides; federal government attorneys were excluded from the sample.

[7] The specific districts were:

5th Circuit	7th Circuit	9th Circuit
S.D. Texas	N.D. Illinois	C.D. California
N.D. Mississippi	W.D. Wisconsin	D. Montana
W.D. Louisiana	S.D. Indiana	E.D. California
		D. Arizona
		D. Oregon

[8] The survey was administered by the University of Wisconsin's Letters and Sciences Survey Center.

We do this for two reasons. First, the concept was initially advanced as a vehicle for explaining differences in patterns of "delay" in the courts that could not be explained by factors such as caseloads, community size, calendaring systems, or seriousness of cases. Church and his colleagues turned to the local legal culture explanation (Church et al. 1978:54):

> It is our conclusion that the speed of disposition of civil and criminal litigation in a court cannot be ascribed in any simple sense to the length of its backlog, any more than it can be explained by court size, caseload, or trial rate. Rather, both quantitative and qualitative data generated in this research strongly suggest that both speed and backlog are determined in large part by established expectations, practices, and informal rules of behavior of judges and attorneys. For want of a better term, we have called this cluster of related factors the "local legal culture." Court systems become adapted to a given pace of civil and criminal litigation ... These expectations and practices, together with court and attorney backlog, must be overcome in any successful attempt to increase the pace of litigation. Thus most structural and caseload variables fail to explain inter-jurisdictional differences in the pace of litigation.

Second, as suggested by the quote above, modifying those expectations that are not attributable to specific structural or contextual factors presents particular problems for court reformers, and determining the degree to which some aspect of judicial process reflects the narrower notion of local legal culture is important in predicting the likely impact of efforts to change that process.

Because Rule 11 relies primarily, though not exclusively,[9] on the action of attorneys for its enforcement, we expected that local norms and practices would influence substantially the application of and reference to the rule. While we recognized that our unit of analysis—federal judicial district—is larger than the "local community" examined in some (but not all—see Church et al. 1978:55-57) other studies that have applied the local legal culture construct, we believe that it is the relevant unit for purposes of analysis of actions in the federal trial courts. Furthermore, when we examined the gross pattern of Rule 11 use across the 11 federal judicial districts we surveyed, we found significant variation among the districts on each of our measures. Can these variations be accounted for by factors such as circuit precedents or size of the community served? If not, what evidence is there that these differences do reflect "local legal culture" in the narrow sense? These are the questions that motivated the analysis presented below.

In our original design of the research, we had not anticipated looking at a local legal culture explanation for our findings. However, in our initial analyses of our data, we found significant differences among the federal judicial districts in our sample, which alerted us to the need to consider local legal culture (in the

---

[9] While judges may refer to or initiate Rule 11 sanctions without the Rule being raised by one of the attorneys, the judges are, by and large, members of the same local legal culture as the lawyers; they might also be part of a separate "judicial culture" (see Kagan et al. 1977:123, 55)—a phenomenon we do not consider in our analysis.

narrow sense) as a potential factor accounting for the observed variation. A major potential problem for us was that we had not sought to specifically measure local norms and expectations in our survey, which would make it potentially very difficult to develop an independent measure of the local legal culture. However, as the analysis below will show, we are able to account for observed variations across the districts without resort to the residualized version of local legal culture. In Section I, we briefly review the history and use of the concept of local legal culture. Section II describes the measures of Rule 11 activities and discusses the types of variables other than local legal culture that might account for variations in Rule 11 activities. Section III presents our statistical analysis.

I. LOCAL LEGAL CULTURE

As noted previously, the concept of "local legal culture" was introduced by Tom Church and his colleagues (Church et al. 1978:54) to account for the perplexing finding that obvious factors such as backlog, court size, caseload, or trial rate failed to account for the pace of criminal case disposition. Church et al. suggest that "speed and backlog are determined in large part by established expectations, practices, and informal rules of behavior of judges and attorneys. ... Court systems become adapted to a given pace of civil and criminal litigation." In follow-up work, Church (1985:449; see also Church 1982) moved to the broader definition of local legal culture: "common practitioner norms governing case handling and participant behavior in court." In this later research, which looked specifically at practitioner attitudes in four criminal courts, Church did not concern himself with whether the attitudes and norms simply reflect the structural and legal realities practitioners must deal with as opposed to local expectations that evolve independent of structural and legal imperatives. Not surprisingly, Church found support for the proposition that there are distinct attitudes concerning procedural issues and practices (e.g., pace of litigation, necessity for trial) in the four large urban jurisdictions he examined (Pittsburgh, Miami, Bronx, and Detroit), and that these attitudes tend to parallel actual practice (e.g., "patterns of actual trial utilization parallel attitudinal orientations of practitioners regarding preferred mode of disposition for the hypothetical case set [1985:480]"). In this follow-up research, because of the small number of jurisdictions examined, Church was not able to consider whether the attitudes and norms might be attributable to structural and legal factors or if the patterns of local culture, in whole or in part, arose independent of such factors.

Nonetheless, a variety of research lends support to an argument that within the criminal justice context, case processing, and expectations concerning case processing, may not simply reflect structural and legal imperatives. For example, while most criminal courts are dominated by guilty plea dispositions, Schulhofer (1984, 1985) reports that Philadelphia, both at the misdemeanor and felony levels, disposes of large proportions of cases through bench trials that he argues are not simply "slow pleas."[10] Schulhofer is not able to identify any types of structural or legal factors that might account for the apparent anomaly. In their study of criminal courts in nine smaller cities, Eisenstein et al. (1988) describe what they label "court communities" that incorporate locally defined expectations about the proper handling and disposition of criminal cases; their research design, which involved looking at three cities in each of three states and three different types of cities within each state, provides a measure of control over both structural and legal factors. Similarly, Levin (1972, 1977) reports sharp differences in the perspectives of the occupants of the local benches in Pittsburgh and Minneapolis, although he relates these differences more to political cultures[11] than to what Church labels local legal culture. Heumann (1978) shows how practitioners come to share views on how cases should be handled (e.g., trial versus guilty plea).

Given the emphasis on the impact of local legal culture on case processing, it seems logical to extend this to the handling of civil cases as well as criminal cases; in fact, one of the key findings that originally led Church to the "local legal culture" explanation was the correlation in disposition times in civil cases between state and federal courts in the same city (Church et al. 1978:56).[12] While some other work has considered other aspects of civil process across a number of federal and/or state courts,[13] little, if any, effort has been made to link patterns to local legal culture.

II. DATA AND VARIABLES

In our survey of attorneys, we asked about Rule 11 activities both in court and out of court during the preceding 12 months:

- Cases in which sanctions were imposed ("sanctioned")
- Cases in which sanctions were formally proposed but not imposed ("motioned")
- Cases in which reference was made to Rule 11 in court or in papers filed with the court but no formal motion was made ("in-court")
- Cases in which reference was made to Rule 11 by one side to the other side outside of court ("out-of-court" or "out-court")
- Cases in which no reference was made to Rule 11 by the opposing side, but

---

[10] White (1971:442) defines a "slow plea" of guilty as involving a proceeding that is formally labeled a bench trial in which "the defendant's counsel facilitates the presentation of evidence and ... admits that the defendant is guilty of some offense, but does not enter a formal plea." Schulhofer's argument is intriguing in light of Mather's observation (1973:214n7) that the term originated in Philadelphia and Pittsburgh.

[11] See Grossman and Sarat (1971), Kritzer (1979), and Grossman et al. (1982) for discussions of political culture (as distinct from local legal culture) applied to the study of the courts.

[12] However, Grossman et al. (1981), who found some sharp contrasts in state/federal patterns of pace of litigation in the five federal judicial districts they examined, question the applicability of the local legal culture explanation.

[13] For example, see Kritzer (1982) on intervention of judges in case management and settlement; Clermont and Eisenberg (1992) on the choice between jury and bench trials; and Friedman and Percival (1976) or Daniels (1990) on the evolution of case mix over time.

Rule 11 was considered in choosing a course of action—an anticipatory response to the possibility of Rule 11 coming up ("anticipatory response" or "affected")

- Cases declined because of a concern about potential sanctions ("declined").

We refer to these different situations as "level" of Rule 11 activity. The exact wording of each of these questions is shown in Figure 8.1; when an attorney reported more than one case involving a particular level of Rule 11 activity, we asked the attorney to focus on only the most recent case involving that level in responding to follow-up questions. In addition to gathering information on Rule 11 practices and experiences, we asked the attorneys about their practices and experiences more generally, including such things as practice setting (firms of varying size, solo practice, etc.), substance of practice (percentage devoted to each of a number of legal areas), usual side represented, percentage of practice devoted to federal litigation, and number of years in practice.

As we noted previously, 3,358 attorneys responded to our survey. However, because we are specifically interested in local effects, we excluded from our analysis here those attorneys who reported federal litigation practices in more than one federal judicial district or who reported that their practices were not primarily in one of the districts in our sample. This eliminated about one-third of our respondents, leaving 2,421 for analysis.

III. ANALYSIS

Table 8.1 shows the percentage of attorneys in each district who reported having had each of the six types of Rule 11 experiences during the 12 months prior to the survey. The χ^2 values shown at the bottom of the table indicate that for all six variables there are significant variations among the districts. The differences among the districts are not just "statistically significant," they are substantial; the ratio of highest to lowest percentage for each type of experience is around 2 to 1 for motions, in-court, out-of-court, and anticipatory responses, and around 3 to 1 for sanctions and declining cases. There is one clear pattern in the table that might account for the significant differences among districts: the large urban districts (Central California, Southern Texas, and Northern Illinois) tend to be on the high end of the percentages. Table 8.2 collapses the districts into three types (large urban, urban, and nonurban), and shows that with the exception of declining cases, lawyers in large urban districts are more likely to report each of the various Rule 11 experiences than are lawyers in the other types of districts;[14] the ratio comparing large urban to the other districts (except for declining cases) tends to be on the order of 3 to 2. Given Donald Landon's (1985, 1990) work on nonurban legal practice,[15] it is interesting that it is the large

---

[14] One simple explanation for this might be that Rule 11 experiences are concentrated in the very large firms that are concentrated in large urban areas; however, if respondents from large firms 50 or more lawyers) are omitted from Table 8.2, the pattern is unchanged.

[15] Landon (1985:95) argues that there are strong norms of comity among lawyers practicing in nonurban areas; this is captured nicely in the comment of one of his respondents who reported that he told clients at their first meeting, "You can hire me to fight your case, but you can't hire me to hate the opposing attorney."

Figure 8.1: Measures of Rule 11 Activity

Sanction Imposed

In the last 12 months, have you been counsel or co-counsel in a case in any federal district court in which sanctions were imposed under Rule 11 of the Federal Rules of Civil Procedure?

Motion for Sanction

In the last 12 months, have you been counsel or co-counsel in a federal district court case in which Rule 11 sanctions were formally proposed, through a written or oral request (e.g., a motion by counsel) or through a show cause order (or equivalent), but no sanction was imposed?

In-Court Reference

In the last 12 months, have you been counsel or co-counsel in a federal district court case in which no formal Rule 11 sanction request or procedure (e.g., a motion, show cause order, or equivalent) was initiated, but some explicit warning or threat of a request for Rule 11 sanctions was made in court or judge's chambers, or some other clear reference was made to Rule 11 in papers filed-with the court (e.g., a specific mention of Rule 11 or use of Rule 11 language—"the claim is not well grounded in fact and is not warranted by existing law or a good faith argument...")?

Out-of-Court Reference

In the last 12 months, focusing exclusively on cases in which the only Rule 11 activity, expressed or implied, was outside of court, have you been counsel or co-counsel in a federal district court case in which, in the course of conversation or correspondence outside of court (and judges' chambers), counsel for one of the parties raised the issue of a Rule 11 violation with counsel for another party?

Anticipatory Response

During the last 12 months, in preparing a case that was, or could have been, filed in federal district court, excluding cases you described in response to prior questions, have you specifically done something, or consciously decided not to do something, because of concerns about potential sanctions under Rule 11, even though there was never an explicit reference to Rule 11 by opposing counsel or a judge (or magistrate)? Here we are thinking of things such as omitting or modifying specific claims or defenses, deciding not to file particular documents, choosing to file in state court rather than federal court, seeking to remove to federal court from state court, undertaking additional investigation or research, etc.

Declined a Case

We are also interested in knowing about cases that were never filed primarily because of concerns about sanctions under Rule 11. During the last twelve months did you, primarily because of Rule 11:

- advise a client not to pursue a lawsuit that you thought had some merit?
- advise a client to settle a case to avoid a suit that would be difficult to defend?
- decline representation of a paying client in a particular matter?
- decline representation of a pro bono client?

Table 8.1: Frequency of Rule 11 Events and Actions by District

Usual District of Practice	% Sanctioned	% Motioned	% In-Court	% Out-Court	% Affected	% Declined
S. Texas	7.8	34.1	26.8	41.8	38.8	20.5
	(295)	(293)	(291)	(292)	(291)	(297)
N. Mississippi	7.7	26.9	18.6	30.2	26.6	29.2
	(130)	(130)	(129)	(129)	(128)	(130)
W. Louisiana	8.4	15.3	22.9	42.0	35.8	16.8
	(190)	(190)	(188)	(188)	(190)	(191)
Arizona	4.1	18.7	17.2	22.8	25.7	20.7
	(268)	(268)	(267)	(267)	(269)	(270)
Montana	3.7	17.5	16.5	19.7	22.5	16.8
	(191)	(189)	(188)	(188)	(187)	(191)
Oregon	5.7	23.5	20.8	32.7	21.7	16.6
	(246)	(247)	(245)	(245)	(244)	(247)
California	5.6	18.3	20.3	33.1	23.8	10.3
	(126)	(126)	(123)	(124)	(126)	(126)
C. California	10.3	31.5	27.9	39.2	30.9	13.3
	(262)	(260)	(262)	(260)	(262)	(264)
N. Illinois	11.5	24.3	35.4	43.9	39.5	22.0
	(347)	(345)	(345)	(342)	(344)	(350)
W. Wisconsin	8.1	14.3	20.3	24.3	21.6	18.9
	(148)	(147)	(148)	(148)	(148)	(148)
S. Indiana	9.2	21.2	20.4	35.4	26.1	14.5
	(207)	(203)	(206)	(206)	(207)	(207)
Total	7.7	23.3	23.6	34.3	29.7	18.3
χ^2	21.88	53.02	47.74	70.23	53.97	28.66

Note: The χ^2 was computed on a table formed from the column under which it is shown; the table was 11 rows by 2 columns (the second column containing the complement of the percentage in the column actually shown above). All have 10 degrees of freedom, and all are statistically significant at the .02 level or better.

urban districts that stand out as higher rather than the nonurban districts that stand out as lower.

There is another statistically significant, albeit much weaker and less consistent,[16] pattern in the data: differences among the circuits. These patterns are captured in Table 8.3. As that table shows, there are statistically significant differences among the circuits for all six of the Rule 11 experiences; however, the only clear pattern here is for the Ninth Circuit to have the lowest percentage of respondents reporting an experience (the one exception is motions that do not lead to sanctions, and here the Ninth Circuit is only slightly above the Seventh

---

[16] The pattern would be clearer if it were not for the District of Central California in the Ninth Circuit, which stands prominently as the highest of the five Ninth Circuit districts on all indicators of Rule 11 activity except declined cases.

Table 8.2: Frequency of Rule 11 Events and Actions by Type of District

Type of District	% Sanctioned	% Motioned	% In-Court	% Out-Court	% Affected	% Declined
Large urban	10.0	29.6	30.4	41.8	36.8	19.0
	(904)	(898)	(898)	(894)	(897)	(911)
Urban	6.5	19.6	20.1	32.4	26.4	16.5
	(1,037)	(1,034)	(1,029)	(1,030)	(1,036)	(1,041)
Nonurban	6.2	19.1	18.3	24.1	23.3	20.9
	(469)	(466)	(465)	(465)	(463)	(469)
Total	7.7	23.3	23.6	34.3	29.7	18.3
χ^2	10.21	32.49	37.24	45.63	35.84	4.60

Note: The χ^2 was computed on a table formed from the column under which it is shown; the table was 3 rows by 2 columns (the second column containing the complement of the percentage in the column actually shown above). All have 2 degrees of freedom, and all are statistically significant at the .05 level or better.

Table 8.3: Frequency of Rule 11 Events and Actions by Circuit

Circuit	% Sanctioned	% Motioned	% In-Court	% Out-Court	% Affected	% Declined
Fifth	8.0	26.8	23.8	39.4	35.3	21.2
	(615)	(613)	(608)	(609)	(609)	(618)
Seventh	10.1	21.3	27.8	37.2	31.8	19.1
	(702)	(695)	(699)	(696)	(699)	(705)
Ninth	6.0	22.6	20.8	29.6	25.3	16.1
	(1,093)	(1,090)	(1,085)	(1,084)	(1,088)	(1,098)
Total	7.7	23.3	23.6	34.3	29.7	18.3
χ^2	10.04	5.99	11.32	20.24	20.77	7.29

Note: The χ^2 was computed on a table formed from the column under which it is shown; the table was 3 rows by 2 columns (the second column containing the complement of the percentage in the column actually shown above). All have 2 degrees of freedom, and all are statistically significant at the .05 level or better.

Circuit). Elsewhere, we considered whether there were any clear differences in the "law of the circuits" that might account for circuit-level differences. We could identify no precedential patterns that might account for differences among the three circuits; however, we did find differences in the *tone* of the appellate court decisions that could affect the attorneys' perceptions of whether the federal courts were interested in aggressively *applying* Rule 11.[17]

---

[17] We eliminated one other explanation for the lower level of activity in the Ninth Circuit. Recall that we included one of each type of district (large urban, urban, and nonurban) in each circuit but added two extra urban districts for the Ninth Circuit; this means that compared to the Fifth and Seventh Circuits, our sample under represents practitioners in the large urban district from the Ninth Circuit. Given the pattern of greater frequency of Rule 11 experiences in the large urban districts as shown in Table 8.2), the lower apparent rate in the Ninth Circuit might just have meant that we have fewer large urban practitioners in our Ninth Circuit sample. To test for this, we applied a crude weighting scheme to discount the over-inclusion of lawyers from urban districts in our Ninth Circuit sample; when this was done, the pattern shown in Table 8.3 was virtually unchanged, indicating that we cannot dismiss the Ninth Circuit pattern as an artifact of our sample design.

A variety of other factors might influence Rule 11-related experiences:

- Practice setting (firms of varying size, solo practice, etc.)[18]
- Substance of practice (is 50% or more of the lawyer's practice in civil rights, personal injury, commercial litigation?[19])
- Usual side represented (plaintiffs, defendants, mixed)
- Percentage of practice devoted to federal litigation
- Number of years in practice.[20]

Because a number of these factors are likely to be correlated with the type of district (e.g., lawyers in nonurban districts are more likely to have a varied practice and be in small firms or solo practices, while lawyers in large urban districts might specialize in federal litigation and be in large firm practices), controls must be included for these other variables.

The standard statistical technique for introducing controls of this type is linear regression analysis; because all our dependent variables are dichotomous, we used logistic regression rather than ordinary least squares regression. The central question for our statistical analysis was whether, after controlling for the variables listed above plus circuit and type of district, individual districts still differed significantly from one another; if significant differences remained, we would then need to explore the local legal culture explanation. Because type of district and circuit are directly confounded with individual districts, we could not simply include ten separate dummy variables for district differences; given our coding of circuit and type of district, we had to identify the appropriate sub-set of dummy variables to capture variations among the individual districts— six dummy variables were required to capture these differences.[21] In addition to

---

[18] We operationalized this variable as a trichotomy: solo practice and firms of 3 or fewer lawyers ("tiny"), larger firms with more than 50 lawyers ("big firm"), and other.

[19] We used these categories because they are the dominant ones involving Rule 11 as well as comprising the largest identifiable categories of civil litigation in federal courts once government collection cases and prisoner petitions are omitted.

[20] One variable we omitted from the analysis, because earlier work had shown no consistent pattern of relationship (see Marshall et al. 1992), was size of community in which the lawyer's practice was based. The lack of relationships for federal litigation patterns is not surprising because, as we noted previously, federal litigation is district-centered rather than immediate community-centered, and lawyers in a given case often come from different towns or communities.

[21] The districts for the dropped dummy variables were captured by the following combinations:

Northern Illinois	Seventh Circuit
Central California	Ninth Circuit
Southern Texas	constant term
Northern Mississippi	nonurban
Western Louisiana	urban

Table 8.4: Selected Logistic Regression Results

	Sanction Imposed		Motion for Sanction		In-Court Reference	
	b	s(b)	b	s(b)	b	s(b)
District	5.394		13.972		5.657	
Arizona	-1.027	.535	.412	.348	-.561	.335
Montana	-.824	.612	-.335	.359	-.346	.378
Oregon	-.972	.512	.525	.337	**-.658**	.330
E. California	-.796	.597	.299	.393	-.425	.373
W. Wisconsin	-.124	.567	-.359	.411	-.341	.389
S. Indiana	-.366	.475	**1.057**	.345	**-.676**	.328
Usual Circuit	.876		12.569		3.890	
Seventh	.274	.294	-.686	.195	.377	.193
Ninth	.190	.317	-.272	.201	.171	.209
District Type	1.009		9.552		1.560	
Urban	.358	.367	**-.797**	.262	.245	.246
Nonurban	.077	.435	-.140	.266	-.094	.291

	Out-of-Court Reference		Anticipatory Response		Declined a Case	
	b	s(b)	b	s(b)	b	s(b)
District	7.666		7.352		16.577	
Arizona	**-.714**	.302	-.228	.300	.957	.370
Montana	-.394	.341	.157	.340	.015	.384
Oregon	-.440	.292	**-.608**	.303	.631	.373
E. California	-.198	.328	-.271	.339	.087	.445
W. Wisconsin	-.023	.347	-.130	.356	-.474	.388
S. Indiana	-.221	.289	-.474	.296	-.207	.369
Usual Circuit	.699		4.774		9.172	
Seventh	-.046	.177	-.134	.177	.104	.211
Ninth	-.152	.191	**-.414**	.193	**-.595**	.250
District Type	6.343		3.455		4.121	
Urban	.161	.215	.113	.215	-.228	.267
Nonurban	-.493	.253	-.375	.256	.366	.273

Note: Figures shown in *italics* are Wald statistics; figures shown in **bold** are statistically significant at the .05 level or better.

circuit, type of district, and district, controls were included for each of the variables mentioned above (practice setting, substance of practice, usual side represented, concentration on federal litigation, and years of practice).[22] Six separate logistic regression equations were estimated, one for each dependent variable.

---

[22] Most of the predictor variables were included as sets of dummy variables; the two exceptions were years of practice and percentage of practice devoted to federal litigation, both of which

The portions of the logistic regression results that are relevant for the local legal culture issue are shown in Table 8.4; the table shows in italics a series of Wald statistics; this is a χ^2-distributed test statistic that tests whether a set of coefficients taken together are statistically different from zero (i.e., whether or not the set of parameters, taken together, accounts for any of the variation in the dependent variable). The relevant test for each of our measures of Rule 11 experience is the Wald statistic (6 d.f.) for the row in the table labeled "District," which indicates whether or not any of the variation in the dependent variable is accounted for by the district after all the other variables in the regression equation are taken into account (including circuit and type of district, which are shown in Table 8.4). Only for unsuccessful motions and for declining cases are there significant variations among districts that cannot be accounted for by the other variables in the model.[23] The failure of the significant district effects to cluster around a particular setting such as in-court activities (i.e., sanctions, motions, and in-court references) casts doubt on there being any type of strong local legal culture effects *beyond those that might be explainable by structural or legal factors*. In fact, the pattern of signs of the coefficients suggests no consistency of district effects; for example, for in-court references, all the coefficients are negative, while for motion for sanction there is a mix of positive and negative signs (interestingly, the district with the strongest positive effect on motions, Southern Indiana, has the strongest negative coefficient on in-court references). If there were local legal culture effects operating here, we would expect to find some consistency in the pattern of individual district coefficients.

IV. CONCLUSIONS

When we undertook this analysis, we started from the empirical result that there appeared to be significant variations among the eleven federal districts in our study in the frequency of Rule 11-related activities. We posed for ourselves the question whether these differences might be attributable to local legal culture, a question that made sense in light of the earlier work reporting a link between local legal culture and procedural aspects of case processing (see Church 1982, 1985). Despite these theoretically based expectations, our analysis shows that much, if not most, of the observed variation among the districts is attributable to factors that can be distinguished from local legal culture narrowly defined. It is certainly likely that some of the variation reflects broader cultural influences, but those influences are captured in structural or contextual variables such as "urbanness of the district." This is not to rule out the existence of some specific local effects, whether based on cultural norms, practices of local

---

were included in a nonlinear form (the natural logarithm of years of practice and the square root of percentage of practice devoted to federal litigation were used as the transformations). Because of the particular concern raised about the impact of Rule 11 on civil rights plaintiffs, a specific interaction term was included for civil rights plaintiffs' attorneys.

[23] Some individual districts differ significantly for motions, in-court references, and anticipatory responses, but these few individual differences are insufficient to support an argument that something on the order of local legal culture is an important factor in explaining these Rule 11 practices.

judges, or some other factor; rather, one need not turn to this type of explanation to account for the overall pattern of variation. Assuming that our conclusion is correct (we will note several alternative interpretations of our results below), why is local legal culture at best a minor factor in the phenomenon we are studying?

The most obvious explanation is that our assumption that federal judicial districts constitute an appropriate unit of analysis for examining local legal culture in federal civil litigation is wrong. Some of our districts cover entire states (e.g., Oregon) and, with the possible exception of the District of Central California (Los Angeles), all our districts have multiple communities (typically including at least two cities of reasonable size). We do not have data available to try to identify the specific community of practice for every attorney in our sample; even if we did, the judges generally serve entire districts not specific communities (although in some districts federal judges may be assigned to particular "divisions" based in specific cities), and it is common for attorneys from the same district who are litigating a case to be from different cities or towns. In summary, federal judicial districts may not be local enough for local legal culture to function.

This is a tempting explanation, but it runs directly counter to the initial work of Church and his colleagues that led to the development of the local legal culture construct. Specifically, the core statistical analysis that Church et al. (1978:56) used as a tentative validation of local legal culture was a comparison of pace of civil litigation in state and federal courts. For each of 17 large cities, the civil disposition time and time to trial for the state court were correlated with the corresponding figures for the federal judicial district that contained the city; the resulting correlations were .603 (r^2 = .364) for disposition and .493 (r^2 = .243) for trial. Several of these federal judicial districts were statewide (e.g., Oregon, Arizona, New Jersey), and all of them included areas much wider than those of the urban state court.

This early analysis of delay seems to suggest both that federal judicial districts are appropriate units for studying local legal culture and that local legal culture is a useful construct for understanding at least some aspects of the civil justice system. Unfortunately, there is a flaw in this statistical analysis that undermines such a conclusion. After reexamining Church et al.'s data,[24] we have doubts as to whether those data actually show a relationship between pace (either disposition time or time to trial) in state court and pace in federal court. For each of their two indicators Church et al. had only 17 observations, and they failed to consider the possibility that the apparent relationships resulted from one or two extreme cases. When we applied a set of tools for identifying influential observations, referred to as "regression diagnostics" (see Fox 1991), to the same data, we discovered that for each measure of pace, there was a single extreme case that accounted for the statistically significant correlation; when we dropped out those cases (Boston for the civil disposition time indicator and Bronx County for the time to trial indicator), the r^2s dropped

---

[24] These data appear in their report (Church et al. 1978:56).

precipitously (to .143 for the time to disposition and .100 for the time to trial indicator), neither of which is statistically significant.[25] Thus, we find that there is not a correlation between pace in state courts and pace in federal courts.[26] The absence of such a correlation brings us right back to the dilemma of whether there is a problem in our selection of geographic units.

The following speculations lead us to the hypothesis that the important distinction here is not unit of analysis but important differences in the civil and criminal justice systems. The thrust of much of the research on criminal courts over the decade and a half prior to our research (see Eisenstein et al. 1988; Eisenstein and Jacob 1977; Flemming et al. 1992; Heumann 1978; Mather 1979; McIntyre 1987; Nardulli 1978; Nardulli et al. 1988; Utz 1978) was on the relatively small group of core players who work with one another on a regular, day-in, day-out basis. This type of structure facilitates, perhaps even ensures, that a common set of expectations will develop among the regular participants. We expect that if one focused on the criminal side of the federal justice system, one would find something closely resembling the local legal cultures or "court communities" described in previous research on state criminal courts: there is a small group of judges, prosecuting attorneys (assistant U.S. attorneys), and public defenders who interact on a very regular basis who have evolved a set of expectations concerning appropriate ways of handling cases; furthermore, there was almost certainly movement of personnel across the prosecution/defense line on a regular basis. Thus, it is probably not the nature of the geographic community that affects formation of local legal cultures; rather, it is the regularity of interaction and the movement of players among different roles.

This type of highly regularized, day-in, day-out interaction is not a feature of civil litigation in federal courts (and, with the possible exception of divorce cases, probably not in state courts either), resulting in the absence of the type of small group of core players who dominate the work of a criminal court.[27] Civil practitioners tend to be independent entrepreneurs (usually organized into firms—see Kritzer 1990:44), as opposed to having strong "sponsoring organizations" (see Eisenstein et al. 1988; Eisenstein and Jacob 1977) ; and the judges do not need to be involved at all in the disposition of cases, unlike at least the formal requirement of sentence ratification in criminal cases.[28] While some research on the civil justice system has suggested individual-to-individual linkages (e.g., plaintiffs' lawyer and claims adjuster—see Carlin 1962:78; Ross

---

[25] If one looks at r^2s adjusted for degrees of freedom, the drop is even sharper: from .32 to .08 for disposition time and from .19 to .04 for time to trial.

[26] Our analysis is consistent with that reported by Grossman et al. (1981), which did not find evidence of consistency in the pace of litigation in the state and federal courts of the five federal judicial districts they examined.

[27] This is not to say that there are no coherent groups that might form a "community"; plaintiffs' lawyers in a particular state court may well comprise a community, but the community does not encompass the full group of players Nardulli (1978) labeled the "courtroom elite."

[28] One exception might be divorce litigation, where the court must formally approve the settlement and grant the divorce decree, but this type of litigation does not occur in the federal courts.

1980:82), even that work has not gone to the level of suggesting the existence of workgroups or communities.[29] In fact, there is a clear literature suggesting conflictual relationships between plaintiffs' lawyers and the civil defense bar (see Jackson and Riddlesperger 1991; Lipson 1984; Watson and Downing 1969);[30] there is little or no research on the criminal justice system suggesting a hostile relationship between prosecutors and defense attorneys.[31] Lastly, while there is, or at least was, substantial movement between criminal defense and prosecution work, there is little similar movement among civil litigators, perhaps due to the tendency for a lawyer doing civil work to come to identify with the side he or she regularly represents (with a concomitant perception that the other side is often unreasonable). Thus, it is likely that the kinds of conditions in the criminal justice system that lead to the formation of "local legal cultures" do not exist, at least to the same degree, on the civil side.[32]

Of course there are alternative ways of interpreting the statistical results we have reported. Perhaps actions connected to Rule 11 are not related to local legal culture while other factors in the civil justice system, such as damage amounts or pace of litigation, are. Particularly in light of our reanalysis of Church et al.'s data, we know of no evidence showing a local legal culture effect for the pace of civil litigation. And, with regard to "going rates," in the civil arena it is not the members of the court community (if one can be said to exist) but outsiders—jurors—who establish the going rates. While yet other aspects of civil practice (e.g., settlement styles, pleading and motions practices, etc.) might be linked to local legal culture, we know of no evidence of such linkages.

One might look at our results and point to the types of activities where district level effects remain (filing motions and declining cases) and argue that they do constitute evidence of a need to look for local legal culture effects. Perhaps local legal culture operates in very specific ways, and rather than looking at the failure of most of the types of Rule 11 activities to be related to district after controlling for the other variables, we should focus on the fact that some effects do show up—why dismiss what might be a half-full glass? In fact, in Table 8.1 we showed what amounted to an almost full glass, and it was our ability to empty

---

[29] While Kritzer (1990:68-76) uses the "workgroup" terminology in his study of litigators, he reports little that approaches the strong linkages found in the criminal justice arena.

[30] One minor indicator of this in our own data is found in the response to our open-ended question, "What is the biggest impact, if any, of the sanctioning provisions of Rule 11 on your practice?" Among those lawyers responding to this question who indicated that they largely represented plaintiffs, 21.7% said that civility had decreased and only 7.4% said that civility had increased; in contrast, among defense lawyers, almost equal numbers said that civility had increased (15.9%) and that civility had decreased (15.3%).

[31] Even where there is no workgroup, as in white-collar defense (see Mann 1985), there appears to be little hostility, perhaps because of the pattern of movement from prosecution to defense work (i.e., prosecutors and defense lawyers are likely to be former colleagues).

[32] The one point where there does appear to be some indication of localized expectations has to do with the appropriate pace of civil litigation. As we noted earlier, the core finding that Church et al. (1978:56) cite is the correlation between disposition time in civil cases in state and federal courts; Sherwood and Clarke (1981) report consistent attitudes about appropriate pace, but they look at only one locale, so it is difficult to assess whether this is a function of local legal culture.

much of it that we found most impressive. Without more data, we cannot definitively dismiss the possibility that the declining of cases due to Rule 11 or the filing of Rule 11 motions is at least partly a product of local legal culture.

In fact, our analysis suggests a number of interesting questions concerning local legal culture, and its applicability to the analysis of civil justice process:

- Within the criminal justice context, can local legal cultures, or court communities, exist in fairly large geographic areas such as federal judicial districts? Can the types of findings produced by research in state criminal courts be replicated in the federal criminal courts?

- Can we find evidence of local legal cultures or court communities operating in state court civil justice systems in either large or moderate size urban communities?

- What types of behaviors can and cannot be influenced by local legal cultures or the informal norms of court communities?

These and other questions suggest opportunities for research on the criminal and civil justice systems.

PART III

THE IMPACT OF
HOW LAWYERS ARE PAID

9

FEE ARRANGEMENTS AND NEGOTIATION[1]

INTRODUCTION

Research from the Civil Litigation Research Project (Kritzer 1990; Kritzer et al. 1985) provides solid empirical evidence that the much-discussed linkage between fee arrangements and lawyer effort (Clermont and Currivan 1978; Franklin et al. 1961; Johnson 1980–81; MacKinnon 1964; Rosenthal 1974; Schwartz and Mitchell 1970; See 1984) does in fact exist, although in a somewhat more complex form than theoretical and empirical analyses had suggested. There is no reason that the impact of fee arrangement should be limited to the amount of time lawyers devote to cases. In this research note, I will show that fee arrangement has important implications for the settlement process, an area of the civil justice system that has been a frequent target for proposed reforms (Bedlin and Nejelski 1984; Rosenberg et al. 1981; Haltom and McCann 2004).

My central argument is that discussions of the settlement process, and particularly of manipulations of that process, must consider the interests of all involved in litigation. Regular participants in litigation are well aware of this point. In my series of interviews with corporate lawyers and their clients in Toronto regarding the impact of fees and fee shifting (Kritzer 1984c), a number of respondents mentioned the importance of taking into account the interest of the opposing lawyer. For example, a litigation partner in a firm with one hundred lawyers said, "If you can satisfy the lawyer [with regard to his fee], you'll be a lot closer to settlement." A lawyer for a large retailer similarly stated that to achieve settlement, "you need to provide an incentive for the [opposing] lawyer." Yet despite the evidence that litigation lawyers do not selflessly ignore their own interests, little attention has been paid to how these interests affect settlement and negotiation.

[1] This chapter originally appeared in *Law & Society Review* 21 (1987), 341-48; it is the revised portion of a paper that had been presented at the Conference on Frontiers of Research on Civil Litigation, Institute of Legal Studies, University of Wisconsin Law School, Madison, September 20, 1985; sections of this paper were also presented at the Workshop for Researchers Studying Judicial Promotion of Settlements, American Bar Foundation, Chicago, November 7–8, 1985. The research was supported by NSF Grant No. SES–8320129; the collection of the data was funded by United States Department of Justice Contract JAOIA–79–0040 and National Institute of Justice Contract J–LEAA–003–82, with supplemental support from the University of Wisconsin Graduate School and the University of Wisconsin Law School. Some references have been updated to refer to later publications rather than to unpublished papers, and some new citations have been added.

I am not suggesting that lawyers engage in questionable actions for financial gain. The argument is more subtle: Lawyers, like all of us, when forced to make a choice for which there is no definitive answer, will tend to select the option that is in their own interest. In other words, the financial incentives of their work will often influence the decisions, and it is not coincidental that they will personally benefit from these choices. Thus, although the plaintiffs' bar may truly believe that the contingency fee is the poor man's key to the courthouse door, this belief is shaped by the fact that the key to the courthouse also brings clients—and therefore a livelihood—to the plaintiffs' lawyers. Elsewhere (Kritzer 1984b [see Chapter 4 in this volume]) I have pointed out that the relationship between lawyers and clients is shaped by professional, personal, and business considerations, the last, at their most basic, meaning income (and income streams). But what is the significance of this type of analysis for settlement and negotiation?

Several recent bits of evidence suggest ways in which the settlement-related behavior of lawyers is affected by fee considerations. The *National Law Journal* (August 19, 1985:4) reported a problem that arose from modifications in the schedule of fees paid to court-appointed counsel in criminal cases before courts in Detroit and Wayne County (these modifications were ordered by the chief judges of the courts involved). A lawyer's daily fee for trial work was reduced from $300 to $150, while the fee paid for appearing in court with a client entering a guilty plea was simultaneously increased from $100 to $150. One of the judges reportedly said that he was concerned about a significant increase in the number of bench trials in his court, which he attributed to lawyers foregoing guilty pleas in favor of unnecessary trials that brought an easy $300 fee. A spokesperson for one of the bar groups opposed to the new fee schedule conceded that some lawyers did "go to trial when a guilty plea might be more appropriate," but attributed this at least partly to aspects of the county prosecutor's policy vis-à-vis plea bargaining.

The *National Law Journal* (July 8, 1985) also published a long feature on fee awards (i.e., the process by which judges set fees in certain types of cases, such as class actions, in which the judge serves as a guardian of the interests of the members of the class who are not present in court). One element of controversy over fee awards concerned the bases by which such awards are set. One approach is a simple extension of the percentage, or contingency, fee used in most cases involving individual plaintiffs (outside of divorce and other family matters). The problem with this approach, particularly in large class actions, is that such fees can yield what some see as windfall payments to lawyers for relatively little work. On the other hand, these sums do encourage lawyers to seek the best settlement possible. The alternate method of fee calculation is the so-called lodestar system in which the lawyer is compensated with an hourly rate, adjusted by some multiplier to reflect the quality of the work or the degree of risk involved. However, this approach can be criticized for creating an incentive for plaintiffs' lawyers to delay settlement and to pad their time by engaging in allegedly unnecessary pretrial maneuvering. This is particularly a problem in class action or mass tort cases (e.g., in the Agent Orange litigation), in which there is no real possibility for significant plaintiff input into the decisions of their lawyers.

I. THE SEARCH FOR BETTER APPROACHES TO NEGOTIATION

In the early- to mid-1980s there was increasing attention on the means of improving the negotiation process. The most prominent work in this area is by the Harvard Project on Negotiation, including such well-received books as those by Fisher and Ury (1981) and by Raiffa (1982), and the launch of the *Negotiation Journal* (1985). Work that is more directed to the legal sphere in general and the litigation (or dispute-resolving) sphere in particular includes Williams's (1983) examination of negotiator "effectiveness" and Menkel-Meadow's (1984) argument that lawyers should move from an "adversary" (zero sum or distributive) mode of bargaining toward a "problem-solving" (positive sum or integrative) mode of negotiation.

None of this literature took into account one of the central facts of everyday litigation in the United States: that some lawyers work on an hourly fee basis while others work on a contingency or percentage fee basis. While contingency fees are most often thought of in regard to personal injury cases, they are in fact widely used in most cases in which an individual as plaintiff is seeking monetary compensation, the major exception being domestic relations. Under a contingency fee, the lawyer is paid a portion of the recovery (plus expenses), and the recovery is often sent directly to the lawyer (who then extracts her fee and expenses, passing the balance on to the client) or jointly to the lawyer and the client. My argument is that the contingency arrangement has very important implications for the lawyer-negotiator.

In my introduction to this chapter, I alluded to the theoretical argument that contingency fee lawyers in cases with modest amounts at stake have an incentive to arrive quickly at a settlement, even if that settlement is not the best for the client. Whether this means that the fee arrangement directly affects the amount of time the lawyer spends on settlement negotiations (although I was unable to find any systematic difference in time spent on such activities comparing hourly and contingency fee lawyers), the same theoretical considerations apply to the content of the actual negotiation. Specifically, since the contingency fee lawyer is to receive a share of the ultimate recovery, she has an incentive to see to it that the recovery can in fact be shared.

Menkel-Meadow (1984:772-73) provides an example that illustrates this argument:

> Ms. Brown buys a car from Mr. Snead, a used car salesman. After a short period of time the car ceases to function, despite repeated attempts by Ms. Brown to have the car repaired. Ms. Brown, therefore, sues Mr. Snead for rescission of the sales contract, claiming misrepresentation in the sale of the car or, in the alternative, breach of warranty, with consequential damages including lost income from the loss of a job due to repeated lateness and absences as a result of the malfunctioning car. Mr. Snead counterclaims for the balance due on the car [plus attorneys' fees as permitted under the sales contract], claiming

that the warranty period has ended and the dealership was given insufficient time in which to cure any possible defects.

As Menkel-Meadow points out, although the lawsuit is over concerns that can be relatively easily monetized, the parties both really want more than just dollars and cents: Ms. Brown wants reliable transportation and her job; Mr. Snead wants to retain his profit on this sale and for Ms. Brown (and her friends) to buy cars from him in the future. One can easily imagine an outcome that satisfies both parties yet differs from the typical damages-oriented lawsuit: Mr. Snead provides Ms. Brown with another car from his large inventory and gives her an extended warranty on that car in compensation for her difficulties; he can then repair the car he originally sold to Ms. Brown and sell it to another customer.

However, what would happen if a contingency fee lawyer entered the Brown-Snead case? If that lawyer is a graduate of UCLA Law School and has taken a course in negotiation from Professor Menkel-Meadow, she could see a variety of ways of settling the case without directly exchanging money. However, she is in the law business to make a living and thus will recognize that Ms. Brown cannot pay a lawyer on an hourly basis and that a lawyer cannot take one-third of a car as a percentage payment. It is highly instructive that the example of Ms. Brown and Mr. Snead is based on a hypothetical case developed by the Legal Services Corporation, Office of Program Support, for training legal services attorneys (Menkel-Meadow 1984:772n). A contingency fee lawyer who sought nonmonetary resolutions of her clients' cases, even if those resolutions were better from the clients' perspective, would soon go out of business unless some alternate payment method were available for such settlements (e.g., fee shifting, whereby the defendant pays the plaintiff's attorney for his time, or a central fund, created by "taxing" contingency fees, from which the lawyer could receive compensation).

II. ANALYSIS

In actual cases, are contingency fee lawyers more concerned with money during their negotiations than are lawyers paid on an hourly fee or some other basis (such as flat fees or salaries)? In its survey of lawyers, the Civil Litigation Research Project (CLRP) obtained information on up to three offers or demands directed at resolving the case (see this chapter's appendix for a brief description of the research design and the data). Using only the data on what the respondent offered or demanded (i.e., ignoring the offers or demands of the opposing party), I classified the content of negotiation as "monetary" (when the demand was for either a specific or nonspecific sum of money), "nonmonetary" (when the demand or offer was not explicitly monetary),[2] or "mixed" (when there was a combination of monetary and nonmonetary demands or offers). This third category includes situations in which an individual demand or offer contained both monetary and nonmonetary elements and those in which the demands or offers changed in nature from one exchange to another.

---

[2] See Kritzer (1991b:46-47) for details on the nonmonetary demands and offers.

Table 9.1: Negotiation Content by Fee Arrangement
(All Respondents)

Fee	Monetary	Nonmonetary	Mixed	N
Hourly	51%	19%	29%	547
Contingency	77%	3%	20%	349
Other	44%	28%	28%	109

x^2 = 90.55; p < .001

Table 9.2: Negotiation Content by Fee Arrangement
(Only Respondents Who Monetized Stakes)

Fee	Monetary	Nonmonetary	Mixed	N
Hourly	63%	5%	32%	370
Contingency	78%	1%	21%	300
Other	62%	8%	30%	60

x^2 = 27.04; p < .001

Table 9.1, which reports the content of the negotiations as reported by respondents, clearly shows the overriding importance of money in the demands of the contingency fee lawyer: Only 3% of the lawyers retained on a contingency fee basis reported making demands that contained no monetary element (and one must wonder how those lawyers expected to be paid) compared to 19% of the hourly fee lawyers; 77% of the demands of contingency fee lawyers were entirely monetary compared to 51% for the hourly fee lawyers. There is no doubt that an element of self-fulfilling prophecy is operating here, since contingency fee lawyers will normally refuse cases that are not amenable to a monetary recovery. Still, in Table 9.2, which shows only those cases in which the lawyer-respondent was able to express stakes in clearly monetary terms, the basic relationship remains clear, although it is somewhat muted because the negotiations of the lawyers paid on other than a contingency fee basis are more monetary in their orientation than those cases shown in Table 9.1.

III. CONCLUSION

This brief analysis provides further evidence of the impact of economic incentives on lawyer behavior. Although lawyers are professionals who are concerned with the needs and interests of their clients, their behavior is nonetheless influenced (note the use of influenced rather than determined) by the forces of economic rationality or necessity or both, and this influence is felt as well in the lawyers' means of negotiating. If we want lawyers to consider actively what Menkel-Meadow calls the problem-solving approaches to negotiation, we must ensure that their livelihood is not dependent upon adversary approaches to negotiation. There is an interesting parallel here to certain issues that have arisen in regard to discovery. Brazil (1978) pointed out that civil discovery is substantially based on a nonadversarial image of a litigation process that is inherently adversarial; he further suggested that as long as the trial lawyer relies upon a reputation as a strong advocate for his or her client's interest as a means of attracting and holding clients, it would be difficult for the discovery process to conform more closely to the ideal that was behind its widespread introduction in the 1930s. Some mechanism might indeed eliminate the economic incentives that tend to push lawyers away from an adversarial, money-oriented stance in negotiation, but the issues that such mechanisms raise are both practically and politically troubling. Given the stridency of physicians' opposition to socialized medicine, the intensity of the bar's opposition to a proposal for socializing the practice of law can only be imagined.

IV. APPENDIX

The data presented above were collected by the CLRP in a survey of 1,382 lawyers representing parties in 1,649 randomly sampled court cases drawn from seven state and five federal courts in five federal judicial districts around the country (Eastern Wisconsin, Eastern Pennsylvania, Central California, South Carolina, and New Mexico); all of the cases were terminated during calendar year 1978. The sample was limited to cases involving a claim of at least $1,000 or some significant nonmonetary demand; certain types of cases (e.g., prisoner petitions and certain kinds of labor law issues were excluded from the sample, and one type, domestic relations, was included in a limited fashion (see Kritzer 1980–81:512). Each of the 1,382 lawyers was interviewed by telephone about the specific case selected for the sample; the interviews averaged one hour in length. Additional details on the CLRP and the data it collected can be found in Trubek et al. (1983a; 1983b), Kritzer (1980–81, 1984a), Kritzer et al. (1984b), and Kritzer (1990).

10

FEE REGIMES AND THE COST OF CIVIL JUSTICE[1]

INTRODUCTION

Why is it that despite all of our efforts, we cannot lick the demon of high costs for civil justice? There are many possible answers to that question, but the focus of this chapter is on one explanation: those proposing and implementing changes directed at reducing the cost of civil justice have failed to grasp the complexities involved in the single most important aspect of those costs: what and how we pay for legal representation. To make clear these complexities, I use the idea of "fee regime," which combines three factors: how lawyers' fees are computed; who pays the lawyer's fee; and how lawyers' fees are regulated and reviewed.[2]

Complaints about the cost of securing (civil) justice are probably as old as formalized procedures for securing that justice. The same can probably be said for the single biggest cost of securing justice in most cases: the costs associated with legal representation. Over a period of about 25 years, England saw three major inquiries related to litigation cost, all of which ended with recommendations and changes that had implications for legal fees. In the 1980s there was the Civil Justice Review and a set of changes, the 1990s saw an inquiry by the Master of the Rolls, Lord Woolf resulting in another set of reforms, and about 15 years later, an inquiry conducted by Lord Jackson of the Court of Appeal, and yet another set of reforms that became effective in 2013.

---

[1] This chapter is a slight updating and reformatting of an essay of the same title that appeared in *Civil Justice Quarterly* 28 (2009), 343-66. At the time the essay was written, England was beginning to consider significant changes to the rules governing the financing of litigation generally and specifically whether restrictions forbidding the use of percentage fees should be revised or eliminated. I have made some changes to the essay to reflect key changes that did occur (permitting percentage fees, limiting what costs could be recovered from the losing side, and eliminating fee shifting for certain groups of plaintiffs). In preparing the original essay I benefited from the opportunity to present the argument in this paper at the Faculty of Law, Australian National University, Canberra, and at the University of Minnesota Law School. I would also like to thank Michael Zander, Richard Moorhead, and Adrian Zuckerman for their comments and suggestions; any errors remain my responsibility.

[2] Another explanation for the seemingly unending discussion of the high cost of civil justice may be that for many people any costs incurred to secure justice is too much. While businesses may see legal and other costs as simply part of doing business, ordinary citizens probably do not have a view more akin to, "why should I have to bear this cost, I didn't do anything wrong." And, while businesses may see legal costs as routine, businesses no doubt prefer those costs to be as low as possible.

Concerns about costs of justice and lawyers' fees more generally are by no means confined to England. In the United States, the issue of adopting a loser pays rule has reemerged yet again as a topic of discussion,[3] being pushed by conservative think tanks such as the Manhattan Institute (see Gryphon 2011) and Common Good.[4] Major American corporations were again in 2009 talking about alternatives to paying their outside lawyers by the hour.[5]

The dilemma for those who would change how the costs of civil justice are computed and paid, or more specifically how the costs of representation are computed and paid, is the fact that all arrangements for costs and fees create incentives. Some of those incentives will be positive but others will be perverse. Predicting how the positive and perverse incentives will balance out is complex and difficult. The difficulty is increased by the fact that while reformers think specifically about the positives they seek to achieve, identifying the possible perverse incentives is difficult and often overlooked.

A simple example of the difficulties can be seen in the effects of England's Access to Justice Act 1999. A major goal of this law was to reduce dependence on government funded legal aid. Several years earlier England had adopted a kind of no-win, no-pay fee system that was called a "conditional fee." Under this system the solicitor would forego his or her usual fee if the case was unsuccessful but could charge an uplift of up to 100% of the usual fee (but no more than 25% of the client's recovery) if the claim was successful. Under the English "loser pays" fee shifting system, a plaintiff was still at risk of having to pay the defendant's costs if the claim was unsuccessful; to deal with this risk insurers devised a system of "after-the-event" (ATE) insurance to cover that risk.[6] The problem this system created was that it reduced the claimant's recovery by the cost of the uplift and the ATE insurance premium, and this discouraged those eligible for legal aid from using the conditional fees. To encourage a shift away from legal aid, the 1999 Act made the conditional fee uplift and ATE insurance premium payable by the losing defendant. The positive incentive intended by this change was to increase the willingness of potential plaintiffs to retain lawyers on a conditional fee basis, particularly plaintiffs who otherwise would qualify for legal aid and who would prefer legal aid where they paid the lawyer nothing to the prospect of having to pay the lawyer up to 25 per cent of their recovery plus the ATE premium. Moving people with claims eligible for conditional fees off civil legal aid would, the Government hoped, reduce very substantially the cost of legal aid. What was not anticipated was that while before the Access to Justice Act 1999 defendant insurers had no reason to care about the size of the uplift or the cost of ATE, once those insurers were obligated

---

[3] There was a wave of discussion on fee shifting (loser pays) in the U.S. in the early 1980s (see, for example, Rowe 1984b).

[4] For the Common Good discussion, see http://newtalk.org/2008/08/would-loser-pays-eliminate-fri.php (last accessed February 4, 2009).

[5] I say "again talking" because this was a theme much discussed about 20 years ago (see Kritzer 1994).

[6] This was called "after-the-event" insurance because it was purchased by the claimant after the injury had occurred.

to pay those costs in most cases (because most cases do result in payment to the claimant), they were very concerned about what they had to pay as the uplift and for the ATE premium.[7] The result was intense conflict over both the size of the uplift and the ATE premium, including whether it was appropriate pay any ATE premium in cases where liability was clear. This issue was fought out through a series of cases that became known as the "costs wars."[8]

I. UNDERSTANDING THE COMPLEXITIES OF FEES AND COSTS

How might we develop a better understanding the complexities in the ways that fees and costs are structured? As suggested previously, I employ the concept of "fee regime" which I define as:

> The structure of attorney compensation for contentious work, includ-
> ing litigation, arbitration, administrative adjudication, and settlement
> of claims in the absence of third-party processing.

While lawyers' fees do not comprise the sum total of the costs of civil justice, for most cases they constitute such a large percentage that understanding the complexities of fees is the central issue.

Fee regimes involve three distinct dimensions:

1. who pays the fee;
2. how the fee is computed;
3. how fees are regulated and reviewed.

The complexities of fee regimes come from the variety one finds within each of the three dimensions and more importantly from the myriad ways that the dimensions interact. In the sections that follow, I will specify in some detail the three dimensions that comprise fee regimes. In the subsequent sections I will discuss some of the complexities of how the dimensions interact.

A. WHO PAYS THE FEE

While I label this dimension "who pays the fee," it more broadly represents who covers the cost of legal representation.[9]

The first alternative in answer to the "who pays" is that each side pays its own lawyers. This is the traditional "American" rule. Normally, when we think of the American rule, we think in terms of a litigant hiring a lawyer and paying that lawyer's fee. However, there are other ways we might think about each

---

[7] It may also be that after the premium became recoverable, ATE providers no longer felt the same need to compete for business by setting premiums at true market rates. Accident Line Protect, which at the time was the largest ATE insurer doubled its premiums just about the time that the Access to Justice Act 1999 was passed by Parliament (see Robins 1999a).

[8] The costs wars generated too many cases to cite, but sampling would include *Callery v. Gray (No.1)* [2002] UKHL 28; [2002] 1 W.L.R. 2000; *Callery v. Gray (No.2)* [2001] EWCA Civ 1246; [2001] 1 W.L.R. 2142; *Claims Direct Test Cases, Re* [2002] EWHC B717, [2003] EWCA Civ 136; *Halloran v. Delaney* [2002] EWCA Civ 1258; [2003] 1 W.L.R. 28; *Sawar v. Alam* [2001] EWCA Civ 1401; [2002] 1 W.L.R. 125; the cost wars were continuing in the late 2000s; see *Gloucestershire CC v. Evans* [2008] EWCA Civ 21; [2008] 1 W.L.R. 1883.

[9] One can also include within this dimension other costs of litigation including filing fees, travel, expert fees, etc.

party covering the cost of representation. Specifically, litigants-in-person (what is referred to as the *pro se* litigant in the United States) is a form by which the party covers its own cost of representation, even though that "cost" involves no out-of-pocket payment; instead the party covers the "cost" by its own time and effort. For the corporate party or a governmental party, representation by an in-house, salaried lawyer (or other in-house staff person in tribunal situations) is another way that a party covers its own cost of representation.

The second way that fees might be paid is by the losing party in a contentious matter, the English Rule, or more generically by "fee shifting." Losers might be obligated to pay all of the reasonable costs incurred by the winner or only some portion of those costs. There may be two-way fee shifting or one-way fee shifting whereby only a losing defendant incurs costs obligations vis-à-vis its opponent, a situation that plays out for plaintiffs receiving legal aid.[10]

Payment by a third party is the third answer to the "who pays" question. Most familiar here is the liability insurer that as part of a liability policy pays its insured's legal expenses, although one might argue that it is the insurance company who is the "real" defendant in terms of what is at stake in the case. A second form of insurance is before-the-event legal expense insurance which might be sold as a stand-alone product, be included as part of some other insurance (home, motor, or the like), or be offered as a benefit of employment either directly by an employer or as part of the benefits of belonging to a union (Blankenburg 1982-83; Kilian 2003; Kilian and Regan 2004). A third form of insurance is the ATE insurance that developed in conjunction with conditional fees in the mid-1990s.

Another form of third-party payment is legal aid. In the United Kingdom legal aid is largely seen as something funded by the government, although there are also specialized legal aid providers that exist as charities. In some countries legal aid originally developed in the form of privately-funded charities, and in some American states this type of legal aid continues to be of some importance. A third way that legal aid is funded is through interest on client accounts, what in some countries is referred to as "interest on lawyers' trust accounts" or IOLTA, a system that is found in both Canada and at least some of the American states. Lastly, legal aid might be funded by the legal profession itself, either through lawyers' pro bono work or contributions made in lieu of donating time.

A final form of third-party payment, long forbidden under the law of champerty and maintenance, is the litigation funding company which provides nonrecourse funding (i.e., the funding is repaid only if damages are paid by the defendant) to lawyers and possibly to the litigants themselves (Steinitz 2011; Rubin 2011; Abrams and Chen 2013). For example, in the United Kingdom, Juridica Investments obtained a capitalization of £80 million in 2007 with the goal of "a diversified portfolio of investments in claims." In the United States,

---

[10] One could argue that American style contingency fees, some commentators in England refer to as "damage-based contingency fees" (see Moorhead 2003) actually constitute a form of one-way fee shifting, because in practice it is the loser who pays the plaintiff's/claimant's fee. Some have argued that American juries in civil cases factor in the percentage to be paid to the plaintiff's lawyer when setting damage awards (see Hans and Vidmar 1986:161).

one finds companies such as LawCash and Law Capital Enterprises (1-877-Fund-My-Case); in Australia there are a number of companies including IMF.[11] Litigation funding companies might be seen as a form of "reinsurance" when the lawyer is being paid on a no-win, no-fee basis because lawyers working on a no-win, no-pay fee basis are providing a form of insurance to their clients (Kritzer 2004b: 16). Obtaining support from a litigation funding company spreads the risk just as is done with reinsurance.

B. How the Fee is Computed

There are many ways that fees can be computed, and most require little or no explanation:

- time;
- flat/fixed;
- percentage of recovery;
- item of service (task-based);
- value to client (value-based);
- set by court schedule or statute;
- per diem;
- salary or covered as part of an ongoing retainer.

Several of these do merit comment. Item of service usually refers to very specific discrete tasks (e.g., writing a letter, preparing a motion, making a court appearance, taking a deposition); however, it could also refer to what I have heard referred to as "phase billing," where a fee is set for each phase of an action, perhaps with the specific fee depending upon the complexity of the specific case. The "value to client" approach is rather vague but in a sense reflects the traditional considerations of amount of effort involved, level of expertise required, importance of the matter to the client, and results achieved; in a sense, it is the old "for services rendered" without explanation bill. Set by court schedule or statute is the method that has been described as being used in Germany; essentially, the fee reflects the amount that is claimed to be in controversy, with the interesting result that a plaintiff who significantly inflates a claim might end up owing fees to a defendant if only a modest amount is recovered because the defendant spent on the defense amounts consistent with what was claimed by the plaintiff (see Leipold 1995; Pfennigstorf 1984; Zuckerman 1996). What I label "per diem" is a fee system where the client is billed based solely on the length of time the file is open; the fee may be computed by counting days, months, or quarters. The amount of work that is done does not affect the fee; the fee depends solely on the length of time from when the case is referred to the lawyer until the case is closed. The final method, salary or

---

[11] "IMF is a publicly listed company providing funding of legal claims and other related services where the claim size is over $2 million. IMF has brought together the major participants in the litigation funding market in Australia to become the largest litigation funder in Australia and the first to be listed on the Australian Stock Exchange." See http://www.imf.com.au (last accessed February 5, 2009).

ongoing retainer, is most commonly the form of "payment" when the case is handled by someone on the staff of the litigant (i.e., an in-house lawyer). However, it could also reflect an arrangement whereby the client pays the lawyer a monthly retainer in return for handling whatever matters arise; some months there may be no work and others there may be a lot. I could also imagine an arrangement where a client contracts with a firm to purchase a fixed amount of time from the firm (i.e., a certain number of FTE's of lawyer effort), and pays the firm on a contract basis; in a sense, this would be a kind of outsourcing of an in-house lawyer type arrangement.

In addition there are myriad ways that these might be combined or enhanced; some examples include:

- contingent hourly (time plus risk enhancement/"uplift"—the conditional fee that was adopted in England in the 1990s);
- fixed fee plus bonus for success;
- reduced-rate hourly plus bonus for success;
- flat fee for all work up until trial preparation; hourly for trial preparation and trial itself;
- time-capped flat fee in which the flat fee covers up a maximum amount of time (typically more than what the expected hourly rate would cover) with anything above the cap billed hourly;
- item of service for specific tasks (e.g., per deposition/witness statement), hourly for other tasks.

I am aware of examples of all of the above. For example, a lawyer in a large U.S. firm recently told me that his firm is now doing some kinds of cases on a fixed fee plus bonus basis. The firm where I observed some years ago had some arrangements of the form of a flat fee prior to trial preparation with subsequent work on an hourly fee basis.

The motivations for trying various fee arrangements are to modify incentives to the advantage of the lawyer or the client, and perhaps even both. However, as I have discussed elsewhere, the revised incentive structures may produce undesired effects, and often firms and their clients retreat to previously existing arrangements (Kritzer 2006:2060-68 [see Chapter 6 in this volume]).

C. FEE REGULATION AND REVIEW

The third element of a fee regime is the nature of any regulation of fees and any mechanism for reviewing fees to determine if they are appropriate. England, Canada, and Australia have long had a structure for reviewing fees because of fee shifting. Costs judges, taxing masters, assessment officers, taxing officers, legal services commissioners, legal ombudsmen, and similar officials have expertise in norms and regulations about fees, and employ those norms and regulations in assessing fees for reasonableness. How this is done has changed over time so that in England now there is a mixture of "fixed costs," "summary assessment" of costs and "detailed assessment" of costs, with costs judges dealing primarily with "detailed assessments" or disputes arising from other methods.

In contrast, the United States has had no systematic structure for fee reviews. Courts have an inherent power to review fees, but this is seldom used except perhaps in certain special circumstances such as when the client is not legally competent due either to age or mental condition. Some states have statutes authorizing judges to review contingency fees but there is little evidence that many such reviews occur, nor when it does happen, what types of standards or bases are used to assess the reasonableness of fee.[12] In these states there is no requirement of review; reviews occur at the court's discretion or by request of one or both of the parties. Judges review fee petitions and formally approve or set fees in class actions and one-way fee shifting cases (see Eisenberg and Miller 2004, 2010; Lynk 1990; Task Force on Contingent Fees 2006). American judges have no particular expertise on fees, and I expect that the judges hate this task. In some states, the bar association and/or the state court system provides what amounts to an arbitration procedure to resolve fee disputes (see, e.g., Gervasi and Lebovits 2009); it is not clear how often they are used or what types of expertise or norms are employed in resolving disputes.

Business clients, who in the past undoubtedly at least looked at bills to see if they seemed reasonable, have turned to systematic methods of reviewing the bills they receive from their outside lawyers. Most prominent has been the use by insurance companies of outside fee auditing companies to review the bills they receive from their own lawyers (see Kritzer 2006:2070 [Chapter 6 in this volume]). Lawyers in some states have challenged this, at least in cases where insurers were paying lawyers to represent insureds (*ibid.*, 2071n38). Lawyers have to some degree learned to live with this or have gotten out of insurance defense as an area of practice (*ibid.*, 2072-76). Firms who directly represent corporations are beginning to see external fee audits. Those firms have long had to deal with questions about their bills raised by the in-house lawyers who are their liaison with the corporations,[13] but the use of outside fee auditing companies changes the nature of the review substantially. One obvious question is how the corporation is paying the fee auditing company. Paying the auditing company a percentage of any savings achieved creates an incentive to cut bills significantly; even if the auditing company is paid on some other basis, the incentive is to find cuts because why else would the corporation want to pay to have the bills audited?

One broad issue regarding fee review and regulation is the issue of what standards are appropriate for determining if fees are appropriate. Arguably, this depends in part on who is paying the fee. One set of standards may be appropriate when a losing party is obligated to pay the winning party's fees. A second set of standards may be appropriate for assessing the reasonableness of what a lawyer is asking his or her own client to pay. And a third set of standards might be employed in the situation where a third party is paying the lawyer's fees. Traditionally in some countries there were explicit standards, including "party-and-party" costs, "solicitor-and-client" costs, and (at least in some Canadian

---

[12] Sloan and Chepke (2008:148) report that for medical malpractice cases, "eight states have enacted a process of review of attorney fees."

[13] I suspect that inside lawyers enjoy reviewing fees just about as much as do judges who must review fee petitions.

provinces) "solicitor-and-own-client" costs. Since 1986 there have been two standards used in England, "standard basis" and "indemnity basis" with the only difference being how doubt is resolved, favoring the paying party on "standard basis" and the receiving party on "indemnity basis."

What about when a third party is paying the fee? In England, fees paid by Legal Aid are set according to a complex system that includes standardized flat rates for many kinds of work as well as some work done on an hourly fee basis and other work governed by a graduated fee plan.[14] A common complaint when some form of legal aid is paying the lawyer's fee is that the payment is too low (see Moorhead 2004:159); this has been a particular issue in criminal defense, particularly in the United States. But there is a broader question of whether there should be some standard to address the potential problem that a third-party payer is limiting payment in a way that constrains the lawyer to an inadequate level of effort. What standard should apply in assessing whether a fee is adequate, particularly when that fee determines the level of effort the lawyer devotes to the case? The client may want the lawyer to do everything necessary to win even if the level of effort is very high relative to what the client might gain or lose; the client may want vindication regardless of the cost. Should the standard be what the client would be willing to pay the lawyer if the client could afford the costs and had to weigh the cost/return trade-off?

A last element focuses on "rates," particularly when the fee is based on the amount of time devoted to a matter. What kinds of rates are appropriate and who determines this? Can the market set the rate when someone other than the consumer of the service is paying the fee? How efficient is the market in determining rates, particularly for services provided to infrequent users of legal services? Should the rate depend on who's paying the fee? All of these are issues that need to be addressed in the context of fee regulation and fee review.

II. THE MULTIPLE WORLDS OF LITIGATION

It is not possible to dissociate the nature of the fee regime and its potential impact from the type of litigation. There are at least three worlds of litigation (see Hensler et al. 1987). The first is the world of the routine: the everyday cases with modest to moderate amounts at stake; these are epitomized by claims arising from road traffic accidents. The second is high value litigation involving individual claims that are not part of what Galanter referred to as "case con-gregations" (Galanter 1990b). Defining where the routine ends and the high value world begins can only be imprecise, but one arbitrary line that might be drawn would define this world as including cases where it makes sense for the costs of the litigation itself to get into six figures for one or more parties. This

---

[14] At one time, the fees recovered by lawyers handling cases for Legal Aid were paid not to the lawyer but to the Legal Aid fund; the Legal Aid fund would then pay the lawyer, using a scale that was somewhat less than what lawyers could charge a privately paying client. In addition, all such fees were subject to a "statutory charge" which effectively was a further 10% reduction of the fee (Genn 1988:89). Solicitors sometimes handled cases they believed to be "sure things" on an informal contingency fee basis as a way of avoiding this charge (ibid., 109-10). I found somewhat similar practices in Ontario in the early 1980s, a time when contingency fees were not permitted in that Canadian province (see Kritzer 1984c:130-31).

would include major injuries regardless of their source (traffic accidents, premises, professional negligence, products liability, business torts, major commercial despites, and the like). Such cases may or may not be "high risk." The third category is what I label "large scale" litigation.[15] It includes mass torts, class actions, what Galanter called "case congregations" which in the United States often involve "multi-district litigation" (MDLs) or possibly wind up in bankruptcy proceedings, and what is sometimes called "bet-your-company" litigation where the future of the company itself is at stake (certain mass torts, major anti-trust cases, etc.). The implications of specific fee regimes depend on which of these worlds one is considering.

This can be seen by contrasting issues of fees and costs in routine versus high value cases. The costs and returns for both lawyers and litigants in high value litigation change how the parties look at the process in ways that turn very heavily on the fee structure. Defendants will spend more and give lawyers more leeway particularly if there is no insurance company standing between the defendant and the lawyer (i.e., the defendant is paying its lawyer itself rather than relying on third-party payment by an insurer). Plaintiffs' lawyers working on a no-win, no-pay basis need deep pockets to finance high value litigation, which is the major reason that medical malpractice and products liability tend to be specialized areas of practice. This is clearly illustrated in the story of attorney Jan Schlichtmann as told in Jonathan Harr's book *A Civil Action* (1995); the defendants in that case were able to outlast the plaintiffs' lawyers' financial resources.

The nature of potential conflicts of interest between lawyers and clients can change depending on whether one is considering a routine or high value case. In the former, the percentage fee lawyer's short-run interest is to secure a quick settlement with relatively modest amounts of time invested; this may mean only a fractional recovery of damages to the client. As I have argued elsewhere, the lawyer's long-run interest is likely to be different (Kritzer 2004b:222-23), and even in the short-run the percentage fee lawyer has an incentive to try to push settlement offers up because the marginal return to the lawyer for a small amount of effort can be quite good.[16] If the client is paying the lawyer's fee on an hourly basis, win or lose, the client is not likely to want the lawyer to make an all out effort. However, in a fee shifting regime, or where the lawyer is paid by a third party, the lawyer's interest and the client's interest might align nicely, although there may be conflict with a third-party payer of the lawyer's fee who might question whether the cost was commensurate with the amount recovered.

In a high value case, a (percentage) contingency fee lawyer's short-run economic interest will readily align with that of the client; it is easily worth it to the lawyer to invest more time because the potential return for that investment, even discounted for risk, is very attractive. However, a lawyer handling a high

---

[15] My third category is somewhat broader than that discussed by Hensler et al. (1987); their third category was limited to mass torts (in part because they were focused specifically on tort litigation).

[16] Even modest increases in settlement figures can produce very good marginal returns to the lawyer (see Kritzer 2004b:159).

value case has more at stake (more of an investment to lose), and this risk may for some lawyers shift them toward being at least somewhat risk averse. Also, at some point, a client in a high value case may see a substantial settlement that is nonetheless considerably less that the case is likely to bring at trial as so attractive that the client will prefer to take what is on the table because the client has only one shot at the "game." Under a fee regime where the plaintiff is paying his or her own lawyer win or lose, the plaintiff's attitude toward settlement may change as the sunk costs increase.

Since 1995 solicitors in England have been permitted to charge on the basis of a conditional fee. As described above, this is a form of no-win, no-pay fee in which the lawyer foregoes a fee if the case is unsuccessful and is paid the normal fee plus a percentage "uplift" if a recovery is made. A conditional fee may be preferable from the lawyer's perspective for smaller, routine cases because the damages limit the amount that can be earned on a percentage basis. In contrast, for large cases, the lawyer would probably prefer a percentage fee structure because of the potential "profits." From the perspective of the plaintiff with a very modest claim, a conditional fee arrangement may be better, particularly from the perspective of securing representation. However, evidence from the United States shows that percentage fee lawyers often handle large numbers of cases that are not profitable, and which the lawyer knows up front are not likely to be profitable because handling such cases can help build a referral network of prior clients. Whether a similar pattern will develop in England given the adoption of a system permitting percentage fees system effective in 2013 is, as of 2014, not yet clear.

III. FEE REGIMES, INCENTIVES, AND CONFLICTS: FURTHER THOUGHTS

The previous section considered multiple worlds of litigation and how the elements of fee regimes interact within the different worlds. Much of that discussion focused on incentive issues. Here I turn to a more general discussion of incentives as they relate to fees and fee regimes.

Fee regimes affect the value of cases. Fee shifting can either increase or decrease the value of a case depending on the level of risk or uncertainty involved. For cases that are low risk from the plaintiff's perspective, fee shifting increases case value from the perspective of the defendant and possibly from the perspective of the plaintiff as well, although for the latter it depends on other aspects of the fee regime equation. From the defendant's perspective, the value of a case is the expectation of the total of its defense costs, what is paid in damages, and what is paid for the plaintiff's costs; this equals the total of the costs multiplied by the probability of having to pay minus the probability of defense costs times the probability of the defense winning. Without fee shifting, the defendant's case value is its costs plus the amount of damages times the probability of having to pay those damages. For low risk cases, the case valuation from the defendant's perspective is almost certainly higher with fee shifting than without. Whether the total cost to the defendant increases or decreases will depend on the mix of low risk and high risk cases; if most cases are low risk (from the claimant's perspective), then overall costs to the defendant will increase. Note that this analysis does not need to take into account the shifting of uplifts and after-the-event insurance premiums, although including those should further increase the value of cases. A study of fee shifting in the one American state that has a fee regime that includes fee shifting, Alaska, found that when asked about the impact of fee shifting, many defense lawyers identified increasing the value of cases, particularly when the central issue in the case was quantum rather than liability, as perhaps the most significant effect (Di Pietro et al. 1995:110-11).

The analysis for the plaintiff is somewhat more complex because it depends not just on whether there is fee shifting but also on whether the plaintiff is directly at risk for the fee shift. Plaintiffs may not be directly at risk for two possible reasons: the plaintiff does not have the financial resources to pay the defendant's costs should the defendant prevail, or the plaintiff has insurance against those costs. The state of Florida briefly had fee shifting in medical negligence cases; adopting a fee shifting system was strongly backed by the medical establishment. However, the system was quickly repealed at least in part after it became apparent that a successful defendant was seldom able to recover its costs because most plaintiffs had little or no resources available to pay those costs (see Snyder and Hughes 1990:356).

As one would expect, the incentives for litigants are greatly affected by the risks they face, both in terms of whether they have to pay their own lawyer as a case progresses and whether they are at risk for the other side's costs. This was most clearly illustrated for me by the comments of a small town solicitor whom I interviewed in 1987. This solicitor handled cases for both privately-paying clients and for clients who had before-the-event legal expense insurance. How he dealt with cases depended on who was paying him (Kritzer 1991b:110):

> I do a lot of motor claims and the [legal insurance program] makes a difference in how I pursue them. Because insurance companies are very, very slow to handle claims, and where I have a client who is privately paying, I will write half a dozen letters to the insurance company virtually begging them to get on with it, and threatening to sue, but not doing it because I need to say to the client, "Bring me in £45 for the plaint fee," and he doesn't want to. Whereas when I've got the [legal insurance], I give the insurers 14 days in which to get going, and if they don't I'll just put it straight into court. It's a lot faster procedure, and it's all because of finance. Clients are happy to go ahead when they are not looking at the bill.

This solicitor went on to illustrate the impact of the insurance by referring to a specific case he was handling at the time of interview:

> This man has instructed me to pursue it. I've actually written to [the legal insurance plan] to get their authority to pursue it because we are under instruction to do so. And they wrote back to me and sort of said, "Well, if you think there is a good chance of success then go ahead." I wrote back again and said, "I've already told you I don't think there's a good chance. Please confirm." And I fully expect them coming back and refusing it, because this bloke has nothing to lose, really, other than that cost [the other side's expenses] which I don't

> think he'd get stuck with. If he was privately paying, it wouldn't have got this far. No way. Because I would have said, "Right, you've got less than a 50–50 chance, and it's going to cost you X pounds to try it," and he wouldn't pursue it.

Incentive issues from the litigant's perspective involve a combination of risk preference and simple cost-benefit analysis. A plaintiff who is paying a lawyer on an hourly basis will be very cognizant of the cost relative to what might be recovered. This is the same calculation that everyone makes when deciding whether to make expenditures on things like repairs, some types of health care, and the like: is the benefit worth the cost, particularly compared to possible alternatives? From the defendant's perspective, one often hears in the United States that decisions to settle are driven not by the merits of the case but by the cost of litigating the case, because the defendant will not be able to recover its costs if the defendant is successful. As I have discussed elsewhere, estimating the effects of fee shifting is complex (Kritzer 2002b:1947-48 [see Chapter 11 in this volume]). There is some evidence that it weeds out some weaker claims, but at the same time it may increase the intensity (i.e., cost) of litigation for stronger claims as well as increasing the amounts paid in settlement for those stronger claims (Hughes and Snyder 1995:243-48).

Incentives for lawyers depend on the fee regime as well. A lawyer working on a no-win, no-pay basis will make choices that are different from those made by a lawyer working on an hourly basis. A lawyer who is being paid by a third-party will deal with cases differently than a lawyer who is being paid directly by the client. Not surprisingly, if the lawyer's fee is based on the amount recovered (or saved), the lawyer will want to focus on money in settlement negotiation, while a lawyer who is paid hourly, a fixed fee, or is on salary will be more inclined to entertain settlements with a significant nonmonetary component (Kritzer 1987 [Chapter 9 in this volume]). One might imagine that plaintiffs who are paying their lawyer on some basis other than a percentage-based contingency fee would also be more willing to consider nonmonetary resolutions when the litigation costs were to be recovered from the defendant if the matter were to be settled out of court.

Deciding *which* cases to pursue will depend heavily on who is paying and how the fee would be computed. As discussed previously, many cases that can be handled on an hourly basis with the loser paying would not be financially viable on a percentage fee basis because the amount at issue is too small. As I have described elsewhere, insurance companies and their outside lawyers have tried a variety of alternatives to the hourly fee; while the goal is typically that the lawyers will continue to work on the cases in more or less the same way that they did on an hourly basis, the firms and the clients quickly realize that both the lawyer and the insurer change how they approach cases when the fee arrangement changes (Kritzer 2006:2060 [Chapter 6 in this volume]). When the lawyer's fee is paid by a third-party, particularly a third-party such as an insurance company with which the lawyer has an ongoing relationship, the lawyer has to balance the interests of the actual client to whom the lawyer owns his or her *professional* loyalty with the interests of the payer of the lawyer's fee to whom the lawyer is likely to have an *economic* loyalty (Kritzer 2012:148). This may be further complicated if the lawyer who is representing an insured is a direct employee of the insurer, a situation that is increasingly common in the United States with the growth of "staff counsel" offices and "captive" law firms. An intriguing question is whether the lawyer in a staff counsel office or captive law firm might actually be better positioned to make choices more in the interest of the client that impose costs on the insurer than would be the outside lawyer? The logic here is that the insurer has to be more careful in making demands on the staff or captive firm lawyer because of potential legal consequences (e.g. claims of bad faith on the part of the insurance company directing the lawyer) than with the outside lawyer whom the insurer can simply decide not to retain in the future if the lawyer does something not to the insurer's liking, an issue that lawyers heavily dependent on particular sources of work cannot help but be sensitive to.[17]

From extant research, we do know that lawyers who have clients who are protected from costs can be more aggressive bargainers. This was a central point in Hazel Genn's seminal book, *Hard Bargaining* (1988). Additional research in England, looking at cases prior to the introduction of conditional fees and the subsequent changes that made uplifts and ATE premiums shiftable, has looked at the likelihood that insurers will make offers, and found that when faced with solicitors who have clients not at risk for costs, insurers were more likely to make settlement offers (and to make subsequent offers if an initial offer is refused) than when dealing with a solicitor whose client was paying on a private basis (Fenn and Vlachonikolis 1990; Swanson and Mason 1998). From my own research, I have seen evidence that the lawyers' having a direct stake in the outcome can, at least at the margins, push them to produce better outcomes for clients. One example is the effort by plaintiffs' lawyers to keep trying to push up a settlement offer even if what is on offer is acceptable for the client; a small amount of additional time can produce a nice return to the lawyer. A second example was in a study of social security disability claims which lawyers often handle on a no-win, no-pay basis; both salaried nonlawyers and salaried or pro bono lawyers also handle these cases. I found that the most effective lawyers were those handling cases on a no-win, no-pay basis, and I argued that these lawyers' greater success was probably attributable to the incentive structure created by the no-win, no-pay fee (Kritzer 1998b:146-47).[18]

---

[17] I was told by one former staff counsel lawyer that he felt more able to do things he thought his insurance company employer would prefer he did not do than was true as a private practitioner, because the insurance company would not want to risk the negative fallout that would occur if it became known that he had be ordered not to do something he felt was appropriate to do (Kritzer 2012:148). See Silver (1997) regarding some of the ethical issues facing staff counsel/captive firms.

[18] There is a long-standing debate over the question of whether lawyers working on a contingency fee basis will tend to settle cases at less than optimal amounts (see Johnson 1980–81). This issue is at the heart of the analysis in my book on contingency fee practice (Kritzer 2004). One of the challenges of analyses testing this argument is what outcomes should be compared to: what a litigant would be willing to pay for on an hourly basis (even contingent hourly), what a litigant totally unconcerned about costs would want, or what? The interesting point in my

The basis on which any service provider's fee is calculated affects incentives vis-à-vis the service provider's efficiency. For lawyers this incentive is very clear: payment by the hour creates incentives for extra care and extra work; as one observer noted, looking under every stone makes sense if you are being paid by the stone.[19] On the other hand, if payment is by a fixed fee set in advance, the incentive is to devote as little time as possible (see also Fenn et al. 2007; Tata and Stephens 2007). A damage-based contingency fee falls somewhere in between because the lawyer's incentive is to invest time as long as the marginal return to the lawyer exceeds the opportunity cost of the lawyer's time (see Johnson 1980–81). As noted above, the lawyer's long-term interest will often mitigate these incentives: the hourly fee lawyer working for a repeat client must be mindful of the need to keep that client, and excessive bills arising from excess investment will likely have negative long-term consequences. The flat fee or contingency fee lawyer working for one-off clients usually needs those clients as a source of future referrals; short changing effort on clients' cases is likely to be harmful to the lawyer's future ability to secure clients. However, the incentives structure choices as to *how* a lawyer does something with the fee leading the lawyer to make choices with an eye to efficiency or lack thereof. For example a lawyer being paid on the basis of something other than the amount of effort might employ informal means of fact investigation while a lawyer being paid hourly would probably be inclined to use more formal methods which also require more of the lawyer's time and possibly more of the court's time as well (Kritzer 2004b:137-38, 2006; Tata and Stephens 2007).

One area where the contrasting incentives of time-based and recovery-based fees has been extensively debated is with regard to American class actions. Here the concern is in part that recovery-based fees may seem out of proportion to the effort plaintiffs' lawyers have devoted to a case, particularly when combined with the level of risk the lawyers faced. However, the alternative hourly fee enhanced by a risk factor, what is called a "lodestar" fee creates potential incentives for inefficiency and dragging cases out because the plaintiffs' lawyers must build up their hours to justify a significant fee.[20] A less dramatic example can be found in the incentives created by a per-diem fee where the lawyer is paid based solely based on the length of time from when the lawyer receives the case until the lawyer closes the case; the lawyer has a strong incentive to keep the case open at least long enough to cover the opportunity cost of the time the lawyer actually spent on the case.

As one would expect, fee regimes create and modulate conflicts between litigants and their lawyers. This is the classic principal-agent problem. Every fee structure has the potential for conflicts of interest as does the issue of who is actually paying the fee. The nature and degree of conflicts differ depending on

---

analysis of social security disability appeals is that there is no settlement option; the case is either won or lost, which provides an interesting test of the impact of the lawyers' incentives.

[19] "[M]ost lawyers will prefer to leave no stone unturned, provided, of course, they can charge by the stone" (Rhode 1985:635).

[20] See Silver (1992) for a discussion of these issues.

whether one takes a short run or long run perspective. Moreover, clients differ in their ability to monitor their lawyers' actions and the less able one is to monitor, the more likely that the conflict will work to the detriment of the client.[21] Often the conflicts created by fee regimes reflect differences between lawyers and their clients with regard to risk, with usually the lawyer more toward the risk neutral position; this may change when the lawyer has his or her own "investment" in the case, which could lead the lawyer to be more risk averse than the client, particularly if the lawyer is concerned about recovering sunk costs.

IV. THE EMBEDDED NATURE OF FEE REGIMES

Fee regimes are deeply embedded in legal systems and become part of the broad legal culture encompassing potential litigants, lawyers, and adjudicators. That is, fee regimes shape the understanding and expectations of participants. Whatever the existing system is, it comes to be seen as normal and appropriate. English legal academics have reported to me that they have had conversations with solicitors who told them that there is no conflict of interest between the solicitor and the solicitor's clients created by fees because the solicitor simply charges by the hour (see Moorhead and Cumming 2008:67). As stated previously, *all* fee arrangements create actual and potential conflicts; only the nature of the conflicts differs. Awareness of the conflicts may be lacking, but that does not mean they do not exist.

Solicitors in England were long among the most strident opponents of any type of no-win, no-pay fee (see, e.g., Law Society 1970). Actually, this is an overstatement because solicitors opposed no-win, no-pay fees in a somewhat selective fashion. Specifically, they opposed such fees in the kinds of cases likely to be initiated by individuals, such as torts, disputes over contracts and property, and the like. Solicitors did not object to no-win, no-pay fee arrangements for at least some of the work undertaken on behalf of business entities, most notably actions to recover debts where the fees are, and have for some time been, routinely calculated as a percentage of the amount recovered (*ibid.*). Even in Canadian provinces where such fees were permitted, in at least one province for over 125 years,[22] there is little evidence that Canadian lawyers commonly made use of no-win,[23] no-pay fees, although that *may* have started to change in

---

[21] Rosenthal (1974) provides the classic discussion of the monitoring issue in the context of the American contingency fee. See Wessel (1976) for a discussing of monitoring effort in corporate litigation practice.

[22] See Kritzer (2004b:258). The final province to permit contingency fees was Ontario, and that happened within the past 10 years. The first province to permit such fees was Manitoba, which has allowed them since 1890 (Minish 1979:69), although such fees appear to have been used infrequently during the first 80 to 90 years they were permitted.

[23] An unpublished report drawing on a survey of practitioners in British Columbia conducted in the mid-1990s found that 78.8% of respondents described "the normal litigation fee arrangement [as] payment contingent on successful work based on a percentage of recovery"; one must be cautious here because the survey upon which this is based had a response rate of 16.4% (Cumming 1996).

the early years of the 21st century.[24]

The embeddedness of fee regimes is also reflected in the ways that procedural rules interact with those regimes to affect how cases are handled. A clear example of this from England is what was traditionally called "payment into court" whereby a defendant could make an offer to settle by depositing the proposed settlement with the court, and if that settlement was declined the plaintiff was put at risk for the defendant's cost subsequent to the offer if the plaintiff failed to better the offer at trial.[25] The rationale for this system was that if a plaintiff had a sure (or near sure) win and could recover all of its costs by winning at trial, the plaintiff would have no incentive to negotiate a settlement or consider a compromise. There was no reason not to go to trial in hopes of receiving a maximum award.

As originally developed, the system of payment into court worked only for a defendant making an offer. Ontario adopted a variation that made it possible for a plaintiff to make a settlement offer that put the defendant at risk for paying significantly more in costs. This system turned on the fact that the Ontario fee shifting system provided only partial reimbursement of the winning party's legal costs; the normal standard for assessing costs was "party-and-party" which comprised only about half of the typical costs leaving the client to pay the balance. A defendant making a settlement offer that the plaintiff failed to beat at trial was entitled to its party-and-party costs from the date of the offer. Given that a plaintiff who was successful at trial would normally receive party-and-party costs, some other, higher standard was needed for the plaintiff to have a similar option; hence, if a plaintiff made an offer to settle and the defendant did not beat it at trial, the plaintiff was entitled to "solicitor-and-client" costs (covering most, if not all, of the plaintiff's costs) subsequent to the date of the offer. Ontario was able to develop this system because it used only partial fee shifting and had multiple standards for assessing lawyer's fees. England created two standards for fee shifting, the "standard basis" and the (higher) "indemnity basis"; subsequent to the creation of these two standards, England was able to change its system and now has "Part 36" offers and payments, with the incentive for the defendant in terms of having to pay costs according to the higher "indemnity standard" plus paying a high rate of interest on the damage award.

The embedded nature of fee regimes also makes it difficult to think outside the box. Consider the following issue. One of the tensions that exist in many systems is between an alleged tortfeasor and the tortfeasor's insurance company (see Kritzer 2012:141-49). Often there is no conflict: the alleged tortfeasor simply wants to hand everything over to the insurance company and have as little as possible to do with the matter. However, there are situations where the interests

---

[24] While the move to permit contingency fees in Ontario was highly visible, there is no information available (as this is written) on how widely they have been adopted by practitioners.

[25] Under the Woolf reforms of the 1990s, payment into court became "offers to settle" either through a "Part 36 Payment" (after proceedings had started) or a "Part 36 Offer" (which could be made before or after the initiation of proceedings). Changes were also made such that it was possible for a plaintiff to make an offer to settle.

conflict: the alleged tortfeasor desires to be vindicated while the insurance company wants to dispose of the case at the least cost, both in terms of defense costs and damage payments. Some types of insurance policies may include a "consent-to-settle" clause, whereby the insured must consent before the insurer can enter into a settlement agreement with the plaintiff. An alternative system, which to my knowledge exists nowhere, would be to unbundle insurance for damages and insurance for litigation defense. The latter could be offered in two forms: the insurer completely controls the defense or the insurer must have its insured's permission to settle, probably with higher rates for policies with a consent-to-settle clause. The former might also be offered in multiple forms specifying under what conditions the damages insurer could or could not reject offers of settlement. This unbundling would greatly change the incentive structure surrounding decisions to settle or go to trial, undoubtedly producing a combination of positive and perverse incentives. I have not done any detailed analysis of this proposal so I cannot speak to the balance between those incentives. I suggest simply as an example of trying to think outside the box.

CONCLUSION

Central to the idea of fee regimes is the ways in which the various aspects interact. Fee shifting requires a form of regulation and review that is not needed when parties pay their own costs. Fee shifting, particularly in systems where the costs payable by the loser approach full indemnification of the successful party, seems most easily aligned with fees calculated based on either hours worked or item of service; they may be most problematic for a percentage-based fee system because of the potential complexities in setting the fees to be shifted. Fee shifting creates incentives for losers to litigate over the fees they have to pay to the successful side, something that does not happen if the fee comes out of the winning side's recovery even if the fee is subject to review and approval by the court as is typically the case in American class actions. How should fee shifting be dealt with if a winning party has employed a salaried staff lawyer, as may be the case with in-house lawyers in a corporation or government, or possibly a salaried lawyer working for a legal insurance plan? Should the loser be required to pay a fee based on market hourly rates for private practitioners, the salary of the staff lawyer, the salary of the staff lawyer plus overhead, item-of-service, or what? Is there a limit to the hourly rates which a losing party should be required to pay, and if so how is that set?

During the first decade of the 21st century there was an on-again, off-again discussion in England of moving to a system of damage-based contingency fees (see Zander 2002), a question that came to the fore as part of Lord Jackson's review of civil costs at the end of that decade (Jackson 2009). An important issue was whether damage-based contingency fees should exist alongside the then current conditional fee including the recoverability from the defendant of the uplift and the after-the-event insurance (ATE) premium? In the end, Jackson's recommendation was to retain conditional fees but also allow contingency fees computed as a proportion of damages recovered. His recommendation called for modifying conditional fees by eliminating the recoverability of both the uplift and the ATE insurance premium for most kinds of cases; he proposed that the elimination of the latter be mitigated by moving from the traditional English rule of two-way fee shifting to "qualified one-way fee shifting" whereby most individual claimants would not face the threat of having to pay a winning defendants legal fees; in addition, the uplift for conditional fees was to be limited to a maximum of 25% of the recovery of general damages and past losses (excluding amounts subject to subrogation).[26]

These aspects of Lord Jackson's proposal went into effect in the spring of 2013.[27] As this is written (about 18 months after the changes went into effect), it is unclear whether there has been significant adoption of damage-based fees. There are reasons why such fees would not be widely used. First, while a client might prefer a damage-based fee in a smaller case, the lawyer would prefer a conditional fee arrangement, and while a lawyer might prefer a damage-based fee in a large case, the client would prefer a conditional fee; there might be a class of cases that are high risk, high value that neither lawyers nor clients would not want to handle on a conditional fee basis but for which a percentage fee would be attractive. Second, English solicitors probably have not grasped the portfolio logic of a percentage fee practice whereby a lawyer handles a many unprofitable cases as a means of creating a referral network among former clients that brings in the small number of highly profitable cases (see Kritzer 2004b).[28]

There have been repeated calls over the years to adopt a loser-pays rule in the United States. Importantly, a loser pays rule has two purposes. First, it is intended to compensate the winning party for the costs incurred to obtain vindication. Secondly, it serves to make potential litigants, particularly potential plaintiffs, consider the risks associated with losing and to be cautious in initiating legal actions. Most of the advocates of adopting two-way version of fee shifting are more interested in the second goal than in the first. What the advocates fail to realize is that in practice both of these goals end up getting modified. First, many plaintiffs may be unable to pay a cost award if their actions prove to be unsuccessful. In some systems there are procedures to require certain plaintiffs, or plaintiffs in certain cases, to post security for costs; this can be a bar to bringing any action. Secondly, when fee shifting is only partial, the fee award lessens the costs of obtaining vindication but does not provide full compensation for those costs. Thirdly, public policy may provide what amounts to one-way fee shifting, either explicitly or de facto. In the United States there are many specific one-way fee shifting statutes, which often have the goal of encouraging private parties to enforce public policy or to hold

---

[26] In addition general damages were increased by 10% (damages in England are set by the judge based on a set of guidelines).

[27] Ontario, which was the last of the Canadian provinces to allow any form of no-win, no-pay fees, now permits a damage-based (i.e., percentage) contingency fee; under Ontario law, plaintiffs can recover the *greater* of party-and-party costs computed in the traditional fashion or the percentage of damages specified in the retainer agreement with the plaintiff's lawyer (Solicitor's Act 1990 as amended 2002 s.20.1).

[28] The difficulty of grasping this logic was evident at a hearing I participated in as part of Lord Jackson's inquiry.

the government accountable (see Fein 1984; Olson 1994; Zemans 1984). In England, in many (perhaps most) cases if a party who has Legal Aid loses an action, the winning party is not permitted to recover its costs, either from the losing party or from the Legal Aid fund.[29] The system of ATE insurance in England meant that a successful defendant could recover its costs, but it was not the plaintiff who had to pay those costs; thus, with this system the first function was operational but the second was not. While specific practices varied, most solicitors did not ask a claimant to pay the cost of the ATE insurance when an action was initiated, and at least some, perhaps many, did not seek to collect that cost from the client if an action failed. If the client was not paying the ATE cost in unsuccessful actions, then it was the solicitor who was effectively paying the successful defendant its costs. Actually, one might argue that if most ATE premiums were recovered from the defendant because there are very few unsuccessful actions, there was really already only a one-way fee shift effectively operating because it was the defendants' payment of the ATE premium that was being used to cover the defendants' costs in the small proportion of cases in which the defendant prevailed.[30]

Thinking about one element of fee regimes without taking into account the other aspects is a dangerous business. The complex interactions inherent in fee regimes present problems for reform which often involves importing some aspects of a fee regime in use in another jurisdiction. These problems are nicely illustrated by the brief-lived experience with two-way fee shifting system for medical negligence cases in Florida. The system was quickly abandoned because no one had considered either how the fee would be computed if the plaintiff won or who would actually pay the fee if the defendant won, given that most plaintiffs were effectively judgment proof. Experience between 1995 and 2010 in England provides further evidence of these kinds of problems. While in the 1990s England did not want to adopt an American-style contingency fee system whereby fees are computed as a percentage of recovery (Abel 2001), changes that were made failed to anticipate the complexities that were being introduced. As best I can tell, no one anticipated the development of after-the-event insurance at the time conditional fees were authorized by the Courts and Legal Services Act 1990. It was only as the actual implementation of conditional fees approached that the Law Society announced that it had developed a plan for low cost (£85) ATE, with a number of insurers quickly jumping into the market with

---

[29] If an individual who has legal aid for an action loses and that individual had been required to make a contribution toward the legal aid fees, the individual might be ordered to pay at least some of the winning party's costs. Legal Aid will only pay trial costs of a successful opposing party if that party is an individual who can demonstrate financial hardship arising from the costs of the litigation and that receiving costs would be just and equitable. Payments of costs from Legal Aid to an opponent who succeeds on appeal are handled differently (see Simons 2004). Courts sometimes make what I would label "contingent" cost orders against legally aided parties; the orders are "contingent" in the sense that they may become enforceable at a future time if the legally aided party's financial circumstances happen to change radically (e.g., winning the lottery).

[30] I have been told that it might have been that some ATE insurers only collected a premium in the case of successful actions where the premium is in the end paid by the defendant. If this is true, then the effective system is a one-way fee shift.

their own offerings (Moorhead 2000a). No one appears to have anticipated the massive satellite litigation, the "costs wars," that arose in the wake of the Access to Justice Act 1999 making the ATE premium and the "uplift" recoverable from the defendant.[31] Under the 1995 system, uplift and ATE premiums were matters between solicitors and their clients. After the uplift and ATE became payable by the defendants, the defendants' insurers who actually had to pay those costs cared very strongly about the question of what uplift for success was appropriate and the amounts being charged for ATE insurance.

The embeddedness of fee regimes in procedure, practice, and culture, combined with the interaction among the three dimensions of fee regimes make change and/or importation very tricky. If a country imports one aspect (e.g., fee shifting into the United States), how does that interact with other aspects of the existing fee regime (e.g., the percentage fee structure)? As England has learned, if the success fee and other types of expenses become shiftable, those who have to pay those costs will have incentives to police the amounts being charged. Could a flat fee system be designed that would work with fee shifting, or are the two elements incompatible? How should fee shifting work when lawyers are salaried employees of the organizational litigants—on what basis should a fee shift be computed?

Even if one thinks about the multiple elements, the complexity of the interactions makes it difficult to predict exactly what changes might ensue if significant changes are made in an existing fee regime. A central challenge then is to design pre-change inquiries that adequately anticipate the effects beyond those specifically intended. A first step is to think deeply about what *is not* being changed and how those aspects relate to what *is* being changed. One can employ the tools of economic analysis and game theory, although they can only go so far because the results they yield are often very sensitive to the assumptions that are made.[32] A second step should be in-depth interviews with key actors laying out a broad range of hypotheticals and scenarios, and asking those actors what they might do differently if a specific new regime were to be adopted. This might involve role playing experiments employing experienced system actors to see how they behave under the new system. Even with these kinds of efforts there will be unanticipated results, but such inquiries have the potential of producing a better understanding of what might happen if changes are implemented.

---

[31] A brief editorial comment by Moorhead (2000b) around the time that uplifts and ATE premiums became recoverable discussed the likelihood of conflict between lawyers and insurers, but the conflict he foresaw was between solicitors and ATE insurers, not the defendants' insurers. One study of the period (White and Atkinson 2000) reported a series of structured interviews conducted around the time that the Access to Justice Act 1999 was being considered by the House of Commons; while the respondents noted a variety of issues raised by the changes under consideration, no one was quoted as seeing the potential conflict that came about. Richard Abel's detailed account of the passage of the Access to Justice Act makes no reference to any concerns about the potential for litigation over costs issues. A search of the popular and legal press turned up only a single reference to the possibility of litigation over costs in the wake of making uplifts and ATE premiums shiftable, and that was by plaintiffs' solicitor Martyn Day (1998).

[32] See Kritzer (2002b:1947-48 [Chapter 11 in this volume]) for a discussion of this problem in reference to fee shifting.

11

LAWYER FEES AND LAWYER BEHAVIOR IN LITIGATION: WHAT DOES THE EMPIRICAL LITERATURE REALLY SAY?[1]

"O'er lawyers' fingers, who straight dream on fees."
Romeo & Juliet, Act 1, Scene 4

"Then 'tis like the breath of an unfee'd lawyer."
King Lear, Act 1, Scene 4

"[M]ost lawyers will prefer to leave no stone unturned, provided, of course, they can charge by the stone."
Deborah L. Rhode (1985:635)

"Billing by the hour is fine, provided I get to define what constitutes the hour."
Source unknown

INTRODUCTION

Lawyers' fees and lawyers' billing practices are the subject of much commentary, humorous and otherwise. Given that the size and nature of lawyers' fees are of great importance to lawyers, to their clients, and to the larger public, this comes as no surprise. In this chapter, I review the empirical literature that provides evidence of the impact of legal fees and fee regulation, both on lawyers and on their clients. My assumption is that impacts on clients and impacts on lawyers are one and the same, and any distinction between the two is primarily due to the lens through which one is looking.

I focus on two particular topics: how fees are computed and who actually pays the fees. There are many questions one could ask about the impact of legal fees, even limited to these two broad topics. The empirical literature, however, is quite thin, which substantially limits what we actually know based on systematic research. In introducing the core sets of research, I will also make selective reference to theoretical analyses of fee arrangement issues. These theoretical perspectives typically draw on the tools of economic analysis, starting from the

---

[1] This chapter originally appeared in the *Texas Law Review* 80 (2002), 1943-83. The references have been reformatted and some footnotes have been omitted.

standard economic assumption of rational decision making. The analyses then examine the expected behavior of an economically rational actor.

I. THE ORGANIZING DIMENSIONS

A. Methods of Computing Legal Fees

Lawyers are nothing if not creative, and this creativity manifests itself in the many different ways lawyers have devised for calculating their fees. The vast array of fee calculations can be grouped into six general types of computation:

- fixed fees where the lawyer specifies a fee in advance, typically for routine work where the tasks are well defined and predictable;
- time-based fees where the lawyer tracks his or her time and calculates the fee by multiplying the time by some hourly rate;
- task-based fees where the lawyer charges fixed amounts for subtasks—writing a letter, making a telephone call, etc.—much like a physician who charges by procedure or an auto mechanic who relies upon the book rate to specify the time for various tasks;
- statutory, or other law-based, fee schedules typically tied in some way to the value of the transaction or the amount in controversy;
- commission-based fee arrangements in which the lawyer's fee is based on some percentage of the amount recovered or the value of the matter being handled (in probate work, for example, the fee is often computed based on the value of the estate); and
- value-based fee systems, in which the lawyer makes a judgment about what the work and result were "worth" to the client and sets the fee accordingly (what the client is willing to pay may of course exert some influence on the fee ultimately charged).

Missing from the above list are the "no-win, no-pay" fee, the "contingency fee," the "conditional fee," and the "lodestar fee." Except for the commission-based fee, which, in contentious work, is by nature a contingency fee, these are not methods of calculation. A lawyer can incorporate an increase or reduction based on outcome into any of the first three methods of calculation. Success bonuses and failure discounts are inherent in the last two arrangements. I will discuss the contingency element of fee calculation as a subtopic of fee computation.

B. Who Pays for Legal Services

The question of who pays the lawyer's fee, or alternatively, who covers the cost of the lawyer's services, is more straightforward. There are essentially four "pure" options:

- the user of legal services pays the fee out of the user's own resources;
- the opposing party pays the fee;
- some third party pays the fee or otherwise covers the cost of the lawyer's services; or

- the lawyer performs the work at no fee (i.e., the lawyer covers the cost of the lawyer's services).

The first of these, "private payment," takes on three forms:

- paying a private-practice lawyer using resources in hand;
- paying a private-practice lawyer using funds recovered from an opposing party (e.g., some proportion of a recovery); and
- paying the salary of a lawyer employed by the user of legal services.

The second system, in which the opposing party pays the fee, occurs in three situations:

- where there is a general fee-shifting rule, which is the case in most countries other than the United States;
- when a specific statute requires the losing party to pay the winner's fees, as is the case for a limited number of claims in the United States; or
- when a pre-existing contractual agreement provides for the recovery of legal fees.

Third-party payment can also take one of several forms:

- an "insurer" pays the fee of a private-practice lawyer,
- the government or "legal aid fund" pays the fee of a private-practice lawyer; or
- the services are provided by a salaried lawyer working for a legal services agency, which can be either privately funded or publicly funded.

The final form of "payment" is no payment at all. I do not include in this category contingency fee arrangements in which the lawyer is paid only for a successful result. Rather, I refer to legal services undertaken without an expectation of receiving a fee (pro bono).

While most instances of representation use only one of the four pure forms of fee payment, it is possible to combine the forms in various ways. In fee-shifting regimes, it is quite common for the loser to pay only part of the winner's legal expense, with the winner paying the balance. Many lawyers perform what might be called "de facto pro bono" when they write off, or reduce, fees charged to private clients because the client cannot pay the lawyer's customary fee. For organizational consumers of legal services, there may be many instances when the legal work is shared by in-house legal staff, which is on salary, and outside counsel charging fees according to some alternative plan.

II. WHO PAYS

A. FEE SHIFTING

Fee shifting refers to the requirement that the losing party in litigation pay some or all of the winning party's legal expenses, including lawyers' fees. The principal purpose of a fee-shifting regime is to make winning parties whole.

In the common law world, there are two general approaches to fee shifting: the "English Rule," which shifts some or all of the winner's costs of legal representation to the loser, and the "American Rule," which does not shift fees, leaving each side responsible for its own lawyers' fees regardless of who wins. Outside the United States, some form of the English Rule is the norm.[2] In the United States, with the exception of the state of Alaska, the American Rule applies unless explicitly abrogated by statute or unless there is a pre-dispute contract providing for some form of fee shifting. In civil law countries, such as those on the European continent, fee shifting is the norm in litigation (see Pfennigstorf 1984).

Most of the statutes that abrogate the American Rule in the United States introduce a "one-way" fee-shifting regime, whereby a successful plaintiff may recover some or all of its attorneys' fees from the losing defendant, but a winning defendant cannot recover attorneys' fees from the losing plaintiff (see Note 1984). The best known of these one-way fee-shifting provisions is the Equal Access to Justice Act,[3] which allows a prevailing nongovernmental party to recover some of its legal expenses in a variety of actions involving federal agencies (see Mezey and Olson 1993; Percival and Miller 1984). A number of states have enacted similar statutes (Olson 1994).

B. THEORETICAL ANALYSES

The impact of fee shifting has been the subject of extensive theoretical work by law and economics scholars.[4] These scholars have considered the impact of fee shifting on:

- the filing of frivolous lawsuits (Bebchuk 1988; Bebchuk and Chang 1996; Polinsky and Rubinfeld 1993, 1998; Rosenberg and Shavell 1985);;
- decisions to settle rather than go to trial (Beckner and Katz 1995; Bowles 1987; Donohue 1991a, 1991b; Gravelle 1993; Hause 1989; Miller 1986; Posner 1977; Reinganum and Wilde 1986; Shavell 1982; Smith 1992);
- the impact of settlement-related fee-shifting rules, such as Rule 68 of the Federal Rules of Civil Procedure or payment into court (Anderson 1994; Chung 1996; Miller 1986; Shapard 1984, 1995);
- the overall volume of litigation (Conard 1984:269; Katz 1987);
- the number of injury-producing events (Hylton 1993b; Rickman 1995);
- the development of the law (Prichard 1988; Saltzman 1986).

There is surprisingly little agreement among those who have undertaken these theoretical analyses. Some analysts argue that fee shifting should increase the

---

[2] Even in England, however, the English Rule does not operate in anything approaching a pure form (see Kritzer 1992:54; Woodroffe 1998:346-48). [Starting in 2013, England changed to a one-way fee shifting regime for many, perhaps most, cases involving individuals as plaintiffs.]

[3] 5 U.S.C. § 504 (2000); 28 U.S.C. § 2412(d)(a) (2000).

[4] There are a number of surveys of the theoretical predictions regarding the impact of fee shifting (see Anderson 1996; Braeutigam et al. 1984; Cooter and Rubinfeld 1989; Rickman 1995; Rowe 1984a).

likelihood of settlement (Davis 1996:65-69), while others argue that it will increase the likelihood of cases going to trial (Posner 1986; Shavell 1982). Some argue that fee shifting will decrease the number of cases filed (Conard 1984), while others argue that the numbers of cases will increase (Shavell 1982). This second difference reflects, in part, the consideration of different types of cases. For example, a strong modest-value case is more likely to be filed than a weak case. Avery Katz (2000:64-65) nicely summarizes the uncertainty:

> [T]he current state of economic knowledge does not enable us reliably to predict whether a move to fuller indemnification would raise or lower the total costs of litigation, let alone whether it would better align those costs with any social benefits they might generate. The reason for this agnostic conclusion is straightforward. Legal costs influence all aspects of the litigation process, from the decision to file suit to the choice between settlement and trial to the question whether to take precautions against a dispute in the first place. ... The combination of all these external effects are too complicated to be remedied by a simple rule of "loser pays." Instead, indemnity of legal fees remedies some externalities while failing to address and even exacerbating others.

As I will show in the following discussion, the empirical literature confirms that the effects of fee shifting are complex and difficult to ascertain.

C. THE EMPIRICAL LITERATURE

In contrast to the extensive theoretical research on the question of fee shifting, there has been relatively little empirical research on the actual impact of fee shifting on lawyers, litigants, and litigation. In significant part, there are few studies of the impact of fee shifting because few American states have fee-shifting regimes for some or all civil cases, and it is therefore difficult to assess their impact in a rigorous fashion. Cross-national studies, such as a study comparing the United States (generally governed by the American Rule) and Canada (generally governed by the English Rule), are problematic because of other substantive legal differences between the countries. With this in mind, there are three general types of studies that have been conducted:

- statistical studies comparing groups differentially affected by fee-shifting rules or comparing patterns before and after changes to fee-shifting rules;
- simulation studies involving experiments in which the fee-shifting rules can be manipulated; and
- impressionistic studies within a particular system where key actors are asked to assess the impact of fee shifting.

D. STATISTICAL STUDIES

1. The Florida Medical Malpractice Study

The most interesting statistical study of fee shifting has taken advantage of the adoption and subsequent repeal of fee shifting in medical malpractice cases in Florida from 1980 to 1985. In a pair of articles, Edward Snyder and James

Hughes (Hughes and Snyder 1995; Snyder and Hughes 1990) employ data for cases disposed of before, during, and after the period in which the English Rule governed attorneys' fees in Florida medical malpractice cases. In the first article, the authors employ data for 10,325 cases disposed of in the periods from 1975 to 1978 and from October 1985 to June 1988. In the second article, the sample increases to 16,404 cases by extension of the study period through September 1990; 58% of the first group of cases and 45% of the second were governed by the English Rule. The authors employ sophisticated statistical methods to analyze this large data set and, based on that analysis, come to the following conclusions about the impact of the English Rule:

- Medical malpractice claimants are more likely to drop claims under the English Rule. The authors interpret this result as indicating that weak claims are less likely to be pursued.

- Those claims that are pursued are more likely to be litigated than settled when the English Rule governs attorneys' fees. The authors interpret this finding as reflecting optimistic litigants who anticipate recovering attorneys' fees.[5]

- Those cases that do go to trial are more likely to result in plaintiff verdicts, probably reflecting that weak cases are less likely to be pursued and that the expectation of recovering attorneys' fees increases the value of the case.

- Plaintiffs obtain larger settlements under the English Rule, which is consistent with the argument that the value of strong cases increases under the English Rule.

- The average defense cost is higher under the English Rule.

Overall, they conclude that the English Rule encourages some plaintiffs (those with strong cases) to pursue their claims while discouraging others (those with weak cases). The result is to reduce the frequency of low-merit claims. However, it was the Florida Medical Association, which had backed the adoption of the English Rule, that ultimately sought its repeal, partly because of early cases awarding the full contingency fee percentage to the plaintiff as the fee shift,[6] and partly because the defendants came to realize the difficulty in collecting the shifted fee when the plaintiff had no resources from which to pay it.[7]

2. The Alaska Rule 82 Study

The only other statistical study of the effect of fee shifting in the United States was conducted in Alaska—the only state to use a form of the English Rule routinely (Di Pietro and Carns 1996). Specifically, Alaska's Civil Rule 82 entitles

---

[5] Actually, in their first analysis of the data, the authors come to the opposite conclusion.

[6] Snyder and Hughes (1990:356) note that the Florida Supreme Court ultimately ruled in *Florida Medical Center, Inc. v. Von Stedna*, 436 So.2d 1022 (1983), that a successful plaintiff was not entitled to recover the full contingency fee from the defendant.

[7] Daniels and Martin (2015) report a similar outcome from provisions in a Texas tort reform measure (HB4 passed in 2003) imposing elements of fee shifting in medical malpractice cases in that state.

a prevailing party in a civil lawsuit to partial compensation for that party's attorney's fees from the loser. The primary category of cases excluded from the provision is domestic relations cases. Cases where attorneys' fees are governed by contract are also excluded. Prevailing parties who pay their attorneys on a percentage basis are entitled to recover attorneys' fees in the amount of 20% of the first $25,000 of a judgment after a contested trial, plus 10% of any judgment over the first $25,000. The percentage is reduced in cases without a contested trial. Prevailing parties not paying on a percentage basis are entitled to 30% of actual "reasonable" fees after a contested trial and 20% otherwise.

In 1994, the Alaska Judicial Council undertook a study of how Rule 82 was working in Alaska and what impact it was having.[8] The study looked at case filings, case records, and responses of attorneys to a survey. The authors of the study were unable to draw strong conclusions about whether fee shifting affected rates of filings in Alaska compared to other states without fee shifting. Overall, the rate of tort filings in Alaska seemed similar to other jurisdictions, perhaps a little lower. In Anchorage, there did seem to be a higher rate of tort cases going to trial, but the authors were not willing to attribute this to fee shifting. One surprising finding was that fee awards were made in only about one-half of the state cases surveyed and one-quarter of the federal diversity cases where they were authorized by Rule 82. A partial explanation for this infrequency might have been the existence of post-judgment settlements in which the prevailing party agreed to forego a fee award in return for the losing party's agreement not to file an appeal. A second surprise was that only a small portion of fee awards came in tort cases. Perhaps less surprising, given that we know that most cases seek relatively modest judgments (see DeFrances and Litras 1999),[9] is that the size of fee awards was relatively modest: the median in state court was $2,240, 39% were under $1,000, and only 27% exceeded $5,000 (Di Pietro et al. 1995:95).

Of more interest are the possible effects of Rule 82 on case filing, settlement, and litigation strategy. Unlike the Florida study, there were no data available for comparison. Instead, the authors explored these questions by interviewing attorneys and judges, which essentially provided information on the perceptions of these actors. Based on the interviews, the authors reported that only 35% of the attorneys could recall even a single instance in which Rule 82 played a significant role in a prospective client's decision not to file a suit or assert a claim. One reason for this small impact is that many individual plaintiffs are judgment proof and would not be able to pay a Rule 82 award. Any concern about fee-shifting rules came from clients who would be able to pay such an award. In other words, those potential plaintiffs with assets sufficient to satisfy a fee award were more likely to evidence risk aversion because they had something to lose. Individuals of modest means and corporations of substantial

---

[8] See Di Petro et al. (1995) for the full report of the study, or Di Pietro (1996) for a brief summary.

[9] See Cohen and Smith (2004) or Langton and Cohen (2008) for more recent, similar studies showing essentially the same.

means were not fazed by the rule. To the extent that there was a perceived effect, it was most clearly associated with weaker or more subjective claims.

About one-third of the attorneys reported that Rule 82 affected their litigation strategy. This effect was typically strongest in the choice between federal or state court, post-trial strategy, or formal settlement offers which under Alaska Rule 68 could modify the fee-shifting burden (Di Pietro et al. 1995:103-11). Each attorney was asked to describe two recent cases, and then asked whether Rule 82 affected their settlement strategy in either of the cases. Only 37% reported an impact on their settlement strategy. Rule 82 was viewed as increasing the value of a case when the defendant's liability was clear and the dispute was over valuation rather than liability. In the words of one defense attorney, "It's just an extra 10% added to the amount my client will pay in the end." In four cases described by defense attorneys, Rule 82 increased the settlement value beyond the face value of the insurance policy limit. One plaintiffs' attorney recalled several specific situations where clients "with assets" who had good claims settled for less than the claims were worth due to concerns about a Rule 82 award. Some attorneys felt that Rule 82 provided an incentive to settle earlier. In strong cases, it reduces the incentive of the defense to drag the case out, particularly when the damages are significant. Additionally, defense lawyers reported that a threat of a Rule 82 award was a good device to get a plaintiff with a weak case to accept an early settlement offer. Finally, the lawyers reported a number of cases in which an appeal was forgone in return for a waiver of attorneys' fees.

One problem with assessing these findings is the absence of a reliable basis for comparison. There are, however, some comparisons internal to the study that do generate confidence in some of the findings. In particular, the attorneys surveyed often drew comparisons between individuals with and without significant assets and between relatively strong or relatively weak claims. To the extent that these factors distinguished the cases, the effects on things such as case value or willingness to settle described by the surveyed attorneys are consistent with the study's results. For the other findings, such as forum selection or post-trial settlement, the significance of the purported effects is less clear.

3. Federal Cases

Two statistical studies have included an examination of the impact of fee shifting in federal cases. One study looked at eighteen different types of cases (with "type of case" defined in terms of the Administrative Office's standard case coding scheme) involving disputes over contracts, real property, personal-injury torts, and property rights (Fournier and Zuehlke 1989). The authors of the study selected a sample of cases involving only monetary remedies filed during the 1979 to 1981 fiscal years for which it was possible to determine unambiguously whether the case had settled or been resolved by trial. The dependent variables of interest were whether the case settled or went to trial, and for those cases that settled, the "settlement demand." The authors included a variable indicating whether the case was governed by the "British rule" or the American rule. The authors found no statistically discernible evidence that the fee-shifting regime influenced either the likelihood of settlement or the settlement demand. However, the authors never identify the cases governed by the "British rule" or the basis for this determination (i.e., whether the parties have agreed by contract to fee shifting). Perhaps the lack of discernible influence results from inaccurate designation of cases as governed by a fee-shifting rule. It is also possible that too few cases in the data set involved a potential fee shift for an effect to be statistically discernible.

The second study of federal cases (Schwab and Eisenberg 1988) focused on constitutional tort litigation involving governmental defendants. These cases are subject to a one-way fee-shifting rule. This study looked at cases in three federal districts: the Central District of California, the Eastern District of Pennsylvania, and the Northern District of Georgia. The authors tried to assess the impact of fee shifting by examining patterns in filing rates and trial rates, comparing constitutional torts to other cases for periods both before and after the passage of the Civil Rights Attorney Fee Award Act in 1976 (42 U.S.C § 1988). Based on this trend data, the authors find no clear evidence that the availability of fee awards led to an increase in the number of cases filed. They do find evidence that a higher proportion of cases were litigated after fee awards were made available, but the evidence also indicates that the rate of success for litigated cases actually declined. This indicates that the availability of fee awards did not increase the willingness of litigants and lawyers to try strong modest cases; rather, it suggests that plaintiffs probably changed their bargaining behavior in a way that resulted in fewer settlements.

4. Studies of Federal Rules of Civil Procedure Rule 11

The 1983 version of the Federal Rules of Civil Procedure contained an important fee-shifting element. Rule 11 provided that lawyers who filed cases or motions that did not meet a minimum standard of support or justification could be sanctioned by the court. The sanction was commonly calculated as a function of the cost incurred by the opposing party to respond to the defective case or motion, and this amount was payable to the opposing party. This version of Rule 11 was very controversial and was eventually modified in 1993 to eliminate the fee-shifting component. Part of the controversy concerned the rule's impact on lawyers' willingness to accept certain types of cases. Opponents of the rule argued that it had a chilling effect on lawyers who represented plaintiffs in discrimination or civil rights cases because of the difficulties of proof in such cases and because, it was argued, lawyers in these cases were particularly vulnerable to the hostility of some judges to discrimination claims (see Tobias 1992). While no empirical studies of the case screening and selection practices of various types of lawyers exist, one study of the imposition of Rule 11 sanctions did find support for the argument that civil rights plaintiffs' lawyers faced a greater risk of sanctions (Kritzer and Zemans 1993 [Chapter 8 in this volume]). A survey of lawyers found a variety of specific reported effects of Rule 11 (Marshall et al. 1992). These included:

- declining one or more cases;
- discouraging clients from pursuing a case or defense;

- not filing particular claims, papers, or motions; and
- engaging in extra review.

Whether these effects[10] should be attributed to concerns about a fee effect (i.e., a fee shift from one side's lawyer to the other side) or to concerns unrelated to fees, such as reputation (i.e., not wanting to be "sanctioned") cannot be distilled from the analysis.

5. Two English Studies

The only other statistical studies of fee-shifting effects were both conducted by researchers in England, one by Timothy Swanson (1990:199-201; see also Swanson 1998) and one by Paul Fenn and Ioannis Vlachonikolis (1990), during the 1980s.[11] Swanson's study focuses on the impact of the repeat player in English litigation and considers 220 case histories of civil tort disputes filed with the High Court of England. Swanson's study indicates that the likelihood that the defendant will make an initial offer decreases as the plaintiff's level of risk increases. Risk to the plaintiff is measured by how the plaintiff is funded and whether the plaintiff is at risk for having to pay the other side's costs (as well as, at least in theory, the plaintiff's own costs) if the plaintiff loses the case. This analysis draws on the fact that, as I discuss in more detail in a later section of this chapter, many plaintiffs are backed by their unions (even in non-work-related cases) and, in that situation, the union assumes the risk of having to pay the other side's fee. Many other plaintiffs have, or at least used to have, legal aid, which puts them, at most, partially at risk for the other side's costs. Most of the remaining plaintiffs are "privately funded," meaning that they are fully at risk. Swanson finds that the likelihood of an offer of settlement being made is greatest when the plaintiff is union-supported (offers in 90% of such cases), least when the plaintiff privately funds the litigation and is thus fully at risk (offers in 53% of such cases), and somewhere in between when the plaintiff receives legal aid and is thus only partially at risk (offers in 66% of such cases). Even stronger support for Swanson's argument comes from the fact that the figures are more or less unchanged in subsequent stages of the bargaining process. That is, if the plaintiff refuses the first offer, the likelihood of receiving a second offer is virtually the same as the likelihood of receiving a first offer. This remains true for third offers if the plaintiff refuses a second offer.

The Fenn and Vlachonikolis analysis is similar to Swanson's in its focus on the likelihood that an insurance company defendant will make an offer. The authors rely on 224 cases collected as part of a large compensation study conducted by a team at the Centre for Socio-Legal Studies at Oxford. They use probit analysis to examine the effect of a number of variables on the estimated probability that an offer will be made. They also look at the factors affecting the decision by the plaintiff to reject that offer (which they presume is indicative of

---

[10] Generally similar findings were reported in other empirical studies of the 1983 version of Rule 11 (see Hess 1992; Nelken 1990; Wiggins et al. 1991).

[11] A summary of Swanson's unpublished study can be found in Kritzer (1991b:93-95).

the offer falling below the plaintiff's minimum ask). One of their results shows that the likelihood of an offer is a function of the way the solicitor representing the plaintiff is being paid. The likelihood of at least one settlement offer, controlling for damages, appears to be least if the plaintiff is unrepresented (88%). It then goes up in increments, first if the plaintiff has retained a solicitor at his or her own expense (96%), next if the solicitor is retained by a trade union (98%). An offer will most likely be made if the solicitor has obtained legal aid on behalf of the plaintiff (99%). These findings are generally consistent with Swanson's analysis described above, though the last two categories are reversed. One major difference, however, is that offers of settlement appear to be more frequent in data set used by Fenn and Vlachonikolis than in Swanson's. This probably reflects the fact that Swanson's analysis included only those cases where a formal legal action had been filed and had led to substantial conflict.

Taken together, these studies indicate that in a fee-shifting regime, a repeat-player insurance company has an enhanced advantage vis-à-vis a one-shot plaintiff. If the plaintiff can be protected in some way from the risks of paying the other side's fee, the defendant will be more willing to make a settlement offer. When the plaintiff is fully at risk, the defendant can refuse to make an offer in the hope that the plaintiff will withdraw the claim rather than run the risk of a cost award.

E. LABORATORY EXPERIMENTS

"Laboratory" experiments typically involve having a group of people—lawyers, students, or others—consider a hypothetical case.[12] The researcher varies key features of the case or the rules to see what effect those features have on how the research subjects deal with the case. At least three such studies exist that are relevant to fee shifting.

Coursey and Stanley (1988) designed an experiment intended to mimic key features of litigation bargaining. Pairs of students were given one hundred tokens, each worth two cents ($0.02), to bargain over. In other words, in each game a total of $2.00 was at stake. If the students reached an agreement as to how to divide the pot within five minutes, the parties kept their agreed shares. If no agreement was reached, a division was imposed on the players, with that division being randomly drawn from a distribution that had been made known to the students in advance of the game. In games played without fee shifting (the American Rule), each side was charged twenty tokens if a division was imposed. In games with fee shifting (the English Rule), whichever side received less than half of the allocation was charged fifty tokens while the side with more than half was not charged. Two different distributions were used for the imposed outcome, one based on a fifty-fifty split and the other centered around a seventy-thirty split (with the players knowing which side was favored). Four pairs of

---

[12] Laboratory experiments constitute one type of simulation. A second type of simulation, which I do not view as "empirical," in the sense I use that term, refers to simulation models in which various parameters are applied to mathematical models of the litigation process to see what results those models predict (see generally Donohue 1991a; Hause 1989; Hersch 1990; Hughes and Woglom 1996; Hylton 1993a; Katz 1987).

students repeated the game ten times with the students randomly paired for each play, thus producing a total of forty trials.

Coursey and Stanley found that the English Rule produced more settlements (97.5% and 72.0% for the two distributions, respectively) than did the American Rule (60.0% and 62.5%), suggesting that the higher risk of paying the opponent's costs under the English Rule encouraged settlement. In terms of settlement amounts, the rule regarding fee shifting did not seem to have any effect when the fifty-fifty distribution was used. When the seventy-thirty distribution was used, the player on the 30% side was more disadvantaged under the English Rule than under the American Rule. This suggests that parties with stronger cases are advantaged more under the English Rule than under the American Rule.

Two studies have examined the potential impact of attorney fee shifting in the context of settlement offers under Rule 68.[13] Under the existing version of Rule 68, which is something like what used to be called "payment into court" in the English system, parties can put the opposing party at risk for certain costs by making a formal settlement offer. These costs do not include attorneys' fees. Both studies examined the impact of adding attorneys' fees to what can be recovered under Rule 68. The approach of both studies involved a simulation where the recoverability of attorney fees was varied. One study (Rowe and Vidmar 1988) involved only law and business school students and used a paper and pencil format, while the other (Anderson and Rowe 1995) involved a mixture of advanced law students and practitioners in a computerized simulation. The form of statistical analysis differed for the two studies, reflecting the complexity of the sample design, but the conclusions were similar: incorporating an attorney fee shift into a formalized offer of settlement such as Rule 68 increased the maximum amount that defendants were willing to pay and decreased the minimum amount that plaintiffs were willing to accept. The result should be an increase in settlements due to the increased likelihood that a zone of overlap would exist between what the defendant would pay and the plaintiff would accept.

F. A NONSTATISTICAL STUDY

A final study, which relied upon open-ended interviews rather than statistical analyses of actual cases, involved fee shifting in Ontario, Canada (Kritzer 1984c). In 1982, I conducted a series of interviews with corporate lawyers and corporate officials in and around Toronto. A key theme of the interviews was the perceived impact of fee shifting. Respondents differentiated the impacts of fee shifting along two dimensions: the size of the case (small versus large) and the type of litigant (individual versus corporation). Simply put, for corporations, fee shifting was part of the business calculation in deciding whether to bring a case and when to settle a case. In very large cases, the issue of fees was clearly secondary to the larger stakes involved, and as cases got smaller, the fees and fee shift became an increasingly important consideration. According to

---

[13] These studies are summarized in Rowe and Anderson (1996).

respondents, the net effect of fee shifting was to encourage settlement when the corporation was a defendant and to discourage bringing a suit, particularly when there were doubts about the case, when the corporation was a plaintiff. For individuals, my respondents saw effects of fee shifting as straightforward in that "fee shifting serves to discourage persons from pursuing cases they otherwise might litigate or to encourage them to accept settlements that are smaller than they might be able to get at trial." While not expressed in these terms, it was clear that the respondents saw individual litigants as tending to be risk averse. Some lawyers qualified this concern by noting that, for many individuals, the threat of having to pay the other side's costs really has no teeth because those individuals have no assets out of which to pay those costs. As succinctly stated by one respondent, "Litigation is the sport of the very rich or very poor."

Importantly, the impacts described by my respondents accrue to the potential litigants rather than to the lawyers representing those litigants. One of the system's possible effects on lawyers, according to the lawyers interviewed, is a practice among personal injury plaintiffs' lawyers to forego any fees they were entitled to in unsuccessful cases. This practice is based in part on the assumption that their clients would have enough trouble paying the opposing party's costs and would have nothing available to pay their own lawyer.

The Ontario interviews raised one other very important point regarding fee shifting: how fee shifts are handled in settlement. In England, the settling defendant typically agrees to pay the plaintiff's costs at the "party-and-party" rate with the option of asking to have the costs "assessed" (meaning having the costs claim reviewed by an officer of the court). However, it appears that in other settings the question of costs is either not explicitly part of the settlement (as is the case in Alaska, except perhaps in post-trial settlements where costs are given up in return for dropping an appeal) or is essentially a part of the negotiation. The latter appears to be the pattern in Ontario. In the interviews I conducted in 1982, I was told that the question of costs in settlement is treated as part of the settlement package, with some litigators believing that it is best to include an explicit "costs" component in the settlement and others finding it best to simply cite a single settlement figure and leave it to the lawyer and the client to resolve the question of fees. At least one person I interviewed, who typically worked on the defense side, indicated that for many cases the first question to be resolved in achieving a settlement was the costs issue so that the plaintiff's lawyer would be assured of receiving his or her fee. Essentially, this person suggested that if you could satisfy the lawyer's own interest you could settle the case. To what degree this suggestion is accurate, or how widespread this view is, I could not determine.

G. FEE SHIFTING AND POLITICAL/POLICY LITIGATION

Fee shifting can have specific policy implications for politically motivated litigation. Charles Epp (1998) has forcefully argued that a key factor in the rise of certain types of cases onto the agendas of supreme courts in several countries around the world is the support available for interest groups and their lawyers to bring such cases. Fee shifting is an important source of such support. In the United States, there are a number of legal provisions at both the state and federal level that allow for successful parties to recover attorneys' fees in a "one-way" regime (see Mezey and Olson 1993; Olson 1994). Certain types of parties, such as plaintiffs in civil rights cases and parties challenging federal administrative action, can recover fees if they prevail while their opponents are not given this right. The evidence that the availability of fee awards has influenced the willingness of lawyers to bring cases of significant policy import takes the form of broad patterns rather than analysis of specific decisions, but the documented patterns do support the existence of such an effect (Epp 1998:60-61; Greve 1989; O'Connor and Epstein 1985). Furthermore, the interest expressed by lawyers in statutes and court decisions that affect the recoverability and computation of fees confirms that lawyers themselves believe that fee recovery does make a difference.[14] Finally, it must be noted that two-way fee-shifting systems may also encourage policy-based litigation, particularly if there are mechanisms that provide at least some protection against the risks faced by certain groups that might bring such cases (Harlow 1995:116-19).

H. THIRD-PARTY PAYMENT

Fee shifting is only one way by which a party may avoid legal fees; another significant means is third-party payment. Third-party payment arises through two mechanisms: legal insurance (either through a benefit provided through employment or membership of some sort, or through an individual insurance purchase) or legal aid (i.e., need-based programs provided either through government funding or charitable funding).

The best piece of empirical research on the impact of third-party payment is probably Hazel Genn's (1988) study of bargaining in personal injury cases in England. This study involved extensive interviews with solicitors during the mid-1980s. At that time, no-win, no-pay fees were formally banned in England, and after-the-event insurance for the risk of having to pay the other side's costs had not yet been developed. There were in practice at least four different funding mechanisms in England: privately funded litigation, legally aided litigation, union-funded litigation, and private insurance-funded litigation. In addition to dictating how the litigant's own lawyer was to be paid, these systems had (and still may have) implications for how fee shifting operated in practice.

When litigation was privately funded, both parties were "actually" at risk for the costs of the litigation. I put the word "actually" in quotation marks because, in reality, solicitors representing a private individual of modest means may have difficulty collecting fees if the client's case is unsuccessful (at least when fees have not been paid "on account" as the case progresses). Moreover, Genn found

---

[14] One key issue for these lawyers is whether the computation of the fee should take into account the contingency factor—i.e., that the lawyers will not be paid if the case is not successful (Leubsdorf 1981). Generally, the Supreme Court has tended to frown upon any consideration of contingency and has endorsed statutory provisions that set hourly rates substantially below the market rate; see *City of Burlington v. Dague*, 505 U.S. 557 (1992); *Pierce v. Underwood*, 487 U.S. 552 (1988); *Pennsylvania v. Delaware Valley Citizens' Council for Clean Air*, 483 U.S. 711 (1987).

evidence of what amounted to an informal contingency fee; that is, solicitors may take cases knowing that they will, in all probability, be unable to collect their fee from the client if they are not successful. Regardless of whether solicitors assume they will not be paid if they lose the case, or whether they simply recognize the difficulties in collecting, both practical and interpersonal, there is a substantial incentive for solicitors to achieve settlements, thus having their fees paid by the defendants. Settlement permits the lawyer to avoid the problems that might arise regarding payment of attorneys' fees.

Genn's analysis suggests that solicitors working on a privately funded basis tend to be less than aggressive negotiators, particularly those solicitors who do not specialize in personal injury work. These solicitors are likely to view the settlement process as a cooperative enterprise rather than as a conflictual one, and Genn suggests that claims inspectors (equivalent to claims adjusters in the United States) for insurance companies are ready and willing to take advantage of this kind of solicitor when the opportunity presents itself. Genn argues that, given the insurance company's natural desire to maximize profits by minimizing amounts paid in settlement, a solicitor who approaches negotiations expecting a cooperative attitude by the claims inspector is asking to be taken advantage of.

There are two pieces of evidence that tend to support the view that privately-funded cases settle without a lot of give and take, or without getting particularly close to the door of the courthouse. First, Harris and his colleagues (1984:94) report that almost two-thirds of the claimants who settle out of court (and virtually all claims are settled rather than tried) accept the very first offer that is made, typically on the advice of their solicitor. Unfortunately, these data are not broken down by method of funding, but Genn (1988:110) estimates that over half of the litigation at that time was privately funded, permitting the inference that a significant portion of the cases settling on the first offer involved private funding. Second, and more specific to the question of private funding, Genn found that the barristers she interviewed "were of the opinion that it was very rare for a plaintiff to be privately funded" (1988:110). This suggests that even though half of the personal injury claimants were privately funded, only a small fraction of their claims progressed to the point at which a barrister was actually briefed by the solicitor. This can only mean that privately funded claimants have a high likelihood of either settling relatively early or abandoning their claims altogether.

At least through the 1980s, the incentives for solicitors in legal aid cases were very different. Solicitors were under an ethical obligation to alert clients to their possible eligibility for government-funded legal aid, but once a client received assistance from legal aid, it imposed costs on the solicitor.[15] The first cost consisted of delay and administrative overhead. At various junctures in a case, it was necessary for the solicitor to obtain the approval of those responsible for legal aid before proceeding, and the solicitor was required to make a full report of the case to the legal aid authorities when the case was concluded. The

---

[15] [Legal aid policies started changing in the 1990s, and by 2014 when this volume is being produced, it has virtually disappeared for money claims.]

second cost was in terms of reduced fees. While a defendant was still obligated to pay the legal fees of a prevailing plaintiff, a legally aided plaintiff's fees were paid into the legal aid fund, and legal aid paid the solicitor directly. The fees paid by legal aid tended to be lower than those that the solicitor might have expected if the case were funded privately. At the time Genn wrote, solicitors were expected to give the legal aid fund what amounts to a 10% discount, and for some (perhaps many) solicitors, the schedule of fees paid by the fund was somewhat lower than they could expect to charge a private client.

There was one exception to the expectation that the legally aided client's solicitor accept payment from the legal aid fund with the required 10% reduction. If the case was settled before the initiation of a court action, the 10% reduction did not apply, but the solicitor still had to be paid by the fund rather than directly by the opposing party. Assuming that a solicitor had other work that paid more than the reduced legal aid fees to fill his time, it was to his or her advantage to settle a legally aided case without initiating a formal legal action.

Another aspect of the rules regarding legal aid can put pressure on the other side (i.e., the defendant) to settle where it might otherwise be prepared to fight a smaller case. When a legally aided litigant loses a case against an opponent with substantial financial resources (e.g., an insurance company), the prevailing party is not permitted to recover its costs either from the losing party or from the legal aid fund, which effectively removes cost-based threats that certain defendants could otherwise use as bargaining chips. While the reduced legal aid fees create an incentive to settle for solicitors who have more remunerative work available, solicitors in marginal practices might be very happy to accept the level of fees that legal aid offers. Moreover, those solicitors need have no concerns about being paid if the case is ultimately unsuccessful. Thus, if a settlement is not arrived at easily, a solicitor in this position has little to lose by pursuing it as far as necessary. Hence, it is not surprising that barristers handling personal injury work find that legally aided clients comprise a larger proportion of their caseload than is true for solicitors.

The third form of financing of personal injury litigation is through the trade unions. Historically, one benefit offered by trade unions in England was the assurance that if a member were injured on the job, the union would fight to see that he or she received compensation for that injury. What this has meant is that for workplace injuries (and for members of some unions, injuries suffered outside the work setting), the trade union would retain a solicitor for the member and cover any costs associated with the case. For example, if the member's case was unsuccessful, the union would pay both the fees of the member's solicitor and the other side's cost. Thus, a solicitor retained by a trade union need not have any concern about being paid and need not worry about the client's fears about losing and having to pay the opponent's fees. As a result, union solicitors can refuse offers that others might accept without too much concern about the costs and risks of having to go to trial if necessary. In Genn's analysis, it is the union solicitor, well-insulated both from concerns about being paid and from client fears about losing and having to pay costs, who is consistently the most successful advocate.

In the 1980s, the fourth form of financing, legal expense insurance, was available to a small number of injury victims. At that time a variety of plans were available, particularly in connection to injuries arising from motor vehicle accidents. For as little as £5 a year, motorists could obtain coverage up to £25,000, for both their own legal fees and for costs that they might have to pay if they lost a court action (see Kritzer 1991b:109). This removed the disincentives associated with fee shifting—the potential plaintiff no longer needed to worry about the downside risk of losing and having to pay both lawyers—and made potential litigants much more willing to contact a solicitor in the first place.

[Here I quote the solicitor previously quoted in Chapter 10 about his perceptions of the impact of legal expense insurance on how he handled cases. I have omitted that material to avoid repetition.]

III. HOW ARE FEES COMPUTED

The second major dimension of fee arrangement is the mechanism for computing the fee. As with any payment system, the computation of a price affects the incentives of both the buyer and the seller. This impact is most apparent in contrasting the incentives created by fees computed on a time-expended basis and those computed on a fixed-price basis. On a "one-off" case basis (i.e., ignoring other uses of the seller's time and long-run considerations regarding future business), the hourly fee computation creates an incentive for the seller to maximize the time devoted to the case and an incentive for the buyer to minimize time. In other words, the seller wants to sell as much as possible and the buyer wants to buy as little as necessary. In contrast, the fixed price or fixed fee arrangement creates an incentive for the seller to minimize the time devoted to the case while the buyer wants the seller to put in whatever amount of time produces the best possible result.

The other two common types of fee computation are prepayment and percentage or commission. I use the term "prepayment" to refer broadly to situations where the lawyer works on a salaried basis and the client does not have to pay on a fee-for-service basis. This method effectively captures the various forms of legal aid where the lawyer is a salaried employee of the legal services agency as well as insurance-based systems where the lawyer is paid on a "per capita" basis (i.e., payment is on the number of insureds serviced rather than on a service-provided basis). The percentage fee arises in both transactional and litigation work. In the latter, it is what is commonly referred to as a contingency fee in the United States: if no recovery is obtained, the fee works out to be zero. The incentives for the prepaid system are much like those of the fixed fee system: the client wants as much as he or she can get and the lawyer wants to provide as little as necessary. The incentives for the percentage fee are more complex because they depend heavily on the amount upon which the percentage is to be based. If additional effort will increase the base amount, the lawyer may have an incentive to put in more time. Whether or not this is the case will depend upon the lawyer's opportunity cost (i.e., what other fee-generating uses the lawyer has for his or her time). Where the opportunity cost is high and the effect of additional effort on the base amount is modest, a conflict will arise between the lawyer, who will not want to put in additional time because the marginal return is not worth the marginal effort, and the client, for whom any marginal gain is a plus.

The potential conflict between lawyers and clients arising due to fee arrangements is an agency problem (Hay 1996a, 1997; Miller 1987).[16] The nature of the incentives have been discussed extensively on a theoretical basis, often specifically in connection with settlement processes (Clermont and Currivan 1978; Danzon 1983; Dover 1986; Gravelle and Waterson 1993; Johnson 1980–81; MacKinnon 1964; Micelli and Segerson 1991; Rickman 1994; Rubinfeld and Scotchmer 1993; Schwartz and Mitchell 1970). The actual empirical research base assessing the theoretical arguments, however, is relatively small.

One of the first empirical studies that looked at the incentives created by contingency fees was Douglas Rosenthal's analysis of personal injury cases (1974). Based on interviews with litigants and lawyers, he concluded that lawyers tended to slight the relatively routine personal injury cases in his sample. He argued that clients needed to monitor their lawyers very closely and demand that lawyers put in the work necessary to obtain good results. One problem with Rosenthal's analysis was that it did not have a good basis of comparison. For relatively modest cases, it is unlikely that clients would want lawyers to put in significant effort if the client was paying on an hourly basis because the costs would rapidly devour any recoveries that might be obtained. The real question is whether a lawyer paid on an hourly fee basis would actually put in more time than the contingency fee lawyer, assuming reasonable client monitoring of what the lawyer was doing.

This specific question was partially examined by myself and others using data from a large study of litigation in the United States circa 1980 (Kritzer et al. 1985). Using regression methods that employed an array of control variables, we estimated regression models predicting the amount of time devoted by a lawyer to samples of cases handled on an hourly fee basis and handled on a percentage fee basis. The results suggested that contingency fee lawyers in smaller cases did devote less time than hourly fee lawyers. This difference was statistically discernible only for cases involving $6,000 or less, but it might exist for cases involving up to $30,000. While no differences were statistically significant above $30,000, if there were differences in effort it was that the contingency fee lawyer put in more time than hourly fee lawyers. This same analysis found that fee arrangements did not directly impact the amount of time that lawyers devoted to cases as much as they influenced the way that other factors influenced the amount of time. In my book, *The Justice Broker*, I summarized this effect as follows (Kritzer 1990:117):

> [F]ee arrangement has a substantial impact on the process by which lawyers allocate time to cases. Contingent fee lawyers appear to be highly sensitive to the potential productivity of their time and they are

---

[16] Overbilling, which is the incentive created by hourly fees, also creates significant ethical issues (see Lerman 1999; Lerman 1994; Ross 1991, 1996).

less affected by craft-oriented factors. This effect can be seen most clearly in two variables: commitment to craft and response to opposing party's briefs. The contingent fee lawyer does spend time in response to the opposing side's briefs, but that response involves half as much time per brief as the response of hourly fee lawyers. While the hourly fee lawyer is strongly influenced by commitment to craft, the contingent fee lawyer does not appear to be so influenced. On the other hand, the level of effort of contingent fee lawyers goes up at a faster rate as the level of stakes increases than it does for the hourly fee lawyer. The contingent fee lawyer appears sensitive to the potential return to be achieved from a case, which is closely related to the stakes. The hourly fee lawyer's return from a case is not as tied up with the stakes, and other types of considerations (e.g., the client's goals, the nature of the forum, etc.) have a greater influence. This broad comparison suggests that the contingent fee lawyer's behavior in terms of the amount of resources put into the case is controlled primarily by the exigencies of the case; those factors also influence the hourly fee lawyer's behavior but are modified in important ways by other considerations. Given that the contingent fee lawyer's return on the investment in a case is directly determined by the case's characteristics and the processing of the case that leads to an eventual outcome, it is not surprising that other factors have relatively little impact.

A second way in which fee computation influences lawyers' behavior is in the content of the negotiation. If lawyers are being paid on a commission or percentage basis (i.e., out of the proceeds of a recovery), lawyers will focus on money in the negotiation process. It is not surprising then that percentage fee lawyers, when they describe exchanges of offers and demands, report that those demands focus on money (Kritzer 1987 [Chapter 9 in this volume]). Rarely (in 1–3% of cases) do percentage fee lawyers report that money is not part of a demand or offer, and in over three-quarters of the cases, the demands and offers are entirely in terms of money. Lawyers being paid on an hourly fee basis, on the other hand, are less likely to report offers and demands expressed exclusively in terms of money and more likely to report the nonmonetary content of offers and demands.

More broadly, one might hypothesize that the fee arrangement affects the content of lawyers' work. One might expect that hourly fee lawyers would be inclined to devote more time to things like legal research and writing briefs-activities that could build up hours [see Chapter 5 in this volume]. Contingency fee lawyers might be expected to devote more time to getting the case settled. However, the one analysis that looked at this question found no evidence supporting differences in work content that was related to the fee arrangement (Kritzer 1990:121-23).

One area where the difference in incentives between hourly and percentage fee arrangements has been extensively discussed in the United States is in connection with class-action litigation, in which the lawyer's fee may be computed on an hourly basis (a "lodestar") or on a percentage basis.[17] Both of these are forms of contingency fees because the lodestar is paid only if the suit is successful and includes a risk multiplier (see generally, Braun and Dobie 1996; Cavanagh 1988; Feinberg and Gomperts 1986; Silver 1992; Solovy and Saunders 1985). The issue is fairly straightforward: the hourly fee gives lawyers an incentive to drag out cases in order to increase the hours for which they will be compensated, at least to the extent that the lawyers believe a judge making the eventual fee award will allow. In class actions, the percentage fee creates a potential incentive for a relatively quick settlement that may not be in the class's best interest. In class actions, the fees, regardless of how computed, are set by the court and paid out of the "common fund" (i.e., the settlement). The availability of such fees encourages law firms to seek clients to bring such cases (Alexander 1991:535). Given that lawyers initiate many of these lawsuits, the potential reputational constraints that mitigate problematic incentives for routine contingency fee cases may not operate in the context of large class action cases. But the presence of the alleged effects can be supported only anecdotally, and it may not be clear that there is in fact that much difference in the fees obtained by lawyers.[18] One could imagine a study of institutional plaintiffs in class action litigation to determine on what basis those plaintiffs chose or supported the choice of a particular law firm as lead counsel.

A final question related to the incentives associated with hourly fees concerns the ability of the purchaser of legal services to obtain an hourly rate below that which a lawyer might be able to get for other work. I say "might" because if a lawyer could definitely get other work, the lawyer would be unlikely to take a case at below-market rates. One area where lawyers are sometimes forced to accept below-market rates is in criminal defense cases, where courts may appoint counsel for indigent defendants and essentially force a lawyer to accept the appointment even though the compensation falls substantially below what the lawyer earns for other work (Cox 2002). Even if lawyers volunteer to accept such appointments, there may be consequences to accepting hourly rates below the prevailing market rate. While one can find many anecdotal or journalistic discussions of the consequences of such practices (see, for example, Fritsch 2001),[19] I know of no systematic empirical research providing evidence of their impact on lawyer behavior. It might reasonably be expected that the lawyer would have an incentive to minimize the time commitment to such below-market work in order to minimize any losses from turning away work that was paid at market rates. High-volume purchasers of routine legal services may also be able to obtain discounted rates from private-practice lawyers. A good example is routine insurance defense work (see Kritzer 2006 [Chapter 6 in this

---

[17] See Lynk (1990) or Macey and Miller (1991) for a theoretical analysis of the implications of contingency fees in class actions.

[18] See Lynk (1994) or Eisenberg and Miller (2004, 2010) for empirical studies of fees in class action litigation that examine the factors that predict the fee that is awarded.

[19] Often these discussions are in the context of death penalty defense.

volume]);[20] plaintiffs' lawyers perceive such practices as creating incentives for defense lawyers to "churn" files in order to be sure that cases generate adequate fees. Whether "churning" actually occurs is hard to determine (no lawyer is going to admit to that practice or other types of practices that might be ethically questionable), but I have been told by defense lawyers that clients paying "wholesale" rates (i.e., insurers) will not get the same kinds of breaks on bills that may be given to clients paying "retail." One lawyer I spoke with reported that, if he has to travel out of town on a matter for an insurance company client, he will bill portal-to-portal at the full rate where he might use a lower rate for travel time (or not bill at all for that time) with a client paying a higher hourly rate. Similarly, this lawyer indicated he might discount time that proved to be unproductive (i.e., a deposition that failed to yield any useful information) for the noninsurance client while not discounting in the same situation for an insurance company client.[21]

A. MITIGATING CASE-BY-CASE INCENTIVES

Most analyses of the impact of fee-arrangement-generated incentive structures examine the incentives on a case-by-case basis. The only typical recognition that lawyers do not have only one case at a time is the incorporation of the idea of opportunity cost, whereby the analysis takes into account the alternative uses of the lawyer's time. An important mitigating factor, seldom discussed, is that lawyers are concerned not only with the income generated by a particular case, but with a stream of income. For lawyers with an ongoing representation of a client in a series of matters, this means that hourly fee lawyers must reign in the temptation to overwork a case. If the client senses that the bills are too high relative to what the case is worth or relative to the client's assessment of what should have been required to deal with the case, the client may decide to shift its future business to another firm. In the interviews that I conducted with corporate lawyers and corporate officials in Toronto, this concern for maintaining the continuing relationship, and the impact of that concern on billing-related issues, was mentioned repeatedly (Kritzer 1984b [Chapter 4 in this volume]). This does not mean that the concern about fees and how they are computed is not a significant issue for corporate lawyers and their clients, but rather that the search for alternative billing relationships that best align the interests of the lawyers and their corporate clients seems to be an ongoing, and probably never-ending, struggle (Banks 1983; Richert 1994; Wessel 1976).

My own work on contingency fee practice in the United States (Kritzer 2004 [see also Chapter 12 in this volume]) shows how these long-run concerns restrained the incentive of a lawyer being paid on a percentage basis to turn small cases over too quickly. Lawyers depend heavily on their reputations, both among other lawyers and among potential clients, for a flow of clients. A lawyer who garners a reputation for settling cases in ways that do not benefit clients

---

[20] See Silver (1997) for a discussion of the issues created by insurers' tight control over billing by their outside lawyers.

[21] [My subsequent study of insurance defense practice (Kritzer 2006 [Chapter 6 in this volume]) cast questions on some of these kinds of assertions.]

may encounter problems in obtaining future clients, particularly clients with good cases. Lawyers want clients to go away satisfied with the results the lawyer achieves and to stay satisfied—satisfied clients tend to be the best advertisement. If clients later learn from conversations with friends that the result the lawyer achieved was not very good, the lawyer's long-run interest will be harmed (Johnson 1980–81:591; Kritzer 1998a:814; Kritzer and Krishnan 1999:366). For many, and perhaps most, lawyers, the effect of these long-term reputational concerns is to provide an economic check on the worst of the perverse incentives often associated with the contingency fee.[22]

B. FIXED FEES

While the incentives for fixed fees are fairly clear-cut (turn the work out with maximum efficiency), there is almost no empirical research examining whether this is in fact what happens. The one study that addresses this is a study of high volume "franchise" law firms. In that study, Van Hoy interviewed lawyers in such firms and spent time observing the work process in the firm (Van Hoy 1995). He found both a focus on efficiency and an emphasis on providing standardized products that could often be turned out by nonprofessional staff. Often, the primary role of the lawyer in the firm was not so much producing the work as selling the firm's standardized services to the client who came in the door. The more work that could be done by staff, the more profitable the practice.

Fixed fees are often used in divorce practice, particularly with clients of very limited means (Ravdin and Capps 1999:394-97). The impact of such fees is to push lawyers away from the formal tools of litigation and toward emphasizing informal negotiation to minimize the amount of time required to handle a case (Mather et al. 2001:140-42). Lawyers working with clients of limited means are also more likely to offload work onto the clients themselves as a way of minimizing their time commitment. Lawyers doing this work also feel pressure to maintain a high caseload in order to generate an adequate stream of fees. One frequent impact of the limited time lawyers are able to put in on an individual case is a perception by the client that the lawyer is inattentive. In a real sense, this perception is accurate, because the lawyer is minimizing the attention devoted to cases whenever possible.

While my focus has been largely on lawyer behavior in civil litigation, another area where the issue of fixed fees has come up is in the area of criminal defense. Many routine cases in criminal defense are handled on a fixed fee basis, particularly where there is an understanding between lawyer and client that the case will not go to trial. In fact, one of the problems for criminal defense lawyers is that there is often relatively little they can do for their clients other than help them through the process of pleading guilty and being sentenced (Blumberg 1967). Lawyers know that they need to get paid before the case comes to an end because the client has little incentive to pay after the lawyer has done what little

---

[22] Of course, economic incentives are by no means the only influence on lawyer behavior. Concerns about professional craft and professional ethics also put a brake on self-dealing (see Johnson 1980–81:591).

the lawyer can do on behalf of the client. However, whether the way that criminal defense attorneys are paid makes any difference in the way that they handle cases is far from clear from the existing empirical research. One study examined two measures of outcome (whether the attorney obtained a charge reduction and an indicator of sentence severity) in nine medium-sized counties in three states. That study found that whether the attorney was privately retained (which I would presume was mostly on a fixed fee basis) or publicly paid (varying by county with some salaried attorneys, some on fixed fee, and some on a contract basis) had little or no impact on case outcomes (see also Eisenstein and Jacob 1977:285; Nardulli et al. 1988:355-59).[23]

C. NO-WIN, NO-PAY FEES

While many people equate contingency fees with American-style percentage fees,[24] there are other types of no-win, no-pay fees (or from the lawyer's perspective, no-win, no-payment fees). The most common such fee arrangement is one where the fee is computed in the same way that it would be on a non-contingency basis, but is payable only if the lawyer succeeds on behalf of the client (Yarrow and Abrams 1999:112-13). Such fees may include some type of enhancement whereby the basic fee is increased by a percentage to reflect the lawyer's assumption of risk. These fee arrangements also produce incentives that may put the lawyer and client in conflict. Depending on the enhancement and the lawyer's risk preference, a lawyer may want to take a case to trial because of the potential for a much larger fee, while a client may prefer to settle. In smaller cases, the lawyer may prefer to settle to secure the payment of a fee (particularly if the fee is based on the lawyer's time), while the client might prefer to go to trial and try for a larger recovery. In some situations, a lawyer may prefer to go to trial purely for reputational reasons that do not directly benefit the client (Gross and Syverud 1996:53; MacKinnon 1964:74-76). There is no systematic evidence concerning the frequency of such divergent preferences or the question of whose preference prevails. Consequently, these effects must remain speculative.

One study suggests that there may be situations in which lawyer and client interests align very closely, and that in such cases the alignment enhances the lawyer's performance. In a study of social security disability appeals, lawyers were marginally more successful than specialist nonlawyers. The best explanation of the difference in success is not in terms of experience or expertise but in terms of incentives. The nonlawyers typically worked on a salaried basis for

---

[23] These are by no means the only studies that look at the impact of the type of attorney. However, the studies have the advantage of considering a combined total of twelve different communities (three large cities in one and nine medium-size communities in the other), with separate analyses carried out for each of those communities. See Wice (1978:202-04) for a summary of several other studies showing similar results.

[24] While percentage fees are best known in the United States, there are other countries that employ such fee arrangements. Two examples are Greece (Skordaki and Walker 1994:57) and the Dominican Republic (Pastor and Vargas 2000). Percentage fees are also permitted in a number of Canadian provinces. [Starting in 2013 percentage fees are permitted in England; see Chapter 12 for information on additional countries that permit percentage based fees.]

social service organizations, while the lawyers typically worked on a contingency fee basis whereby they were paid only if the appeal was successful. Moreover, the nature of the system was such that lawyers could not typically negotiate a compromise settlement for their clients—either they won the case or they lost it. In this situation, the interests of lawyers and clients coincided, and it worked to the clients' benefit (Kritzer 1998b:146-47).

Putting the lawyer at risk provides strong incentives to screen cases. In certain types of cases, such as medical malpractice, lawyers turn away the vast majority of cases that potential clients bring (Dietz et al. 1973:95-101). More generally, a survey of contingency fee lawyers in Wisconsin found that they turned away roughly half the cases that were presented to them, and that this figure rose to 80-90% for lawyers who aggressively sought out cases using media advertising (Kritzer 1997).[25] The lawyers indicated that most of the cases declined had problems with liability. While the folklore of the legal profession is that lawyers routinely advise clients not to pursue a matter (Glendon 1994:37, 75), there is no evidence of the frequency with which lawyers billing on an hourly- or fixed-fee basis turn away clients presenting matters within the lawyer's usual area of practice.

The other side of this coin is that contingency fees can create incentives to take cases that a lawyer would not otherwise take or that a litigant would not otherwise bring. Analyses of the returns from contingency fee practice show that in a large proportion of cases, lawyers actually make substantially less on a per hour basis than they would from work for which they could charge prevailing hourly rates (Kritzer 1998c:291-93). The median case for most lawyers produces a return at best marginally better than the prevailing hourly rate (*ibid.*, 272-81).[26] For most lawyers handling contingency fee work, the real profits come from a very small segment of cases. While a few lawyers and law firms can "cherry pick" cases so that their case portfolio is largely composed of high profit cases, most lawyers need to take a range of cases to establish a network of referral sources (former clients and other lawyers) that will bring in the occasional high-profit case. One lawyer who turned over as many as 200 cases a year told me that two-thirds of his gross fees (and hence his "profits") came from perhaps a dozen cases each year; the other cases essentially covered his overhead. This lawyer took large numbers of cases primarily to keep his name out in the community. From my own observations of contingency fee lawyers at work, I would also surmise that knowing which cases will be profitable and

---

[25] A study of plaintiffs' lawyers in Texas (Daniels and Martin 2002) found a roughly similar level of screening, with lawyers reporting accepting around a third of cases during the period covered by the Wisconsin survey (but also reporting a drop to accepting only about a quarter of cases by the end of the decade.

[26] A leading critic of contingency fees, Lester Brickman, has repeatedly asserted that contingency fee work routinely produces what amounts to windfall returns to the lawyer (Brickman 1989:32-33, 1992:1838, 1994; see also Brickman et al. 1994). While there are certainly examples of what some would reasonably label "windfall" fees, there is no evidence that such fees are a matter of routine. Furthermore, even when there are very large fees, such as in the case of the tobacco litigation brought on behalf of the states, making a judgment of whether these fees constitute "windfalls" is not straightforward: what looks like a windfall after the fact, may have looked like a huge gamble when the case was first undertaken.

which will be money losers is not something a lawyer knows up front. The actual damages and the investment that will be required to obtain a recovery cannot be known with any certainty until well into a case.[27]

In the early 1990s, Stock and Wise (1993) examined the contingency fees charged by a national sample of lawyers who belonged to the Association of Trial Lawyers of America (ATLA). They argue that the degree of risk that lawyers handling cases on a contingency fee basis are willing to accept depends upon the magnitude of the risk and the lawyer's ability to diversify risk across a portfolio of cases. The ability to diversify risk is in turn a function of the size of the lawyer's firm and the resources available to the firm. They also argue that risk increases with case size, not necessarily in terms of the likelihood of winning and losing, but in terms of the amount at stake for the lawyer (i.e., the amount of time the lawyer will have to devote to the case). Looking at a sample of large antitrust and securities cases, they show that the risk multipliers increase as the amount at stake increases. They conclude that "firms will bear risk if they are compensated for the risk, [and that] [m]ore risk requires greater compensation" (*ibid.*, 601).

D. SALARIED LAWYERS

While the situation of salaried lawyers has been the subject of empirical study (Spangler 1986), the existing research has little to say about the impact of a salaried position on lawyer behavior. Salaried lawyers often find themselves in situations of extremely heavy demands for their time, either because of heavy caseloads or because of the pressures of a partnership track in a large law firm (Galanter and Palay 1990, 1991). In a sense, these demands reflect the incentives of those who hire and pay these salaried lawyers. From the perspective of the employer, the marginal cost of the time of lawyers already on staff is essentially zero except for the opportunity cost of that time. Faced with heavy time demands, lawyers who are neither paid by the hour nor generate fees by the hour want to categorize and process cases with dispatch and minimize what they see as unproductive uses of their time, such as extensive interaction with clients (Hosticka 1979).

There is one very interesting theoretical analysis of the implications of this kind of salaried fee arrangement for the incentives of the lawyer to devote time to a case (Johnson 1980–81:600-02). What this analysis shows is that for the lawyer working in a salaried setting, there is an important distinction drawn between an effort calculation that focuses solely on the instant case and a calculation that considers the benefit of the same effort distributed across an entire caseload. Particularly in settings where a lawyer is handling a set of similar cases, spending more time than is strictly rational from the perspective

---

[27] A somewhat related issue, about which I know of no empirical work, is the impact of referring cases to other lawyers in return for a portion of the fee that the receiving lawyer eventually earns. While "referral fees" are often debated as raising ethical questions for lawyers, there are good reasons that such fees might work to the benefit of the client as well the referring lawyer (see Hay 1996b).

of the individual case can yield benefits to other cases that make that investment a rational choice. This benefit may come in the form of establishing precedents through a test case. The consequences of winning an important test case can produce a substantial benefit for a large group of potential clients who may not need to become clients because of the changes wrought by the test case. While one might think of this effect primarily in terms of lawyers in legal services or legal aid practices, it also makes a lot of sense for a lawyer working as an inside counsel handling employment-related issues. In this situation, the goal may be to establish a reputation as a means of deterring certain types of cases in the future, as well as that of trying to win a favorable precedential decision.[28] While this argument makes intuitive sense, I know of no empirical research that examines the issue. There is systematic evidence that insurers can lower their claims processing costs by using in-house lawyers,[29] but whether this lower cost is the result of incentive effects, simple caseload demands, systematic differences in cases handled by inside and outside counsel, or simply lower per hour costs is not clear.

E. ETHICAL FAILINGS RELATED TO FEE ARRANGEMENT

Legal fees create incentives for lawyers to misbehave. Surprisingly, we know little about the frequency of such misbehavior. Authors have discussed the ethical issues raised by various fee arrangements (Jay 1989; MacKinnon 1964; Ross 1991, 1996; Society of Advanced Legal Studies 2001), but these closely track the incentive issues previously discussed. Where authors have discussed examples, or purported examples, of unethical behavior related to fees, the discussions have been largely anecdotal (Brickman 1989; Lerman 1999, 1998). What little we know from systematic empirical research tends to link unethical behavior not to any particular fee arrangement but to issues such as marginality of practice, client pressures, practice context (i.e., what courts or agencies a lawyer practices before), and the social context of a particular law firm (Arnold and Hagan 1992; Carlin 1966). Thus, there is no empirical evidence that any type of fee arrangement increases the likelihood of unethical behavior, although the specific nature of unethical conduct most likely does vary depending on the type of payment structure.

---

[28] Generally, the desire to "play for rules" can modify the impact of standard incentive calculations (Albiston 1999; Galanter 1974:101-02). This effect is not limited to salaried lawyers. Individual fee-for-service lawyers may themselves choose to "play for rules." While for hourly fee lawyers this requires a willing or blind client, the contingency fee lawyer may be relatively free to pursue rules-oriented outcomes. An opponent of the contingency fee lawyer might, however, put cross-pressures on the lawyer by offering to drop an appeal in return for a payment, which the contingency fee lawyer's risk-averse client may be very tempted to accept.

[29] Studies by the Insurance Services Office (1996:16, 1998:18) of cases arising from commercial liability policies show that the cost of inside counsel as a proportion of the paid loss may be as little as about 50% of the cost of outside counsel.

IV. CONCLUSION: DO FEE ARRANGEMENTS ACCOUNT FOR BROAD CROSS-NATIONAL DIFFERENCES IN LITIGATION PATTERNS?

The discussion throughout this chapter has focused largely on the micro-level effects of fee arrangements on lawyers and their clients. In closing, it is worthwhile to consider briefly what macro-level effects can be attributed to fee arrangement. The common-sense answer is that fee arrangement has significant effects. The United States is often held up as an example of a highly litigious country, and this characterization is attributed in large part to the impact of fee arrangements. In interviews I conducted in Canada, respondents were quick to identify the absence of contingency fees as explaining their belief that litigation was less common in Canada (Kritzer 1984c). During the debate over adopting the conditional-fee form of contingency fees in England, critics pointed to the United States as evidence of the negative impact such arrangements would have—one English expatriate warned against putting "an American hamburger stand into the middle of St. Paul's Cathedral" (Abel 2001; see also Atiyah 1997:27).[30] Others attribute differences in litigiousness to the incentives and disincentives created by fee shifting or the lack thereof (Watson et al. 1991:419). Of course, one can also see the combination of the absence of contingency fees and the presence of fee shifting as a kind of "double whammy."

There are two problems in assessing the truth of the proposition that fee arrangement affects broad patterns of litigiousness, including the aggressiveness with which lawyers seek out cases. First, it is difficult to find good data comparing litigation patterns across countries (Galanter 1983:51). Second, even if one finds data that allows comparison, sorting out the factors that might account for differences is by no means straightforward.

On the litigiousness issue itself, patterns are not as clear as the popular perception might suggest. In his study of law and disputes in Morocco, Lawrence Rosen (1989:64) observed that "one seldom meets an American who has been involved in an actual lawsuit and almost no Moroccan who has not." My own comparative work on propensity to sue suggests that broad statements about differences in propensity have to be conditioned by the type of issue involved (see also Kritzer 2008b; Kritzer et al. 1991b). While it may be the case that persons in the United States are more likely to bring claims and suits for personal injury, Britons may be equally likely to seek redress for consumer problems and perhaps more likely to pursue claims related to employment and rental residences (Kritzer 1991c:403-05; Kritzer et al. 1991a:507; Kritzer et al. 1991c:885; Jacob et al. 1996:127-32). Finally, the most comprehensive effort to compile cross-national data on litigation rates that includes the United States (Wollschläger 1998:587-88) shows that the United States is not the most litigious nation, nor is the United States all that different from England and Wales. Moreover, the availability of percentage fees, such as the American contingency fee, does not clearly lead to higher levels of litigation. If this were

---

[30] The assumption that litigiousness is partly explained by the availability of no-win, no-pay fees is by no means new (see Atiyah 1987:1017).

the case, one would expect to find Greece, where percentage fees are available, to be roughly as litigious as the United States. Furthermore, if the presence of fee shifting discourages litigation, it is hard to account for the higher litigation rates in Germany, Sweden, and Austria compared to the United States.[31]

It is almost certainly the case that lawyers in the United States are more entrepreneurial than are lawyers in England, but is this because of the availability of percentage fees in the United States, or does it reflect broader patterns of economic and legal culture?[32] The English legal profession has traditionally not been as economically motivated as the American profession; professionalism for lawyers in England has been much more entwined with social status than with economic status (Burrage 1996:49-51). The legal profession in England has not been aggressive in trying to open new areas of practice. It might be that the solicitors' profession was able to earn such a comfortable living throughout much of the early 19th and 20th centuries from its conveyancing monopoly that it simply did not feel a need to seek out other income sources (Abel-Smith and Stevens 1967:382-405). It is certainly worth noting that the longstanding opposition of solicitors to any form of no-win, no-pay fee first began to subside after the demise of the conveyancing monopoly (Kritzer 2001a:242). Attributing cross-national differences in patterns of professional behavior entirely to the presence or absence of specific fee rules is highly questionable.[33]

In the end, both at the macro and micro level we are hard pressed to find strong differences in behavioral patterns that can be tied to fee arrangements. This does not mean that fee arrangements do not matter; rather, it is indicative of the complexity of the effects of fee arrangements. The various effects tend to cross-cut in significant ways. The result is often that clear evidence of effects is difficult to find.

---

[31] See Pfennigstorf (1984:44-65) regarding the rules governing fee shifting in these countries. One explanation for the high litigation rate in Germany is fee-related: the wide use of legal expense insurance (see Markesinis 1990:392). However it is not clear whether legal expense insurance preceded or followed a high level of litigation. Legal expense insurance is also widely available in Sweden as is legal aid. But "[n]either legal aid, nor legal-expenses insurance ... had any noticeable effect in increasing the number of cases taken to court..." (see Boyle 2000: 1196).

[32] See Kagan (2001:55-57) or Daniels and Martin (2001) regarding the entrepreneurialism of the American legal profession.

[33] The opposition from the profession is evident in reports issued by the Law Society (Law Society 1970, 1987a).

12

SEVEN DOGGED MYTHS CONCERNING CONTINGENCY FEES[1]

INTRODUCTION

One of the hallmarks of litigation in the United States is what we call the contingency fee. Given the alleged litigation explosion in the United States (Bok 1983; Glendon 1994; Lieberman 1981; Manning 1977)[2] and the supposed litigiousness of the American populace,[3] the contingency fee is a frequent target of the proponents of so-called tort reform[4] who seek to reduce both the exposure to lawsuits and the amounts paid out in damages.[5] One example targeted by

---

[1] This chapter originally appeared in the *Washington University Law Quarterly* 80 (2002), 739-94. The original research reported in this chapter was supported by a grant from the National Science Foundation's Law and Social Science Program (Grant No. SBR–9510976); additional support was provided by the University of Wisconsin Graduate School. Research assistance was provided by J. Mitchell Pickerill, Jayanth Krishnan, Lisa Nelson, and Ian Crichton. I would like to thank the Administrative Office of the United States Courts and the RAND Corporation for making available to me data from RAND's evaluation of the Civil Justice Reform Act; Nicholas Pace (at RAND) and James Kakalik (retired from RAND) were generous in assisting me by answering questions as I worked with those data. The conclusions I drew from those data are of course my own and do not represent the views of either the Administrative Office or the RAND Corporation. I would also like to thank Stephen Daniels of the American Bar Foundation for making available some unpublished results from the survey of Texas plaintiffs' lawyers that he conducted in collaboration with Joanne Martin. The references in this article have been reformatted from law review style to in-text citations, and many essentially repetitive footnotes have been omitted; some small sections have been updated to reflect changes that have occurred since the original publication. The original article also included an appendix which provided a more detailed analysis of the fees that lawyers receive from their contingency fee work; readers interested in that analysis should consult the original article or my book, *Risks, Reputations, and Rewards* (2004b).

[2] See Abel (1988a), Catenacci (1989), Daniels (1985), or Galanter (1983, 1986) for critiques of the litigation explosion argument.

[3] A variety of evidence suggests that the United States may not be uniquely litigious (see Markesinis 1990; Wollschläger 1998).

[4] The leading critic of the contingency fee is Lester Brickman (1989, 1996a, 2011; see also Brickman et al. 1994). Professor Brickman published a critique of this chapter when it originally appeared (Brickman 2003) to which I responded (Kritzer 2004a).

[5] A good example can be found in the Republican Contract with America, which was the cornerstone of Newt Gingrich's successful effort to lead Republicans to the control of Congress in the 1994 election; the ninth bill on the "We Will Pass" list was "The Common Sense Legal Reform Act." In 1996, a series of initiatives on the California ballot would have limited contingency fees, imposed fee shifting in shareholder litigation, and mandated a no-fault auto insurance system (see Passell 1996).

critics was the huge fees received by lawyers representing states in the health-care cost tobacco litigation.

The goals of these supposed reformers were clearly brought home to me in December 2001. I received a telephone call from an attorney representing a large American corporation. The company had produced a product that had caused a significant number of deaths in several countries outside the United States. Importantly, as the lawyer described the situation to me, there was no real question about liability; the concern was to minimize the damages to be paid out. This had become important because a number of American attorneys were seeking to sign clients from these countries to contingency fee retainer agreements in order to sue the American company in courts in the United States. The lawyer who contacted me was trying to find someone to whom public relations people working on behalf of his client could refer media representatives from the foreign countries; the lawyer's intention was to get the word out about "how bad contingency fees were for the clients" and "how it was often the case that clients ended up with very little after paying the lawyers their exorbitant fees." I told the lawyer who called me that I would be happy to talk to any media people who contacted me, but I would not be able to convey the message his client wanted to get into circulation.[6]

Proponents of so-called reform have propounded a variety of criticisms of contingency fees, along the way creating a variety of myths about the nature and operation of contingency fees. In this chapter, I demonstrate that the most frequently advanced myths are just that—myths. In particular, in the pages that follow, I examine the following assertions:

- Contingency fees are peculiarly American.
- There is in reality little risk to the attorneys in most contingency fee cases because most cases result in some recovery for the client.
- The use of modern advertising techniques by contingency fee lawyers has produced a flood of clients seeking compensation.
- Contingency fee lawyers accept most cases that potential clients bring to them.
- Contingency fee lawyers charge a "standard" fee of one-third of the recovery.
- Lawyers routinely obtain windfalls from contingency fee cases.
- The interests of contingency fee lawyers and their clients are routinely in conflict.

A. DATA SOURCES

In the discussion that follows I draw upon a variety of sources of data, both published and unpublished. My most important source of unpublished data is a

---

[6] There can be cases in which clients receive relatively small portions of the defendant's payment; however, when this happens in individual cases (other than class actions), it is usually not so much a function of the fees and expenses of the lawyer but rather a function of other claims against the settlement, such as those from medical providers, health insurers, or workers' compensation insurers.

study I have conducted of contingency fee practice in Wisconsin (Kritzer 2004b). I also draw on data from the RAND Corporation's evaluation of the 1990 Civil Justice Reform Act (see Kakalik et al. 1996). Before turning to the seven myths, I briefly describe these two studies.

1. The Wisconsin Contingency Fee Study

My primary source of original data is my study of contingency fee practice in Wisconsin. To obtain direct and current information on contingency fees, this study involved a variety of types of data collection:

- a structured survey of contingency fee practitioners to obtain basic descriptive information about the lawyers' practices and information on a sample of cases handled by the lawyers;
- observation of lawyers at work to obtain an in-depth understanding of key processes such as case screening and negotiation; and
- semi-structured interviewing to ascertain whether the observational findings were *sui generis*.

The mail survey of contingency fee practitioners, which was carried out during the fall of 1995, relied upon a sampling frame defined by the Litigation Section of the State Bar of Wisconsin.[7] Lawyers provided a total of 511 usable responses representing an estimated response rate of 48%.[8] To obtain information on a sample of actual cases, the survey requested data on up to three cases: the case closed most recently after a trial had begun, the case closed most recently after filing but before the start of trial, and the case closed most recently before filing. Requesting data on the "most recent" cases in each category provides an approximation to random sampling, and the three different disposition stages provide for stratification along the key dimension of when a case is closed.[9] Overall, lawyers provided information on 989 cases (332 unfiled, 390 filed but not tried, and 267 that went to trial).

My observations in law offices during 1996 involved three different practices.[10] I was excluded from very little that was relevant to my work.[11] The three

---

[7] After removing government lawyers and others clearly not engaged in contingency fee practice, the sample included a total of 1,850 target respondents.

[8] I say "estimated" because the survey was mailed to a sample that included many lawyers not involved in contingency fee practice. I included with the survey a postcard which respondents could return indicating that they did not do any contingency fee work. Of the 1,850 lawyers who received the questionnaire, 1,192 provided some kind of response. In order to estimate the number of contingency practitioners among the 658 who did not respond, a research assistant called about 200 law offices and asked whether the lawyer handled cases on a contingency fee basis. Putting this all together, I estimate that 1,072 of the 1,850 lawyers receiving the questionnaire did at least some contingency fee work.

[9] To further frame the sample of cases, I asked only about cases that the lawyer had closed during the preceding twelve months (or previous fiscal year, if that was easier). I also collected information on the number of cases the lawyer had closed in each of those categories during the time period; this made possible the development of a weighting scheme to adjust for the relative frequency of different types of dispositions and the lawyer's practice volume.

[10] Only one of the four lawyers I approached turned me down. The first two lawyers I contacted said "yes," the third said "no," and the fourth said "yes."

settings were very different. One was a specialist plaintiffs' firm, one was a contingency fee plaintiffs' specialist in a medium-sized general practice firm, and the other was a litigation (broadly defined to include criminal, civil, and family litigation) specialist in a small general-practice firm.

Finally, I conducted a total of forty-seven semi-structured interviews, twenty-eight with contingency fee practitioners, thirteen with litigation defense lawyers, and six with current or retired insurance claims adjusters. I conducted the interviews between May and October 1996. I drew the sample of contingency fee practitioners using a combination of legal directories and Yellow Pages advertisements. These interviews averaged about one hour in length, and all were tape recorded and transcribed. I identified the defense-side respondents from directories and in the course of interviews with other respondents.[12] These interviews were conducted by telephone and were also, with one exception, tape recorded and transcribed.

2. Civil Justice Reform Act Evaluation Study

The second source of unpublished data that I use is a study conducted by the RAND Corporation of federal civil cases. RAND conducted this study under contract with the Administrative Office of the U.S. Courts as an evaluation of the impact of the Civil Justice Reform Act (CJRA). For my purposes, I have employed data from two separate samples drawn by RAND.[13] The first sample is from cases terminated during 1991 (up to December 15); the second is from cases filed in 1992 (and in some situations 1993). Cases were taken from twenty federal districts around the country, some of which were involved in pilot projects under the CJRA and some of which served as comparison districts. Samples were stratified to include adequate numbers of cases for each of the types of case-processing interventions adopted in response to the CJRA and to include adequate numbers of cases in each of the three categories of work burdens placed on federal judges; asbestos cases were specifically omitted from the study. RAND constructed sample weights to take into account variations in sampling rates. Each of the two samples (1991 terminations and 1992–93 filings) contained approximately 5,000 cases. Surveys of the lawyers involved in each case were then carried out (omitting the 7% of cases from the 1992–93 sample that were still pending as of January 1996 when the final surveys were sent out); the response rate from lawyers was around 50%.[14] A total of 742 respondents from the 1991 sample reported being paid on a contingency fee basis, and as did 603 respondents for the 1992–93 sample.

---

[11] I was excluded from a firm business meeting in one practice, a trip to talk to an expert in another, and a number of noncontingency fee-related events in the third.

[12] In my interviews with contingency fee practitioners, I solicited names of defense lawyers and adjusters with whom I might speak. From the defense lawyers, I solicited names of additional adjusters, focusing on individuals who had recently retired (on the assumption that they would feel less constraint than would individuals currently employed by insurance companies).

[13] See Kakalik et al. (1996:95-129) for details on the complex design employed by RAND.

[14] There are differing ways to compute the response rate; hence the somewhat ambiguous figure provided above (see Kakalik et al. 1996:117).

Impact of How Lawyers are Paid

Questions on the lawyer survey captured information on the amount of time spent by lawyers on the case (Question 9A); legal fees paid by the lawyer's client excluding expenses (Question 27A); the amount at stake ("the best likely monetary outcome"—Question 16B); the numbers of years the lawyer had been practicing law (Question 28); the percentage of the lawyer's practice devoted to federal district court litigation during the previous five years (Question 29); and the size of the lawyer's firm (Question 30).[15] The ways some of the questions were asked would tend to provide underestimates of the amount of lawyer effort involved (some respondents could not provide estimates of the hours worked by all attorneys for their client and hence provided only partial estimates of lawyer effort, and lawyers were instructed to exclude the number of hours devoted to proceedings before administrative agencies or in state courts involving the dispute in the federal court case), and/or overestimates of the fees they received (the fee question asked for the fees paid for all lawyers for their client). The result is that effective hourly rates and mean hourly returns (both defined below) may be overestimated in the analysis based on the CJRA data that I report below. The information on hours and fees required for analysis was available for 392 (weighted) respondents from the 1991 sample and 297 (weighted) respondents for the 1992-93 sample.[16] In addition to the data from the lawyer survey, I was able to draw on data RAND researchers coded from the court records. The key variables from the court records are the type of case as indicated by the plaintiff's lawyer at the time of filing and the stage of processing when the case was terminated.

I. MYTH 1: CONTINGENCY FEES ARE A UNIQUELY AMERICAN PHENOMENON[17]

Contingency fees have a long history in the United States. One scholar has found evidence of such fees as far back as the early nineteenth century (see Karsten 1998), although the widespread use of such fees did not come until much later (see Bergstrom 1992). A popular perception both inside and outside the United States is that it is contingency fees that set the United States apart from the rest of the world with regard to civil litigation (Kritzer 1984c).

In fact, contingency fees—by which I mean "no win, no pay" fees—are not unique to the United States. Some form of legally accepted "no win, no pay" fee exists in an increasing number of other countries:

- **Australia:** Australian courts began to recognize the appropriateness of "no win, no pay" fee arrangements in 1960, although it was not until 1994 that such fee arrangements started to be available for potential litigants in certain types of cases (e.g., product disputes) in any type of routine way (Bolt 1999; Cannon 1998). By 2010 conditional fee arrangements (no win,

---

[15] See Kakalik et al. (1996:281-85) for the full questionnaire.

[16] The results reported in this section all employ the sampling weights prepared by the RAND staff.

[17] This section has been substantially updated to reflect developments since the publication of this chapter as an article. Also, the country-by-country discussion is now in alphabetical order.

no pay with a premium charged if the claim is successful) are described as a "common billing arrangement" (Cameron 2010:206).

- **Canada:** All provinces of Canada now permit such fees (Knutsen and Walker 2010:246; Melnitzer 2004; Skordaki and Walker 1994:36). Ontario was the last province to allow such fees with a legal change in 2004; some provinces have allowed contingency fees for over 100 years (Minish 1979; Swartz 1996) and some permit percentage-of-recovery contingency fees.[18] It is not clear how often various forms of contingency fees are actually used in Canada.

- **Denmark**: Conditional-type fee arrangements (no win, no pay, with a premium over the normal fee if successful) are permitted but rare (Svenningsen et al. 2010:282).

- **Dominican Republic:** The Dominican Republic allows percentage fees much like those in the United States; such fees, called *cuota litis*, are limited to no more than 30% of the recovery (Pastor and Vargas 2000:17).

- **England & Wales:** Starting in 1995, English solicitors could charge clients in a growing variety of cases on a "conditional fee" basis in which the client pays nothing if no recovery is obtained and pays an "uplift" of up to 100% over the normal fee if there is a recovery (Yarrow 1998, 2000, 2001). In 1999, the government moved to greatly expand the use of conditional fees in order to reduce the cost of legal aid (Lord Chancellor's Department 1998; Zander 1998), and under provisions of the Access to Justice Act 1999, successful plaintiffs could recover the "uplift" from the defendant (Robins 1999b; Underwood 1999). Furthermore, in a 1998 decision, the Court of Appeal in England ruled that it was not contrary to law for English solicitors to act on a contingency basis whereby the solicitor would forgo some or all of his or her normal fee if the case was not successful.[19] A further change took effect in April 2013; for cases filed after that change, the uplift was no longer recoverable from the defendant, and solicitors could charge based on a percentage of the recovery rather than using the conditional fee form (Gretton 2013; Hurst 2014).[20] Throughout this period solicitors were able to charge what one observer labeled a "damage-based contingency fee" (i.e., a percentage fee) in cases that would not come to court, particularly cases decided by the Employment Tribunal (see Moorhead 2010).

- **France:** In France, major Paris law firms are using contingency fees increasingly (Skordaki and Walker 1994:61), and they are now being permitted to base fees in part on results achieved (Sheridan and Cameron 1992:France-15; Tuil and Visscher 2010:45; Villedieu 2010:344).

---

[18] See *McIntyre Estate v. Ontario*, 53 O.R.3d 137 (2001).

[19] See *Thai Trading Co. v. Taylor* [1998] 1 Q.B. 781, C.A. While England was long noted as a country where contingency fees were not permitted, in a 1998 decision, the Court of Appeal noted: "It is not uncommon for solicitors to take on a case for an impecunious client with a meritorious case, knowing that there is no realistic prospect of recovering their costs from the client if the case is lost, without thereby waiving their legal right to their fees in that event. As every debt collector knows, what is legally recoverable and what is recoverable in practice are not the same" (*id.* at 788-89).

[20] The 2013 change also modified the traditional fee shifting rule so that most individual plaintiffs were no longer at risk for the defendant's costs should the case be unsuccessful.

- **Germany:** Until a ruling of the German Constitutional Court in late 2006, result-based fees were not permitted; in the wake of that ruling, German law was modified to allow no-win, no-pay fees with an uplift over the normal (statutorily-set) fee for clients "who would not have access to justice without entering into a contingency fee or any other result-based fee" (Hess and Hübner 2010:354-55; Tuil and Visscher 2010:43-44).

- **Greece:** Greece permits percentage fees much like the American contingency fee, but with a limit of 20% of the amount recovered (Skordaki 1990:57); Greece also allows lawyers to consider the result achieved in setting a fee (Kerameus and Koussoulis 1999; Sheridan and Cameron 1992: Greece-10).

- **Irish Republic:** In the Irish Republic, banisters take cases on a "no goal, no fee" basis, in which the barrister receives his or her normal fee unless no recovery is obtained (Skordaki and Walker 1994:43). There is some evidence that in practice fees are tied to the amount of recovery (see Tuil and Visscher 2010:46).

- **Israel:** Contingency fees are common in Israel, and resemble fees in the U.S. in being based on a percentage of recovery and sometimes involving a different percentage depending on the stage of resolution; it may be that the percentages tend to be slightly lower than in the U.S. (Zamir and Ritov 2010:255-65).

- **Japan:** While few auto accident cases in Japan lead to law suits, in those cases that do go to court, the lawyers (*bengoshi*) representing the claimant normally charge on a contingency ("no win, no fee") basis (Tanase 1990; but see Sugawara and Osaka 2010:376-77).

- **New Zealand:** In New Zealand, both barristers and solicitors may charge on a speculative basis (Skordaki and Walker 1994:33).[21]

- **Northern Ireland:** In Northern Ireland, "speculative fee arrangements have operated unofficially, for many years" (Skordaki and Walker 1994: 29).

- **Russia:** "Advocates often work *only* [emphasis added] for success fee agreed with a client, which will usually be close to 10 per cent of the amount of the claim" (Maleshin 2010:486).

- **Scotland:** Scotland has long permitted lawyers to act on a "speculative basis." If the plaintiff wins, he or she pays the lawyer the normal fee, but the plaintiff pays nothing if he or she loses (Skordaki and Walker 1994: 26).

- **Spain:** Success fees and percentage fee arrangements are valid in Spain; the latter became allowed by a 2008 decision of the Spanish Supreme Court (Medina et al. 2010:492).

- **Taiwan:** Various forms of contingency fee arrangements are permitted, including percentage-based fees (Shen and Chen 2010:530).

- **Other countries:** Other countries that permit fees based on a percentage of recovery include Estonia, Finland, Hungary, Italy, Lithuania, Slovakia,

---

[21] In New Zealand, personal injury claims are handled through a no-fault regime administered by the Accident Compensation Commission.

and Slovenia (Hodges et al. 2010:132-33). Several countries permit elements of contingency (i.e., fees based in part on results achieved). In Italy this supplementary fee is called the *palamario* (Sheridan and Cameron 1992:Italy-20). Other countries that permit this include Luxembourg (Sheridan and Cameron 1992:Luxembourg-12), and Portugal (Sheridan and Cameron 1992:Portugal-13). Brazil allows fees that include a contingency/percentage element (Bermudes 1999). In a number of Latin American countries lawyers frequently enter into private, non-enforceable arrangements with their clients for fees based on a percentage of recovery (Gómez 2010: 397).

As the above listing shows, each country's system is somewhat different. Nonetheless, the assertion that contingency fees are peculiarly American is clearly false. Moreover, even an assertion that the percentage-based contingency fee is specific to the United States is not correct.

II. MYTH 2: MOST CONTINGENCY FEE CASES INVOLVE LITTLE RISK FOR LAWYERS

While there are some areas of litigation where lawyers face substantial risk of nonrecovery and hence no fee if a case is being handled on a contingency fee basis,[22] most contingency fee cases do yield some recovery and hence some fee. However, this assertion misses the real contingencies of contingency fee practice. For both the lawyer and the client, recovery or no recovery is only one part of the uncertainty inherent in litigation. The other contingencies faced by the lawyer (and the client) include:

- uncertainty about the amount that will be recovered (and hence the fee the lawyer will receive);
- uncertainty about what it will cost, in both effort and expenses, to obtain the recovery; and
- uncertainty about how much time will pass before the recovery is obtained.

In fact, for most cases the real contingencies are not whether there will be a recovery but these other areas of uncertainty.

It is easy to understand the importance of uncertainty over the amount to be recovered and the cost of obtaining the recovery by imagining a first meeting between a lawyer and a potential client. Perhaps there is no issue at all of liability; the lawyer's client was a pedestrian on the sidewalk who suffered a soft-tissue injury and bruises while dodging a car driven by a well-insured driver who was convicted after the accident of driving under the influence. The lawyer might say to the client at the first meeting (ignoring ethical strictures against such a statement), "I can guarantee that I will get a recovery for you." The lawyer then asks the client whether she would rather pay the lawyer on an hourly basis at $125 per hour due monthly or on a percentage basis at 33%

---

[22] Two such areas are medical malpractice (see Vidmar 1995:49-92) and job discrimination (see Walsh 1990), although the situation regarding job discrimination may have eased after the passage of the Civil Rights Act of 1991 (see Farhang 2009, 2010).

payable at the conclusion of the case.[23] Almost certainly the client would then ask the lawyer two questions: "How much would your fee be on an hourly basis? How much do you think you will recover for me?" To this, the lawyer might well respond, "I can't say with a lot of certainty either how much the fee would be on an hourly basis because that will depend on how difficult the other side is in settling the case, and whether we have to file suit. I also can't say for sure what the recovery will be; you are still in treatment, and the recovery will depend on whether you have any continuing problems or fully recover from your injuries." The client might then ask the lawyer for a worst-case scenario, to which the lawyer might say that the recovery could be as little as $5,000 if the client's medical condition resolves itself quickly and there is no residual problem. The lawyer would also respond that, if it is necessary to file suit, that would involve at least twenty to twenty-five hours of the lawyer's time, and two or three times that if the case actually has to go to trial. A little quick arithmetic on the part of the client would show that with a trial (albeit this is very unlikely)[24] the lawyer's fee could exceed the amount recovered. Even without a trial, the client could end up with very little after paying the lawyer $125 per hour. Moreover, the client has to come up with the lawyer's fee as the case progresses, rather than waiting until the end. With all of these considerations, most clients would choose the contingency fee over the hourly fee.

While I have presented the above from the viewpoint of the client choosing between hourly and contingency fees, it also serves illustrate the uncertainty for the lawyer taking the case on a contingency fee. The lawyer needs to be prepared to accept a fee that yields a low return on the lawyer's investment. One of the lawyers I observed settled a case on the eve of trial for $60,000, having started out with a demand for $200,000. The lawyer, who had a nominal billing rate of $175 per hour, had devoted about 300 hours to the case. While the lawyer did receive a fee of $20,000, about $8,000 of this went into time devoted to the case by the lawyer's paralegal. In the end, the lawyer netted about $40 per hour. From the viewpoint of the lawyer, this case was a clear loser.

III. MYTH 3: PLAINTIFFS' LAWYERS OBTAIN A SIGNIFICANT PORTION OF THEIR CLIENTS THROUGH ADVERTISING, PARTICULARLY MEDIA ADVERTISING AND DIRECT MAIL

The Supreme Court decision in *Bates v. State Bar of Arizona* (433 U.S. 350 [1977]) freed lawyers from traditional strictures on advertising. Within the legal profession, personal injury specialists have probably been the most aggressive in using advertising. This has produced a bonanza in revenue for the telephone companies that put out Yellow Pages, and in every major media market one sees significant television advertising by lawyers seeking personal injury clients. Most controversial has been direct mail solicitation where lawyers mine publicly available reports of traffic accidents to identify potential clients and then send

---

[23] The median hourly rate reported by lawyers in the 1995 survey who did at least some work on an hourly basis was $125/hour.

[24] A trial on damages could occur even if the defendant stipulated as to liability.

241

letters to these individuals telling them about the possibility of obtaining compensation and inviting them to contact the lawyer for a no-cost consultation.[25]

Given the amount of advertising done by lawyers, one might expect that advertising is the dominant vehicle through which most lawyers get personal injury clients. This is not in fact true. In my survey of Wisconsin contingency fee practitioners,[26] I asked them what percentage of their clients come from each of a variety of sources including:

- referrals from other lawyers;
- referrals from other clients;
- advertisements in Yellow Pages;
- advertising in other media;
- existing clients;
- community contacts and word-of-mouth;
- direct mail advertising;
- other; and
- unknown.

Table 12.1 summarizes the responses, showing the mean percentage obtained from each source and breaking this down between those lawyers who are personal injury specialists and those who are not. The only advertising source that produces a significant proportion of clients across the respondents is advertisements in the Yellow Pages. The dominant sources of cases are the traditional ones of client referrals, referrals from other lawyers, and referrals through community contacts. One surprising source, at least for the personal injury specialists, is "current clients." I interpret this as referring to repeat clients; as one personal injury lawyer described it to me, a surprising number of clients come back with new cases.

One might question whether this analysis obscures the possibility that a small group of lawyers, those who invest the most into media advertising and direct mail, are highly dependent on these sources. In fact, only 8 of the 471 respondents in my survey of Wisconsin practitioners reported that they were currently using direct mail, and only one of those reported getting more than 15% of his clients through his direct mail efforts. One of the lawyers I interviewed had been an aggressive user of direct mail, and he reported that despite all of his efforts he never got more than 20% of his clients through this medium; most of his clients were referrals from former clients or from other lawyers.

---

[25] A number of states have tried to ban any such contacts, but in 1988 the Supreme Court in *Shapero v. Kentucky Bar Association* (486 U.S. 466 ([1988]), ruled that states could not do so. In a later case, *Florida Bar v. Went-For-It, Inc.* (515 U.S. 618 [1995]), the Court ruled that states could bar lawyers from sending such solicitations for thirty days, and a number of states have implemented such a limitation.

[26] See Kritzer and Krishnan (1999) for a more detailed analysis.

Table 12.1: Sources of Cases: Wisconsin

Source	All respon- dents	Personal Injury Specialists	Non-Personal Injury Specialists
Lawyer referrals	19.4%	19.1%	19.6%
Client referrals	25.3	27.7	25.2
Existing client	19.2	11.4	23.0
Yellow Pages advertising	10.6	16.0	7.9
Other media advertising	3.0	7.7	0.6
Direct mail	0.2	0.5	<0.1
Community contacts	15.4	13.6	16.3
Other and unknown	6.9	5.9	7.4
(n)	(471)	(153)	(318)

Cell entries are the mean percentage reported for the source.
Source: Krtizer & Krishnan (1999:351)

A significant minority (37%) of personal injury specialists do use advertising other than the Yellow Pages. Among those who do use advertising in Yellow Pages, most obtained less than one-third of their clients through it (and almost none obtained one-half or more of their clients this way). Lawyers in one firm that was a heavy user of television advertising reported that when their advertisements were running, they could expect ten or more calls per day. Most of the calls concerned cases which had no significant fee potential or issues that they did not handle (or could not be handled on a contingency fee basis). The lawyers in this firm were happy if a week's worth of phone calls yielded two or three cases. One lawyer in this firm estimated that advertising (both in media and in Yellow Pages) directly produced only about one-quarter of his revenue, although he attributed another one-quarter to indirect effects of advertising (i.e., referrals from former clients who themselves originally came in as a result of the advertising).

Are these findings peculiar to Wisconsin? Stephen Daniels and Joanne Martin have been engaged in a study of the personal injury plaintiffs' bar in Texas. Their study has involved both semi-structured interviews and a mail survey. Based on ninety-five semi-structured interviews, they found that only 10% of the respondents obtained more than one-half of their clients through "direct marketing," which included all forms of advertising (Yellow Pages, television, radio, newspaper, billboards, direct mail, etc.). In contrast, 27% obtained more than one-half of their clients through client referrals, and 51% obtained more than one-half of their clients through lawyer referrals (Daniels and Martin 1997). Daniels and Martin's mail survey produced responses from 552 plaintiffs' lawyers practicing in Texas (Daniels and Martin 2002). They split their respondents into four groups depending on the types of cases the lawyers handled: Bread and Butter I (handling the most routine cases); Bread and Butter II; Heavy Hitters I; and Heavy Hitters II (handling the largest, most complex cases). Table 12.2 shows the average percentage of clients in each category from

Table 12.2: Sources of Cases: Texas

Source	All respondents	Bread & Butter I	Bread & Butter II	Heavy Hitter I	Heavy Hitter II
Referrals from other plaintiffs' lawyers	18.3%	10.0%	14.2%	21.5%	27.5%
Referrals from other lawyers	19.1	10.5	17.7	20.7	27.8
Referrals from former clients	28.9	36.4	34.1	26.2	18.2
Other referrals	12.8	13.8	11.8	14.4	11.3
All advertising	12.3	20.0	13.0	9.2	6.9
Yellow Pages advertising	8.4	14.8	9.3	6.0	3.2
Television advertising	2.6	3.8	2.2	1.8	2.8
Direct mail	0.3	0.2	0.2	0.2	0.5
Other advertising	1.1	1.2	1.3	1.2	0.4
Other sources	6.3	6.9	5.7	5.4	6.9
(n)	(540)	(138)	(141)	(134)	(139)

Cell entries are the mean percentage reported for the source.

Source: Daniels & Martin (2000); additional detail provided by Stephen Daniels

each source listed in Daniels and Martin's questionnaire. Advertising in general accounts for about 12% of clients, and two-thirds of this 12% comes generally from Yellow Pages advertising. Advertising is least important for those at the top end of practice and most important for those toward the bottom; however, even for those in the group most dependent on advertising, only an average of about 21% of their clients are obtained in this way, and again, two-thirds of those come from Yellow Pages advertising. Thus, even for the group most dependent on advertising, no more than about 6% of clients come from a combination of television and direct mail.

Despite all of the prominence of modern advertising, most lawyers representing clients on a contingency fee basis get the vast majority of those clients through the tried-and-true means of referrals, largely from satisfied clients and from other lawyers.[27] What these analyses cannot measure is whether the advertising prompts people to seek out lawyers through one of these traditional means. For example, it is certainly possible that someone receiving a direct mail solicitation from a lawyer after an accident would be prompted to seek out a recommendation for a lawyer and then consult that lawyer, even if the solicitation did not draw the individual into the office of the lawyer who sent the solicitation.[28] Likewise, television advertising may have sensitized injury victims

---

[27] This does not mean that there are no firms that depend largely on advertising for their client base; Engstrom (2009; 2011) describes firms that she labels "settlement mills" which do appear to rely on advertising.

[28] A study of direct mail solicitation recipients in Wisconsin found that only 5% hired a lawyer from whom they received a letter, while 10% of the respondents who read the letter found it helpful (see Kritzer and Krishnan 1999:354).

to the availability of compensation. However, it is hard to firmly link any changes in patterns of contacting a lawyer to these developments, first because it is not clear that there have been changes in those patterns, and second because there is no good baseline against which to compare earlier patterns to present patterns.

IV. MYTH 4: LAWYERS ACCEPT AS CLIENTS MOST OF THOSE INDIVIDUALS WHO CONTACT THEM WITH POTENTIAL CLAIMS

One popular image of plaintiffs' lawyers is that they are so anxious to get clients that they will represent virtually anyone who calls on the telephone or walks in the door. In *A Nation Under Lawyers*, Mary Ann Glendon argues that, at least in the past, good lawyers did as much to discourage litigation as to advance it; she quotes an observation attributed to Elihu Root that "[a]bout half of the practice of the decent lawyer consists in telling would-be clients that they are damned fools and should stop" (Glendon 1994:37). The press furthers the image of contingency fee lawyers as stirring up litigation in reports of swarms of lawyers gathering whenever there is some major event that could produce litigation.[29] Even without such reports one should not be surprised that contingency fee lawyers have a reputation of stirring up trouble given the apparent logic of the contingency fee: the lawyers get a cut of whatever they recover, and without cases there is no cut to get.

Undoubtedly, there are lawyers who push the edge of the liability frontier or who engage in practices pejoratively referred to as ambulance chasing or operate as what some have labeled "settlement mills" (Engstrom 2009, 2011). However, the day-to-day reality of most contingency fee legal practices is very different from these images. While virtually every contingency fee practitioner wants to find highly lucrative cases, such cases are relatively rare. Many cases presented to lawyers are not winnable or do not offer a prospect of even a moderately acceptable fee. The contingency fee practitioner seeks to choose cases that offer a high probability of providing at least an acceptable return and hopes to find some fraction of cases that present the opportunity to generate a significant fee (Crane 1988). Lawyers evaluate potential cases in terms of the risks involved and the potential returns associated with those risks. An attorney will reject cases that do not satisfy the attorney's risk-to-return criteria. Thus, contingency fee lawyers resemble portfolio managers, choosing to "invest" (their time) in risky cases hoping to obtain adequate or better returns.

What does this mean in terms of actual practice when a potential client contacts a contingency fee lawyer? In my survey of Wisconsin practitioners, I asked my respondents how many contacts they had received from potential clients in the prior year and how many of those contacts had led to a retainer agreement. There are at least two ways to convert these figures into acceptance rates. First, we can look at it from the perspective of the lawyer by asking what is the typical

---

[29] On the 1984 disaster in Bhopal, India, see Galanter (1990a; see also Riley 1984); on Enron, see Barboza (2002).

proportion of potential cases lawyers accept? This involves looking at mean or median acceptance rates across the sample of lawyers. Alternatively, from the viewpoint of the potential client, one can ask what is the likelihood that a randomly selected client calling a randomly selected lawyer will have his or her case accepted by that lawyer? To look at this, the best estimate involves aggregating across lawyers: adding up the number of cases accepted across all of the lawyers and the number of contacts received across all of the lawyers and dividing the two figures. Table 12.3 shows both types of estimates.

Table 12.3: Acceptance Rates: Wisconsin

Number of contacts	Number of respondents (weighted)	Mean percent accepted	Total number of contacts	Total number of cases accepted	Percent of total cases accepted
1-10	236	51%	1,513	764	50%
11-25	279	54%	5,403	2,868	53%
26-75	251	53%	10,830	5,602	52%
76-200	125	35%	15,707	5,469	35%
201-1000	47	37%	19,831	7,616	38%
Over 1000	7	7%	16,700	1,295	8%
All	945	49%	53,584	23,614	34%

Results based on weighted data; unweighted n is 455.

Overall, lawyers reported accepting cases from a mean of 49% (median 50%) of the potential clients who contacted them; the first and third quartiles are 25% and 75%, respectively. Aggregating across the 455 lawyers,[30] the lawyers accepted 23,614 of 69,984 cases for an acceptance rate of 34%. Eliminating the seven respondents reporting 1,000 or more contacts gives an aggregate acceptance rate of 42%. As shown in Table 12.3, there appears to be a fairly clear linkage between volume and selectivity. For those lawyers or firms receiving about one-and-one-half or fewer contacts per week, the acceptance rate tends to be on the order of 50%; for those with 1.5 to about 20 contacts per week (1,000 cases per year), the acceptance rate is under 40%. For the very high-volume practices with more than twenty contacts per week, the acceptance rate drops off sharply to 8%.

I also asked lawyers why they declined cases, asking them to estimate the percentage of uses declined for the following reasons:

- questions about liability;
- low damages;
- a combination of questionable liability and low damages;
- outside of the lawyer's area of practice; and
- other.

Table 12.4 shows that the dominant reason for refusing cases involves questions of liability.

---

[30] Weighting brings the nominal n up to 945, which is the figure shown in Table 12.3.

Table 12.4: Reasons for Declining Cases

	All respon- dents	Omitting respondents with more than 1,000 contacts	0 to 75 contacts	76 to 1,000 contacts
	Aggregate Percentages			
Lack of liability	47%	41%	35%	43%
Inadequate damages	17%	22%	23%	22%
Both lack of liability and inadequate damages	13%	15%	20%	13%
Outside lawyer's area of practice	11%	10%	12%	10%
Other reasons	11%	12%	11%	12%
	Mean Percentages			
Lack of liability	36%	36%	34%	44%
Inadequate damages	18%	18%	17%	20%
Both lack of liability and inadequate	20%	20%	21%	13%
Outside lawyer's area of practice	10%	10%	10%	9%
Other reasons	13%	13%	13%	14%

Results based on weighted data.

Again, one might ask whether these patterns are peculiar to Wisconsin. They are not. In their survey of Texas plaintiffs' lawyers, Daniels and Martin (2002:8-17) asked the lawyers to estimate the percentage of calls from potential personal injury clients that lead to a signed contingency fee agreement. Table 12.5 shows the pattern both for all respondents and broken down into the same four categories of lawyers discussed previously.[31] Overall, the typical respondent reports that about one-quarter of calls lead to representation. For lawyers handling the most routine cases, this figure rises to about one-third, and for those lawyers handling the biggest cases, the figure drops to under 20%. Based on these data, my findings for Wisconsin, if anything, overstate the acceptance rates.[32]

---

[31] I compiled Table 12.6 from figures reported in Daniel and Martin's text.

[32] It is possible that some of the differences between Wisconsin and Texas reflect changes in the approximately five years between my survey and the Texas survey. Daniels and Martin also asked their respondents to estimate the number of calls per month and the percentage of cases accepted five years prior to their survey. The lawyers reported both a drop in the number of calls and a drop in the percentage of cases accepted. Five years earlier, the mean and median percentage accepted at the firm level were 35.9% and 30%, respectively; for the individual lawyers, the mean and median five years ago were 36.4% and 30%, respectively. However, even these higher figures are lower than the figures in Wisconsin.

Table 12.5: Acceptance Rates: Texas

Source	All respondents	Bread & Butter I	Bread & Butter II	Heavy Hitter I	Heavy Hitter II
Calls/month, Firm					
Mean	36.2	37.8	35.3	38.6	33.6
Median	15	18	20	20	20
Calls/month, Respondent					
Mean	18.9	21.9	18.3	18.5	16.8
Median	10	12.5	10	10	8
Percent accepted, Firm					
Mean	25.4%	35.1%	26.7%	24.2%	16.6%
Median	15%	30%	15%	15%	10%
Percent accepted, Respondent					
Mean	26.7%	35.1%	27.0%	26.8%	17.9%
Median	20%	30%	20%	20%	10%
(n)	(540)	(138)	(141)	(134)	(139)

Cell entries are the mean percentage reported for the source.
Source: Daniels & Martin (2000); additional detail provided by Stephen Daniels

V. MYTH 5: CONTINGENCY FEES ARE STANDARDIZED AT A RATE OF 33%

I frequently hear comments about the "standard, one-third contingency fee."[33] In my interviews with Wisconsin practitioners, many did in fact say that they normally charged one-third (unless statutes or regulations limited the percentage in some way[34]); however, others reported much less standardization in fees, and many of these lawyers who reported that they had a "normal" fee of one-third indicated that in some circumstances they would deviate from the standard fee.

My survey of Wisconsin practitioners makes it clear that there is substantial variation in the contingency fees that lawyers charge. In my survey, I asked the lawyers to tell me about three specific cases: the most recent case settled without filing, the most recent case settled or disposed after filing but before trial, and the most recent case disposed by trial. For each of these cases, I asked the lawyers to describe the contingency fee arrangement they had with their client. Table 12.6 summarizes the responses.

---

[33] "Standard contingency fees are typically at least one-third, forty and even fifty percent in cases settled before trial and often more than fifty percent [of the net recovery] in cases which go to trial" (Brickman 1996a:268).

[34] Wisconsin limits percentage fees in medical malpractice cases (33% or 25% of the first $1 million depending on whether the liability is stipulated within a statutory deadline, and 20% of any amount over $1 million). Wis. Stat § 655.013 (1986). In worker's compensation cases, attorney's fees are limited to 20% of disputed benefits. Wis. Stat. § 102.26(2) (1993). In federal social security cases, fees are typically limited to no more than 25% of back benefits up to a maximum of $4,000, see 42 U.S.C. § 406(a)(2); see also Baughman (1997).

Table 12.6: Variation In Contingency Fees: Wisconsin

Fee arrangement	Percent of cases	Range of percentage fees charged for variable percent	
		Maximum	Minimum
Flat third	57%		
Flat quarter	3%		
Other flat percent	1%		
Flat, percent unknown	4%		
Variable percent	31%		
No lawsuit		33%	15%
No trial		43%	20%
Trial		50%	25%
Appeal		50%	33%
Other	5%		
(n)	(822)		

Based on weighted data.

Excluding those types of cases for which fees are specifically governed by statutes or regulations, 64% of the cases in my sample involved retainers specifying a fee as a flat percentage of the recovery; 31% employed a variable percentage; and 5% employed some other type of contingency arrangement. Of the cases with a fixed percentage, a contingency fee of one-third was by far the most common, accounting for 88% of those cases. Five percent of the cases called for fees of 25% or less, 1% specified fees around 30%, less than 1% specified fees exceeding one-third of the recovery; the exact percentage was not ascertained for 4% of the cases. Thus, on the order of 60% of the cases employed the so-called "standard" one-third contingency fee.

The most common pattern for those cases employing a variable percentage called for a contingency fee of one-quarter if the case did not involve substantial trial preparation (or, in some cases, did not get to trial) and one-third if the case got beyond that point; the contingency fee rose to 40% or more if the case resulted in an appeal. For cases not involving a lawsuit, the contingency fee percentage could be as low as 15% or as high as 33%. The range for those cases involving a suit but not trial was 20% to 43%. For those going to trial, the range was from 25% to as high as 50%. One of the lawyers told me that he would consider taking certain types of risky cases which he saw as having a high likelihood of going to trial only if the contingency fee percentage was 50% if the case went to trial. Another lawyer explained that he would consider quoting a fee that might involve a percentage as high as 50% in cases where the potential client came in with an offer in hand. In these cases, the fee would be based only on any recovery over and above the offer in hand, with the fee being the lesser of 50% of the additional recovery or 33% of the total recovery.

Thirty-four cases in the sample involved a fee with a contingency element that did not conform to the standard percentage fee arrangement. The variations included:

- An hourly fee paid until an initial settlement offer is obtained, and then 50% of anything over and above that offer.
- An hourly fee capped at 33% of the recovery.
- A flat retainer plus a percentage.
- An hourly retainer plus a percentage once that time is exhausted.
- An hourly fee up to a set maximum with a percentage if that maximum is exceeded.
- A premium hourly rate with no fee if there is no recovery.
- A reduced hourly rate plus a bonus based on recovery.
- A reduced hourly rate plus a reduced percentage.
- A capped hourly rate plus a percentage.

In my interviews, it was clear that some lawyers were very open to negotiating individualized retainer agreements, while others were very firm in offering only specific types of arrangements. Some lawyers expressed a willingness to negotiate with the client to get a case that they viewed as good; others rejected any idea of such negotiations. Others told me that they specifically laid out the choice of an hourly fee versus a contingency fee.[35] Another lawyer, whose practice was exclusively contingency fee, told me that in a case of clear liability, severe injury, and a relatively low policy limit, he would charge 5% or less (e.g., $5,000 on a $100,000 recovery) if he was able to get the insurer quickly to tender its policy limits.

Again, one can ask whether the variation in fees is peculiar to Wisconsin. Some evidence from the RAND CJRA survey of federal cases shows that this is not the case, although that study does not provide the same level of detail found in the Wisconsin survey.[36] Specifically, the question asked by the RAND CJRA survey did not allow respondents to describe a fee that varied depending on the stage of disposition or that involved alternative types of contingency arrangements. Of the cases handled under a contingency fee in the RAND survey, 55% involved a one-third contingency fee, 25% involved a contingency fee of less than one-third of the recovery, and 20% involved a contingency fee of more than one-third of the recovery. This pattern is both similar and different from the Wisconsin pattern. It is similar in the percentage of cases that involved a one-third fee; it is different in that the RAND survey showed a substantially larger proportion of cases involved a contingency fee of more than one-third of the recovery. Despite these differences, it is clear that while the average contingency fee may be on the order of one-third, there is significant variation from this supposed "standard."[37]

---

35 Wisconsin law specifically requires this for medical malpractice cases. Wis. Stat. § 655.013(2) (1986).

36 In this section, I report my own analysis of data collected by RAND; see Kakalik et al. (1996) for RAND's report of its analysis.

37 Further evidence on this point is provided by a 1991 national survey of Association of Trial Lawyers of American (ATLA) members that found that only 54.3% of respondents reported that they always stated fees as a fixed percentage of recovery (see Stock 1992:app. B, question 12).

My research in Wisconsin revealed a number of other important variations worth noting. First, while the fee is usually described as being based on the gross recovery (i.e., before the lawyer is reimbursed for expenses), some lawyers in Wisconsin treat the gross recovery for fee-computation purposes as the recovery less any payments to subrogated interests. Even when they do not do this, lawyers typically seek to get the subrogated parties to take a reduced payment, which serves as a way of netting more for the client (or as a way of having the subrogated party pay a share of the attorney's fee).

Second, it is not at all uncommon for lawyers to reduce the percentage that they are entitled to under the retainer agreement. In the survey, I asked lawyers if the final fee differed from the fee specified in the retainer. In 18% of the cases for which the respondents obtained some recovery for their clients, the final fee was less than what they could have taken under the terms of the contingency fee agreement. The survey did not include questions as to why these reductions occurred. Follow-up interviews suggested that two primary elements drove the decision to take a lower fee. First, there was a perception on the part of the lawyer that taking a smaller fee would facilitate a settlement. For example, a lawyer might feel that the client would be more likely to go along if the legal fee was cut from 33% to 30% or 25% or even 20%. A large proportion of the re-ductions were from one "round" figure (e.g., 33% or 25%) to another (e.g., 30% or 25% or 20%). Second, some lawyers expressed the view that the lawyer should not walk away with more than the client. In cases in which substantial payments had to be made to subrogated parties, lawyers often reduced their fee to a level that they split with their client what was left after paying the subrogat-ed claims. Occasionally, when the case yields a minimal payoff, the lawyer will simply waive any fees owed. Sometimes a lawyer will waive a fee on a small case as a means of generating good will, particularly if the client is in a good position to refer future potential clients to the lawyer.

VI. MYTH 6: LAWYERS ROUTINELY RECEIVE WINDFALL FEES FROM CONTINGENCY FEE WORK

There is no doubt that on occasion lawyers handling cases on a contingency fee basis obtain very large fees, whether you measure those fees in absolute terms or against the time the lawyer devoted to the case. What is important in considering changes to the types of fees that are allowed is the nature of typical contingency fees. Changes that fail to recognize the day-to-day reality of con-tingency fees are likely to impact the system in ways that deny redress to those harmed by the actions of others. In thinking about returns from contingency fees, the first issue to deal with is measurement. I consider that issue before turning to estimates of returns.

A. MEASUREMENT

The first measure that I employed was the "effective hourly rate" (EHR): the fee received by the lawyer divided by the amount of time the lawyer had to expend to obtain that fee. This measure captures the various elements of the contingencies facing the lawyer:

$$EHR = \text{fee received} / \text{hours}$$

This measure is useful because it is precisely this figure that some critics of contingency fees have attacked, suggesting that lawyers are frequently able to obtain "effective hourly rates of thousands and even tens of thousands of dollars" (Brickman 1989, 1996b). While there are some cases that do earn lawyers' fees that translate into rates of $1,000 or more per hour, we know little or nothing about the frequency of such cases or, more importantly, what the typical effective hourly rate looks like. Economists would argue that the economically rational lawyer would demand to do better, on average, from contingency fees than from hourly (or flat) fees because the contingency fee lawyer is providing additional services to the client which merit compensation (see Posner 1977:448-49; Schwartz and Mitchell 1970:1150-54). However, this type of economic rationality presumes an opportunity cost analysis in which the contingency fee lawyer has alternative uses for his or her time which will provide a known level of compensation; in situations where a lawyer has otherwise unused time, the lawyer may be willing to accept cases where the lawyer expects the compensation to be less than what the lawyer would like to believe is the value of the time involved (see generally Carlin 1962).

One problem with the effective hourly rate measure is that it measures returns at the level of the individual investment, not at the level of what might be called the lawyer's overall portfolio. Short of a complete audit of a lawyer's cases over a period of time, there is no ready way to measure the overall performance, or "yield," on a portfolio. One might be tempted to view the mean effective hourly rate or the median effective hourly rate as a measure of portfolio performance, but that is flawed. Using such a measure would presume that all cases should be treated equally. It is a bit like the situation where a stock investor with $25,000 to invest puts $1,000 into a penny stock and the remaining $24,000 into three stocks costing $8,000 each. If the investor sells all of the stock a year later, receiving $5,000 for the penny stock and $9,000 for each of the mainstream stocks, the total received on the $24,000 is $32,000 for a yield of $8,000 or (33.33%) of the original $24,000. However, the individual returns are 400% on the penny stock and 12.5% on each of the mainstream stocks. If one were to average these returns, the average would be 109%. Which measure makes more sense as an overall indicator of yield on the portfolio?

While I do not have the data needed to look at the portfolio return for individual lawyers, I can obtain estimates of the yield from what I will label the "meta-portfolio." By this I mean returns across sets of cases using information from sets of respondents. This would be something like taking all of the stocks listed on the New York Stock Exchange, the total dividends paid out by the companies for these shares (i.e., multiplying the dividend by number of shares for each company, and adding these up), computing the total capitalization of each company's listed stock (the selling price times the number of shares, and adding these up), and then dividing the total dividends by the total capitalization. The same operation can be done for definable subsets of stocks (e.g., the thirty industrial companies in the Dow Jones Index, banks, technology companies, insurance companies, etc.) as a way of getting an average return for the subset.[38]

In the case of yields for contingency fee portfolios, I compute the meta-portfolio returns by adding up the fees received across the sampled cases and adding up the hours worked; the resulting total fees can be divided by the total hours to produce what I label "mean hourly return" (MHR) which is a measure of the yield for the meta-portfolio:

$$MHR = \sum fees \, / \sum hours$$

As with the stock example, this procedure can be applied to meta-portfolios defined along various dimensions (e.g., unfiled cases, filed cases, tried cases, auto accident cases, etc.). The advantage of the mean hourly return figure is that a very high return for a relatively small case will not dominate the calculation because the computation is effectively weighted to reflect the size of a case.

B. Establishing an Appropriate Basis for Comparison and Other Estimation Issues

To understand and assess the returns lawyers earn for contingency fee work requires some base for comparison. There are many possible comparisons that one could make. For example, what types of effective hourly rates do various types of physicians earn? About the time of the data collection, I had a minor dermatological procedure carried out. The fees by the physician came to $195 for ten to fifteen minutes of his time (and the clinic billed another $112 for the use of its facilities); the hourly rate then was something between $800 and $1,200. More recently, one of my adult children had a three-hour surgical procedure for which the surgeon billed over $12,000, or more than $4,000 per hour.

Alternatively, one might compare to the effective hourly rate charged by a good automotive service operation [these figures are circa 2002]. There the stated hourly rate for the mechanic might be $45; however, the billing is based on the "book time," and a good mechanic can beat the book time by 25% to 50%; to that, one needs to add the markup on the parts that the shop sells to its customers. All together, a good auto repair shop might generate $75 to $100 per mechanic-hour after covering the wholesale value of the replacement parts.

One good potential comparison is to the hourly rates charged by lawyers with comparable training and experience. An examination of the hourly rates reported by insurance defense lawyers in the economic surveys of state bars during the mid-1990s showed that these rates tended to be in the $80- to $100-per-hour range. If anything, this is probably a low-end estimate of comparable hourly rates because insurance companies have sufficient purchasing power that they are able to keep the hourly rates paid to outside counsel at the low end of market rates. In a sense, the insurance companies are able to buy outside legal

---

[38] In fact, there is an investment trust, SPDR Dow Jones Industrial Average ETF Trust, that is intended to produce a yield that mirrors the Dow Jones Industrials (https://www.spdrs.com/product/fund.seam?ticker=DIA).

services wholesale and pay wholesale rather than retail rates (see Silver 1997; Kritzer 2006 [Chapter 6 in this volume]).[39]

Probably the best comparison would be to the hourly rates actually charged by the lawyers who responded to my survey. As it turns out, most of the lawyers (85%) had done at least some work on an hourly basis during the previous year. In my survey, I asked them for the hourly rate quoted for the most recent matter they accepted on an hourly basis. A total of 389 lawyers provided information on that hourly rate; the median hourly rate was $125 per hour and the mean was $124 per hour. This then provides one baseline for comparison in the discussion that follows.

A second baseline comes from the RAND CJRA data. While the focus of my analysis is on the returns from contingency fee work, a much larger proportion of the lawyers who responded to the RAND survey were working on an hourly fee basis. These lawyers were asked to report the hourly rate they were charging for the sample case.[40] Information on hourly rates was requested from those lawyers handling cases on an hourly basis; 41.5% and 43.3% of the respondents provided that information for the 1991 and 1992–93 surveys, respectively. Based on a frequency distribution published by RAND (Kakalik et al. 1996:283), I estimate the mean hourly rates for the two sets of cases (1991 and 1992–93) as $136 per hour and $144 per hour, respectively; the corresponding medians are $125 per hour and $133 per hour, respectively.[41] These figures represent a second baseline for comparison.

C. ESTIMATION ISSUES

In making comparisons between the contingency fee lawyers' fees and the rates charged by lawyers billing on an hourly basis, it is necessary to be careful to exclude from the fees obtained by contingency fee lawyers components that hourly fee lawyers would typically bill separately. Under both fee arrangements, expenses such as copying, travel, witness fees, and filing fees are normally handled as separate billable expenses. In contrast, while most hourly fee lawyers also bill separately for paralegal time, this is an expense absorbed within the typical contingency fee. Consequently, to estimate the effective hourly rate of

---

[39] The above figures may be less comparable that they appear to be at first glance. Insurance defense lawyers bill for everything at the full rate, including things that they might be inclined to discount for clients paying "retail" rather than "wholesale" rates. As one defense lawyer described this to me, for a "retail" client he might decide to discount his charges for a trip to take an out-of-town deposition, particularly if the deposition proved to be unproductive; however, he would not discount this for an insurance company client paying "wholesale" rates. This same lawyer pointed out that with insurance defense work, time is more productive in that relatively little effort needs to be devoted to acquiring business, unlike other areas of practice (particularly plaintiffs' work).

[40] For cases extending over a period of years, the hourly rates may have changed over the course of the case. If more than one lawyer worked on the case, the respondent was directed to provide the average rate.

[41] The RAND survey used a closed-ended question in which the respondents were asked to choose from among the following categories: $75 or less, $76–$125, $126–$175, $176–$250, or more than $250. I estimated the means and medians using standard methods described in Blalock (1979:61-66).

contingency fee lawyers, it is necessary to deduct from the gross fee the equivalent of what would be charged for any paralegal time devoted to the case. A second issue is that many lawyers do not maintain time records for their work on contingency fee cases. Interestingly, the majority of the lawyers who responded to my survey reported that they did keep time records, but only about one-quarter of the respondents actually consulted those records. Even if all of the lawyers did keep time records and did consult those records, my observations of the lawyers at work (two of whom did keep time records) made clear that the nature of contingency fee practice (i.e., constant shifting from one case to another) makes tracking time, at best, an effort at approximation. This same problem may apply to many hourly fee lawyers as well. The result is that it is typically necessary to rely upon estimates of effort; this means that a specific figure for an individual case might involve some significant error, but if the errors are essentially random, they will cancel out across a set of cases. As a check, I do present below an analysis of the effective hourly rates obtained by those lawyers who kept time records and who reported that they referred to those records in completing the survey.

D. Effective Hourly Rates and Mean Hourly Returns in Wisconsin

How do contingency fee lawyers do in terms of the effective hourly rates that they earn from contingency fee legal practice? I was able to compute an effective hourly rate for 878 cases. About 4% of these rates exceeded $1,000, and 1% exceeded $2,000; in three of the cases, the rate exceeded $3,000, with the highest single rate at $4,473. In contrast, in about 11% of the cases the effective hourly rate was negative or zero. One lawyer had an effective hourly rate of −$2,617 and another's rate was −$1,225; these negative figures arise because of the costs of paralegal time spent on the case. Thus, if one uses $1,000 as the "jackpot," lawyers were 2.5 times as likely to be total losers than they were to win the jackpot.[42] A final indicator of the variability is that the standard deviation for effective hourly rate is extremely high ($430) reflecting the fact that the distribution of effective hourly rates is highly skewed toward a small number of very large figures.

One problem with the figures above is that they do not adjust for the characteristics of my sample, where cases handled by high-volume lawyers are underrepresented, cases handled by general practitioners are underrepresented, and cases going to trial are overrepresented. If I weight my sample to try to approximate the population of cases in Wisconsin, the figures shift somewhat: just under 8% of effective hourly rates exceeded $1,000 and about 2% exceeded $2,000; only about 7% were zero or negative. With the weighting, the variability of effective hourly rates is even greater, with a standard deviation of $631.

The variability, and the potential of "jackpots," is not surprising. That is, in one sense, the essence of the contingency fee. However, how do lawyers do in the "typical" case? How we define "typical" becomes important. The presence of

---

[42] If one uses $500 per hour as the "jackpot" figure, then the chances of being complete losers and winning the jackpot are about equal.

a small number of very high hourly rates leads to the result that we will see very different things depending on whether we look at the median (the middle case) or the arithmetic mean (the common average). In fact, as I will argue below, the gap between the median and the mean tells us important things about the nature of contingency fee practice. If I simply take all of the cases in my sample, without considering the lawyer's caseloads or the way I designed the sample (i.e., oversampling cases that went to trial, undersampling general practitioners), I find that the median effective hourly rate is $132, which is almost the same as the mean/median hourly rate that these same lawyers report charging for their hourly fee work; in fact, $125 falls at the 49th percentile. Thus, in about one-half of the cases in my sample, lawyers did better than the median hourly rate for hourly fee work and in about one-half of the cases they did worse.

If this were the end of the story, an economist would probably conclude that contingency fee lawyers were not pursuing an economically rational course of action given that the economist expects the contingency fee lawyer to extract higher fees to reflect the risks the lawyer bears and the financing services the lawyer provides. These higher fees appear in the mean effective hourly rate, which is considerably higher: $242, which corresponds to the 72nd percentile of what the lawyers report charging for their hourly fee work. That is, in the typical case, the contingency fee lawyer does not do better than the median hourly rate, but across a set of cases, the lawyer will do better. This was best expressed by one lawyer I interviewed who had a very high-volume practice. He told me that 60% to 70% of his gross fees came from perhaps a dozen of the cases he closes each year; in most of his cases, he was lucky if he met the costs of running his practice. Eliminating the top 10% of the cases from the sample leaves the mean effective hourly rate for the remaining 90% of the sample at $136, which is virtually the same as the overall median.[43]

One additional refinement is needed. The results need to be adjusted to take into account the sample structure (i.e., the oversampling of tried cases and the undersampling of cases handled by general practitioners and high-volume practitioners). With the appropriate weighting, the median effective hourly rate rises to $167, and the mean goes up to $345, reflecting the fact that it is the upper tail that is pushing up the mean. Eliminating the top 10% of cases reduces the weighted mean effective hourly rate to $181.

What type of overall picture emerges from focusing on the "mean hourly return" (estimated by adding up all of the hours reported on the cases in the sample and all of the fees received, adjusted for the costs of paralegal time, and dividing these two figures)? The result, unadjusted for the sampling structure, is $169. As with the mean effective hourly rate, this estimate is greatly influenced by relatively small numbers of extremely profitable cases. Dropping the most profitable 10% of cases from the sample leaves a 10%-trimmed sample-wide mean hourly return of $104; dropping only the most profitable 5% of cases lends to a mean hourly return of $137, virtually identical to the median. This pattern

---

[43] The median for this "right-trimmed" sample is $113. Because generally the medians are not affected greatly by the trimming, I will not report trimmed medians in the tables or discussion.

reemphasizes the role of a relatively small portion of cases as generating the "profits" across a portfolio of contingency fee cases. Again, the pattern is different if we rely on the weighted data. There, the mean hourly return is $207 and the 10%-trimmed sample-wide mean hourly return is $147.

1. The Record-Keeping Issue

As noted previously, one of the possible problems with the estimates above is that, even though many of the attorneys in the sample did keep time records, only a small fraction of those who had such records referred to their records in responding to the survey. One might expect that attorneys overestimate their time, either remembering it incorrectly or responding strategically in order to make their per-hour return look more acceptable.

When I was first thinking about doing the current study, I had the impression that virtually no lawyers working on a contingency fee basis maintained time records. In conversations with several local attorneys, I became aware that there were at least some lawyers who did keep track of their time while doing work on a contingency fee basis. Drawing upon a list of attorneys who were likely to be in practices where this was true (provided to me by several local persons knowledgeable about various practices), I conducted an unscientific survey where I asked these attorneys to provide me with information on contingency fee cases closed over a recent time period.[44] These lawyers provided me with information on a total of ninety-two cases, with gross fees received ranging from $0 to $910,000 and lawyer effort ranging from 3 hours to 7,000 hours.[45] Dividing net fee by lawyer-hours produced an estimate of the effective hourly rate. The median was $125;[46] the mean effective hourly rate was $189.[47]

In the sample from the systematic Wisconsin survey, there were 151 cases with information on effective hourly rate for which the lawyers reported having consulted their case files where those files contained time records;[48] this is only 17% of the entire sample, and consequently the data need to be treated with caution. For these 151 cases, the median effective hourly rate was $111 and the

---

[44] The time frame varied from lawyer to lawyer, depending upon his or her case volume.

[45] In addition to attorney-hours, I asked each respondent to provide information on paralegal hours. Many cases involved no paralegal time, but others consumed substantial quantities. To adjust for this, I subtracted an estimate of the cost of paralegal time (I assumed that the gross cost was $30 per hour). With this adjustment, two of the cases actually yielded negative net fees; the median adjusted fee was $6,550, with the first and third quartiles at $2,600 and $15,000.

[46] The first and third quartiles are $61 and $250.

[47] The mean hourly return—obtained in the usual way by summing all of the hours reported, summing all of the fees (after adjusting for paralegal time), and dividing these two sums to get the per hour fee—was $160.

[48] The questionnaire did not specifically ask the lawyers whether they consulted their time records; rather, if asked only if they consulted their case files and if those files contained time records.

mean was $170, both somewhat less than the corresponding figures for the overall sample.[49]

Taken together, both the earlier unscientific sample and the subsample from the 1995 survey show that, if anything, the absence of time records may have led to an overestimation of the effective hourly rates that lawyers are earning from contingency fee work, most likely reflecting underestimates of the number of hours the lawyers spent on the cases identified in my survey.[50]

E. EFFECTIVE HOURLY RATES IN FEDERAL CASES: THE CJRA DATA

One obvious question from the analysis above is whether the patterns I report are peculiar to Wisconsin and Wisconsin practitioners. Ideally, one would like to have closely comparable data drawn from a nationwide sample. I do not have such data, but the CJRA evaluation conducted by the RAND Corporation provides information for a sample of cases handled in the federal district courts in the early to mid-1990s.

Before turning to the results from the CJRA data, there are two key differences between the cases represented in the CJRA data and the Wisconsin cases discussed above. First, all of the cases in the CJRA sample were filed in court; unlike the Wisconsin data, there are no cases that were resolved prior to court filing. Second, the federal cases involve substantially higher monetary stakes. Specifically, about 20% of the CJRA cases involved a potential recovery of $50,000 or less compared to 73% of the Wisconsin cases; only 17% of the Wisconsin cases involved potential recoveries of over $100,000 compared to more than 50% of the CJRA cases; and only 5% of the Wisconsin cases involved potential recoveries of over $300,000 compared to over 20% of the CJRA cases.[51]

One additional difference in the data should also be noted. With the Wisconsin data, I was able to adjust the returns to take into account the cost of paralegal time. I can make no such adjustment with the CJRA data, which means that, compared to the Wisconsin data, I am overestimating the returns based on the CJRA data.

Table 12.7 shows the returns contingency fee lawyers report for cases in the two CJRA samples. One striking feature of the table is the generally much higher values shown for 1991 compared to 1992–93. Recall that the 1991 sample is of cases terminated in 1991 while the 1992–93 is of cases filed in 1992 or 1993 and terminated by January 1996; approximately 7% of the cases originally included in the 1992–93 sample had not terminated by January 1996 and were

---

[49] These figures are derived from the unweighted data (i.e., I have made no adjustments for sample structure). Looking separately at the unfiled, filed, and tried cases, the respective medians and means are $146 and $224 (n=51), $109 and $170 (n=61), and $95 and $99 (n=39).

[50] Such an underestimate would be consistent with what I was told by lawyers working on an hourly basis about the difficulty of capturing the hours they spent on various matters, and by comments by a senior lawyer who described the surprise that occurred when his firm first started keeping systematic time records and they discovered they were spending a lot more time on matters than they thought was the case (Kritzer 2006:2061 [Chapter 6 in this volume]).

[51] These comparisons are rough because the two surveys measured stakes using different questions.

Table 12.7: Returns from Contingency Fee Cases: CJRA Data

	Mean EHR[a]	Median EHR	Mean Hourly Return	10%- Trimmed Mean EHR	10%- Trimmed Mean Hourly Return
Federal cases, 1991	$425	$127	$215	$209	$160
Federal cases, 1992–93	$236	$108	$157	$125	$110

[a]EHR = Effective Hourly Rate

excluded from the final surveys. One possible explanation for the difference between the two samples is that the high-return cases are those that are in the last 7% of cases terminated. However, this does not completely explain the difference in results for the two samples; excluding the slowest 7% of cases from the 1991 sample does not bring the figures for that sample into line with the figures for the 1992–93 sample. In the following discussion I reference both figures, showing the lower 1992–93 figures in parentheses.

Overall, I assess the patterns for the CJRA data as quite consistent with the Wisconsin data. Table 12.8 shows the comparison across the samples. In terms of overall level, the median effective hourly rate, mean effective hourly rate, and mean hourly return for the CJRA data are $127 ($108), $425 ($236), and $215 ($157). If one compares these to the overall (weighted) figures for Wisconsin— $167, $365, and $207 for the three statistics respectively—the differences cut both ways, with Wisconsin higher for some and the CJRA data (from the 1991 sample) higher for others. If one limits the comparison to the Wisconsin cases with $50,000 or more at stake, the Wisconsin data show considerably higher returns than do the federal cases from around the country: $285, $239, and $261. One can further refine the comparison by limiting the Wisconsin cases to those that were filed in court. For this subset of cases, the median effective hourly rate, mean effective hourly rate, and mean hourly return for Wisconsin are $155, $281, and $218; further limiting this subset to only those cases involving $50,000 or more creates comparable figures of $310, $497, and $274, respectively. Table 12.8 also shows figures for the federal cases involving $50,000 or more (in about 20% of the federal cases, the respondents report stakes as $50,000 or less);[52] this does not affect the inferences to be drawn from the patterns in the data. The general conclusion from this overall analysis is that the figures from the Wisconsin survey are not significantly out of line with patterns that one would expect to find from national studies.[53]

---

[52] Stakes are not measured in the same way in the two surveys, so the controls for amount at stake are only approximate.

[53] One other partial comparison is possible. The appendix to Stock's report of the survey of ATLA members (Stock 1992) includes some summary data from the survey. Specifically, the respondents were asked about their "last contingency fee case, whether successful or not." Included among the questions were the fee received and the hours invested; the means of the

Table 12.8: Returns from Contingency Fee Cases:
Wisconsin and CJRA Compared

	Mean EHR[a]	Median EHR	Mean Hourly Return	10%-Trimmed Mean EHR	10%-Trimmed Mean Hourly Return
Federal cases, 1991	$425	$127	$215	$209	$160
without cases involving less than $50,000	$506	$147	$225	$213	$174
Federal cases, 1992–93	$236	$108	$157	$125	$110
without cases involving less than $50,000	$262	$120	$163	$135	$118
All Wisconsin cases	$365	$167	$207	$184	$147
without cases involving less than $50,000	$739	$285	$261	$196	$162
All Wisconsin cases that were filed in court	$281	$155	$218	$182	$156
without cases involving less than $50,000	$497	$310	$274	$237	$181

[a]EHR = Effective Hourly Rate

F. COMMENTS: THE RETURNS FROM CONTINGENCY FEE WORK

Clearly, there are profits to be made from contingency fee work. While it is the top 10% of cases that tend to produce the most significant profits, the typical contingency fee practitioner can expect even the remaining 90% of cases to produce over a portfolio of cases a fee premium amounting to 25% to 30% over what hourly fee work generates. Contingency fee work can be very lucrative, particularly for those lawyers who develop expertise and processes for handling large numbers of cases. The high profitability comes from locating a small segment of the cases that produce extremely good returns on the lawyer's investment of time. Some lawyers are able to "cherry pick" the good cases; others handle large volumes of cases in order to find the occasional very profitable case. Relatively few lawyers ever see "the really big one." One of the lawyers I observed had been doing plaintiffs' contingency fee work for twenty

---

responses to these two questions are $65,700 and 279.4 respectively. This yields a mean hourly return of $235.

years, had a very successful practice, and had never collected a fee of over $100,000 on a case.[54]

VII. MYTH 7: THE INTERESTS OF CONTINGENCY FEE LAWYERS AND THEIR CLIENTS ROUTINELY DIVERGE

A frequent critique of contingency fees is that the interests of lawyers and clients may diverge (Clermont and Currivan 1978; Danzon 1983; Gravelle and Waterson 1993; Hay 1996a, 1997; Johnson 1980–81; MacKinnon 1964; Miller 1987; Rickman 1994; Rosenthal 1974; Rubinfeld and Scotchmer 1993; Schwartz and Mitchell 1970). Lawyers may want to settle cases too quickly and for lower amounts than a client might prefer, or lawyers may prefer to accept higher risk, taking a case to trial in the hopes of a large verdict while the client would prefer to settle and be assured of compensation. A simple example makes it clear how the former situation might happen. A lawyer handling a case with a maximum payment of $25,000 comes out better by settling the case for $10,000 after ten or twenty hours of work (investigating the claim, collecting documentation, drafting a demand letter, and negotiating a settlement) than by taking the case to trial and winning $25,000 after 100 or 150 hours of work. With the settlement, a lawyer receiving a 25% fee earns $125 to $250 per hour; with the trial, even with a 33% fee, the lawyer earns only $55 to $83 per hour.

The problem arises for two reasons. First, for modest cases, the rational client paying on an hourly fee basis will make very different choices than the rational client paying on a percentage basis. The hourly fee client would want to limit the amount of time the lawyer put into the case and would probably opt to accept a lower gross settlement because the client will obtain a higher net. The percentage fee client does not care about what it costs in terms of lawyer-hours to obtain a result; all the client cares about is maximizing recovery (discounting for risk preference).[55]

The second source of the problem of conflict arises because the client is not well situated to evaluate whether a settlement offer is a good one. How does the client assess an offer? A client could try to locate jury verdict reporters or literature on case valuation and use this to come to an independent estimate of the case value. Alternately, a client could pay another lawyer a fee specifically to evaluate a settlement offer. However, such things virtually never happen. Few clients are willing to bear the expense of an independent evaluation, and relying on published sources would at best provide a sense of the range of values into which the client's case probably falls. Moreover, lawyers have a variety of ways of manipulating clients' expectations and assessments (Kritzer 1998a).

---

[54] A conversation with this lawyer more than five years after I had observed in his practice revealed that the "big one" had finally come in, and he had settled a case that generated a fee in excess of $250,000.

[55] It is also important to note that using an hourly fee arrangement does not eliminate the conflict of interest between lawyer and client, it only changes the nature of that conflict (see Johnson 1980–81:575-82).

It is undoubtedly true that most lawyers handling cases on a contingency fee basis are extremely mindful of their own interests as they negotiate settlements. However, this does not mean they are not very concerned about the interests of their clients.[56] The key here is that for the lawyer, it is not the outcome of a single case that typically matters but the outcomes across the set of cases. This means that the lawyer has to be concerned not only about his or her return from current cases but of the prospect of getting future cases.

One way to think about this is that the lawyer must take into consideration the entire set of cases currently in the lawyer's portfolio and what implications a specific case might have both for the current portfolio and for cases that might come into the portfolio later. Consequently, lawyers do not always handle a given case in the manner one would predict of someone who was seeking to profit-maximize on a case-by-case basis. The lawyer must consider both the short-term payoffs from current cases and the long-term reputational issues, both with regard to future clients and future opponents. It was extremely clear during my observation that the three lawyers I observed are very cognizant of their reputations, and the issue of reputation came up repeatedly in my subsequent interviews.

The typical view is that a lawyer must be recognized as someone who would be willing and able to take cases to trial because insurance adjusters and defense attorneys are less inclined to make top-dollar settlement offers to a lawyer with a reputation for wanting to settle quickly. The best way to get quick, good settlements is to have a reputation for being an aggressive trial lawyer— aggressive both at trial and in negotiation. Interestingly, the lawyers who have reputations for being most aggressive in moving toward trial may also be the lawyers who are most able to turn over cases quickly once a client's medical situation has become clear; if an insurer knows that a lawyer is moving to get a case ready for trial, the insurer has an incentive to get the case settled.

But reputational issues are not just important for settling cases. They are also important for getting clients. First, a reputation for being an effective negotiator and litigator is crucial to obtaining referrals from other lawyers. This is most obvious when a referring lawyer will receive a referral fee; the referring lawyer wants to maximize the referral fee, and this will lead the referrer to consider the receiving lawyer's reputation (see Hay 1996b).[57] Even when no referral fee is paid, from my observation, lawyers making such referrals are mindful of the expertise and success of the lawyers to whom they make referrals.

Second, the other major source of clients for most contingency fee lawyers is satisfied clients who will refer friends, family members, or coworkers who in the future need a lawyer, or even come back themselves with a new case. It is not helpful to a lawyer's long-term financial interest to have clients later realize that a coworker or neighbor who had a similar injury received a much

---

[56] In this discussion, I focus only on economic incentives. The behavior of lawyers can also be constrained by professional norms and formal rules of conduct.

[57] One way to think about the referring lawyer is as a sophisticated client who is able to make a good assessment of the worth of a case. This provides strong motivations for lawyers wanting referrals from other lawyers to insure that they obtain good results.

larger settlement check.[58] How is this the case for former contingency fee clients who do not have sophisticated knowledge of what cases are worth? Very simply, clients talk about their experiences and compare their experiences with those of their friends. A client who obtained a settlement of $2,000 or $3,000 for a serious injury such as a broken leg is likely to hear things from others that suggest that the injury was substantially undercompensated. Contingency fee lawyers want their clients to leave satisfied with the result the lawyer obtained on their behalf; more importantly, the lawyers want the clients to stay satisfied. A lawyer who settles cases too cheaply may have trouble maintaining the reputation necessary to create the flow of potential clients that is in the lawyer's long-term interest.

The emphasis on satisfied clients as a source of referrals was very evident at one of the practices where I observed. The lawyer always wanted to be present when the client picked up the settlement check. The typical routine was for the lawyer to hand the client the check and his business card and say to the client something like, "Hopefully, you won't need me again. If you know anyone who does [need me], please send them in."[59] Lawyers want their clients not only to leave the case satisfied but also to stay satisfied as they discuss their experiences with family, friends, neighbors, and coworkers.

Particularly those lawyers who handle the most routine cases want clients to be satisfied because a surprising number of clients may be repeaters. In one of the practices where I observed, one of the partners estimated that 10% to 15% of the firm's clients are repeaters (consistent with the broader patterns described above). He emphasized that some of his firm's practices with regards to setting the final fee are geared specifically to making sure that clients leave satisfied; in particular, he believes that it is not in the firm's long-term interest to take a fee that exceeds the net to the client, even though there are no ethical strictures against such fees and the firm's contingency fee retainer agreement would clearly permit such fees in some circumstances (e.g., when a large subrogation claim had to be paid from the recovery). The role of reputation through word-of-mouth and repeat clients is important for a successful practice, even for practices that aggressively seek clients through media or direct mail advertising. The head of a firm that makes extensive use of direct mail to auto accident victims told me that 80% of his firm's cases come from repeat clients and prior client referrals; only 15% to 20% of the cases come from direct mail.

The result of all of these considerations is that lawyers do not simply manipulate clients to maximize their own short-term economic benefits. Lawyers

---

[58] A good reputation among former clients can reflect things in addition to the recovery: responding well to client contacts (i.e., returning telephone calls), keeping the client abreast of developments, and interacting positively and effectively with the client. See Kritzer (2004b: 219-52) for a discussion of the various roles of reputation for contingency fee practitioners.

[59] The desire to encourage clients to refer others was evident in other ways in this lawyer's practice. First, the lawyer looked much more carefully at potential cases that came as referrals than as cold calls; he was more likely to take a marginal case on a referral because he wanted to encourage the referrer to refer additional potential clients. Second, if a past client had referred others, the lawyer was willing to handle matters for that referrer that he would not otherwise handle, and even to do so without charging any fee at all for a very small matter.

regularly accept fee reductions and push cases beyond the point that their own immediate economic interest would suggest was rational. Furthermore, the lawyers are extremely attentive to the way that their clients see what has been accomplished on their behalf.

CONCLUSION

Myths and misinformation abound in connection with the American contingency fee. Many of the myths contain elements of reality, but the reality is usually more complex and nuanced than the myths would lead one to expect.

Central to the reality of the contingency fee is that the repeat-player contingency fee attorney is able to act as a risk-neutral agent on behalf of the client, essentially providing a kind of insurance against the range of contingencies involved in the case. The most important of these contingencies concern not whether the lawyer will be paid, but rather how much the lawyer will be paid and how much time and other resources the lawyer will have to invest to obtain that fee. The latter uncertainty has relatively little to do with the nature of the case—or even the clarity of the case—but rather with the actions of the opposing side.

My goal in this analysis has not been to show that contingency fees always produce reasonable returns to lawyers. Rather, it seeks to provide a more accurate portrait of the realities of contingency fees in typical cases. This is important because proposals for change do not try to single out in any way the small subset of cases where returns are extremely high—"excessive" or "windfall," in the words of advocates of reform. The types of proposals advanced would affect contingency fee practice in general without regard for whether the kinds of cases impacted are the types that raise problems, and without regard for the realities of contingency fee practice.

One proposal advanced during the 1990s would have limited the fees that could be collected for "early" settlements to 10% of the damages recovered up to $100,000 and 5% of any amounts over $100,000 (see Brickman et al. 1994). An early settlement offer is any offer made within sixty days from receipt of a demand for settlement from a plaintiff's counsel. The proposal failed to take into account that a significant proportion of cases handled on a contingency basis are quite small. Data collected from automobile claims closed in 1997 show that the median case involving a represented claimant produced a bodily injury payout of $7,500; 25% of the cases involved a payout of $4,000 or less.[60] Assuming an hourly rate of $125 and a 10% cap, the median case could never cover more than six hours of a lawyer's opportunity cost. Moreover, such proposals reflect a lack of understanding of what representation of injured parties entails. From my observation, the lawyers move reasonably promptly to settle routine cases as soon as the client's medical condition has reached a suitable state; through that time, the lawyer has been monitoring the client's medical situation, collecting

---

[60] This figure is based on my own analysis of data collected by the Insurance Research Council as part of its series of periodic surveys of closed automobile injury claims; for details on this survey, see Insurance Research Council (1999).

documentation related to expenses and other losses, and counseling the client to be sure that there is documentation and that the client has obtained appropriate treatment (see Chapter 5 in this volume). By the time the case is ripe for settlement, the lawyer will have put in a nontrivial amount of time. The time required to prepare a demand letter with the relevant documentation of loss and to negotiate the actual settlement will, for a significant proportion of cases, represent a time investment worth considerably more than 10% of the recovery.

While some might assert that insurers would have settled the case without the lawyer's involvement for more than the claimant will net after paying a lawyer's fee, I find the claim highly dubious. Insurers may happily pay a claimant based on the expenses the claimant documents, but the typical claimant does not know what is compensable, nor does he or she know how to document all the expenses that a lawyer would present to an insurer (for many cases, this is in fact the lawyer's most important contribution). Insurance claims adjusters are not paid to help personal injury claimants identify all compensable elements of their claims; they are paid to dispose of claims quickly and economically, and this means a claims adjuster will not tell a claimant to wait to settle in case the injury does not fully heal. An adjuster will also not tell a claimant when the claimant has overlooked some obvious (to the adjuster) element of damages. Turning again to the data on closed automobile accident injury claims, I isolated all cases in which the most serious injury was a fracture of a weight-bearing bone. There is no obvious reason to assume that there are systematic differences in these cases based on whether there was or was not attorney representation. However, with lawyer representation, the insurer paid the limits of the policy in significantly more cases: 43% compared to only 31% when there was no lawyer representation ($\chi^2 = 7.297$, $p = 0.026$).

If lawyers are in fact systematically overcompensated in personal injury cases, the alternative to restricting contingency fees is to modify the market for representation of personal injury claimants. Insurance claims adjusters handle claims just fine for insurance companies. Why should there not be "plaintiffs' claims adjusters" available to represent injured parties in negotiating settlements?[61] There are independent adjusters who work with persons and companies who have sustained a casualty loss in assessing the amount of that loss; these adjusters also negotiate on behalf of their clients with the casualty insurer. Is there any reason to suppose that an individual with significant experience as a claims adjuster handling personal injury claims would not be able to document and present a claim on behalf of clients? The plaintiffs' bar would argue that nonlawyers would not be able to bring suit if an insurer balked at making a reasonable settlement; in such cases, a lawyer could be hired to handle the case. More importantly, if there are cases that do not merit paying a lawyer a one-third contingency fee because they can be easily settled, then such cases could be handled by nonlawyers; nonlawyers who handled only such cases would be able to charge fees considerably lower than those charged by lawyers.

---

[61] The equivalent of the plaintiffs' claims adjuster does exist in England (Blackwell 2000; Jacob et al. 1996:142).

In other words, if the real goal is to protect the injured parties from greedy, overcharging lawyers, then the route is not to restrict contingency fees. Rather, the route is to let the market find the appropriate level for such fees by removing artificial controls that allow lawyers to allegedly overcharge in a clearly identifiable subset of cases.

PART IV

LAWYERS' LEGAL PRACTICE
IN THE 21st CENTURY

13

FROM LITIGATORS OF ORDINARY CASES TO LITIGATORS OF EXTRAORDINARY CASES: STRATIFICATION OF THE PLAINTIFFS' BAR IN THE 21st CENTURY[1]

INTRODUCTION

The legal profession is a popular icon in American and other western cultures. As such, it is often associated with what is wrong or problematic about society. Political leaders and commentators who draw on the profession's iconic value typically present the profession as a unitary body that stands in opposition to many of the interests of the broader society. So, for example, the profession is often attacked for simply defending the interests of lawyers at the cost of the larger society. In his 2000 campaign for the presidency of the United States, George W. Bush took aim at the profession as clearly stated in the Republican Party Platform:

> Reform of the legal profession is an essential part of court reform. Today's litigation practices make a mockery of justice, hinder our country's competitiveness in the world market and, far worse, erode the public's trust in the entire judicial process. ...
>
> Avarice among many plaintiffs' lawyers has clogged our civil courts, drastically changed the practice of medicine, and costs American companies and consumers more than $150 billion a year. ...
>
> We fully support the role of the courts in vindicating the rights of individuals and organizations, but we want to require higher standards for trial lawyers within federal jurisdiction, much as Governor Bush has already done in Texas—and as we encourage other States to do within their own legal codes. To achieve that goal, we will

[1] This chapter originally appeared in the *DePaul Law Review* 51 (2001), 219-40. It is a revision of a paper that was prepared for the Seventh Annual Clifford Symposium on Tort Law and Social Policy, DePaul University College of Law, April 5–6, 2001; an expanded version, including more extensive material on developments in England, was presented at the W.G. Hart Workshop at the Institute for Advanced Legal Studies, London, June 26–28, 2001 (which was subsequently published in the *International Journal of the Legal Profession* 8 [2001], 225-50). I would like to thank John Heinz and Rebecca Sandefur of the American Bar Foundation for making available some unpublished materials from the 1995 survey of the Chicago Bar. I would particularly like to thank Rebecca Sandefur for running some statistical analyses of those data. The article has been reformatted to become this chapter; some references have been updated and some citations have been omitted.

strengthen the federal rules of civil procedure to increase penalties for frivolous suits and impose a "Three Strikes, You're Out" rule on attorneys who repeatedly file such suits. ...

To protect clients against unscrupulous lawyers, we will enact a Clients' Bill of Rights for all federal courts, requiring attorneys to disclose both the range of their fees and their ethical obligation to charge reasonable fees and allowing those fees to be challenged in federal courts. Because private lawyers should not unreasonably profit at public expense, we will prohibit federal agencies from paying contingency fees and encourage states to do so as well. Even more important, we will require attorneys to return to the people any excessive fees they gain under contract to States or municipalities.[2]

While the target was often plaintiffs' lawyers, these attacks typically referred to lawyers, rather than to "trial" lawyers.[3] Similarly, Marc Galanter's analysis of lawyer jokes and humor often places lawyers in particular settings, but the jokes seldom recognize differences among lawyers (Galanter 1998b:830; see also Galanter 2005).

While the public does not typically draw a lot of distinctions among groups within the legal profession, other than occasional distinctions between "my" lawyer who is trying to help me versus the "other guy's" lawyer who is trying to screw me,[4] scholars have long recognized that the legal profession is far from a politically or economically united interest. Recognized lines of stratification include social class and ethnic origins, as well as clientele.

This essay suggests that it is time to recognize a new line of stratification, one that exists within what is commonly labeled the "plaintiffs' bar." While there have always been important lines of differentiation among those lawyers who handle personal injury claims for injury victims, changes in the nature of some areas of personal injury litigation, epitomized by the spectacular success of litigation targeting tobacco companies, have created very significant lines of cleavage that either did not previously exist or that could be submerged within a broader common interest of the plaintiffs' bar. Thus, where in the past prominent lawyers such as Joe Jamail or Phil Corboy might be admired for their

---

[2] Republican National Committee, Republican Platform available at http://www.rnc.org/GOPInfo/Platform/2000platform7 (last visited September 3, 2001).

[3] While campaigning for the presidency in 1992, George H.W. Bush singled out the plaintiffs' bar:

> You know I'm not anti-lawyer, but let me tell you something. We spend up to $200 billion every year on direct costs to lawyers. Japan doesn't spend this; Germany doesn't. And I want to take on those ambulance chasers and reform our lawsuit-happy legal system. You see, when doctors are afraid to practice, when people are afraid to help somebody along the highway, when coaches are afraid to coach Little League, my message is this: As a nation, we must sue each other less and care for each other more.

George H.W. Bush, Remarks to the Community in Holland, Michigan (October 12, 1992) available at http://www.bushlibrary.tamu.edu/papers/l1992/92101203.html (last visited August 31, 2001).

[4] Some people are just plain "anti-lawyer"; see, for example, the website of the "Anti-Lawyer Party" at http://wevote.com/pages/antilaw.html (last visited August 31, 2001).

success in litigating high profile and high fee cases,[5] in recent years, lawyers such as Stanley Chesley, Joe Rice, Walter Gauthier, Robert Habush, Michael Ciresi, and John O'Quinn have become controversial figures within the plaintiffs' bar, as well as beyond it.

I. CLEAVAGE AND STRATIFICATION WITHIN THE LEGAL PROFESSION

As noted above, while much of the public may view the legal profession as a unitary group, thoughtful observers and scholars have long recognized that the profession is highly fractured. In fact, the legal profession as a single entity is a relatively recent development. Within England, there is still a formal distinction between solicitors and barristers (Abel-Smith and Stevens 1967:14-17). Those two branches of the profession emerged through an evolutionary process of merger among a wide variety of specialized groups, including attorneys, scriviners, conveyancers, King's Counsel, serjeants-at-law, and proctors, as well as barristers and solicitors. While merger and evolution within the English legal profession left only the two branches at the beginning of the nineteenth century,[6] solicitors and barristers remained highly distinct in terms of both class origins and training. The solicitor's branch was a means of attaining professional status for the sons of the merchant and middle class, largely through a system of apprenticeship. In contrast, the barrister's branch was an occupational outlet for the sons of the gentry (particularly second and later sons who would not inherit the family estate). Such preparation typically involved first obtaining a classical education through "public" schools and degrees from elite universities, followed by a period of gentlemanly association at the Inns of Court where the barristers-to-be attended dinners to listen to barristers tell them about the art of advocacy. While today, entry into both branches is typically through a university education in law (Abel 1988b:263-66),[7] elements of these distinctions, particularly the class-related aspects, remain.

A. TRADITIONAL APPROACHES

In the United States, class and ethnicity have been a central line of cleavage within the profession at least since the latter part of the nineteenth century. In the first fifty to seventy-five years after independence from England, the legal profession was represented by the image of lawyers like Abraham Lincoln who learned the law through personal study and apprenticeship.[8] By the latter part of

---

[5] Jamail received a reported $300 million or so from his representation of Pennzoil in its suit against Texaco (Blum 1988).

[6] Actually, there is a small, relatively unique third profession, scrivener-notaries (see Shaw 2000). [By 2014 additional professions have emerged including legal executives and costs specialists.]

[7] [By 2014 there was some evidence that the apprenticeship route of entry was starting to re-appear.]

[8] This is not to say that the public perception of lawyers was necessarily positive. One aspect of the Jacksonian period was strong opposition to a legal profession as contrary to democratic principles as envisioned by the Jacksonians (see Hurst 1950:251; Pound 1953:236-39).

the century, the growth of the corporation and the demands for legal services it created led to growing distinctions between lawyers who served the corporate interests and those who worked on behalf of individuals and small businesses. This coincided with the growth of university-based legal education, the organization of the American Bar Association, and pressures to regularize legal training and control entry into the profession. During this period, one saw developments such as the case-method of legal education and the beginnings of the "Cravath" system for corporate law firms. In some ways, the growing rift within the profession between those lawyers who championed the interests of workers and the common man and those who derived their income from corporations was epitomized by the controversy over Louis Brandeis's nomination to become the first Jewish person to sit on the United States Supreme Court. Brandeis represented the rise of the immigrant class, although, in fact, Brandeis was from a German-Jewish family that immigrated to the United States before the Civil War (Strum 1984:1-4). Until well after World War II, it was common to explicitly exclude Jews (and other undesirables) from the "white shoe" corporate firms (Galanter and Palay 1992:39; Smigel 1964:44). Even in the late twentieth century and the beginning of the twenty-first century, these firms are much more likely to draw from the ranks of white Anglo-Saxon Protestants than is the profession as a whole (Heinz and Laumann 1982:136).[9]

The most extensive research on stratification in the American legal profession is the work of John Heinz, Edward Laumann, and Robert Nelson. Heinz and Laumann's seminal study of the Chicago bar as of 1975 showed that among lawyers one could identify two distinct "hemispheres," one oriented toward serving large corporate clients (and their wealthy owners and executives) and one oriented to "personal services" (or "personal plight"), including the needs of small family businesses (Heinz and Laumann 1982:127-39).[10] Lawyers in the corporate-services hemisphere were more likely to come from "establishment" backgrounds, while those in the personal services sector came more from ethnic, working class, and lower middle class backgrounds. The former were likely to have attended elite or near-elite law schools, while the latter were likely to have attended state university law schools or law schools associated with other local universities. A replication of the 1975 study, twenty years later, showed that the basic cleavage persisted (Heinz et al. 1998:770-74). Perhaps the most important change was that the corporate hemisphere is consuming an increasing share of legal effort. Where corporate services comprised just over half of legal effort in 1975; by 1995, it consumed about two-thirds of legal effort.

A second change noted by Heinz and his colleagues relates to another line of distinction among lawyers, fields of specialization. The Cravath system marked the beginning of specialization within the American bar as we have come to know it today. Heinz and his colleagues report that substantive fields were more

---

[9] In a later study Heinz et al. (2005:60-62) found that the amount of cleavage along "ethno-religious" lines declined between 1975 and 1995 within the Chicago bar, but had by no means disappeared.

[10] Observers of the profession had noted this cleavage early in the twentieth century (see Reed 1921:237-39).

distinct in the 1990s than they were in the 1970s, an indicator of ever increasing substantive specialization among lawyers.[11] There is a fairly clear pecking order among specializations with fields most closely linked to work for large corporations (securities, tax, anti-trust, patents) at the top and fields like divorce and landlord-tenant at the bottom (Heinz and Laumann 1982:91; Sandefur 2001: 386-87).

In an analysis of the 1995 Chicago data, Sandefur and Heinz suggest that the market for legal services is becoming more competitive and may be moving toward a "winner-take-all" market (Sandefur and Heinz 1999). Winner-take-all markets have two distinguishing characteristics: high rewards are highly concentrated in the hands of a relatively small group of top performers, and those rewards are distributed on the basis of relative, as well as absolute, performance. Sandefur and Heinz presented evidence showing a huge difference in incomes between the top 10% of performers (mean income $537,000) and the middle 10% (mean income $82,000). Drawing on national census data to compare 1970 and 1990, they reported that the skew (measured as the ratio of the mean to the median) is increasing, going from 1.13 to 1.28; for their own Chicago bar data, the corresponding ratio for 1995 is 1.56. Sandefur and Heinz also reported that the impact of income on lawyers' satisfaction with their income is linked to market position with those lawyers working in settings with clear pathways of advancement, such as partnership in a corporate law firm, less affected by current income than those in less predictable settings (i.e., practices focused largely on personal services). Using logistic regression, the authors found that the odds of being satisfied or very satisfied with income is multiplied by 1.11 for lawyers in "high business fields" for each additional $10,000 of income, 1.13 for lawyers in "middle business fields," and 1.20 for lawyers in "low business fields."[12] Using these results, they estimated that 42% of those making $45,000 while working in a "high business field" are satisfied or very satisfied with their incomes, compared to only 32% of those in "low business fields"; for those making $162,500, 71% and 80% respectively are satisfied or very satisfied in "high" and "low" business fields. The authors found an even larger gap in looking at a second question dealing with the lawyers' satisfaction concerning their chances of advancement; on this question, there is relatively little variation dependent on income for lawyers in practices with high or middling business content (spread from 48% satisfied to 60% satisfied), but quite substantial variation for lawyers in practices in "low business fields" (spread from 39% satisfied to 80% satisfied).

---

[11] For lawyers with substantial practice in some areas, the substantive area is the primary basis of distinction rather than client base. In those areas, it is common for lawyers to have both business and nonbusiness clients, although the business clients may be of the family business variety.

[12] These multipliers were obtained by exponentiating the logistic regression coefficients reported by the authors in their Table 6.

B. TRADITIONAL PERSPECTIVES ON STRATIFICATION IN THE PLAINTIFFS' BAR

While most research on stratification in the legal profession has distinguished among lawyers from different types of backgrounds or serving different types of clients, a number of scholars have recognized that there are distinctions to be drawn within the plaintiffs' bar itself. While not specifically focused on the plaintiffs' bar per se, Jerome Carlin's (1962:71-91) study of solo practitioners devoted significant attention to lawyers handling personal injury claims. Carlin distinguishes between what he calls the "lower" and "upper" segments of the solo bar handling personal injury cases. Lawyers in the lower segment drew their clients largely from a neighborhood or ethnic base and were most likely to handle personal injury cases in the context of a general practice; lawyers in this lower segment were very concerned about competition for clients. In contrast, the "upper" segments of the solo personal injury bar tended to be specialists who frequently drew clients through "suppliers," including referrals from other lawyers; these lawyers were much less concerned about competition for clients. Ross's study (1980:73-78) of the settlement of automobile accident claims also found a clear distinction between lawyers who handled these cases as part of a general practice and those who specialized in negligence cases. In his analysis of claims outcomes, Ross found that specialists, which he defined in terms of membership in the predecessor to the Association of Trial Lawyers of America [now the American Association for Justice], obtained recoveries that on average were considerably higher than those obtained by other lawyers. Rosenthal, in his study of representation in personal injury claims (1974:134), again found specialists to be more likely (67%) to obtain a "good" result than non-specialists (47%). The difference between specialists and non-specialists is by no means limited to the American context, as clearly shown by Genn's study of personal injury claims in England (1988).[13]

More recent studies of the plaintiffs' bar have emphasized the role of "markets" and link markets to specialization. During the period that Carlin, Ross, and Rosenthal were writing, the market for legal representation for injured persons was essentially local. While there were some occasional exceptions, they typically came through networks of lawyer referrals for fairly rare and high profile cases, such as those arising out of air crash disasters. Advertising and modern communication has changed that. Today, markets for legal services are bounded largely by limitations on legal practice, such as admission to state bars. In-state regional or statewide marketing by plaintiffs' lawyers is now commonplace. Furthermore, certain types of plaintiffs' litigation, most prominently medical malpractice, have come to require increasing levels of substantive expertise combined with significant resources for experts and trial preparation. The result is that the market for personal injury representation is now tiered

---

[13] I should note, however, that my own analysis of plaintiffs' success in cases actually filed in court, albeit in a study not limited to personal injury cases or personal plight cases, did not show any impact of lawyer specialization or lawyer experience; specialization did improve success from the viewpoint of the contingency fee lawyer (Kritzer 1990:135). However, in another study, which did include contingent fee lawyers in one setting, I did find that specialization was a very significant factor in effectiveness (1998b:170-86).

along several dimensions: geography, size of claim, and substantive expertise. This is most clearly explicated in Van Hoy's study of the plaintiffs' bar in Indiana; Van Hoy (1999:357-62) distinguished among lawyers who have a local versus statewide client base, lawyers who handle special areas such as medical malpractice and products liability who tend to be statewide in their practices, and lawyers who limit their practices to "significant" injuries, which he defined as those involving damages of $15,000 or more, versus those whose practices are primarily composed of "moderate-value injuries." While moderate-value, personal injury practices tend to be local in their geographic markets, this is by no means necessarily the case, particularly for high volume firms that rely on extensive advertising. Many of the patterns reported by Van Hoy are also described by Daniels and Martin (1999:380-82; 2015) in their study of the Texas plaintiffs' bar.

II. The Changed Nature of the Plaintiffs' Bar

The dimensions of market, specialization, and substantial versus moderate injuries only begin to capture the nature of the stratification that has emerged in the plaintiffs' bar during the 1990s. While the vast majority of claims handled by lawyers are well below six figures, in recent years we have seen cases that can involve nine, ten, or eleven, or in the case of the tobacco litigation, twelve figures: $206,000,000,000 in the national tobacco settlement (Meir 1998) or $145,000,000,000 in punitive damages awarded by a jury in a Florida class action jury verdict (Fisk 2001b). While these are extreme, they do epitomize the gap that has developed between routine and even very significant litigation, such as "bad baby" medical malpractice cases, and extraordinary cases. What is significant here is that the biggest are getting so big as to represent a different world entirely, different even from what Deborah Hensler (1993:141) has characterized in terms of multiple worlds of tort litigation; rather than "multiple worlds" of litigation, perhaps we need to start thinking about "multiple solar systems" or "multiple universes."

In its 2001 survey of the largest jury verdicts for the year 2000, the *National Law Journal* listed sixteen verdicts, not including the Florida tobacco case, ranging from a low of $32.9 million to $122.59 million, with an average of $63 million (Fisk 2001a). Data reported by Jury Verdict Research (JVR) showed that about 12% of personal injury verdicts exceed $1 million, and that percentage is growing; JVR also found that the median personal injury verdict has been stable over the last seven years at $50,000 (Harris 2001). This is particularly noteworthy given that JVR's database tends to be slanted toward larger cases because of its manner of data collection.[14] Research has shown clearly that verdicts reported in the press are skewed toward the larger cases (Bailis and MacCoun 1996:66; Chase 1995:772-74); most people realize that typical jury verdicts

---

[14] A study of jury verdicts in the 75 largest counties in the United States for 1996 found the median verdict in tort cases to be $31,000, and that only 5.8% of the tort verdicts exceeded $1 million (DeFrances and Litras 1999). These figures actually constitute a decline from 1992, when the comparable figures for the same counties were $51,000 and 7.8% (DeFrances et al. 1995).

are in the thousands rather than the millions (Kritzer 2001c). However, the visibility of large, and now occasionally astronomical, verdicts highlights that there is something different going on in at least some types of litigation.

A. PATTERNS OF CHANGE

One of the first indicators that change in structure of the plaintiffs' bar is evident is the growth of bureaucratic structures in a small segment of the bar. This growth is actually happening at both the bottom and the top of the case universe. At the bottom, there are now firms designed specifically to process high volumes of low value cases. Van Hoy (1999:345) describes one such firm in Indiana:

> Greg operates a mass advertising, mass production personal injury practice that is focused almost completely on the firm's home market. The firm employs "about seven secretaries that we train ourselves" who screen the 75-100 calls the firm receives each day from the local television, radio, and telephone book advertising. The secretaries, who are supervised by Greg and one associate attorney, are responsible for working most case files until settlement.

My own interviews with plaintiffs' lawyers in Wisconsin involved contact with lawyers in several such firms; one of those lawyers described how his practice operated by tracing a hypothetical case:

> After our initial interview you would go into an interview room. Now I turn it over to a paralegal. She takes the background, she fills out a bunch of forms, finds out all the doctors, where you live, medical background, medical authorizations, has you sign a retainer agreement, wage authorizations, takes pictures of injuries, and then the file goes into our, for lack of a better term, assembly line. We put it into a fairly sophisticated assembly line. Someone takes the interview; it gets entered into a computer system. It starts then going to various different places. If your case, which in a case like this would need investigation, the file including the interview and police report would go to one of the investigators who would immediately try to get statements and interviews, and pin down the facts. We would set it up; we would confirm the insurance. All the people working on the case at this point are nonlawyers ... the interviewer is a nonlawyer, investigator is a nonlawyer, and everyone is given the following mission: Number one, look at the case, look at the case, look at the case. What risk do we take, what is the assessment of the risk. These persons are trained to look at the files because lawyers will take cases because they want numbers, they want to say I'm a big rainmaker, I've got a lot of cases. So, the paralegals are trained to go to our managing partner and say this is a case I'm involved in and I don't think it looks like a good liability situation, I don't think it looks like a good risk, I don't think there's insurance, I don't think there's a mode of recovery here, the person doesn't appear that injured, and they are told to bring to us and review with us what they think of the case. They know cases as

well as lawyers know cases. And we find that clients will tell them [paralegals] stuff that they won't tell us [lawyers].[15]

While these firms are bureaucratic in how they operate, they typically involve a small number of lawyers. Galanter (1998a:471) has attributed the small size of plaintiffs' firms to a combination of factors, including the personality of lawyers who are very successful as contingency fee litigators ("the 'alpha male' characteristics of many of the most successful plaintiffs' lawyers") and the nature of the capital involved in plaintiffs' firms, which typically has been highly dependent on the name of an individual lawyer.

However, at the top end of the spectrum, this is changing. One aspect of this change is the shift from the individual charisma of the star litigator toward what is more equivalent to "brand names" tied to a firm rather than to an individual lawyer. A firm that has accomplished this in Wisconsin is Habush, Habush, Davis, and Rottier (HHDR). HHDR, with ten offices around Wisconsin and over thirty attorneys,[16] relies upon a large advertising budget, along with a well-earned reputation for successful representation.[17] However, while most lawyer advertising focuses on showing pictures of the lawyers, HHDR's advertising tends to focus on satisfied clients by showing pictures of smiling families. HHDR uses a combination of television, radio, and Yellow Pages advertising,[18] and a significant fraction of the Wisconsin population will spontaneously name the Habush firm as a law firm to contact in case of accidental injury (Kritzer and Krishnan 1999:355). In fact, a report about a baseball park construction accident noted that one of the victims of the accident had specifically told his wife some days before his death, in a premonition of what was to happen, "If anything ever happens to me, I want you to call Bob Habush" ("Robert L. Habush, A 'Typically Relentless' Approach Wins Big" 2001). HHDR's prominence in Wisconsin is further reflected in the fact that it was one of three firms, probably the lead firm, representing the State of Wisconsin in the tobacco litigation that led to the $206 billion multi-state settlement, earning a third or more of the resulting $75 million fee.

Law firms that litigate huge, complex cases, such as tobacco, breast implant, and the like, require staff and financial resources beyond the scale of the traditional plaintiffs' firms. It is no accident that HHDR was involved in the tobacco litigation; it could bankroll the litigation and even absorb a loss if that had been the end result. It is also no accident that around the country, it was firms such as Robins, Kaplan, Miller & Ciresi in Minnesota, or Ness, Motley, Loadholt, Richardson & Poole in South Carolina, that played lead roles in the

---

[15] See Chapter 11 in this volume, for details of the study from which this interview is drawn.

[16] Information from the firm website, available at http://www.habush.com (last visited March 14, 2001). [The firm is now known as Habush, Habush and Rottier.]

[17] One of the cases listed among the *National Law Journal*'s top verdicts of 2000 was a $99 million dollar award arising from a construction accident at a new baseball park in Milwaukee. Robert Habush was the lawyer who won that award.

[18] It has an advertisement on the back cover of the telephone book in most larger towns and cities in Wisconsin.

tobacco litigation. These firms have both experience in complex litigation and the extensive resources, both in terms of people and money, to handle such cases and their attendant risks. For example, Ness Motley built its resources through its major role in the asbestos litigation that burst onto the national scene in the 1980s. It is an area that continues to be a major part of the firm's practice. Ness Motley was a firm of over seventy lawyers, with a sizeable support staff and a practice of national proportions.[19] Robins Kaplan, a firm of two-hundred lawyers, three-hundred support personnel, and offices in five states and Washington, D.C., is somewhat different in that its practice goes well beyond personal injury to include business litigation and other areas of business practice; in 2002, Robins Kaplan listed sixty-six lawyers as practicing in the areas of personal injury, medical malpractice, mass torts, and catastrophe litigation.[20] Unlike Ness Motley, Robbins Kaplan has long approached plaintiffs' practice in a way that resembles a corporate firm more than the traditional small plaintiffs' firm headed by a single star litigator. At the time that named partner Michael Ciresi was handling hundreds of Dalkon Shield and Copper-7 IUD cases in the 1980s, the firm already had two hundred lawyers, and the importance of these resources was beginning to be recognized; in the words of another lawyer handling large numbers of Copper-7 cases, "Robins, Kaplan is a big firm, and it had the resources to stand toe to toe with Searle. ... They were able to make the case. We weren't" (Sier 1988). The importance of the resources of a firm like Robins Kaplan was captured in a news article about the hiring of a top litigator, Jim Fetterly, a specialist in catastrophe cases such as the MGM Grand fire in Las Vegas. Fetterly closed his own ten-attorney boutique firm because the resources required to represent clients had begun to exceed the firm's ability to finance cases (Phelps 2001).

While in some ways Robins Kaplan is unique, in others it is not. There is an increasing number of firms that specialize in litigation in a way that includes both large scale commercial litigation (typically done on an hourly basis) and high visibility plaintiffs' class action done on a contingency basis. Such firms include Boies, Schiller & Flexner with offices in ten cities (Goldhaber 2001), and Susman Godfrey with more than fifty lawyers headquartered in Houston.[21] In addition, there are firms that specialize in plaintiffs' class action such as Lieff, Cabraser, Heimann & Bernstein with forty-five lawyers based in San Francisco and Waite, Schneider, Bayless & Chesley with sixteen lawyers based in Cincinnati.

Central to all of these firms is resources: the ability to bring to bear substantial legal effort and to deal with the cost of extended, monster-scale litigation. These are repeat players in the truest sense of the concept (Galanter 1974:97-98). Like the traditional repeat players on the defense side, they are in the game

---

[19] While the firm has offices in only four states, lawyers in the firm are licensed to practice in 20 states.

[20] Information obtained from the Robins Kaplan website, available at http://www.rkmc.com (last visited March 13, 2001).

[21] Information from firm website, available at http://susmangodfrey.com/Defaulth.htm (last visited March 14, 2001).

for the long term and have the resources to sustain cases that, until recently, would have bankrupted virtually any lawyer or plaintiffs' law firm (Harr 1995: 123-32). While in the past, one might have started with the assumption that the defendant had the resources to swamp the plaintiff, these firms have accumulated sufficient capital through major victories in cases such as asbestos, tobacco, Dalkon Shield, etc., so that it may well be the plaintiff that is in the stronger resource position. Having greater resources does not ensure victory, as evidenced by the lack of success in recent cases brought against the gun industry by lawyers bankrolled with tobacco winnings (Amon 2000; Duffy 2001; Levy 2000; Turbin 1999; Van Voris 1998), but losing is something these firms can now afford.

III. THE IMPACT OF THE DIVISIONS WITHIN THE PLAINTIFFS' BAR

While competition is nothing new within the plaintiffs' bar, it now functions in a way that differs from competition of the past. The plaintiffs' firms with large bankrolls have a capability to dominate the market for profitable cases in a way that was not previously possible. The largest of the bankrolls accrued to the firms that took on the tobacco cases, which then used those bankrolls to open new avenues of litigation.

Traditionally, within a highly competitive market for clients and cases, the plaintiffs' bar has nonetheless seen itself as sharing common interests: the need for sympathetic judges (Champagne and Cheek 1996; Watson and Downing 1969), the need for rules that favor plaintiffs (Lipson 1984), restrictions on client solicitation and advertising, and general opposition to various aspects of tort reform, such as limitations on the contingent fee, limitations on various types of damages such as punitive damages and noneconomic damages, changes to the American rule on fee shifting, eliminating joint and several liability, and statutes of repose. The general assumption is that if a change might hurt some plaintiffs' lawyers' clients and, thus, hurt those lawyers themselves, it must be bad for all plaintiffs and all plaintiffs' lawyers. In fact, what is in the interest of one segment of the plaintiffs' bar need not be in the interest of other segments.

A. INCOME STRATIFICATION

The "winner-take-all" market discussed above presents one line of cleavage within the bar. Recall Sandefur and Heinz's (1999) analysis of the relationship between income and satisfaction with income: they estimated that 40% of those making $45,000 working in a "high business field" are satisfied or very satisfied with their incomes, compared to only 32% of those in "low business fields"; for those making $162,500, 72% and 80% respectively are satisfied or very satisfied in "high" and "low" business fields. At my request, Rebecca Sandefur reran the analysis for lawyers who devoted 25% or more of their practice to plaintiffs' personal injury work and for those who devoted 50% or more to this area. While the number of respondents was small, forty-eight and thirty-seven for the two groups respectively, the impact of income was much greater than for even the low business fields group looked at by Sandefur and Heinz. For those whose practice was 50% or more plaintiffs' personal injury, an estimated 15% of those making $45,000 were satisfied with their income compared to 97% making $162,500; expanding the group to include those with 25% or more plaintiffs' personal injury produced corresponding figures of 23% and 93%.

One interpretation of these figures is that those at the lower end of the income range among plaintiffs' personal injury practitioners look at those who are doing extremely well and feel an acute sense of relative deprivation. This is consistent with the "winner-take-all" image. It may also reflect a sense that the chances for moving up significantly in income do not seem particularly positive; however, it might also mean that the lawyers in this area are very ambitious in terms of income and simply have not begun to achieve their expected goals.

B. DIRECT MAILERS VERSUS THE BRAND NAMES

One clear example of conflict with the plaintiffs' bar involves the limitations on client solicitation. Those law firms that have invested heavily in advertising and have, through that medium, established themselves as a "brand name" have a strong incentive to try to limit the ability of other lawyers to reach out to clients via direct mail contacts in the wake of an injury producing accident. The "brand name" firms want potential clients to think of them first; receiving a mail solicitation from another firm has a significant likelihood of diverting the potential client to the mailer when, otherwise, the potential client might have called the "brand name" firm.

It may well be the case that the kinds of clients that the "brand name" firm wants differ from those of the direct mailer. That is, the brand name and direct mailer firms may not actually be in all that much competition for clients most of the time; however, the "brand name" wants first crack at the client. Moreover, the kinds of clients the "brand name" wants (i.e., clients with significant damages and fairly clear liability) are more likely to want to see a lawyer before considering a settlement than many, if not most, of the direct mailer's potential clients; those clients, with relatively lesser damages and less clear liability, are prime targets for quick and early settlements offered by a seemingly friendly and sympathetic insurance adjuster. Most limitations on direct mail bar such contacts by attorneys for thirty days after an injury producing accident; this is prime time for insurance adjusters to contact injury victims and try to reach a quick, and almost certainly advantageous from the insurer's perspective, settlement.[22] The injury victims most likely to settle at this stage are the bread-and-butter clients of the direct mailers, but may be of much less importance to the "brand name" firms. Of course, the "brand name" firms will express their opposition to direct mail not in terms of their own interests, but rather in terms of professional dignity or concerns about "ambulance chasing."

---

[22] Insurance adjusters are also under pressure to close claims quickly simply as a measure of productivity (Ross 1980:59-60).

C. THOSE HANDLING SPECULATIVE LITIGATION VERSUS THOSE HANDLING ROUTINE LITIGATION

More important, particularly in terms of understanding the impact of litigation such as the tobacco litigation on the plaintiffs' bar, is the distinction between high risk, high return, speculative litigation, and low risk, low return, routine litigation. The lawyers who undertook tobacco cases in the 1990s were incurring significant risks: no one had ever prevailed in personal injury cases against the tobacco industry when the injury arose from the long-term exposure to tobacco products. In fact, it was not until 2001 that any individual had actually collected money as compensation for an injury caused by their own smoking. The lawyers who undertook these suits combined a kind of risk sharing pool and significant firm-specific resources to make the litigation viable. States turned to contingency fee arrangements as a way of eliminating their own risks of having to devote substantial dollars or other resources to the litigation. The tobacco industry poured many millions of dollars into legal fees and expert consultant fees to fight the cases brought against them. Imagine what difference it might have made if the states or their contingency fee lawyers had been at risk of having to pay a significant portion of the tobacco industry's legal expenses? It is hard to imagine that the litigation could have gone forward under that circumstance.

1. Fee Shifting

Generally, it is assumed that fee shifting rules are bad for plaintiffs; I have made that argument in my own writing (Kritzer 1984c:136-37, 1992). However, the little real empirical research that has been done on the subject in the U.S. context of contingency fees shows that the picture is more complex (Di Pietro 1996:89; Di Pietro et al. 1995:100-23; Hughes and Snyder 1995:234-48).[23] While fee shifting does create disincentives to litigate, particularly for persons in the middle class who have assets that could be used to satisfy a fee award, it also strengthens the hand of the plaintiff who has a good case by effectively increasing the value of the case. Furthermore, one can imagine fee shifting regimes that include insurance for plaintiffs against the downside risk of losing and having to pay the other side's fee.[24]

For example, imagine a system where the lawyer agreed to bear the plaintiffs' downside risk in return for receiving the "shifted" fees in addition to the commission fee that we call a contingency fee. We already know that most contingency fee lawyers decline most relatively risky cases, and the key risk contingency fee practitioners face is in terms of how much of their time a case will require and how much of a fee they will actually receive (Kritzer 1998c:267). A significant percentage of cases are declined because the amount that the lawyer estimates can be recovered will not yield a fee sufficient to cover the

---

[23] [See Chapter 10 in this volume for a discussion of these complexities.]

[24] These kinds of insurance schemes were developed in England in the late 1990s in conjunction with the introduction of a form of contingency fee that is labeled a "conditional fee" (see Papworth 1998; Lord Chancellor's Department 1998; Yarrow and Abrams 1999:10).

lawyer's time (Kritzer 1997:22). If the lawyer's fee were to include both the percentage of the recovery and an amount paid by the defendant, the calculation changes. While the defendant's ability to recover some of its costs from the plaintiff or the plaintiff's lawyer, if a case results in a verdict for the defendant, will lead some defendants in some cases to litigate rather than settle, it is also true that the ability to recover costs from the defendant if the case goes to trial will make a plaintiff's lawyer's threat to go to trial more credible in a modest case. Furthermore, the additional fee will mean that many valid cases that today are not economical for a lawyer to handle will have the potential of producing a satisfactory fee. Some of these cases may be quite significant and relatively clear on liability, but simply uneconomical given current defendant practices (e.g., modest but reasonably clear cut medical malpractice cases).

A lawyer-financed fee shifting system would be very problematic for lawyers who handle speculative cases that produce fees in eight figures or more. This litigation is speculative simply because of the risks involved. Settlements occur, in part, because the defendants perceive the potential cost of losing as being so high that they make a considered business judgment about the potential costs of losing and litigating and the risks associated with them.[25] Plaintiffs' lawyers can pursue these cases because what they put at risk is considerably less than it would be under a fee-shifting system where they covered their clients' downside risk. For the lawyers handling high risk cases, a fee shifting regime such as I describe would make such cases much less attractive.

2. Damage Caps

The plaintiffs' bar has been united in its opposition to caps on punitive damages and other types of noneconomic damages, such as compensation for pain and suffering. Typical caps that have been proposed have been on the order of $250,000 and/or some link to the amount of economic loss (Greenlee 1997: 726). For most lawyers handling personal injury cases, these caps are essentially irrelevant. For such caps to be relevant, two conditions are necessary; the injuries must be such that the lawyer can justify either a large punitive award or a large pain and suffering award, and there must be a source of payment for a large award.

Punitive awards in personal injury cases are quite uncommon, and even when they do occur, they tend toward the modest side; in 1992, less than 1% of plaintiff verdicts in tort cases in a sample of the seventy-five large counties produced punitive awards exceeding $250,000 (DeFrances et al. 1995:8), and in 1996, the figure was considerably less than 1% (DeFrances and Litras 1999:9).

As for pain and suffering awards, economic damages drive most awards and settlements, combined with a source of compensation. The most common source of compensation is another driver's insurance policy, and most of these

---

[25] An excellent example of this kind of decision can be seen in the litigation over Bendectin (see Sanders 1998:35-39). Ultimately Merrill Dow prevailed but the company sought to avoid the costs of litigation and the potential costs of losing by agreeing to a $180 million settlement. The litigation proceeded because the class certification that was central to that settlement was thrown out by the Sixth Circuit Court of Appeals.

have damage limits well below the caps that have been discussed. The problem for most lawyers is making a case for significant pain and suffering damages. One could readily imagine reforms in noneconomic damages that would actually work to the advantage of most lawyers: place some limits at the upper end, but permit plaintiffs' lawyers to prove pain and suffering through per diem arguments; or alternatively, set some statutory guideline for noneconomic damages in routine cases that is indexed to the cost of living. The idea that some mechanism other than juries would be used to set noneconomic damages is an anathema to most plaintiffs' lawyers, but for those working with low end, routine injuries something other than the "shadow of the jury" might be more effective and actually produce increased compensation for injuries where pain is a major component. While there is an assumption that juries are more favorable to plaintiffs than are judges, empirical evidence calls that assumption into question (Clermont and Eisenberg 1992:1125-26; Eisenberg et al. 2006; Eisenberg et al. 2002; Glaberson 2001).[26]

These arguments may also apply for major medical malpractice cases. The cases in which the largest damages are paid are not driven by pain and suffering but by the high cost of long-term intensive medical care. The standard line about punitive damages and noneconomic damages is that it is the threat of huge awards that convince defendants and insurers to make realistic settlement offers for economic damages. However, in most types of cases, the threat of massive economic damages associated with long-term medical care is more than enough to convince a defendant to settle these cases. Again, the assumption that juries are the key to reasonable compensation may not be true in medical malpractice cases. In 1996, the median medical malpractice award by a judge was $454,000 compared to about half that ($254,000) by a jury. Similarly, judges found for plaintiffs in 38% of medical malpractice trials compared to juries, which found for plaintiffs in only 23% of trials (DeFrances and Litras 1999:6).

Given that the controversy over damage caps is often tied to "out of control juries," one might imagine a situation where a compromise over damage caps might be that such caps would apply only to jury trials requested by plaintiffs. That is, if a plaintiff agreed to have a case tried by a judge, then no cap would apply. A defendant could insist on a jury trial, but in doing so, the defendant would waive any damage caps.[27]

This type of compromise might be very attractive to lawyers handling large cases other than what I have termed "speculative" cases. It is in the most speculative cases where the uncertainty about extreme jury verdicts is most

---

[26] I have been told by a number of plaintiffs' lawyers that, in today's [circa 2002] climate, they would just as soon try a routine soft tissue injury case to a judge than to a jury. In fact, 1996 verdict data from the 75 largest counties in the U.S. (DeFrances and Litras 1999:8) show that in automobile tort cases, the median award by judges was higher ($20,000) than the median award by juries ($18,000), and that judges' verdicts were more likely to exceed $250,000 (12.2% versus 8.4%) or $1 million (7.1% versus 3.0%) than were juries.

[27] I am not proposing this as a system change. There are a variety of side impacts that would need to be examined, the most obvious of which would be the increased role of judges, and the implications of that for judicial selection processes.

important, and the type of limitation I described would be most threatening to those lawyers.

CONCLUSION

The legal profession in the United States is heterogeneous along many dimensions, ranging from social background to clientele. While members of the profession ostensibly share a background of legal training and an interest in the well-being of the profession, this commonality is eclipsed by cleavages that range from economic interest to political outlook. Within the swirl of diverging views and interests, the plaintiffs' bar, a.k.a. "trial lawyers," might seem to be a group of lawyers with a strong shared core of interests and outlooks. Politically, the organized plaintiffs' bar has supported politicians, most often Democrats, who oppose changes in the civil justice system that, on first view, seem anti-plaintiff. How real is this supposed commonality of interest?

In this chapter, I have discussed developments that raise questions about the commonality of interests within the range of lawyers who represent plaintiffs on a contingency basis. The kinds of cases handled by identifiable subgroups within the plaintiffs' bar differ in ways that reflect conflicts of interest with other plaintiffs' lawyers rather than commonalities. I have illustrated these conflicts by looking at a variety of issues on most of which the plaintiffs' bar has traditionally taken a united stand:

- fee shifting (losers pay)
- damage caps
- right to jury trial
- client solicitation

In discussing these various issues, I have outlined ways in which changes might be made that would be advantageous to some segments of the plaintiffs' bar and their clients, but disadvantageous to other segments. Some of the "proposals" I have advanced would be significant departures from current practice, and none of them are by any means fully developed as policy proposals to be considered in the immediate future. However, they do provide a prism to help us think about the conflicts within the plaintiffs' bar.

What difference will it make when and if the plaintiffs' bar begins to realize the nature of these conflicts? One possible insight into that question is the one example listed above where conflict has already occurred: client solicitation. Generally, the "establishment" of the plaintiffs' bar, lawyers who tend to be extremely successful practitioners who have no need to rely upon direct mail, has sought to take the supposed "high" road by endorsing strictures on direct solicitation. The primary defenders of direct mail are those who do use it, or think they might use it at some point in the future. Most plaintiffs' lawyers sit on the sideline of this battle, if for no other reason that a letter from an unknown plaintiffs' lawyer may lead someone to contact them based upon their local reputation because the injured person was prompted by the letter to "ask around" for an idea of lawyers to contact.[28] In other words, the split within the plaintiffs' bar is right where one would expect to find it: in the wallet. There is no reason to expect differing responses should some of the other issues I have outlined arise.

The practice of law is "a changin'," to paraphrase Bob Dylan. The economic structures that have governed the work of the personal services sector are shifting in significant ways in the United States and in other countries as well.[29] While the underlying causes of change are complex, the result is the transformation of the economics of personal services practice. The common result will be increasing stratification and conflict among lawyers who previously shared a set of interests because of the common plight of their client base.

---

[28] In fact, one survey of recipients of direct mail found that only 11% of those recipients who hired a lawyer actually hired a lawyer from whom they had received a mailing. Some significant percentage beyond the 11% undoubtedly were prompted to contact a lawyer by the letter (see Kritzer and Krishnan 1999:353).

[29] See Kritzer (2001a) for an extension of the argument in this chapter to England.

14

THE PROFESSIONS ARE DEAD, LONG LIVE THE PROFESSIONS: LEGAL PRACTICE IN A POSTPROFESSIONAL WORLD[1]

INTRODUCTION

The American legal profession is facing challenges that are sending tremors through its institutional foundations. On the one hand, U.S. lawyers appear to be wielding ever increasing power as reflected in victories in litigation with such powerful groups as cigarette manufacturers. At the same time, the profession finds its traditional prerogatives under increasing challenge with the push for multidisciplinary professional practices, direct encroachment by a variety of service providers (accountants, consultants, paralegals, etc.), and mounting political attacks on the profession for its apparent greed (e.g., huge fees from the tobacco litigation) and apparent arrogance (Glaberson 1999). Much as the businesses and governments who bear the bulk of health care expenses forced major restructuring of health care delivery, the large consumers of legal services (which are consuming an ever larger share of legal services; see Heinz et al. 1998) are seeking means of limiting and monitoring the costs of those services (*ibid.*; Kritzer 1994). Lawyers increasingly find themselves working not as independent professionals but as employees of bureaucratically organized law firms, corporations, and government. The dynamics of this change, combined with shifts in where legal effort is directed, have attracted the attention of scholars (Galanter and Palay 1991; Heinz et al. 1997; Heinz et al. 1998; Seron 1996; Spangler 1986; Van Hoy 1997).[2]

[1] This chapter originally appeared in *Law & Society Review* 33 (1999), 713-59; earlier versions were presented at the 1999 Law and Society Annual Meeting, May, Chicago, and at the 1999 Legal Aid Board Research Unit Conference, Legal Aid in a Changing World, November 4–5, London. Hilary Sommerlad, William L.F. Felstiner, Austin Sarat, Howard Erlanger, Neil W. Hamilton, Susan Silbey, Nancy Reichman, and two anonymous reviewers provided helpful comments on an earlier draft of this essay. I also benefited by comments and discussion at a faculty seminar at William Mitchell College of Law where the paper was presented. I would like to also acknowledge the series of grants from the Law and Social Science Program of the National Science Foundation (SES–8320129, SES–8511622, SES–9212756, and SBR–9510976) that have supported my research over the years and that, in turn, have greatly shaped my understanding of and thinking about the legal profession. This version includes some minor updates to reflect changes that have occurred since the original publication.

[2] The number of lawyers in the United States increased 142% between 1975 and 1995 (Carson 1999:1). This kind of growth has been a phenomenon throughout much of the developed world (Abel and Lewis 1989:142-47); for example, in England and Wales, the number of practicing

Although revolutionary changes are still nascent for the legal profession, change has been very dramatic in the American medical profession. In less than a decade, American doctors were brought into a structure of institutional and corporate medicine that contrasts sharply to the professional structure that had developed and thrived during most of the twentieth century (see Brame 1994; McKinlay and Stoekle 1988).[3] Services that were once the exclusive preserve of licensed professionals are being delivered by specialized nonprofessionals who may or may not work under the nominal supervision of a professional (see also Beardwood 1999). Sellers of products such as pharmaceuticals pitch directly to consumers rather than limiting their marketing to the medical practitioners who must prescribe the product for the consumer to have access to it. Consumers turn to information sources unavailable before the mid-1990s to obtain information that once was the virtual preserve of the professional service provider, and they can access that information without having to first learn a complex system of categorization of the type customarily used to organize specialized information (but see Brody 1999; Davis and Miller 1999; Miller 1999). In

---

solicitors increased by 50% during the 11-year period of 1983–1984 through 1994–1995 (Wall and Johnstone 1997:99), the legal profession in West Germany increased by 158% between 1961 and 1990, and the legal profession in the Netherlands increased by 87% between 1970 and 1990 (Blankenburg 1998:9). Within the practice of law, an ever increasing portion of legal services is consumed by large corporate enterprises. Where in 1960 sole practitioners comprised 64% of private practice lawyers in the United States, by 1995 only 47% of lawyers practiced in this type of setting; this percentage is actually a slight increase from 1991, when the corresponding figure was 45%, and by 2005 the figure had increased slightly to 48.6%. At the other end of the spectrum, I estimate that in 1960, less than 2% of U.S. lawyers in private practice were in firms of 50 or more lawyers; by 1991, this percentage had grown to 18%, and to 20% by 2005. Between 1988 and 1992, the total number of law (solicitor) practices in England was virtually unchanged; only the largest practices (those with 20 or more principals) increased, and that increase was more than 50%, although these firms still only comprised less than 2% of all practices (Bowles 1994:25). Put another way, while the legal profession in the U.S. grew 58% between 1980 and 1995, the growth in "large" firms (51 or more lawyers) has been 287% compared with only 49% for groupings of five or fewer lawyers. Not surprisingly, the change in the large firms is even more stunning if we push the comparison point back to the 1960s. Galanter and Palay (1991:22) report that in the early 1960s there were only 38 firms with 50 or more lawyers. Assuming that the average size among these firms was 75 lawyers, a total of about 2,850 lawyers were in such firms. By 1981, this figure had grown to 27,200, and by 1991, to 105,236. The growth from circa 1960 to 1991 was an astounding 3,592%. Although "large" law firms in England are typically smaller than large law firms in the United States, the largest English firms exceed 1,000 lawyers (Brennan 1998b:A15), and there are substantial pressures toward such growth (see Lee 1992). Using data from their study of the Chicago bar in 1975, Heinz and his colleagues estimate that at that time, 53% of total legal effort served the corporate client sector and 40% served the personal/small business sector, a ratio of 1.33 to 1; in their 1995 replication of the earlier study, the corporate sector's consumption of legal effort had grown to 64%, whereas the personal/small business sector was down to 29%, a ratio of 2.21 to 1 (Heinz et al. 1998:21).

[3] Between 1983 and 1994, the percentage of patient care physicians practicing as employees rose from 24.2% to 42.3%, whereas the percentage in solo practices fell from 40.5% to 29.3% (Kletke et al. 1996:555); by 1997, solo practitioners had fallen further to 26% (see Stolberg 1998). Between 1980 and 1996, the proportion of office-based, patient care physicians working in group practices rose from 27.9% to 46.4% (computed from Randolph 1998:43). By 1997, 92% of physicians had at least one contract with a managed care organization (Stollberg 1998). Although the rate of change has accelerated since the mid-1980s, the shift toward "bureaucratic medicine" and the issues this change raised were recognized as early as the mid-1970s (Mechanic 1976:49-57; see also Ritzer and Walczak 1988).

addition, consumers can connect with other consumers to share experiences and information and to provide support to one another (Bly 1999a, 1999b).

We are moving into a period in which the role of professions such as law and medicine as they are known in the Anglo-American world is radically changing and may be in sharp decline (Abel 1986). Although I hesitate to add another "post-xxx" to a lexicon now overflowing with "posts" (postmodernism, post-structuralism, postmaterialism, postindustrialism, post-Soviet, post-this, and post-that), a concept that begins to capture the full dimensions of these developments is postprofessionalism.[4] In the discussion that follows, I focus on this idea; I do not seek to provide a comprehensive review of either the concept of "profession" or of recent developments in legal professions around the world.[5] Rather, I describe what I see as key major developments, both within and outside the profession, that are driving changes in the way the lawyers practice and how consumers, broadly defined, access legal services in the Anglo-American world. My intention is to provoke reexamination of some of our assumptions about the legal profession as an institution. As suggested by the title of this chapter, the changes wrought by postprofessionalism will not mean the extinction of professions, but rather a wholesale reshaping of this institution as we now know it, hence my suggestion, "the professions are dead, long live the professions."

I. PROFESSIONALISM AND POSTPROFESSIONALISM

What specifically do I mean by postprofessionalism? The starting point to answer this is a definition of "profession."

A. PROFESSIONS: MULTIPLE CONCEPTIONS

One problem with thinking about professions is that the term profession can be defined and conceptualized in many different ways (Barker 1992), three of which I label the common parlance definition, the "historical" definition, and the sociological definition, with the first as the most inclusive and the last as the least. My focus is on the sociological, but it is important to recognize that there are a variety of meanings attributed to the concept.

Profession, according to the "lay definition," is almost synonymous with "occupation" and is distinguished primarily by means of its antonym, "amateur." As commonly used in lay parlance, a "professional" can refer to a fire-

---

[4] My efforts to locate previous uses of this concept identified only two. The first is as the title of a chapter, "Useful Unemployment and Its Professional Enemies," in Ivan Illich's book (1977); Illich seems to use the term postprofessionalism to refer the deprofessionalized world he advocates (see Illich et al. 1977). The other is a book entitled *PostProfessionalism: Transforming the Information Heartland* (Cronin and Davenport 1988), which focuses on developments in the "information professions."

[5] For example, one important theoretical and practical issue in the analysis of professions that I do not consider is that of gender. This issue has been very prominent in the literature on professions generally (see, for example, Hearn 1982; Witz 1992) and in the literature on the legal profession specifically (some notable examples include Dixon and Seron 1995; Hagan et al. 1991; Hull and Nelson 1998; Menkel-Meadow 1989; Pierce 1995; Seron and Ferris 1995; Sommerlad 1994; Sommerlad and Sanderson 1998).

fighter, a plumber, an auto mechanic, a secretary, a teacher, a salesperson, a social worker, a lawyer, a doctor, or a member of the military as well as many other occupations. Members of all these occupations often choose to pride themselves on their "professionalism," and by referring to themselves as a "professional" (e.g., a "professional secretary" or a "professional firefighter"), they mean that they perform a particular line of work as a means of earning a livelihood and are committed to what they view as a set of standards of performance. As this discussion makes clear, there is an important distinction to be made between the occupational category of "professional" and what might be described as an ideological commitment to "professionalism," referring to expectations of work performance. The term professionalism can also be used to refer to possessing the occupational status of a "profession" (in any of the senses of profession discussed here) without regard to what might be labeled as the ideology of professionalism.[6] In my concept of postprofessionaism, the "ism" is used in the latter sense (in the same sense as the "ism" in "postindustrialism").

Professions, according to the "historical" definition, include a broad class of occupations that are characterized by "trained expertise and selection by merit, a selection made not by the open market but by the judgment of similarly educated experts" (see also Bell 1973; Perkin 1989:xiii).[7] These professions are built on human capital, and typically involve some recognition of qualifications and some sort of career hierarchy (Perkin 1989:2). Some occupations are able to restrict entry by enforceable licensing rules based on recognized expertise (such restrictions can extend from physicians and lawyers to insurance agents and stock brokers, both of which are licensed through a testing procedure). Others may be able to achieve a recognition of a strong credentialing process outside a state-based enforcement structure (e.g., librarians, engineers, college professors). Still other occupations have no licensing process and at best a weak credentialing process, but nonetheless are associated with an expertise that has led to the appellation "professional" (e.g., managers, computer programmers).[8] The key elements to professionalism in this broad sense are the creation of and recognition of trained expertise and the structuring of occupations around this expertise. Within developed economies, professionalism of this type is endemic and is one of today's key features (Perkin 1996). I refer to professions defined in this sense as "general professions."

The sociological definition uses "professional" in a still more restrictive sense.[9] As with the historical definition, professional occupations are a feature of a particular stage of economic development. Professions are specific occupational groups that are at a minimum defined as "exclusive occupational groups

---

[6] A closely related term or concept is professionalization, which refers to achieving the status of a profession.

[7] A similar definition can be found in Lipartito and Miranti (1998:303): "Professionals [are] purveyors (and creators) of expertise."

[8] The role of formal credentialing varies from country to country. For example, Britain seems to rely more on training programs that produce credentials than does the United States, where employers are primarily concerned about experience.

[9] On the problem of, and importance of, definition, see Freidson (1983).

applying somewhat abstract knowledge to particular cases" (Abbott 1988:8). Two key elements to this definition go beyond the historical definition: exclusive occupational groups and the application of abstract knowledge.[10] As noted above, many occupational groups enjoy exclusivity (through licensing or union structures), and abstract knowledge is today applied by many technical occupations (e.g., computer programmers, electronic repair technicians). It is the combination of recognized exclusivity with the application of abstract knowledge that defines what sociologists label as professions. Professions in the sociological sense have further distinguished themselves by adding notions of altruism, regulatory autonomy through peer review processes, and autonomy vis-à-vis the service recipient (i.e., the professional tends to control the relationship with and the service provided to the client/patient/customer). By combining these characteristics with their abstract knowledge-based expertise, these professions have regularly asserted claims of independence that other occupational groups have never successfully advanced (Larson 1977).[11] And although there have always been issues of degree of autonomy, control, and expertise, it is the future of professionalism defined in these terms that is the focus of this essay. For purposes of clarity, I will refer to these as "formal professions." As should be obvious, formal professions are a subset of general professions. Also, formal professions tend to conflate the two different meanings of "professionalism"; that is, achieving the status of profession is equated with maintaining the ideology of professionalism as reflected in the definitional elements of formal professions.

Although general professions reflect a particular stage of economic development, formal professions as I am considering them are even more embedded in a particular social, economic, and political structure. The occupations that compose the formal professions in Anglo-American countries exist in some form in all developed societies, but the position of these occupations in English-speaking countries is not found in all other developed societies (Dezalay and Garth 1997). In particular, parallel occupations do not necessarily possess the kinds of prestige and autonomy possessed by the formal professions. For example, the formal professions of England and the United States tend to stand at the top of the occupational prestige hierarchy. In France, in contrast, the graduates of the *grandes écoles* (e.g., École Normale Supérior, École Nationale d'Administration, or École Polytechnique) stand at the top of the status hierarchy; these schools "do not prepare specifically for professional careers but offer a general education to a social elite" (Perkin 1996:79), and it is state employment in the grand corps (most of whose members are recruited from the *grandes écoles*) that constitutes the top of the employment hierarchy. The

---

[10] Professionals are typically required to demonstrate their mastery of this abstract or "formal" knowledge to secure a license to practice their profession as an occupation.

[11] Alternatively, it might be asserted that "in return for access to their extraordinary knowledge in matters of great human importance, society has granted [professionals] a mandate for social control in their fields of specialization, a high degree of autonomy in their practice, and a license to determine who shall assume the mantle of professional authority" (Schön 1988:7).

members of the grand corps constitute general professionals, but are not necessarily members of formal professions as I am using the concept.

Even the formal professions differ in important ways across national settings. Although mindful of its economic well-being, the English legal profession was strongly embedded in a status system that placed an emphasis on particular types of legal services (e.g., transfer and ownership of property, whether by sale [conveyancing] or inheritance [succession]) that was associated with both wealth and status (Abel-Smith and Stevens 1967; Sommerlad 1995:165; Sugarman 1996:108-12). This system led to the neglect of many areas of potential legal practice; for example, throughout much of the twentieth century, lawyers ceded areas such as taxes and much corporate work to accountants (Sugarman 1995). This ignoring of areas of potential practice has deep roots in the English legal professions; in fact, at times the professions have seemingly abandoned areas of practice that were not consistent with the status image they were seeking (Burrage 1996:46; see also White 1976). In contrast, the legal profession in the United States has been more entrepreneurial. Although some elements of the profession focused on status and prestige (see Powell 1988), these elements were never able to achieve a dominant role, and new entrants to the profession worked hard to expand the opportunities for income.

The medical profession is another example of differences. In the United States, a career in medicine is a path to substantial economic well-being. Even as the government became increasingly involved as a funder of medical services (through Medicare and Medicaid), the system of funding actually served to increase income of physicians because it was initially based on a fee-for-service model. In contrast, the socialization of the English medical system after World War II meant that medicine was not a route to high income (comfortable perhaps) except for a small group of physicians who worked largely outside the government-funded system. Medicine remains a prestigious occupation in England, but it lacks the economic opportunities that have been the case for American physicians since World War II. The economic constraints imposed by the English system significantly changed the nature and degree of autonomy enjoyed by physicians, while at the same time meaning that for many patients, options that were not affordable before socialized medicine are now available.

The sharp growth in the role of legal aid in England had an impact on the legal profession not entirely unlike what happened previously to the medical profession. Legal aid used to fund a significant portion of legal services in England (although now largely limited to criminal cases), but subjects the lawyers providing those services to a variety of kinds of controls that reduce their autonomy (Genn 1988; Sommerlad 1996). At the same time, the availability of legal aid (and increasingly private legal insurance) has meant that the potential client pool grew. One result was increased conflict between the legal profession and the government that must fund legal aid. Another result has been radical changes in what is deemed to be acceptable forms of funding legal services; although the legal profession had long adamantly opposed contingency fees, even as recently as the late 1970s (Benson 1979), by the mid-1980s, the profession was looking seriously at this option (Law Society 1987a), and in the late 1990s, the government embraced a form of no win, no pay fee (calling them conditional fees) as a means of reducing legal aid expenses.[12]

In this essay, I seek to find some broad generalizations. Yet, even as I do so, I fully recognize the limitations of context, both geographical and chronological. The argument I advance must be considered within the reality of these limitations.

B. POSTPROFESSIONALISM

Postprofessionalism refers to the combination of three elements:

- the formal professions' loss of exclusivity (Abel 1986; Commission on Nonlawyer Practice 1995; Kritzer 1998b);
- the increased segmentation in the application of abstract knowledge through increased specialization (Ariens 1994; LoPucki 1990; Podgers 1993);[13]
- the growth of technology to access information resources (Calhoun and Copp 1988; Clark and Economides 1988; Katsh 1989; Susskind 1998; Wall and Johnstone 1997).

The end result is that services previously provided only by members of formal professions can now be delivered by specialized general professionals or nonprofessionals (see Clark 1992; Hartmann 1993). The type of political and economic power that members of the formal professions and their organizations were able to wield to secure their control through much of the twentieth century (Johnson 1972; Larson 1977) cannot withstand the pressures created by the combination of segmentation of tasks and improved access to information.[14] Equally important is that although at one time professions might have been able to control what information was available through the control of journals sponsorship, editorial control, peer review processes, and the like (Freidson 1994:134), the Internet and the World Wide Web have reduced much of that control.

Part of what is happening is that the formal professions are losing their uniqueness and are being eclipsed by professions in the much more general sense (hence, "the professions are dead, long live the professions"). If this were the extent of what was occurring, it would probably make sense to label the

---

[12] England began embracing contingency fees at the same time that contingency fees were under unprecedented attack in the United States (see Brickman 1989; Brickman et al. 1994).

[13] Specialization, or perhaps more accurately, "hyperprofessionalization," can at the same time increase the role of those professionals who achieve particularly high levels of specificity in their knowledge so that they are able to deal with extremely complex situations that call for particularly high levels of judgment and experience.

[14] Since the 1970s, sociologists have debated the issue of whether professions are best understood as motivated primarily by power concerns (Freidson 1986; Johnson 1972) both vis-à-vis clients and markets (Larson 1977) or as occupations that combined a set of unique traits that required special treatment by the state and the market (Halliday 1987; Parsons 1954b), what Parker nicely labels "communities of competence" (Parker 1997a:390-91). Although this debate is important, the core of my argument is that technological developments are effectively mooting its relevance. Moreover, the developments I project will also alter the terms of the debate over regulation of professions (*ibid.*).

developments "new professionalism." An earlier literature spoke of "deprofessionalization," which Haug (1973:197; see also Toren 1975) defines as "a loss to professional occupations of their unique qualities, particularly their monopoly over knowledge, public belief in their service methods, and expectations of work autonomy and authority of the client"[15] (more recent literatures have considered "deskilling," which means that nonprofessionals are assuming increasing numbers of tasks that were the preserve of professionals). Neither "new professionalism" nor "deprofessionalization" fully captures the nature of current developments. I choose the label "postprofessionalism" because of the complexities of these developments and the multiplicity of ways in which they are being manifested: changing patterns of political influence, rationalization of knowledge,[16] and the growth of technology as a tool of accessing this knowledge (compare to Krause 1996:283-84).

How has postprofessionalism come about, and what are its implications for legal practice in the twenty-first century? The next section discusses in more detail the forces pushing generally toward postprofessionalism. A discussion of the specific forces operating on the legal profession follows. I then turn to the implications of postprofessionalism for the legal profession and legal practice.

II. MOVING INTO THE POSTPROFESSIONAL WORLD

Today, a key driving force is a change in the role of knowledge. Although he sees the most apparent change in the shift from production of goods to production of services, Daniel Bell once argued that the growth in the professional and technical occupations was the "most startling change" (1973:17). The work of these occupations revolves around knowledge, and it is around knowledge that what Bell called the "postindustrial" society is organized. Bell observed that knowledge has been "necessary for the functioning of any society," but went on to argue that what distinguishes knowledge in the postindustrial society is the centrality of "theoretical knowledge—the primacy of theory over empiricism and the codification of knowledge into abstract systems of symbols" (*ibid.*, 20).

Bell failed to see one implication of the codification of knowledge that is changing the role of occupations such as the formal professions today. The codification of knowledge makes possible the subdivision of expertise in ways that allow persons with much less than traditional professional training to deliver services that rely on sets of abstract knowledge previously the province of formal professionals. The codification and general systematization of knowledge and information also make it possible to develop new ways of imparting and accessing that knowledge. Furthermore, the more that knowledge can be converted to or expressed in terms of information and decision-making rules, the more the tools of information technology can be brought to bear in accessing and using that knowledge.

---

[15] For discussions of deprofessionalization as it relates specifically to the legal profession, see Rothman (1984) and Anleu (1992).

[16] Wilensky (1964:149-50) anticipated the problem that increased rationalization of knowledge would have for the formal professions.

As noted above, ideas of practitioner independence and autonomy lie at the core of the standard image of the formal professional. Over a 15-year period (1980 to 1995), the percentage of private practice lawyers working in firms of six or more went from 29% to 38% [a figure that was essentially unchanged in 2005]. Increasingly, we are coming to see formal professionals, not just lawyers, as working in institutional or bureaucratic settings that are designed to control workers rather than to foster autonomy (see Galanter and Palay 1991; Spangler 1986; Van Houtte 1999). This change does not necessarily come as a surprise, having been described in the 1970s as part of what some observers labeled deprofessionalization (Haug 1973; Toren 1975). This bureaucratization is closely connected to the rationalization and compartmentalization of knowledge.[17]

The traditional image of the formal professional as having substantial control over the substance and conditions of his or her work has increasingly come to be questioned (Abel 1989). Although some might argue that the degree of control was never as great as the professional image might suggest (Auerbach 1976:40–73; Carlin 1962; Heinz and Laumann 1982:360–65), the lament that the practice of law has become "just a business" has become common, and the struggle to recapture the supposed spirit of professionalism is a theme that has regularly recurred (American Bar Association 1998; Commission on Professionalism 1986; Glendon 1994; Gordon and Simon 1992; Kronman 1993; Linowitz 1994; Solomon 1992).[18] Abel has characterized the loss of control experienced by the legal profession as the "decline of professionalism." Drawing on the work of Larson (1977), Abel (and others) argues that professions are largely economic entities designed to limit entry ("control the production of producers") and limit competition from within and without ("control the production by producers"). In the late twentieth century, Abel argues, the legal profession in particular lost these kinds of controls (Abel 1986).[19] As I discuss in detail elsewhere (Kritzer 1998b:6–14), the struggle for control over production has gone on throughout the twentieth century in the United States, and the profession has never had the level of control that it wanted; in other common-law countries

---

[17] At least in the United States, the implications of bureaucratization are beginning to be evidenced in such places as the Federal Rules of Civil Procedure. The 1993 revision of Rule 11, which deals with the obligations of attorneys and the potential of sanctions for certain types of behavior, includes the following provision (FRCP 11(c)(1)(A)): "Absent exceptional circumstances, a law firm shall be held responsible for violations committed by its partners, associates, and employees."

[18] Solomon (1992) argues that the crisis of legal professionalism is a recurring theme that goes back at least as far as the 1920s. In a discussion of the apparent longing for a lost "golden age" of professionalism, Galanter quotes condemnations of the commercialization and deprofessionalization of the big lawyers by such 1930s luminaries as Harlen Fiske Stone and Karl Llewellyn (Galanter 1996:556–58). In fact, the question of whether law is a business or a profession has been debated since the first decades of the twentieth century, as indicated by a book published in 1916 entitled *The Law: Business or Profession?* (Cohen 1916).

[19] Another element, more important in some countries than in others and for some professions than others, is the increasing role of the government as a source of access to and funding for professional services (Krause 1996:272). This element is most evident in systems of socialized medicine or large-scale government medical insurance (e.g., Medicare in the United States), but it is also true in other professions, such as law in Britain, where legal aid pays, or until recently did pay, a significant portion of the country's legal bill.

such as England, the professions have typically had control over only a very narrow range of what in the United States is deemed to be the practice of law (Abel-Smith and Stevens 1967; Sugarman 1996).

A. AN HISTORICAL PARALLEL

Of course, professions are not the only entities that served to limit competition, nor are they the only entities that have lost that control. One can see parallels between what happened to skilled craftspeople during the Industrial Revolution and what is happening to the professions (Krause 1996; Posner 1993:6-13). Prior to the modern factory, craftspeople produced most nonagricultural goods for sale. Becoming a craftsperson was typically a process that involved several years, usually achieved by serving an apprenticeship. The craftsperson usually possessed a number of interrelated skills that together were necessary to produce a type of product. Over time, the guild structure, which typically involved a master craftsperson with a group of apprentices and journeymen working in the master's workshop, developed. In addition, the craft guilds relied on their relationship with the state to maintain monopolistic control over the production of specific products (Kramer 1927), although the state's endorsement was probably most important for the monopolies held by the various merchant guilds; in addition, it is doubtful that the ending of state support was central to the eventual demise of the guilds (Kramer 1905:587-89). In return for state protection, guilds served as a source of revenue and took on civic responsibilities that the rudimentary governmental apparatus could not handle.

Eventually, many crafts evolved increasing levels of differentiation within the production process, which in turn led to increasing differentiation between the masters and those in apprentice and journeymen roles. In some crafts, journeymen began creating their own organizations to meet workplace and social needs.[20] The rationalization of the production process, combined with the invention of machines, eventually led to the development of the factory. Industrialists were able to isolate the individual tasks needed for production and then hire workers each with just enough skill to carry out one or several of those tasks. The result was cheaper production of goods, a shift from human capital in the form of skilled craftspeople to industrial capital, and the effective end of many crafts except for highly specialized or artistic applications (Ashley 1906: 218-22; Schneider 1969:34-46).

Much as today one function of formal professions is to insulate and protect their members, prior to industrialization the guilds provided the kind of protections for their members that Abel describes as the underlying rationale for the professions (Krause 1996; Posner 1993:6-11). Just as formal professions in the English-speaking world have enjoyed substantial autonomy,[21] craftspeople

---

[20] Many of these organizations evolved into the forerunners of today's craft unions (Howell 1878:73-105; Unwin [1904] 1963).

[21] Whether professions have really had as much autonomy from the clients as the image of the professional suggests is debatable (see Cain 1979; Heinz and Laumann 1982; Johnson 1972; Sarat and Felstiner 1995).

enjoyed considerable autonomy through the guild structure (Black 1984:12-26). The guilds lost power and control not just because previously independent, skilled workers were brought into situations of dependence, but because the nature of the work itself was fundamentally reorganized. The development of the factory model of production played an important role, serving to replace the dominance of commercial capital with industrial capital (Unwin [1904] 1963: 70-102). By combining technology with a process of rationalization, industrialists were able to eliminate the kind of craft-based skills required for preindustrial production of goods. The resulting division of labor meant that industrial workers needed only very narrow skills to carry out their role in the production process (Posner 1993:12). Employers could impart the skills necessary with relatively little expense. A small number of persons with high levels of skill continued to be needed to design factories and production modalities, but the typical level of skill needed in the production process was greatly reduced.

At the same time, the political protections enjoyed by the guilds began to disappear, in part from developments in the structure of the state and in part from the growing role of trade beyond local communities and individual nations. The state came to depend less on the guilds for revenue as other forms of taxation developed, and the state evolved its own infrastructure to take on the civic functions that the guilds had handled.[22] At the same time, improved transportation made communities less dependent on local producers and made it more difficult for local guilds to enforce monopoly rights (Kramer 1927:185-210).

Postprofessionalism involves a similar phenomenon, but rather than the production of specialized goods, it concerns the production of specialized services. Much as craftspeople were displaced by early technological developments and the division of tasks into relatively simple elements, formal professionals are being displaced by service providers organized around highly specialized tasks who may, when needed, draw upon modern technological tools to access information. Just as craftspeople viewed this new form of goods production as a threat to their livelihood, members of formal professions are having to deal with the economic threats posed by specialized service providers. Where industrialization helped to shatter the then-current economic role of persons skilled in the use of their hands, equivalent developments for those skilled in the use of their heads are evident today. The changing nature of work combined with loss of state patronage and the globalization of economic activity constitute the conditions for postprofessionalism.

III. WHY THE PROFESSIONS ARE LOSING CONTROL

As Abel has observed, the legal profession has lost control over both the production of producers and the production by producers (Abel 1986). Abel argues that the development, and now the decline, of the professions reflected a

---

[22] My description here is clearly Eurocentric and is most applicable to England. The guild system appears to have endured much later in other countries, particularly Germany (Black 1984:123-25; Walker 1971:73-107).

historical "trajectory of professionalism"; that is, professions are "historically specific institutions for organizing the production and distribution of services" (Abel 1986:7; Crompton 1990; see also Sommerlad 1995). As suggested by the historical parallel discussed above, one can see the decline as arising from many of the same types of historical forces that characterized industrialization and the decline of the craft/guild system. Three primary forces lead to the loss of control: the changing nature of work, challenges to professional autonomy and control, and globalization of the professional services sector.

A. CHANGING NATURE OF WORK

The decline of the crafts arose from two key workplace developments (which were at the core of industrialization): rationalization of work and technological developments. Similar changes are today evident in the professional's workplace.

1. Rationalization

Rationalization of the professional workplace involves three elements: the formalization and systematization of the distribution of knowledge, the development of standardized procedures, and the segmentation of professional practice. The impact of rationalization is evident both with regard to the production of producers of professional services and the production of those services by producers.

The rationalization of entry processes for the professions has radically altered the production of producers of professional services (Kritzer 1991a:547-50). Historically, professions such as medicine and law (at least in the common-law world[23]) controlled entry through a process akin to apprenticeship. The apprenticeship model was highly personalistic and particularistic, with decision making resting largely in the hands of individuals who had incentives to limit entry, both in terms of who was permitted entry and how many were permitted entry. Over the course of the twentieth century, however, entry moved to a system of formal education (see Dhavan et al. 1989), and at the same time access to educational opportunities was no longer limited to members of the social and economic elite (Fulton 1989; Sommerlad 1995:166). Control over entry has shifted from the professionals themselves to educational authorities whose incentives are to increase, not control, enrollments; thus, although few people in the United States would contend that the country is experiencing a shortage of lawyers, the number of law schools continue to increase as new units within existing universities and as free-standing institutions. The overall effects of these developments is to rationalize the process around "objective" criteria (grades, examinations, etc.) as opposed to the more personalized criteria of the apprentice system and to increase the opportunities to enter the profession radically.

---

[23] The university was much more important in training professions n Europe than in other parts of the world (Krause 1996:1-13, 127-28, 175, 226).

Rationalization is also evident in the production of services. Traditional controls such as limits on advertising, mandatory fee schedules, and the like have either disappeared or have been greatly relaxed. Professional practice is increasingly marked by a combination of specialization and delegation. In significant part, specialization is attributable to the codification of knowledge that underlies the work of the formal professions. Where we once thought of doctors or lawyers, we now have doctors who describe themselves as allergists, cardiologists, dermatologists, endocrinologists, nephrologists, neurologists, pediatricians, obstetricians, oncologists, ophthalmologists, orthopedists, radiologists, rheumatologists, urologists, and a whole host of surgeons, and among legal practitioners we now have specialists in the fields of criminal defense, divorce and family, elder law, insurance defense, labor law, litigation, patents and trademarks, personal injury, real estate, environmental law, mergers and acquisitions, workers compensation, and wills and estates. Although in contrast to what has happened in the medical profession the American legal profession has resisted formalizing specializations, the reality is that all but the small town lawyer and the most marginal of urban practitioners have come to specialize in the services that they offer.[24] These specializations are evident in both the corporate services and the personal services sectors. In the former, specialization (and stratification related to specialization) has long been the norm (see Nelson 1988; Slovak 1980; Smigel 1964). In the latter, successful practitioners have come to see their work as revolving around some type of either substantive (real estate) or process (court-oriented) specialization (see Seron 1996).[25]

As professionals have recognized the quality and efficiency gains of specialization, they have built on the identification of tasks within their specialized areas of work to delegate to nonprofessionals or general professionals. Many of these tasks are extremely routine, but not always. In some areas of practice, professionals are able to design their practices so that relatively little of the client or patient contact is directly with the professional. As clients and patients increase in sophistication (through education, access to information, etc.),[26]

---

[24] Many countries have formalized certain types of specialization among legal practitioners through the formation of multiple legal professions. To the English-speaking world, the best known of these is the division of the English legal profession into barristers and solicitors (Abel 1988b), which is more of a functional than a substantive division. In the civil law world, the separate profession of notaries has long provided many services provided by lawyers in the common-law world (Arruñada 1996; Closen and Dixon 1992; Malavet 1996; Olgiati 1994; Suleiman 1987), and remnants of this separation can be found in some common-law jurisdictions (Brockman 1997; Shaw 2000).

[25] A 1998 issue of the *Wisconsin Lawyer* (vol. 61, no. 6, p. 18) ran an in-house ad for the State Bar's organized sections. The ad was headlined, "Burger law? Generally, we're all specialists."

[26] In *Disabling Professions*, Illich et al. (1977) base much of their critique of the professions on the assumption that clients lack the sophistication to use professional services in a fashion that does not create a relationship of dependence (see Illich et al. 1977, particularly McKnight's essay). At no point do they deal with (1) the situation of sophisticated, corporate consumers of professional services or (2) the increasing educational level of the general population. Their failure to see the revolution in access to information is not surprising, however, given that they were writing in the 1970s.

they begin to demand direct access to lower-cost, nonprofessional providers of specific services previously the domain of professions. Some of these nonprofessional specialties were effectively created by professionals as means of increasing efficiency. The result is that professionals have themselves created many of the conditions for postprofessionalism to take hold.

2. Information Technology

The second major force is information technology and the resulting changes in how knowledge is accumulated and then distributed in society. Whereas industrialization grew as a result of the invention of machines to carry out repetitive tasks that previously required skilled craftspeople, today it is the rise of information technologies that can be readily employed to access codified forms of knowledge. Given the very close linkage between information and knowledge, the rapidly improving tools for accessing information reduce the need to rely on highly trained individuals who have acquired extensive information as part of their training. Whereas over the first half century of the information age the developments revolved around information processing, the next half century will see developments in knowledge processing (Susskind 1998:56-59).

Take, for example, the ways of delivering support for complex technological tools such as computer hardware and software. At one time, most sellers of these tools hired experienced professionals to provide user consulting; support staff needed to have a thorough understanding of the software (and frequently the hardware it ran on) to be able to diagnose and solve user problems. Over time, information tools have emerged that allow technology companies to build sophisticated databases of information that persons with relatively small amounts of training and experience can access to deal with many, if not most, user questions and problems.

Among providers of legal services, the traditional tools for accessing legal information (i.e., case law) was a sophisticated set of categories closely tied to a variety of legal concepts. These categories, developed by West Publishing Company, form the West "Key Number" system, which in turn is integrated into the West Digests. To access case law effectively, one needed training in the central concepts that lie at the core of the category system. Modern information technology has led to an alternative system for accessing case law: free text searches using massive electronic databases (most prominently Westlaw and LEXIS). The result is to make it possible for persons with a much less sophisticated understanding of legal categories and principles to perform at least rudimentary legal research. As a result of these developments, lawyers regularly delegate research tasks to paralegals and legal assistants.[27]

---

[27] I do not want to overstate either the former complexity or the current simplicity. Even without electronic tools, it was possible to teach law students fairly quickly how to use the paper-based tools. And, even with the electronic tools, good legal research still requires substantive knowledge as well as knowledge of how to do a computer-based search.

B. CHALLENGES TO PROFESSIONAL AUTONOMY AND CONTROL

Modern formal professions in the English-speaking world have often enjoyed the protection of the state. These protections (e.g., licensing laws, unauthorized practice laws) have been the primary device used to exclude potential competitors from domains considered to belong to members of a profession. Whereas in the guild system, the state granted protections in return for money and services, the protections enjoyed by the professions have been justified primarily in terms of the "public interest" or "public protection." As evidence mounts that nonprofessionals can deliver quality services often at lower cost (see, for example, Commission on Nonlawyer Practice 1994; Kritzer 1998b; Moorhead et al. 2003; Parker 1997a), it is becoming more difficult to maintain those protections.

As tasks become specialized and it becomes possible for persons to acquire the limited set of knowledge necessary to deliver highly specific services traditionally the domain of a member of a formal profession, it becomes increasingly difficult for the profession to maintain any exclusivity over those tasks. A common claim by formal professionals seeking to protect their domain is that someone without the level of training required to be a full member of the profession will not be able to recognize the complex interrelationships and subtle issues raised in a specific case. This argument is used by lawyers seeking to ban nonlawyers from handling real estate closings and by ophthalmologists seeking to limit the tasks that can be carried out by optometrists. Yet whenever previously restricted tasks have been opened to new providers, the problems predicted by the profession opposing relaxation of restrictions have failed to materialize in significant numbers, if at all.

To date, the medical profession, at least in the United States, has succeeded in maintaining control over most nonprofessionals who might be potential competitors for routine service delivery. Health maintenance organizations and other organizational providers of medical care use specialized paraprofessionals for an increasing number of tasks.[28] Although it still appears that the professional physician is formally in control, that control is shifting from the physician to the organization and even directly to the paraprofessional (see Freudenheim 1997). As part of this shift, the paraprofessional providers may be achieving elements of autonomy, from physicians if not from organizational employers, that they had not previously enjoyed. Whereas before the paraprofessional was limited to roles that supplemented physicians, they are today increasingly supplanting physicians, which in turn reduces the number of physicians needed (see Kilborn 1997). These changes reflect the health care providers' needs to obtain economies. As physicians lose jobs within these organizational medical providers, they will have to deal with the pressures of postprofessionalism.[29]

---

[28] Accountancy is another profession that has recognized the usefulness of delegation to paraprofessionals (see Compton 1993; Hicks and Rymer 1990).

[29] The accountancy profession continues to have certain elements of protection (created by statutes requiring audits for certain entities); the institutional structure of accounting, however, has long been built on large-scale entities, and the large accounting firms have been relatively quick to seize opportunities beyond the traditional accounting role. Another of the

C. GLOBALIZATION OF THE PROFESSIONAL SERVICES SECTOR

The last development has been the globalization of the professional services sector (Aharoni 1993; Dezalay and Sugarman 1995; Flood 1995, 1996; OECD Workshop on Liberalisation of Trade Services 1997). Here I use the term globalization very broadly to encompass the widening geographic horizons of how professional services are provided. At one time, professional services were delivered almost exclusively on a local basis: doctors, lawyers, and accountants practiced locally, drew clients locally, and relied on local institutions (courts, hospitals, etc.). Accountants were the first of the professions to develop nationally (and then internationally), primarily because they serviced large corporations with operations in many locales and many countries. The corporate sector of the legal profession was next, as it too devised new ways to meet the needs of large corporate clients; developments such the European Union have spurred these developments along (Whelan and McBarnet 1992).[30] In recent years, elements of the personal services sector of the bar have also begun to reach out beyond their local communities; one now finds statewide law firms advertising for personal injury clients, securities specialists seeking clients around the country, and mass tort specialists flying off to sign up clients at the most recent international disaster. The development of large hospital corporations has moved medical practice into a wider geographic base, although the idea of regional specialty-center hospitals has been around for some time.

The geographic widening of the market for professional services reflects the combination of improvement in transportation, communication technology, and information technology. Today, a physician in Istanbul can consult with a specialist at the internationally-known Mayo Clinic in Rochester, Minnesota, almost as easily as with someone in Istanbul. Communication technology allows the local physician to share test results, medical histories, and so on, and that same technology allows instantaneous transmission of electronic data (EKG, digital imaging, etc.) that at one time would have necessitated the patient traveling 10,000 miles. Similarly, information technology allows lawyers in New York, London, and Singapore to work simultaneously on documents needed for a complex financial transaction in Hong Kong. A personal injury lawyer in Charleston, South Carolina, can obtain copies of previous depositions by an opposing expert witness electronically, or via overnight courier if they are not available for electronic transmission, from an attorney in Portland, Oregon. Or, a solicitor in England working on tobacco-related cases can access key documents obtained from American tobacco companies via the Internet.

---

classic "professions," the clergy, has been forced to come to grips with elements of postprofessionalism for radically different reasons: the inability to recruit sufficient numbers of individuals to join the profession. This issue has led to two developments: the opening of the clergy of many religions to persons previously excluded (i.e., women) and an increased reliance on laypersons to carry out duties previously the responsibility of members of the clergy.

[30] The European Union also presents an interesting example of globalization forcing the creation of a profession that previously had been subsumed within another profession: dentistry in Italy (see Orzack 1981).

Once it becomes difficult to control competition from players beyond a professional group's area of political influence, the ability to maintain the group's professional monopoly is doomed. It is only a matter of time before competition from within the local community (i.e., nonprofessionals) will join the competition from without.

IV. LAWYERS CONFRONT POSTPROFESSIONALISM

For the lawyers, postprofessionalism is real and immediate:

- Although corporate lawyers have for many years been very attentive to the demands of their fee-paying clients, corporations have become increasingly sophisticated in their use of legal services (Banks 1983; Brennan 1998a; Morrison 1998; Wessel 1976).[31] In the 1970s, corporations might have automatically turned to "their" outside law firm, but today corporations often rely on a panel of law firms (Coates et al. 2011) or may even put work out for bid, inviting interested firms to participate in a "beauty contest." Furthermore, corporations regularly demand that their outside law firms consider alternatives to hourly billing in pricing their services (Barrett 1996; Leibowitz 1998; Richert 1994). More generally, lawyers are having to recognize and deal with growing consumer consciousness, particularly in the United States but increasingly elsewhere as well (Flood 1991; Goriely 1994; Hanlon 1997:813; Henning 1992; Jones 1988:686; Sherr et al. 1994; Sommerlad 1995).

- Until recently, a lawyer who achieved partner status in a large corporate law firm could look forward to a secure position and many years of a substantial income, but today corporate legal practice has become a world of change and turmoil. Employment structures have radically changed to include a variety of types of positions, and firms regularly shed partners,[32] dissolve (see, for example, Kumble and Lahart 1990), and merge (Galanter and Palay 1992:50-56; Galanter and Henderson 2008). Life in a large corporate law firm increasingly resembles life in the management sector of any large business.

- In the 1980s and 1990s, a number of bar-related groups and commissions were appointed to examine the issue of whether it is time for the legal profession to come to grips with the reality of nonlawyers providing a wide range of legal services; typically, the resulting report recommended finding a way to accommodate (and regulate) the competing providers (Commission on Nonlawyer Practice 1994, 1995; Ianni 1990; Public Protection Committee 1989).

- We are beginning to see the development of computer-based "expert systems" that can be employed to handle routine cases such as valuing personal injury claims or uncontested divorces (Archer 1996; Wall and Johnstone 1997:109-11; Webster 1994).

---

[31] Concerns about billing by corporate law firms can only be heightened by research showing large-scale billing frauds by lawyers (including managing partners) in such firms (Lerman 1999).

[32] Although news reports in specialized periodicals (e.g., *National Law Journal*) of partners being dismissed are quite common, I know of no hard data on the actual frequency of these events—though such reports were common during the Great Recession.

The response by the legal profession to these and other developments has been to try to hold onto an outmoded image of professionalism. Compared with other professions, the legal profession may have had a stronger ally in the state because of its close connection to state functions (Krause 1996:253; Rueschemeyer 1989). Nonetheless, although lawyers have avoided coming to grips with the "brave new world" of postprofessionalism, that avoidance has not prevented that new world from emerging.

A. RESISTING COMPETITORS

The legal profession's continued resistance to the tides of postprofessionalism is nowhere more evident today than in their efforts to retain control over the market for legal services (Baker 1999). Segments of the bar have strenuously opposed any opening of what they deem to be legal practice to nonlawyers (see France 1995a), even though nonlawyer practice is already common in many areas (Commission on Nonlawyer Practice 1995; Kritzer 1998b); to date, they have largely succeeded, at least in terms of formal rules.[33] Whether the bar can successfully resist significantly increased intrusion of nonlawyers into areas previously claimed by lawyers much longer is doubtful.[34] The strategies (see Witz 1992) previously pursued by lawyers and other professions simply are ceasing to be as effective as they once were, and the number (and vigor) of actual and potential competitors is sharply increasing.

On the political side, observers have pointed out that U.S. legislatures are relatively unique in the high proportion of lawyers among their members. One might argue that lawyers have only maintained their control over delivery of legal services because of their political strength. This argument, however, neglects that professional monopolies have involved fields other than law (Krause 1996; Larson 1977). Furthermore, the conflicts within the legal profession, both in the United States and elsewhere, are deep and longstanding (see Auerbach 1976; Krause 1996:191), and given the depth of the conflicts, there is no reason to expect that the profession itself would be united over the issue of what constitutes legal practice.

What else besides politics might be holding back the postprofessional tide in the legal services market? It might be that clients value the professional/client relationship in ways that will make moving toward paraprofessionals difficult. Seron argues that the solo and small-firm lawyers she studied perceived that the

---

33 This is still largely true as of 2014, although there are some cracks showing as evident by such developments as the creation of limited license legal technicians in Washington (see Chambliss 2014).

34 One might ask whether there was ever any validity to the arguments used by the legal profession in support of limits on who could provide legal services, or did the success of the profession in asserting a broad monopoly simply reflect the political power of the profession? Studies of complaints about "unauthorized practice" show that the source of complaints is not predominantly dissatisfied consumers, but lawyers concerned about competition (Johnstone 1955:3-4; Rhode 1981:29-38). Furthermore, what systematic empirical research there is consistently provides little or no support for the arguments of the professionals seeking to protect their turf (see Bogart and Vidmar 1989; Genn and Genn 1989; Kritzer 1998b; Moorhead et al. 2003), in no small part reflecting that much of legal practice does not draw upon technical legal knowledge (Kritzer 1990:90-105; Rueschemeyer 1973:23, 194).

relationship they had with a client was very important from the client's perspective (Seron 1996:106-26). Interestingly, in the cases where this relationship is probably the most true—divorce cases—many of the practitioners are uncomfortable with the nature of client expectations for the lawyer/client relationship. They see the client as expecting a relationship that the lawyer either cannot guarantee to deliver, the knight-in-shining-armor advocate, or is not trained to deliver, the social worker/therapist (but see Cotts 1998; Sarat and Felstiner 1986).

Although many clients do want a "relationship" with the provider of "professional" services, others see the professional simply as a service provider from whom they want an efficiently delivered service. Expectations vary among clients and patients in the same way that expectations vary among consumers generally. Just as some consumers value the product of the craftsperson and will choose that over the more standard industrial product despite the increased cost, some consumers may prefer a relationship with a professional and be willing to pay for it. This pattern exists in today's medical marketplace. There is a lot of discussion of the breaking of the traditional doctor-patient relationship.[35] Although many people are forced by employers or others to obtain medical services through one specific organization, others have a choice. Typically, that choice involves paying a premium for the traditional fee-for-service medical service or having access to a wider range clinics; just as some fraction of consumers of products pay for the "handmade" or "custom" item produced by a craftsperson, some people are willing to pay a premium to maintain a traditional doctor-patient relationship and to increase their flexibility of choice among medical service providers. In 100 years, it will be interesting to look back and see if the expectations associated with the doctor-patient relationship have disappeared as those who remember, probably in somewhat idealized terms, "the way it used to be" pass from the scene.[36]

At the other end of the spectrum, the corporate hemisphere continues to resist moving toward multidisciplinary practices (Lee 1992:39-42; Van Duch 1999a), even as pressures to do so mount (Van Duch 1999b). This resistance continues even though large international accounting firms have moved into areas previously the preserve of lawyers (see Dezalay 1992:165-201; Dezalay and Sugarman 1995). To some degree, recent patterns reflect global developments; that the definition of formal professional domains varies sharply from one country to another means that nonlawyers in some countries have handled tasks that in other countries are the preserve of the legal profession (Abbott 1988:275-78; Abel-Smith and Stevens 1967:401-02). The big accounting firms have the resources and muscle to chart new directions in methods of delivering professional services to the corporate community. Leaders of the legal profession raise alarms about these developments (see Fox 1998), pointing to professional standards (e.g., conflict of interest rules) that differentiate lawyers from

---

[35] What most people are actually referring to is the general practitioner-patient relationship; few people have long-standing relationships with their surgeon!

[36] As this is revised in the fall of 2014 and the second round of enrollment under the Affordable Care Act is ongoing, these changes are probably well underway.

accountants. Even while bar leaders raise such alarms, however, some of the traditional "advantages" of the legal profession erode. In the 1998 legislation reforming the U.S. Internal Revenue Service (IRS), accountants and others authorized to practice before the IRS were granted the equivalent of attorney-client privilege in noncriminal tax matters (Johnson 1998). Previously, lawyers could use their privilege, which was not held by accountants, as a means of attracting tax clients. Although lawyers still have a privilege advantage in criminal cases, for large corporations that has seldom been an issue although it may have become more important in the years after the Enron meltdown and financial crisis that occurred in the latter part of the first decade of the 21st century.

Whereas previously the legal profession lost control over the production of producers to the legal academy, the near future is likely to see substantial erosion in the profession's control over the production by producers. This erosion will come from challenges by potential competitors (other professions such as accounting and paraprofessionals), from economic pressures to reduce the cost of legal services, and from politicians seeking to capitalize on the apparent public disaffection with lawyers (Ballard 1999). What specific changes might we see in the legal profession? Let us now turn to that question.

V. THE NEXT ROUND OF CHANGES IN LEGAL PRACTICE

A. SPECIALIZATION

The issue of specialization, which is by no means new,[37] continues to be extremely controversial (see Rosen 1990). Anglo-American legal professions cling to the image of the general practitioner, and there are many such practitioners at work across the country, particularly in smaller cities and towns (Economides 1992; Landon 1985, 1990), but they are increasingly the exception. In addition to the general structure of corporate legal firms, some substantive areas (e.g., tax and intellectual property) have long been the province of specialists.

Only since the 1970s has the issue of specialization begun to produce any formal developments, with the California bar adopting the first state-level system for certifying some specialists in 1973 (LoPucki 1990:53) and private groups such as the National Board of Trial Advocacy creating their own specialist certification systems. In the United States, the specialization issue has been closely tied up with the question of lawyer advertising: under what circumstances should a lawyer be permitted to hold himself or herself out as a specialist in a particular area (see Podgers 1993)? The ABA Model Rules of Professional Conduct prohibit lawyers from claiming specialization except in officially recognized categories (*ibid.*, 2). In the wake of the United States Supreme Court's 1977 decision striking down absolute bans on lawyer advertising, *Bates v. State Bar of Arizona* (433 U.S. 350 [1977]), the ABA moved to

---

[37] Ariens (1994) recounts the history of the debate over specialization, which dates from at least the 1920s.

create model standards for specialty areas, adopting a plan developed by the Standing Committee on Specialization in 1979 (see Rosen 1990:3).

Only a minority of states have actually adopted systems for certifying specialists (ABA Standing Committee on Specialization 1993; LoPucki 1990:53), and proposals for such systems have often been controversial (see also Gherty and Dietrich 1991; LoPucki 1990:1-2):

> Would recognizing specialties give some lawyers an advantage over others in getting clients?
>
> Would uncertified lawyers who actually practice in an area be more at risk for claims of malpractice in the event of a negative outcome?
>
> Would specialization drive up fees?

Added to the controversy over the impact of recognizing specialization is the dilemma of which dimensions of specialization to recognize. In addition to substantive areas of law (tax, admiralty, real estate), there is the question of task-oriented specialties (litigation, administrative process, etc.) or venue-oriented specialties (IRS, Securities and Exchange Commission, federal court, U.S. Supreme Court, etc.).[38] There are a range of programs to certify specialists in various fields, but relatively few lawyers seek out such certification.[39]

Generally, the developments with regard to specialization have been experience related rather than training related.[40] Unlike the medical profession,[41] where one enters a formal training program (a residency) to become a specialist, a lawyer works in the field to become certified as a specialist. Only after a number of years of experience can the lawyer seek such certification. One can argue that training for a specialization today is where legal training was at the beginning of the twentieth century: it is essentially an apprentice system (but often without the guidance of an experienced mentor). Just as legal training moved from the law office to the law school, it may be time that specialized training made a similar move.

Yet even absent either formal training programs or much in the way of formal certification programs, specialization is a reality within the practice of law. The range of legal issues that a client may bring, whether that client is a corporation or a college professor, is beyond the competence of a single lawyer. A lawyer whose practice focuses on residential real estate transactions may be

---

[38] England has long recognized forum-based specialization (barristers held a monopoly in the higher courts), but this specialization has partly broken down with the certification of solicitor advocates (Barnard et al. 1999; Zander 1997). Yet although the traditional structure of specialization is under attack, the certification process shows that the recognition of specialization is not.

[39] As of 2012, less than 40,000 lawyers were certified in one or more areas, see http://www.americanbar.org/content/dam/aba/administrative/professional_responsibility/2012_national_certification_census.authcheckdam.pdf (last visited November 16, 2014).

[40] This approach to specialization, either certified or informal, seems to be the norm within common-law systems; see, for example, Stager and Arthurs (1990:199-201).

[41] On the development of specialization within the medical profession, see Stevens (1971:74-289).

able to prepare a simple will for a client whom the lawyer represented on a home purchase or sale, but that lawyer may be well beyond his or her competence in preparing a will that anticipates the complexities of a six- or seven-figure estate. It would take a specialist in trusts and estates, whether a lawyer or an accountant or possibly an estate planner, to deal with the issues involved. The profession has to confront the realities of specialization in practice, and the legal academy needs to incorporate that reality into formal legal education.[42]

B. DISSOLVING DISCIPLINARY BOUNDARIES: THE COMING RISE OF MULTI-DISCIPLINARY PRACTICES

Although specialization will increasingly define the nature of legal practice, pressures also work in the opposite direction. One is the development of multidisciplinary practices and partnerships. Until very recently, the American (and English) legal professions staunchly maintained the position that lawyers must not work in private practice situations where they are under the supervision or control of nonlawyers. Among other things, this position means that all partners in a private practice who provide legal services must be lawyers. The stated rationale for these restrictions turns on the types of ethical obligations lawyers have that do not apply to nonlawyers: the attorney-client privilege, conflict of interest rules, the lawyer's role as an officer of the court, and so on (see Law Society 1987b).

Among formal professions, only lawyers have succeeded in maintaining these types of distinctions.[43] Large medical practices today involve a variety of professions and paraprofessions (medicine, optometry, podiatry, midwifery, physical therapy, social work, etc.). Similarly, the large accounting firms include, in addition to CPAs, information professionals and non-CPA tax specialists. Some American law firms have gotten around restrictions on multidisciplinary practices by spinning off as separate firms units providing services that require the expertise of professionals other than lawyers (see Gibbons 1989; Van Duch 1998). Pressure to deal more systematically with the multidisciplinary needs of clients has grown sharply in the last ten to fifteen years (Van Duch 1999b), in part as a response to other professions, such as accounting, which increasingly are recognized as providing services previously thought of as in the domain of the legal profession (Hayes 1998). On the corporate side, this pressure will be particularly intense as legal practice globalizes (Brennan 1998b), with the necessity of dealing with national differences in the boundaries among professions. Legal professions have come to recognize the necessity of confronting this issue:

- At its 1999 summer meeting, the American Bar Association considered proposals from a commission created to consider the issues raised by mul-

---

[42] See Kritzer (1998b:209-16, 2002a) or Van Alstyne et al. (1990:112-25) for discussions of how specialized training might be incorporated into the legal academy.

[43] Some forms of multidisciplinary practice by lawyers—for example, lawyers who themselves offer a variety of both legal and nonlegal (e.g., insurance, real estate sales, title, accounting) services—have long been accepted (Wolfram 1999).

tidisciplinary practices (Commission on Multidisciplinary Practice 1999; Gibeaut and Podgers 1998; Molvig 1999; Van Duch 1999a).

- The prior year, leaders of the Law Society of Upper Canada (Ontario) debated relaxing existing bans on such practices (Rose 1998a), and in 1999, several committees for the Canadian Bar Association and the Federation of Law Societies of Canada came down in favor of rules to permit fee sharing arrangements (Rose 1999).

- In 1998, the Paris bar voted to accept a form of multidisciplinary partnership (Rose 1998c).

- The Law Council of Australia voted on a draft policy statement concerning multidisciplinary practices in December 1998 (Rose 1998a).

- The English Law Society (the organization of solicitors) engaged in a consultation to try to find some workable arrangement for multidisciplinary partnerships (Rose 1998d), and the Legal Services Act 2007 included provisions allowing solicitors to practice in an "alternative business structure" that might involve ownership and management by nonlawyers.

- The Dutch bar has engaged in negotiations with international accounting firms over permitting multidisciplinary practices in the Netherlands (Rose 1998b).

- The International Bar Association, at its 27th biennial conference in 1998, passed a resolution concerning the regulation of multidisciplinary practices (Rose 1998e, 1998f).

Thus, in the late 1990s, the long-standing barriers against lawyers working in partnerships with other professionals appeared to be on the verge of collapse but it was a decade later before legislation was passed in England permitting "alternative business structures" and another several years before the legislation was implemented.

In the years to come, the lines among professions, both formal and general, as they were known throughout the 20th century will become much less distinct and will perhaps begin to disappear. The groupings of services will probably be less along the lines of professions as defined today and much more along substantive or client lines. Thus, for a corporation, rather than turning to (1) a law firm to handle labor negotiations, (2) a specialized service firm to handle unemployment compensation issues, and (3) an insurance company to handle workers' compensation, one might see a generalized employee services firm that serviced all those areas with a combination of lawyers, mediators, accountants, risk managers, and so on. Similarly, where today a residential property purchase might involve a real estate broker, an attorney, a title insurer, an engineering firm to inspect a property, an insurance broker to provide casualty insurance and a home buyer's warranty, and a mortgage company to provide a mortgage, in the future all these services might be grouped into a single "home buyers' service corporation"; one already sees effective combinations of many of these services, both in the United States and other common-law countries. How far these kinds of combinations will extend is the unanswered question.

C. CHANGING STRUCTURES OF FIRMS

For those law firms that remain focused solely on law, the structure of the firms will almost certainly change (see Galanter and Henderson 2008). In the large corporate arena, this issue has been discussed extensively, particularly in terms of the dynamics promoting increasing size (see particularly Galanter and Palay 1992). The changes, however, will not be limited to the big corporate firm. Two changes are already obvious.

The first is the changing status of lawyers within firms. The modern American law firm developed along the distinction between lawyers who were partners (owners) and those who were associates (employees). The corporate firm today has myriad categories: equity partner, nonequity partner, of counsel, associate (partner track and nonpartner track), contract lawyer, and so on. These categories have developed in significant part to allow firms to be more responsive to client needs. The traditional partner/associate model effectively locked firms into particular patterns of staff and services. The more diverse set of categories allows firms to be more responsive to the needs of clients and the flow of work.

Outside the corporate firm, it is increasingly common for lawyers to speak about positions in terms of "owners" ("shareholders") and "employees." Most often, these terms reflect the reality that in small firms the expectation is often that a lawyer-employee (a nonowner) will work in the firm for a period of time to gain experience and then move on; the labels avoid any suggestion of an expectation of partnership. In other situations, a law practice may be built around the reputation of the "owner," which is probably most common in more entrepreneurial areas of practice such as plaintiffs' personal injury. Often, these practices stay relatively small, in part because of the owner's dominance and in part because the work does not itself require large groupings of lawyers. In either case, the "owner"/"employee" distinction sees the law practice in a more clearly business-oriented mode. Despite the frequent cries of members of the legal profession that the practice of law is becoming "too much like a business," this trend will in fact only increase in the future.

One way the "business" pressures will be evident will be in increasing pressure to find cost-efficient ways to deliver legal services. For both corporate and personal services firms, one route will be in the increasing use of nonlawyer staff, whether called paralegals, legal assistants, legal secretaries, or something else. These staff members will handle routinized aspects of the legal work, including basic computerized legal research, review of documents, drafting of relatively standard documents, interaction with outside parties (experts, service firms, etc.), and anything else the lawyers believe that a particular paralegal is capable of handling. The pressures for efficiencies will break down many of the traditional barriers. As noted earlier, in England it is already common for "legal executives" (roughly equivalent to paralegals) to handle many aspects of criminal court work (see McConville et al. 1994), which has been a result of pressures to reduce the cost of providing criminal defense services. These types of patterns will become more widespread.

A second way that business, or "commercial," pressures on corporate law firms is already evident is in the shift from departmental structures based largely on substantive areas of law (e.g., property, finance, contracts, tax, trusts and estates, litigation) to structures based on the industries of the targeted clients. Today large law firms commonly have groups organized around major client groups such as the computer industry, healthcare, pharmaceuticals, transportation. Although such organization is not entirely new (it has long been common for some large firms to have large departments focused on banking), there does appear to be something of a shifting emphasis toward defining practices based along commercial lines rather than along legal-professional lines (Hanlon 1997:809-10).

D. CHANGING DEMANDS ON (CORPORATE) FIRMS

Increasingly, the concern of legal practitioners is one of efficiently delivering their product in a way that ensures quality. Previously, large firms viewed the partner/associate system as a vehicle for achieving these ends, but firms today are confronting corporate clients who demand efficiencies and accountability that are the anathema of the "Cravath" system. These clients no longer rely on strong ongoing relations with a single (or primary) outside law firm; rather corporations today look to outside lawyers for "specialized services on a case-by-case, transaction-by-transaction basis" (Nelson and Nielson 2000:458), though they may do this by employing a panel of law firms (see Coates et al. 2011). Thus, the corporate client might once have seen a value to subsidizing "their" outside law firm's development of new legal talent, but that is no longer the case.

One impact of this change is that the organizational language of a large firm practice today looks very much like the language of other large organizational providers of services: teams, accountability, total quality management, information technology, and so on (see Henning 1992, 1997; Landis 1997; Sommerlad 1995). Another impact is that where previously firms recruited at only the entry level and promoted from within, firms today seek legal talent across the experience spectrum; this type of staff recruitment is also an important means of securing clients by recruiting experienced lawyers who bring their existing clients with them to their new firm. The emphasis within the firms is less on professional development and professional autonomy, and increasingly on marketing (Galanter and Palay 1992:53) and delivering the kind of service for which wealthy clients are prepared to pay.[44]

The result of these developments is that large corporate firms seek out ways to deliver services that provide flexibility and reduce costs. The former is accomplished by creating new forms of employment of lawyers that avoid the commitments of the partner/associate system; the use of paralegals and legal

---

[44] There is a danger here that I am overstating the degree of change (but see Galanter and Palay 1991:20-30). Whether there was ever some golden age when the big firms did not keep a very close eye on the bottom line is doubtful. The emphasis, however, has almost certainly changed, perhaps best reflected in the concern about generating billable hours (Galanter and Palay 1991; Landers et al. 1996).

assistants to perform routine tasks previously assigned to entry-level lawyers and sometimes nonroutine tasks of the type one would expect to be handled by more senior lawyers[45] is a key approach to the goal of reducing costs. Where once the cost of training new attorneys was typically shifted directly onto clients, today firms have to find other ways of providing experience and training (see France 1995b).[46]

E. SUBCONTRACTING ELEMENTS OF LEGAL SERVICES

One way that industrial production has been rationalized is through subcontracting. Rather than producing every element of a product, manufacturers turn to subcontractors to produce major elements that can be incorporated into their products. This case is particularly true when the product has highly specialized elements that must be produced in a manner that is tangential to the primary manufacturer's production process. In the health arena, one sees this in a number of areas. At one time, individual dentists produced "appliances" such as dentures and crowns for their patients. Today, most dentists in the United States rely on specialized suppliers to produce the individualized products; these suppliers have highly skilled technicians and equipment that permit much more efficient production that can be done by the individual dentist.

Although it is common today for lawyers to refer cases and clients to other lawyers, either because a case is outside a lawyer's areas of expertise or because of the resources needed to handle a case, it is unusual for lawyers to subcontract elements of a case to other law firms (although tasks such as litigation management are already being subcontracted). As the demands for efficiencies increase, one might expect to see specialized service providers develop that concentrated on very specific aspects of a case. Legal research and legal writing are possible examples. If a lawyer needed a brief on a particular issue, a specialized legal research firm employing skilled paralegals, legal writers, and editors might be employed to produce the brief.

F. CONNECTING LAWYERS AND CLIENTS

One side effect of the technology that is pushing change in legal practice will affect the "marketing" of legal services. Large corporations have long had the ability to seek legal counsel in a national market. Clients on the "personal services" side (Heinz and Laumann 1982; Heinz et al. 1998; Heinz et al. 2005),

---

[45] In the late 1990s, I attended a meeting where the major law firm involved in the case was represented not by one of the firm's partners, or even by an associate, but by a senior paralegal. A study of criminal representation in England reported that it was common for nonlawyers to appear in court on behalf of criminal clients (McConville et al. 1994), and 1998 legislation allows nonlawyers to handle certain in-court functions for the Crown Prosecution Service (Verkaik 1999; White 1998); both internal and external evaluations of the use of "lay presenters" have been very positive (Crown Prosecution Service Inspectorate 1999; Ernst & Young 1999).

[46] One method of training litigation associates used by some larger firms is to assign young trial attorneys to work at the district attorney's office (or some similar agency) for a time so that they quickly obtain substantial courtroom experience while simultaneously fulfilling the firm's pro bono obligations (see Williams 1994).

however, have relied almost exclusively on the local market. In turn, although some lawyers have used modern advertising techniques to attract clients, most have continued to rely on traditional word-of-mouth referrals from prior clients, repeat clients, and referrals from other local lawyers (Daniels and Martin 1999; Kritzer and Krishnan 1999; Van Hoy 1999). The Internet provides a vehicle for potential clients to locate lawyers in a wholly new way, particularly if the potential client has some sort of fairly esoteric legal problem (e.g., an injury arising from the use of a particular machine or tool). By using a site that searches lawyer directories or an online lawyer referral service, potential users of lawyers' services can find lawyers purporting to work in the area of the person's needs. More general searches of the Internet allow the potential client to find others outside his or her own community with similar problems and to get information on and recommendations regarding lawyers. Lawyers, in turn, are provided with a new advertising medium. Well-designed websites can provide "hits" on searches made by potential clients. Legal referral services that have a presence on the Internet (Leibowitz 1999a) are another vehicle for connecting lawyers and clients.

Although there are still major issues concerning who may practice law where, information technology is radically changing markets from local to national and even international. Particularly where practice does not require a physical presence including where "appearance" may be made remotely over an electronic hookup, which is now practical through various services, lawyers are no longer bound to a relatively small area, with the result that potential clients have a wider range of lawyers from which to choose.

G. INCREASED ROLE OF ELECTRONIC TOOLS IN LEGAL RESEARCH AND PRACTICE

Information tools such as Westlaw and LEXIS have radically altered how lawyers can carry out legal research. However, for many years the cost of using these tools was quite high and was often prohibitive for the provider of services to clients without the resources of a large corporation. The cost of accessing electronic research resources has been plummeting, both through free or low-cost services on the Internet and through competitors to Westlaw and LEXIS that provide CD-ROM-based services at much lower cost.

In the United States, one nagging problem for many such alternatives had been the control over citations exercised by West Publishing. The pressures arising from demands by alternative producers have begun to crack this control. A number of states have adopted "vendor neutral" citation systems (typically involving a combination of year, state name, case number, paragraph number). More important, West Publishing effectively lost its copyright over pagination (and its system of "star pagination" in electronic versions of decisions) as a result of several 1998 court decisions (Ebbinghouse 1999). These developments have served to reduce the cost of electronic research tools further and thus increase their use by lawyers (and others doing legal research).

These types of research tools are familiar to all practitioners and researchers. What will lead to more change are other types of services that started to become available in the 1990s. Take CyberSettle.com, for example. This service was marketed as a tool to assist in settlement processes by allowing parties to make a series of settlement offers confidentially and then letting the service provider determine whether there is a settlement based on a set of matching rules.[47] Another example of an online service that broke new ground was VirtualJury.com; this site provides an online focus group type of review of cases similar to what jury consultants do on a face-to-face basis.

H. ACCESS TO LEGAL SERVICES

Legal services is a broad concept, encompassing a wide range of activities. The legal professions of various countries differ significantly in the range of activities over which they have tried and succeeded in asserting control (e.g., there are no legal limits in England and Wales on who may provide legal advice, in contrast to the very stringent limits in the United States). In those areas of legal services where lawyers have obtained control, access to services depends on a combination of fee structures, client resources, and availability of legal aid. Opening previously controlled legal services for delivery by those who do not possess the full credentials of a legal professional has the potential of greatly widening access to legal services. This access will come in a variety of different ways.

The first will be a greatly expanded structure of standardized legal services offered through firms headed by lawyers but with services actually provided by specialized nonlawyers. Storefront, franchise law firms that partially used such a model (see Van Hoy 1997) existed for a period in the 1980s and 1990s, but they failed to live up to the owners' expectations and were largely gone by sometime in the early 2000s. However, one can still imagine a "legal services" firm (as distinct from a "law firm") that used staff with varying levels of training to handle routinized matters; the staff would rely heavily on information-based tools to produce "products" for the firm's clients. These firms would be able to deliver standardized services at relatively low costs. Central to the success of such legal services firms would be the acceptance of the idea of "standardized services" by the potential client population.[48] In some areas, nonlawyers routinely deliver such standardized services already (e.g., standardized home purchase contracts completed by real estate agents). If highly standardized services became widely accepted, legal services firms would not have to employ any lawyers unless required by law to do so.

The second way by which access to legal services would be increased is through delivery of legal services by nonlawyers working for social service or similar agencies. This situation is already happening in many areas (Kritzer

---

[47] As of 2014 CyberSettle.com is still in operation, and appears to have developed a line of work resolving disputes over healthcare charges. In the original version of this chapter, I speculated that over time CyberSettle.com might develop a large database of cases with the kind of information that would allow the valuing of claims which could then be marketed both to lawyers and to claimants themselves; this does not appear to have happened.

[48] I suspect that part of the reason that franchise law firms failed was their need to try to maintain the fiction of individualized services (see Van Hoy 1995).

1998b; Moorhead et al. 2003), most often in fields that private practice lawyers do not now find lucrative (e.g., unemployment compensation appeals, welfare benefit appeals). For example, the Legal Aid Society of San Francisco has a program to provide representatives for claimants in unemployment compensation appeals. The representatives include "law students, recent graduates, practicing attorneys, union representatives, and legal workers," and the program has a very high success rate, 84% compared with the 35% to 40% success rates of claimants statewide (Employment Law Center undated). In several states, advocates working through organizations such as parent information centers assist parents of disabled children in conflicts with educational authorities (Baker 1999). In England, the single largest providers of legal advice are probably the Citizen Advice Bureaux, which are actually staffed primarily by lay volunteers (Baldwin 1989; Goriely 1996:231-32; Richards 1989). Thus, in the future, one will find nonlawyers increasingly employed in various settings filling significant gaps in the provision of legal services.

Nonlawyers, however, will not work only in those areas neglected by lawyers, but will move into various specialized areas in direct competition with lawyers. The impact of this competition will be to reduce the costs of fee-based legal services. In the 1980s in England, the Thatcher government moved to open conveyancing work to specialized nonlawyers; one impact of this change was a rapid decrease in the fees charged for conveyancing work (Domberger and Sherr 1989). In Ontario, nonlawyers routinely provide representation in traffic court, charging fees below those charged by lawyers (Bogart and Vidmar 1989; see also Ianni 1990). Estate planning is often done by financial planners. One can image a variety of other areas where nonlawyers could effectively provide services: routine wills, uncontested divorces, routine auto accident claims, domestic violence injunction hearings, benefit claim hearings, and so on; this is the idea behind the limited license legal technician program in Washington slated to go into operation in 2015. Assuming that the current barriers can be overcome, the key to success of such alternative service providers will be the recognition by the public that sources of effective, affordable assistance are available. Information sources such as the Internet may play an important role in spreading the word about such services.

As my own research has shown, high-quality specialist nonlawyers can acquire the same types of reputational advantages that lawyers possess today, along with the same types of informal "system" (i.e., people) knowledge (Kritzer 1998b). Thus, although at one time one might have argued that lawyers do more than just give legal advice and that it is the combination of skills and knowledge that set them apart from nonlawyers (e.g., a lawyer can get phone calls returned when a nonlawyer might not be so lucky), those advantages disappear as other types of service providers are recognized as effective players.

I. INCREASED RELIANCE ON SELF-HELP

As discussed previously, one important implication of information technologies is the relatively easy access to information that was previously the exclusive domain of the professional. The amount of information readily available from a computer keyboard is staggering. In years past, it took significant training to learn how to access technical, including legal, information, but today, any junior high school student with access to the Internet can find much of that information. Specialized presses, such as Nolo Press, combined with software vendors and specialized websites that provide automated legal forms represent resources that are designed for self-help users, and lawyers in some states view such materials as a clear threat to their monopoly on legal practice (Carvajal 1998; Leibowitz 1999a, 1999b). Groups such as the American Pro Se Association (www.legalhelp.org) are proliferating (providing what they label as "legal help" rather than "legal advice"). Websites such as Lawyers.com and FindLaw.com provide links to many legal self-help sites and publications.

Finding information and knowing how to use it are two different things. I would not expect the hypothetical junior high school student to know how to put the information together to answer a significant legal question, but an intelligent nonlawyer will be able to use these tools (e.g., Findlaw.com) to answer quickly many questions that previously required the services of a lawyer. As people recognize this capability, there will be an increase in the availability of simple training regimes that give nonlawyers (or laypersons vis-à-vis other professions) the basic knowledge to assimilate the information they can access. Already one can find such courses in areas such as family law, auto insurance, consumer rights, and workers' compensation (see Stein 1998). In addition, people who find information on the Internet may also turn to the Internet to seek out individualized legal advice, either through lawyer referral services or through some sort of online legal consultation; for example, one lawyer, disbarred in 1998 by the Arizona Supreme Court, has set up an online service that will, among other things, answer "legal questions for $24.95 and up, payable by credit card" (Van Voris 1999).

I use the "self-help" phrase broadly to encompass any activity that customarily has been the province of the professional service provider. One could imagine a service that collected information on verdicts and settlements and made that information to claimants who could then use that information to assess a settlement offer made either through an attorney or directly by an insurance adjuster. iCourthouse.com is another web-based service; the goal of this system is to provide a kind of online trial (probably closer to arbitration), with "jurors" recruited from among web users; the creators of this site appear to have the goal that people will eventually have predispute contractual agreements to use their service if a dispute arises (much like today's arbitration clauses in contracts).[49] More generally, individuals might access "legal guidance systems" (Susskind

---

[49] In a period of about 15 minutes in 1998 I was able to locate three sites offering some sort of online arbitration system, typically in somewhat specialized areas. These include the World Intellectual Property Organization Arbitration and Mediation Center, which originally focused on domain name disputes, but has moved into other types of commercial issues (http://arbiter.wipo.int/arbitration/online/index.html?); CyberArbitration, which focuses on cyberspace-related disputes including domain name issues (http://www.cyberarbitration. com/arbitration.htm); and CyberTribunal, a project based at the Centre de recherche en droit public, which also focuses on "cyber-conflicts" (http://www.cybertribunal.org/english/html/ project.asp).

1998:xxiv) that lead them through the tasks involved in making basic decisions and presenting their claim to the insurance adjuster. In the medical arena, pharmaceutical companies rely on something of a self-help ethic in their advertising of prescription drugs directly to consumers, who then ask their physicians about the potential of the drugs. Although there is nothing directly analogous in the legal field, such advertising is just one more indication of what may be a rising self-help ethic.

Self-help will not eliminate the need for legal professionals or other legal practitioners, except perhaps in the simplest, most routinized of legal tasks (see Carvajal 1998). My own research (Kritzer 1998b) makes it clear that specific experience is important in dealing with certain types of legal matters and that experience cannot normally be acquired through self-help. The impact of self-help activities is going to be less in terms of eliminating the service provider and more in changing the types of services provided and modifying the relationship between the service providers and the recipients of the providers' services. With better information available, someone who previously sought professional-level services might feel more comfortable using a nonprofessional (in the formal sense) service provider. The user of that provider's services would be in a better position to make some judgments about the quality of the services being provided.

Better information will also change the relationship between formal professionals and the users of their services. The kinds of "information asymmetries" (Paterson 1996:156-58) that have been crucial for defining the professional/client relationship are undergoing drastic changes. The customary image of the professional-client/patient relationship clearly puts the professional in the superior position. Part of the autonomy of the formal professional is in deciding what is best for the client and then proceeding benevolently (or paternalistically) to do what the professional has identified as best.[50] Heinz and Laumann (1982:360-65) have shown that autonomy of this type is lacking in the corporate services sector of the legal profession. To the degree that the personal services lawyer has enjoyed the autonomy described by writers on the professions such as Heinz and Laumann, the growing self-help movement, and the information it makes available, will shift the balance more in the direction of the client.

J. REDUCED REGULATORY AUTONOMY

One aspect of the traditional claims for professions is regulatory autonomy. The lessening of information asymmetries between professionals and their clients (and possibly other interested persons) also serves to reduce the validity of the claim, central to regulatory autonomy, that only another professional can evaluate a professional's performance. Although professional disciplinary bodies have often included at least token laypersons, those bodies have almost always been under the control of members of the profession. This arrangement contrasts with licensing and regulatory bodies for many "nonprofessional"

---

[50] Although the image of the "paternalistic" professional persists, a variety of research raises challenges to this view (see, for example, Cain 1979; Rosenthal 1974; Sarat and Felstiner 1995).

occupations. It will become increasingly difficult for professionals to maintain control over regulation of their members as the claims to exclusive knowledge become increasingly untenable.

These developments can already be seen. In Australia, where the state-level law societies traditionally exercised self-regulatory authority of practitioners, one state (Victoria) has moved that authority to governmental agencies (Legal Practice Act 1996), and the issue has been raised in at least one other state (Campbell 1997; see also Parker 1997b). In England, what was known as the Clementi review led to the Legal Services Act 2007 which moved authority of regulating legal professions from the professional organizations themselves to a new Legal Services Board (LSB) which in turn has authorized specific regulators for various elements of the English legal professions.

Another example of decreased regulatory autonomy has to do with changes in the administration of government-funded legal aid. In Britain, legal aid was administered for many years by the profession itself through the Law Society. In the late 1980s, this responsibility was moved to the independent Legal Aid Board which was replaced by the Legal Services Commission in 2000, and then by the Legal Aid Agency in 2013. Ontario has followed a similar pattern, starting with a legal aid plan administered by the Law Society of Upper Canada, but moving in 1997 to a system administered by an independent agency, Legal Aid Ontario/Aide Juridique Ontario. These independent agencies have seen their role as providing legal services rather than as providing lawyers' services and have been very active in seeking out ways of employing service providers outside the legal profession to meet the needs of their constituencies (Steele and Bull 1996; Steele and Seargeant 1999; Zemans 1999).

CONCLUSION

I am sure that the types of developments described only scrape the surface of what postprofessionalism will mean for the legal profession, the practice of law, and the provision of legal services. To the degree that recent changes resulted from the combination of increased rationalization in knowledge and the growing power of information technology, the shape of the world with which today's formal professionals will have to cope will depend on yet unseen developments in that rationalization process and the information technologies that have exploded recently.

In this new world, "professionals" will continue to be central, but the special place of the traditional professions will wither. Although I have called this development postprofessionalism, others might choose to label it professionalism, referring not to the withering of the formal professions but to the growth in what I referred to as general professions (Perkin 1996). Whatever the label, professionalism as Anglo-American societies have known it is fading. The new professionalism will be much more dynamic, reflecting the rapidity of change in the workplace and the accompanying demands of the market.

The professions are dead. Long live the professions.

15

THE FUTURE ROLE OF "LAW WORKERS": RETHINKING THE FORMS OF LEGAL PRACTICE AND THE SCOPE OF LEGAL EDUCATION[1]

INTRODUCTION

Change does not come easily to professions. Professionals invest heavily in education and training, and devote years to gaining the experience and expertise that allows them to demand significant fees from the clients who seek to access that expertise. While professionals welcome new developments in their particular fields of knowledge, because clients will keep coming to take advantage of these developments, they are less welcoming, and often fearful, of other developments that provide new avenues for accessing the expertise that is traditionally their exclusive province. Yet, the late twentieth century witnessed precisely these developments that cause concern to professionals.

In a previous essay (Kritzer 1999 [Chapter 14 in this volume]), I argued that these changes are leading toward a phenomenon that I labeled "postprofessionalism." I describe postprofessionalism as involving the combination of three elements:

A profession's loss of exclusivity;

The increased segmentation in the application of abstract knowledge through increased specialization; and

The growth of technology to access information resources.

The combination of these developments has made it possible for services that were previously provided only by members of what we commonly call the

[1] This chapter was originally published in the *Arizona Law Review* 44 (2002), 917–38, copyright © 2002 by Herbert M. Kritzer and the Arizona Board of Regents, and is reprinted here with permission of the author and publisher. It was presented at the conference on The Future Structure and Regulation of Law Practice sponsored by the James E. Rogers College of Law, University of Arizona, Tucson, Arizona, February 22–23, 2002. I also had the opportunity to present this paper to colloquiums at the University of Wisconsin Law School and the William Mitchell College of Law. I would like to especially thank Ted Schneyer for inviting me to the conference and for pushing me to develop further some of the arguments that I had advanced in previous articles. This version has been reformatted to use social science style citation; some references have been omitted, and a few others have been updated.

professions to be delivered by specialized nonprofessionals. The combination of developments with regard to the production and delivery of professional services is somewhat analogous to what happened vis-à-vis production by craftspeople with the development of the factory and automation. Specifically, the decline of guilds (for controlling access), the rationalization of production (by dividing the production process into very discrete, simplified tasks), and the development of machinery, led to factories employing relatively unskilled laborers, replacing the traditional craft-oriented form of production.[2]

In this chapter, I sketch an image of the future world of "law workers":[3] those who are involved in the production and delivery of legal services, other than persons who perform strictly clerical or support tasks (i.e., typists/word processing operators, filing clerks, computer technicians, bookkeepers, etc.). In terms of the occupations that we know today, law workers include lawyers, paralegals, legal assistants, and possibly law librarians. As I have shown in my study of nonlawyer advocacy (Kritzer 1998b), law workers also include tax preparers (enrolled agents), accountants, unemployment compensation specialists, union agents, and specialized advocates who handle welfare appeals, social security disability appeals, domestic violence cases, workers' compensation claims, immigration issues, and so on. If our goal is to understand categories in terms of competencies and the services that can be delivered, those categories have ceased to be useful and we need to find new ways of conceptualizing the occupations that comprise the broad category of "law workers."

Traditionally, being admitted to the practice of law was supposed to indicate that a lawyer was competent to provide legal services to clients. Today, being admitted to practice, and hence licensed to provide any type of legal service within the geographic area of admission, has little to do with competence to practice. In fact, the most recent ABA "statement" regarding legal education from the profession itself, the "MacCrate Report" (MacCrate 1992) speaks not in terms of competence, but in terms of skills and values, with the goal of attaining competence relegated to a "fundamental value" to be instilled, rather than something the law school experience is supposed to produce. A person whose lawyer proves "incompetent" actually has little recourse unless that incompetence constitutes "negligence." In practice, the profession itself does little or nothing to ensure competence, and there is little that others can do either. This point was driven home to me in a conversation that I had with an official of the New York State Workers' Compensation Board, which requires nonlawyers to pass an examination on workers' compensation law and procedures before being

---

[2] While craft-oriented production remains for a limited market, even that often involves a more rationalized form of production than was the tradition. For example, I ordered a new dining room table from a local store that purchased from Amish "craftsmen"; in discussing my order, I was told that I could also order matching chairs, although they would actually be made, not by the person who made the table, but by someone else who specialized in chairs. When I said I was concerned about the stain matching if the pieces came from different sources, I was told not to worry because the finishing was actually done by a third person who specialized in this task, so the stain used on all pieces would actually be the same.

[3] Compare to "law-jobs" (Llewellyn 1940), or "law experts" (Arthurs and Kreklewich 1996:34-35).

allowed to appear as representatives, and has established procedures for disciplining those whom it licenses. As part of my study of nonlawyer advocacy, I had contacted the official to obtain information on the Board's experience in disciplining the advocates that it licenses. The official told me that the Board initiates disciplinary proceedings against "very few" nonlawyers; the official then went on to tell me that the problems that the Board saw were generally not with the nonlawyers that it licenses but with nonspecialist lawyers. The problem from the Workers' Compensation Board's viewpoint is that any lawyer licensed in New York may handle a workers' compensation matter, and that the Board has no regulatory authority over lawyers who appear before it; furthermore, the New York Bar has no inclination to deal with the incompetence that the Board encounters.

In the nineteenth century, the practice of law was a much more limited undertaking. It dealt largely with a few types of issues (criminal law, property, contracts, and occasionally torts—the areas of law that continue today to comprise the core first-year curriculum in American law schools). With the growth of the administrative and welfare state, and with the rise of the large corporate enterprise, the legal field has expanded beyond anything that could have been envisioned 150 years ago. While this development may have originally manifested in what Heinz and Laumann have labeled the corporate hemisphere (Heinz and Laumann 1982; Heinz et al. 1998; Heinz et al. 2005), it is by no means limited to those who practice in large firms. While the idea of "general practice" might have once meant dealing with anything that came through the door, general practice today is really a label for a kind of limited range practice that involves a small number of traditional areas. Even those areas are often limited to a relatively routinized subset of issues. This growing complexity and the corresponding explosion of legal knowledge and information are making it difficult, probably impossible, to sustain the image of *the* legal profession (Arthurs 1995). Globalization, and the demands that it has placed on law, legal institutions, and legal professions, adds a further dimension to this growing complexity (Arthurs 1997; Kritzer 1999:730-31).

My goal is not to propose rules or policies that improve the competency of those who deliver legal services. Rather, I want to begin to reconceptualize what it means to deliver legal services and to prepare those who will do the delivering. To this end, I want to describe three distinct roles for law workers, and then discuss what law schools need to do to educate and train these different types of workers.

I. LAW WORKERS: TODAY AND TOMORROW

A. VARIETIES OF LEGAL OCCUPATIONS TODAY

While, at least in the formal sense, there is only one "legal profession" in the United States, the reality is much more complex. There is a wide variety of "law workers," broadly defined to include all individuals who deliver services of a legal nature. Many of these law workers provide very specialized, specific services, such as property title transfers, tax preparation and tax law consultation, or legal document preparation assistance (see Arthurs and Kreklewich 1996:42-44; Bernstein 2002; Commission on Nonlawyer Practice 1994; Hines 2001). Others, such as legal assistants and many paralegals, work under the formal guidance of licensed lawyers and handle most of the tasks that lawyers handle, other than actually appearing in court.[4] Even in the area of formal advocacy, at least outside the courts, nonlawyers regularly appear in a wide variety of venues.

Not only are there many types of nonlawyer law workers in the United States, but efforts to assess the quality of their work, or to compare the quality of that work to that of licensed lawyers, indicate that the general quality of these services is quite good, and may even, in certain circumstances, be better than that provided by lawyers (Rhode 2000:135-41). For example, the American Bar Association's Commission on Nonlawyer Practice found no evidence that nonlawyers delivered poor services (Commission on Nonlawyer Practice 1995). My own study comparing lawyer and nonlawyer advocates in four different venues showed that nonlawyers could, and often did, provide high quality representation. In certain circumstances, the typical lawyer was better. In other circumstances, the typical nonlawyer was better. In still other circumstances, there was no apparent difference between lawyers and nonlawyers (see Kritzer 1998b). The findings of research in the United States parallel those of studies in Ontario and England that show that specialist nonlawyers can and do provide quality representation (Bogart and Vidmar 1989; Genn and Genn 1989; Moorhead et al. 2003).[5] In England, the Law Society (the national organization of solicitors) has long decried and criticized nonlawyer "claims assessors" who represent injured persons in settling damage claims on a commission basis (Law Society 1970). However, an effort to determine what, if any, problems exist with regard to the results achieved by claims assessors was unable to identify any systematic issues, although it did raise the possibility of applying some form of regulatory scheme to this now unregulated group of service providers (Blackwell 2000).

---

[4] Even in the court context, there may now be some exceptions. For example, in Wisconsin, it is possible for a nonlawyer to appear in court as an advocate for victims of domestic violence; victims have a right to have such "service representatives" present with them in court to assist them (unless a victim is represented by counsel or is actually testifying) and, with the permission of the court, to address the court. Wis. Stat. § 895.73(2) (2002). An exception may also depend on the meaning of "court"; certain nonlawyers, either accountants or "enrolled agents," may appear as advocates in the U.S. Tax Court. In England, it is now common for nonlawyer legal executives, formally under the supervision of solicitors, to routinely appear in court for the early stages of criminal proceedings, and since 1998 have some rights to conduct litigation (Francis 2002). In Ontario, nonlawyers who work without the supervision of lawyers can appear as advocates in at least some types of minor criminal cases, such as driving while intoxicated (see Bogart and Vidmar 1989:4).

[5] In fact, the apparent success of a California teenager who provides basic legal advice on the website AskMe.com might raise questions about whether significant specialized expertise is needed for much of what passes for legal advice; maybe all that is needed is basic common sense and a bit of self-confidence (see Lewis 2001).

B. THE STRUCTURE OF LEGAL OCCUPATIONS IN THE TWENTY-FIRST CENTURY

Richard Susskind has written extensively on the impact of information technology on the practice of law (Susskind 1998, 2001, 2008, 2013). Much of his writing has dealt with how information technology can be integrated into the day-to-day functioning of legal practice, particularly large scale, corporate practice. He envisions new roles in what he calls the "client service chain." For example, one of these roles is the "legal infomediary," who assists the client in identifying the kinds of legal expertise and service providers that he or she needs. Susskind also sees clients increasingly gaining access to legal resources provided by the law firm through its extranet and intranet services (the former being publicly available and the latter being selectively available to paying clients, either on a fee-for-access basis or as part of the rebundled service provided by the firm). A second new role that Susskind envisions is the "legal information engineer" or LIE (my abbreviation, not Susskind's). In Susskind's vision, the LIE's role is to build legal information systems that systematize work that is currently done manually. For example, reasonably good software already exists for handling routinized legal tasks; the most widely used programs are popular tax preparation software packages, such as TaxCut [now H&R Block Tax Software] and TurboTax. One can imagine many areas to which such tools can be expanded, with the crucial caveat that for matters governed by state law, there will have to be separate solutions for each state (just as TaxCut and TurboTax offer separate packages for each state's income tax).

Susskind's work illustrates a way to think about the future structures of legal services delivery and the different roles that will ensue. I envision three primary roles:

> **Legal Information Engineers** (LIEs) who design and maintain systems to routinize legal service delivery and facilitate access to legal information. Thus, LIEs' roles are not limited to building the kinds of straightforward systems envisioned by Susskind but go beyond those to implement protocols developed by Legal Consultants, design triage systems to properly route users, and build access tools that allow both end recipients and Legal Processors to access appropriate bases of expertise.

> **Legal Consultants** (LCs) who both deal with highly specialized matters and develop protocols to be implemented by a combination of LIEs and Legal Processors.

> **Legal Processors** (LPs) who perform two key roles: engaging in protocol-based triage procedures to determine whether they are the appropriate providers of services and delivering those relatively routine services that cannot be automated or are needed by clients who choose not to use the automation tools available. LPs will refer complex or otherwise nonfitting matters to the Legal Consultants (LCs), both for the purpose of allowing the LCs to service those clients and to provide input to the LCs for developing and improving existing service protocols.

Figure 15.1 graphically displays the model that I envision. In the next section, I discuss in detail the roles of each of the components of this "legal services triad," starting from the bottom of the list above.

Figure 15.1: The Legal Profession Triad

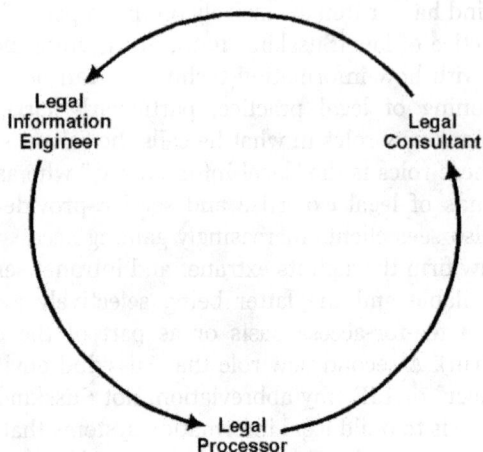

II. THE LEGAL PROFESSION TRIAD

A. LEGAL PROCESSORS

In 1996, I spent three months observing in the offices of three different lawyers whose work involved cases taken on a contingency fee basis (see Kritzer 2004b). The practices of two of those lawyers concentrated on this type of work while the third lawyer's practice combined contingency fee cases with other court-oriented work (criminal, divorce, and simple commercial litigation). In one of the offices, the lawyer that I observed clearly preferred some aspects of his work to others, and he delegated the tasks that he did not enjoy to a paralegal. Those tasks included legal research and legal drafting; he focused on interacting with clients, negotiating with opposing parties, and spending time in court. The work that he did himself drew largely on his people skills and less on the formal skills that he learned in law school. In the second office, the lawyer told me point blank that most of the work that he did could readily be done by a nonlawyer with the appropriate specialized training (and as discussed above, in some states, the workers' compensation cases that he handled could have been handled by nonlawyers).[6]

While each case handled by these lawyers was unique in certain ways, the cases were marked much more by their commonalities. As a result, the work became heavily repetitive. The lawyers paid careful attention to detail in order to avoid problems and challenges, and there were only occasional opportunities for creative solutions or arguments. Still, neither the care required nor the nature of the creativity that might be exercised was closely tied to legal training as we know it today. As I watched these lawyers work, I could easily imagine how one might create written protocols that would guide a trained nonlawyer in handling

---

[6] Circa 1980, twenty out of fifty states permitted nonlawyers to represent workers' compensation claimants (see Rhode 1981).

the tasks required by a case. The key elements, in addition to following routines and recognizing key issues (e.g., determining the nature of insurance coverages available for compensation), were (1) keeping up with important changes in the law, such as new judicial interpretations of insurance policy provisions (i.e., knowing when a routine needs to be modified), and (2) knowing the other players in the system in order to communicate effectively with them.

While I focused on contingency fee cases (largely personal injury and workers' compensation cases), much of the work in the personal services/personal plight sector of the market could be similarly handled by trained nonlawyer specialists working with protocols or from specialized experience. Relevant areas of practice might include writing wills and estate planning, handling noncomplex estates, divorce and child custody cases, property transfers, welfare and benefits claims, consumer cases, routine criminal matters (for either the prosecution or defense), personal bankruptcy and debt (including debt collection), and guardianship matters.

One could see appropriate protocols programmed into a software tool that requires the entry of key elements of information, and then cross-checks for particular problems and issues in order to alert the service provider to possible issues that had been overlooked or additional information that should be sought.[7]

A key issue for LPs would be licensing and regulation.[8] Clearly, some level of training (or comparable experience) would be needed. Who would determine what those requirements would be for a given type of practice? Who would regulate such providers? What kinds of recourse would disgruntled clients have? I hesitate to specify in detail what might be required because that could vary significantly by specific practice area. For example, in Ontario, Canada, one type of provider of specialized services handles defense of driving while intoxicated cases; many of these providers are former members of the Ontario Provincial Police and, as a result, have extensive experience in court as witnesses and know the issues that are involved in drunk driving cases. While this experience does not necessarily mean that a former officer will be an effective representative, the experience is probably more directly related to handling these cases than is the general law school experience. A second example, in the area of representing persons with personal injury claims, would be former insurance adjusters; in evaluating claims, an experienced adjuster will know the issues and what is

---

[7] In fact, hospitals are increasingly using such protocols to reduce the possibility of medical errors. A good example is medication delivered to patients. While an ordering physician is supposed to keep track of other medications that a patient is taking in order to avoid harmful drug interactions, frequent failures to detect such contraindications have led to computer-based systems—Computerized Physician Order Entry (CPOE) systems—that monitor the medications that are prescribed for patients and issue alerts when a newly ordered medication may interact with a previously ordered one. These systems also check dosage amounts against patient characteristics like age and weight (see Kaushal and Bates 2001). Such systems are part of a larger set of developments under the rubric of Clinical Decision Support Systems (CDSS), which are computer-based systems that assist and guide physicians in medical diagnosis and treatment (see Hunt et al. 1998).

[8] See Wolfson et al. (1980:165-69) for a general overview of approaches to regulation; Wilkins (1992) provides a good discussion of contemporary issues concerning the regulation of lawyers.

needed both in the way of documents and arguments.[9] Both of these examples turn largely on related experience rather than on formal training.

In other areas, the relevant approach may involve more formal educational requirements combined with some type of specialized examination. Some existing voluntary programs have already adopted this approach. For example, the Certified Financial Planner (CFP) Board of Standards is an "independent professional regulatory organization" that sets requirements and offers examinations to individuals who wish to describe themselves as "certified financial planners."[10] The CFP Board, in turn, is accredited by the National Commission for Certifying Agencies (NCCA), which is the accrediting arm of the National Organization for Competency Assurance (NOCA). NOCA accredits a number of different "certifying agencies," most dealing with providers that are connected to medical care.

In 1998, California passed SB1418, creating the formal occupation of Legal Document Assistant (LDA).[11] The law, which became fully effective on January 1, 2000, allows a licensed LDA to distribute published materials written or approved by an attorney, prepare documents under the direction of the customer, and file the documents in the appropriate court. To be licensed, a Legal Document Assistant must meet one of the following educational requirements:

1. A high school diploma or general equivalency diploma, and either a minimum of two years of law-related experience under the supervision of a licensed attorney, or a minimum of two years' experience, prior to January 1, 1999, providing self-help service.

2. A baccalaureate degree in any field and either a minimum of one year law-related experience under the supervision of a licensed attorney, or a minimum of one year of experience, prior to January 1, 1999, providing self-help service.

3. A certificate of completion from a paralegal program that is institutionally accredited but not approved by the American Bar Association, and that requires successful completion of a minimum of twenty-four semester units, or the equivalent, in legal specialization courses.

4. A certificate of completion from a paralegal program approved by the American Bar Association.

To become licensed, an LDA must be bonded in the amount of $25,000 or more (or post a bond of that amount with the county clerk who issues the license). In addition to specific limitations on the services that an LDA may provide, an LDA must have a written contract with each client, specifying what the LDA will do and for what fee. An LDA who violates any of the provisions of the regulatory

---

[9] At least some of the claims assessors in England who do this work previously worked as "claims inspectors," the English equivalent of claims adjusters (see Kritzer 1998b:3).

[10] See http://wwv.cfp-board.org/main-abtus.html (last visited January 10, 2002).

[11] After the enactment of this law, the California Association of Independent Paralegals was renamed the California Association of Legal Document Assistants (CALDA). Background information on LDAs, requirements for practice, services offered, and similar information can be found on CALDA's website, http://vww.calda.org (last visited September 12, 2014).

and licensing statute may be charged with a misdemeanor punishable by a fine of up to $2,000 and imprisonment for up to one year. These regulations also apply to nonlawyers licensed as Unlawful Detainer Assistants (i.e., individuals who provide services in connection with eviction proceedings).

In 2012 the Washington Supreme Court adopted rules to allow practice by limited license legal technicians (LLLT), although actual licensing has not gone into effect as this is written [November 2014]. According to those rules, an LLLT will be authorized to complete the following tasks within the particular legal areas that the LLLT has qualified to work in:

1. Obtain relevant facts, and explain the relevancy of such information to the client;

2. Inform the client of applicable procedures, including deadlines, documents which must be filed, and the anticipated course of the legal proceeding;

3. Inform the client of applicable procedures for proper service of process and filing of legal documents;

4. Provide the client with self-help materials prepared by a Washington lawyer or approved by the [LLLT] Board, which contain information about relevant legal requirements, case law basis for the client's claim, and venue and jurisdiction requirements;

5. Review documents or exhibits that the client has received from the opposing side, and explain them to the client;

6. Select and complete forms that have been approved by the State of Washington, either through a governmental agency or by the Administrative Office of the Courts or the content of which is specified by statute; federal forms; forms prepared by a Washington lawyer; or forms approved by the Board; and advise the client of the significance of the selected forms to the client's case;

7. Perform legal research and draft legal letters and documents beyond what is permitted in the previous paragraph, if the work is reviewed and approved by a Washington lawyer;

8. Advise a client as to other documents that may be necessary to the client's case (such as exhibits, witness declarations, or party declarations), and explain how such additional documents or pleadings may affect the client's case;

9. Assist the client in obtaining necessary documents, such as birth, death, or marriage certificates.

LLLTs are governed by the LLLT Board which began operating in 2013. To become an LLLT one will have to meet certain educational requirement, pass a subject-specific examination; LLLTs will be subject to a set of rules of professional conduct approved by the Washington Supreme Court; LLLTs will need to meet continuing education requirements, pay an annual licensing fee, and carry what amounts to liability insurance. The first area authorized for LLLTs is domestic relations. The first LLLTs are expected to start practicing in 2015.[12]

The model developed in California does not go as far as the Washington model. The California approach was a political compromise between segments of the bar that adamantly opposed any legislation legitimizing or recognizing nonlawyer practice and groups that advocated broad recognition of law workers other than lawyers.[13] The Washington approach is similar to those that allow for a specific venue to adopt licensing or certification procedures for those who appear before it (e.g., "enrolled agents" before the IRS). Typically, systems allowing for nonlawyer practice include provisions that protect consumers from incompetent or unscrupulous practitioners by requiring them to post a bond or carry liability insurance. One implication is that if nonlawyers providing limited legal services are required to be insured or bonded, then why shouldn't lawyers also be required to provide such protections to their clients? Only one state, Oregon, currently requires that lawyers carry malpractice insurance in order to be licensed to practice in the state (Commission on Nonlawyer Practice 1995: 129n441).[14]

B. LEGAL CONSULTANTS

While a significant portion of legal matters are routine and lend themselves to alternative approaches to service delivery, a lot of legal work is not appropriate for such an approach. This work will typically involve some combination of significance (i.e., amount at stake, precedential implications, etc.), uniqueness, and complexity. The key that makes such cases different is the need for creativity on the part of the practitioner; thus, the distinction between the legal processor and the legal consultant might be summed up by whether or not their cases call for what is sometimes labeled "creative lawyering." The issue here is not so much one of presence or absence of creativity, but rather one of degree. The legal processor will occasionally encounter a case that needs creative lawyering, and should realize that such cases need to be referred to a legal consultant. For the legal consultant, a large percentage of his or her cases will require creative lawyering; in a sense, creativity will be part of the routine of the legal consultant's work.

---

[12] For more on LLLTs in Washington, see Chambliss (2014) or https://lib.law.washington.edu/content/guides/llltguide (last visited November 16, 2014).

[13] There was also substantial conflict between different groups of nonlawyers, with one preferring a model where paraprofessionals work only under the direct supervision of lawyers and another wanting the recognition of independent practice. While the nomenclature is by no means unambiguous, "legal assistants" typically prefer the former model, while those who prefer the latter model use the label "paralegals."

[14] Legal malpractice insurance is not the only possible form of protection for clients. Lawyers in some jurisdictions must make payments into a fund to compensate clients for unscrupulous behavior such as embezzlement from trust funds; however, such funds typically do not provide for compensation for incompetent representation, only for unethical behavior. Also, firms that organize as LLPs or LLCs may be required by state law to carry liability insurance.

Since many matters are inappropriate for routinized handling, one role of LPs is to recognize when they have such cases and refer those cases to Legal Consultants. This is why Figure 15.1 shows an arrow from the LPs to the LCs.

One of the lawyers that I observed had a practice that was dominated by the kinds of cases I envisioned going to legal consultants. For example, one of his clients had suffered a disabling injury on the job. The lawyer sought compensation, not just through workers' compensation, but also from third parties who were responsible for the situation that caused the injury. The case raised complex issues of what constituted reasonable precautions on the part of the client, the employer, and the third parties. Framing the issues and establishing relevant proofs required extensive investigation and creativity. Ultimately, the case concluded with a seven figure settlement.

While all three of the lawyers whom I observed as part of my study of contingency fee practice had some cases that required creative handling or raised unusual issues, the bulk of the other two lawyers' work was very routine in nature; their work involved important knowledge and skill, but it could have been readily handled by a trained non-JD specialist. Most of their work involved assembling information (largely medical records to document treatment and loss), reviewing that information for uncertainties and problems, presenting that information as the core of a demand, and working toward a final settlement figure. The lawyers needed to know how to handle a specific range of legal issues and, more importantly, how to communicate the dimensions of a claim to the opposing side. The specific legal knowledge required could readily be acquired through training (or experience) that falls well short of a standard law school education. While my research focused on contingency fee practice, the same argument could be made regarding other routinized areas of work, such as probate, special areas of criminal defense (e.g., driving while intoxicated), or divorce (Mather et al. 2001; Sarat and Felstiner 1995). The key is the nature of the mix of work for various types of legal practice.

In addition to handling cases that do not fit the standardized protocols, a legal consultant has an important role in developing these protocols. In part, this happens over time as new issues arise and get worked out, or as new areas of practice develop. For example, *Goldberg v. Kelly*[15] held that a person whose welfare benefits were to be reduced or terminated is entitled to due process in the form of a "fair hearing." In the immediate wake of *Goldberg*, there was much uncertainty as to what the parameters and requirements of such hearings would be, and what standards of proof and judgment the adjudicators would employ. During this period, effective representation called for significant creativity and a broad understanding of legal concepts and advocacy. However, over time, the hearings became routinized as evidentiary issues and other legal questions were resolved; while a unique situation may occasionally arise, most issues are sufficiently straightforward that specialized nonlawyer advocates can be effective representatives (see Simon 1988). This by no means eliminates the role of lawyers; having a lawyer with a broader background available as a trainer

---

[15] 397 U.S. 254 (1970).

and a resource, and to take over cases that raise unusual or complex issues, almost certainly improves the overall quality of representation.[16]

The legal consultants of tomorrow will be specialists and this fact raises the important issue of acquiring and certifying specialized expertise.[17] The general legal profession has been reluctant to formalize specialization, with the obvious exceptions of multiple legal professions, such as solicitors and barristers in England. The issue of specialization has been on the legal profession's agenda for some time.[18] Some areas of the law, such as tax and intellectual property, have long been the province of specialists. The organization of the large corporate law firm has been based on specialization for most, if not all, of the twentieth century (see Galanter and Palay 1991; Laumann and Heinz 1977; Nelson 1988; Smigel 1964). However, it was not until the 1970s that the issue of specialization had begun to produce any formal developments, with the California bar adopting the first state-level system for certifying some specialists in 1973 (LoPucki 1990), and private groups such as the National Board of Trial Advocacy creating their own specialist certification systems.[19] The ABA Model Rules of Professional Conduct prohibit lawyers from claiming specialization, except in officially recognized categories, and it was not until 1979 that the ABA created model standards for specializations, adopting a plan developed by the Standing Committee on Specialization earlier that year (Rosen 1990:3).[20]

Surprisingly, only a minority of states has actually adopted systems for certifying specialists,[21] and proposals for such systems have often been controversial, raising such questions as (LoPucki 1990:1-2):

> Would the recognition of specializations favor some lawyers over others in attracting clients?

---

[16] The idea of a hierarchy of knowledge or specialization is not limited to the multi-occupation model that I am describing. Even within today's legal profession, lawyers routinely refer cases to other lawyers with more specialized practices, or contact such lawyers for advice and information. "Lawyer-to-lawyer" consultation networks are common, and a significant amount of "legal research" is actually conducted not by reading law books but by calling other lawyers for a quick read on an issue.

[17] In fact, I adopted the label "legal consultants" based on the term used in England to refer to medical specialists, "consultants."

[18] See Rosen (1990) for a bibliography of commentaries and other writings on specialization.

[19] In significant part, the specialization issue has been closely tied to the question of lawyer advertising: under what circumstances should a lawyer be permitted to hold himself or herself out as a specialist in a particular area? In *Peel v. Attorney Registration and Disciplinary Commission of Illinois*, 496 U.S. 91 (1990), the Supreme Court struck down an Illinois ban on the communication (advertising) of certification and provided some impetus to the development of certification plans. See Podgers (1993) for a review of relevant Supreme Court decisions.

[20] This development came in the wake of the U.S. Supreme Court's 1977 decision to strike down absolute bans on lawyer advertising in *Bates v. State Bar of Arizona*, 433 U.S. 350 (1977). In 1987, the ABA Standing Committee on Specialization published a revised version of the Model Standards for Specialty Areas, which contained model standards for twenty-five areas of practice, from admiralty to workers' compensation.

[21] By 1990, only fourteen states had adopted plans to certify specialists (most were rather limited) and one state, Georgia, had abandoned its plan (LoPucki 1990:53). By 1993, eighteen states had adopted such plans (ABA Standing Committee on Specialization 1993:i).

Would uncertified lawyers who practice in a particular specialization be more at risk for claims of malpractice in the event of adverse outcomes?

Would specialization drive up fees?

The controversy over the impact of recognizing specialization is complicated by the dilemma of which dimensions of specialization to recognize. In addition to substantive areas of law (e.g., tax, admiralty, real estate), there is the question of task-oriented specialties (litigation, administrative process, etc.) or venue-oriented specialities (Internal Revenue Service, Securities and Exchange Commission, federal court, U.S. Supreme Court, etc.).[22]

Specialization has generally been experience-related, rather than training-related.[23] Unlike the medical profession, where a physician enters a formal training program (a residency) to become a specialist, a lawyer works in the field to become certified as a specialist. A lawyer can seek such certification only after acquiring a number of years of experience. Legal specialization today is where legal training was ninety years ago; it is essentially an apprentice system (but often without guidance from experienced mentors).

Although the roles of the legal processor and the legal consultant are distinct, they could clearly be combined into a single practice. Both roles turn on the concept of specialized legal expertise. This structure may resemble a contemporary practice, where one or two lawyers supervise a group of paralegals who handle the routine work,[24] but it is potentially quite different. While there is a hierarchy of expertise, there need not be a hierarchy of control; there is no reason why the firm must be managed by, or owned by, the legal consultants. This concept has been adopted in England by "claims management companies." These firms handle routine personal injury claims with a combination of solicitors and claims assessors (adjusters). Although there were some problems with some of these companies, they were related to a combination of startup issues and overly ambitious goals (see Inman 2001; Walsh 2001).

C. LEGAL INFORMATION ENGINEERS

The third leg of the triad is the legal information engineer (LIE). Richard Susskind created the concept of the legal information engineer (Susskind 1998:270). In Susskind's vision, legal information engineers will be those members of the legal profession "whose knowledge forms the basis of legal

---

[22] These specialties mirror three types of expertise that I have identified as crucial to effective representation: substantive, procedural, and insider expertise (Kritzer 1998b:14-15). There are other dimensions of specialization as well: type of client, type of industry, side represented, size of matter, and geographical area (Hagglund and Bimbaum 1984; LoPucki 1990:11).

[23] This approach to specialization, either certified or informal, seems to be the norm within common law systems (see, for example, Stager and Arthurs 1990:199-201).

[24] In my study of contingency fee practice, I came across several law firms that functioned this way. American "franchise" law firms also functioned this way, producing routine materials with the supervising lawyer largely handling intake and overseeing the work of the nonlawyer staff (see Van Hoy 1997).

information services" (*ibid.*, 291).[25] My image is more specific: LIEs will use information technology and, where possible, artificial intelligence (AI) to design software tools and other systems that will guide legal processors and/or actual users of legal services in dealing with routinized legal tasks and in accessing legal information.

Artificial intelligence will be an important element of what will come in the future developments. Susskind has been writing about the role of artificial intelligence in the delivery of legal services since the 1980s (see Susskind 1987). In addition to Susskind, other people have been working on such topics as automated legal reasoning and "legal knowledge engineering" (Kralingen et al. 1996; Valenta 1995). One early effort to use this technology in the U.S. focused on claim valuation in personal injury cases (Waterman and Peterson 1984). The idea behind this system was to draw on a large body of information about jury verdicts in a given area to identify key factors that influenced the amounts awarded (Chin and Peterson 1983; Peterson 1983, 1987; Peterson and Priest 1982), and then build a model of the claims evaluation process (Peterson 1984). Combining the model and the data leads to a system that can take corresponding information in new cases to estimate valuations. There are already a variety of online tools for handling other tasks, such as simple wills, uncontested divorces, etc.

The role of the legal information engineer is to design and maintain two kinds of systems: those intended for direct client use and those intended for practitioner use (the latter systems are reflected in Figure 15.1 by the arrow that goes from the legal information engineer to the legal processor). Such systems automate routine work, provide access to legal information data sources, guide simple legal analysis, and provide tools for detecting errors and issues that might otherwise be overlooked. The operational models for consumer-oriented systems and practitioner-oriented systems are likely to differ because the latter will assume a core level of knowledge that allows shortcuts for information entry and more sophisticated cross-checking. While a typical system for consumer use would probably be built around a "questionnaire" or "interview" model, with the user responding to specific questions,[26] a system for practitioner use would probably use a more efficient "form" or "screen" model that presumes that the user knows the reason particular information was needed and understands the nature of the information to be provided on a particular form.

---

[25] Susskind divides future providers of legal services into two groups: what he calls "legal specialists," who are akin to my notion of "legal consultants," and legal information engineers, who would combine some aspects of the roles that I ascribe to legal processors (perhaps because in England, the term "engineer" refers to technicians who handle routine repair and maintenance tasks) and legal information engineers. Susskind describes the main task of the legal information engineer as "that of an analyst ... [whose role is] to interpret and repackage the formal sources of law ... and articulate it in a structured format suitable for implementation as part of a legal information service" (1998:207).

[26] Popular tax preparation software such as TurboTax uses this approach.

The legal information engineer combines the skills of a systems analyst with a body of core legal knowledge.[27] The core of the LIE's expertise is in designing systems that automate and/or guide the completion of legal tasks. To this end, the LIE is neither a programmer nor necessarily an expert in a particular area of the law. The engineer relies on a legal consultant for substantive guidance in designing and maintaining a system for a particular legal area or task. Thus, in Figure 15.1, an arrow goes from the legal consultant to the legal information engineer. The interaction between the legal information engineer and the legal consultant occurs both in the initial design phase and in system maintenance. This latter point is crucial: the law changes and the viability of expert systems in law depend upon those systems keeping up with the changes as they occur. Therefore, a key role of the legal consultant is to alert the legal information engineer to changes in the law that require modification to a system. Some changes might require nothing more than "tweaking" the system while others may require a major overhaul. As a result, a key to effective design of these systems will be ease of modification to adapt to the dynamic character of the law. One could imagine different groups of legal information engineers, with one group specializing in initial development and design, and another specializing in the maintenance of existing systems.

One obvious complication, at least in federal systems such as the United States, is the variation from state to state in the law. Even systems that deal with federal law may have to account for significant differences among the circuits. It may be possible to design systems that deal with groups of states that have similar law on a given topic, but some variations will undoubtedly be so significant that purely state-specific systems must be designed. The economic viability of such systems will substantially depend on the potential volume of use. As a result, a wide range of systems may be available for a large state such as California, but not for a small-population state such as North Dakota.

D. SUMMARY

Law workers of the future will be comprised of different groups with different kinds and levels of training. Legal consultants will be the providers of the future who handle the work that requires highly customized analysis and service. Legal processors will handle the routine work that today is often delegated to paralegals and other support staff, as well as work that could readily be delegated to such persons. Legal information engineers will design and maintain information systems that provide access to bodies of legal information and facilitate the completion of many standardized legal tasks. As suggested by the arrows in Figure 15.1, these three groups of law workers will interact in a regular, structured fashion.

Legal consultants will provide substantive input to legal information engineers. Legal information engineers will create task completion and information

---

[27] In this regard, legal information engineers are similar to today's law librarians, who typically combine knowledge about the law with knowledge about legal information sources and search tools.

retrieval tools to be used by legal processors, as well as lay persons engaged in self-help activities. Legal processors will identify and forward to legal consultants matters that are inappropriate for the routine services that the processors offer. As law workers, all three groups will share a core level of legal knowledge and a legal vocabulary.

III. THE ROLE OF THE LAW SCHOOL IN THE FUTURE WORLD OF LAW WORKERS

So where does the law school fit into this model? Figure 15.2 illustrates the role that I see for the future law school: it will occupy the center of the world of law workers, providing training (both initial and ongoing) to legal processors, legal consultants, and legal information engineers.

Imagine a redesigned legal curriculum where the first year remains similar to what it is today, with a focus on the traditional areas of the common law plus perhaps some elements of statutory interpretation. The first year will introduce future law workers to core legal concepts and the basics of legal analysis. The first year might differ only slightly for each group of future law workers. Those planning to become legal consultants might take a course in legal writing (with the assumption that a significant portion of their future work will involve the preparation of original legal documents). Those planning to become legal processors might take a course on client interviewing and case management. Those planning to become legal information engineers might take a course on the basics of systems analysis. The training for each group would diverge after the first year.

Figure 15.2: The Law School and the Legal Profession Triad

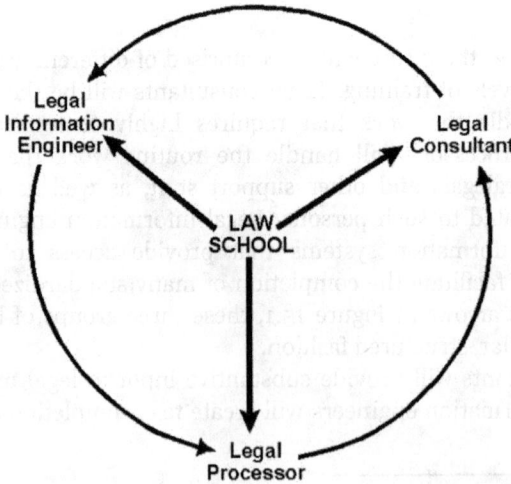

A. LEGAL CONSULTANTS

In the second year, legal consultants would continue with courses that are designed to hone core legal knowledge and legal analysis skills. The third and fourth year would be devoted to training in a chosen specialty. Ideally, there would be a significant "clinical" element to this part of the training. This clinical element might mean that law schools will specialize in the particular fields that they offer to legal consultants, reflecting the availability of clinical opportunities in a given area. Perhaps law schools in a given region could form a consortium, with students moving to the appropriate school for the last two years. An important issue here would be the development of some way to certify specializations at the completion of the fourth year. This might be accomplished through specialized bar exams (different exams for different specialties) and perhaps a voluntary certification system for more fine-grained specialties.

B. LEGAL PROCESSORS

In the second year, legal processors would move on to course and clinical work in their chosen specialties. The course work would be geared to the day-to-day, nitty-gritty of a specialty (e.g., divorce, welfare benefits and advocacy, injury compensation, etc.). At the end of the year, these students would take an examination that tests them on both broad legal skills (from the first year) and the specifics of their specialties (compare to Arthurs 1996:220). Once in practice, a legal processor would be authorized to make court or administrative tribunal appearances in his or her specialty, at least at the trial level; appellate work might be restricted to legal consultants who are certified in a given area.

There might be an alternative one-year track for those legal processors who have relevant experience in a field. For example, a person who has previously worked as an insurance adjuster might be allowed to sit for the examination on injury compensation after taking the core first-year sequence, on the assumption that the prior experience provides an adequate background in the specialty.

Thus, in terms of academic content, future legal processors and future legal consultants will share the same basic first-year experience. Since a law school would probably offer tracks for both groups, and they may share some classes during the initial years, there might be a good role here for "online" law schools (see Oliphant 2000). While I am skeptical of the online model's ability to develop high-level legal analysis and legal reasoning skills, it may be a viable way to instill the basic level that legal processors need. The online approach might be particularly useful to those who seek to transfer to legal processor careers from backgrounds that have already provided significant experience and expertise.[28]

---

[28] Oliphant's former institution, William Mitchell College of Law, obtained approval from the ABA in 2014 for a program that combines face-to-face and online instruction (see Janus et al. 2014). It will be several years before the success of the program can be judged, either in terms of bar exam passage or in terms of graduates securing positions in law firms or other practice settings.

C. LEGAL INFORMATION ENGINEERS

As indicated above, legal information engineers would take the same core curriculum during the first year. The only non-core first-year course should probably introduce students to the conceptual elements of systems analysis. After the first year, the training of legal information engineers will diverge sharply from that of either legal consultants or legal processors.

The second, and possibly third, year of training for legal information engineers would focus largely on the skills and knowledge needed to design and maintain both client-use and provider-use systems. This program should involve both training in system design and training that enables legal information engineers to understand how target audiences actually use their systems. While the substance of legal information systems will be different from those in other areas, their basic functions will undoubtedly resemble systems in other fields. Therefore, the training of legal information engineers could readily be part of a joint enterprise of the future law school, the school of library and information science, and perhaps the department of operations research in the business school.

Because legal information engineers will not directly interact with consumers, I doubt that there will be a need for formal examinations or licensing structures for this group of law workers. On the other hand, certification might lend legitimacy to LIEs. The best form of certification would probably be a voluntary system based on the completion of specific coursework.

D. GENERAL ISSUES

The changes to legal education described above will not come easily.[29] They evoke the ongoing tension between liberal educational goals and vocational training goals. At top universities, prestige tends to accrue not to those who serve vocational needs, but to those engaged in research and writing that adheres more closely to the traditional model of liberal education. American legal education has long been torn between the goal of teaching students "to think like a lawyer" and the goal of serving the practical needs of the future practitioner (see Johnson 1991; Rhode 2000:185-92, 196-205; Schlegel 1995).[30] One commentator expressed this conflict nicely: "legal education has been and is still almost entirely about law and is only incidentally and superficially about lawyering" (Lopez 1988-89). While the clinical aspect of legal education in the U.S. has grown over the last decade or two, it is still the step-child of the typical law school, with "clinical" faculty often possessing a lower status than that of "regular" faculty; clinical programming is more likely to employ faculty on a low-paid, adjunct basis, and seldom offers the security of tenure.[31]

---

[29] A limited step in the direction of these kinds of changes might be found in the planned training for limited license legal technicians who are slated to begin practicing in the state of Washington in 2015 (see Chambliss 2014).

[30] This issue is not limited to American legal education; regarding Canada, see Arthurs (1998), and regarding England, see Fitzgerald (1993:14).

[31] As this chapter is being revised in 2014, there appears to be a growing trend to grant full-time clinical faculty tenured status.

Some of the tensions between the clinical and nonclinical side of American legal education may be attributed to the lack of a department structure within the law school. Contrast the structure of the law school to that of medical school, where there are departments in such areas as anatomy and specialists who teach first- and second-year medical students some of the basics that they will need to become practitioners. One could imagine a redesigned law school with multiple departments, some focusing on the basic analytical skills taught during the first year (and the second year as well for students in the legal consultant track), and others focusing on substantive specialties or practical skills.

CONCLUSION

This chapter assumes that the world in which legal practice is situated has changed. Some of these changes are technological developments that affect a wide range of occupations and professions, while others, such as the explosion of law itself, are more internal. Legal education continues to be structured around two roles: the general practitioner and the lawyer who enters a large corporate firm that will provide specialized training on the job. A smaller and smaller proportion of lawyers are engaged in general practice (see Heinz et al. 1998:765),[32] and the economic pressures on corporate law firms may be bringing to an end the time when those firms could assume a major training function (see France 1995b). Moreover, the self-help movement and competing providers are challenging the traditional providers of legal services, and this challenge is not going to go away.

While the changes upon which my analysis is based are substantial, there are important continuities as well. Fundamental to my argument is growing differentiation within legal practice. However, the idea that legal practice, and the legal profession, are stratified is not new (see Kritzer 2001a [Chapter 13 in this volume]; Kritzer 2001b). Moreover, the idea that stratification and differentiation imply that there should be different training provided to prospective providers of legal services is not new. As far back as the early twentieth century, the potential for differentiation was recognized. In 1913, the Committee on Education of the American Bar Association requested that the Carnegie Foundation for the Advancement of Teaching undertake an investigation "into the conditions under which the work of legal education is carried on in this country" (Reed 1921:xviii). Since this was a period in which the ABA was encouraging a model of education in which it would play a prominent role in the accreditation of law schools, one might surmise that the ABA intended to find that the large number of unaccredited, part-time, and evening law schools provided a substandard legal education. According to Alfred Reed, the author of the Carnegie Endowment study, the issue of the future of part-time legal

---

[32] Heinz et al. do not actually refer to "general practice" in their statistics, but they do show that the proportion of legal work devoted to the personal services sector has declined from 40% in 1975 to 29% in 1995. In their 1975 study, Heinz and Laumann reported (1982:325) that 70% of their respondents had described themselves as having a specialization. According to data provided to me by John Heinz, this figure rose to 75% in 1995 (see also Heinz et al. 2005: 37-38).

education was linked to "the perpetuation of the theory of a unitary bar, whose attainments are to be tested by uniform examinations" (*ibid.*, 77). In the conclusion of his study, Reed (*ibid.*, 417) argued that the legal profession was not in fact unitary, that the differentiation among practitioners was functional and would continue to exist, and that developments in legal education should take into account the reality of this differentiation. History proved that the ABA, perhaps in concert with the economic stresses produced by the Depression, largely succeeded in driving part-time, proprietary legal education out of business (although part-time legal education re-emerged in the last decade of the twentieth century). It is, in a sense, ironic that the developments of the closing decades of the twentieth century started a reconsideration of some of the developments of the early decades of the century.

Clearly, the image that I have sketched does not return us to an earlier time. Rather, it moves us forward, based on an understanding that has different foundations. It is important to ask whether the specific structure that I have outlined is actually going to come about. I would estimate that the probability of that occurring is one out of three. Major changes will happen—they have happened in England as a result of changes in legal aid, the less exclusive role possessed by the legal profession, and changing norms of professional regulation (Moorhead 1998, 2004; Steele and Bull 1996; Steele and Seargeant 1999),[33] but they will look substantially different from the model that I have outlined. I do expect a bifurcation in legal services providers, with some resembling what I have labeled legal consultants and some resembling legal processors. Whether they will share some basic educational experiences, according to my vision, is harder to say. Still, the myth of the unitary legal profession—the goal of reformers a century ago—will finally be demolished.

---

[33] Under the provisions of the Legal Services Act 2007, the traditional legal professions of solicitors and barristers have now been joined by a number of regulated providers of legal services, including licensed conveyancers, legal executives, patent attorneys, trademark attorneys, costs lawyers, notaries, and chartered accountants; see http://www.legal servicesboard.org.uk/can_we_help/approved_regulators/ (last visited October 6, 2014).

REFERENCES

ABA Standing Committee on Specialization (1993) "Specialization State Plan Book." Chicago, IL: American Bar Association.

Abbott, Andrew (1988) *The System of Professions: An Essay on the Division of Expert Labor*. Chicago, IL: University of Chicago Press.

Abel, Richard L. (1986) "The Decline of Professionalism." 49 *Modern Law Review* 1-41.

_____. (1988a) "The Crisis Is Injuries, Not Liability," in Walter Olson, ed., *New Directions in Liability Law*. New York: Academy of Political Science.

_____. (1988b) *The Legal Profession in England and Wales*. Oxford, UK: Basil Blackwell.

_____. (2001) "An American Hamburger Stand in St. Paul's Cathedral: Replacing Legal Aid with Conditional Fees in English Personal Injury Litigation." 51 *DePaul Law Review* 253-313.

Abel, Richard L. and Philip S.C. Lewis [eds.] (1989) *Lawyers in Society: Comparative Theories*. Berkeley, CA: University of California Press.

Abel-Smith, Brian and Robert Stevens (1967) *Lawyers and the Courts: A Sociological Study of the English Legal System, 1750–1965*. Cambridge, MA: Harvard University Press.

Abrahamse, Allan F. and Stephen J. Carroll (1999) "The Frequency of Excess Claims for Automobile Personal Injuries," in Georges Dionne and Claire Laberge-Nadeau, eds., *Automobile Insurance: Road Safety, New Drivers, Risks, Insurance Fraud and Regulation*. Norwell, MA: Kluwer Academic Publishers.

Abrams, David and Daniel L. Chen (2013) "A Market for Justice: A First Empirical Look at Third Party Litigation Funding." 15 *University of Pennsylvania Journal of Business Law* 1075-1109.

Agar, Michael H. (1980) *The Professional Stranger: An Informal Introduction to Enthography*. New York: Academic Press.

Aharoni, Yair [ed.] (1993) *Coalitions and Competition: The Globalization of Professional Business Services*. New York: Routledge.

Albiston, Catherine (1999) "The Rule of Law and the Litigation Process: The Paradox of Losing by Winning." 33 *Law and Society Review* 869-910.

Alexander, Janet Cooper (1991) "Do the Merits Matter? A Study of Settlements in Securities Class Actions." 43 *Stanford Law Review* 497-598.

American Bar Association (1998) "Promoting Professionalism: ABA Programs, Plans, and Stategies." Chicago, IL: American Bar Association.

Amon, Elizabeth (2000) "Cincinnati Gun Suit Fires a Dud." *National Law Journal*, September 4, A10.

Anderson, David A. (1994) "Improving Settlement Devices: Rule 68 and Beyond." 23 *Journal of Legal Studies* 225-46.

_____. [ed.] (1996) *Dispute Resolution: Bridging the Settlement Gap.* Greenwich, CT: JAI Press Inc.

Anderson, David A. and Thomas D. Rowe, Jr. (1995) "Empirical Evidence on Settlement Devices: Does Rule 68 Encourage Settlement?" 71 *Chicago-Kent Law Review* 519-45.

Anleu, Sharyn L. Roach (1992) "The Legal Profession in the United States and Australia: Deprofessionalization or Reorganization?" 19 *Work and Occupations* 184-204.

Archer, Ray (1996) "Do-It-Yourself Center Lets People Do Legal Legwork." *Arizona Republic*, October 20, H1.

Ariens, Michael (1994) "Know the Law: A History of Legal Specialization." 45 *South Carolina Law Review* 1003-61.

Arnold, Bruce L. and John Hagan (1992) "Careers of Misconduct: The Structure of Prosecution of Professional Deviance among Lawyers." 57 *American Sociological Review* 771-80.

Arruñada, Benito (1996) "The Economics of Notaries." 3 *European Journal of Law and Economics* 5-37.

Arthurs, Harry W. (1995) "A Lot of Knowledge is a Dangerous Thing: Will the Legal Profession Survive the Knowledge Explosion?" 18 *Dalhousie Law Journal* 295-309.

_____. (1996) "Lawyering in Canada in the 21st Century." 15 *Windsor Yearbook of Access to Justice* 202-25.

_____. (1997) "Globalization of the Mind: Canadian Elites and the Restructuring of Legal Fields." 12 *Canadian Journal of Political Science* 219-46.

_____. (1998) "The Political Economy of Canadian Legal Education." 25 *Journal of Law and Society* 14-32.

Arthurs, Harry W. and Robert Kreklewich (1996) "Law, Legal Institutions, and the Legal Profession in the New Economy." 34 *Osgoode Hall Law Journal* 1-60.

Ashley, William (1906) *An Introduction to English Economic History and Theory: Part II, The End of the Middle Ages.* New York: Longmans, Green.

Atiyah, Patrick S. (1987) "Tort Law and the Alternatives: Some Anglo-American Comparisons." 1987 *Duke Law Journal* 1002-44.

_____. (1997) *The Damages Lottery.* Oxford, UK: Hart Publishing.

Auerbach, Jerold S. (1976) *Unequal Justice: Lawyers and Social Change in Modern America.* New York: Oxford University Press.

Babcock, Linda and Greg Pogarsky (1999) "Damage Caps and Settlement: A Behavioral Approach." 28 *The Journal of Legal Studies* 341-70.

Bailis, Daniel S. and Robert J. MacCoun (1996) "Estimating Liability Risks with the Media as Your Guide." 80 *Judicature* 64-67.

Baker, Debra (1999) "Is This Woman a Threat to Lawyers?" *ABA Journal*, June, 54-57.

Baldwin, John (1989) "The Role of Citizens Advice Bureaux and Law Centres in the Provision of Legal Advice and Assistance." 8 *Civil Justice Quarterly* 24-44.

Ballard, Mark (1999) "'Lawyer' Label Hurts at Polls." *National Law Journal*, November 22, A1, A7.

Banks, Robert S. (1983) "Companies Struggle to Control Legal Costs." 61 *Harvard Business Review* 168-70.

Barboza, David (2002) "Enron Cases Await; Let the Swaggering Begin." *New York Times*, March 23, B1.

Barker, Stephen F. (1992) "What Is a Profession?" 1 *Professional Ethics* 73-99.

Barker, William T. (2004) "Laying the Foundation for Staff Counsel Representation of Insureds." 39 *Tort Trial & Insurance Practice Law Journal* 897-946.

Barnard, Matt, Linda Tsang, and Veronica Cowan (1999) "All Bar None—With the Access to Justice Bill Sweeping Away the Last Obstacles, the Stage Is Set for Solicitor Advocates to Shine." *Law Society Gazette*, June 30, 20-24.

Barrett, Paul M. (1996) "Companies Make Little Headway Curbing Lawyers' Billable Hours." *Wall Street Journal*, December 2, B11.

Barzun, Jacques and Henry F. Graff (1992) *The Modern Researcher* [5th Edition]. Boston: Houghton Mifflin.

Baughman, M. Wade (1997) "Reasonable Attorney's Fees Under the Social Security Act: The Case for Contingency Agreements." 1997 *University of Illinois Law Review* 253-78.

Beardwood, Barbara (1999) "The Loosening of Professional Boundaries and Restructuring: The Implications for Nursing and Medicine in Ontario." 21 *Law & Policy* 315-43.

Bebchuk, Lucian Arye (1988) "Suing Solely to Extract a Settlement Offer." 17 *Journal of Legal Studies* 437-50.

Bebchuk, Lucian Arye and Howard F. Chang (1996) "An Analysis of Fee Shifting Based on the Margin of Victory: On Frivolous Suits, Meritorious Suits, and the Role of Rule 11." 25 *Journal of Legal Studies* 371-403.

Becker, Howard S. (1978) "Arts and Crafts." 83 *American Journal of Sociology* 862-89.

Beckner, Clinton F., III and Avery Katz (1995) "The Incentive Effects of Litigation Fee Shifting When Legal Standards Are Uncertain." 15 *International Review of Law and Economics* 205-24.

Bedlin, Howard and Paul Nejelski (1984) "Unsettling Issues About Settling Civil Litigation: Examining 'Doomsday Machines', 'Quick Looks', and Other Modest Proposals." 68 *Judicature* 9-29.

Bell, Daniel (1973) *The Coming of Post-Industrial Society: A Venture in Social Forecasting*. New York: Basic Books.

Bensman, Joseph and Robert Lilienfeld (1991) *Craft Consciousness: Occupational Technique and the Development of World Images* [2nd Edition]. New York: Aldine de Gruyter.

Benson, Henry (1979) "The Royal Commission on Legal Services: Final Report." London: HMSO.

Bergstrom, Randolph E. (1992) *Courting Danger: Injury and Law in New York City, 1870–1910*. Ithaca, NY: Cornell University Press.

Bermudes, Sergio (1999) "Administration of Civil Justice in Brazil," in Adrian A.S. Zuckerman, ed., *Civil Justice in Crisis: Comparative Perspectives of Civil Procedure*. Oxford, UK: Oxford University Press.

Bernstein, David E. and Jeffrey D. Jackson (2004) "The *Daubert* Trilogy in the States." 44 *Jurimetrics Journal* 351-66.

Bernstein, Fred (2002) "Being of Sound Mind, and a $55 Consultation." *New York Times*, May 16, E1, E6.

Black, Anthony H. (1984) *Guilds and Civil Society in European Political Thought from the Twelfth Century to the Present*. Ithaca, NY: Cornell University Press.

Blackwell, Brian (Chairman) (2000) "The Report of the Lord Chancellor's Committee to Investigate the Activities of Non-Legally Qualified Claims Assessors and Employment Advisors." London: Lord Chancellor's Department.

Blalock, Hubert M., Jr. (1979) *Social Statistics* [2nd Edition]. New York: McGraw-Hill.

Blankenburg, Erhard (1982-83) "Legal Insurance, Litigant Decisions and the Rising Caseloads of Courts: A West German Study," Madison, WI: Disputes Processing Research Program Working Paper, University of Wisconsin Law School.

_____. (1998) "Patterns of Legal Culture: The Netherlands Compared to Neighboring Germany." 46 *American Journal of Comparative Law* 1-41.

Blasi, Gary (1995) "What Lawyers Know: Lawyering Expertise, Cognitive Science and the Functions of Theory." 45 *Journal of Legal Education* 313-97.

Bloch, Marc (1953) *The Historian's Craft*. Translated by Peter Putnam. New York: Vintage Books.

Blum, Andrew (1988) "The $400 Million Man?" *National Law Journal*, September 26, 2.

Blumberg, Abraham (1967) "The Practice of Law as a Confidence Game: Organizational Cooptation of the Profession." 1 *Law & Society Review* 15-39.

Bly, Laura (1999a) "A Netword of Support: Patients Find Emotion, Practical Advice-- and Each Other." *USA Today*, July 14, D1.

_____. (1999b) "Personal Hunt for Help Finds Advice, Rants, Friends." *USA Today*, July 14, D4.

Bogart, W.A. and Neil Vidmar (1989) "Empirical Profile of Independent Paralegals in the Province of Ontario." Windsor, Ontario: University of Windsor Law School.

Bok, Derek C. (1983) "A Flawed System." 85 *Harvard Magazine* 38-45, 70-71.

Bolt, Cathy (1999) "WA Canola Farmers in Class Action over Seeds." *Australian Financial Review*, January 21, 2.

Boon, Andy (1995) "Ethics and Strategy in Personal Injury Litigation." 22 *Journal of Law and Society* 353-73.

Bowles, Roger (1987) "Settlement Range and Cost Allocation Rules: A Comment on Avery Katz's 'Measuring the Demand for Litigation: Is the English Rule Really Cheaper?'" 3 *Journal of Law, Economics, and Organization* 177-84.

Boyle, Elizabeth Heger (2000) "Is Law the Rule? Using Political Frames to Explain Cross-National Variation in Legal Activity." 79 *Social Forces* 385-418.

Braeutigam, Ronald, Bruce Owen, and John Panzar (1984) "An Economic Analysis of Alternative Fee Shifting Systems." 47 *Law and Contemporary Problems* 173-86.

Brame, R. G. (1994) "Professionalism, Physician Autonomy, and the New Economics of Medicine." 171 *American Journal of Obstetrics & Gynecology* 293-97.

Braun, Bruce R. and W. Gordon Dobie (1996) "Litigating the Yankee Tax: Application of the Lodestar to Attorneys' Fee Awards in Common Fund Litigation." 23

Florida State University Law Review 897-916.

Brazil, Wayne D. (1978) "The Adversary Character of Civil Discovery: A Critique and Proposals for Change." 31 *Vanderbilt Law Review* 1295-361.

Brennan, Lisa (1998a) "How Should Companies Pick Firms?" *National Law Journal*, August 24, B1-B2.

_____. (1998b) "Linklaters Merger Is Just a Start." *National Law Journal*, August 10, A1, A15.

_____. (1998c) "Outside Fee Audits Draw Bar Dissent." *National Law Journal*, August 3, A6.

Brickman, Lester (1989) "Contingent Fees Without Contingencies: Hamlet without the Prince of Denmark?" 37 *UCLA Law Review* 29-137.

_____. (1992) "The Asbestos Litigation Crisis: Is There a Need for an Administrative Alternative?" 13 *Cardozo Law Review* 1819-89.

_____. (1994) "On the Relevance of the Admissibility of Scientific Evidence: Tort System Outcomes Are Principally Determined by Lawyers' Rates of Return." 15 *Cardozo Law Review* 1755-97.

_____. (1996a) "ABA Regulation of Contingency Fees: Money Talks, Ethics Walks." 65 *Fordham Law Review* 247-335.

_____. (1996b) "Contingency Fee Abuses, Ethical Mandates, and the Disciplinary System: The Case Against Case-By-Case Enforcement." 53 *Washington and Lee Law Review* 1340-73.

_____. (2003) "Effective Hourly Rates of Contingency-Fee Lawyers: Competing Data and Non-Competitive Fees." 81 *Washington University Law Quarterly* 653-736.

_____. (2011) *Lawyer Barons: What Their Contingency Fees Really Cost America.* New York: Cambridge University Press.

Brickman, Lester, Michael Horowitz, and Jeffrey O'Connell (1994) "Rethinking Contingency Fees." New York: Manhattan Institute.

Briggs, Charles L. (1986) *Learning How to Ask: A Sociolinguistic Appraisal of the Role of the Interview in Social Science Research.* New York: Cambridge University Press.

Brockman, Joan (1997) "'Better to Enlist Their Support than to Suffer Their Antagonism': The Game of Monopoly between Lawyers and Notaries in British Columbia, 1930-81." 4 *International Journal of the Legal Profession* 197-234.

Brody, Jaen E. (1999) "The Health Hazards of Point-and-Click Medicine." *New York Times*, August 31, D1, D6.

Bruni, Frank (2005) "My Week as a Waiter." *New York Times*, January 25.

Buchman, Jeremy (2007) "The Effects of Ideology on Federal Trial Judges' Decisions to Admit Scientific Evidence." 35 *American Politics Research* 671-93.

Burrage, Michael (1996) "From a Gentlemen's to a Public Profession: Status and Politics in the History of English Solicitors." 3 *International Journal of the Legal Profession* 45-80.

Cain, Maureen (1979) "The General Practice Lawyer and the Client: Towards a Radical Conception." 7 *International Journal of the Sociology of Law* 331-54.

Calhoun, Craig and Martha Copp (1988) "Computerization in Legal Work: How Much Does New Technology Change Professional Practice," in Richard L. Simpson and Ida Harper Simpson, eds., *Research in the Sociology of Work: High Tech Work* [Vol. 4]. Greenwich, CT: JAI Press.

Cameron, Camille (2010) "Australia," in Christopher Hodges, Stefan Vogenauer, and Magdalena Tulibacka, eds., *The Costs and Funding of Civil Litigation*. Oxford, UK: Hart Publishing.

Campbell, Roderick (1997) "Disciplinary Plan for Lawyers; Will Incident Prompts MLA's Move." *Canberra Times*, August 30, A6.

Cannon, Michael (1998) *That Disreputable Firm: The Inside Story of Slater and Gordon*. Carlton, Victoria: Melbourne University Press.

Carlin, Jerome E. (1962) *Lawyers on Their Own: A Study of Individual Practitioners in Chicago*. New Brunswick, NJ: Rutgers University Press (rept. 2011, Quid Pro).

_____. (1966) *Lawyers' Ethics: A Survey of the New York City Bar*. New York: Russell Sage Foundation.

Carroll, Stephen, Allan Abrahamse, and Mary Vaiana (1995) "The Costs of Excess Medical Claims for Automobile Personal Injuries." Santa Monica, CA: RAND Institute for Civil Justice.

Carson, Clara (1999) *The 1995 Lawyer Statistical Report*. Chicago, IL: American Bar Foundation.

Carvajal, Doreen (1998) "Lawyers Are Not Amused by Feisty Legal Publisher." *New York Times*, August 24, D1, D4.

Casper, Jonathan D. (1972) *American Criminal Justice: The Defendant's Perspective*. Englewood Cliffs, NJ: Prentice-Hall.

Catenacci, Richard D. (1989) "Hyperlexis or Hyperbole: Subdividing the Landscape of Disputes and Defusing the Litigation Explosion." 8 *Review of Litigation* 297-324.

Cavanagh, Edward D. (1988) "Attorney's Fees in Antitrust Litigation: Making the System Fairer." 57 *Fordham Law Review* 51-110.

Chambers, David L. (1997) "25 Divorce Attorneys and 40 Clients in Two Not So Big but Not So Small Cities in Massachusetts and California: An Appreciation." 22 *Law & Social Inquiry* 209-30.

Chambliss, Elizabeth (2014) "Law School Training for Licensed 'Legal Technicians'? Implications for the Consumer Market." 65 *South Carolina Law Review* 579-610.

Champagne, Anthony and Kyle Cheek (1996) "PACs and Judicial Politics in Texas." 80 *Judicature* 26-27.

Chase, Oscar G. (1995) "Helping Jurors Determine Pain and Suffering Awards." 23 *Hofstra Law Review* 763-90.

Cheng, Edward K. and Albert H. Yoon (2005) "Does *Frye* or *Daubert* Matter? A Study of Scientific Admissibility Standards." 91 *Virginia Law Review* 471-513.

Chesebro, Kenneth J. (1993) "Galileo's Retort: Peter Huber's Junk Scholarship." 42 *American University Law Review* 1637-726.

Chin, Audrey and Mark A. Peterson (1983) "Fairness in Civil Jury Trials: Who Wins, Who Loses in Cook County." Santa Monica: RAND Institute for Civil Justice.

Chung, Tai-Yeong (1996) "Settlement of Litigation under Rule 68: An Economic Analysis." 25 *Journal of Legal Studies* 261.

Church, Thomas W. (1982) "Examining Local Legal Culture: Practitioner Attitudes in Four Criminal Courts." Williamsburg, VA: National Center for State Courts.

Church, Thomas W., Jr. (1985) "Examining Local Legal Culture." 1985 *American Bar Foundation Research Journal* 449-518.

Church, Thomas W., Jr., Alan Carlson, Jo-Lynne Lee, and Teresa Tan (1978) "Justice Delayed: The Pace of Litigation in Urban Trial Courts." Williamsburg, VA: National Center for State Courts.

Cicourel, A.V. (1964) *Method and Measurement in Sociology.* New York: Free Press.

Clark, Andrew (1992) "Information Technology in Legal Services." 19 *Journal of Law and Society* 13-30.

Clark, Andrew and Kim Economides (1988) "Technics and Praxis: Technological Innovation and Legal Practice in Modern Society." 15 *Sociolgia del diritto* 41-67.

Clermont, Kevin M. and J.D. Currivan (1978) "Improving on the Contingent Fee." 63 *Cornell Law Review* 529-639.

Clermont, Kevin M. and Theodore Eisenberg (1992) "Trial by Jury or Judge: Transcending Empiricism." 77 *Cornell Law Review* 1124-77.

Closen, Michael L. and G. Grant Dixon, III (1992) "Notaries Public from the Time of the Roman Empire to the United States Today." 68 *North Dakota Law Review* 873-96.

Coates, John C., Michele M. DeStefano, Ashish Nanda, and David B. Wilkins (2011) "Hiring Teams, Firms, and Lawyers: Evidence of the Evolving Relationships in the Corporate Legal Market." 36 *Law & Social Inquiry* 999-1031.

Cohen, Julius Henry (1916) *The Law: Business or Profession?* New York: Banks Law Publishing Company.

Cohen, Thomas H. and Steven K. Smith (2004) "Civil Trial Cases and Verdicts in Large Counties, 2001." Washington, DC: Bureau of Justice Statistics.

Commission on Multidisciplinary Practice (1999) "Report to the House of Delegates." Chicago, IL: American Bar Association.

Commission on Nonlawyer Practice (1994) "Nonlawyer Practice in the United States: Summary of the Factual Record Before the American Bar Association Commission on Nonlawyer Practice." Chicago, IL: American Bar Association.

_____. (1995) "Nonlawyer Activity in Law-Related Situations: A Report with Recommendations." Chicago, IL: American Bar Association.

Commission on Professionalism (1986) "'... in the Spirit of Public Service': A Blueprint for the Rekindling of Lawyer Professionalism." Chicago, IL: American Bar Association.

Compton, Ted R. (1993) "The Emerging Role of the Paraprofessional." 63 *CPA Journal* 71-72.

Conard, Alfred F. (1984) "Winnowing Derivative Suits Through Attorneys' Fees." 47 *Law and Contemporary Problems* 269-92.

Conley, Janet (2001) "Fight over Auditing Coming to an End." *National Law Journal*, April 23, A1.

Connolly, Paul R., Edith A. Holleman, and Michael J. Kuhlman (1978) "Judicial Controls and the Civil Litigative Process: Discovery." Washington, DC: Federal Judicial Center.

Converse, Jean M. and Howard Schuman (1974) *Conversations At Random: Survey Research As Interviewers See It.* New York: John Wiley and Sons.

Cooter, Robert D. and Daniel L. Rubinfeld (1989) "Economic Analysis of Legal Disputes and Their Resolution." 27 *Journal of Economic Literature* 1067-97.

Cotts, Cynthia (1998) "They're Psych Ph.D.s and J.D.s." *National Law Journal*, August 31, A1, A17.

Coursey, D.L. and L.R. Stanley (1988) "Pre-Trial Bargaining Behavior Within the Shadow of the Law: Theory and Experimental Evidence." 8 *International Review of Law and Economics* 161-79.

Cox, Gail Diane (1997) "Insurance Defense: A Shakeout." *National Law Journal*, January 3, 1997, A1.

_____. (2002) "Indigent Defense as a Road to Indigency." *National Law Journal*, April 22, A22.

Crane, Mark (1988) "Lawyers Don't Take *Every* Case." *National Law Journal*, January 25, 1, 34.

Crompton, Rosemary (1990) "Professions in the Current Context." [Special Issue] *Work, Employment & Society* 147-66.

Cronin, Blaise and Elisabeth Davenport (1988) *Post-Professionalism: Transforming the Information Heartland*. London: Taylor Graham.

Crown Prosecution Service Inspectorate (1999) "Report on the Evaluation of Lay Review and Lay Presentation." London: Home Office.

Cummings, Douglas J. (1996) "An Empirical Perspective on the Interplay Between Contingency Fees and the Legal System." Toronto: York University.

_____. (2001) "Settlement Disputes: Evidence from a Legal Practice Perspective." 11 *European Journal of Law and Economics* 249-80.

Danet, Brenda, Kenneth Hoffman, and Nicole Kermish (1980) "Obstacles to the Study of Lawyer-Client Interaction: The Biography of a Failure." 14 *Law & Society Review* 905-22.

Daniels, Stephen (1985) "We Are Not a Litigious Society." 24(2) *The Judges' Journal* 18-22.

_____. (1989) "The Question of Jury Competence and the Politics of Civil Justice Reform: Symbols, Rhetoric and Agenda-Building." 52 *Law and Contemporary Problems* 269-310.

_____. (1990) "Caseload Dynamics and the Nature of Change: The Civil Business of Trial Courts in Four Illinois Counties." 14 *Law & Society Review* 299-320.

Daniels, Stephen and Joanne Martin (1995) *Civil Juries and the Politics of Reform*. Evanston: Northwestern University Press.

_____. (1997) "'That's 95% of the Game, Just Getting the Case': Markets, Norms, and How Texas Plaintiffs' Lawyers Get Clients." Paper presented at Law & Society Association Annual Meeting, St. Louis, MO, May 26-June 2.

_____. (1999) "'It's Darwinism—Survival of the Fittest': How Markets and Reputations Shape the Way in Which Plaintiffs' Lawyers Obtain Clients." 21 *Law & Policy* 377-79.

_____. (2001) "'We Live on the Edge of Extinction All the Time': Entrepreneurs, Innovation and the Plaintiffs' Bar in the Wake of Tort Reform," in Jerry Van Hoy, ed., *Legal Professions: Work, Structure and Organization*. New York: JAI/Elsevier Science Ltd.

_____. (2002) "It Was the Best of Times, It Was the Worst of Times: The Precarious Nature of Plaintiff's Practice in Texas." 80 *Texas Law Review* 1781-828.

_____. (2015) *Tort Reform, Plaintiffs' Lawyers, and Access to Justice.* Lawrence, KS: University Press of Kansas.

Danzon, Patricia M. (1983) "Contingent Fees for Personal Injury Litigation." 14 *Bell Journal of Economics* 213-24.

Davis, Joshua P. (1996) "Toward A Jurisprudence of Trial and Settlement: Allocating Attorneys' Fees by Amending Rule of Civil Procedure 68." 48 *Alabama Law Review* 65-142.

Davis, Robert and Leslie Miller (1999) "Millions Scour the Web to Find Medical Information." *USA Today*, July 14, A1-A2.

Day, Martin (1998) "Success Fees Set to Soar." *The Lawyer*, July 28, 2.

DeFrances, Carol J. and Marika F.X. Litras (1999) "Civil Trial Cases and Verdicts in Large Counties, 1996." Washington, DC: Bureau of Justice Statistics, U.S. Department of Justice.

DeFrances, Carol J., Steven K. Smith, Patrick A. Langan, Brian J. Ostrom, David B. Rottman, and John A. Goerdt (1995) "Civil Jury Cases and Verdicts in Large Counties." Washington, DC: Bureau of Justice Statistics, U.S. Department of Justice.

DeShaw, Aaron (undated) "Colossus: What Every Trial Lawyer Should Know." http://www.theinjuryspecialists.com/upload/Colossus.pdf, last visited August 10, 2014.

Dezalay, Yves (1992) *Marchands de droit.* Paris: Fayard.

Dezalay, Yves and Bryant Garth (1997) "Law, Lawyers and Social Capital: 'Rule of Law' versus Relational Capital." 6 *Social & Legal Studies* 109-41.

Dezalay, Yves and David Sugarman [eds.] (1995) *Professional Competiton and Professional Power: Lawyers, Accountants and the Social Construction of Markets.* London: Routledge.

Dhavan, Rajeez, Neil Kibble, and William Twining [eds.] (1989) *Access to Legal Education and the Legal Profession.* London: Butterworths.

Di Pietro, Susanne (1996) "The English Rule at Work in Alaska." 80 *Judicature* 88-92.

Di Pietro, Susanne and Teresa W. Carns (1996) "Alaska's English Rule: Attorney's Fee Shifting in Civil Cases." 13 *Alaska Law Review* 33-93.

Di Pietro, Susanne, Teresa W. Carns, and Pamela Kelley (1995) "Alaska's English Rule: Attorney's Fee Shifting in Civil Cases." Anchorage, AK: Alaska Judicial Council.

Dietz, Stephen, C. Bruce Baird, and Lawrence Berul (1973) "The Medical Malpractice Legal System," in *Appendix: Report of the Secretary's Commission on Medical Malpractice.* Washington, DC: Department Health Education, and Welfare [OS 73-89].

Dingwall, Robert (1997) "Accounts, Interviews and Observations," in Gale Miller and Robert Dingwall, eds., *Context and Method in Qualitative Research.* London: Sage Publications.

Dixon, Jo and Carroll Seron (1995) "Stratification in the Legal Profession: Sex, Sector, and Salary." 29 *Law & Society Review* 381-412.

Dixon, Lloyd and Brian Gill (2001) *Changes in the Standards for Admitting Expert*

Evidence in Federal Civil Cases Since the Daubert Decision. Santa Monica, CA: RAND Institute for Civil Justice.

Dobbin, Shirley A., Sophia I. Gatowski, James T. Richardson, Gerald P. Ginsburg, Mara L. Merlino, and Veronica Dahir (2002) "Applying *Daubert*: How Well Do Judges Understand Science and Scientific Method?" 85 *Judicature* 244-7.

Domberger, Simon and Avrom Sherr (1989) "The Impact of Competition on Pricing and Quality of Legal Services." 9 *International Review of Law and Economics* 41-56.

Donohue, John J., III (1991a) "The Effects of Fee Shifting on the Settlement Rate: Theoretical Observations on Costs, Conflicts, and Contingency Fees." 54 *Law and Contemporary Problems* 195-222.

_____. (1991b) "Opting for the British Rule, or If Posner and Shavell Can't Remember the Coase Theorem, Who Will." 104 *Harvard Law Review* 1073-119.

Douglas, Jack D. (1985) *Creative Interviewing.* Beverly Hills, CA: Sage Publications.

Dover, Michael A. (1986) "Contingent Percentage Fees: An Economic Analysis." 51 *Journal of Air Law and Commerce* 531-66.

Duffy, Shannon P. (2001) "Philly Loses Its Gun Maker Suit." *National Law Journal,* January 8, A4.

Ebbinghouse, Carol (1999) "West Loses Copyright Claim over Page Numbers." *Information Today,* July 1, 20.

Economides, Kim (1992) "The Country Lawyer: Iconography, Iconoclasm, and the Restoration of the Professional Image." 19 *Journal of Law and Society* 115-23.

Eisenberg, Theodore, Paula L. Hannaford-Agor, Michael Heise, Neil LaFountain, G. Thomas Munsterman, Brian Ostrom, and Martin T. Wells (2006) "Juries, Judges, and Punitive Damages: Empirical Analyses Using the Civil Justice Survey of State Courts 1992, 1996, and 2001 Data." 3 *Journal of Empirical Legal Studies* 263-95.

Eisenberg, Theodore, Neil LaFountain, Brian Ostrom, David Rottman, and Martin T. Wells (2002) "Juries, Judges, and Punitive Damages: An Empirical Study." 87 *Cornell Law Review* 743-82.

Eisenberg, Theodore and Geoffrey P. Miller (2004) "Attorney Fees in Class Action Settlements: An Empirical Study." 1 *Journal of Empirical Legal Studies* 27-78.

_____. (2010) "Attorney Fees and Expenses in Class Action Settlements: 1993–2008." 7 *Journal of Empirical Legal Studies* 248-81.

Eisenstein, James, Roy B. Flemming, and Peter F. Nardulli (1988) *The Contours of Justice: Communities and Their Courts.* Boston: Little Brown & Co.

Eisenstein, James and Herbert Jacob (1977) *Felony Justice: An Organizational Analysis of Criminal Courts.* Boston: Little, Brown & Co.

Eisikovits, Zvi and Jerome Beker (2001) "Beyond Professionalism: The Child and Youth Care Worker as Craftsman." 30 *Child & Youth Care Forum* 92-112.

Employment Law Center (undated) "The Claims Project." San Francisco, CA: Legal Aid Society of San Francisco.

Engstrom, Nora Freeman (2009) "Run-of-the-Mill Justice." 22 *Georgetown Journal of Legal Ethics* 1485-547.

_____. (2011) "Sunlight and Settlement Mills." 86 *New York University Law Review* 805-86.

Epp, Charles E. (1998) *The Rights Revolution: Lawyers, Activists, and Supreme Courts in Comparative Perspective.* Chicago, IL: University of Chicago Press.

Ernst & Young (1999) "Reducing Delay in the Criminal Justice System: Evaluation of the Pilot Schemes." London: Home Office.

Farhang, Sean (2009) "Congressional Mobilization of Private Litigants: Evidence from the Civil Rights Act of 1991." 6 *Journal of Empirical Legal Studies* 1-34.

_____. (2010) *The Litigation State: Public Regulation and Private Lawsuits in the U.S.* Princeton, NJ: Princeton University Press.

Federal Judicial Center (1991) "Rule 11: Final Report to the Advisory Committee on Civil Rules of the Judicial Conference of the United States." Washington, DC: Federal Judicial Center.

Fein, Bruce (1984) "Citizen Suit Attorney Fee Shifting Awards: A Critical Examination of Government-'Subsidized' Litigation." 47 *Law and Contemporary Problems* 211-32.

Feinberg, Kenneth and John S. Gomperts (1986) "Attorneys' Fees in the Agent Orange Litigation: Modifying the Lodestar Analysis for Mass Tort Cases." 14 *New York University Review of Law & Social Change* 613-32.

Feldman, Martha S. (1995) *Strategies for Interpreting Qualitative Data.* Thousand Oaks, CA: Sage Publications.

Felstiner, William L.F. (2001) "Synthesizing Socio-Legal Research: Lawyer-Client Relations as an Example." 8 *International Journal of the Legal Profession* 191-201.

Felstiner, William L.F., Richard L. Abel, and Austin Sarat (1980–81) "The Emergence and Transformation of Disputes: Naming, Blaming, Claiming..." 15 *Law & Society Review* 631-54.

Felstiner, William L.F. and Austin Sarat (1992) "Enactments of Power: Negotiating Reality and Responsibility in Lawyer-Client Interactions." 77 *Cornell Law Review* 1447-98.

Fenn, Paul, Neil Rickman, and Alastair Gray (2007) "Standard Fees for Legal Aid: An Empirical Analysis of Incentives and Contracts." 59 *Oxford Economic Papers* 662-81.

Fenn, Paul and Ioannis Vlachonikolis (1990) "Bargaining Behaviour by Defendant Insurers: An Economic Model." 14 *Geneva Papers on Risk and Insurance* 41-52.

Fisher, Roger and William Ury (1981) *Getting to Yes: Negotiating Agreement Without Giving in.* Boston, MA: Houghton-Mifflin.

Fisk, Margaret Cronin (2001a) "Despite 2000 Slump, Juries Remain Bullish." *National Law Journal*, February 19, C3, C26.

_____. (2001b) "Husband-Wife Team Take on Goliath and Walks Away with a Monster Jury Award." *National Law Journal*, February 19, C14.

Fitzgerald, Maureen (1993) "Stirring the Pot of Legal Education." 27 *The Law Teacher: Journal of the Association of Law Teachers* 4-35.

Flemming, Roy B. (1986) "The Client Game: Defense Attorney Perspectives on Their Relations with Criminal Clients." 1986 *American Bar Foundation Research Journal* 253-77.

Flemming, Roy B., Peter F. Nardulli, and James Eisenstein (1992) *The Craft of Justice: Politics and Work in Criminal Court Communities.* Philadelphia, PA: University of Pennsylvania Press.

Flood, John (1991) "Doing Business: The Management of Uncertainty in Lawyers' Work." 25 *Law & Society Review* 41-72.

_____. (1995) "The Cultures of Globalization: Professional Restructuring for the International Market," in Yves Dezalay and David Sugarman, eds., *Professional Competition and Professional Power: Lawyers, Accountants and the Social Construction of Markets*. London: Routledge.

_____. (1996) "Megalawyering in the Global Order: The Cultural, Social and Economic Transformation of Global Legal Practice." 3 *International Journal of the Legal Profession* 169-214.

_____. (2013) *What Do Lawyers Do? An Ethnography of a Corporate Law Firm*. New Orleans, LA: Quid Pro Books.

Fournier, Gary M. and Thams W. Zuehlke (1989) "Litigation and Settlement: An Empirical Approach." 71 *Review of Economics and Statistics* 189-95.

Fox, Lawrence J. (1998) "Fee Fie Foe Firm: Big Four Gobble Up Lawyers." *National Law Journal*, July 27, A22.

France, Mike (1995a) "Bar Chiefs Protect the Guild." *National Law Journal*, August 7, sec. A, p. 28.

_____. (1995b) "Dilemma: Who Will Teach Associates?" *National Law Journal*, November 20, A1, A22.

Francis, Andrew M. (2002) "Legal Executives and the Phantom of Legal Professionalism: The Rise and The Rise of the Third Branch of the Legal Profession?" 9 *International Journal of the Legal Profession* 5-25.

Franklin, Marc A., Robert H. Chanin, and Mark Irving (1961) "Accidents, Money and the Law: A Study of the Economics of Personal Injury Litigation." 61 *Columbia Law Review* 1-39.

Freidson, Eliot (1983) "The Theory of Professions: State of the Art," in Robert Dingwall and Philip S.C. Lewis, eds., *The Sociology of the Professions: Doctors, Lawyers and Others*. London: Macmillan (rept. 2014, Quid Pro).

_____. (1986) *Professional Powers: A Study of the Institutionalization of Formal Knowledge*. Chicago, IL: University of Chicago Press.

_____. (1994) *Professionalism Reborn: Theory, Prophecy, and Policy*. Chicago, IL: University of Chicago Press.

Freidson, Eliot (2001) *Professionalism, the Third Logic: On the Practice of Knowledge*. Chicago, IL: University of Chicago Press.

Freudenheim, Milt (1997) "As Nurses Take on Primary Care, Physicians Are Sounding Alarms." *New York Times*, May 30, A1.

Friedman, Lawrence M. and Robert V. Percival (1976) "A Tale of Two Courts: Litigation in Alameda and San Benito Counties." 10 *Law & Society Review* 267-301.

Fritsch, Jane (2001) "Pataka Rethinks His Promise of a Raise for Lawyers to the Indigent." *New York Times*, December 24, A12.

Fulton, Oliver (1989) "Access to Higher Education: A Review of Alternative Policies," in Rajeez Dhavan, Neil Kibble, and William Twining, eds., *Access to Legal Education and the Legal Profession*. London: Butterworths.

Galanter, Marc (1974) "Why the 'Haves' Come Out Ahead: Speculations on the Limits of Legal Change." 9 *Law & Society Review* 95-160.

_____. (1983) "Reading the Landscape of Disputes: What We Know and Don't Know (and Think We Know) About Our Allegedly Contentious and Litigious Society." 31 *UCLA Law Review* 4-71.

_____. (1984) "Worlds of Deals: Using Negotiation to Teach About Legal Process." 34 *Journal of Legal Education* 268-76.

_____. (1986) "The Day After the Litigation Explosion." 46 *Maryland Law Review* 3-39.

_____. (1990a) "Bhopals, Past and Present: The Changing Legal Response to Mass Disaster." 10 *Windsor Yearbook of Access to Justice* 151.

_____. (1990b) "Case Congregations and Their Careers." 14 *Law & Society Review* 371-95.

_____. (1993) "News from Nowhere: The Debased Debate on Civil Justice." 71 *Denver University Law Review* 77-113.

_____. (1996) "Lawyers in the Mist: The Golden Age of Legal Nostalgia." 100 *Dickinson Law Review* 549-62.

_____. (1998a) "Anyone Can Fall Down a Manhole: The Contingency Fee and Its Discontents." 47 *DePaul Law Review* 457-77.

_____. (1998b) "The Faces of Mistrust: The Image of Lawyers in Public Opinion, Jokes, and Political Discourse." 66 *University of Cincinnati Law Review* 805-45.

_____. (2005) *Lowering the Bar: Lawyer Jokes & Legal Culture.* Madison, WI: University of Wisconsin Press.

Galanter, Marc and William D. Henderson (2008) "The Elastic Tournament: The Second Transformation of the Big Law Firm." 60 *Stanford Law Review* 1867-1929.

Galanter, Marc and Thomas Palay (1992) "The Transformation of the Big Law Firm," in Robert L. Nelson, David M. Trubek, and Rayman L. Solomon, eds., *Lawyers' Ideal/Lawyers' Practices: Transformations in the American Legal Profession.* Ithaca, NY: Cornell University Press.

Galanter, Marc and Thomas M. Palay (1990) "Why the Big Get Bigger: The Promotion-to-Partner Tournament and the Growth of Large Law Firms." 76 *Virginia Law Review* 747-814.

_____. (1991) *Tournament of Lawyers: The Transformation of the Big Law Firm.* Chicago, IL: University of Chicago Press.

Galluccio, Nick (1978) "The Rise of the Company Lawyer: Government Red Tape Costs Consumers Plenty But It Is Creating New Opportunities for Law School Graduates." *Forbes*, September 18, 168-81.

Garfinkel, Harold (1967) *Studies in Ethnomethodology.* Englewood Cliffs, NJ: Prentice-Hall.

Gatowski, Sophia I., Shirley A. Dobbin, James T. Richardson, Gerald P. Ginsburg, Veronic B. Dahir, and Mara Merlino (2001) "Asking the Gatekeepers: A National Survey of Judges on Judging Scientific Evidence in a Post-*Daubert* World." 25 *Law and Human Behavior* 435-58.

Gawande, Atul (2002) *Complications: A Surgeon's Notes on an Imperfect Science.* New York: Henry Holt and Company.

Genn, Hazel (1988) *Hard Bargaining: Out of Court Settlement in Personal Injury Actions.* Oxford, UK: Oxford University Press.

Genn, Hazel and Yvette Genn (1989) *The Effectiveness of Representation at Tribunals: Report to the Lord Chancellor.* London: Queen Mary College, Faculty of Laws.

Gervasi, Michael V. and Gerald Lebovits (2009) "Part 137: The Attorney-Client Fee-Dispute Program." 8 *Richmond County Bar Association Journal* 7-10, 23.

Gherty, Terrence M. and Dean R. Dietrich (1991) "Specialization: Pro and Con." *Wisconsin Lawyer*, November, 10-13.

Gibbons, Thomas F. (1989) "Branching Out: At Least 45 Law Firms Have Opened Non-Law Business." 75(11) *ABA Journal* 70-75.

Gibeaut, John and James Podgers (1998) "Feeling the Squeeze: Commission Appointed to Assess Threat from Accountants." 84(10) *ABA Journal* 88.

Glaberson, William (1999) "Lawyers Contend with State and Federal Efforts to Restrict Their Rising Powers." *New York Times*, August 5, A15.

_____. (2001) "A Study's Verdict: Jury Awards Are Not Out of Control." *New York Times*, August 6, A9.

Glendon, Mary Ann (1994) *A Nation Under Lawyers: How the Crisis in the Legal Profession Is Transforming American Society*. New York: Farrar, Straus and Giroux.

Golan, Tal (2004) *Laws of Men and Laws of Nature: The History of Scientific Expert Testimony in England and America*. Cambridge, MA: Harvard University Press.

Goldhaber, Michael D. (2001) "Boies Schiller's Big Year." *National Law Journal*, February 12, A1, A17.

Gómez, Manuel A. (2010) "Latin America: A Regional Report," in Christopher Hodges, Stefan Vogenauer, and Magdalena Tulibacka, eds., *The Costs and Funding of Civil Litigation*. Oxford, UK: Hart Publishing.

Gordon, Robert W. and William H. Simon (1992) "The Redemption of Professionalism?" in Robert L. Nelson, David M. Trubek, and Rayman L. Solomon, eds., *Lawyers' Ideals/Lawyers' Practices: Transformations in the American Legal Profession*. Ithaca, NY: Cornell University Press.

Goriely, Tamara (1994) "Debating the Quality of Legal Services: Differing Models of the Good Lawyer." 1 *International Journal of the Legal Profession* 159-72.

_____. (1996) "Law for the Poor: The Relationship between Advice Agencies and Solicitors in the Development of Poverty Law." 3 *International Journal of the Legal Profession* 215.

Gravelle, H.S.E. (1993) "The Efficiency Implications of Cost-Shifting Rules." 13 *International Review of Law and Economics* 3-18.

Gravelle, Hugh and Michael Waterson (1993) "No Win, No Fee: Some Economics of Contingent Legal Fees." 103 *Economic Journal* 1205-20.

Greenlee, Mark B. (1997) "*Kramer v. Java World*: Images, Issues, and Idols in the Debate over Tort Reform." 26 *Capital University Law Review* 701-38.

Gretton, Ed (2013) "Jackson—An Overview." *Law Society Gazette*, March 25.

Greve, Michael S. (1989) "Environmentalism and Bounty Hunting." 97 *The Public Interest* 15-29.

Gross, Samuel R. and Kent D. Syverud (1996) "Don't Try: Civil Jury Verdicts in a System Geared to Settlement." 44 *UCLA Law Review* 1-64.

Grossman, Joel B., Herbert M. Kritzer, Kristin Bumiller, and Stephen McDougal (1981) "Measuring the Pace of Litigation in Federal and State Trial Courts." 65 *Judicature* 86-113.

Grossman, Joel B., Herbert M. Kritzer, Kristin Bumiller, Austin Sarat, Stephen McDougal, and Richard E. Miller (1982) "Dimensions of Institutional Participation: Who Uses the Courts and How?" 44 *Journal of Politics* 86-114.

Grossman, Joel B. and Austin Sarat (1971) "Political Culture and Judicial Research." 1971 *Washington University Law Quarterly* 177-207.

Gryphon, Maryie (2011) "Assessing the Effects of a Loser Pays Rule on the American Legal System: An Economic Analysis and Proposal for Reform." 8 *Rutgers Journal of Law and Public Policy* 567.

Guthrie, Chris, Jeffrey J. Rachlingski, and Andrew J. Wistrich (2001) "Inside the Judicial Mind." 86 *Cornell Law Review* 777-830.

Hagan, John, Marjorie Zatz, Bruce Arnold, and Fiona Kay (1991) "Cultural Capital, Gender, and the Structural Transformation of Legal Practice." 25 *Law & Society Review* 239-62.

Hagglund, Clarence and Robert Bimbaum (1984) "Legal Specialization: The Need for Uniformity." 67 *Judicature* 436-47.

Halliday, Terence C. (1987) *Beyond Monopoly: Lawyers, State Crises, and Professional Empowerment*. Chicago, IL: University of Chicago Press.

Haltom, William and Michael McCann (2004) *Distorting the Law: Reform Politics, Mass Media, and the Litigation Crisis*. Chicago, IL: University of Chicago Press.

Hammersley, M. (1992) *What's Wrong with Ethnography: Methodological Explorations*. London: Routledge.

Hanlon, Gerard (1997) "A Profession in Transition? Lawyers, the Market, and Significant Others." 60 *Modern Law Review* 798-822.

Hans, Valerie P. and Neil Vidmar (1986) *Judging the Jury*. New York: Plenum Publishers.

Harlow, Carol (1995) "Why Public Law Is Private Law: An Invitation to Lord Woolf," in Adrian A.S. Zuckerman and Ross Cranston, eds., *Reform of Civil Procedure: Essays on 'Access to Justice'*. Oxford, UK: Clarendon Press

Harr, Jonathan (1995) *A Civil Action*. New York: Random House.

Harris, Andrew (2001) "Report Maps Million Dollar Verdict States." *National Law Journal*, February 12, A4.

Harris, Donald, Mavis Maclean, Hazel Genn, Sally Lloyd-Bostock, Paul Fenn, Peter Corfield, and Yvonne Brittan (1984) *Compensation and Support for Illness and Injury*. Oxford, UK: Oxford University Press.

Hartmann, Michael (1993) "Legal Data Banks, the Glut of Lawyers, and the German Legal Profession." 27 *Law & Society Review* 421-41.

Hastie, Reid., David A. Schkade, and John W. Payne (1999) "Juror Judgments in Civil Cases: Effects of Plaintiff's Requests and Plaintiff's Identity on Punitive Damage Awards." 23 *Law & Human Behavior* 445-70.

Haug, Marie R. (1973) "Deprofessionalization: An Alternative Hypothesis for the Future." 20 *Sociological Review Monograph* 195-212.

Hause, John C. (1989) "Indemnity, Settlement, and Litigation, or I'll Be Suing You." 18 *Journal of Legal Studies* 157-79.

Hay, Bruce L. (1996a) "Contingent Fees and Agency Costs." 25 *Journal of Legal Studies* 503-33.

_____. (1996b) "The Economics of Lawyer Referrals." Cambridge, MA: Harvard University, Center for Law, Economics, and Business.

_____. (1997) "Contingent Fees, Principal-Agent Problems, and the Settlement of Litigation." 23 *William Mitchell Law Review* 43-79.

Hayes, Arthur S. (1998) "Bean Counters Win." *National Law Journal*, August 10, A4.

Hazard, Geoffrey C., Jr. (2000) "Lawyers Not Private Eyes." *National Law Journal*, April 10, A23.

Hearn, Jeff (1982) "Notes on Patriarchy, Professionalization and the Semi-Professions." 16 *Sociology* 184-98.

Heckman, Candace (2003) "Does Insurance Company 'Low-ball' Pain and Suffering? Industry's Use of Colossus, a Service to Judge the Worth of Claims, Comes Under Fire." *Seattle Post-Intelligencer*, May 15, A3.

Heinz, John P. (1983) "The Power of Lawyers." 17 *Georgia Law Review* 891-911.

Heinz, John P. and Edward O. Laumann (1982) *Chicago Lawyers: The Social Structure of the Bar*. New York: Russell Sage Foundation.

Heinz, John P., Edward O. Laumann, Robert L. Nelson, and Paul S. Schnorr (1997) "The Constituencies of Elite Urban Lawyers." 31 *Law & Society Review* 441-72.

Heinz, John P., Robert L. Nelson, Edward O. Laumann, and Ethan Michelson (1998) "The Changing Character of Lawyers' Work: Chicago in 1975 and 1995." 32 *Law & Society Review* 751-75.

Heinz, P. John, Robert L. Nelson, Rebecca L. Sandefur, and Edward O. Laumann (2005) *Urban Lawyers: The New Social Structure of the Bar*. Chicago, IL: University of Chicago Press.

Henning, Joel F. [ed.] (1992) *Total Quality Management for Law Firms*. New York: Practising Law Institute.

_____. (1997) *Maximizing Law Firm Profitability: Hiring, Training and Developing Productive Lawyers* [Release 6]. New York: Law Journal Seminars-Press.

Hensler, Deborah R. (1993) "Reading the Tort Litigation Tea Leaves: What's Going on in the Civil Liability System?" 16 *Justice System Journal* 139-54.

Hensler, Deborah R., Mary E. Vaiana, James S. Kakalik, and Mark A. Peterson (1987) "Trends in Tort Litigation: The Story Behind the Statistics." Santa Monica, CA: RAND Institute for Civil Justice.

Hensler, Deborar R., Bonnie Dombey-Moore, Beth Giddens, Jennifer Gross, Erik K. Moller, and Nicholas M. Pace (1999) *Class Action Dilemmas: Pursuing Public Goals for Private Gain*. Santa Monica, CA: RAND Institute for Civil Justice.

Hersch, Philip L. (1990) "Indemnity, Settlement, and Litigation: Comment and Extension." 19 *Journal of Legal Studies* 235-42.

Hess, Burkhard and Rudolf Hübner (2010) "Germany," in Christopher Hodges, Stefan Vogenauer, and Magdalena Tulibacka, eds., *The Costs and Funding of Civil Litigation*. Oxford, UK: Hart Publishing.

Hess, Gerald F. (1992) "Rule 11 Practice in Federal and State Court: An Empirical, Comparative View." 75 *Marquette Law Review* 313-68.

Heumann, Milton (1978) *Plea Bargaining: The Experiences of Prosecutors, Judges, and Defense Attorneys*. Chicago, IL: University of Chicago Press.

Hicks, Margaret and Victoria S. Rymer (1990) "Paraprofessionals in Public Account-ing—Current State of Use." 60 *CPA Journal* 84-86.

Hines, Crystal Nix (2001) "Chain of Legal Self-Help Centers Is Expanding." *New York Times*, July 31, 2001, C1.

Hinsz, Verlin D. and Kristin E. Indahl (1995) "Assimilation to Anchors for Damage Awards in a Mock Civil Trial." 25 *Journal of Applied Social Psychology* 991-1026.

Hodges, Christopher, Stefan Vogenauer, and Magdalena Tulibacka (2010) "The Oxford Study on Costs and Funding of Civil Litigation," in *The Costs and Funding of Civil Litigation*. Oxford, UK: Hart Publishing.

Hosticka, Carl J. (1979) "We Don't Care About What Happened, We Only Care About What is Going to Happen: Lawyer-Client Negotiations of Reality." 26 *Social Problems* 599-610.

Howell, George (1878) *The Conflicts of Capital and Labour Historically and Economically Considered*. London: Chatto and Windus.

Huber, Peter W. (1991) *Galileo's Revenge: Junk Science in the Courtroom*. New York: Basic Books.

Hughes, Everett C. (1971) "Studying the Nurse's Work," in *The Sociological Eye: Selected Papers on Work, Self, & the Study of Society*. Chicago, IL: Aldine Atherton.

Hughes, James W. and Edward A. Snyder (1995) "Litigation and Settlement under the English and American Rules: Theory and Evidence." 38 *Journal of Law and Economics* 225-50.

Hughes, James W. and Geoffrey R. Woglom (1996) "Risk Aversion and the Alloca-tion of Legal Costs," in David A. Anderson, ed., *Dispute Resolution: Bridging the Settlement Gap*. Greenwich, CT: JAI Press.

Hull, Kathleen E. and Robert L. Nelson (1998) "Gender Inequality in Law: Problems of Structure and Agency in Recent Studies of Gender in Anglo-American Legal Professions." 23 *Law and Social Inquiry* 681-705.

Hunt, Dereck L., R. Brian Haynes, Steven E. Hanna, and Kristina Smith (1998) "Effects of Computer-based Clinical Decision Support Systems on Physician Performance and Patient Outcomes: A Systematic Review." 280 *Journal of the American Medical Association* 1339-46.

Hunting, Roger Bryand and Gloria S. Neuwirth (1962) *Who Sues in New York City? A Study of Automobile Accident Claims*. New York: Columbia University Press.

Hurst, James Willard (1950) *The Growth of American Law: The Law Makers*. Boston, MA: Little, Brown.

Hurst, Peter (2014) "The English System of Costs: Life After the Jackson Reforms." 25 *European Business Law Review* 565-85.

Hylton, Keith N. (1993a) "Fee Shifting and Incentives to Comply with the Law." 46 *Vanderbilt Law Review* 1069-1128.

_____. (1993b) "Litigation Cost Allocation Rules and Compliance with the Negli-gence Standard." 22 *Journal of Legal Studies* 457-76.

Hyman, Jonathan M., Milton Heumann, Kenneth J. Dautrich, and Harold L. Rubenstein (1995) *Civil Settlement: Styles of Negotiation in Dispute Resolution*. New Brunswick, NJ: New Jersey Administrative Office of the Courts.

Ianni, Ron W. (1990) "Report of the Task Force on Paralegals in Ontario." Toronto: Ontario Ministry of the Attorney General.

Illich, Ivan (1977) *Towards a History of Needs*. New York: Pantheon Books.

Illich, Ivan, Irving Zola, John McKnight, and Harley Shaiken (1977) *Disabling Professions*. London: Marion Boyars.

Inman, Phillip (2001) "Compensaion: Adding Insult to Injury for Accident Victims." *The Guardian*, February 10, 2.

Insurance Research Council (1994) "Auto Injuries Claiming Behavior, and Its Impact on Insurance Claims." Oak Brook, IL: Insurance Research Council.

_____. (1996) "Fraud and Buildup in Auto Injury Claims." Malvern, PA: Insurance Research Council.

_____. (1999) "Injuries in Auto Accidents: An Analysis of Auto Insurance Claims." Malvern, PA: Insurance Research Council.

Insurance Services Office (1996) "Closed Claim Survey for Commercial General Liability: Survey Results, 1995." New York: ISO Data, Inc.

_____. (1998) "Closed Claim Survey for Commercial General Liability: Survey Results, 1997." New York: ISO Data, Inc.

Jackson, Donald W. and James W. Riddlesperger, Jr. (1991) "Money and Politics in Judicial Elections: The 1988 Election of the the Chief Justice of the Texas Supreme Court." 74 *Judicature* 184-89.

Jackson, Rupert (Lord) (2009) "Review of Civil Litigation Costs: Final Report." London: TSO.

Jacob, Herbert, Erhard Blankenburg, Herbert M. Kritzer, Doris Marie Provine, and Joseph Sanders (1996) *Courts, Law and Politics in Comparative Perspective*. New Haven, CT: Yale University Press.

Janus, Eric S., Greg M. Duhl, and Simon Canick (2014) "William Mitchell College of Law's Hybrid Program for J.D. Study: Answering the Call for Innovation." *Bar Examiner*, September, 28-36.

Jay, Stewart (1989) "The Dilemmas of Attorney Contingent Fees." 2 *Georgetown Journal of Legal Ethics* 813-84.

Johnson, Alex M. (1991) "Think Like a Lawyer, Work Like a Machine: The Dissonance Between Law School and Law Practice." 64 *Southern California Law Review* 1231-60.

Johnson, David Cay (1998) "New I.R.S. Law: A Guide to Shifting Burdens." *New York Times*, July 26, B10.

Johnson, Earl, Jr. (1980–81) "Lawyer's Choice: A Theoretical Appraisal of Litigation Investment and Decisions." 15 *Law & Society Review* 567-610.

Johnson, Terence J. (1972) *Professions and Power*. London: Macmillan.

Johnstone, Quintin (1955) "The Unauthorized Practice Controversy: A Struggle Among Power Groups." 4 *University of Kansas Law Review* 1-57.

Jones, James W. (1988) "The Challenge of Change: The Practice of Law in the Year 2000." 41 *Vanderbilt Law Review* 683-95.

Kagan, Robert A. (2001) *Adversarial Legalism: The American Way of Law*. Cambridge, MA: Harvard University Press.

Kagan, Robert A., Bliss Cartwright, Lawrence M. Friedman, and Stanton Wheeler (1977) "The Business of State Supreme Courts, 1870–1970." 30 *Stanford Law Review* 121-56.

Kahneman, Daniel, Paul Slovic, and Amos Tversky (1982) *Judgement Under Uncertainty: Heuristics and Biases*. Cambridge, UK: Cambridge University Press.

Kakalik, James S., Terence Dunworth, Laural A. Hill, Daniel McCaffrey, Marian Oshiro, Nicholas M. Pace, and Mary E Vaina (1996) "An Evaluation of Judicial Case Management Under the Civil Justice Reform Act." Santa Monica, CA: RAND Institute for Civil Justice.

Karsten, Peter (1998) "Enabling the Poor to Have Their Day in Court: The Sanctioning of Contingency Fee Contracts, a History to 1940." 47 *DePaul Law Review* 231-60.

Katsh, M. Ehtan (1989) *The Electronic Media and the Transformation of Law*. New York: Oxford University Press.

Katz, Avery (1987) "Measuring the Demand for Litigation: Is the English Rule Really Cheaper?" 3 *Journal of Law, Economics, and Organization* 143-76.

Katz, Avery W. (2000) "Indemnity of Legal Fees," in Boudewijn Bouckaert and Gerrit De Geest, eds., *Encyclopedia of Law and Economics, Volume V: The Economics of Crime and Litigation*. Cheltenham, UK: Edward Elgar.

Kaushal, Rainu and David W. Bates (2001) "Computerized Physician Order Entry (CPOE) with Clinical Decision Support Systems (CDSSs)," in Kaveh G.Shojania, Bradford W. Duncan, Kathryn M. McDonald, and Robert M. Wachter, eds., *Making Health Care Safer: A Critical Analysi of Patient Safety Practices*. Rockville, MD: Agency for Healthcare Research and Quality, U.S. Department of Health and Human Services.

Kerameus, K.D. and S. Koussoulis (1999) "Civil Justice Reform: Access, Costs, and Delay. A Greek Perspective," in Adrian A.S. Zuckerman, ed., *Civil Justice in Crisis: Comparative Perspectives of Civil Procedure*. Oxford, UK: Oxford University Press.

Kilborn, Peter T. (1997) "Doctors Organize to Fight Corporate Intrusion." *New York Times*, July 1, A12.

Kilian, Matthias (2003) "Alternatives to Public Provision: The Role of Legal Expenses Insurance in Broadening Access to Justice: The German Experience." 30 *Journal of Law and Society* 31-48.

Kilian, Matthias and Francis Regan (2004) "Legal Expenses Insurance and Legal Aid—Two Sides of the Same Coin? The Experience from Germany and Sweden." 11 *International Journal of the Legal Profession* 233-55.

King, Gary, Robert O. Keohane, and Sidney Verba (1994) *Designing Social Inquiry: Scientific Inference in Qualitative Research*. Princeton, NJ: Princeton University Press.

Kirk, Jerome and Marc L. Miller (1986) *Reliability and Validity in Qualitative Research*. Beverly Hills, CA: Sage Publications.

Kletke, Phillip R., David W. Emmons, and Kurt D. Gillis (1996) "Current Trends in Physicians' Practice Arrangements: From Owners to Employees." 276 *Journal of the American Medical Association* 555-60.

Knutsen, Erik S. and Janet Walker (2010) "Canada," in Christopher Hodges, Stefan Vogenauer, and Magdalena Tulibacka, eds., *The Costs and Funding of Civil Litigation*. Oxford, UK: Hart Publishing.

Krafka, Carol, Meghat A. Dunn, Molly Treadway Johnson, Joe S. Cecil, and Dean Miletich (2002) "Judge and Attorney Experiences, Practices, and Concerns Regarding Expert Testimony in Federal Civil Trials." 8 *Psychology, Public Policy, and Law* 309-32.

Kralingen, R.W. van, H.J. van den Herik, J.E.J. Prins, M. Sergot, and J. Zelznikow [eds.] (1996) *Legal Knowledge Based Systems: Foundations of Legal Knowledge Systems*. Tilburg, Netherlands: Tilburg University Press.

Kramer, Sheila (1905) "The English Craft Gilds and the Government: An Examination of the Accepted Theory Regarding the Decay of the Craft Gilds." 23 *Studies in History, Economics, & Public Law* 445-595.

_____. (1927) *The English Craft Gilds: Studies in Their Progress and Decline*. New York: Columbia University Press.

Krause, Elliott A. (1996) *Death of the Guilds: Professions, States, and the Advance of Capitalism, 1930 to the Present*. New Haven, CT: Yale University Press.

Kritzer, Herbert M. (1979) "Political Cultures, Trial Courts, and Criminal Cases," in Peter F. Nardulli, ed., *The Study of Criminal Courts: Political Perspectives*. Cambridge, MA: Ballinger Publishing Company.

_____. (1980–81) "Studying Disputes: Learning from the CLRP Experience." 15 *Law & Society Review* 503-24.

_____. (1982) "The Judge's Role in Pretrial Case Processing: Assessing the Need for Change." 68 *Judicature* 28-38.

_____. (1984a) "The Civil Justice Research Project: Lessons for Studying the Civil Justice System," in Alan Gelfand, ed., *Proceedings of the Second Workshop on Law and Justice Statistics 1983*. Washington, DC: U.S. Justice Department, Bureau of Justice Statistics.

_____. (1984b) "The Dimensions of Lawyer-Client Relations: Notes Toward a Theory and a Field Study." 1984 *American Bar Foundation Research Journal* 409-28.

_____. (1984c) "Fee Arrangements and Fee Shifting: Lessons from the Experience in Ontario." 47 *Law and Contemporary Problems* 125-38.

_____. (1987) "Fee Arrangements and Negotiation: A Research Note." 21 *Law & Society Review* 341-48.

_____. (1990) *The Justice Broker: Lawyers and Ordinary Litigation*. New York: Oxford University Press.

_____. (1991a) "Abel and the Professional Project: The Institutional Analysis of the Legal Profession." 16 *Law & Social Inquiry* 529-52.

_____. (1991b) *Let's Make a Deal: Negotiations and Settlement in Ordinary Litigation*. Madison, WI: University of Wisconsin.

_____. (1991c) "Propensity to Sue in England and the United States: Blaming and Claiming in Tort Cases." 18 *Journal of Law and Society* 400-27.

_____. (1992) "The English Rule: Searching for Winners in a Loser Pays System." 78(11) *ABA Journal* 54-58.

_____. (1994) "Lawyers' Fees and the Holy Grail: Where Should Clients Search for Value?" 77 *Judicature* 186-90.

_____. (1997) "Contingency Fee Lawyers as Gatekeepers in the Civil Justice System." 81 *Judicature* 22-29.

_____. (1998a) "Contingent-Fee Lawyers and Their Clients: Settlement Expectations, Settlement Realities, and Issues of Control in the Lawyer-Client Relationship." 23 *Law & Social Inquiry* 795-822.

_____. (1998b) *Legal Advocacy: Lawyers and Nonlawyers at Work*. Ann Arbor, MI: University of Michigan Press.

_____. (1998c) "The Wages of Risk: The Returns of Contingency Fee Legal Practice." 47 *DePaul Law Review* 267-319.

_____. (1999) "The Professions Are Dead, Long Live the Professions: Legal Practice in a Postprofessional World." 33 *Law & Society Review* 713-59.

_____. (2001a) "The Fracturing Legal Profession: The Case of Plaintiffs' Personal Injury Lawyers." 8 *International Journal of the Legal Profession* 225-50.

_____. (2001b) "From Litigators of Ordinary Cases to Litigators of Extraordinary Cases: Stratification of the Plaintiffs' Bar in the Twenty-first Century." 51 *DePaul Law Review* 219-40.

_____. (2001c) "Public Perceptions of Civil Trial Verdicts." 85 *Judicature* 78-82.

_____. (2002a) "The Future Role of 'Law Workers:' Rethinking the Forms of Legal Practice and the Scope of Legal Education." 44 *Arizona Law Review* 917-38.

_____. (2002b) "Lawyer Fees and Lawyer Behavior in Litigation: What Does the Empirical Literature Really Say?" 80 *Texas Law Review* 1943-83.

_____. (2002c) "Seven Dogged Myths Concerning Contingency Fees." 80 *Washington University Law Quarterly* 739-94.

_____. (2004a) "Advocacy and Rhetoric vs. Scholarship and Evidence in the Debate over Contingency Fees: A Reply to Professor Brickman." 82 *Washington University Law Quarterly* 477-507.

_____. (2004b) *Risks, Reputations, and Rewards: Contingency Fee Legal Practice in the United States*. Stanford, CA: Stanford University Press.

_____. (2006) "The Commodification of Insurance Defense Practice." 59 *Vanderbilt Law Review* 2053-94.

_____. (2007) "Toward a Theorization of Craft." 16 *Social and Legal Studies* 321-40.

_____. (2008a) "Daubert in the Law Office: Routinizing Procedural Change." 5 *Journal of Empirical Legal Studies* 109-42.

_____. (2008b) "To Lawyer, or Not to Lawyer: Is That the Question?" 5 *Journal of Empirical Legal Studies* 875-906.

_____. (2009) "Fee Regimes and the Cost of Civil Justice." 28 *Civil Justice Quarterly* 344-66.

_____. (2012) "Betwixt and Between: The Ethical Dilemmas of Insurance Defense Practice," in Leslie C. Levin and Lynn Mather, eds., *Lawyers in Practice: Ethical Decision Making in Context*. Chicago, IL: University of Chicago Press.

Kritzer, Herbert M. and Jill K. Anderson (1983) "The Arbitration Alternative: A Comparative Analysis of Case Processing Time, Disposition Mode, and Cost in the American Arbitration Association and the Courts." 8 *Justice System Journal* 6-19.

Kritzer, Herbert M., W.A. Bogart, and Neil Vidmar (1991a) "The Aftermath of Injury: Cultural Factors in Compensation Seeking in Canada and the United States." 25 *Law & Society Review* 499-543.

_____. (1991b) "Context, Context, Context: A Cross-Problem, Cross-Cultural Comparison of Compensation Seeking Behavior." Paper presented at Law and Society Association Annual Meeting, Amsterdam, Netherlands, June 26–30 [http://netfiles.umn.edu/users/kritzer/www/research/LSA-1991.pdf].

Kritzer, Herbert M., William L.F. Felstiner, Austin Sarat, and David M. Trubek (1985) "The Impact of Fee Arrangement on Lawyer Effort." 19 *Law & Society Review* 251-78.

Kritzer, Herbert M., Joel B. Grossman, Elizabeth McNichol, David M. Trubek, and Austin Sarat (1984a) "Courts and Litigation Investment: Why do Lawyers Spend More Time in Federal Cases?" 9 *Justice System Journal* 7-22.

Kritzer, Herbert M. and Jayanth Krishnan (1999) "Lawyers Seeking Clients, Clients Seeking Lawyers: Sources of Contingency Fee Cases and Their Implications for Case Handling." 20 *Law and Policy* 347-75.

Kritzer, Herbert M., Austin Sarat, David M. Trubek, Kristin Bumiller, and Elizabeth McNichol (1984b) "Understanding the Costs of Litigation: The Case of the Hourly Fee Lawyer." 1984 *American Bar Foundation Research Journal* 559-604.

Kritzer, Herbert M., Neil Vidmar, and W.A. Bogart (1991c) "To Confront or Not to Confront: Measuring Claiming Rates in Discrimination Grievances." 25 *Law & Society Review* 875-87.

Kritzer, Herbert M. and Frances Kahn Zemans (1993) "Local Legal Culture and the Control of Litigation." 27 *Law & Society Review* 535-58.

Kronman, Anthony T. (1993) *The Lost Lawyer: Failing Ideals of the Legal Profession.* Cambridge, MA: Belknap Press of Harvard University Press.

Kumble, Steven J. and Kevin J. Lahart (1990) *Conduct Unbecoming: The Rise and Ruin of Finley, Kumble.* New York: Carroll & Graf.

Landers, Renée M., James B Rebitzer, and Lowell J. Taylor (1996) "Rat Race Redux: Adverse Selection in the Determination of Work Hours in Law Firms." 86 *American Economic Review* 329-48.

Landis, Benjamin (1997) *The Governance of Law Firms.* Littleton, CO: Big Bison Press.

Landon, Donald D. (1985) "Clients, Colleagues, and Community: The Shaping of Zealous Advocacy in Country Law Practice." 1985 *American Bar Foundation Research Journal* 81-112.

_____. (1990) *Country Lawyers: The Impact of Context on Professional Practice.* Westport, CT: Praeger Publishers.

Langton, Lynn and Thomas H. Cohen (2008) "Civil Bench and Jury Trials in State Courts, 2005." Washington, DC: U.S. Department of Justice, Bureau of Justice Statistics.

Larson, Magali S. (1977) *The Rise of Professionalism: A Sociological Analysis.* Berkeley, CA: University of California Press.

Laumann, Edward O. and John P. Heinz (1977) "Specialization and Prestige in the Legal Profession: The Structure of Deference." 1977 *American Bar Foundation Research Journal* 155-216.

Law Society (1970) "Memorandum on Maintenance and Champerty: Claims Assessors and Contingency Fees." London: Law Society.

_____. (1987a) "Improving Access to Civil Justice: The Report of the Law Society's Working Party on the Funding of Litigation." London: Law Society.

_____. (1987b) "Multi-Disciplinary Partnerships and Allied Topics." London: Law Society.

Lee, R. G. (1992) "From Profession to Business: The Rise and Rise of the City Law Firm." 19 *Journal of Law and Society* 31-48.

Leibowitz, Wendy R. (1998) "Not Snow, Nor Sleet, Nor Gadget Boom Will Kill the Billable Hour." *National Law Journal*, August 31, B13.

_____. (1999a) "Lawyers, $15.95 a Box." *National Law Journal*, February 22, A18.

_____. (1999b) "Regulators Crack Down on 'Cyberlawyers.'" *National Law Journal*, February 22, A5.

Leipold, Dieter (1995) "Limiting Costs for Better Access to Justice—The German Experience," in Adrian A.S. Zuckerman and Ross Cranston, eds., *Reform of Civil Procedure: Essays on 'Access to Justice'*. Oxford, UK: Clarendon Press.

Lepore, Jill (2015) "On Evidence: Proving *Frye* as a Matter of Law, Science, and History." 124 *Yale Law Journal* 1092-1158.

Lerman, Lisa (1999) "Blue-Chip Bilking: Regulation of Billing Expense Fraud by Lawyers." 12 *Georgetown Journal of Legal Ethics* 205-365.

Lerman, Lisa G. (1994) "Gross Profits? Questions About Lawyer Billing Practices." 22 *Hofstra Law Review* 645-53.

_____. (1998) "Scenes From a Law Firm." 50 *Rutgers Law Review* 2153-88.

Leubsdorf, John (1981) "The Contingency Factor in Attorney Fee Awards." 90 *Yale Law Journal* 473-513.

Levin, Martin A. (1972) "Urban Politics and Judicial Behavior." 1 *Journal of Legal Studies* 193-221.

_____. (1977) *Urban Politics and the Criminal Courts*. Chicago, IL: University of Chicago Press.

Levy, Robert (2000) "Blackmail of Gun Makers." *National Law Journal*, January 31, A20.

Lewis, Michael (2001) "Faking It: The Internet Revolution Has Nothing to Do with the Nasdaq." *New York Times Magazine*, July 15, 15.

Lieberman, Jethro K. (1981) *The Litigious Society*. New York: Basic Books.

Linowitz, Sol M. (1994) *The Betrayed Profession: Lawyering at the End of the Twentieth Century*. New York: Charles Scribner's Sons.

Lipartito, Kenneth J. and Paul J. Miranti (1998) "Professions and Organizations in Twentieth-Century America." 79 *Social Science Quarterly* 301-20.

Lipson, Albert (1984) "California Enacts Prejudgment Interest: A Case Study of Legislative Action." Santa Monica, CA: RAND Institute for Civil Justice.

Llewellyn, Karl (1940) "The Normative, the Legal and the Law-Jobs: The Problem of Juristic Method." 40 *Yale Law Journal* 1335-1400.

Lopez, Gerald (1988–89) "Training Future Lawyers to Work with the Political and Socially Subordinated: Anti-Generic Legal Education." 91 *West Virginia Law Review* 305-87.

LoPucki, Lynn M. (1990) "The De Facto Pattern of Lawyer Specialization." Madison, WI: Institute for Legal Studies, University of Wisconsin Law School.

Lord Chancellor's Department (1998) "Access to Justice with Conditional Fees." London: Lord Chancellor's Department.

Lynk, William J. (1990) "The Courts and the Market: An Economic Analysis of Contingent Fees in Class-Action Litigation." 19 *Journal of Legal Studies* 247-60.

_____. (1994) "The Courts and the Plaintiffs' Bar: Awarding the Attorney's Fee in Class-Action Litigation." 23 *Journal of Legal Studies* 185-209.

Macaulay, Stewart (1963) "Non-Contractual Relations in Business: A Preliminary Study." 28 *American Sociological Review* 55-67.

MacCrate, Robert (1992) "Legal Education and Professional Development—An Educational Continuum: Report of the Task Force on Law Schools and the Profession: Narrowing the Gap ['MacCrate Report']." Chicago, IL: American Bar Association, Section of Legal Education and Admissions to the Bar.

Macey, Jonathan R. and Geoffrey P. Miller (1991) "The Plaintiffs' Attorney's Role in Class Action and Derivative Litigation: Economic Analysis and Recommendations for Reform." 58 *University of Chicago Law Review* 1-118.

Mack, Michael A. (1995) "Insurance Companies Move Defense In-House." *National Law Journal*, November 13, 1995, C38-C39.

MacKinnon, F.B. (1964) *Contingent Fees for Legal Services: A Study of Professional Economics and Responsibilities*. Chicago, IL: Aldine Publishing Co.

Malavet, Pedro A. (1996) "Counsel for the Situation: The Latin American Notary, a Historical and Comparative Model." 19 *Hastings International and Comparative Law Review* 389-488.

Maleshin, Dmitry (2010) "Russia," in Christopher Hodges, Stefan Vogenauer, and Magdalena Tulibacka, eds., *The Costs and Funding of Civil Litigation*. Oxford, UK: Hart Publishing.

Mann, Kenneth (1985) *Defending White-Collar Crime: A Portrait of Attorneys At Work*. New Haven: Yale University Press.

Manning, Bayless (1977) "Hyperlexis: Our National Disease." 71 *Northwestern University Law Review* 767-82.

Markesinis, Basil S. (1990) "Litigation-Mania in England, Germany and the USA: Are We So Very Different." 102 *Studi Senesi* 372-433.

Marshall, Lawrence C., Herbert M. Kritzer, and Frances K. Zemans (1992) "The Use and Impact of Rule 11." 86 *Northwestern Law Review* 943-86.

Mather, Lynn M. (1973) "Some Determinants of the Method of Case Disposition: Decision-Making by Public Defenders in Los Angeles." 8 *Law & Society Review* 187-216.

_____. (1979) *Plea-Bargaining or Trial: The Process of Criminal-Case Disposition*. Lexington, MA: Lexington Books.

Mather, Lynn M., Richard J. Maiman, and Craig A. McEwen (1995) "'The Passenger Decides on the Destination and I Decide on the Route': Are Divorce Lawyers 'Expensive Cab Drivers'?" 9 *International Journal of Law and the Family* 286-310.

Mather, Lynn M., Craig A. McEwen, and Richard J. Maiman (2001) *Divorce Lawyers at Work: Varieties of Professionalism in Practice*. New York: Oxford University Press.

McConville, Mike, Jacqueline Hodgson, Lee Bridges, and Anita Pavlovic (1994) *Standing Accused: The Organisation and Practices of Criminal Defence Lawyers in Britain*. Oxford, UK: Clarendon Press.

McCracken, Grant (1988) *The Long Interview*. Newbury Park, CA: Sage Publications.

McIntyre, Lisa (1987) *The Public Defender: The Practice of Law in the Shadows of Repute*. Chicago, IL: University of Chicago Press.

McKenna, Judith A. and Elizabeth C. Wiggins (1998) "Empirical Research on Civil Discovery." 39 *Boston College Law Review* 785-807.

McKinlay, John and John Stoekle (1988) "Corporatization and the Social Transformation of Doctoring." 18 *International Journal of Health Services* 191-205.

Mechanic, David (1976) *The Growth of Bureaucratic Medicine: An Inquiry into the Dynamics of Patient Behavior and the Organization of Medical Care.* New York: John Wiley & Sons.

Medina, Maria Aránzazu Calzadilla, Carlos Trujillo Cabrera, and Alejandro Ferreres Comella (2010) "Spain," in Christopher Hodges, Stefan Vogenauer, and Magdalena Tulibacka, eds., *The Costs and Funding of Civil Litigation.* Oxford: Hart Publishing.

Meir, Barry (1998) "Cigarette Makers and States Draft a $206 Billion Deal." *New York Times*, November 14, A1.

Melia, Kath M. (1997) "Producing 'Plausible Stories': Interviewing Nursing Students," in Gale Miller and Robert Dingwall, eds., *Context and Method in Qualitative Research.* London: Sage Publications.

Melnitzer, Julius (2004) "Ontario Officially Ends Prohibition on Contingency Fees." *Corporate Legal Times*, November, 28-29.

Menkel-Meadow, Carrie (1984) "Toward Another View of Legal Negotiation: The Structure of Problem Solving." 31 *UCLA Law Review* 754-842.

_____. (1989) "Exploring a Research Agenda of the Feminization of the Legal Profession: Theories of Gender and Social Change." 14 *Law & Social Inquiry* 289-319.

Menkel-Meadow, Carrie and Robert G. Meadow (1983) "Resource Allocation in Legal Services: Individual Attorney Decisions in Work Priority." 5 *Law & Policy Quarterly* 237-56.

Mezey, Susan Gluck and Susan M. Olson (1993) "Fee Shifting and Public Policy: The Equal Access to Justice Act." 77 *Judicature* 13-20.

Micelli, Thomas J. and Kathleen Segerson (1991) "Contingent Fees for Lawyers: The Impact on Litigation and Accident Prevention." 20 *Journal of Legal Studies* 381-400.

Miles, Matthew B. and A. Michael Huberman (1994) *Qualitative Data Analysis: An Expanded Sourcebook* [2nd Edition]. Thousand Oaks, CA: Sage Publications.

Miller, Gale and Robert Dingwall [eds.] (1997) *Context & Method in Qualitative Research.* London: Sage Publications.

Miller, Geoffrey P. (1986) "An Economic Analysis of Rule 68." 15 *Journal of Legal Studies* 93-125.

_____. (1987) "Some Agency Problems in Settlement." 16 *Journal of Legal Studies* 189-215.

Miller, Leslie (1999) "Guidelines, Libraries Offer Cures for Web Confusion." *USA Today*, July 14, D5.

Minish, Loraine (1979) "The Contingency Fee: A Re-Examination." 10 *Manitoba Law Journal* 65-77.

Mintz, Morton (1985) *At Any Cost: Corporate Greed, Women and the Dalkon Shield.* New York: Pantheon.

Molvig, Dianne (1999) "Multidisciplinary Practices: Service Package of the Future?" *Wisconsin Lawyer*, April, 10-13, 44-45.

Moorhead, Richard (1998) "Legal Aid in the Eye of a Storm: Rationing, Contracting, and a New Institutionalism." 25 *Journal of Law and Society* 365-87.

_____. (2000a) "Conditional Fee Agreements, Legal Aid and Access to Justice." 33 *University of British Columbia Law Review* 471-90.

_____. (2000b) "Lawyers and Insurers: The Next Conflict? [Editorial]." 7 *International Journal of the Legal Profession* 93-94.

_____. (2003) "Access or Aggravation? Litigants in Person, McKenzie Friends and Lay Representation." 22 *Civil Justice Quarterly* 133-55.

_____. (2004) "Legal Aid and the Decline of Private Practice: Blue Murder or Toxic Job?" 11 *International Journal of the Legal Profession* 159-90.

_____. (2010) "An American Future? Contingency Fees, Claims Explosions and Evidence from Employment Tribunals." 73 *Modern Law Review* 752-84.

Moorhead, Richard and Rebecca Cumming (2008) "Damage-Based Contingency Fees in Employment Cases: A Survey of Practitioners." Cardiff, UK: Cardiff University.

Moorhead, Richard, Avrom Sherr, and Alan Paterson (2003) "Contesting Professionalism: Legal Aid and Nonlawyers in England and Wales." 37 *Law & Society Review* 765-808.

Morrison, Rees W. (1998) *Law Department Benchmarks: Myths, Metrics, and Management.* Little Falls, NJ: Glasser Legal Works.

Mullenix, Linda (1994a) "Discovery in Disarray: The Pervasive Myth of Pervasive Discovery Abuse and the Consequences of Unfounded Rulemaking." 46 *Stanford Law Review* 1393-445.

_____. (1994b) "The Pervasive Myth of Pervasive Discovery Abuse: The Sequel." 39 *Boston College Law Review* 683-89.

Nagareda, Richard A. (2006) "FDA Preemption: When Tort Law Meets the Administrative State." 1 *Journal of Tort Law* [online journal].

Nardulli, Peter F. (1978) *The Courtroom Elite: An Organizational Perspective on Criminal Justice.* Cambridge, MA: Ballinger Publishing Co.

_____. (1986) "Insider Justice: Defense Attorneys and the Handling of Felony Cases." 77 *Journal of Criminal Law & Criminology* 379-417.

Nardulli, Peter F., James Eisenstein, and Roy B. Flemming (1988) *The Tenor of Justice: Criminal Courts and the Guilty Plea Process.* Urbana, IL: University of Illinois Press.

Nelken, Melissa (1990) "The Impact of Federal Rule 11 on Lawyers and Judges in the Northern District of California." 74 *Judicature* 147-52.

Nelson, Robert L. (1981) "Practice and Privilege: Social Change and the Structure of Large Law Firms." 1981 *American Bar Foundation Research Journal* 95-140.

_____. (1983) "Practice and Privilege: The Social Organization of Large Law Firms." Ph.D. Dissertation, Sociology, Northwestern University, Evanston, IL.

_____. (1988) *Partners with Power: Social Transformation of the Large Law Firm.* Berkeley, CA: University of California Press.

Nelson, Robert L. and Laura Beth Nielson (2000) "Cops, Counsel, and Entrepreneurs: Constructing the Role of Inside Counsel in Large Corporations." 34 *Law & Society Review* 457-94.

Nelson, Robert L., and Rebecca Sandefur, with John P. Heinz, and Edward O. Laumann (2005) "From Professional Dominance to Organisational Dominance: Professionalism, Inequality, and Social Change Among Chicago Lawyers, 1975–1995," in William L.F. Felstiner, ed., *Reorganisation and Resistance: Legal Professions Confront a Changing World.* Oxford, UK: Hart Publishing.

Neustadter, Gary (1986) "When Lawyer and Client Meet: Observations of Interviewing and Counseling Behavior in the Consumer Bankruptcy Law Office." 35 *Buffalo Law Review* 177-284.

Note (1984) "State Attorney Fee Shifting Statutes: Are We Quietly Repealing the American Rule?" 47 *Law and Contemporary Problems* 321-46.

O'Connor, Karen and Lee Epstein (1985) "Bridging the Gap Between Congress and the Supreme Court: Interest Groups and the Erosion of the American Rule Governing Awards of Attorneys' Fees." 38 *Western Political Quarterly* 238-49.

OECD Workshop on Liberalisation of Trade Services (1997) *International Trade in Professional Services: Advancing Liberalisation through Regulatory Reform*. Paris: Organisation for Economic Co-operation and Development.

Olgiati, Vittorio (1994) "The Latin-Type Notary and the Process of European Unification." 1 *International Journal of the Legal Profession* 253-68.

Oliphant, Robert E. (2000) "Will Internet Driven Concord University Law School Revolutionize Traditional Law School Teaching?" 27 *William Mitchell Law Review* 841-79.

Olson, Susan M. (1994) "How Much Access to Justice from State 'Equal Access to Justice Acts'?" 71 *Chicago-Kent Law Review* 547-82.

_____. (1992) "Studying Federal District Courts Through Published Cases: A Research Note." 15 *Justice System Journal* 782-800.

Orzack, Louis (1981) "New Profession by Fiat: Italian Dentristry and the European Common Market." 15A *Social Science & Medicine* 807-16.

Packer, Herbert L. (1964) "Two Models of the Criminal Process." 113 *University of Pennsylvania Law Review* 1-68.

Papworth, Jill (1998) "Policies to Stop You Footing the Bill After the Damage Is Done." *Guardian*, May 30, 7.

Parikh, Sara (2001) "Professionalism and Its Discontents: A Study of Social Networks in the Plaintiff's Personal Injury Bar." Ph.D. thesis, Sociology, University of Illinois at Chicago, Chicago, IL.

Parker, Christine (1997a) "Competing Images of the Legal Profession: Competing Regulatory Strategies." 25 *International Journal of the Sociology of Law* 385-409.

_____. (1997b) "Converting the Lawyers: The Dynamics of Competiton and Accountability Reform." 33 *Australia-New Zealand Journal of Sociology* 39-55.

Parsons, Talcott (1954a) "The Professions and Social Structure," in *Essays in Sociological Theory*. New York: Free Press.

_____. (1954b) "A Sociologist's Look at the Legal Profession," in *Essays in Sociological Theory*. New York: Free Press.

_____. (1962) "Law and Social Control," in William Evan, ed., *Law and Sociology*. New York: Free Press.

Passell, Peter (1996) "California Propositions Are Anti-lawyer, and No Joke." *New York Times*, February 8, D2.

Pastor, Santos and Carmen Vargas (2000) "La Justicia Civil en la República Dominicana." Washington, DC: World Bank (Banco Mundial).

Paterson, Alan A. (1996) "Professionalism and the Legal Services Market." 3 *International Journal of the Legal Profession* 137-68.

Percival, Robert V. and Geoffrey P. Miller (1984) "The Role of Attorney Fee Shifting in Public Interest Litigation." 47 *Law and Contemporary Problems* 233-48.

Perkin, Harold (1989) *The Rise of the Professional Society: England since 1880.* London: Routledge.

_____. (1996) *The Third Revolution: Professional Elites in the Modern World.* London: Routledge.

Peterson, Mark A. (1983) *Compensation of Injuries: Civil Verdicts in Cook County.* Santa Monica, CA: RAND Institute for Civil Justice.

_____. (1984) "Evaluating Claims: Theory and Practice." Santa Monica, CA: RAND Institute for Civil Justice.

_____. (1987) *Civil Juries in the 1980s: Trends in Jury Trials and Verdicts in California and Cook County, Illinois.* Santa Monica: RAND Institute for Civil Justice.

Peterson, Mark A. and George L. Priest (1982) *The Civil Jury: Trends in Trials and Verdicts, Cook County, Illinois, 1960–1979.* Santa Monica, CA: RAND Institute for Civil Justice.

Pfennigstorf, Werner (1984) "The European Experience with Attorney Fee Shifting." 47 *Law and Contemporary Problems* 37-124.

Phelps, David (2001) "Robins, Kaplan Catastrophic Group Adds Firepower of Top Litigator Jim Fetterly." *Star Tribune*, January 28, D1, D4.

Pierce, Jennifer L. (1995) *Gender Trials: Emotional Lives in Contemporary Law Firms.* Berkeley, CA: University of California Press.

Plous, Scott (1993) *The Psychology of Judgment and Decision Making.* Philadelphia, PA: Temple University Press.

Podgers, James (1993) "Recent Developments in Specialization: The Relationship between Specialization and Advertising," in ABA Standing Committee on Specialization, *Specialization Desk Book.* Chicago, IL: American Bar Association.

Pogarsky, Greg and Linda Babcock (2001) "Damage Caps, Motivated Anchoring, and Bargaining Impasse." 30 *Journal of Legal Studies* 143-59.

Polinsky, A. Mitchell and Daniel L. Rubinfeld (1993) "Sanctioning Frivolous Suits: An Economic Analysis." 82 *Georgetown Law Journal* 397-435.

_____. (1998) "Does the English Rule Discourage Low-Probability-of-Prevailing Plaintiffs?" 27 *Journal of Legal Studies* 519-35.

Posner, Richard A. (1977) *Economic Analysis of Law* [2nd Edition]. Boston: Little, Brown and Co.

_____. (1986) *Economic Analysis of Law* [3rd Edition]. Boston: Little, Brown and Co.

_____. (1993) "The Material Basis of Jurisprudence." 69 *Indiana Law Journal* 1-37.

Pound, Roscoe (1953) *The Lawyer from Antiquity to Modern Times.* St. Paul, MN: West Publishing.

Powell, Michael J. (1988) *From Patrician to Professional Elite: The Transformation of the New York City Bar Association.* New York: Russell Sage.

Prichard, Fred (2005) *Experts in Civil Cases: An Inside View.* New York: LFB Scholarly Publishing.

Prichard, J. Robert S. (1988) "A Systematic Approach to Comparative Law: The Effect of Cost, Fee, and Financing Rules on the Development of Substantive Law." 17 *Journal of Legal Studies* 451-75.

Public Protection Committee (1989) "Report of the Public Protection Committee." San Francisco, CA: State Bar of California.

Raiffa, Howard (1982) *The Art and Science of Negotiation*. Cambridge, MA: Belknap Press of Harvard University Press.

Randolph, Lillian (1998) "Physician Characteristics and Distribution in the U.S., 1997–1998 Edition." Chicago, IL: American Medical Association.

Ravdin, Linda J. and Kelly J. Capps (1999) "Alternative Pricing of Legal Services in a Domestic Relations Practice: Choices and Ethical Considerations." 33 *Family Law Quarterly* 387-418.

Reed, Alfred Z. (1921) *Training for the Public Profession of the Law*. New York: Carnegie Foundation for the Advancement of Teaching.

Reed, John P. (1969) "The Lawyer-Client: A Managed Relationship?" 12 *Academy of Management Journal* 67-80.

Reinganum, Jennifer F. and Louis L. Wilde (1986) "Settlement, Litigation, and the Allocation of Litigation Costs." 7 *RAND Journal of Economics* 557-66.

Rhode, Deborah L. (1981) "Policing the Professional Monopoly: A Constitutional and Empirical Analysis of Unauthorized Practice Prohibitions." 34 *Stanford Law Review* 1-112.

_____. (1985) "Ethical Perspectives on Legal Practice." 37 *Stanford Law Review* 589-652.

_____. (2000) *In the Interests of Justice: Reforming the Legal Profession*. New York: Oxford University Press.

Richards, Jean M. (1989) *Inform, Advise and Support: The Story of Fifty Years of the CAB*. London: Lutterworth Press.

Richert, David [ed.] (1994) "Legal Billing: Seeking Alternatives to the Hourly Rate [Symposium]." 77 *Judicature* 186-202.

Rickman, Neil (1994) "The Economics of Contingency Fees in Personal Injury Litigation." 10 *Oxford Review of Economic Policy* 34-50.

_____. (1995) "The Economics of Cost-shifting Rules," in Adrian A.S. Zuckerman and Ross Cranston, eds., *Reform of Civil Procedure: Essays on 'Access to Justice.'* Oxford, UK: Clarendon Press.

Riley, John (1984) "U.S. Lawyers Court Disaster in Bhopal." *National Law Journal*, December 31, 3.

Risinger, D. Michael (2000) "Navigating Expert Reliability: Are Criminal Standards Being Left on the Dock." 64 *Albany Law Review* 99-152.

Ritzer, George and David Walczak (1988) "Rationalization and the Deprofessionalization of Physicians." 67 *Social Forces* 1-22.

Robbennolt, Jennifer K. and Christina A. Studebaker (1999) "Anchoring in the Courtroom: The Effects of Caps on Punitive Damages." 23 *Law & Human Behavior* 353-73.

"Robert L. Habush, A 'Typically Relentless' Approach Wins Big." (2001) *National Law Journal*, July 16, C9.

Robins, Jon (1999a) "Accident Protection Insurance." *Law Society Gazette*, October 27.

_____. (1999b) "The Price of Success." *Law Society Gazette*, January 7, 14-15.

Robinson, Robert (2004) "A Tale of Two *Dauberts*: The Selective Application of Scientific Scrutiny for the Admissibility of Expert Testimony." Ph.D. Dissertation, Political Science, University of Wisconsin, Madison, WI.

Rose, Neil (1998a) "Australian Lawyers Head for MDP Freedom." *Law Society Gazette*, October 28, 10.

_____. (1998b) "Dutch Crisis over MDP Dispute with Andersen." *Law Society Gazette*, September 30, 6.

_____. (1998c) "French Lay Down MDP Guidelines." *Law Society Gazette*, July 15, 6.

_____. (1998d) "Society in Bid to Find MDP Formula." *Law Society Gazette*, October 21, 1, 5.

_____. (1998e) "Trade Official Clears MDP Path." *Law Society Gazette*, September 23, 6.

_____. (1998f) "World Lawyers in MDP Change of Heart." *Law Society Gazette*, September 16, 1.

_____. (1999) "Canada Joins Clamour for MDPs." *Law Society Gazette*, August 25, 6.

Rosen, Lawrence (1989) *The Anthropology of Justice: Law as Culture in Islamic Society*. New York: Cambridge University Press.

Rosen, Nathan Aaron (1990) "Lawyer Specialization: A Comprehensive Annotated Bibliography of Articles, Books, Court Decisions and Ethics Opinions." Chicago, IL: American Bar Association, Standing Committee on Specialization.

Rosen, Robert Eli (2002) "'We're All Consultants Now': How Change in Client Organizational Strategies Influences Change in the Organization of Corporate Legal Services." 44 *Arizona Law Review* 637-83.

Rosenberg, David and Steven Shavell (1985) "A Model in Which Suits Are Brought for Their Nuisance Value." 5 *International Review of Law and Economics* 3-13.

Rosenberg, Maurice, Peter F. Rient, and Thomas D. Rowe, Jr. (1981) "Expenses: The Roadblock to Justice." 16 *Judges' Journal* 42-47.

Rosenthal, Douglas E. (1974) *Lawyer and Client: Who's in Charge*. New York: Russell Sage Foundation.

Ross, H. Laurence (1980) *Settled Out of Court: The Social Process of Insurance Claims Adjustment* [2nd Edition]. New York: Aldine Publishing Co.

Ross, William G. (1991) "The Ethics of Hourly Billing by Attorneys." 44 *Rutgers Law Review* 1-100.

_____. (1996) *The Honest Hour: The Ethics of Time-based Billing by Attorneys*. Durham, NC: Carolina Academic Press.

Rothman, David J. and Sheila M. Rothman (1984) *The Willowbrook Wars: A Decade of Struggle for Social Justice*. New York: Harper & Row.

Rowe, Thomas D., Jr. and Neil Vidmar (1988) "Empirical Research on Offers of Settlement: A Preliminary Report." 51(4) *Law and Contemporary Problems* 13-40.

Rowe, Thomas D., Jr. (1984a) "Predicting the Effects of Attorney Fee Shifting." 47 *Law and Contemporary Problems* 139-72.

Rowe, Thomas D., Jr. [ed.] (1984b) "Symposium: Attorney Fee Shifting." 47 *Law and Contemporary Problems* 1-354.

Rowe, Thomas D., Jr. and David A. Anderson (1996) "Empirical Research on the Success of Settlement Devices," in David A. Anderson, ed., *Dispute Resolution:*

Bridging the Settlement Gap. Greenwich, CT: JAI Press.

Rubin, Paul H. (2011) "Third-Party Financing of Litigation." 38 *Northern Kentucky Law Review* 673-85.

Rubinfeld, Daniel L. and Suzanne Scotchmer (1993) "Contingent Fees for Attorneys: An Economic Analysis." 24 *RAND Journal of Economics* 343-56.

Rueschemeyer, Dietrich (1973) *Lawyers and Their Society: A Comparative Study of the Legal Profession in Germany and the United States.* Cambridge, MA: Harvard University Press.

_____. (1989) "Comparing Legal Professions: A State-Centered Approach," in Richard L. Abel and Philip S.C. Lewis, eds., *Lawyers in Society: Comparative Theories.* Berkeley, CA: University of California Press.

Saks, Michael J. and David L. Faigman (2005) "Expert Evidence after *Daubert*." 1 *Annual Review of Law and Social Science* 105-30.

Saltzman, Andrea (1986) "Incorporating Statutes Into the Common Law: The Judicial Response to Statutes Shifting Attorneys' Fees." 30 *Saint Louis University Law Journal* 1103-50.

Sandefur, Rebecca L. (2001) "Work and Honor in the Law: Prestige and the Division of Lawyers' Labor." 66 *American Sociological Review* 382-403.

Sandefur, Rebecca L. and John P. Heinz (1999) "Winner-Take-All Markets for Legal Services and Lawyers' Job Satisfaction," Chicago, IL: American Bar Foundation Working Paper Series.

Sanders, Joseph (1998) *Bendectin on Trial: A Study of Mass Tort Litigation.* Ann Arbor, MI: University of Michigan Press.

Sanders, Joseph and Craig Joyce (1990) "'Off to the Races': The 1980s Tort Crisis and the Law Reform Process." 27 *Houston Law Review* 207-95.

Sarat, Austin and William L.F. Felstiner (1986) "Law and Strategy in the Divorce Lawyer's Office." 20 *Law & Society Review* 93-134.

_____. (1989) "Lawyers and Legal Consciousness: Law Talk in the Divorce Lawyer's Office." 98 *Yale Law Journal* 1663-88.

_____. (1995) *Divorce Lawyers and Their Clients: Power and Meaning in the Legal Process.* New York: Oxford University Press.

Scheingold, Stuart and Austin Sarat (2004) *Something to Believe In: Politics, Professionalism, and Cause Lawyering.* Stanford, CA: Stanford University Press.

Schiller, Stephen A. and Peter M. Manikas (1987) "Criminal Courts and Local Legal Culture." 36 *DePaul Law Review* 327-41.

Schlegel, John Henry (1995) "Law and Endangered Species: Is Survival Alone Cause for Celebration." 28 *Indiana Law Review* 391-411.

Schneider, Eugene V. (1969) *Industrial Sociology: The Social Relations of Industry and the Community.* New York: McGraw-Hill.

Schön, Donald A. (1983) *The Reflective Practitioner: How Professionals Think in Action.* New York: Basic Books.

_____. (1988) *Educating the Reflective Practitioner.* San Francisco, CA: Jossey-Bass Publishers.

Schulhofer, Stephen J. (1984) "Is Plea Bargaining Inevitable?" 97 *Harvard Law Review* 1037-1107.

_____. (1985) "No Job Too Small: Justice Without Bargaining in the Lower Criminal Courts." 1985 *American Bar Foundation Research Journal* 519-98.

Schwab, Stewart J. and Theodore Eisenberg (1988) "Explaining Constitutional Tort Litigation: The Influence of the Attorney Fees Statute and the Government as Defendant." 73 *Cornell Law Review* 719-84.

Schwartz, Murray K. and Daniel J.B. Mitchell (1970) "An Economic Analysis of the Contingent Fee in Personal Injury Litigation." 22 *Stanford Law Review* 1125-62.

See, Harold (1984) "An Alternative to the Contingent Fee." 1984 *Utah Law Review* 485-509.

Seron, Caroll and Kerry Ferris (1995) "Negotiating Professionalism: The Gendered Social Capital of Flexible Time." 22 *Work and Occupations* 22-47.

Seron, Carroll (1996) *The Business of Practicing Law: The Work Lives of Solo and Small-Firm Attorneys*. Philadelphia, PA: Temple University Press.

Shapard, John E. (1984) "The Influence of Rules Respecting Recovery of Attorneys' Fees on Settlement of Civil Cases." Washington, DC: Federal Judicial Center.

_____. (1995) "Likely Consequences of Amendments to Rule 68, Federal Rules of Civil Procedure." Washington, DC: Federal Judicial Center.

Shavell, Steven (1982) "Suit, Settlement, and Trial: A Theoretical Analysis Under Alternative Methods for the Allocation of Legal Costs." 11 *Journal of Legal Studies* 55-81.

Shaw, Gisela (2000) "*Notaries* in England and Wales: Modernising a Profession Frozen in Time." 7 *International Journal of the Legal Profession* 141-55.

Shen, Kuan-Ling and Helena H.C. Chen (2010) "Taiwan," in Christopher Hodges, Stefan Vogenauer, and Magdalena Tulibacka, eds., *The Costs and Funding of Civil Litigation*. Oxford, UK: Hart Publishing.

Sheridan, Maurice and James Cameron (1992) *EC Legal Systems: An Introductory Guide*. London: Butterworths.

Sherr, Avrom, Richard Moorhead, and Alan Paterson (1994) "Assessing the Quality of Legal Work: Measuring Process." 1 *International Journal of the Legal Profession* 135-58.

Sherwood, David R. and Mark A. Clarke (1981) "Toward an Understanding of Local Legal Culture." 6 *Justice System Journal* 200-17.

Siegelman, Peter and John J. Donohue, III (1990) "Studying the Iceberg from Its Tip: A Comparison of Published and Unpublished Employment Discrimination Cases." 24 *Law & Society Review* 1133-70.

Sier, Julia Flynn (1988) "Liability Litigator: Michael Ciresi; Winning with Hard Work and Histrionics." *New York Times*, October 9, 6.

Silver, Charles (1992) "Unloading the Lodestar: Toward a New Fee Award Procedure." 70 *Texas Law Review* 865-970.

_____. (1997) "Flat Fees and Staff Attorneys: Unnecessary Casualties in the Battle over the Law Governing Insurance Defense Lawyers." 4 *Connecticut Insurance Law Journal* 205-57.

Silver, Charles and Kent Syverud (1995) "The Professional Responsibilities of Insurance Defense Lawyers." 45 *Duke Law Journal* 255-363.

Silverman, David (1993) *Interpreting Qualitative Data: Methods for Analysing Talk, Text and Interaction*. Thousand Oaks, CA: Sage Publications.

Simon, William H. (1978) "The Ideology of Advocacy: Procedural Justice and Professional Ethics." 1978 *Wisconsin Law Review* 29-144.

_____. (1988) "An Innovative Model Providing High Quality Legal Assistance for the Elderly in Wisconsin." Madison, WI: Center for Public Representation.

_____. (1991) "Lawyer Advice and Client Autonomy: Mrs. Jones's Case." 50 *Maryland Law Review* 213-26.

Simons, Jonathan (2004) "Recovering Costs from the Legal Services Commission." *New Law Journal*, October 15, 1528.

Skordaki, Eleni (1990) "European Lawyers and the Single Market." Paris: Conseil Supérieur du Notariat Français.

Skordaki, Eleni and Danielle Walker (1994) *Regulating and Charging for Legal Services: An International Comparison.* London: The Law Society.

Sloan, Frank A. and Lindsey M. Chepke (2008) *Medical Malpractice.* Cambridge, MA: MIT Press.

Slovak, Jeffrey S. (1980) "Giving and Getting Respect: Prestige and Stratification in a Legal Elite." 1980 *American Bar Foundation Research Journal* 31-68.

Smigel, Erwin O. (1964) *The Wall Street Lawyer: Professional Organization Man?* Bloomington, IN: Indiana University Press.

Smith, Bradley L. (1992) "Three Attorney Fee-Shifting Rules and Contingency Fees: Their Impact on Settlement Incentives." 90 *Michigan Law Review* 2154-89.

Snyder, Edward A. and James W. Hughes (1990) "The English Rule for Allocating Legal Costs: Evidence Confronts Theory." 6 *Journal of Law, Economics, and Organization* 345-80.

Society of Advanced Legal Studies (2001) "Report of the Working Party on the Ethics of Conditional Fee Arrangments." London: Society of Advanced Legal Studies.

Solomon, Rayman L. (1992) "Five Crises or One: The Concept of Legal Professionalism, 1925–1960," in Robert L. Nelson, David M. Trubek, and Rayman L. Solomon, eds., *Lawyers' Ideals/Lawyers' Practices: Transformations in the American Legal Profession.* Ithaca, NY: Cornell University Press.

Solovy, Jerold S. and Terry Rose Saunders (1985) "When the Court Awards Fees." *National Law Journal*

Sommerlad, Hilary (1994) "The Myth of Feminisation: Women and Cultural Change in the Legal Profession." 1 *International Journal of the Legal Profession* 31-54.

_____. (1995) "Managerialism and the Legal Profession: A New Professional Paradigm." 2 *International Journal of the Legal Profession* 159-85.

_____. (1996) "Criminal Legal Aid Reforms and the Restructuring of Legal Professionalism," in Richard Young and David Wall, eds., *Access to Justice: Legal Aid, Lawyers & the Defence of Liberty.* London: William Gaunt & Sons.

Sommerlad, Hilary and Peter Sanderson (1998) *Gender, Choice and Commitment: Women Solicitors in England and Wales and the Struggle for Equal Status.* Aldershot, UK: Ashgate Publishing.

Southworth, Ann (1996) "Business Planning for the Destitute? Lawyers as Facilitators in Civil Rights and Poverty Practice." 1996 *Wisconsin Law Review* 1121-73.

Spangler, Eve (1986) *Lawyers for Hire: Salaried Professionals at Work.* New Haven, CT: Yale University Press.

Spiegel, Mark (1979) "Lawyering & Client Decision-making: Informed Consent and the Legal Profession." 128 *University of Pennsylvania Law Review* 41-140.

Spradley, James P. (1979) *The Ethnographic Interview*. New York: Holt, Rinehart and Winston.

_____. (1980) *Participant Observation*. New York: Holt, Rinehart and Winston.

Stager, David A.A. and Harry W. Arthurs (1990) *Lawyers in Canada*. Toronto: University of Toronto Press.

Steele, Jane and Gillian Bull (1996) "Fast, Friendly and Expert? Legal Aid Franchising in Advice Agencies Without Solicitors." London: Policy Studies Institute.

Steele, Jane and John Seargeant (1999) "Access to Legal Services: The Contribution of Alternative Approaches." London: Policy Studies Institute.

Stein, Lisa (1998) "Law School for Nonlawyers Is Expanding Nationwide." *National Law Journal*, August 3, A9.

Steinitz, Maya (2011) "Whose Claim Is This Anyway? Third Party Litigation Funding." 95 *Minnesota Law Review* 1268-338.

Stern, Gerald M. (1976) *The Buffalo Creek Disaster: How Survivors of One of the Worst Disasters in Coal-Mining History Brought Suit Against the Coal Company—and Won*. New York: Random House.

Stevens, Rosemary (1971) *American Medicine and the Public Interest*. New Haven, CT: Yale University Press.

Stevens, William K (1984) "U.S. Lawyers Are Arriving to Prepare Big Damage Suits." *New York Times*, December 12, A10.

Stock, James H. (1992) "Compensation for Nonpayment Risk in Legal Cases Taken on Contingency: Economic Framework and Empirical Results." Cambridge, MA: Harvard University, Kennedy School of Government.

Stock, James H. and David A. Wise (1993) "Market Compensation in Class Action Suits: A Summary of Basic Ideas and Results." 16 *Class Action Reports* 584-604.

Stollberg, Cheryl Gay (1998) "As Doctors Trade Shingles for Marquee, Cries of Woe." *New York Times*, August 3, A1, A14.

Strauss, Anselm L. (1987) *Qualitative Analysis for Social Scientists*. New York: Cambridge University Press.

Strum, Phillipa (1984) *Louis D. Brandeis: Justice for the People*. Cambridge, MA: Harvard University Press.

Sugarman, David (1995) "Who Colonized Whom? Historical Reflections on the Intersection between Law, Lawyers and Accountants in England," in Yves Dezalay and David Sugarman, eds., *Professional Competiton and Professional Power: Lawyers, Accountants and the Social Construction of Markets*. London: Routledge.

_____. (1996) "Bourgeois Collectivism, Professional Power and the Boundaries of the State. The Private and Public Life of the Law Society, 1825–1914." 3 *International Journal of the Legal Profession* 81-136.

Sugawara, Ikuo and Eri Osaka (2010) "Japan," in Christopher Hodges, Stefan Vogenauer, and Magdalena Tulibacka, eds., *The Costs and Funding of Civil Litigation*. Oxford, UK: Hart Publishing.

Suleiman, Ezra N. (1987) *Private Power and Centralization in France: The Notaires and the State*. Princeton, NJ: Princeton University Press.

Susskind, Richard E. (1987) *Expert Systems in Law: A Jurisprudential Inquiry.* Oxford, UK: Clarendon Press.

_____. (1998) *The Future of Law: Facing the Challenges of Information Technology.* Oxford, UK: Clarendon Press.

_____. (2001) *Transforming the Law: Essays on Technology, Justice, and the Legal Marketplace.* Oxford, UK: Oxford University Press.

_____. (2008) *The End of Lawyers? Rethinking the Nature of Legal Services.* New York: Oxford University Press.

_____. (2013) *Tomorrow's Lawyers: An Introduction to Your Future.* New York: Oxford University Press.

Svenningsen, Kristine, Jan-Erik Svensson, and Anders Ørgaard (2010) "Denmark," in Christopher Hodges, Stefan Vogenauer, and Magdalena Tulibacka, eds., *The Costs and Funding of Civil Litigation.* Oxford, UK: Hart Publishing.

Swanson, Timothy M. (1990) "A Review of the Civil Justice Review: Economic Theories Behind the Delays in Tort Litigation." 43 *Current Legal Problems* 185-217.

Swanson, Timothy M. and Robin Mason (1998) "Nonbargaining in the Shadow of the Law." 18 *International Review of Law and Economics* 121-40.

Swartz, Jean V. (1996) "Lawyer Contingent Fee Agreements in Canada." Washington, DC: Library of Congress, Law Library.

Tanase, Takao (1990) "The Management of Automobile Accident Compensation in Japan." 24 *Law & Society Review* 651-92.

Task Force on Contingent Fees (2006) "Report on Contingent Fees in Class Action Litigation." 25 *Review of Litigation* 459-96.

Tata, Cyrus and Frank Stephens (2007) "When Paying the Piper Gets the 'Wrong' Tune: The Impact of Fixed Payments on Case Management, Case Trajectories, and 'Quality' in Criminal Defence Work," in Pascoe Pleasence, Alexy Buck, and Nigel J. Balmer, eds., *Transforming Lives: Law and Social Process* London: Legal Services Commission/TSO.

Taylor, Gary (1991) "Party's Over in Insurance." *National Law Journal*, September 23, 1, 26.

Tobias, Carl (1992) "Civil Rights Plaintiffs and the Proposed Revision of Rule 11." 77 *Iowa Law Review* 1775-93.

Toren, Nina A. (1975) "Deprofessionalization and Its Sources." 2 *Sociology of Work and Occupations* 323-37.

Trubek, David M., Joel B. Grossman, William L. F. Felstiner, Herbert M. Kritzer, and Austin Sarat (1983a) "Civil Litigation Project Final Report [3 volumes]." Madison, WI: Disputes Processing Research Program, University of Wisconsin Law School.

Trubek, David M., Austin Sarat, Wiliam L. F. Felstiner, Herbert M. Kritzer, and Joel B. Grossman (1983b) "The Costs of Ordinary Litigation." 31 *UCLA Law Review* 72-127.

Tuil, Mark and Louis Visscher [eds.] (2010) *New Trends in Financing Civil Litigation in Europe: A Legal, Empirical, and Economic Analysis.* Cheltenham, UK: Edward Elgar.

Turbin, Richard (1999) "Gun Manufacturers in Plaintiffs' Sights." *National Law Journal*, August 9, B20.

Tversky, Amos and Daniel Kahneman (1974) "Judgment Under Uncertainty: Heuristics and Biases." 185 *Science* 1124-30.

Underwood, Kerry (1999) "Conditional Fees in Practice." 143 *Solicitors Journal* 1000-01, 1032-33, 1066-67, 1092-93.

Unwin, George ([1904] 1963) *Industrial Organization in the Sixteenth and Seventeenth Centuries.* London: Frank Cass.

Utz, Pamela (1978) *Settling the Facts: Discretion and Negotiation in Criminal Court.* Lexington, MA: Lexington Books.

Valenta, A. (1995) *Legal Knowledge Engineering: A Modelling Approach.* Amsterdam, Netherlands: IOS Press.

Van Alstyne, W. Scott, Joseph R. Julin, and Larry D. Barnett (1990) *The Goals and Missions of Law Schools.* New York: Peter Lang.

Van Duch, Darryl (1998) "Bullish on Spinoffs." *National Law Journal*, August 10, A1, A14.

_____. (1999a) "ABA Honchos Differ over MDP Vote." *National Law Journal*, August 23, A6.

_____. (1999b) "MDPs Get International Support." *National Law Journal*, July 12, A4.

_____. (1999c) "Test Case for Insurers' Billing Rules: Ethics at Issue." *National Law Journal*, January 24, A1.

Van Houtte, Jean (1999) "Law in the World of Business: Lawyers in Large Industrial Enterprises." 6 *International Journal of the Legal Profession* 7-25.

Van Hoy, Jerry (1995) "Selling and Processing Law: Legal Work at Franchise Law Firms." 29 *Law & Society Review* 703-29.

_____. (1997) *Franchise Law Firms and the Transformation of Personal Legal Services.* Westport, CT: Quorum Books.

_____. (1999) "Markets and Contingency: How Client Markets Influence the Work of Plaintiffs' Personal Injury Lawyers." 6 *International Journal of the Legal Profession* 345-66.

van Maanen, John (1988) *Tales of the Field: On Writing Ethnography.* Chicago, IL: University of Chicago Press.

Van Voris, Bob (1998) "Gun Cases Use Tobacco Know-How; the Sequel." *National Law Journal*, December 7, A1.

_____. (1999) "Disbarred, Unbowed." *National Law Journal*, November 15, A1, A11.

Verkaik, Robert (1999) "Anger over 'Lay Prosecutors' Plans." *The Independent*, August 20, 9.

Vidmar, Neil (1995) *Medical Malpractice and the American Jury: Confronting the Myths about Jury Incompetence, Deep Pockets, and Outrageous Damage Awards.* Ann Arbor, MI: University of Michigan Press.

Villedieu, Anne-Laure (2010) "France: The Rules on Funding and Costs," in Christopher Hodges, Stefan Vogenauer, and Magdalena Tulibacka, eds., *The Costs and Funding of Civil Litigation.* Oxford, UK: Hart Publishing.

Walker, Mack (1971) *German Home Towns: Community, State, and General Estate, 1648–1871.* Ithaca, NY: Cornell University Press.

Wall, David S. and Jennifer Johnstone (1997) "The Industrialization of Legal Practice and the Rise of the New Electric Lawyer: The Impact of Information Technology on Legal Practice in the U.K." 25 *International Journal of Sociology of Law* 95-116.

Walsh, Conal (2001) "Claims Direct Cash Crunch." *The Observer*, July 22, 9.

Walsh, Sharon (1990) "The Vanishing Job-Bias Lawyers: Attorneys, Law Firms Say They Can't Afford to Try Rights Cases." *Washington Post*, July 6, C1.

Wasserstrom, Richard A. (1975) "Lawyers as Professionals: Some Moral Issues." 5 *Human Rights* 1-24.

Waterman, Donald A. and Mark A. Peterson (1984) "Evaluating Civil Claims: An Expert Systems Approach." 1 *Expert Systems* 65-76.

Watson, Garry D., W.A. Bogart, Allan C. Hutchinson, Janet Mosher, and Kent Roach (1991) *Civil Litigation: Cases and Materials* [4th Edition]. Toronto: Emond Montgomery.

Watson, Richard A. and Rondal G. Downing (1969) *The Politics of the Bench and Bar: Judicial Selection Under the Missouri Nonpartisan Court Plan*. New York: John Wiley & Sons.

Webster, Guy (1994) "Quickcourt Kiosks Earn Praise from Users, Court System." *Arizona Republic*, August 21, H4.

Wessel, Milton R. (1976) *The Rule of Reason: A New Approach to Corporate Litigation*. New York: Addison-Wesley Publishing Co.

Whelan, Christopher and Doreen McBarnet (1992) "Lawyers in the Market: Delivering Legal Services in Europe." 19 *Journal of Law and Society* 49-68.

White, Edward (1998) "Crime, Disorder—and Suitable Case Workers." *Solicitors' Journal*, April 3, 297.

White, R.H.H. (1976) "The Distasteful Character of Litigation for Poor Persons," in Neil MacCormick, ed., *Lawyers in Their Social Setting*. Edinburgh, UK: W. Green & Son.

White, Robin C.A. and Rachel Atkinson (2000) "Personal Injury Litigation, Conditional Fees and After-the-Event Insurance." 19 *Civil Justice Quarterly* 118-35.

White, Welsh S. (1971) "A Proposal for Reform of the Plea Bargaining Process." 119 *University of Pennsylvania Law Review* 439-65.

Wice, Paul B. (1978) *Criminal Lawyers: An Endangered Species*. Beverly Hills, CA: Sage Publications.

Wiggins, Elizabeth C., Thomas E. Willging, and Donna Stienstra (1991) "The Federal Judicial Center's Study of Rule 11." #2 *FJC Directions* 3-40.

Wilensky, Harold L. (1964) "The Professionalization of Everyone." 70 *American Journal of Sociology* 137-58.

Wilkins, David B. (1992) "Who Should Regulate Lawyers?" 105 *Harvard Law Review* 799-888.

Willging, Thomas E., Donna Stienstra, John Shapard, and Dean Miletich (1998) "An Empirical Study of Discovery and Disclosure Practice under the 1993 Federal Rules Amendments." 39 *Boston College Law Review* 525-96.

Williams, Gerald R. (1983) *Legal Negotiation and Settlement*. St. Paul, MN: West Publishing.

Williams, Lois G. (1994) "Professional Development for Litigators," in *In-House Training: Maximizing Your Lawyers' Professional Potential*. Philadelphia, PA: American Law Institute.

Witz, Anne (1992) *Professions and Patriarchy*. London: Routledge.

Wolfram, Charles W. (1986) *Modern Legal Ethics*. St. Paul, MN: West Publishing Company.

_____. (1999) "Multidisciplinary Practice of Law: The Dawn of a New Age." St. Paul, MN: William Mitchell College of Law (talk presented November 9).

Wolfson, Alan D., Michael J. Trebilcock, and Carolyn J. Tuohy (1980) "Regulating the Professions: A Theoretical Framework," in Simon Rottenberg, ed., *Occupational Licensure and Regulation*. Washington, DC: American Enterprise Institute for Public Policy Research.

Wollschläger, Christian (1998) "Exploring Global Landscapes of Litigation Rates," in Jürgen Brand and Dieter Strempel, eds., *Soziologie des Rechts: Festschrift für Erhard Blankenburg zum 60 Geburtstag*. Baden Baden, Germany: Nomos.

Woodroffe, Geoffrey (1998) "Loser Pays and Conditional Fees—An English Solution." 37 *Washburn Law Journal* 345-57.

Yarrow, Stella (1998) *The Price of Success: Lawyers, Clients and Conditional Fees*. London: Policy Studies Institute.

_____. (2000) "Just Rewards? The Outcome of Conditional Fee Cases [Summary]." London: University of Westminster School of Law.

_____. (2001) "Conditional Fees," in *The Settlement of Legal Disputes: An Assessment of Recent Reform Measures* [Hume Papers on Public Policy, Volume 8, No. 3]. Edinburgh, UK: Edinburgh University Press.

Yarrow, Stella and Pamela Abrams (1999) "Nothing to Lose? Clients' Experiences of Using Conditional Fees." London: University of Westminster, School of Law.

Yin, Robert K. (1994) *Case Study Research: Design and Methods* [2nd Edition]. Thousand Oaks, CA: Sage Publications.

Zamir, Eyal and Ilana Ritov (2010) "Revisiting the Debate over Attorneys' Contingent Fees: A Behavioral Analysis." 38 *Journal of Legal Studies* 245-88.

Zander, Michael (1997) "Rights of Audience in the Higher Courts in England and Wales since the 1990 Act: What Happened?" 4 *International Journal of the Legal Profession* 167-95.

_____. (1998) "The Government's Plans on Legal Aid and Conditional Fees." 61 *Modern Law Review* 538-50.

_____. (2002) "If Conditional Fees, Why Not Contingency Fees?" *New Law Journal*, May 24, 797.

Zemans, Frances Kahn (1984) "Fee Shifting and the Implementation of Public Policy." 47 *Law and Contemporary Problems* 187-210.

Zemans, Fred (1999) "The Community Legal Clinic QAP: An Innovative Experience in Quality Assurance in Legal Aid." Paper presented at Legal Aid in a Changing World [Conference Sponsored by the Legal Aid Board Research Unit], London, November 4-5.

Zuckerman, Adrian A.S. (1996) "Lord Woolf's Access to Justice: Plus ça change...." 59 *Modern Law Review* 773-96.

INDEX

ABOUT THE AUTHOR

HERBERT KRITZER holds the Marvin J. Sonosky Chair of Law and Public Policy at the University of Minnesota Law School. He has conducted extensive empirical research on the work of lawyers in the American civil justice system, and is internationally recognized for his work writing on a range of civil justice-related issues. His books include *Justices on the Ballot: Continuity and Change in State Supreme Court Elections* (Cambridge University Press, 2015); *Risks, Reputations, and Rewards: Contingency Fee Legal Practice in the United States* (Stanford University Press, 2004); *The Justice Broker* (Oxford University Press, 1990); *Let's Make a Deal* (University of Wisconsin Press, 1991); and *Legal Advocates: Lawyers and Nonlawyers at Work* (University of Michigan Press, 1998), and he is one of the coauthors of *Courts, Law and Politics in Comparative Perspective* (Yale University Press, 1996). He is the editor of the multi-volume *Legal Systems of the World* (ABC-CLIO, 2002), and coeditor of *In Litigation: Do the Haves Still Come Out Ahead* (Stanford University Press, 2003) and the *Oxford Handbook of Empirical Legal Research* (2010). He has published extensively in professional journals, including leading journals in political science, interdisciplinary legal studies, and law.

Over the last 35 years Kritzer has conducted research on the American civil justice system dealing with legal malpractice, contingency fee legal practice, insurance defense practice, the impact of Rule 11 sanctions, scientific and technical evidence after *Daubert*, news coverage of civil justice by local television and local newspapers, and alternative forms of advocacy and representation. Research with a cross-national element has included writing on the English Rule, propensity to sue, the frequency of criminal and civil trials in England and Canada, and politics in the English judicial system. Other areas of recent work have included Supreme Court decision making, public attitudes toward the courts, and changing patterns in state supreme court dockets. From 2003 to 2007 he served as editor of the *Law & Society Review*.

Kritzer has served as a consultant and analyst for the Wisconsin Supreme Court's Office of Court Operations on a "consumer perspective" survey of users of its circuit courts; as a consultant to the State Bar of Wisconsin on its studies of jury verdicts, pro bono activities, and legal needs; as a consultant to the Alaska Judicial Council for its study of fee shifting practices; and as a consultant to the World Bank for docket profiling studies in Latin America. He was a member of the Wisconsin Equal Justice Task Force, which examined issues of gender equity in the state's court system. Between 2012 and 2014 he served as an international member on the principal social science panel overseeing the UK's Research Excellence Framework 2014 (REF2014).

At the University of Minnesota he teaches tort law, courses on legal professions in the United States and countries around the world, and several law and social science courses.

www.ingramcontent.com/pod-product-compliance
Lightning Source LLC
Chambersburg PA
CBHW061232220326
41599CB00028B/5401